A World to Win

A World to Win

*The Life and Works
of Karl Marx*

Sven-Eric Liedman

Translated by
Jeffrey N. Skinner

VERSO
London • New York

First published in English by Verso 2018
First published as *Karl Marx: En Biografi*
© Albert Bonniers Förlag 2015
Translation © Jeffrey N. Skinner 2018

Every effort has been made to secure permission for images appearing herein
that are under copyright. In the event of being notified of any omission,
Verso will seek to rectify the mistake in the next edition of this work.

1 3 5 7 9 10 8 6 4 2

Verso
UK: 6 Meard Street, London W1F 0EG
US: 20 Jay Street, Suite 1010, Brooklyn, NY 11201
versobooks.com

Verso is the imprint of New Left Books

ISBN-13: 978-1-78663-504-4
ISBN-13: 978-1-78663-507-5 (US EBK)
ISBN-13: 978-1-78663-506-8 (UK EBK)

British Library Cataloguing in Publication Data
A catalogue record for this book is available from the British Library

Library of Congress Cataloging-in-Publication Data
A catalog record for this book is available from the Library of Congress

Typeset in Sabon by MJ & N Gavan, Truro, Cornwall
Printed in the UK by CPI Group (UK) Ltd, Croydon, CR0 4YY

Contents

Preface

It is a great joy for me that my biography of Marx, originally published in Swedish in September 2015, has now reached the English-speaking world. Prior to the translation, the text was updated and a few mistakes in the original have been corrected. The great majority of references to Swedish and other Scandinavian literature have been removed. On the other hand, the German, French – and to some extent Italian – books and articles remain. I think it important that substantial portions of international Marx research are taken into consideration.

There are two crucial reasons why I – having worked on Marx, and Engels as well, from the 1960s until now – took on the task of writing a major biography of Marx in the second decade of the twenty-first century.

First, a quarter-century after the fall of the Berlin Wall and the dissolution of the Soviet Union, it has finally become possible to provide a portrait of Marx unobscured by what happened after his death. Quite simply, we have an opportunity to assess the whole of Marx's multifaceted work in a way that would have been impossible only a few years ago.

The second reason is a little more down-to-earth: the major critical edition of the *Marx-Engels-Gesamtausgabe* has now come so far that the greater part of his work – including important, previously unpublished manuscripts and excerpts – has been edited in an exemplary manner. It is now possible, for example, to compare Engels's editing of the third volume of *Capital* with Marx's own manuscript in a completely new way. In excerpts of his reading, with accompanying commentary, Marx's prodigious literary consumption becomes apparent in both its breadth and depth.

In the first chapter of this book, I take a position on a great number of prominent representations of Marx. Since 2015, however, an important English-language biography has become available, namely Gareth Stedman Jones's *Karl Marx: Greatness and Illusion*. It has earned glowing reviews from many quarters and deserves a few words here; I have to be able to explain why another sweeping biography of Marx is needed.

To begin with, it should be said that Stedman Jones's work deserves a lot of praise. It is an extremely thorough study that clarifies important parts of the background to Marx's work. In particular, he has mapped out in detail the confusing diversity of the generally short-lived workers' movements, from the Chartists up to the time of Marx's death, when various social democratic parties had begun to take shape. There is hardly anything to be added in this regard. In my own biography, these movements have been dealt with to the extent that they are important to understanding Marx's activities, and no further.

Stedman Jones has also very energetically elucidated many important sources of inspiration for Marx. Not infrequently, he does so in such detail that Marx's own writing is actually overshadowed. For my own part, I have certainly provided an account of the literature that influenced Marx. I examine a broader sphere of influence, such as the natural scientists Marx eagerly studied.

But, for me, it was important first of all to present Marx's work in all its breadth. My estimation of Marx as an author is a world away from Stedman Jones's assessment of him. He depicts a relatively brief period when Marx was successful both as a theoretician and a politician: the years from 1864 to 1869, when he completed the first volume of *Capital* and simultaneously played a decisive role in the development of the International Workingmen's Association. It is natural to consider this a high point. But for me, the whole body of his work – everything from the early years up to the last incomplete manuscripts – amounts to a towering achievement, though the great majority of it never went to print during his lifetime.

Stedman Jones sums up rather neatly the original thinking

found in the *Communist Manifesto*, but as regards the *Economic and Philosophic Manuscripts* he is significantly more reserved. The noteworthy aspects of the substantial preparatory work for *Capital*, known as the *Grundrisse*, do not emerge. He judges the text 'clumsy and disjointed' and the presentation 'chaotic', and perhaps with good reason. But certain pages are brilliant all the same; there – as he so often does – Marx succeeds in throwing light on his theory with elegant aphoristic incisiveness. In particular, he provides in glimpses a vision of the working life of the future found nowhere else in his oeuvre. Generally speaking, the *Grundrisse* opens up a broader perspective than the first volume of *Capital*.

In contrast to Stedman Jones, I am profoundly concerned with the last few decades of intensive research concerning the *Grundrisse* and in particular *Capital*. It is striking how names such as Hans-Georg Backhaus, Michael Heinrich, and Andrew Kliman are conspicuous by their absence in Stedman Jones's work. As a result, he does not succeed in providing an up-to-date reading of *Capital*.

The notion that Marx was unproductive after 1870 has a long history, one familiar from many previous biographies. But newer studies have painted a very different picture. At the end of his life, Marx was of course physically much weaker but as restlessly active as ever, deepening and broadening his already voluminous reading. Most of it stopped at detailed, often extremely interesting excerpts. But he also authored a number of manuscripts, some of which attained lasting significance. The *Critique of the Gotha Programme* belongs here, of course, but so too does the text that formed the basis for Engels's widely read book *The Origin of the Family, Private Property, and the State*. The drafts of his responses to Vera Zasulich are another item of great importance. Teodor Shanin, a specialist in this period of Marx's output, even distinguishes a 'late Marx', to sit alongside the established 'young' and 'mature' Marx. In this biography, I follow my subject all the way to the end.

My own background in the history of philosophy and science is of some relevance. I have analysed Marx with regard to the thinking of his time, and this line of inquiry has unearthed previously unnoticed facts regarding his relationship to the natural sciences. In a comprehensive study of Engels, published in Swedish in 1977 and in an abbreviated translation in German in 1986 (*Das Spiel der Gegensätze*) – but unfortunately not in English – I could map out in detail the surprising origins of the curious doctrine (which often had fateful consequences) called dialectical materialism, which culminated in a 'dialectics of nature'. I can now supplement this picture and highlight all kinds of previously unnoticed facets.

It has been possible to bring a greater understanding to the tension in *Capital* between, on the one hand, a dialectic with roots in Hegel and, on the other, a struggle for exactitude inspired by the era's triumphs in physics and chemistry.

In summary, Stedman Jones provides an ambitious and detailed picture of Marx's political achievements, albeit one marked by his own ideological preferences. Yet, it is remarkable that he completely ignores important works such as Wolfgang Schieder's *Karl Marx als Politiker*. The thinker, empirical researcher, and author who takes shape in Jones's biography is an unsatisfying portrayal, the features of which rely on research that has long been overplayed. This is fatal, since it is in these capacities that Marx can actually inspire us today. The political game has changed numerous times over the last hundred and fifty years. The tools Marx developed for his analysis of society and history are still sharp but lie unused far too often, despite the fact we live in a period of striking similarity to Marx's own.

With this biography, I have attempted to explain not only who Marx was in his time, but why he remains a vital source of inspiration today. Whether the endeavour has been a success is a matter for the reader to decide.

1

The Great Project

When I was young, it was my good fortune to make the acquaintance of an old German Jew who was dying, here in London,
from the effects of long hardship and privation, of overwork and
poverty. I did what I could to save, to prolong his life. I got him
sent to Algeria, to the south of France, and got the most brilliant
young physician on Harley Street to look after him. But it was too
late. In the short time I knew him, he taught me more than all other
teachers, dead or living. He saw more clearly than any other man
the disease that was killing the world. His name was Karl Marx.

The man who spoke these words was named E. Ray Lankester.
He was one of Great Britain's foremost biologists at the turn
of the twentieth century, and one of the few present at Marx's
funeral.[1]

But this book is not about Dr Lankester. It is about Marx.

Karl Marx lived from 1818 to 1883. By the autumn of 1850, half
of his life had passed. He was truly a man of the 1800s, rooted
in his century. Today he belongs to the distant past, yet his name
constantly crops up.

The collapse of the Soviet Empire at first appeared to bury him
in its rubble, in the oblivion that surrounds the hopelessly obso-
lete. Marx was only the first in a series of repugnant figures who
now, fortunately, had been consigned to the history books: everything that had been realized in the Soviet Union and China had
been designed first in Marx's imagination.

This is a notion that is still widely prevalent. But it soon turned out that Marx had an active afterlife, independent of the disintegration of empires. More than a few regretted his demise.

The most influential of these was Jacques Derrida, the French philosopher, who played an important role in the intellectual life of the twentieth century. In 1993, he published *Specters of Marx*, in which he conceded that Marx was indeed dead, but nevertheless haunted a world of growing injustices like a ghost.[2]

Another French philosopher, Étienne Balibar, also published an ingenious little book in which he asserted that Marx's thought was extremely relevant to today's world, while the philosophy trumpeted from the Soviet Union had no actual connection with Marx.[3]

A few years later, around the turn of the century, Marx became topical in a more spectacular fashion. The *New Yorker* named him the most important thinker of the coming century,[4] and in a vote organized by the BBC, he came out top among philosophers as the greatest thinker of the last millennium.[5] In his last book, *How to Change the World* (2011), the great Austro-British historian Eric Hobsbawm spoke about a meeting with George Soros, the famous investor. Soros asked him about his position on Marx; anxious to avoid a quarrel, Hobsbawm responded evasively, whereupon Soros replied: 'That man discovered something about capitalism 150 years ago that we need to take advantage of.'[6]

These anecdotes may seem trivial. Someone who is a celebrity, a public figure people readily refer to, does not need to be influential in a serious sense. It is more telling that Marx is constantly part of the discussion of the fateful questions of our time. When French economist Thomas Piketty caused a sensation in 2013 with his voluminous *Capital in the Twenty-first Century*, Marx's name dominated the flood of commentary the book gave rise to. Traditional economists ascribed to Piketty all the sins for which they routinely blame Marx, and enthusiasts took the promise in the book's punning title quite literally: a new *Capital* for the twenty-first century. In fact, the distance between Piketty and Marx is quite large. Piketty is not interested in the duel between labour and capital; his focus is on finance capital. The similarity lies in the long historical perspective, as well as in the attention paid to the growing – and in the long run catastrophic – division between the few who hold more and more power through their riches, and the many who are thereby rendered powerless. Piketty himself is eager to emphasize Marx's significance. Marx's thesis on the unending accumulation of capital is as fundamental for economic analysis in the twenty-first century as it was for the nineteenth, Piketty says.[7]

Sociologist Göran Therborn attacks the growing division in the world from another direction in his 2013 book, *The Killing Fields of Inequality*. He points out that the growing inequality cannot be measured only by widening gaps in income and wealth. Differences in health and lifespan – and people's opportunities in general to develop in an adequate manner – are also appearing. Therborn perceives a particular existential inequality that concerns rights, dignity, respect, and degrees of freedom, for example. It turns out that this inequality, in all its aspects, is now rapidly accelerating even in Europe, especially in the Nordic countries.[8]

Therborn himself has a background in Marxism and, by all appearances, now considers himself a post-Marxist – that is, remaining in the tradition but free from all ties to previous groups. Indeed, one of his later books, from 2008, is titled *From Marxism to Post-Marxism?*[9]

In the face of another fateful question of the age – the environmental crisis in general and the climate crisis in particular – Marx's name sometimes comes up. This may seem surprising: the empire that had its ideological origins in Marx – the Soviet Union – caused unparalleled environmental destruction. But those who go directly to Marx without detouring through Stalin, Khrushchev and Brezhnev find that he certainly cared about the environment. Material production for him was an interaction between nature and humanity that had been eliminated as a result of capitalism. The person who has most emphasized this (and to some extent overemphasized it) is American sociologist John Bellamy Foster, above all in his 2000 book *Marx's Ecology*.[10] Foster's perspective turns up in Naomi Klein's 2014 grand general scrutiny of the relationship between capitalism and climate, *This Changes Everything*.[11]

Marx is also present in discussions about the new class society that developed in the decades around the turn of the twenty-first century. British economist Guy Standing perceived a new social class in the world of that era. He published a widely discussed book about it in 2011: *The Precariat: The New Dangerous Class.* He considers people of today who are living in an incessantly uncertain financial situation as belonging to the precariat. He perceives three different layers: workers who, through deindustrialization, have lost their jobs and have no prospect for employment; refugees from the world's hotbeds of crisis who have been forced out into the margins of society; and, finally, well-educated people who are reduced to temporary, equally uncertain, positions that are interspersed with periods of unemployment. This is a diversity that is perhaps entirely too large for the term to be manageable. But there is an important unifying link here that has to do with the labour market and the conditions of employment. More and more people are relegated to a diffuse borderland between temporary jobs and no jobs at all. The relative security that the workers' movement fought for is becoming more and more restricted, and the social safety net is growing thinner or being torn to shreds in recurring crises.[12]

It is natural that the crisis that crossed the world in 2008 and 2009 aroused a new interest in Marx, and for *Capital* in particular. With the fall of the Berlin Wall in 1989, many said with pleasure that not only the Soviet Empire, but Karl Marx too would thereby lose all relevance they had had so far. It is fitting that the Soviet Union was sent to the past once and for all after 1991, but not Marx. And why not Marx?

To approach the question, we must first take a step back. The societal change that characterized Marx's work more than any other was industrialization, and with it the development of a workers' movement. Today, those developments appear distant and close at the same time. In countries where mass production once began, we have entered into a post-industrial society. The nineteenth-century sweatshops that Marx had in mind are now found chiefly in countries such as China, Indonesia, and the Philippines. In Europe and the United States, other class divisions than those of the 1800s and 1900s are getting wider and deeper.

A large number of economists who portray the reality of the early twenty-first century as the best – indeed, the only natural – one are doing everything they can to convince ordinary people that they belong to the great capitalist community of interest. 'It's everyone's money that's at stake,' they chant. Their own theory is built on the notion of an eternal equilibrium in a world of restless change. We could call it a new kind of more prosaic Platonism. Something eternal exists beyond the chaotic diversity that the senses (and the charts) bear witness to.

What could be more natural in a situation like this than to summon Karl Marx back from the shadows? No social theory is more dynamic than his. No one speaks more clearly about widening class divisions than he does.

It is impossible to read the introductory, stylistically razor-sharp and rhetorically perfect first pages of the *Communist Manifesto* without recognizing the society that is ours. The bourgeoisie 'has drowned the most heavenly ecstasies of religious fervour, of chivalrous enthusiasm, of philistine sentimentalism in the icy water of egotistical calculation'.

Are we not again living in that society? Have we not come back to the reality of the 1840s, even if more globalized and technologically more advanced? The free flow of commodities is the norm that forces other norms to shrink into insignificance.

Marx can, sometimes, come almost painfully close to describing our current world. Today, a brutal economism dominates many minds to the extent that it has become invisible for them. It is often called neoliberalism, after the school that Milton Friedman became the symbol of in the 1970s. But the name does not matter. The important thing is that many of Friedman's ideas have become everyday life; the market dominates every detail, and even states and municipalities are run like businesses.

Friedman's spiritual forefathers – the representatives of the Manchester School – lived in Marx's time, with John Bright and Richard Cobden leading the way. For them too, free trade would solve all problems. Marx harboured a reluctant admiration for the Manchester liberals, seeing them as heralds for a development that had to precede the society he himself was fighting for. At the same time, he attacked them heatedly when they claimed to represent the whole of the people – the workers as well – against the aristocracy.

Marx wrote much about Cobden and Bright and their followers, especially in his articles in the *New York Daily Tribune*.

The Marx of the twenty-first century must brace himself against the reality that has been created since the 1980s.

Today, Marx may be discussed and often cited, but he has only a fraction of the influence he – apparently, at least – had fifty or a hundred years ago. In a way, this is paradoxical. His vision of society would seem to appear less pertinent then than it does now. The Soviet Union, which was supposed to be following in his footsteps, was characterized by many things, from censorship, forced labour camps, and rule by the bosses to schools and universities for everyone and guaranteed support for a non-modernistic culture – indeed, a 'philistine sentimentalism', to use the words of the *Manifesto*. In the other Europe, where Marx is also found in the family tree, certain politicians could talk about democratic socialism, and there – despite many shortcomings and injustices – moderate social security prevailed for most. The economy blossomed, preparing the ground for reforms that made life more tolerable for ordinary folk. Of course, there were still class divisions, but not as precipitous as a hundred years earlier.

Marx's analysis of his time thus makes better sense today than it did fifty years ago. Its accuracy applies, above all, to the way capitalism works.

But Marx had not counted on capitalism's ability to constantly renew itself and develop new productive forces. Today, capitalism appears more dominant than ever. In the only large country where Marx still has a place of honour – China – he has to put up with constantly being drenched in the 'icy water of egotistical calculation'. Communism has become the 'Sunday best', tight as a straitjacket. Everyday life is marked by a race for market shares, as ruthless as it is successful. Marx's analysis of the way capitalism works is being brilliantly confirmed. But for him, it would have been inconceivable that a country that quotes him would drive capitalism to its utmost extremes.

It is in this paradoxical situation that entering deep into the study of Marx becomes important.

Going this deep requires that, from the beginning, we settle accounts with a range of fallacies about Marx circulating in the general public and making a reasonable understanding of his life and work more difficult. These fallacies, large and small, will turn up in their natural contexts further on in the text. Here, it is only a question of relieving the reader, from the beginning, of unnecessary ballast.

Misconceptions and Exaggerations

Several of the most common assertions about Marx are quite simply false. The claim that he wanted to dedicate the first volume of *Capital* to Darwin belongs here. He never dreamed of it. On the other hand, he did send a printed copy to the great biologist, who thanked him for the kindness but at the very most read the first few pages.

Another fallacy is that Marx said that religion is opium for the people. He never said that; he said it is an opium *of* the people. There is a big difference. Religion is not something that the malicious powers that be dispense to the people. It is the people themselves who seek relief and comfort in religion.[13]

Other common ideas about him can be questioned with good reason. One of the most widespread is that he was a determinist. Societal development would inexorably progress from one stage to another. Socialism would follow capitalism with the necessity of natural law.

This idea arises more naturally, as the Marxism that came after him often expressed itself this way. What is more, there are phrases in the works of Marx himself that are easily interpreted in this direction. But research over the last few decades – the research that could be conducted on his core texts in the condition he left them – has shown that he spoke more of tendencies than an inevitable development. According to him, there were far too many uncertain factors. He himself spoke of the power of accidental circumstances.

Sometimes, he is painted as a hypocrite for trying – often in vain – to live like a Victorian bourgeois. But he was not ashamed of that. He didn't follow any ascetic attitude to life, but indulged everyone – himself included – in the advantages that were still only possible for a small minority.

The Marx found beyond the clichés is a living figure occupying a time as full of revolutionary news and social change as our own. This is the man, and the world he lives in, that we will now encounter.

But this book is not the first about Marx – only the latest in a nearly endless succession. What function will this particular book fulfil, then? To attempt an answer to this question, we have to cast a glance over the vast literature that exists. The main stress, of course, lies on the biographies – the books that in one way or another claim to deal with the complete Marx, his life and his works.

The Diversity of the Books

Eleanor Marx, his youngest daughter, was the first person who intended to write a biography of Karl Marx. But, apart from a few early articles, there were only incomplete notes, for reasons we will come back to. The notes are of great value as eyewitness accounts by a person who was intimately familiar.[14]

The earliest full-scale biography is by Franz Mehring, and was published in 1918. Mehring's book is solid; in addition, its particular strength lies in its historical proximity – Mehring knew Friedrich Engels personally. But his book, by today's standards, has its inevitable limitations in that relatively few of Marx's written works were yet known in 1918.[15]

The shadow of actually existing socialism falls over the literature that came out during the more than seventy years of the Soviet Union's history. Marx is either held up as the first great inspiration, or he is spared responsibility for what happened. The succession of more or less official biographies in the Soviet Union and the GDR had to be brought into harmony with the current regime. This did not prevent knowledgeable, well-balanced accounts from coming out in such an environment. Heinrich Gemkow's 1967 work, *Karl Marx: eine Biographie* should be held up in particular here.[16]

In Western Europe and the United States, many good biographies came out alongside bitter propaganda efforts. Some of them attempted to directly counteract both the devout tributes and the demonization of Marx. One example is Maximilien Rubel and Margaret Manale's 1975 work *Marx Without Myth*. The American author Allen Wood concentrated on Marx's works, and dealt with the biographical details in only a few pages in his 1981 book *Karl Marx*.

Another American, Jerrold Siegel, went in the opposite direction. In his book from 1978, *Marx's Fate: The Shape of a Life* he tried above all to capture Marx the man. It is an interesting personal portrait that nevertheless does not seem fully convincing. In his 1973 work *Karl Marx: His Life and Thought*, British author David McLellan strives to find a balance between the man and his works. It is an equally serious and ambitious biography that provides much important information. Marx's works are treated conscientiously, but closer textual analyses are often set behind a swarm of lengthy citations.

One lucid, easily accessible – but also cursory – work is German author Werner Blumenberg's 1962 book *Marx in Selbstzeugnissen und Bilddokumenten*, an English translation of which came out in 1972.

'Analytical Marxism' represents a special kind of interpretation of Marx. It aims at understanding and criticizing Marx's works with the tools of modern analytical philosophy. Norwegian author Jon Elster is the only one of the central representatives of the school who has written something that could resemble a biography of Marx: his 1986 work *An Introduction to Karl Marx*. It is a handy little book in which Marx's life is dealt with in a few pages, and the author keeps his works at arm's length, certain of what is valuable and what is worthless in it. Elster's book has the usual virtues of analytical philosophy – order and clarity – but also its shortcoming, an attitude of looking down at the object of study from on high.[17]

Back in the 1960s, the most comprehensive work about Marx's early development came out, in which Engels's childhood and youth were also dealt with: French author Auguste Cornu's *Karl Marx et Friedrich Engels: leur vie et leur œuvre* (1955–1970). Despite its four volumes, the work does not cover more than the time up until 1846, when Marx was twenty-eight and Engels twenty-six. It is written in the orthodox tradition but abounding in a wealth of detail, and it stays close to the sources. Anyone seeking the most certain information about Marx's background and earlier development can turn with confidence to Heinz Monz's 1973 book *Karl Marx: Grundlagen der Entwicklung zu Leben und Werk*.

After the Soviet epoch, the biographies changed their character. There is no longer a politically sanctioned tradition of interpretation to concur with or to repudiate. The relationship to Marx has also become more direct. British author Francis Wheen's 1999 contribution to the genre, *Karl Marx: A Biography*, is marked by a certain infectious rashness and enjoyed international success. Wheen wallows in both the comical and the tragic details of Marx's life, but only by way of exception does he go deeper into the reason Marx still arouses interest: his ideas and his works.

Less easygoing is American author Jonathan Sperber, who in his extensive 2013 biography *Karl Marx: A Nineteenth-century Life* prefers to paint its grey on grey. While most are astounded over the hunger for learning that pushed Marx further, as they are over the singular, colourful, and highly tragic in his life story, Sperber does not let himself be impressed. He absent-mindedly devotes half a page at the end of his account to Marx's literary appetite, which was aimed at everything from Aeschylus to Balzac. The metre-high stacks of excerpts that Marx produced under an intense life of readership elicit only a comment from him that it was terribly untidy in Marx's workroom with all those disorganized notes.[18]

Sperber's dour image of Marx may well be contrasted with the glowing colours in a biography a few years older – that of the famous French economist, author, and political adviser Jacques Attali's light and elegant 2005 work, *Karl Marx – l'esprit du monde*. Attali's chief merit is that he does justice to the many facets of Marx in an enjoyable way. But despite everything, even this is a book that deals more with his life than with his works. Descriptions form a beautifully shimmering diversity, but do not really create any idea of why this old German would still be topical.

Anyone who wants a genuinely penetrating introduction to Marx's works has reason to turn to a somewhat older book that nevertheless comes out in constantly new, reworked, and expanded editions: Michael Heinrich's 1991 work, *Die Wissenschaft vom Wert* (The Science of Value). The entire great project of *Capital* is in focus there. In this way, it joins a hard-to-grasp and rapidly growing specialized literature, which will here be presented in its given context. But Heinrich's actually follows Marx's development in its entirety, and can therefore also be seen as an intellectual biography that places great demands on its reader, but also yields bountiful rewards.

The once-vigorous Italian literature on Marx and Marxism has more or less run dry since the Italian Communist Party passed into being a general party of the left. There are exceptions, however. Philosopher Stefano Petrucciani wrote a handy 2009 biography simply titled *Marx*.[19] Since then, he has gone further with a more inspired 2012 study titled *A lezione da Marx* (Taking Lessons from Marx),[20] in which he discusses how we can approach Marx's texts today.[21]

A number of introductions to Marx's works have come out over the past few years, intended to initiate new readers into the old master's world of ideas. The foremost example is Thomas Petersen's and Malte Faber's solid, thought-provoking 2015 book, *Karl Marx und die Philosophie der Wirtschaft* (Karl Marx and the Philosophy of Economics), the third edition of which has already come out.[22]

Finally, I would like to mention a few short pamphlets by the celebrated British literary scholar Terry Eagleton. In 1999, he published *Marx*, a very small biography – in format, a longer essay – and in 2011, the somewhat more extensive *Why Marx Was Right* followed. The latter is not as apologetic as the title hints at, but is primarily an attempt to explain why Marx is still a current thinker in the twenty-first century.

That is an ambition that also inspires this book.

∼

After this review of the literature – in which many more titles could have been mentioned and where the selection is also marked by my ignorance of a number of important languages – it may seem odd to write yet another biography of this man who already has had so much written about him.

There is a crucial reason that I did it, after all. I believe myself capable of bringing something new in relation to previous biographies. One important reason is that I have devoted greater attention than usual to Marx's work in the biographical literature about him. His life history is also included here, in both its grand and its trivial details. But it is his writings that make Marx memorable, influential, and still important. I have carefully gone through everything he left behind, both complete documents and manuscripts. I have even reviewed the things that most researchers of Marx browsed past with a reflexive flick of the thumb. As regards the important works – with the great project bearing the name of *Capital* in the centre – I have tried to summarize current research and have also provided an overview that is entirely my own.

On a number of points, I feel I am capable of renovating the image of Marx the thinker and scholar. I show that the concept of alienation has a changed, but still central, place in his later works as well. It thereby also becomes possible to elaborate his little-developed theory of ideology. In general, I believe myself capable of explaining his relationship to his philosophical predecessors, particularly Hegel and his central conceptual framework. At the same time, I can indicate the significance of a broad cultural – and in particular, literary – structure for the whole body of Marx's work. I can derive his rapidly changing political position from his view of the relationship between political and social change. I can locate the border between him and his followers – yes, even between him and Engels: what is called Marxism, I argue, should by rights be called Engelsism.[23] Marx did not create a system. As a scholar and author he is more of a Faustian figure, constantly on the way deeper into the endless world of knowledge.

The Marx I wish to depict is firmly anchored in the nineteenth century. Its horizons were also his. At the same time, he stands out as a suitable red-hot critic of the capitalism that rules the world of the twenty-first century.

A Great, Unfinished Body of Work

Only a small part of what Marx wrote was printed during his lifetime. Most of it remained lying in incomplete manuscripts. Since then, posterity has gradually published what he left behind. Engels was first with the continuation of the only volume of *Capital* that Marx himself allowed the world to study. He not only reproduced Marx's text but also, by his own accord, filled in the gaps his friend left open.

Later publishers largely reproduced what Marx wrote. This was so when the *Economic and Philosophic Manuscripts* (also called the *Paris Manuscripts*) were published around 1930, showing a Marx that deviated from the standard picture being punched out at the time. So also a few decades later when another, equally astounding manuscript – the *Grundrisse* – surprised faithful readers of Marx with its existence.

An attempt at a critical edition of both Marx's and Engels's works was launched in Germany around 1930 (in connection with the *Economic and Philosophic Manuscripts* first being published). But Adolf Hitler put a stop to the project's continuation in 1933.

The first major edition of both Marx's and Engels's works was the *Marx-Engels-Werke*, or MEW, which was published in East Germany from 1956 onwards. It was not a critical edition. Works in French or English were reproduced in German translation; the long introductions were highly tendentious and carefully adapted to the prevailing political climate in the Soviet Union, and the text editions themselves had their shortcomings. Works considered dangerous to the official ideology – such as the *Economic and Philosophic Manuscripts* and the *Grundrisse* – were boxed off in supplementary volumes or only published much later.

These shortcomings would be rectified in and through the critical edition – the *Marx-Engels-Gesamtausgabe* – which, through its name, was already directly linked to the incomplete project from the 1930s. Its first volume came out in 1975, but after forty years the work is still far from completed. The gigantic proportions are a part of the explanation: the edition will eventually comprise approximately 120 volumes with accompanying extensive critical apparatus. Another contributing reason is the collapse of the

GDR and the Soviet Union. It took a while before the project got another backer (the Berlin-Brandenburg Academy of Sciences and Humanities). Now volume after volume is being published at a fairly rapid pace.

A critical review shows that the early volumes of MEGA have certain shortcomings that an observant reader must bear in mind.[24] The same sharp gaze has not been directed towards later parts of the edition. Nothing human is perfect. What shortcomings there may be are no longer due to the bad influence of the machineries of power in the GDR and the Soviet Union.

In any case, MEGA is the most outstanding edition, in principle containing everything (except the irretrievably lost) that Marx and Engels put down on paper. Much that previously lay inaccessible and hard to interpret in the archives is now available, and provides a richer, more complex image of both men than previously.

But important parts of the totality are still missing. A number of central works by Marx are, for the time being, only in the *Marx-Engels-Werke* or some other reasonably reliable edition.

On the other hand, *Capital* and all its preliminary work back to the *Grundrisse* have now been published in MEGA. It is possible for the first time to distinguish between Marx's own texts and Engels's contributions – something that is important, particularly as regards the third volume of *Capital*, to which Engels made extensive changes and supplements to what Marx wrote.[25]

In this case, we can know exactly what Marx wrote in his own hand. This is so for most of his texts. For a long time, Jenny Marx, his wife, made clean copies of his hard-to-read handwriting, but so far as can be determined, she made no additions of her own. There is, however, one notable exception: she made, by all appearances, her own small but not insubstantial contribution to her husband's manuscript for the *Communist Manifesto*.[26]

As regards the many newspaper articles Marx wrote in the *New York Daily Tribune*, it is sometimes difficult to precisely distinguish Engels's share, particularly concerning the purely linguistic formulation in English. As luck would have it, Marx's and Engels's styles of writing differ in a fundamental way. This makes it easy to determine when Marx, in all essentials, is the author of the articles.

The intent of this book is not only to provide an all-round picture of Marx and above all his work. It is also to entice into further reading. Marx is an exciting writer, sometimes brilliant, sometimes carefully investigative, often polemically razor-sharp – and occasionally coarse, or biased, or thoughtless. His repertoire of knowledge is substantial, his frames of reference are broad.

Texts by Marx have been my reading matter for more than fifty years now. In 1965, I published my first selection of writings from his youth – *Människans frigörelse* (The Liberation of Mankind) – and three years later came a book about the young Marx, *En värld att vinna* (A World to Win). In the 1970s, I became engrossed in Engels's philosophy and its relation to nineteenth-century scientific and ideological development. The result was a two-volume work published in 1977: *Motsatsernas spel* (The Play of Contradictions).

Over all the years that have passed since then, I have come back again, off and on, to questions about Marx and Engels, about Marxism and socialism and communism. In 2003, together with Björn Linnell, I published a selection of central Marx texts.

The book the reader now holds in their hands is the most extensive I have written about Marx. In principle, I try to cover all the important things Marx wrote. Against this background – before I give an account of the book's contents – it may be reasonable for me to say something about the most appropriate path into the world of Marx's ideas. These recommendations cannot be anything but highly personal.

The best beginning is the brilliant first section of the *Communist Manifesto*. The *Manifesto* as a whole is marked by the problems of the 1840s, by dreams of the future, and especially by the disputes among various factions of the left. But it is as if the prelude were written for our own time.

After that, it would be good to follow with the *Economic and Philosophic Manuscripts*. Marx soon abandons the ideas about human nature he brings forward there, but he holds on to the crucial ideas about what human life should be and what prevents it from being so in capitalist society.

It is best if the path into Marx's great theory of society goes through his little pamphlet *Value, Price, and Profit*, which originally was a few lectures he gave for the London members of the International Workingmen's Association – the famous First International – where he himself soon began setting the tone. It was at the same time as he was completing the first volume of *Capital*, and the lectures are an easily accessible introduction to several of the main thoughts there.

From there the path to *Capital* should lie open – this remarkable, powerful foundation of the theory, as eternally incomplete as Gaudí's Sagrada Família in Barcelona. The *Grundrisse* also lies within reach, as with everything else Marx left behind in the form of books, manuscripts, newspaper articles, excerpts, and letters. It should be a pleasure to read Marx – an intellectual and emotional adventure.

If I succeed in infecting any of my readers with this love of adventure, I will be satisfied.

A Guide Through the Work

The first chapter briefly depicts the historical background of Marx's life: the path from the industrial and political revolutions of the late 1700s to the age when electricity transformed the world and the social democratic parties began to be established.

The following four chapters cover Marx's life up through the revolutions of 1848–49. They deal first with his childhood and youth up until his marriage with the baroness Jenny von Westphalen and their departure from Germany.

After that it is the nineteenth-century capital of Paris that will come into focus both for the young family and for this account. Paris of the 1840s is a magnificent environment, and young Karl will become acquainted with both luxury and poverty, with both the finest salons and the dark places where rebellious journeymen gather and hammer out insidious plans. In this environment, he also begins the great project that would gradually be given the name of *Capital*.

But German (or more precisely, Prussian) police spies were on his trail all the time, and finally got him deported from Paris. He was forced to take refuge in Brussels, a considerably less colourful city. He and his new-found friend, Friedrich Engels, nevertheless created a small rebellious centre there and soon came into contact with like-minded people in London. From there, they were both tasked with working out a programme for the Communist League, which had now taken shape. Engels wrote the model for the *Communist Manifesto*, but it was Marx who completed the text and gave it its brilliant stylistic formulation.

The *Manifesto* came out just as a long-heralded revolution broke out, first in Paris and then in many other parts of Europe. Marx could have returned to Paris in triumph, though it was not in Paris that his strengths were needed most but in Cologne, where the rebellion was also in full swing. In Cologne, he became a celebrated journalist: like a red flag to a bull for some, a guiding star for others. But this time as well, the vigilant censorship was too much for him, and his paper – the *Neue Rheinische Zeitung* – had to be shut down. As always, Marx fought using only words, in newspaper columns or in other revolutionary organizations, but never with weapons. His friend Engels also tried his luck on the barricades. But the revolution was soon put down and reaction triumphed.

Now there was only one European country Marx could seek refuge in: Great Britain. It was in London that the rest of his and his family's lives would take place. The remaining chapters of the book deal with his activities there. This account is more systematic than chronological.

But the first terribly dark and heavy years in London deserve a particular description. The financial problems seemed to be too much, and the only possibility was a steady stream of money from Engels, who was now working in the family company of Ermen and Engels in Salford, outside Manchester. But Engels's money could not prevent several of the Marx children from falling ill and dying. For Jenny and Karl Marx, the pain was dreadful.

The situation was not improved by Karl most likely having had an affair with the family's maid, Helene Demuth, behind his wife's back. The result was a son, who was immediately given up.

At the same time, Marx tried to continue working as a journalist and author. The newspaper and journal articles are given their own chapter here. In particular, I look at his collaboration

with the *New York Daily Tribune*. Engels sometimes got to step
in as his ghostwriter, as Marx himself was occupied with his great
project on *Capital*. But he wrote most of them himself; the articles
unmistakably bear his mark, and on the other hand it is often
magnificent journalism and an important source for anyone who
wants to know how he concretely assessed the age in which he
lived. The picture of Marx and his works would be incomplete if
these articles are left out.

Nonetheless, his labour on the great theory of society was and
remains the backbone of his work. The first grand example of his
plans is a more than 700-page manuscript that he quickly compiled over a few months at the end of the 1850s, exhilarated by an
international economic crisis that he saw as a forerunner to social
revolution. This is known to posterity as the *Grundrisse* (the
'Outlines'), and it is a partially chaotic but in long parts extremely
profound, sometimes completely brilliant and thoroughly original
account. A thoroughgoing exposition is devoted to it here.

But Marx himself was not satisfied with the open form of the
Grundrisse and went over instead to a significantly more austere
setup. This became *Capital*, the first volume of which came out in
1867. More volumes were to have come, but Marx was never finished; it was Engels who, after Marx's death, completed Volumes
II and III. In particular, he put his mark on the third volume. Now
Marx's own text exists in a critical edition, and it thereby becomes
possible to make comparisons. The differences, as we shall see, are
significant.

Capital is the subject of an enormous amount of literature.
Interpretation often stands against interpretation. This diversity
will be illustrated as comprehensively as possible here, at the same
time as my own preferences are indicated. The chapter on *Capital*
is the most extensive, and perhaps also the most intensive, in the
book. Readers who tire out can be glad of the opportunity for
getting a good rest in the chapter's final section, 'The unknown
masterwork.'

Marx cannot be thought of without Engels, nor Engels without
Marx. In the literature about them, the issue of differences and
similarities is extremely controversial. Sometimes they are represented as intellectual twins, and sometimes it is said that Engels

completely misinterpreted his friend. Here, I attempt to provide a nuanced response. They were two distinctly different personalities united by a long, deep friendship complicated by Marx's financial dependency; at the same time, Engels never questioned that it was Marx who was the groundbreaking thinker and researcher. Their scientific interests coincided partially, but not completely. Marx was well acquainted with Engels's ambition to create a kind of philosophy that resulted in works such as *Anti-Dühring* and *Dialectics of Nature*, but the results made no impression on his own work. On the other hand, as we shall see, a few peripheral notes in *Capital* had unintended consequences both for what Engels achieved and for all of subsequent history. Engels was also the one who above all got to pass on the heritage once Marx was dead. He did it both reverentially and in his own way at one and the same time.

Marx and his politics is a chapter in itself. He was politically active during several important periods of his life; at the same time, he saw politics only as a form for society's real content, which was the way that class societies created and distributed resources among themselves. Political power was a confirmation and reinforcement of the basic relations of power. But it was also there that people became conscious of their own different interests.

Marx's fundamental understanding explains why, in his political activity, he sometimes appears as a man of compromises who wants to assemble a radical left, and sometimes as a caustic polemicist castigating those who do not have the same opinions as he does. Within the International, he succeeds in writing programmes that satisfy a broad spectrum of perceptions about how society should be changed. But when clashes of opinion between his followers and Bakunin's anarchists become sharp, he is again a man of battle and would rather let the organization come to nothing than engage in negotiations. At first, he greets the Paris Commune of 1871 with mistrust, but soon it fills him with enthusiasm. He follows the development of German social democracy with a certain ambivalence: his criticism of the first party programme is merciless but becomes crucial for the future.

With the chapter on his politics, Marx's life and work is illustrated in its various facets; the great question that must finally be asked still remains: what is the relationship between Marx and what is called Marxism? The answer requires a brief exposition of Marxism's varied history. From this it becomes clear that Marx is not a system builder, as both leading German social democrats and Lenin asserted. He was always on the road, never satisfied with the results he had reached, guided by what he himself calls a clue.

At the same time, much can be recognized in his attitude towards those who think differently than he does in the movement he inspired. He could be ruthless in his polemics, driving out those who diverged from organizations where he had a decisive influence. He was certainly not always like that; he could also work for compromises. But dialogue was not his natural medium. He pushed his own positions with unfailing force and energy.

It is nevertheless precisely that force and energy that makes Marx one of the great living classics – a classic that must constantly be brought up to date, especially in an age marked by ruthless capitalism. He is the master of the incomplete work and the excerpt, and he is the perpetual model of the close involvement of journalism and the detachment of *Capital*. He himself should not be regarded uncritically. Both the outstanding and the less tenable – yes, even the purely objectionable – must be held out under the light. This can only happen with a thoroughgoing exposition of what he achieved. Story, account, and analysis must be welded together into a totality.

Nostalgia is not an emotion suitable to Marx studies. We need him for the present, and for the future.

2

The Time of Revolutions

The Industrial Revolution

In many respects, Karl Marx was a child of the French Revolution of 1789. But it was another revolution – slower but even more sweeping – that above all would mark his life and works: the Industrial Revolution.

The term *industrial revolution* was developed by socialist thinkers in the early 1800s. The French radical Louis Auguste Blanqui was, as far as we know, the first person to use it to designate an entire epoch, and Friedrich Engels took over the usage in his 1845 book on the situation of the working class in England. Today, the Industrial Revolution is in history books everywhere.

But simply calling it a revolution can make its precise meaning unclear. The images of political revolutions govern its interpretations; barricades and battle formations appear in the mind's eye. But for the school of thought that Marx would come to leave his mark on, the process of industrialization was the most thorough-going – fundamental, in fact – revolution of another type.

Industrialization, unlike political revolutions, does not have a birth date. It is a process that is only possible to distinguish after it has achieved a certain scale. It had its beginnings in England, Scotland, and Wales during the second half of the eighteenth century and required a long series of prerequisites, such as the expansion of sheep-breeding and wool production and the over-population of the countryside, as well as a series of technological innovations – especially the continuing domestication of steam power.[1] The necessary infrastructure was established: first canals, and then – a few decades into the nineteenth century – railroads that were built for transport of both cargo and people.[2] The villages where this production was located began to grow rapidly and cities became increasingly bloated; factories were constructed wherever there was energy to run them, and coal dominated, quickly causing environmental destruction on a previously unseen scale. But the wheels clattered faster and faster and productivity increased, creating a new kind of more expansive but also riskier wealth than the great landed properties of the aristocracy or the plunder from colonialism. Periods of brilliant economic success were replaced by crises where stock lay unsold, and many of the recently wealthy became destitute. But those who made it through the wringer came out of the crisis strengthened, with enough resources to make use of constantly new technological aids; incessant societal reorganization helped fortunate owners enjoy the fruits of increasingly efficient production.

Cotton was the commodity that set industrialization going in Great Britain. Raw materials were brought from increasingly vast plantations in America, where people stolen from Africa worked under the inhumane conditions of slavery. The damp British climate turned out to be ideal for the cotton trade, and the machines required for processing were relatively cheap. The British, who had recently imported cotton fabrics from India, soon dominated the entire world market.

A few decades later, modern iron production began – heavier, more cost-intensive, but nevertheless brilliantly efficient in comparison with earlier techniques. Now Belgium and France – and soon enough, Germany and the United States – were in on the competition. In some places, industrialization became a state interest.

Iron was produced for consumption only as an exception: nails and kitchen utensils – but rarely iron girders – were bought for household needs. The iron industry provided capital goods. From start to finish, its expansion was associated with the railroads, which left their mark on the nineteenth century. People spoke of railroad mania; the pace of expansion was incredible. In 1830 there were only approximately thirty kilometres of railroad – primarily the Manchester–Liverpool line – and a decade later, 7,200 kilometres. In 1859 that distance had more than quintupled. And it continued until a large part of the world had been linked together in vast railroad networks.

But it was not only through the railroads that iron became important. The world revelled in enormous iron constructions like bridges, with the Eiffel Tower for the 1889 World's Fair the genre's crowning glory.

Steamers were another typical product of the Industrial Revolution that would fundamentally change the transport of commodities and people. The telegraph was yet another. With it, messages could be quickly sent from place to place and from country to country. Before then, trips on horseback had been the fastest transport for both people and messages. Now, horses had been left hopelessly behind.

Newspapers also underwent a great development with the new methods of communication. Using the new rotary press – in operation since 1846 – more and more could be printed in shorter periods of time. Thus, these technical innovations interacted with each other, reorganizing not only the physical world, but also people's thoughts and feelings. Throughout the nineteenth century, the press gained unprecedented power over minds.

Everywhere industrialization advanced, it brought not only new machinery, new forms of communication, and new products. It also transformed societies; its most revolutionary consequence was the production of two new social classes: industrial capitalists and industrial workers.

Capitalism was not born with industry. Merchant capital had already previously developed and was partially bound up with Europeans' combined voyages of discovery and expeditions of conquest. It became profitable to invest money in exports of domestic products and imports of much-coveted exotic goods; companies were formed, often under state management but with individual partners. Vast riches were thus amassed, which were invested in new projects in a widening spiral.

But merchant capital invested in commerce; the capitalists dabbled with trade. Industrial capital dealt, from start to finish, with production. It was a fairly motley crowd who embarked upon competition: from already prosperous bourgeois to mere adventurers. The operations were risky, and many would fold during the recurrent crises. But, gradually, a social class crystallized that despite internal competition was able to form a united front against other social classes. With distaste and fright, the old landowning aristocracy observed how these upstarts not only slapped together factories and flooded the market with new products, but also thereby usurped ever greater economic power. With that power came growing political influence and demands to be given a part of the landowners' privileges.

The other social class the bourgeoisie had to offer resistance to was the industrial workers. Most industrial workers were former agricultural workers driven off the land, but there was also a growing share of craftsmen who had lost their livelihoods in the fight against cheap industrial products. Rapidly growing multitudes of women, men, and children were united in industry. Like their masters, they represented something new in history.

To ensure profits from production, the industrial capitalists had to minimize their workers' wages. The ideal was that the workers would work as many hours as possible for compensation that was only just enough for their own and their children's survival. But with technological development, more could be produced in shorter periods. At first, many workers saw this development of machinery as a threat to their employment and attacked the machines with sledgehammers and other weapons. But this struggle was in vain, and they soon found a tactic that was much more effective. They joined together into what could be called the first unions (or, if you like, the embryo of the first workers' party). These workers were called the Chartists, after the list of demands (or charter) they united around. Their success was limited, and their ambitions of creating a new society were dashed. But the model for solidarity lived on, and despite intense resistance from their opponents the workers now and then succeeded in winning certain minor successes.[3]

The terrible conditions that industrial workers lived and worked in also roused consternation among many observers. Manchester in particular – the centre of the cotton industry – was a place of pilgrimage for a stream of travellers who, with alarm and indignation, witnessed what they assumed would be the future for all of humanity as long as no radical countermeasures were applied. In 1845, Benjamin Disraeli, who would soon stand out as the leader of the conservative British Tory Party, wrote a novel inspired by his observations in Manchester called *Sybil: Or the Two Nations*. In it, he vividly described the glaring differences between the slums the workers lived in and the wealth among the propertied classes. His remedy was a society in which everyone was incorporated into an organic unity where hierarchies were natural but no one lived in want or provocative affluence.

Another critical traveller was Scottish author Thomas Carlyle, who blamed the misery of the city on the disintegration of all natural human relationships, which were replaced by a society united only by money – what he called the *cash nexus*. What should have been miraculous – people being served by machines – was instead producing filth and misery.[4]

Manchester's residents wrote about it, too. James Philips Kay, a government doctor confronted with his city's poverty on a daily basis, described in detail the work, the sanitary conditions, and health in the factory and slum quarters. Friedrich Engels followed in his footsteps – but more on his contributions to the issue later.[5]

The grave working conditions also drew the attention of the government authorities. The British Parliament pushed through legislation shortening the working day to ten hours. The industrial capitalists fought tooth and nail against the reform. But it was carried out, and did not result in the collapse of industries; instead, it became a spur to further accelerating technological development so that more could be produced in a shorter amount of time.

The nineteenth century in which Karl Marx lived was just as revolutionary and changed just as rapidly as the decades that closed the twentieth and opened the twenty-first. Then, as now, people found it difficult to manage getting used to everything new.

Reorganization of the Sciences …

The Latin verb *revolvo*, which forms the basis for our word 'revolution', actually means 'to roll back' – that is, retake an earlier position. As late as the Middle Ages and the sixteenth and seventeenth centuries, the word 'revolution' was used for the constantly repeated movements of the planets.

In the eighteenth century, a completely new meaning set in. Now, revolution meant a thorough change. It was in this sense that people began talking about a revolution in the sciences with figures like Copernicus, Galileo, Kepler, and Newton, who replaced an earlier conception of the world with a new one. From the history of science, the new meaning of the word spread to politics.

The natural sciences have continued to be revolutionized again and again since then, but the designation 'scientific revolution' is still reserved for the changes in the sixteenth, seventeenth, and perhaps eighteenth centuries.[6]

On the threshold of the 1800s, the mechanics that Newton developed a century earlier were perfected. At around the same time, chemistry was given a completely new foundation by French scientist Antoine Lavoisier, who determined that oxygenation is crucial for the combustion process, both in organic substances and in living organisms. Quantitative determinations replaced the old, merely qualitative ones. Chemistry became one of the great conquering sciences of the nineteenth century. It transformed agriculture and became the basis for the dyeing industry and crucial for large parts of the development of medicine – pharmacology in particular. For many, it provided a new basis for a philosophy of life and conception of the world: was not everything – the activity of thinking included – ultimately a chemical process?

In physics, the energy principle – in the beginning called the law of constancy of force – would create a great stir in the middle of the century. Simply put, it meant that what were then seen as nature's fundamental forces could pass into each other. Mechanical movement, electricity, chemical reactions, and heat were thus linked together in a system of equilibrium. German physicist Rudolf Clausius aroused even more wonder in 1850 when he showed that heat can never completely pass into movement. The notion of eternal circulation was thus overthrown. The universe is moving inexorably towards stasis, which means that all processes will ultimately cease. For those who saw development as an endless process of advance, this truth was hard to swallow. The sun will die out and all humanity's achievements will come to naught. Pessimists, if anything, experienced a dull satisfaction.

Equally spectacular, but richer in practical consequences, was the rapid development of knowledge about electricity. As early as 1820, Danish physicist Hans Christian Ørsted had discovered that an electric current created a magnetic field, thereby laying the foundation for the theory of electromagnetism. English physicist Michael Faraday went further, laying out the principles for both the dynamo and the electric motor – or, in layman's terms, how movement is converted to electricity, and electricity into movement. He also became the father of electrolysis by showing how chemical compounds – water, for example – could be broken down with the help of electricity.

These, and a series of other scientific breakthroughs, laid the foundation for what is usually called the second scientific revolution.[7] It began at the end of Marx's life – he himself was fascinated by what he saw of the applications for both electricity and the new chemistry – and culminated prior to the First World War. Electricity was its greatest triumph – everything from the transmission of power over great distances to light bulbs that illuminated cities, workplaces, and homes.

There is an interesting difference between the first and the second industrial revolutions. The first in no way added to the most advanced science of the age. The principle of steam power has been known since antiquity, and the technological innovations required for the cotton industry, the early iron industry, and the coal trade presumed no great scientific breakthroughs. In the second revolution, on the other hand, research and technology met; which is why it also been called the technological revolution.

Developments in biology and medicine played a crucial role in the nineteenth-century conception of the world. At the centre, of course, was Charles Darwin's 1859 book, *The Origin of Species*.

There were many theories before him – going back to antiquity, in fact – that argued that animals and plants had changed over time. The problem was how the change itself was to be explained. In the eighteenth and nineteenth centuries, people generally sought the model in the most perfected scientific theory of the time: mechanics. It could explain how nebulae became planetary systems through the force of attraction. But organisms were so much more complicated.

Darwin went another way entirely. He found the model for his explanation in the breeding of domestic animals. Through cultivating certain desired characteristics, people developed breeds that corresponded to their wishes. Darwin spoke of this as an artificial selection. But he also discerned a natural one. Individual organisms of the same species differed significantly from each other. Certain variations were better suited to the environment where they lived; others succumbed. Changes could occur over time this way.

The Origin of Species created an enormous sensation. It collided with the creation story of the Bible. But it did not answer to the strict scientific requirement for conformity to laws; with Darwin, blind chance ruled.[8]

Those who let themselves be convinced often drew consequences for humanity and its world. Herbert Spencer, the English philosopher who wanted to summarize all knowledge into a system, had supplied Darwin with the watchword 'survival of the fittest' and applied the same thesis to human society. But there, the thesis went from description to norm: the less suited *should* perish – in fact, it was a mercy for them to disappear. From Spencer's ideas, a 'social Darwinism' developed in the United States that saw the ideal society as an arena for merciless competition where only the best survived.[9]

Against this interpretation of Darwinism, socialists and communists emphasized the role collaboration between individuals played in his theory. The Russian anarchist Peter Kropotkin maintained that species development progressed through mutual aid.

Conservative thinkers who accepted Darwin's thesis drew more pessimistic conclusions: humans were one animal among others, and that set limits for what type of society they could live in. Others used Darwin to support racist ideas. Darwin likened species development to a great tree. Could the human races then not be likened to small branches that naturally grew apart? *Should* they not be? Reasoning of this kind had disastrous consequences then, and still does today.

But Darwin was not all of nineteenth-century biology. Even before him, German researchers Matthias Jakob Schleiden and Theodor Schwann had shown that all living things consist of cells. Another German, Rudolf Virchow, deduced illnesses from changes in cells, becoming the father of cellular pathology.[10] French chemist Louis Pasteur proved the role of bacteria in illnesses. Research was nearing the borderlands between organic and inorganic, living and dead. There were biologists who already seemed to glimpse the answer to the question of the origins of life. Some asserted that they had created artificial cells, then as now.

Knowledge dealing specifically with humans, their societies and their history underwent a similarly grand development. Psychology as an independent discipline was created in the late 1800s, though still squeezed between philosophy and biology – and, in fact, even physics.[11] The unconscious depth of the soul had been a theme since the Romantic era, but only around the turn of the twentieth century did it form the centre of Sigmund Freud's psychoanalysis.[12]

Sociology is a child of the nineteenth century. Previously, society had been regarded above all from the point of view of politics. The political concept of *status* was now met by the *class* of sociology. People's collaboration and conflict in their daily lives became the subject of systematic study.

Statistics became important for development within sociology. It had older roots, but had now been made more stringent through the development of probability calculus at the turn of the nineteenth century. The Belgian Adolphe Quetelet created the concept of *l'homme moyen* (the 'average man') and tried to understand society as like a planetary system, in which the average being constituted the centre of gravitation.[13]

Political economy, or economics, played an important role at a time when capitalism was advancing victoriously over Europe and the world. The tradition from Adam Smith's 1776 book, *The Wealth of Nations*, was taken up independently by David Ricardo. But towards the end of the nineteenth century, Smith's central thesis – that the value of a commodity depended on the amount of work put into it – was increasingly abandoned. Instead, the relationship between supply and demand was regarded as crucial.[14]

Even historical research underwent great changes during the nineteenth century. The once-obscure tradition of source criticism gained clarity and conciseness. Textual criticism made similar advances through new, grandiose editions of classic texts and historical documents. Knowledge of the past became more certain as the works of great authors, composers, and artists were made accessible as never before.

… and of Philosophy

The sciences specialized rapidly during the nineteenth century. Fields of specialization became smaller, and new borders were drawn between spheres of authority. What was lost in breadth was gained in depth.

For the science from which nearly all modern disciplines issued – philosophy – specialization posed a challenge. Philosophy did not have obvious triumphs it could point back to. The questions of Plato and Aristotle remained under discussion.

Immanuel Kant, the eighteenth-century thinker who in many respects set the agenda for nineteenth-century philosophy, himself had a background in science and stated that philosophers should not ask questions about the truth of advanced science but instead investigate *why* it was true. Mechanics was constructed in the same way as geometry. It was based on a number of obvious truths (axioms) but nevertheless dealt with reality. With its help, of course, the movements of projectiles and heavenly bodies could be calculated.

Kant's solution was to see the foundations of mechanics, like those of geometry, in people's own understanding. The categories of understanding were also those of reality. The question of what reality is, beyond our knowledge of it, was impossible to ask.

But Kant also held that there *was* a reality independent of us, and his many followers soon discovered that this implied a problem. The category of cause and effect belonged to the categories of understanding, but if there was an outside world that affected us, must it not thereby somehow cause our knowledge of it?

Johann Gottlieb Fichte was among those who argued that we did not need to conceive a reality independent of ourselves. The world *is* our knowledge of it. It was a philosophical solution as productive as it was risky. The field lay open for grandiose speculation and passing fads. Those were the 'wild years' of German philosophy, as cultural and philosophical historian Rüdiger Safranski says. They fused partially with a powerful Romantic current centred on longing and feeling, imagination and creation. From this remarkable situation emerged the philosopher Friedrich Wilhelm Joseph Schelling, who built a bridge between art and biology. His initial successes were spectacular, inspiring a generation of young men and women in everything from literary composition to medicine. One of the most outstanding was his wife, Caroline Schlegel-Schelling, revolutionary and friend of Goethe. When she died prematurely, her husband ceased publishing books.

Another thinker took the German stage instead: Georg Wilhelm Friedrich Hegel. Hegel had the same philosophical background as Schelling, but other sources of inspiration as well, among them more down-to-earth Scottish economic theory. Schelling saw lightning-quick inspiration as the chief source of knowledge. According to Hegel, the road to insight was long and strenuous. He became the philosopher of development above all.

He called his method the *dialectic*, a concept from antiquity that denotes the art of setting argument against argument. According to him, it is not only thinking that advances dialectically, but reality as well. As a matter of fact, reality can only be provisionally distinguished from thought. They are part of an unceasing process characterized by what Hegel calls *Aufhebung*, or sublation.

Such, according to Hegel, is the paradigm of both thought and reality. Something disappears, but reappears in a more complex context. An example: before the French Revolution, royal absolutism prevailed. With the revolution, all the powers that be were overthrown. But it could not rest there; complete freedom passed into the reign of terror. Out of this emerged Napoleon, who under his rule moulded together freedom and authority. Or, in the artificial language of Hegelianism: after the negation follows the negation of the negation (which is called *synthesis* in some popularizations, although Hegel distanced himself from the word with its oblique meaning of 'final result').

For several decades, Hegel had great influence in Germany among both conservatives and radicals. Then came reaction; he was treated as 'a dead dog', as Marx says in *Capital*. But his reputation grew in a number of other countries, especially the United States and Great Britain. In the latter, he had a central role in both philosophy and political thought. Leading liberal thinkers were deeply influenced by him.

But philosophy also took many other paths around Europe and its relationship to the specialized sciences was managed in different ways. In France, Auguste Comte asserted that the philosopher should be a 'specialist in general ideas' who joined together all learning in a single system staking out the path from the simple and abstract (mathematics) to the most complex and concrete (what he called sociology). In England, Herbert Spencer – the man who both inspired and vulgarized Darwin – tried to do something similar.

Others wanted to go back to Kant's strict method, but to avoid the logical difficulty that made Fichte and others abandon him. The result was neo-Kantianism, which dominated philosophy in Germany – and also in part in Sweden – well into the twentieth century.

John Stuart Mill, an older contemporary of Marx, combined traditional British imperialism with influences from German idealism in his own way. Like Marx, he was an economist, but no subverter of the discipline. Politically, he was a radical liberal and wavered between capitalism and socialism. He stood miles away from Spencer's kind of merciless competitive liberalism.

Around the turn of the twentieth century, philosophy took new paths. In England, a few young academics rebelled against the predominant Hegelianism and laid the foundations of what would come to be called analytical philosophy. On the Continent, phenomenology took form. But now we are a good bit away from Marx's lifetime.

The only nineteenth-century philosopher who profoundly affected Marx was Hegel. He regarded the others with absent-minded interest or pure contempt. Nevertheless, they were important elements in the background against which his life and thought played out.

The Revolutions

The French Revolution was an obvious reference point for most Europeans in the 1800s. The mere memory of it struck terror into the privileged classes, and instilled hope among the discontented and rebellious.

It was a contradictory history. In only a few years, it changed its face again and again. It started as a protest against arbitrary royal power, and the powerlessness of the Third Estate against the nobility and the clergy. But its demands were soon radicalized, and new forces took over. Much was redone, from weights and measures and the calendar to schools and universities. Above all, relations among people were transformed. All revolutionaries agreed on greater political equality, even if not on how many would be given the right to vote. As regards social equality – the relation between the rich and the poor – opinions diverged widely.

The necessary background to the revolution was eighteenth-century France's combination of national destitution and brilliant intellectual creativity. The workers and small-scale craftsmen were starving; it was even worse for the immense rural underclass of small farmers and agricultural workers in the countryside. But before 1789, their combined wrath carried little weight against the absolute power that the king and his state apparatus possessed.

Absolute power observed with distaste how new, radical ideas spread in ever wider circles. The representatives of these ideas spoke of enlightenment, which would put superstition and prejudice to flight and question everything that had tradition as its sole support. The chief work of the Enlightenment was the

Encyclopédie of Diderot and d'Alembert, published from 1752 to 1772, in which human reason constituted the sole guiding star and all the facets of reality were analysed.

One of the original contributors to the encyclopaedia was Jean-Jacques Rousseau of Switzerland. But he soon left the project, and became the great naysayer of the Enlightenment. Faith in progress was hideous to him; his ideal was the simple life of a craftsman (but it is a lie that he ever would have wished to go 'back to nature'). At the same time, it was his conviction that the people – all the people – should govern the country.

It was this thought above all that guided the Jacobins, who with their leading representative Maximilien de Robespierre left their mark on the revolution during its most subversive period. It started with King Louis XVI and Queen Marie Antoinette being sentenced to death in 1793 and ended with the fall of Robespierre in July 1794. During their brief heyday, the Jacobins had the support of the more radical 'Hébertists', who under their leader Jacques René Hébert held a dominant position in Paris. But religion became a controversial issue between the Jacobins and the Hébertists. Hébert wanted to worship human reason alone. Robespierre, who believed in a sublime, rational God, could not tolerate that opinion and executed his opponent.

Tens of thousands of other men and women who deviated from Robespierre's line in one way or another shared Hébert's fate during what the Jacobins themselves called *la terreur*, the Reign of Terror. In the end, Robespierre and his closest followers fell victim to the wave of killing they had set in motion.

It is entirely too easy to reduce the period of Jacobin power to blood, tyranny, and executions. But it embraced more. There was a social pathos that was genuine. Property relations in society were to be changed. Everyone would get a portion of the country's welfare. This ambition aroused bitter opposition among social classes that believed they had a right to more than others.

For a short time, the Jacobins also implemented an idea launched back at the start of the revolution – that the right to vote should be linked to citizenship. Previously, it had always been associated with property; it was only property owners who were responsible for how society was governed. The Jacobins ensured the right to vote for all *male* citizens. But there were revolutionaries who wanted to go further and give *all* citizens, even women, the right to vote. There were three pioneers of this thinking: Olympe de Gouges, Anne-Josèphe Théroigne de Méricourt, and Jean Antoine de Condorcet. All three were brutally forced aside by the ruling Jacobins. Olympe de Gouges was among those executed.

After the fall of the Jacobins, a significantly more moderate faction took power. But ever since the beginning of the revolution, revolutionary France had been threatened by other powers, including its own aristocracy that had fled the country. Its enemies were successfully pushed back, but at the price of increasing militarization of the revolution. Ultimately, the cleverest and most successful of all the revolutionary generals took power alone: Napoleon Bonaparte, who after a few years proclaimed himself emperor. In some respects, Napoleon carried out the revolutionary programme; in many others, he broke completely with it. He was careful to keep the large majority of people on his side – for example, it was through a referendum that he ensured absolute power for himself, and he blocked all attempts to restore the privileges that applied before the revolution. He let the Jews – who, thanks to the revolution, could leave the ghettos – remain free; when Black slaves made a revolution similar to the French one in Haiti, however, he met them with brutal military force but was beaten back. He compromised with the Church, and created the modern state bureaucracy after the pattern of the army he so capably led. Above all, he was a warrior who traversed the European continent, victorious until he made the mistake of trying to conquer all of Russia. Weakened after the campaign for Moscow, he was defeated by his many enemies.

The victorious powers let France remain a Great Power, but at the price of the reactionaries' victory; a new king of the same dynasty as the old one was crowned, and the nobility and clergy waited hungrily to regain their privileges. But everything that had been changed during the revolutionary period up through Napoleon's rule could not be undone. The new regime met stiff resistance. Dissatisfaction fermented, and in 1830 the 'July Revolution' broke out. Although craftsmen played a decisive role on the barricades, it was the upper bourgeoisie who won the day.

A new king with limited power was installed, and the leading politician – François Guizot – restricted the right to vote to property owners. To everyone who could not reach the required level of assets, he directed a challenge: 'Get rich! Get rich!' (Charles Baudelaire, the first great poet of modernism, responded with the poem 'Get Drunk!')

Such challenges aroused a growing anger. But it was now not only in France that the sitting regime was threatened, but in almost all of Europe. The 1840s were a remarkable decade, brimming over with new political ideas and programmes. The finale came in February 1848, when revolutions broke out, first in France and then in country after country over a large part of the continent – in fact, the unrest spread all the way up to Scandinavia. The scent of victory was in the air; ordinary people – craftsmen and workers – were full of hope. But the rebellion failed everywhere. France even got a new emperor, a second Napoleon. In Great Britain, the country that had gone the furthest in industrial and economic development, absolutely nothing happened politically.

If anyone had said that these would be the last in the classic suite of revolutions initiated in 1640s England (where a king had also been executed, just as in France 150 years later), not many would have believed them. But that is how it was. Later revolutions on the continent came after devastating wars. Only one of them – the Russian Revolution in 1917 – resulted in a regime that was in existence for a longer period.

The deep economic crisis of 1856–57 did not lead to any political revolutions; afterwards, a prolonged economic boom set in that certainly did not lift the poor out of their poverty but nevertheless soothed their minds. A series of limited wars took place. Prussia emerged victorious from several showdowns with its neighbours, and after the last one – against France – a number of previously separate German states united in 1871 under Prussian supremacy in what was called the German Reich. Up until then, there had been a motley collection of kingdoms, duchies, and of free cities such as Hamburg and Bremen. (Some of the duchies were not much larger than a stage for light opera.) But even after Napoleon's defeat, Prussia had secured a dominant position among the German-speaking states. Its only real counterweight was the great Habsburg Empire, with its political centre in Vienna and an overwhelmingly non-German – Slavic or Hungarian – population. After the revolutions of 1848–49, Hungarian ruling families strengthened their position and the result was the Austro-Hungarian Empire, which existed until the end of the First World War.

But after 1871 the German Reich stood out as the strongest power on the European continent. After its victory against France, it subjugated two important French provinces: Alsace and Lorraine.

In war-torn France, a rebellion broke out in Paris, led by a motley band of craftsmen, workers, intellectuals, and even an officer. The result was the Paris Commune, a political experiment character- ized equally by creativity and confusion, and after two months it was brought to an end with great brutality by the recently defeated troops now led by a strong French bourgeoisie. Order was restored, but the memory of the short-lived experiment in socialism lived on, especially inspiring the revolutionaries in Russia.

The economic boom broke in 1873, but this did not lead to any great disturbances. Europe's Great Powers devoted themselves with renewed energy to subjugating territories in foreign lands – Africa in particular. Colonialism was not a new phenomenon; the Portuguese, Spanish, Dutch, and English had already conquered large territories on other continents – in fact, a number of smaller states had tried to grab some of the overabundance that coun- tries, defenceless against European cannons, offered. But towards the end of the nineteenth century and up to the First World War, this unscrupulous treatment accelerated. New states – above all Germany and Belgium – joined the race.

The world was nevertheless not large enough for the expanding European Great Powers to be satisfied indefinitely. People had long spoken about an impending war that, with Europe's dom- inance at the time, must become a world war. In 1914, this war actually broke out, and now it was European lives that were being obliterated with the same indifference that African lives recently had been.

This lies well beyond Marx's lifetime. Marx only experienced the prolonged economic crisis after 1873, and also the growth of a range of social democratic and socialist parties.

The outlines of his life can be summarized thus: He was born three years after the fall of Napoleon. He was seven when the first train rolled on its rails. He was thirty when the European revolution broke out, and a little over forty when Darwin's epoch-making work was published. He managed to experience several of capitalism's periods of prosperity and its crises. Before he died, both the telephone and the light bulb had been invented. But the First World War still lay far off, and it was even longer until the October Revolution in Russia as well as the first governments led by social democratic parties.

But enough with the preliminaries. Now the story can begin.

3

The Darling of Fortune

Background

Karl Marx was born in Trier, Germany's oldest city, which has its origins in the Roman era. Its most famous building is the Porta Nigra, constructed more than 1,800 years ago. Since then, Trier has passed under many masters. Today, it constitutes Germany's outpost against Luxembourg. When Marx was born, it had just been conquered by Prussia.[1]

As part of the Rhineland, Trier had belonged to France only a few years earlier. French troops had taken the city in 1794, and the laws of the Republic had been introduced. The new regime was greeted joyfully, primarily by the young and well educated, who had been deeply affected by the slogan of liberty, equality, and fraternity. Others viewed French anti-religious policy, which affected both the Catholic majority and the Protestant and Jewish minorities, with horror. For the majority of the people in Trier, living in difficult conditions, the changes did not mean as much as the spokesmen of the revolution had hoped. On the one hand, the great French market was opened to them; on the other, endless war meant great trials.

When Napoleon seized power, he turned the organization of the army into the norm for the whole of society. In the domain of the schools in particular, the military model became a straitjacket. One of its sharpest critics was named Johan Hugo Wyttenbach, a pedagogue who eventually became the headmaster of the high school in Trier – the high school Marx attended. When Wyttenbach became headmaster, Napoleon had already been deposed and Trier had fallen to Prussia. Wyttenbach was among those who greeted the Prussians as liberators, during a period when a previously unknown German nationalism had seized many intellectuals. But, like many, he soon grew disappointed in the new regime when it crushed freedom of speech and turned its back on everything connected with the Enlightenment.[2]

Most in Trier, perhaps, never had any illusions about their northern German masters. A period of reaction set in after the fall of Napoleon. The chief instrument of the reaction was the Holy Alliance, which Prussia had entered into with Russia and the Habsburg Empire. The ideal of revolution had to be combated, and the bonds between political power and religious power were to be fastened again, even more firmly.

This entire atmosphere was foreign to the leading circles of Trier. The new order also meant acute economic difficulties. Now the French market was closed; only the local ones remained. In the countryside outside Trier in particular, poverty had long been severe; now the farmers – especially the grape farmers, creators of the famous Mosel wine – were subject to pure destitution. The prices for agricultural products fell, wine prices hit bottom, and taxes simultaneously became heavier. Even the city dwellers tasted oppression in ample measure. The poor got poorer, craftsmen were reduced to poverty, teachers and priests had less and less to live on, and the standard of living for the previously rather well-to-do markedly worsened. In addition, the least expression of popular dissatisfaction became the subject of repression by the Prussian authorities.

Certainly, there were reasons for unease and suspicion among the new powers that be. Courts and other local authorities were trying to act on their own. Most of the leading circles of the city had been, and remained, adherents of French Revolutionary ideas, interpreted in a more or less radical spirit.

Seditious ideas were also aired in books and newspapers. Ludwig Gall, who worked in the city administration, published a pamphlet in 1825 in which he attacked the egoism of the propertied class and claimed that far too few represented the interests that could bind the entire population together. While the 'capitalists and landowners' were enriching themselves, the majority of the people were sinking into ever deeper poverty. Things were getting worse for the day labourers, the farmers, and the craftsmen. Something now had to be done for their sake!

The *Trierische Zeitung* published lines of thought similar to Gall's. The newspaper had started printing in 1814, radicalizing gradually until it began advocating socialism around 1840.[3]

The Prussian authorities became even more furious when influential men developed ideas that seemed to directly threaten north German supremacy. After the French Revolution, there were various Casino Societies (*Casinogesellschaften*) founded in numerous German cities; one of them was in Trier. Despite its declared political neutrality, the society became a forum for radical sentiments.

The July Revolution of 1830 in France, which overthrew the reactionary king Charles X, roused hopes in the Rhineland of a similar development there. Rumours circulated that war would break out between France and Prussia. One of the heads of the city, Johann Ludwig von Westphalen – Karl Marx's future father-in-law – declared that reactions in the Rhineland would hardly be marked by German patriotism in the event of open conflict.

Even after the military situation calmed down, hope for change in political structures was sustained for many years, finding its most noteworthy expression in a party the Trier Casino Society arranged in January 1834. Everyone was in high spirits, we are told, and the mood climbed even higher when they sang the Marseillaise in unison. The pro–July Revolution song, La Parisienne, evoked rapture. One of the participants pulled out a *tricouleur* flag, stood on his chair, and waved it. This symbol of revolution quickly became the subject – as one observer noted – of 'a nearly religious veneration'. A certain Brixius, a lawyer, declared, 'Without the French Revolution, we would now be eating hay like cattle.'

Those who stood out at the event were primarily lawyers. One of them, Heinrich Marx – Karl's father – acted with greater caution, as far as can be judged. According to reliable witnesses, he left the party before the most provocative demonstrations had begun.[4] At the time, his son Karl was a high school student, barely sixteen years old.

The party inevitably came to the attention of the Prussian authorities. Brixius the lawyer was held primarily responsible for the seditious activity, and was charged with high treason. The court in Trier acquitted him – something the Prussians would not allow, and so appealed the decision. But the higher court in Cologne also found the charge to be groundless, and there the matter rested.

By the standards of the time, Trier was a politically radical city. Lord Mayor Wilhelm Haw, who also had a background as a lawyer, was a Freemason and quickly became a source of annoyance for the foreign masters. He expressed himself frankly in various contexts – on behalf of his office, no less – and was suspected, like many others, of housing sympathies for the new July monarchy in France. At dinners, he would propose toasts for freedom of the press and of humanity, and turn against the monarchy. His defence of the Casino party of 1834 did not endear him to Prussian eyes. Ultimately the contradictions became acute, and those like Haw who demanded the city's autonomy met ever stronger resistance. The situation became intolerable. and Haw resigned at the end of 1840. This did not mean that passive resistance came to an end. But it was the case that Prussia entered a more reactionary phase as a new king, Friedrich Wilhelm IV, ascended the throne.

Family

Karl Marx belonged to a family of rabbis. His uncle Samuel was the chief rabbi of Trier, and his grandfather and a number of ancestors were rabbis before him. Karl's mother was named Henriette, and her maiden name was Pressburg. She was from Nijmegen in the Netherlands, and never learned to speak or write fluent German. Her parents, by all appearances, had come to Nijmegen from Bratislava. Karl's maternal grandfather was said to have been a merchant and money changer. But there were numerous rabbis in Henriette Pressburg's family as well. It is possible that through his mother, Karl was distantly related to the great poet Heinrich Heine, who gradually became his close friend. One of

Karl's aunts married Lion Philips, a successful industrialist and grandfather to the founder of Philips, the large, still-flourishing multinational company.

Henriette Marx bore nine children, but only four survived her (she was born in 1788 and died in 1863): besides Karl, there were three daughters. Tuberculosis put the others into an early grave.[5] Their eldest son, Mauritz David, did not even live to four. The story of Marx's sister Henriette is a gripping one; she fell ill early but persisted in getting married, convinced that marriage would cure her. But she died after a few months. Karl's next younger brother Hermann lived to be twenty-three. He had gone into commerce, first in Amsterdam and then in Brussels. In a letter to Karl, their father exclaimed that Hermann was truly kind-hearted, but lacked talent. Tuberculosis took his life as well.

Youngest brother Eduard's life was even shorter – he was only eleven. 'Write to him as if he were healthy,' Heinrich Marx encouraged his son Karl in a letter the same year Eduard died.[6] The youngest sister, Caroline, died at the age of twenty-two.

Karl's older sister Sophia was the sibling who meant the most to Karl. She admired him immensely and wrote passionate letters to him. In 1842, she married a lawyer in Maastricht, and thus moved to her mother's old native country. She survived her younger brother, dying in 1886.

The spouse of younger sister Louise was also a Dutch lawyer, but the family moved to Cape Town in South Africa in the 1850s. Emilie, on the other hand, kept to the area where she grew up, starting a family with a local civil servant and living out her life in Trier. It was she, the youngest surviving daughter, who as time went on took care of their mother. Emilie, who lived until 1893, was in contact with Karl's family all the time, and claimed herself that in many respects she was similar to her famous brother.[7]

Karl Marx also had problems with his lungs, which excused him from military service. Karl's weak chest sometimes worried his father. For his mother, who otherwise called him *ein Glückskind*, a darling of fortune, her son's health was a constant concern.[8] Karl lived more than sixty years with his bad lungs, though it was a pulmonary illness that ultimately laid him in his grave.

Karl's father, Heinrich Marx, had a French lawyer's education; after his degree, he returned to his hometown of Trier and began to work as a lawyer. When Prussia took over command of the city, it soon became evident that Heinrich's Jewish faith would give him difficulties in his career. He quickly converted to Christianity – specifically, the Evangelical, or Lutheran doctrine. Only a minority of the city belonged to it, to be sure – most were Catholic – but on the other hand it was the state religion of the Prussian masters. There is nothing indicating that this was a big step for Heinrich Marx. He was a child of the Enlightenment in its milder version, in which the ideals of reason and tolerance were united with the belief in a sublime, merciful, and just God.[9] Karl and his siblings were not baptized before 1825, the year in which Karl would begin attending a Lutheran school. Their mother converted even later, and unwillingly.

Heinrich Marx was a successful defence lawyer. Caution characterized everything he did. But he was also a man of principle, and turned emphatically against both usury and exceptional laws for Jews. His private finances were in extremely good order, and he left a small fortune behind.[10]

Heinrich Marx died on 10 May 1838, at the age of sixty-one. His son Karl had been home a few days earlier, celebrating his twentieth birthday on 5 May. On the 7th, he had travelled back to Berlin. Contemporary sources are surprisingly quiet about Karl's reaction to his father's death. Later testimony speaks that much more strongly to the fact that Karl mourned him for as long as he lived. Karl's youngest daughter Eleanor testifies that 'Marx was deeply attached to his father. He never tired of talking about him, and always carried an old daguerreotype of his father with him'. They found this photo in his breast pocket when he died, along with a portrait depicting his wife, Jenny, and his recently deceased eldest daughter. Engels placed the three pictures in Marx's coffin.[11]

It is not surprising that the memory of his father followed him throughout his life. They were very close to each other. Family tradition says that Karl was only seven when his father began having intellectual conversations with him. The most eloquent image of the relationship between father and son comes from the letters between them during the son's student years. We will return to them shortly.

Many disparaging words have been written about Henriette Marx, particularly over the last few decades. Jerrold Siegel, who in his biography of Marx makes partial use of psychoanalytical keys, asserts that she had an excessive need of control and tried for a long time to intrude into Karl's life. It was in his attempts to emancipate himself from her, and from a feeling of power-lessness, that her son developed a habit of sudden outbursts of rage. Francis Wheen calls her 'an uneducated, in fact half-literate woman', obviously without properly considering that she had a native language other than German and that she had never attended a formal school. Wheen also asserts that Karl's relation-ship with her was a poor one, and that for a long time he wished her dead.

On the other hand, the person who dug deepest into Marx's family relations – Heinz Monz – reports nothing about Marx disliking his mother. There is at least one document that men-tions the opposite: a letter Marx wrote as late as 1861 to socialist leader Ferdinand Lassalle. In it, he says that he has been to Trier and visited the then seventy-three-year-old Henriette Marx. He certainly had every reason to be friendly with her, since she had just torn up some old IOUs. But that was no reason to state the following nuanced opinion: 'Incidentally, the old woman also intrigued me by her exceedingly subtle spirit and unshak-able equanimity.' Karl Marx, that singularly honest man, would never have stated such an opinion if he detested or despised his mother.[12]

Student and Poet

We do not know much about Karl Marx's early years. His sisters related a number of anecdotes about him being a real little tyrant, who did things such as making them eat mud pies. Of course, the truth in these stories – which are now standard in Marx biogra-phies – cannot be judged.[13]

Only in 1835, when he was to take his school examination in
Trier, does he become fully visible in the documents. He had been
trained in the kind of high school sketched out by Wilhelm von
Humboldt a few decades earlier, where Latin and Greek dominated the curriculum.

All his student writings have been preserved and are carefully
reproduced in the *Marx-Engels-Gesamtausgabe*.[14] In Latin, it was
a matter of writing a long essay, in one's own words, on a given
subject. Marx and his fellow students were to answer the question
of whether the reign of Augustus could be counted among the
happiest in the history of the Roman Empire. Marx's response
is balanced. The era of Augustus is compared on the one hand
with the old Republic a few centuries earlier, and on the other
hand with the reign of Nero. The latter is quickly and easily dismissed; it was characterized by the most shameful arbitrariness
and murders of its foremost citizens. On the contrary, there was
a lot to be said of the early Republic: the simplicity of its morals,
fulfilment of one's duties, and the altruism of its civil servants.
Spiritual cultivation worthy of the name did not exist, however,
and the era was marked by violent party conflicts between patri-
cian and plebeian. What spoke against the Augustan era was that
every semblance of freedom had disappeared. On the other hand,
Caesar was lenient, and culture blossomed under him. Moreover,
the military successes were superb. In short, the Augustan era is
quite rightly counted among the best. QED.

The essay follows the morals of Latin education of the time.
Cato the Elder's praise of the strict, character-building customs
of times past had to find expression, and Nero's reign of terror
dismissed. The loss of freedom under the empire cannot be left
unchallenged, but it is well outweighed by the culture, the leni-
ency, and the military successes. Marx's opinions, in short, are
flexible towards the prevalent norms. In addition, he shows that
he has a good Latin vocabulary and the ability to write long sentences with many interwoven subordinate clauses.

Latin also required what was known as an *extemporale*, in
which the teacher slowly read a text in German that the students
would translate directly into Latin. In Greek, it was a matter of
turning a few paragraphs from Sophocles' *Women of Trachis*, a

text the class had not previously become acquainted with, into German. The opposite applied in French; a German text was to be translated.

Mathematics was a subject of which Humboldt thought highly. The mathematics teacher in Trier complained about the students not receiving enough instruction in the subject, and he was therefore lenient in grading their efforts. Four problems were to be solved: two in geometry, and two in algebra. Marx only took up three; one that dealt with money, interest, and amortizations (a subject to which he would later devote a great deal of labour) was left unsolved.

The candidates also had to interpret the text concerning a short Bible quotation, and the results inevitably became a small sermon (however difficult it is to think of Karl Marx in the pulpit, his pious interpretation sounds quite convincing). In his German essay, the freedom to express oneself personally was greatest. The prescribed subject was 'Reflections of a Young Man on the Choice of a Profession'. The theme is a classic one: Hercules choosing between the narrow path of duty and the broad path of sin. Marx starts off with one of humanism's central theses of defiance. Whereas other creatures have their given roles in creation, humans are alone in freely being able to choose what they will do with their lives. Of course, the Deity does not leave them alone, Marx says, but the divine voice can easily be drowned out by fantasy and emotions can lead them astray. The important thing is not to shine, but to deserve respect. It is not good enough to be a passive instrument for others; humans must be independently creative. At the same time, it is a matter of being of maximum benefit for others. We should not egoistically search for our own satisfaction; our happiness belongs to the millions.

That last sentence could be interpreted as a presentiment of Marx's later ideas. But, in this case, it is illusory; his classmates expressed similar thoughts, and their inspiration was undoubtedly Wyttenbach, the school's headmaster. His cautious Enlightenment thinking resounded in his students' written compositions.

Incidentally, Wyttenbach himself corrected the essay. He praised its contents but found fault with 'an excessive striving after unusual, flowery expressions' (*ein übertriebenes Suchen nach einem seltenen, bilderreichen Ausdruck*). This was the reaction of a man of the Enlightenment to a text whose author had obviously imbibed a great deal of the style of Romanticism. There were no Romantics in the collegium in Trier.

Both the Latin essay and the one on religion received good marks. In the *extemporale* he made a great deal of blunders, but so did his classmates; it was a difficult task. The translation into French, however, was said to indicate certain shortcomings in diligence, whereas the paper in mathematics was clearly marked as passing. The worst was Greek. The translation of Sophocles was 'mediocre at the most' according to his teacher, Vitus Loers.

All in all, Marx's performances were relatively good. He was only seventeen years old – thereby among the youngest – and placed sixth out of twenty-two students who passed (in addition, ten students failed).

It is hardly likely that Karl Marx would have been a high school student who concentrated entirely on the prescribed lessons in school. Later, as a university student, he devoted at least a rather absent-minded interest in the courses he signed up for. Even as a high school student, he had developed a burning interest in contemporary literature, starting to write his own poetry in the Romantic style.

What is more, his relationship with Vitus Loers, the teacher who found his Greek translation so mediocre, was quite tense. He refused to pay the farewell visit to Loers that, according to etiquette, students should have done with their teachers before they set off to university. Loers was offended, and Marx's father had to try to smooth over the insult. But Heinrich Marx was no admirer of Loers. Loers was the Trojan horse in the high school at Trier. Among his colleagues who preferred to direct their gazes towards Paris rather than Berlin, he was the only one who took the side of the government. The authorities rewarded him by making him headmaster alongside Wyttenbach. Heinrich Marx was shocked.[15]

Karl was a capable student, but all the same not brilliant. He was young, but Edgar von Westphalen – his closest friend in his class – was a year younger and nevertheless got better grades than he did. Both belonged to the ranks of the privileged, for whom high school studies seemed self-evident right from the beginning. They were surrounded by numerous, far older sons of farmers who had had a longer way to go, and who could only hope for a modest future as Catholic priests in the countryside.

Karl Marx's career was also regarded as fairly certain: he would become a lawyer, like his father. He therefore set off for the university in Bonn to study law. It is during this time that we can begin to divine more of his personality. The sources begin to speak through his letters. At that time, he also became a studious poet. To be sure, he had already started to try his luck as a poet at the end of his time in high school. But now the inspiration flowed.

As a poet, Marx was chiefly a Romantic. The leading individuals in Trier stood closer to the Enlightenment. Freedom and reason, and moderate religious faith had still been guiding lights long after the breakthrough of Romanticism. But Edgar von Westphalen's father – Marx's future father-in-law – may have influenced him early on.

In Bonn worked August Wilhelm Schlegel, one of Romanticism's most important advocates. Even in the 1790s, Schlegel had been among the central figures of the small circle in Jena that had given wings to the ideas of Romanticism. Now, several decades later, he stood at the lecturer's desk in Bonn and had the young Karl Marx among his listeners. But it was certainly not he who inspired the young man sitting at his feet to outbursts of Romanticism. Not one line in Marx's poems indicates that he had been influenced by the typical Romantic conception of the world, with its inspiration from nature. It was instead a younger Romantic, marked by abrupt changes from sincerity to scorn and from rapture to despair, who caught his attention. Heinrich Heine was a master of the genre, but Marx was no Heine. He was only one of many students writing poetry in the Bonn of his time. Together with other like-minded students, he lived a typical student life in the manner of the 1830s, with merry parties and pranks. Poetry was an important element of the environment. Over a few years, Marx wrote large quantities of poetry. In the great edition of his collected writings, poetry takes up a total of 234 large, rather dense pages.[16]

Heinrich Marx regarded his son's poetry with a mixture of admiration and alarm. His reactions can be read in the stream of letters he wrote to Karl. 'I have read your poem word for word,' he declares in an early letter, but adds: 'I quite frankly confess, dear Karl, that I do not understand it, neither its true meaning nor its tendency.' It was surely not his son's view that happiness could only be found in abstract idealization, in keeping with his enthusiasm?

It is likely that the poem that frightened him so is called 'Wunsch' (Desire), included in the collection of copies of poems Karl's sister Sophie made, thereby saving it for posterity. It is certainly a discordant, wild poem that expresses a young man's despairing search for something to follow when a 'dark demon' is ravaging his inner being. Heinrich Marx was certainly also shocked about the defiant atheism the poem expresses. It could be the reason he brought up the importance of a belief in God in the same letter. Heinrich himself was no fanatic; his son knew this. But faith is a need in human beings, and there are moments in life when even the atheist has to turn to the Most High.[17]

His father's reactions did not deter Karl from sending him additional works of poetry. 'It is kind of you to send me your poems, although you know I am not of a poetic nature,' writes Heinrich in another letter. He confesses that he himself, even during his first love affair, could not burst out in verse. But he is of course thankful for the poems.[18]

In a letter from the end of 1836, a mild irony can be divined from Heinrich Marx's words. Against his son's poetry, he sets his own prose dealing with money and material security. Karl had evidently hinted that he preferred to aim at a career in academia than one in law. Good, his father says, do so; respectable poetry could perhaps be the first lever in such a career. Although would it not be simpler to be a lawyer? Karl did not have as difficult a path to go on as his father.

When Heinrich Marx turned sixty in April 1837, Karl sent him a full collection 'as a small token of eternal love'.[19] There is a lofty dedication to his father, as well as ballads and romances. But the wild and the beautiful are suddenly broken in a few sarcastic, rather earthy epigrams. In one of them, the German sits in his armchair, 'stupid and dumb', and tries to imagine away the drama that history is playing out, which will soon drag him along in it.[20] In another epigram, the name Hegel turns up for the first time. He is denoted there sometimes with 'he', and sometimes with 'I' – a sign of identification. The third stanza is quite interesting:

> Kant and Fichte soar to heavens blue
>   Seeking for some distant land,
> I but seek to grasp profound and true
>   That which – in the street I find.

The lines are not memorable as poetry, but as the first expression of a form of thinking who would play a crucial role in all of Marx's future writings. We will meet it again and again – heaven set against earth, head against feet, the concrete against the abstract. Hegel is still on the correct, down-to-earth side; in fact, he seems to have woken the young poet up to a new insight. One day, this would sound different.

The epigram, like a number of other poems in the birthday present to his father, suggests a more realistic style in Marx. But the Romantic has not yet been eliminated. The collection concludes with a longer draft of a 'humorous novel', *Scorpion and Felix*.[21]

We know nothing of his father's reaction. As we have already seen, he was moderately entertained by his son's poetry. It could possibly help the boy in an academic career, he thought, but then it had to be solid. The Romantic fittings were foreign in the extreme for Heinrich Marx, a man of the Enlightenment.

Jenny von Westphalen

Another recipient of Karl Marx's poetry appreciated it all the more. Her name was Jenny von Westphalen and she was an older sister of Edgar, Karl's classmate and friend. Through Edgar, Karl became like one of the family in the von Westphalen household.

Like Heinrich Marx, Jenny and Edgar's father Ludwig von

Westphalen was a lawyer. He was a great man in Trier, highly placed in the regional government with responsibility for things such as prisons, the police service, fire protection, and statistics. But despite a considerable salary, his financial position was never as solid as Heinrich Marx's. Both men knew each other well. They were both members of the Casino Society and opponents of Prussia's claim to power. They were also both cautious men.

According to what Karl Marx told his daughter Eleanor much later, Ludwig von Westphalen was the man who awakened young Karl's lifelong interest in literature, Shakespeare and Dante in particular. That was likely the fact of the matter. Heinrich Marx was, as we have seen, a down-to-earth type, a stranger to poetry. It could not have been he, or the old-fashioned teachers at the high school in Trier, who stirred up the poetic vein in Karl.[22]

In the Westphalen household, Karl also found his great love, Jenny, four years his senior. In the beginning, Jenny was somewhat hesitant before Karl's tokens of love – he was still a very young man and she was decidedly more mature. But she was soon captivated by him.

Their love was never without complications. There was a class distinction between them: she was nobility, and he came from a family of rabbis. Moreover, he was a somewhat unruly young man who often had too much of a good time at university. Her significantly older half-brother Ferdinand, who would gradually have a career in grand style and become a reactionary minister of the interior in Prussia, was a furious opponent of the relationship. Eventually, when Karl's opinions swung far to the left, Ferdinand even put police spies on his brother-in-law. But Jenny's and Karl's relationship had unswerving support in her father, who early on had detected Karl's unusual gifts and charm.

In the Marx family, the blossoming romance was at first met with joy and wonder. In a letter that is otherwise brimming with indignation, Heinrich Marx stresses that the young man with his splendid gifts, parents who love him, and 'a girl whom thousands envy you' is a darling of fortune.[23] Karl's sister Sophie was previously a friend of Jenny's and was tremendously pleased with the relationship between her and the brother she adored. Your sisters love you 'beyond all measure', she wrote to him. And Jenny as well! She visits us often, Sophie told him, and she 'wept tears of delight and pain on receiving your poems'.[24]

The poems in question were an extensive collection dedicated to 'my dear, eternally beloved Jenny v. Westphalen'. The title is not modest: *Buch der Lieder* (Book of Songs). Its chief source of inspiration is obviously Heinrich Heine's famous book of poems from 1827, also called *Buch der Lieder*. Compared with this singular masterwork, the eighteen-year-old's attempt falls hopelessly short. On the other hand, the emotions Karl Marx expresses are warm, and his Romantic flame is strong and clear. Here harps resound, and a landscape that could be reminiscent of Caspar David Friedrich's famous painting *Wanderer Above the Sea of Fog* opens out. Cliffs loom large, and under them the fog lies thick. But soon the wanderer stands outside the window of his beloved, and a dialogue à la Romeo and Juliet plays itself out. The young Karl is a good rhymer, and holds rigidly to the meter. He could even write sonnets without trembling at a rhyme or a syllable.

In a poem called simply 'An Jenny' (To Jenny), he professes his boundless love, but also an anxiety and a pain that are so great that he could long for annihilation. These are the usual violent swings of a great love affair, depicted in Goethe's *Egmont* with the unrivalled lines 'Himmelhoch jauchzend, zum Tode betrübt …' (Rejoicing to heaven, grieving to death …).[25]

Jenny now became the natural centre, not only of Marx's poetry but of his life as well. But his relationship with his parents – and his father in particular – mark his early life in another way.

Father and Son

The correspondence between Heinrich and Karl Marx contains much more than Heinrich's reactions to his son's poetry. In fact, it provides a quite eloquent picture – at least of the father's relationship to the son. There is only one letter from Karl preserved: a letter that is much longer, to which we will soon return. Other letters from him we can deduce have been lost, since his father comments on them. But a consistent feature of the correspondence is Heinrich's complaints that his son is so stingy in his letter-writing.

'You know your mother and how anxious she is, and yet you show this boundless negligence!' Heinrich writes in the very first letter, three weeks after his son's departure.[26] Karl must have said something indignant in response to this, and his father tried to calm him down. But the reproaches for his inadequate diligence in writing letters recur again and again.

Another more conspicuous theme is money. In his father's eyes, the young Karl Marx is wasteful. Why does he constantly need more, without saying what he needs it for? His father reminds him that Karl is not the only child in the family. The necessities should be enough, even for a student. Do not forget, a lawyer's income is not unlimited![27]

The son tries to clarify his expenses, but the account makes the father indignant. The figures are completely out of order, he writes. Orderliness must be demanded even from a learned man, to say nothing of a lawyer.[28]

Heinrich Marx soon concluded that student life in Bonn was entirely too attractive for the young Karl. Better that his studies be located in the capital of Prussia – Berlin, with its military and civil servants. That would straighten the boy out. Heinrich wrote a letter of attorney saying that he not only allowed, but also actively wished for his son to change his place of study.[29]

And so it was done. The still only eighteen-year-old Karl Marx moved his studies to Berlin. The university there had just inaugurated a new era in the history of higher education by making research a mandatory part of university teachers' work. Education and research were thereby linked in a single programme of instruction that was nonetheless difficult to realize. But neither did Karl Marx now become the exemplary student his father had hoped for. He gave himself up to philosophy, and was soon lost to any career as a lawyer.

His financial wastefulness did not diminish; quite the contrary. Karl continued to waste unreasonable amounts of money. During his first year in Berlin, he spent almost 700 thalers, his father points out. It was an enormous sum, considering that the richest young men with the same dispositions had to be satisfied with 500. The father was not even managing to pull in as much money as the son was consuming.

There is concern throughout the father's letters that his son will not know how to set limits in his life. This concerned not only money, but lifestyle. Particularly in the beginning of the correspondence, there are many anxious admonitions that Karl not forget to exercise, and moreover to be abstinent with food and drink. His mother, who often wrote small additions to Heinrich's letters, goes into more detail, as officious as she is tender. Order and cleanliness are not side issues, she enjoins him. Scour with soap and a brush! Be careful with wine and coffee, and with pepper as well. Don't go to sleep too late, and get up early, don't catch cold, and don't dance. With the addition: '[Y]ou are the kindest and best.'

The father also worried that in his studies the son would try to take on too much. In Bonn, he had applied to entirely too many colleges. He was spreading himself thin, his father complained, adding: 'The field of knowledge is immeasurable, and time is short.' It was a matter of limiting himself. But it only got worse in Berlin.

The culmination is the long letter Karl wrote to his father in November 1837. It was preceded by correspondence in which only his parents' letters remain. In the first letter, Heinrich Marx appeals to his son's 'better self', to his passion and his tenderness of heart, and to his ability to overcome his stormy idiosyncrasies and his unhealthy sensitivity. There is thus a brief description of the young Karl as his father sees him: passionate and kind-hearted on the one hand, and on the other oversensitive and unbalanced. His hope was in the better self. Did not Karl himself say he was the darling of fortune? Should not he at least think of the girl who was sacrificing her distinguished position and her wonderful future prospects to follow him into a 'greyer future'?

The long letter from Karl in response only added to his parents' worry. In his mind's eye, Heinrich conjured up an image of his son in a dressing gown, in the gloomy light of an oil lamp, unkempt, ruminating over the mysteries of the world without regard for either respectability or his poor father's concerns.

His son could not even write home regularly, Heinrich complained. When he did put something down on paper, the result was a fragment that from beginning to end indicated indecision

and division. Heinrich wrote of *Zerrissenheit* – inner turmoil –
and at the same time confessed how poorly he thought of that
'modern word' that all 'cowards hide behind'. And now Karl was
joining such a contemptible crowd!

Full of indignation, the father – a man of the Enlightenment –
exclaimed: 'Do not blame nature. It has certainly treated you like
a mother. It has given you strength enough, the will is left to man.'
But faced with the first difficulties he met on the way, this darling
of fortune was gripped by *Zerrissenheit* ('shattered heart' in the
Collected Works). It indicated weakness and an unmanly character. On top of it all, Karl was wasting money. This may seem
prosaic to you, Heinrich writes sarcastically. A man who discovers
a new philosophical system nearly every day cannot devote any
attention to trifles like money.

This is the tone of the letters that were now following in quite
rapid succession. But in the last letter to his son, the words are
more lenient. Out of fatigue, I cannot go on, but lay down my
weapons, Heinrich says. He still finds it difficult, however, to put
up with the wastefulness, he adds.[30]

Part of the matter was that during Karl's years in Berlin,
Heinrich had been sick and was getting worse. He as well was
succumbing to the family's curse – tuberculosis. He spent most
of his time visiting spas with his wife Henriette. His cough was
becoming more and more severe, as was his fatigue.

The correspondence indicates that Heinrich Marx thought
highly of his son's talents. It can also be understood, indirectly,
that Karl gladly expressed his positive feelings for his father.
Heinrich Marx is often mildly deprecating before the sentimental
words Karl clearly directed towards him in his letters, now lost.

The relationship between them both was naturally unequal at
heart. Financially, Karl was completely dependent on his father.
In his letters, he had to justify all the money he felt he needed for
his life as a student. He was therefore eager not only to emphasize
how diligently he was studying, but also to point out his devotion.

At heart, father and son were very different. Heinrich Marx
was a cautious man. Life had taught him to navigate carefully.
When Prussia took power over Trier, he found it difficult to realize
his career plans as a lawyer. He was forced to renounce his faith.

Even after he became both a Lutheran and successful in his profession, he knew he was vulnerable. Anti-Semitism had blossomed with German nationalism during the Napoleonic Wars, and it did not halt before an approved profession of faith. He did not betray his ideals, but he avoided demonstratively defying the authorities.

He constantly advised his son to secure a profession, preferably as a lawyer. An academic career could also be possible, but it required patrons.

Karl Marx was anything but cautious. He did not doubt his ability to get by in the world. More than that, in fact; he believed he knew he was going to accomplish something big. He was not afraid of defying the authorities and flouting conventions. He believed he was able to devour tremendous amounts of information, applied to a long series of courses, and threw himself into various activities. And he wasted money.

Nothing depicts the image of the very young Karl Marx so clearly as his only preserved letter to his father.

The Letter to His Father

It was on 10 November 1837 that Karl began his letter. But he was not finished with it until just before four o'clock in the morning of the next day. With it, he offered his father an image of the unkempt youth in a dressing gown, pale and brooding in the shifting light, with the dark Berlin night outside.[31]

It is a long letter; hardly a fragment, as Heinrich Marx alleged. But it certainly indicates *Zerrissenheit* – inner turmoil, a restless chase among different areas of interest and fields of study, endless wrestling with the great questions of philosophy, and moreover a pining for his chosen one, the beautiful baroness back home in Trier, Jenny von Westphalen.

In print, the letter takes up eight large pages. Its style is lofty and fateful. Karl is facing a new phase in his life; a new era is dawning, and as with world history it is a matter for the individual to scrutinize both the present and what has been. It is easy for the individual to become lyrical, 'for every metamorphosis is partly a swan song, partly the overture to a great new poem, which endeavours to achieve a stable form in brilliant colours that still emerge into one another'. Grand words – but Karl had mastered this lofty aesthetic prose to perfection; his sentences are strong, well formed, and rhetorically effective.

In his letter, he summarizes the year in Berlin that has passed. It was first marked by longing for Jenny and the flight from everyday life into lyricism. But this lyricism became 'owing to my attitude and whole previous development ... purely idealistic'. In short, reality faded away and nature with it; mere castles in the air remained. But his feelings were warm, and this can certainly be seen in the three notebooks of poetry he sent to his beloved.

Nevertheless, lyricism had to remain a spare-time occupation – he was going to devote himself to law, he quickly added. He had written extensive extracts from legal literature, in which he had also tried to develop principles of legal philosophy. The contradiction between what is and what should be, so typical of idealism, was then revealed in full force. He ended up in forms devoid of content, and material without order. It was necessary to devote himself completely to philosophy, and he hastily created a complete philosophical system that also turned out to be unsustainable.

But his thirst for activity was not satisfied; he seems to have kept up with it all. He read and took careful notes about works on the history of art and of history, he translated Tacitus and Ovid from the Latin, and he obtained textbooks in English and Italian grammar – though without getting anywhere. But after so much learned drudgery, he had to devote himself completely to literary creation for a time. The results were such things as a draft of the fantastical novel in verse in the style of E. T. A. Hoffmann, *Scorpion and Felix*, which we have already encountered.

The fragment still exists, and it is completely in the style of Hoffmann. A mildly absurd Hoffmannesque spirit rests not only over the narrative, but also over the letter that paints a picture of a young man throwing himself into his many interests, and who seems ready to sacrifice comfort and a bourgeois future in order to make his way to a conclusive insight, regardless of what it is.

Hoffmann had lived in Berlin at the end of his relatively short life. It was not him that the young Marx finally chose as his guiding star, but another great spirit who also passed his final, most successful years in Berlin: the philosopher Hegel. After having floated around in the world of ideas in the company of Kant and Fichte, Karl Marx came to the conclusion that the idea must be sought 'in reality itself'. 'If previously the gods had dwelt above the earth, they now became its centre.' These are thoughts we recognize from the poem about that same Hegel that Marx dedicated to his father. But previously, he now said, he had been repelled by 'the grotesque craggy melody ... which did not appeal to me'. Now he had found his way to it, even if after further digressions into various works of legal and philosophical literature that he sometimes made excerpts from, sometimes translated, and sometimes made the starting point for dialogues in the style of Plato. His many pursuits finally made him sick, and he had to seek out fresh air in the country outside Berlin. The illness was his salvation, because he then managed to acquaint himself with the various parts of Hegel's philosophy, and additionally get to know 'most of his disciples' personally. By those means, he gained entry to a 'Doctors' Club', for whose members Hegel's philosophy was the common denominator.

Faced with these fireworks of thoughts and impulses, his father became thoroughly frightened. His reaction seems rather natural, considering that Heinrich Marx's greatest wish was that his son would choose an education that led to a profession and a secure income. Karl had chosen his own path. But was it a path, and not more or less untrodden terrain?

The Young Hegelians

The 'Doctors' Club' Marx spoke about was no formal association, but a loose amalgamation of young men who met to discuss the great philosophical questions of the time in a free, jovial atmosphere. The designation 'Doctors' Club' is Marx's own, and as far as is known there is no instance of it anywhere else.[32] Marx was not yet a doctor, but the other members he mentioned had their theses behind them. Oldest among them was the leader, Bruno Bauer. He was nine years older than Marx, and already a good bit into an academic career.

Hegel's thinking was the magnet that held the Doctors' Club together. Marx and his friends interpreted Hegel in a radical direction. Hegel was the philosopher of unceasing change, they emphasized. Every stage of history had to create its own antithesis.

An opponent of this radical thinking spoke furiously of 'Hegelings'. But that designation did not stick; instead, the prevalent name soon became 'Young Hegelian'. The name gained currency in 1838, and it was codified in an influential 1841 pamphlet by Bruno Bauer: *Die Posaune des jüngsten Gerichts über Hegel den Atheisten und Antichristen* (The Trumpet of the Last Judgement against Hegel the Atheist and Antichrist). There were Young Hegelians of this kind not only in Berlin, but also in many other places around the German states, and soon after in other quarters as well. A little later, they were given an alternative name: *Die Hegelsche Linke* – the Left Hegelians.

In Berlin, these young leftists held animated conversations in various beer halls in the university quarter near Friedrichstrasse and Dorotheenstrasse. It was here Karl Marx (still only a student) was admitted as a full member – in fact, as a central figure. Bruno Bauer soon saw in him his closest collaborator.

Religion occupied the Young Hegelians' attention. Criticism of the Bible had become an important speciality in Germany of the 1830s, and it did not halt even before the Holy of Holies. David Friedrich Strauss, who learned much from Hegel but left Berlin for Tübingen early on, had by the mid-1830s published *Das Leben Jesu* (The Life of Jesus), a book that enjoyed great public success.[33] Bauer himself was a theologian, and continued along the same path. The Bible was regarded primarily as a historical document and not as holy scripture, and it would thereafter be scrutinized closely. Later, Bauer would go so far as to deny that Jesus ever existed.

But in Prussia, the step from religion to politics was not a long one. Lutheranism was the state religion. The Church was a political power. Criticism of the foundations of Christianity was easily perceived as criticism of the State itself. William J. Brazill, author of a monograph on the Young Hegelians, thus made a mistake when he counted Marx out of the group with the justification that criticism of religion was not his main interest. Politics was very much a concern for the Young Hegelians, and Marx played an important, if brief, role among them.[34]

Even Marx's future friend, Friedrich Engels, would acquaint himself with the group in Berlin for a time. Engels was performing his military service in the city then, and took the opportunity to participate in its intellectual life. He did not meet Marx, who had already left, but he socialized with many of the other Young Hegelians. Engels, a rather talented draftsman, depicted a lively scene from November 1842. At the time, the Berlin group had expanded with several new and important members, and with a temporary visitor named Arnold Ruge as well. Ruge, who at the time was otherwise in Halle or Dresden, stands in one corner of the drawing, gesticulating excitedly. A dispute is obviously playing out between him and Bruno Bauer, also gesticulating. Max Stirner, who a few years later in 1844 would publish *Der Einzige und sein Eigentum* (The Ego and Its Own), also appears to be engaged in the heated conversation. The others present seem to be less interested. A few newspapers are lying on the floor, as well as an overturned chair. A number of glasses are standing on a table, and in the upper left-hand corner, Engels has drawn a squirrel. The squirrel symbolizes the Prussian censor, who signified a constant nuisance for the Young Hegelians. The minister in Prussia who monitored such things as the sanctity of religion and the limits of the printed word, was named Eichhorn – German for 'squirrel'.[35]

By the time he made the drawing, Engels had already published a few articles as well as some pamphlets, either anonymously or under the pseudonym Friedrich Oswald. A letter he wrote to Arnold Ruge a few months before the drawing indicates that he was capable of writing more; his style was already easy and flowing. But now he hesitated. He was still young, he wrote; he needed to study more, and he was no philosopher by profession.

As his drawing shows, he nevertheless continued to socialize in the circle of Young Hegelians. At that time, the Berlin group had begun to appear under the joint name of *Die Freien*, 'The Free'. It was a designation neither Marx nor Engels wanted anything to do with. On the contrary, 'The Free' soon became the subject of their scorn and derision.

The most important thing Engels had written up until then was a series of articles and a few small pamphlets about Friedrich Wilhelm Joseph Schelling, at one time a herald of new thought in Germany but now an older, conservative philosopher of a clearly theistic and Christian hue.

Schelling had been summoned to Berlin with the task of uprooting the 'dragon seed of Hegelian pantheism'. Prussia had a new king, Friedrich Wilhelm IV, and with him a partially new ideology. Many had hoped for a turn to greater liberty. The opposite happened. The king was a Romantic and a deeply Christian conservative, and his closest advisers were of the same type. Hegel and his many disciples, scattered from right to left, were abominations to men with such a conception of the world. God, according to Hegel, was a spirit that was both the driving force and the goal of the development of everything. Early on, many had seen pantheism – the doctrine that God is in everything – in this philosophy. Now, the powers that be in Prussia were talking about the same thing; but unlike Hegel's earlier adversaries, they could put power behind their words. The summons of Schelling to Berlin was one of their measures – if not the most powerful one, then the most spectacular.

On 15 November 1841, Schelling began holding his lectures. Interest was at a boiling point. Approximately four hundred listeners attended; many of them are found in the history books. We can ignore the leading bigwigs of the city, the generals, and other persons of authority whose presence more marked the goodwill of royal power than it did a burning interest in philosophy. But even the aging Alexander von Humboldt, the discoverer and natural scientist, was there, as was the historian Leopold von Ranke and legal historian Friedrich Carl von Savigny. Was it interest that drove them, or courtesy towards a colleague?

Among the younger – and they made up most of the audience – the passion for the free play of ideas was even greater. Many expected something extraordinary. Mikhail Bakunin, the future revolutionary who at the time was quite well incorporated into the group of Young Hegelians in Berlin, was there; Friedrich Engels was as well. Arnold Ruge had travelled up from Halle for the event (in a letter, he described the excitement prior to Schelling's appearance as *unglaublich*, 'unbelievable'). Jacob Burckhardt, who much later would write his epoch-making book on Renaissance culture in Italy, was in the audience. So was a young Danish man, Søren Aabye Kierkegaard, as yet unknown to the world. In fact, only Karl Marx was missing.

Schelling began his lecture by emphasizing 'the significance of the moment'. Implicit in his message: he intended to found an epoch yet again, as he had done in his youth. At the same moment, confusion broke out in the hall. The doors flew open, and new listeners streamed in. No one wanted to miss out on this singular occasion. But the continuation was tamer than expected. Schelling spoke about his great predecessors, Kant and Fichte. He did not mention Hegel, and the reason was not just that he was to uproot the dragon seed of pantheism Hegel had sown, in accordance with his task. It was evident as he went on that he saw Hegel as an imitator, who in his thinking had certainly got into various dead ends but in his best moments echoed Schelling's ideas.

Schelling had named his lecture series *Philosophie der Offenbarung*, 'Philosophy of Revelation', and that title captured the entire philosophical system he had been working on for decades without ever coming to a conclusion. The starting point of the first lecture was the distinction between essence and existence. Through reason we sense the essence of an object – what makes a chair a chair, or a person a person. But existence is a question for experience. It is only with our senses that we can verify whether or not a certain object exists. Schelling calls the philosophy that proceeds from essence *negative*. Like Hegel, he himself had pursued it once. But now he wanted to go the opposite way and start with experience – in short, with what exists.

At least one of his listeners – Kierkegaard – was deeply moved by this first lecture. It was as if Schelling anticipated his own development towards thought in which the bare existence of humanity is the initial, and most important, question of philosophy. But with the following lectures, Schelling disappointed him. Positive philosophy sought existence in mythology. That was not where Kierkegaard wanted to be. In his diary, he wrote disparagingly about the man at the lecturer's desk.

Others had been hostile right from the start, and not only

because they still stood on Hegel's side. For them, Schelling above all was a tool of the repression the new king was exercising. It was in that spirit that Friedrich Engels began to speak. He first did so in a few articles in *Telegraph für Deutschland* in December 1841, and thereafter in two small booklets that came out the following year: *Schelling und die Offenbarung* (Schelling and Revelation) and *Schelling, der Philosoph in Christo* (Schelling, the Philosopher in Christ). Both were published under a pseudonym.

Engels defended Hegel – or rather, the Hegelian school – against Schelling's attacks. He pointed out how unreasonable it was that Schelling, on the one hand, described Hegel as his own epigone, and on the other asserted that Hegel's philosophy is misleading and has dangerous consequences for society. But Engels also took up Schelling's new positive philosophy and its claim to entail a safe defence of Christianity. Engels grew up in a strictly Pietistic home, and was thoroughly conversant with the Bible, as well as with the various tricks in its defence. At the same time, he saw himself as a radical pursuer of the Hegelian project. He was keen to emphasize the kind of power Hegelianism had become after the death of its master.[36]

If we look at the effect the authorities in Berlin had hoped for, Schelling's lectures were a fiasco. The only interest they aroused came from posterity, and the posthumous edition of his *Philosophie der Offenbarung* is now counted among the classics. But a development of this kind was not in the interests of the Berlin powers. In its efforts to annihilate the dragon, it had on hand other, heavier tools than philosophical lectures. Opinions proved impossible to govern, but with the institutions that lay directly in the hands of the state a better attempt could be made.

Hegel was a philosopher of the state. This is often said, but the expression can be misinterpreted. In the 1820s, he witnessed several of his best students being persecuted and even imprisoned in the hunt for enemies of the state. Cautious as always, he nevertheless got involved in their cause.[37] He was already dead when the strict conservative interpretation of his political thought was given a brief official status for a few years in the 1830s. But that interpretation never reigned supreme, and Hegel himself would likely not have been satisfied with the politics that cited him.

If he himself was not a state philosopher, the state had a central place in his thought. He distinguished between different classes (social, not economic) in society. 'Der Mittelstand' – the middle, or general, class – held a unique position. The qualifier 'middle' could mean that the class found itself in the middle of the societal hierarchy, above the business class and under the nobility. But the decisive content was something else: by virtue of its education and its sense of justice, the middle class could constitute an intermediary between different interests, weigh them against each other and choose to represent reason above the combatants. Hegel counted not only the genuine servants of the state, but also university teachers very much among the middle class. It was in fact the professors who developed and conveyed the knowledge crucial for the development of the state.[38]

Hegel thereby ascribed a key role in society to himself and his colleagues. In emphasizing the crucial significance of the middle class, he formed part of an important tradition that had developed in earnest chiefly in Prussia after the catastrophic defeat against Napoleon. All forces had to be gathered. Those in authority concluded that the revolution was a constant threat, but a return to the old way was impossible. Prussia could not match France in military strength, or England in economic vitality. What remained was the path of education and cautious change. In this process, civil servants and academics had to take the lead. It was in that spirit that Wilhelm von Humboldt developed his ideas about a reformed school system and an entirely new kind of university in Berlin. Leading politicians Karl Freiherr vom Stein and Karl August Fürst von Hardenberg agreed.

Modern reformism was born in this environment. Its first standard-bearers were civil servants and professors. Hegel became one of the latter when he was summoned to Berlin in 1816. His disciples, whether conservative or radical, followed his path as far as possible.

It was a thorny path from the very start. After the fall of Napoleon, Prussia joined the Holy Alliance with Russia at its head. Radical forces, especially students, demanded a modern constitution. One student, Karl Sand, took to violence and murdered the author August von Kotzebue, who had been exposed as

a Russian spy. The reaction was violent, with increased censorship
and other freedoms curtailed.

Hegel navigated cautiously in these troubled waters. As a professor, he enjoyed a certain freedom in expressing his opinion
from the lecturer's desk. But as soon as he went to publish, he
was subject to censorship like everyone else. His summary of his
political and philosophical ideas in *Elements of the Philosophy
of Right* from 1821 is a marvel of caution; in it, he turns aside
from the lectures he was holding on the subject at the same time.
'What is rational is real, and what is real is rational,' he says in the
Preface.[39] This could be interpreted as an unquestioning tribute
to the established order of things: everything has already been
arranged in the best conceivable way. Heinrich Heine, who was
among Hegel's enthusiastic students around 1820, claimed that,
in his lectures, Hegel said that the real *becomes* rational and thus
the goal of a process of improvement. Only recently has it been
found that Heine was right. A long series of notes Hegel's students
made when they followed his lectures have been published; they
point in Heine's direction.[40]

Despite the ravages of reaction, Hegel did not abandon his
cautious reformism. In that regard, most of his followers were
faithful to him – at least for as long as they could cherish hopes
of being able to work within the university system. The Young
Hegelians are a good example. From their professorial chairs and
through their writings, they hoped to develop Prussia and the
other German states in a radical direction.

Arnold Ruge and Bruno Bauer, who were both close to Marx
during a crucial period, were among those who aimed to make a
contribution within 'the civil service intelligentsia' (*die beamtete
Intelligenz*). In 1840, Ruge distanced himself from revolutionary
changes, which he associated with Romanticism, and he pointed
out that theory and science offered a less bloody battlefield. It
was there that the battle could be fought with some prospect of
success, and the path of success was that of reforms.[41]

The other Young Hegelians cherished the same kind of hopes.
Bruno Bauer, the leading figure among them, seemed to be on the
way to a professorship at the theological faculty in Bonn. It was
the minister of culture himself, Karl Stein von Altenstein, who

cleared the way for him, and Bauer saw his happiness assured. And not just his! At a university where his own point of view – so common in Berlin – was completely unique, he wanted to see his promising young friend and fellow traveller Karl Marx as his colleague as soon as possible. And Marx was far from unwilling.

A living picture of the course of events comes out of the stream of letters Bauer wrote to Marx.[42] Marx was a much more sluggish letter-writer; Bauer complained about missed responses just as Marx's father had done earlier. Marx obviously wrote something, however, as Bauer's correspondence shows. But the letters no longer remain.

Through Bauer, on the other hand, we are given a lively glimpse inside the university in Bonn. He finds it extremely wretched. His colleagues are narrow-minded, and their prejudices against Hegelianism monumental. He scares them out of their wits by announcing a lecture series on 'The Life of Jesus and criticism of the Gospel according to John'. What chasms opened before their eyes under the word 'criticism'!

Bauer also insistently encourages Marx to rid himself of 'the despicable examination' and finally become a doctor. But it is a matter of being careful in his doctoral thesis. Every indiscretion could be held against the author. You also need to think of your future bride, Bauer admonishes. If you fail to secure a career through some attack, you also cloud her future. But, he adds consolingly, once anyone has captured a professorial chair they can say what they will. The freedom of teaching as prescribed by law protects them.

Caution was not Marx's chief virtue. When he presented his thesis, he took the opportunity to make a few magnificent and deeply untactical attacks. His older friend was shocked. But for a little while longer, there was hope for a future under the protection of the university. Bauer still lingered in Bonn. There was only one problem: the final appointment was late in coming. But it would surely soon come? And with his thesis behind him, Marx could join him.

There is reason to stop a moment before this thesis. It did not determine Marx's destiny. But it says something important about both his educational path and his ideals at the time he wrote it.

The Doctoral Thesis

Marx completed his thesis swiftly and boldly. He began his work in the summer of 1840 and was finished in March the following year. He would defend his degree in Jena. The most important reason for that was that the university there lay beyond the reach of Prussian authority. It was under the protection of a few small duchies in Thuringia, with Sachsen-Weimar at their head. Another reason may have been that the teachers in Jena at the time were considered to be rather indulgent. They caused no trouble for those students who wanted to get on quickly, and Marx – so he still thought – was in a hurry to Bonn.

Only a few decades earlier, Jena had been the centre of a great intellectual development. From his lofty position in the neighbouring city of Weimar, Goethe had kept his hand on the university and seen to it that not only his fellow poet Schiller received a professorship, but also that the philosophers Fichte and Schelling could work there for a few years and gather substantial crowds of listeners below their lecturer's desks. In only a few years, they and other young intellectual heroes had turned Jena into Germany's most famous university towns.

But, with the Napoleonic Wars, Jena sank bank into its earlier obscurity, with mediocre teachers and students whose chief interests seemed to be beer and pranks. The leading philosopher was named Karl Friedrich Bachmann, and he could hardly be said to be particularly bright. He found himself, however, in the immediate vicinity of the best and brightest; he had sat at the feet of Schelling and Hegel, and cultivated his mineralogical interests in Goethe's company. He remained faithful to Jena, and had received an ordinary professorship there back in 1813. Hegel was his principal master, but later on in life he began to estrange himself from the man. In the end, he frontally attacked Hegel's method of identifying thought and being, idea and reality; he did this in 1833 with a publication titled *Über Hegels System und die nochmalige Umgestaltung der Philosophie* (On Hegel's System and the New Transfiguration of Philosophy). It became his most noted work, and the subject of numerous counterattacks from Hegelians.

It was to this man, Bachmann, that Marx turned in a letter of 6 April 1841. The letter was endowed with the then-customary polite phrases of the 'honourable Sir' type, but otherwise it was – to say the least – straight to the point. Marx enclosed a formal letter to the faculty drawn up in Latin, his thesis manuscript, his curriculum vitae, previous examination marks and the mandatory fee, and expressed the desire that in the event his thesis could be approved, his case be expedited so that he could receive his diploma. He could only stay at his address in Berlin – Schützenstrasse 68 – for an additional few weeks, and it was important for him to receive his rank of doctor before his departure.[43]

Bachmann was neither frightened nor annoyed by the young man's resolute tone. Only a week after the letter left Berlin, he was ready to deliver his opinion to the faculty of philosophy in Jena. He called Marx 'a very worthy candidate' and said that the thesis testified to 'as much intelligence (*Geist*) and acumen as wide reading'. There was one little mistake the candidate was guilty of – in the Latin petition to the faculty he spoke of a master's degree. This should be pointed out to him: he was to become a doctor, and that in Latin as well. Bachmann added that Marx had sent in too much money for the diploma. The excess amount would be sent back.[44]

That was how simply Marx earned his Ph.D. He did not need to present himself in Jena, much less defend his thesis against any opponents. In any case, he attended his conferment ceremony. He became 'Doctor Marx'. New adventures now awaited.

The thesis Bachmann approved so quickly is of moderate size, but must still have made up a large package on its way to Jena by mail coach. A part of it has been lost, but the remainder – of which the lion's share consists of notes with long quotes, mostly in Greek but also in Latin and French – still comes to seventy large printed pages in the *Marx-Engels-Gesamtausgabe*. The title is impressive: *Über die Differenz der demokritischen und epikureischen Naturphilosophie* (Difference Between the Democritean and Epicurean Philosophy of Nature).

The subject of the thesis is the atomic theory of antiquity. Epicurus adopted Democritus's idea that the world consists of very small atoms moving about in empty space. In today's history books, it goes without saying that Epicurus deviated from his master by asserting that the movements of the atoms are random, but this difference was not noticed in 1841. Leibniz placed the views of nature in Democritus and Epicurus on an equal footing, Marx pointed out. Hegel, 'the giant (*riesenhafte*) thinker', certainly saw the difference in principle but did not have time and space enough to investigate it.[45] With his thesis, Marx attempted to fully demonstrate what the new thinking in Epicurus consisted of.

Marx became perhaps the first to clearly investigate the difference between the two philosophers. It was an achievement, however, that passed his contemporaries completely by. But Marx saw the work as only one part of a larger project in which Epicureanism, Stoicism, and Scepticism would be brought together. It would largely entail a careful analysis of Greek (and Roman) philosophy after Plato and Aristotle.[46]

There is a purpose for this declaration. To obtain a permanent position in the world of German universities, a doctorate was not enough. It also required a significantly larger, more demanding habilitation thesis. The subject of the study Marx announced would fit here splendidly. In short, he declared that he imagined a future at some university.

But let us return to the doctoral thesis. Marx did not content himself with investigating Democritus's and Epicurus's different conceptions of chance and necessity. He also pointed out that they both had completely different strategies for arriving at knowledge. Democritus says that he wandered throughout large parts of the world. He sought knowledge everywhere, learning from Egyptians, Persians, and Indians. Epicurus, on the other hand, calls himself an autodidact. Democritus, seeing the material world as nothing but appearances and illusion, seeks positive knowledge of it. Epicurus sees the material world as real, but disdains empiricism.

This might lead the reader to think that Marx would now put himself on Democritus's side. But he did not. While Democritus regards nature only from the material side, Marx says Epicurus sees the connection between the material and the spiritual. According to Epicurus, two bodies that repel each other thereby also negate their relationship to each other. The relationship between them is not only real, but ideal.[47]

The line of thought may today seem difficult to follow, but it becomes comprehensible against the background of the philosophical terminology of the time. Like Schelling before him, Hegel had asserted the primacy of the spirit and the intellect at the expense of substance. The material can be explained from the spiritual, and not the other way around (as materialists like Democritus asserted). Even nature is run through with something spiritual, though on a lower level than the human. Simple natural events become comprehensible in terms of the spiritual. Attraction is a primitive analogue to the inclination towards each other that people can feel, and repulsion the opposite.

The material, in other words, has a spiritual side, and the spiritual a material side. Marx appears here as a good Hegelian seeking to meld idealism and realism. In their view of nature, the Left Hegelians do not much differ from the Right. Nature is not the centre of their attention, nor was it Hegel's. Instead there is history, politics, knowledge, art, religion – in general, everything human.

For Marx, nature still appears as a reflection of the spiritual. This is, for me at least, the reasonable interpretation of the text. But there is another, nearly opposite reading. John Bellamy Foster stands by it in the previously mentioned *Marx's Ecology*. According to Foster, the thesis is only Hegelian 'in spirit', not in substance. In other words, Marx gave lip service to Hegel but at heart had already distanced himself from him. In fact, Foster goes further: Marx was never following Hegel, but from the beginning was captivated by the materialist tradition that reached from antiquity up to the Enlightenment thinkers.

In short, the view of society and of history that Marx developed a few years after his doctoral thesis had already been furnished with its permanent foundation in a materialist conception of the world. Foster also sees Darwin as a somewhat unwilling, hesitant materialist who with his theory of evolution filled a gap in Marx's otherwise solid worldview.[48]

As I understand it, this entire interpretation entails a gross simplification. Marx's relationship to Hegel, materialism, and

Darwin was significantly more complex. On the other hand, it
is easy to agree with Foster that with his thesis, Marx joined a
long tradition of reading Epicurus that had gone on – periodically in secret – ever since the old philosopher's own time 2,300
years ago. The aspect of the inheritance from Epicurus that Marx
emphasizes even in the foreword to his thesis is not materialism,
but the revolt against the gods and thereby against religion and
the societal order in general. Marx also engages David Hume,
the eighteenth-century Scottish philosopher. (Typical for the time,
Hume is rendered in German translation and Greek authors in
Greek.)

But the finale itself of the foreword is a quote from one of his
most beloved dramas: *Prometheus Bound*, by Aeschylus. In it,
the rebellious Prometheus, who defied the gods by giving fire
to humanity, refuses to bend his spirit to the will of Zeus. His
punishment is to be chained to a rock, unable to protect himself
against a vulture that eats his liver. Standing helpless, he is visited
by Hermes, the messenger of the gods. Prometheus exclaims
defiantly:

> I can assure you that it is easier
> To be prisoner here than a servant of the gods

Prometheus is the principal saint in the philosophers' calendar,
says Marx.[49] They are truly challenging words, directed against all
types of authority, even the Prussian. But Marx's need for polemics
is not satisfied with this attack. In a particular chapter, he enters
into a highly contemporary discussion concerning the inheritance
from Hegel, and spares no gunpowder there either. It is handled
in a way that allows Marx to draw associations with Plutarch's
depiction of the Roman general Marius, who killed the Cimbri
to the last man, leaving so many corpses that the people around
Marseilles could fertilize their vineyards with them. The resulting
harvest was glorious. In the same way, Marx says, Hegel can serve
entirely different purposes than what he himself intended. He is
accommodated now to the one, now to the other – but always
morally. (Morals, in Hegel's terminology, are always limited and
in that sense abstract; Marx uses them the same way.)

Two extreme parties arise out of the different narrow interpretations of Hegel. One is the positive party, the other is the
liberal (Marx italicizes the word). The one turns into itself; the
other devotes itself to criticism, and its philosophy is thus directed
outward. But both fail to do what they intend to, and are thereby
transformed into Lilliputians who, with the help of megaphones,
try to make themselves into giants.

With this comparison, both burlesque and grotesque, Marx
goes on the attack against not only Right Hegelians and pure
defectors from Hegel, but also against certain Left Hegelians who
wanted to get closer to the Prussian state as it appeared in the
early 1840s. Arnold Ruge, a man Marx would soon collaborate
closely with, belonged to the latter.[50]

Bruno Bauer, his friend who wanted to prepare the way for
his academic career, was thoroughly frightened in the face of
this succession of rebellious notes. 'What sort of berserker rage
(*Berserkerwuth*) has seized you again?!' he exclaimed in a letter.
'What is it that pushes you and worries you?'[51] But he wrote
the warning cries in vain: the thesis was in Jena with Professor
Bachmann. In a way, it is odd that Bachmann did not react to the
attacks. He himself belonged to those who had turned from Hegel,
and should therefore have taken them personally. But perhaps he
was able to disregard things like that and look to the indisputable
qualities of the thesis. Those certainly exist. The author possessed
both wide erudition and intellectual acuity. But the text was also
marked by haste. It is true that Marx had begun gathering notes
on Epicurus a few years earlier, but writing the thesis itself took
him only a little over six months. As often happened, a long period
of incubation was required before his writing took shape.

With his thesis, Marx makes it clear that he does not intend to
become a compliant man of the state. It is true he was aiming for
an academic career, but once there he intends to be uncompromising and follow his own reason wherever it leads him.

Bauer also still hoped that he would be able to link the rebellious
young man to the university in Bonn. But it soon turned out that
the Prussian university was closed, and not only to such provocative candidates as Karl Marx. All Young Hegelians, without
exception, were subjected to the same harsh verdict. Bauer never

got the appointment that seemed self-evident. On the contrary: he had to leave the academic world. The hope for a daring programme of reforms from within the state's own institutions of higher education was extinguished.

Now, only one other, more direct way to mould public opinion remained for those who wished to influence the country's development: newspapers, journals, and books. So, like many of his friends, colleagues, and adversaries, Marx became a man of the press.

The Families

Marx had dedicated his doctoral thesis to Ludwig von Westphalen. His future father-in-law was described as 'an old man who has the strength of youth' who hailed every advance of the time with enthusiasm, and whose entire being was characterized by a real idealism. Marx regrets that he only has an 'insignificant pamphlet' to present to this 'fatherly friend' whose name was so dear to him.[52]

The words are lofty, but their sincerity cannot be doubted. Ludwig von Westphalen had meant much to the young man; after Heinrich Marx's death in particular, he had become like a father to Marx.

The delight in the friendship would be brief, however. Ludwig von Westphalen died on 3 March 1842, less than a year after Marx had finished his thesis. Now there was no man in an older generation who was close to him.

There were two older women, on the other hand: his mother and his future mother-in-law. However relations had been between Henriette Marx and her 'favourite of fortune', and however it developed later, it became tense in the extreme after Heinrich Marx's death. The reasons were financial. Karl had ordered his student life according to the generous remittances from home. However much the father complained, the money turned up and made the son's student life pleasant. After Heinrich's death, nothing was assured. All the same, he must have received something; he continued his studies until his thesis was finished in 1841. The old promissory notes Henrietta tore up in 1861 were certainly from that time.

Karl wanted to get his inheritance as soon as possible. The dream of being successful all at once followed him throughout his life. But the inheritance after his father did not permit easy conversion into hard cash. Most of it was bound up in real estate, and his mother and some of his sisters needed someplace to live.

The situation led to violent scenes. We know this chiefly through some letters Marx wrote to Arnold Ruge in 1842 and 1843 – while he was defending his thesis and the path of academia turned out to be impracticable for him. In the first letter, he speaks of 'the most unpleasant family controversies' due to his family, despite their prosperity, forcing him to live under burdensome financial circumstances for the time being. In another, written in January 1843, he tells Ruge that he has broken with his family and that he has no right to the estate as long as his mother is alive. A few months later, he was ready to get married. He then said that his future bride had had to fight 'the most violent battles' with her 'pietistic aristocratic relatives' who worshiped 'the Lord in heaven' with the same frenzy as 'the lord in Berlin'. But the Marx family had also tormented her. Some 'priests and other enemies of mine' had 'ensconced themselves' and given her problems. Marx sighed that he and his bride had had more conflicts than people three times their age who boasted of their life experience. But still: 'I can assure you, without the slightest romanticism, that I am head over heels in love, and indeed in the most serious way.'[53]

It is difficult to get a clear notion of what their families' opposition looked like. We already know that Ferdinand von Westphalen, Jenny's significantly older half-brother, was from the very start a sworn enemy of the love affair between Jenny and Karl. The sources say nothing about any others. However, we can be sure that Jenny's mother Caroline was not among their opponents.

To all appearances, Caroline von Westphalen was a cultured person who put no obstacles in the way of Jenny's and Karl's future happiness. They lived with her in Bad Kreuznach at the time they married, and it was she who, a few years later, would send Helene Demuth – the woman who would become their indispensable helper – to their household.[54]

It is even more difficult to know what Marx was referring to when he spoke of 'the priests' (*die Pfaffen*) and other negatively disposed people among his relatives that Jenny had to fight against. 'Ensconced themselves' could be interpreted as new in-laws. But it is extremely unlikely that the Maastricht lawyer his older sister Sophie married in 1842 would have played any role in the context. Sophie was the sister closest to both him and Jenny. The younger sisters were still unmarried.

Could the reason have been related to status – that Jenny was too noble a girl? That is unlikely. Even less could the fact that she was not Jewish have played a role. What is likely is that even Jenny – certainly against her will – had been dragged into the turbulence concerning money and inheritance. The Marx family's assets were greater than the Westphalen's, but that did not help very much.

What kind of person was Jenny von Westphalen, then? A beauty, said those who had met her. Certainly, she was more beautiful than the portrait that was painted of her in her youth.[55] Marx tells her in a letter from the 1860s that during a brief visit to Trier, he was constantly asked how things were for the prettiest girl in town. Her husband swelled with pride.

And what about Karl Marx's own appearance? There is a vivid description of him from around the time of his marriage: 'Karl Marx was an energetic twenty-four-year-old whose thick black hair grew on his jaw, his arms, his nose, and his ears. He was dominant, intense, full of grandiose self-confidence, but at the same time very serious, learned, a restless dialectic.'[56] It is not difficult to picture him.

But let us return to Jenny von Westphalen. Posterity only has indirect testimony about her beauty. On the other hand, it can be easily ascertained that she had a brilliant mind and solid schooling from home. Her letters are excellent in every respect: well written, expressive, witty, and full of keen-eyed observations. She could spice them up with expressions in foreign languages, even Latin. One time, she wrote an entire letter to her husband in French, and finally noted with surprise which language she had chosen.[57]

Once she had decided on the four-years-younger Karl Marx – which she did early on – she did not hesitate for a moment. Bruno Bauer, who met her in Trier, could calmly inform Karl that she was prepared to 'endure everything with you', somewhat prophetically adding, 'and who knows what will come?'[58]

At the beginning of the relationship, Karl would have outbursts of jealousy. This was when he was living in Berlin, and Jenny in Trier, and they could only meet occasionally. On Karl's twentieth birthday, he had clearly been gripped by dark suspicions which she passionately repudiated in a letter. She was torn by her feelings; Heinrich Marx had died a few days after Karl's return to Berlin, and she was crushed. First Karl's jealousy, and then the old man's death – it was too much! Barely a month later, she had pulled herself together for a more balanced letter. She tells him how she had sat for hours by the old man's deathbed and spoken about the most important things: religion and love. She wished that Karl could also have been there. And in the Romantic spirit, she exclaimed: 'There is a love that extends over this life and is *infinite*,' and a love like that possessed Heinrich Marx. She placed a lock of his hair in the letter to Karl.

There are many letters from Jenny to Karl from the period of their engagement (those from Karl have been lost). Jenny's description gives an idea of the passion in Karl's feelings: 'Your beautiful, gripping, impassioned love, the indescribably beautiful expressions thereof, your enthusiastic visions.' She did not want to lose these under any circumstances. Karl needed to understand that she could sometimes be fairly merry and mischievous – in short, flirty – with other young men, but it meant nothing. He had on one occasion clearly held out the prospect of wanting to duel with some rival, and the idea filled her with horror. Karl was her great love. No one else meant anything to her.[59]

In the lines concerning her way of chatting lightly with young men and Karl's annoyance over it, a class difference can be divined. She was a fine girl who learned the stylish rules of the social life of the nobility, while he with his simpler background misunderstood the meaning of the flirtation. But Jenny was also a girl who intended to submit to her husband when the time came. She saw that as destiny, and at times regretted it. A few months before she was to be married, she wrote to her future bridegroom: 'We have been condemned to passivity by the fall of man, by Madame Eve's sin; our lot lies in waiting, hoping, enduring, suffering. At most we

are trusted with knitting stockings, with needles, keys, and everything beyond that is evil.'⁶⁰ But despite that, she did not intend to
abdicate completely from her freedom. She put in her veto against
Karl's ideas on transferring the publication of a planned periodical, the *Deutsch-Französische Jahrbücher*, to Strasbourg. She did
not intend to move there, and it soon turned out that her will was
victorious.

Karl Marx and Jenny von Westphalen were married in Bad
Kreuznach, not far from Trier, on 19 June 1843. The wedding
took place in an evangelical church – likely the Wilhelmskirche
and not, as otherwise usually said, in Pauluskirche.⁶¹ The fact that
they chose an evangelical church says nothing about their faith.
All marriages in Prussia were religious, and both bride and bridegroom were Lutheran in name. Otherwise, religion was a closed
chapter for them.

The significance of Jenny Marx in Karl Marx's subsequent life
can scarcely be overestimated. She was not only his beloved wife
all those years, and the mother of his seven children. She was anything but his passive discussion partner, and she was universally
appreciated by all of the couple's guests, who certainly did not
praise her only for her beauty. She was, and remained until her
strength failed her, the first reader of everything he wrote. She
was the one who could decipher his unreadable handwriting, and
therefore made a fair copy of his manuscripts.

Jenny Marx also could endure all the horrors life was to throw
at her and her family over many, many years. She has not left a
single word behind her in which she complains about her husband's inability to provide for her and her children. She only
blames society, politicians, and capitalists.

The Journalist

Once Marx had his doctorate conferred in Jena in April 1841, he
set out immediately for Bonn. He still cherished hopes of a readership at Bauer's side. But his plans were soon dashed, and now only
one path stood open for him as for his Young Hegelian brothers
in misfortune: that of the literary man. If Prussia could not be

reformed from within the body of the state itself, it must be done through opinion. An enlightened public could, at best, force the state into greater openness.

'Public opinion' was a keyword of the times. Rousseau had spoken about it. But with him, *l'opinion publique* was above all a negative concept: a faceless mass deluded by morally lax writers into thinking the same thoughts.[62] Others saw opinion as the force through which society could be changed into something better. No one expressed this optimism better than the Swedish botanist, economist, and bishop Carl Adolph Agardh. Opinion, he said in a newspaper article, was similar to 'electricity, which runs through the chain of citizens who, thereby permeated, feel the same way at the same moment, feel the same pleasant jolt, or the same mild healing warmth'.[63] He had an image of the still-popular experiments with Leiden jars in mind, in which a row of people took each other by the hand and one of them touched a charged jar. Everyone in the row would then give an involuntary little hop.

The same kind of optimism surely drove Marx when he entered into hectic activity as a journalist for a few years. To start with, he and Bruno Bauer planned together to write a continuation of a pamphlet by Bauer we have already encountered, *Die Posaune des jüngsten Gerichts*. Marx was to write about Hegel and art in it, but, as so often happened, he did not finish in time. The censor managed to intervene and confiscated what Bauer had written. Marx instead offered his text for Arnold Ruge's periodical *Anekdota*, published in Switzerland. But he had to rework the article first. He was not satisfied with its 'tone of the *Posaune*' – the part Bauer had already put up – and he complained about the 'irksome constraint of the Hegelian exposition' that he wanted to replace with a 'freer, and therefore more thorough exposition'.[64]

It is clear that, by this time, Marx had already begun to withdraw from Bauer's positions. Instead, he sought connection with a man whom he had castigated in his thesis without mentioning him by name: Arnold Ruge. Ruge had published the Young Hegelians' journal for a few years. Sixteen years older than Marx, he had been among Hegel's students but had been imprisoned for six years in the 1820s, accused of subversive activities. Once released, he established himself as a publisher of periodicals in

Halle. After Friedrich Wilhelm IV's accession to the throne, the censorship became too severe for him and he moved his operations to Dresden in Saxony. There, he published *Deutsche Jahrbücher für Wissenschaft und Kunst* for a time. But even Saxon censorship made his activities impossible; thus he opened the Swiss *Anekdota*. It was there that Marx intended to publish his article on Hegel's aesthetics. But this was not finished either. On the other hand, another contribution Marx published under the pseudonym 'A Rhinelander' was finished, which dealt with the Prussian censorship instruction. The article signified his debut as a journalist.[65]

Expectations among his friends of what he could achieve were great. Marx had an 'eminent head' and was a 'brilliant writer', Ruge wrote in a letter to his publisher. Greater opportunities to satisfy the young man's thirst for activity also soon opened up. In Cologne, a new newspaper had started in January 1842. It was called *Rheinische Zeitung*, and it was an organ for the Rhenish opposition to the Prussian authorities. A range of men with money supported it, including two men on the editorial board Marx knew, Georg Jung and Moses Hess. Both were older than Marx, but admired him for his brilliance. The most enthusiastic was Hess, who wrote in a letter to a friend: 'You should prepare to meet the greatest – perhaps the only real – philosopher of the current generation. Imagine Rousseau, Voltaire, d'Holbach, Lessing, Heine, and Hegel combined in one and the same person – I say combined, and layered upon each other – and you have Doctor Marx.'[66]

Marx was welcome to contribute articles. Several of his old acquaintances, such as Bauer and Ruge, were already contributors. For the first time, a daily paper had become a natural forum for Young Hegelians. By April, the authorities had discovered that the kind of people who had just been driven out of the universities had now turned up in the newspaper columns instead. The censor argued they should also be refused admittance there, but the regional authorities refused to enforce the decision.

Marx contributed his first article in May 1842, which became a long series of articles on the negotiations regarding freedom of the press under the sixth Rhenish *Landtag*, or regional parliament.[67] Freedom of the press and censorship thus remained the centre of his attention. But towards autumn, he turned to a burning social issue far from the Young Hegelians' usual concerns. While Bauer and his peers, to the annoyance of the owners, wrote in an abstract and rather hard to understand manner, Marx took on everyday issues. This strengthened his position in the paper; he was brought into editorial work and soon characterized its political profile. Under his management, *Rheinische Zeitung* became a leading organ of opinion in Prussia. He gained an entirely new, topical subject when he wrote about communism, attacking the *Allgemeine Zeitung* in Augsburg for calling his paper 'communist' after publishing an article on the housing situation in Berlin.

With that, the distance from Bauer and his peers increased; they were now gathered in Berlin under the name *Die Freien*, 'The Free'. Georg Herwegh, a poet who followed in Marx's footsteps, wrote a brief article in which he declared that 'The Free', through their 'political Romanticism, their cult of genius, and their new name, compromised the party of freedom'. Most of the members were excellent people, but as a group 'The Free' were nothing more than a vain attempt at mimicking a French club. Marx edited the text but let the essential parts remain in the paper. The break was definitive.[68] It was Marx, not Bauer, who had taken a new path.

At the same time, the struggle against censorship had become even more intense. At first, certain articles were forbidden, and finally all publication was put to a stop. The last edition of the paper was dated 31 March 1843. It was a decision that roused a storm of protest in Cologne and other cities in the Rhineland. But the decision stood. Marx's first adventure in newspapers was at an end.

He set off for Bad Kreuznach to get married and to write articles, but now for journals. Marx's usual difficulty with finishing what he started again manifested itself when he was to submit these articles. Only as a newspaper writer did he ever manage to deliver what he was supposed to on time – and more besides. It is easy to see that he is an excellent journalist, with a sure sense of style and often brilliant, quick-witted, and all-round knowledgeable. He addresses himself to a circle of readers that has a large vocabulary. At times, he treats himself to a few Latin phrases – something that probably caused problems for the more mercantile readers of *Rheinische*

Zeitung. French, which he sometimes dusts the text with, is a self-evident feature in these border regions and certainly bothered no one. It seemed equally natural for him to quote Goethe, Schiller, and Shakespeare. Even Papageno from Mozart's *The Magic Flute* surely fell within the readers' frame of reference.

It is thus freedom of the press and censorship that was first the focus of Marx's interest when he threw himself into the world of newspapers. Two immense blocks of text are involved: twenty-two large printed pages in Ruge's *Anekdota* and forty equally large pages in *Rheinische Zeitung*.

In the first article, Marx benefited from the fact that he actually studied law. He conducted a sharp, but also amusing, review of the new provisions on censorship formulated under Friedrich Wilhelm IV. They were seemingly more liberal than their predecessors from 1819 – but only seemingly. Marx conducted a merciless examination of the provision that the censorship 'not prevent serious and modest (*beschiedene*) investigations of truth'. The truth – he says as a man of the Enlightenment – is no more modest than light itself. And who should it be modest towards? he wonders. Towards himself? He comes out with a quote from Spinoza: *verum index sui et falsi* – truth is the touchstone of itself and of falsehood. Should one be considerate towards falsehood? Goethe is also brought in to support the attack: 'Only the mean wretch is modest.'[69]

Against the awkwardly formulated censorship provisions, Marx stresses that not only are results part of truth, but the path to them is as well. Truth must be arrived at; in other words, the truth requires a method.

He subjects paragraphs that object to 'frivolous, hostile' attacks on Christianity to the same merciless scrutiny. By that, it turns out, is meant *every* questioning of the adopted religion. What is more, religion and politics slide together; religion serves as protection for the state and its interests.[70]

The series of articles on the debates regarding freedom of the press has a quicker pulse, but also contains a penetrating discussion on the concept of freedom. The contributions from various representatives in the Rhenish Diet are reported concisely and often sarcastically, and form a contrast to the writer's own more clear-cut ideas. Freedom, it turns out, is usually discussed in terms of social classes, and on the other hand not from the perspective of the individual. 'Censorship', it has been said, 'is a lesser evil than excesses on the part of the press.' People are thus devoted to fighting freedom of the spirit, Marx says. One speaker asserts that the shortcomings of the German people are reflected in the shortcomings of the press, and therefore the press needs to be tamed by censorship. Why, Marx wonders, should the Germans be prevented from expressing themselves, their own 'spirit of the people' (*Volksgeist*)?[71]

When Marx wrote his series of articles, he readily used formulations that still qualified him as a good Young Hegelian. Freedom of the press, he explains, forms the idea, freedom, the good. The free press is the 'characterful, rational, moral essence of freedom', the opposite of the censored press 'with its hypocrisy, its lack of character, its eunuch's language'.[72] *Idea, reason, morality*: these are heavy words in Hegel's vocabulary. For Marx, it is still spirit that governs the world.

He also objects to the idea that freedom of the press should be regarded as a subpart of freedom of trade. Of course, it is a more reasonable thought than the spineless idealism of German liberals, who only express a typical German weakness for the emotional. There is, in fact, something common between the right to express oneself freely and the right to freely develop trade, crafts, and industry. They are all *'freedom without any specific name'* – that is, without time-honoured privileges.

But freedom of the press still consists from beginning to end of the freedom not to be any branch of industry. The writer who defers to the demands of industry becomes a legitimate victim of censorship. The attitude of the young aristocratic intelligentsia lies in this thought. 'The press is the most general way by which individuals can communicate their intellectual being. It knows no respect for persons, but only respect for intelligence', Marx writes.[73]

The series of articles also contains a memorable formulation: 'No man combats freedom; at most, he combats the freedom of others.'[74] This is reminiscent of Rosa Luxemburg's famous criticism of Lenin and his view on the dictatorship of the proletariat: 'Freedom is always and exclusively freedom for the one who thinks differently.'[75] This sentence was written a little over seventy-five years later, and without the knowledge of Marx's earlier utterance.

There is also reason to cast a glance at another early article in *Rheinische Zeitung*. It is titled, quite modestly, 'The Leading Article in No. 179 of the *Kölnische Zeitung*' and is a furious polemic against a competing newspaper in Cologne. It constitutes a fiery defence of the right of philosophers to develop their thoughts in public. Philosophy had long been attacked in the press for its lack of respect for state and religion, and at the same time accused of leading youth astray. In fact, Marx says, the newspapers were echoing the philosophical ideas of the time without realizing it. Would it not be better if the feared Leviathan, the monster of philosophy, were allowed to appear in the flesh? Philosophers had been silent long enough in the face of self-satisfied superficiality and stale newspaper phrases. It was now time for them to begin to speak in the press. Previously, journalists had been ignorant, and been satisfied with calming phrases that had not been put through the trial of doubt. Quite the contrary – they demanded blind faith. Now the critical mind was to manifest itself.[76]

There is a large measure of self-confidence in these lines. But with them, Marx is also justifying his own new activities. It is his task to give philosophy a voice in his newspaper. Marx's earliest newspaper articles have an introverted element, in their own way: they deal with freedom of the press and the role of philosophy in the press – concepts related to himself and his activities. It would be something else a few months later, when he scrutinized yet another debate in the Rhenish *Landtag*. This time, it was an issue of a law that affected a completely different kind of person than he himself: small farmers, farmhands, and the poor. Social issues made their entry into Marx's writings when he wrote about the new proposed law, which meant that clearing out dried branches and brushwood from the forest would be placed on a par with theft. Children would be forbidden from picking berries and fruits. The defenders of the law asserted that the new provisions would be practical; anyone who took anything out of the forest would be punished. Marx said ironically that perhaps he himself was impractical, but nevertheless joined those invoking a customary right that the poor and politically powerless masses had been able to enjoy the fruits of for as far back as memory could reach. Gathered wood, like the berries and fruits, were to be regarded as nature's alms for the poor.

But it was a completely different world of ideas that was now making itself heard in the debates of the *Landtag*. In fact, it was a special interest – that of the forest owners – that speaks from within the proposed law. The interest had a 'petty, wooden, mean and selfish soul', Marx said, but this soul was still taking command of the public sense of justice. A person punished with fines for theft in the forest would, if she were unable to pay, be made to perform day labour in the forest, unlike for any other unregulated debts. Prison sentences would also be imposed. The usual effusions about how important it was to have a Christian disposition had to make room here for 'vicious materialism'. An entire social class would be flogged into forestry work. No consideration was made of the fact that it was hunger and other hardships that drove the poor to what would now, without exception, be called 'theft' and judged accordingly.[77]

The dark reality Marx takes up here has been depicted in our times in Edgar Reitz's masterful 2013 film *Die andere Heimat* (*Home from Home*). The environment the film portrays is the Hunsrück region in Pfalz, and the era is the early 1840s, exactly the time in which Marx wrote his articles.

Marx's articles are characterized by passion for justice and great indignation, and, naturally, they roused the particular annoyance of the censors. Indeed, the reaction was more violent than to anything else published in *Rheinische Zeitung*. Prussia had not one, but three ministers tasked with censorship; they exchanged a series of outraged messages and put Rhineland provincial authorities on alert. A paper with such an objectionable tendency constituted a threat to the existing order. Either the newspaper had to be re-formed from the ground up, or prohibited. With Marx at the rudder, a conciliatory attitude was ruled out; as far as is known, none of the newspaper's supporters or readers demanded he be replaced. *Rheinische Zeitung* was sentenced to death.[78]

Nevertheless, the article about the forest thefts is not subversive.

It challenges the *Landtag*, and it critically scrutinizes the forest owner's acquisitiveness. It sharply outlines the horrible destitution of ordinary people. But it only uncovers the circumstances; it does not sketch out how a resistance should be organized. Those who would be disadvantaged by the new legislation – the poor – are not encouraged to take any illegal action. On the contrary, they are portrayed as passive victims of a merciless development in which old feudal relations of dependency are united with exclusive ownership that permits no non-owners to even pick berries or fallen timber.

The series of articles are consistent with the radical liberalism of the time. Marx wanted to change opinions in the country. He still contented himself with the resources of the journalist: it was his words that would rouse minds.

But more lay in wait in his toolbox. This is indicated by an article he published right before the series about the laws on wood theft was inaugurated, and was the first he publicized after he became editor of *Rheinische Zeitung*: 'Communism and the Augsburg *Allgemeine Zeitung*'. The background is simple: *Allgemeine Zeitung* had accused *Rheinische Zeitung* of communism after the latter had both reproduced an article from a communist journal and also covered a conference in France that dealt with the factory workers' situation. Marx was not the one who wrote it, but he was the one conducting the defence. Communism, he said, was spreading in Europe. It was on the agenda in France and England. Since the bourgeoisie had taken the nobility's position, the propertyless now also wanted to have a part of society's riches. These were facts that the newspaper in Augsburg was trying to avoid.

Rheinische Zeitung did not even ascribe a *theoretical reality* to communism, Marx wrote. Even less did they desire it to be realized in practice. On the other hand, it asserted that the writings on the subject – and 'the sharp-witted work of Proudhon' in particular – should be studied thoroughly, and not dismissed with superficial flashes of wit. Only in-depth study could be the starting point for serious criticism. To understand the reality of communism, *Augsburger Zeitung* was not looking back to Plato but to an '*obscure acquaintance*'. By all appearances, this obscure acquaintance was one Gustave d'Eichthal, who was part of creating a small utopian society in which the responsibility for production, as well as profit, was shared equally among all. But, Marx said, it was not this kind of practical experiment that constituted the real danger. If the masses participated in them, those in power could always respond with cannons. It was the *theoretical achievement* – Marx italicized the words – that constituted the real threat. Ideas that conquer our intelligence and capture our minds and our conscience become chains that could not be broken without also bursting our hearts asunder. Ideas could be like demons forcing people into submission. But *Allgemeine Zeitung* ran no risk there, Marx added. The newspaper had neither its own understanding nor its own insights, and thereby did not have its own conscience, either.

Philosophical idealism was still speaking in these lines: it was through ideas that the world could be changed. A small utopian society would lead nowhere as long as it did not have innumerable others like it, and many such societies could be mowed down with cannons. But the ideas![79]

Marx continued his journalistic deeds in the same spirit. He wrote articles about a draft for a law on divorces. Once again, the Hegelian world of concepts appears. The authors behind the proposal did not understand the essence of marriage, but mixed worldly and spiritual conceptions together in an absurd manner, Marx explained. They were not striving for the real reforms needed, but only wanted to revise existing legislation. They did not understand that if the base (*Basis*) of marriage was not the family, then a marriage law would be as little required as a law on friendship. The discretion of neither legislators nor private persons were part of marriage; it was its essence that needed to be expressed. If a marriage dies, then the divorce decree itself should only be regarded as a record of the fact.[80]

With articles so mercilessly critical, it was not surprising that *Rheinische Zeitung* had increasing problems with censorship. More government-friendly newspapers began attacking it for its lack of moderation; that kind of exhortation made Marx even more indignant. The press had to form the connecting link between the head of the state and the heart of civil society, he said. Its task was not just to express itself judiciously and intelligently, but also to temperamentally put the injustices of society into words.

Another criticism Marx encountered concerned the accusation that the articles in his newspaper were anonymous. He declared frankly that '*anonymity* is an essential feature of the newspaper press'. It was only through this that a newspaper got its special *Geist*, its spirit.

What he wrote about the proposed law on forest theft also met with criticism in other newspapers. He responded that the vine-yard workers on the Mosel were living in a *Notzustand* (state of distress) that entailed *Notwendigkeit* (necessity) for the free press. The peasants could not express themselves publicly on their own. It was the duty of the newspapers to put their terrible situation, which was now threatened with becoming even worse through ill-advised legislation, into words.[81]

This would not be the last time Marx linked *Not* and *Notwendigkeit*.

But the censors were not persuaded by these words. On 20 January 1843, the decision came to shut down *Rheinische Zeitung*; Marx would continue his futile struggle against the powers that be for a time. On 17 March, he drew his ultimate weapon. In a brief notice, he explained that the editorial board was giving up their work. It was signed 'Dr. Marx'. It was the first time he appeared over his own name in the newspaper.[82] It was, of course, also the last. His time as a journalist had come to an end, for now.

On the Way Out

It was not easy for Marx to cut his links with Hegel. He was dissatisfied when his own presentation was entirely too reminis-cent of the old philosopher's writing style. But no matter how he tried to liberate himself, relics still remained. In fact, there would always be a more or less distant echo of Hegel in whatever Marx wrote.

The distance increased markedly after his encounter with the writings of Ludwig Feuerbach.

Feuerbach, born in 1804, was himself a student of Hegel and

had long followed in his footsteps. But by the late 1830s he had become more and more critical, and in 1839 he published his book *Zur Kritik der Hegelschen Philosophie* (Towards a Critique of Hegel's Philosophy). Two years later, it was followed by the great work that above all else built his fame: *The Essence of Christianity*. It quickly gained influence and became the subject of equal parts admiration and loathing. Its theses are clear, and rather easy to understand. Against Hegel's speculative thinking, Feuerbach placed an epistemological sensualism. It is thus through our senses that we attain knowledge. But this does not mean the word *essence* disappears from Feuerbach's vocabulary – something even the title of his book testifies to. Evidence from the senses is of course the foundation of all sustainable knowledge. But from this material it is possible to sort out the essential – that which makes something what it is.

In accordance with this method, Feuerbach arrived at the thesis that above all made him and his book famous: It is not God who created humanity; it is humanity which created God. God is the image of humanity that in the best case – in a good society – it itself could be. It is only in a world marked by injustices and need that we can imagine a God apart from humanity.

This thesis also contains, as is evident, a criticism of society. In society as it appears today, a person cannot fully develop. In various ways, she becomes disfigured and must therefore seek comfort in a higher reality. The question is how we can have an idea of the essence of humanity when real, empirical humanity provides no support for it. Feuerbach makes use here of Hegel's concept of alienation (*Entfremdung*). Because of external circumstances, humanity cannot become what it has the possibility of becoming. Instead, people place the ideal they carry with them in a God who is thus actually an ideal human.

This means that our knowledge is not completely limited to what lies open to the senses. Using what we observe, we can also see the potential in reality. Through our study of history, we can see a development that points towards the perfection of our species. Some day we ourselves will resemble the image of God that the pious now create for themselves.

No matter how far Feuerbach distanced himself from Hegel's

philosophy, central elements from it nevertheless remain. It is as
Marx Wartofsky, perhaps his greatest biographer, says,

> In an important sense, Feuerbach remained a Hegelian all his life.
> The unifying theme of his work is the progress of human con-
> sciousness, the unfolding of its self-awareness. And it is Feuerbach
> himself who recognizes that Hegelian philosophy establishes
> the *form* of this development, and suggests the mode of its pro-
> gress (in the dialectic of consciousness with its 'other', in the
> *Phenomenology of Mind*), albeit in 'inverted' or 'fantastic form'.[83]

The Essence of Christianity roused Engels's undivided enthusiasm.
In his polemical pamphlet *Schelling and Revelation*, he declared
that 'a new era has begun'. Much later, in 1886, he remembered
that '[e]nthusiasm was universal: we were all Feuerbachians for a
moment.'[84] He adds that Marx also was enthusiastic – something
that came out in his writing.

But there was a difference between Marx's and Engels's reactions. For Engels, who underwent a long and painful emancipation
from the intensely Pietistic environment of his childhood, *The
Essence of Christianity* was the crucial document that finally clarified the religion he had grown up with. Marx was less rooted
in his faith; his father had had a simple but scarcely demanding
trust in God without emotional outbreaks and threats of hell. His
mother had left Judaism only reluctantly, but certainly did not
influence Karl with her doubts; he became an atheist in his late
teens without any great mental struggle. Instead it was the philosophy of Hegel that became his great passion. We remember
how, in the long letter to his father, he described his adherence
to Hegel in terms of a conversion. Radical Hegelianism posed
no problem as long as he was in a university environment, but it
became obviously less manageable in the world of newspapers. Of
course, Marx adhered stubbornly to his idealism – ideas govern
the world! – but with the reality dominated by the censors, the
wood-owning country squires and impoverished wine growers,
the feeling for the concrete that had once drawn him to Hegel
seemed to demand something more substantial.

Once he had given up the fight with censorship and the future again became an open question, it was primarily a few journal articles by Feuerbach that preoccupied him. Most important for him was 'Principles of Philosophy for the Future'. Its programme was simple and unequivocal. God had just been revealed as an ideal image of humanity. Now it was a question of revealing Hegel's philosophy in a similar manner.[85]

Hegel admitted no transcendent reality. There was no sphere of reality that thought could not grasp and make conceptual. The God that appears in his text cannot be separated from reason. In earlier philosophy, God had been radically separated from humanity, but according to Feuerbach it was not so with Hegel. Briefly put, the thinking person has access to God. Or (a conclusion Feuerbach does not explicitly draw) she actually *becomes* God.

It goes without saying that Feuerbach's interpretation of Hegel was not shared by the Right Hegelians. For them, the reconciliation between Christianity and philosophy was the main question. That was what made their ideas so inviting to the Prussian state authorities in the 1830s. Feuerbach was on the other end of the scale.

In customary theology, the external – or material – world was radically separated from God. God had created the visible world, but it was not itself divine. In Hegel's thinking, matter becomes only a part of the whole, but a different and lower part. In this way, the new Prussian regime's accusations of pantheism were justified. Pantheism is the logical development of Hegelian thinking.

But the centre of this philosophy is the thinking subject. The God of theism is an object for humanity. In speculative philosophy of Hegel's model, God is not separated from humanity. It is precisely on this point that Feuerbach made his decisive thrust. Why call this God? Why speak of it as if it were something other than humanity? The same criticism that he recently directed towards Christianity, he now directed towards Hegel. It is not God who is the creator; it is humanity. Nor is there something divine in thinking; it is something human. Theology becomes anthropology. The centre of philosophy is not the divine but the human.

In Hegel, the evidence of the senses – in short, the empirical – is only a preliminary, and often misleading, preliminary stage for thinking. Only through thinking is what we see and hear given a plausible meaning. On the contrary, according to Feuerbach, the senses are the starting point for all knowledge. He does not deny thinking, but thinking is always secondary. The anthropology he wants to put in place of philosophy is an empirical discipline.

It is not odd that Marx was so directly captivated by Feuerbach's ideas. The transition to his standpoint was certainly not lightning quick. During his time with *Rheinische Zeitung*, the distance from the Young Hegelians' world of ideas had already grown. Bruno Bauer's way of writing and thinking seemed more and more foreign. But it was only when his adventure in newspapers was behind him that he took the decisive step. What set it off was the articles in which the same criticism directed against Christianity now fell upon Hegel's system.

Feuerbach had a powerful influence on his young, radical contemporaries. His mode of expression radiates a remarkable intensity. Not many philosophers had the same talent for aphoristic incisiveness as he did. One only needs to choose a few examples from his article on the philosophy of the future : 'It is by no means only through thinking that man is distinguished from the animal.' 'The *true* dialectic is not a *monologue of the solitary thinker with himself*. It is a *dialogue between "I" and "you"*.' And: 'The essence of speculative philosophy is nothing other than the *rationalized, realized, actualized essence of God*. The speculative philosophy is the *true, consistent, rational theology*.'

Those who were seeking a way out of Hegel's shadow in the early 1840s found an idealistic guide in Feuerbach. The problem was how to go further. Feuerbach nailed Hegel's speculative philosophy with formal simplicity, and he pointed to anthropology as the science that could replace philosophy. But what would constitute the area of study for anthropology? Feuerbach said: '*Truth is only the totality of man's life and being*.' This is not much of an 'only'.[86]

Marx would linger on a few sweeping statements of this kind, but they never confused him in his attempts to master a significantly more concrete reality in his own research.

Jenny and Karl lived in Bad Kreuznach from May to October of 1843. The stylish little spa town – where, according to tradition,

Doctor Faust had once been active – became the scene not only for their marriage but for their diverse social life as well. Bettina von Arnim, one of the great female figures of Romanticism, also lived there. She and Karl had already met in Berlin, and Bettina found great interest in having conversations with the young man whose radical ideas interested her. She saw herself as a Romantic socialist, though she held to her idea of a kind of people's kingdom.

But for the Marxes, Kreuznach could only be a stopping point. Karl had no future in Prussia; Jenny and he therefore had to imagine a future beyond the country's borders. After some hesitation, the choice appeared obvious: Paris!

Meanwhile, Marx and Ruge were developing plans together for a Franco-German journal that would build a bridge between both the cultural and linguistic regions. The plans were grandiose; the best writers would be hired. Feuerbach was one important name. Ruge contacted him for collaboration, and Marx wrote a detailed letter in which he specified what the editors wanted. He seems to have understood that Feuerbach was busy with settling accounts with Schelling's philosophy. Nothing could be better suited, Marx wrote. Feuerbach was 'Schelling in reverse', while Schelling was the favourite of the Prussian censors. It was particularly important that the truth of Schelling's wretchedness be known even in France. There, he had just begun to gain the most unexpected sympathizers. Even 'the gifted Leroux' (a leading socialist) was said to be impressed.[87]

Feuerbach was hesitant. He wrote two different draft letters and also sketched out an article on Schelling. But, in the letter he finally sent, he said no – it was a mistake to ever have occupied himself with Schelling. What he wrote had to have content.[88]

Marx, however, did not give up hope of associating more closely with Feuerbach. Barely ten months later, in October 1844, he sent a new letter to express, 'the great respect and – if I may use the word – love' to the author of 'Philosophy of the Future' and other important articles. These, he said, constituted 'a philosophical basis for socialism' as well as for communism. Feuerbach had pulled the concept of 'the human species' (*Menschengattung*) 'from the heaven of abstraction to the real earth'.[89]

Once again, heaven and earth. Once, Marx had seen Hegel as

the down-to-earth antithesis of Fichte and Schelling. Now it was Feuerbach in comparison to Hegel.

Feuerbach clearly intended to respond to the letter. But he never finished his reply. We do not know why. Perhaps he took fright at the prospect of being regarded as the socialists' and communists' own philosopher.[90] Much later, in any case, he expressed appreciation of Marx's *Capital, Vol. I* (1867) as 'that most interesting and at the same time horrifying and rich work' in which the virtue in capitalism could be seen as 'at best a monopoly of the factory owners, the capitalists'.[91]

But back to Marx's letters. As a sign of his appreciation, he enclosed an article with the title 'Contribution to the Critique of Hegel's Philosophy of Law. Introduction' (*Zur Kritik der hegelschen Rechtsphilosophie. Einleitung*). He had published it in the first and only issue of *Deutsch-Französische Jahrbücher*, which was printed in Paris in February 1844. 'On the Jewish Question' – one of Marx's most controversial articles – also appeared there, as did a few letters between Marx and Ruge, the other publisher.

Hegel's Philosophy of Law, the Jewish Question, and Analysis of the Mystical

During his months in Bad Kreuznach, Marx had been feverishly active. Despite his honeymoon – which he and Jenny spent in Bingen, Hildegard's small town where the poet Stefan George would also be born a few decades later – and despite the time-consuming conversations with Bettina von Arnim, he managed to read and write a copious amount.[92] His most comprehensive work remained incomplete: a criticism of the Hegelian philosophy of law. The manuscript fills 130 printed pages and consists of a review of some fifty paragraphs in Hegel's 1821 work *Grundlinien der Philosophie des Rechts* (Philosophy of Right). It is a milestone in Marx's development. The shorter work included in the *Deutsch-Französische Jahrbücher* is only a variation on the theme he developed in his manuscript.

What is new is not only that he is so evidently influenced by Feuerbach's writings. It was here, above all, that he developed a method of interpretation that he would remain faithful to long after the influence from Feuerbach had faded away.

What he had written so far, apart from the poems, was limited to his doctoral thesis and his journalism in *Rheinische Zeitung*. In his thesis, he is a typical Young Hegelian seeking further radical development of Hegel's philosophical and historical lectures. Marx the journalist writes on the limitations to freedom of the press in Prussia, and on a proposed law that threatens to further worsen the plight of the poor.

In 'Contribution to the Critique of Hegel's Philosophy of Law', he uses some of Feuerbach's central reasoning for the first time. In religion, as in speculative philosophy of Hegel's type, subject and predicate switch places. The concepts of *subject* and *predicate* do not have a grammatical, but a logical sense. In a sentence such as 'All men are mortal', 'all men' is the subject and 'mortal' is the predicate. Something about the subject is expressed explicitly through the predicate, but the subject is the starting point of the sentence and often the active component. But, in speculative philosophy, as in religion, it is the predicate that seems to determine what the subject is. 'God has created humanity' says Christianity, while in fact it is the reverse. Hegel presupposed that the Idea is realized in the history of humanity, whereas it is actually humanity that develops ideas of various kinds. In religion, as in speculative philosophy, concrete humanity appears passive while abstractions such as God or the Idea govern its development. The background to this notorious error of judgement is an existence, as unjust as it is merciless, in which people have no possibility of fundamentally changing their situation.

In the 'Critique of the Hegelian Philosophy of Law', Marx frequently speaks about subject and predicate in this sense.[93] Following Feuerbach, he professes himself an adherent of the world of experiences. Like Feuerbach, he argues that, based on this empiricism, one can come to know the essence of an object – what real, genuine humanity is, for example, or the secret of Christianity.

Marx no more completely abandons Hegel than Feuerbach does. Both would rather find what is valid in Hegel's philosophy at the same time as they show how his method of making abstract quantities such as the Idea or God into the agents of reality is misleading.

The difference between Marx and Feuerbach that first meets the eye is that Marx analyses and criticizes Hegel's texts in a much more detailed fashion. Feuerbach's dispute with this idealist philosophy stops at general statements about Hegel's inability to bridge the contradiction between thinking and being. Marx, on the other hand, reproduces paragraph after paragraph in Hegel's account of the state and tackles the majority of them. Even his general assertions have a foothold in specific sections of text in Hegel. Marx's assiduous excerpting of texts thereby has a direct effect on his criticism of Hegel's philosophy of law, as it did previously in his doctoral thesis.

In one place, he translates Hegel's philosophical rhetorical prose into the language of the common man. Whereas Hegel says 'the *sovereignty* of the state is *the monarch*', everyday prose should be content with the assertion that 'the monarch has sovereign power'. Where Hegel establishes that sovereignty is 'the will's abstract and to that extent *unfounded self-determination* with which lies the final decision', the man on the street could simply say 'sovereignty does what it wills'.[94]

The word *criticism* has a central position in Marx, but not in Feuerbach. Marx distinguishes between vulgar criticism and true criticism. Vulgar criticism is dogmatic and establishes certain alleged truths in contrast to the idea being criticized. It draws out the contradictions that exist in the criticized idea but it does not seek to understand how they could have arisen. This, on the other hand, is what true criticism is devoted to. It is not satisfied with verifying contradictions in the current constitution; 'it *explains* them, it comprehends their genesis, their necessity'.[95] In short, it makes it understandable why people – or at least certain people – must perceive political reality in a certain way, and it investigates what basis their ideas have. Hegel and his followers' view of the state and its relationship to civil or bourgeois society is completely natural – inevitable, in fact – for those who regard society from a certain perspective (here Marx was probably thinking primarily of civil servants, which included university professors).

It is the task of the critic to reveal the 'mysticism' that characterizes the Hegelian view of society. The choice of words is a consequence of Marx, in the spirit of Feuerbach, seeing religion as the paradigm for all kinds of illusions that people can form about reality in all its various facets. Political ideas spring from the same source as religious convictions. Reality assumes a distorted form, which is why it puts people into positions where they cannot see clearly and without illusions – at least without the help of the true critic.[96]

Marx's criticism is not only a criticism of religion or philosophy, like Feuerbach's. It also, and above all, pulls society apart. The society Hegel creates a philosophical refuge for is scrutinized and rejected in Marx's account. Hegel defends not only royal power but the privileges of the nobility as well. It is repugnant that one is born into a certain position in society, Marx objects. More than repugnant, in fact: it creates a false identity between body and soul; the noble body is of a special, more refined type than others. Marx writes contemptuously that '[t]he secret of the nobility is zoology' – they claim to constitute a particular human race. Marx's use of the word 'race' is a sign of how loosely the concept of race could still be used at that time. It is not a question of race in the biological sense. Marx is far from the racial divisions that the German natural scientist Johann Friedrich Blumenbach created at the end of the eighteenth century. Blumenbach distinguished between Caucasians, Mongols, Ethiopians, Americans, and Malays, whereas his followers preferred to use terms of colour (white, yellow, black, red, and brown). The special position the nobility claims, according to Marx, is of a different type.[97]

Hegel's defence of the monarchy and the nobility could lead to the misconception that he was a traditionalist. But Marx did not make that mistake. He emphasizes that Hegel's view of society is modern. Bourgeois society, the society of trade and manufacture and formation of public opinion, constitutes the dynamic force in its development. The task of the state is to settle the disputes that would result in life-and-death competition between different wills.[98] Marx accused Hegel of adapting to actually existing Prussia with its mixture of monarchy, class rule, and incipient modern middle classes. It is ultimately, private property – whether inherited or acquired – that was to be protected in Hegel's state.

Marx professed himself an adherent of democracy. The content he placed in the word cannot be precisely defined apart from the obvious: democracy meant that the people as a whole were involved in governing the country. We know nothing about, for example, whether Marx counted women among 'the people', just as little as whether he was thinking of a representative democracy. But even in 1843, recommending democracy in general terms was a radical standpoint. Not only conservatives or open reactionaries but also most good liberals feared democracy, as everyone would be part of it and make decisions. The fear of the mob – *le peuple* – associated with the excesses of the French Revolution was still strong. But Marx saw democracy as 'the *essence of all state constitutions*' – its highest form. He compared it with Christianity, which in his world of ideas with its European markings constituted the essence of religion.

Marx saw democracy as the only way to overcome atomized, or individualistic, bourgeois society. It is worth quoting what he wrote about individualism: 'Present-day civil society is the real principle of *individualism*; the individual existence is the final goal; activity, work, content, etc., are *mere* means.' These words from 1843 could also have been said about early twenty-first-century society.

Against individualism, Marx asserts 'the communist being in which the individual exists'. While Hegel's state only seemingly included everyone through mistaking the state with the people, this communist essence would actually embrace everyone.[99] It may seem as if Marx, with such words, is only building on the etymology in the word 'communism', from the Latin *communis*, the common. But communism was a movement of the period that soon won new adherents. In *Rheinische Zeitung* he had distanced himself from it. Now, in Bad Kreuznach, he began to change his mind.

Marx's criticism of Hegelian philosophy of law remained unfinished. When, in October 1843, he and Jenny moved to Paris, he was still harbouring plans to finish it and publish it. But in Paris he only wrote one shorter article: 'Contribution to the Critique of Hegel's Philosophy of Right, Introduction'. According to his plans, it was to precede the mass of text we have just scrutinized.

The new article begins with fanfare: the criticism of religion has essentially finished in Germany. Now it was a matter of religion's worldly forms of revelation – in brief, criticism of society. Marx repeated Feuerbach's main idea in the criticism of religion: it is humanity that created religion, and not the other way around. In religion, the essence of humanity is realized in a fantastic (that is, distorted) manner, 'because the *human essence* has no true reality'.

It is thus the shortcomings of earthly life that constitute the breeding ground of religion. Marx expressed this in the wonderful prose that he was capable of when he managed to leave the profusion of details in the excerpts and the dry precision of abstract concepts. He wrote: '*Religious* distress is at the same time the *expression* of real distress and also the *protest* against real distress. Religion is the sigh of the oppressed creature, the heart of a heartless world, just as it is the spirit of spiritless conditions. It is the *opium* of the people.'

It sometimes happens that the final words are incorrectly translated as 'opium *for* the people'. That expression would mean that the powers that be offer regular people a calming drug instead of a good life. But the context, as is evident, is unambiguous. It is a tormented humanity that itself creates a comforting imaginary world. Even in religion, there is a protest against the wretchedness of the world.

Opium had made its entrance into Western consciousness towards the end of the eighteenth century. It had first been regarded as a promising medicine, and played a central role in several fashionable cures. The Scottish doctor John Brown recommended it as a kind of universal cure. His recommendations, and those of other doctors, proved to be particularly effective as regards alleviating pain. Its simultaneously habit-forming, apathy-inducing, and over the long term directly disastrous effects became obvious only after several decades. It was at that time that opium began to play a decisive role in British efforts to make the population of China passive. In the history of imperialism, the drug can really be called an opium *for* the people. But it was long afterwards that

Marx spoke of opium *of* the people. The expression 'opium of the people' had, moreover, been used many times before Marx. Kant had used it, as had Herder, Feuerbach, and Heine. Hegel used it in speaking of Indian religion.[100]

Now that criticism of religion had been completed, it was time to go further to '*the criticism of the vale of tears*, the *halo* of which is religion,' Marx said. More specifically, German reality stood in focus for the work whose introduction he was now publishing. Germany was behind the times. In 1843, it had not yet managed to reach the stage France attained in 1789. The criticism of Hegel's philosophy of right, which was indirectly a criticism of Germany (Marx spoke about Germany although there was no such country yet), was criticism of an outmoded system. It was only a preliminary stage for criticism of *modern* politics and social reality in which the relationship between industry and finance on the one hand, and politics on the other, was the main problem. It is only in philosophy that Germans were contemporary; in philosophy, they could imagine their own future. But it was now a question of making good on the insights of philosophy. In this way, philosophy could be escaped by realizing it.

For Germany's part, it was not yet a question of total liberation, but for the time being only a political revolution that would clear away the old regime. Bourgeois society could thereby liberate itself, and the ruling bourgeois class could for a time be hailed as liberators. But even they had their own definite interests. Only the proletariat had nothing of their own to defend except their own humanity. The hope of human liberation therefore lay with the proletariat.[101]

The hypothetical figure that was the basis for this reasoning would come to be important for Marx. Only the person who owns nothing could stand for universal liberation.

It is obvious that Marx had quickly changed much in his outlook when he arrived in Paris. The difference is already evident in relation to the manuscript for which he planned to use the text as an introduction. Nothing had yet been said there about the proletariat and its role, and nothing about the impending bourgeois revolution in Germany. The contours of a programme had developed out of his criticism. What had happened?

Before we go into this question, another text also published in *Deutsche-Französische Jahrbücher* should be scrutinized: 'On the Jewish Question'. It was placed before the introduction to Hegel's philosophy of right in the journal, but we do not know if it was written before the introduction. Many of the fundamental ideas are the same. But the subject is radically different.

'On the Jewish Question' is Marx's first dispute with Bruno Bauer, who had once led him into the Young Hegelians' world of ideas. Now Marx abandoned his companion and entered into a sharp polemic with him. In a few smaller publications, Bauer had taken up the so-called 'Jewish question', asserting that it would find its solution if the Prussian state stopped demanding a profession of the Christian faith from its citizens. In that case, everyone – both Jews and non-Jews alike – would be on the same level in relation to political power. It was not only the Jews who needed to be emancipated; it was everyone. The privileged position of Christianity had to be abolished.

Marx credited Bauer certain points. He was a splendid theologian. His account of the Jewish faith was excellent. On the other hand, his political analysis was deficient. Bauer believed that the secular state contained the solution. We could then practise our religion for ourselves, and at the same time be good citizens of the state. Bauer thereby contents himself with political emancipation. In and of itself, that was a big step. But it was humanity that needed to be liberated! The origins of religion are not the state, but the distorted lives that workers and capitalists – everyone, in fact – were forced to live. These lives had to be brought into focus. Everyday life was solid ground; the state (like religion) was above it like some distant heaven.

If the state were secularized, it would not mean that humanity's religious faith would wither away. The United States offered a splendid example. There, Marx said, there was no state religion. But 'North America is pre-eminently the country of religiosity'. This was completely natural: when people are liberated from state management of religion, the religious become even more religious. Only when the Americans liberated themselves as humans could they also liberate themselves from their religion. 'The question of the *relation of political emancipation to religion* becomes for us the question of the *relation of political emancipation to human emancipation.*'

This basic idea is completely in agreement with Marx's application of Feuerbach's philosophy. The foundation of religion is a society in which people cannot realize themselves and become completely human. What made the article scandalous in the eyes of posterity (as far as is known, the age in which he lived did not react) is the way in which Marx wrote about Jews, their religion, and their activities. Bauer wanted to solve the Jewish question in Prussia through making the state secular. Then the Jews could become citizens among the others. But Marx objected: it was not enough to regard the Jew as he was on the Sabbath. The everyday Jew devoted himself to endless bartering. It was not enough to open the path to political recognition for Jews. It required the Jews liberating themselves from the tyranny of self-interest. Only then could they become free as people.

But – and here comes the dialectical expression of the article that is far too rarely noticed: 'The Jews have emancipated themselves insofar as the Christians have become Jews.' In the extremely religious United States, God was worshiped with the same ardour as Mammon. Marx leaned towards the British colonel and author Thomas Hamilton, who in his 1833 book *Men and Manners in America* asserted that bartering had become the entire content of a normal American's life; the American 'talks only of interest and profit'. In fact, Hamilton said, even the office of the priesthood had become a commodity.

Similar elements can be found in every country where the bourgeois revolution moved victoriously forward, Marx interjected. Individuals, full of egoism, remained. Christianity is a further development of Judaism and therefore, according to Marx, stands higher as a religion (the idea of progress is an obvious starting point for him). In real life it was still Judaism, practical in its nature, that was victorious. Egoism permeated society. Only in another kind of society could it become better. Only when humanity understands itself in its social being is emancipation complete.[102]

In the article, Marx makes use of the customary vocabulary of anti-Semitism, already worn out in 1843 but still in circulation in the early twenty-first century. Jews barter. They have eyes for nothing but money. Even in their religion, self-interest is allowed to rule. Marx himself was of Jewish origin. As far back as it has been possible to follow his family tree, there has not been a single non-Jew among his relations. His own father had converted to Christianity with his family. But he had not escaped anti-Semitism for it, and his son Karl also experienced it throughout his life.

Posterity can see Marx as one of the first in a brilliant tradition of researchers and authors with a Jewish background. Many of the representatives of that tradition would make their mark not only on the intellectual development of Europe, but of large parts of the world from the mid-1800s onwards. In his superb 1992 book *Redemption and Utopia*, Michel Löwy talks about a '*siècle d'or*', a golden century that met its grisly end in 1933 when the Nazis seized power. He mentions the names 'Heine and Marx, Freud and Kafka, Ernst Bloch and Walter Benjamin', and – as we know – he could have added Einstein and many others. Of course, Marx could have had no idea of the tradition whose beginning he was part of. He was primarily keen on being completely secularized, and he shared that ambition with many of those like him.

But despite such ambitions, many observers in this Jewish tradition have spotted elements of messianism – the belief in a coming historical catastrophe from which a saviour, a Messiah, would come forth. Elements of this tradition have even been seen in Marx. Löwy, who went deeper into the question than most, finds this supposition debatable and shallow, discovering much stronger messianic ideas in other representatives of the tradition.[103]

Marx thus appears as quite thoroughly secularized. But this does not mean that he avoided the taunts of anti-Semitism. This is why it could seem so much more remarkable that he himself takes to the same low vocabulary. How can this be explained? The most far-fetched explanation is given by Arnold Künzli in his book *Karl Marx: eine Psychographie*. Künzli, who in a risky fashion here tried to narrow down Marx's psyche from his life and work (or, more correctly, from certain works), asserted that Marx was characterized by self-hatred. Marx abhorred himself and his origins. Thus these diatribes against Jews.[104]

There is no support for such an interpretation. Marx was a person who, despite many misfortunes in his life, maintained strong self-esteem. He spoke of his father with pride. He never hid the fact that he himself was of Jewish origin. And he objected to all discrimination, social or otherwise, against Jews. But the idea that 'On the Jewish Question' testifies to an explicit anti-Semitism lives on in other, less reasonable forms. Must Marx's words be interpreted in this way?

When he wrote 'On the Jewish Question', no one imagined that Jews formed a biologically specific group, much less a race. The biologistic viewpoint came as a waste product of the broad Darwinist movement. For Marx, as for his contemporaries, Judaism was, from beginning to end, a religious faith – a faith that Marx commented disparagingly on without exception. In addition, he associated this faith with an everyday life that wholly amounted to earning money.

The decisive expression in the article on the Jewish question came, as I have already pointed out, with the sentence: 'The Jews have emancipated themselves insofar as the Christians have become Jews.' The first part of the sentence is equally as important as the second. In the first part, Marx is talking about himself and all the others who left Judaism, thereby liberating themselves. In the second, it is a question of the victory of capitalism in contemporary Christianity. Money now governs the world, as it once governed the lives of the Jewish minority.

It has been pointed out that 'On the Jewish Question' has the form of what was called a *Judenwitz* – a 'Jewish joke' – told by Jews among themselves, the gist of which is the fact that the first person pointed out goes free while someone else entirely is pilloried.[105] It is possible that Marx had this in mind, but we do not know. The important thing is that the article is primarily an expression of anti-capitalism.

That said, the fact remains that Marx was dealing casually with harmful stereotypes. 'On the Jewish Question' is not the only example of this. He also scattered about disparaging and prejudiced taunts about Blacks, the Polish, the Irish, the Indians, and especially the Germans. This did not prevent him from having close Jewish friends and a beloved son-in-law – Paul Lafargue –

who had Black ancestry. He also had lively contacts, marked by appreciation and warmth, with people of every nationality that he otherwise disparaged as less capable.

Ultimately, this kind of verbal abuse can be ascribed to a general incaution that in many areas got him into difficulties. Here, in particular, it was not his contemporaries but posterity that has realized how objectionable his use of slurs against different kinds of groups of people was. Those around him seem to have been blind to what such abuse could lead to. Nor did his many enemies have an eye for them. In fact, they constantly let him know that he was a typical Jew.

The really fatal thing is that so many people in various socialist and communist traditions did not only indulge Marx's linguistic recklessness but became both racists in general and anti-Semites in particular. There is a dark tradition, and within it Marx's text could barely serve as a corrective. On the contrary such anti-Semites have been able to find support above all in 'On the Jewish Question'.

4

————————

In Paris

A Simmering Environment

Marx came to Paris in late October 1843. Under pressure from the Prussians, French authorities deported him in early February 1845. His stay thus lasted barely fifteen months. But they were fifteen months that meant a revolution in his life.

The 1830s and 1840s were exceptionally creative decades. Paris was at the focal point for everything new. Social projects blossomed, at least in ideas and dreams. Most of Saint-Simon's many followers were in Paris, Charles Fourier's visions of the future drew people to the city, and it was here that Étienne Cabet's plans for a new kingdom of happiness enjoyed success. Pierre Leroux, who helped redefine socialism, was in Paris. And another term, 'communism', was also turning up more and more frequently.[1]

The new economic theories from England and Scotland had already made their entry into Paris a few decades earlier, chiefly through Jean-Baptiste Say, who had developed his own Gallic variant. They suited the new kind of society that was now beginning to take form in France as well, both through a modest but increasingly rapid industrialization and a growing finance sector. Those who desired a new kind of society had to take a position on the dynamic development of the economy.

Paris was not just a melting pot in the field of ideologies. Culture in its narrower meaning was in a vital phase. Its literature was rich and lively. Honoré de Balzac was constructing the substantial world of his novels, a singular panorama of contemporary

France. Aurore Dudevant, alias George Sand, was also enjoying great success as an author. Charles Augustin Sainte-Beuve became the first literary critic in the modern sense.

Musical life was equally significant. Paris was the city of Hector Berlioz, and the great composers and musicians of the time stayed there for shorter or longer periods: Franz Liszt, Frédéric Chopin, Richard Wagner, Felix Mendelssohn, Hector Berlioz, and many others. The scope among painters was no smaller: everything from Jean-Auguste-Dominique Ingres's paintings of beautiful, well-dressed society ladies to Honoré Daumier's incomparably nasty caricatures of the men of power was to be found here.

On the other hand, France was politically stagnant after the July Revolution of 1830. The king, Louis Philippe, was satisfied with a system in which money reigned supreme. His understanding was shared by the leading politician, François Guizot, whose most famous utterance to the French has already been quoted: 'Get rich! Get rich!' But social rifts and dissatisfaction were increasing.

In Salons and Cafés

It was this remarkable environment which greeted Marx and his wife Jenny. Jenny was already pregnant, and on 1 May 1844, their daughter Jenny – who would come to be called Jennychen – was born.

Domestic happiness did not prevent the young husband and father from making himself at home in the simmering new environment. He was not the only German who had taken refuge in Paris. There was an entire German colony that included everyone from poets to craftsmen. In Paris, they could live a freer, richer life than they could in their German homelands.

One of them was the great author Heinrich Heine. Marx came to know him in December 1843, and he, Jenny, and Heine began a deep friendship. Through Heine, Marx began to frequent one of the real focal points of Parisian life: the salon of Marie d'Agoult, where many musicians, artists, and authors met. We must stop a moment with Marie d'Agoult and some of her visitors.

Marie d'Agoult was born into the aristocracy, and was married early to a French nobleman who gave her her surname. After a few years, the piano virtuoso and composer Franz Liszt came into her life. With him her existence changed utterly. He became her lover and father to three of her children – among them Cosima, the future wife of Richard Wagner. But Liszt abandoned her after a few years. This did not crush her in the least; she created her own career. Above all, she became a celebrated writer under the pseudonym of Daniel Stern. Her most enduring work is *Histoire de la Révolution de 1848* (History of the 1848 Revolution), written between 1850 and 1853, which is still cited as a well-informed eyewitness depiction.

But Marie d'Agoult also held a salon that gathered many of the great personages of the era. At that time, Paris was the cultural capital of Europe, but it also constituted a centre for new, revolutionary political ideas. Culture and politics met at Madame d'Agoult's.

Many of the more or less regular visitors to the salon were living in exile. Heine was one of them; Marx another.[2] We know nothing in detail of Marx's life at the salon. But he was an exceptionally receptive person who had the ability to fuse together impressions from the most disparate spheres of reality. At Madame d'Agoult's he could, as Jacque Attali has pointed out, meet with several of the great personages we have already mentioned: Franz Liszt and Frédéric Chopin, George Sand, Charles-Augustin Sainte-Beuve, and Jean-Auguste-Dominique Ingres. It is likely that he also met the prose author whom he would rank highest of all throughout his life – Honoré de Balzac.[3] When he left France in 1845, he received reports on Parisian life from Hermann August Ewerbeck, one of his German friends. Clearly, Marx had asked Ewerbeck to deliver something to Heine that concerned 'Frau Gräftin Darg', which must be a distortion of the name d'Agoult. But the efforts, according to the letter, did not lead to the desired result.[4]

Heine's importance to Marx during this momentous time in Paris is often underestimated. It is said that they became good friends in Paris and got on well in each other's company, and it is usually added that Marx deeply admired Heine's poetry, as Heine just as highly appreciated the intelligence and acumen of his twenty-one-year-old friend. But Heine's influence was certainly greater than that. He introduced his young friend to much that could not be found in Trier, Bonn, or Berlin.

Like many other Germans, Heine initially had a positive view of the 1830 revolution in France; in fact, it was the direct reason he settled in Paris in 1831. From there, he also wrote hopeful newspaper reports for a few years. In the art of painter Léopold Robert, he found signs that people were on the way to abandoning their dreams of finding happiness in the life to come and were now instead looking for it in this world. But the more that cold economic calculations prevailed in 1830s France, the darker Heine's image of the times became. He sought escapes from the society of egoism in various socialist and communist ideas. The world of ideas that Marx first came into intense contact with in Paris was thus well known to his new friend, who was significantly older.

Like his new fellow traveller, Heine gladly talked about the need for a revolution. At the same time, his political radicalism was largely aesthetic, if not mostly so. It was in art, literature, and perhaps music in particular, that Heine could most clearly read the need for a new and better society. He was not alone in this. The socialist tendency he sympathized with above all – Saint-Simonism – contained a crucial aesthetic component. In it, the artist was a central figure in the new society of the future taking over the role of the priests.[5]

The interpretation made it easier for many of the artists to let themselves be influenced by Saint-Simon's ideas.[6] Heine was only one of many; Liszt was another and George Sand a third. In this context, George Sand is particularly interesting. It is clear that she and Marx had come into contact with each other in Paris. During the revolution of 1848, she turned to Marx for help with exonerating the anarchist Mikhail Bakunin, who had been accused of being a Russian spy. Marx, who was then editor-in-chief for *Neue Rheinische Zeitung*, published an open letter from her on the subject.[7]

In her enormous autobiography, *Histoire de ma vie* (History of My Life), Sand provides a lively picture of Paris in the 1840s. The name Marx does not turn up, but we get a look into the social life Marx was part of for a time. Great personages pass in review; among them are also politicians rather than artists, like Pierre Leroux, whom we have already met, and Félicité Robert de Lamennais, a Catholic priest who also was a socialist. Heine is there, of course, well integrated in this radical left circle – at least up until the great schism over the revolution of 1848. Sand herself was more consistent than most. A pathos for the hard-working, oppressed masses permeated most of her work. She was also convinced that the greatest minds of the future were among them, and encouraged workers with ambitions to become writers to try their luck. She hoped for a French proletarian literature, but her hopes did not come to pass.[8]

The new revolutionary ideas were readily discussed in d'Agoult's salon, and conversations flowed spontaneously from politics to music and art. Moreover, of course, the gatherings were devoted to rarefied musicianship. An attachment to 'the people's music' and a marked aesthetic elitism apparently got on well there without problem.

Marx did not only move among the salons of Paris. Above all, he sought out craftsmen and workers. In his letters from his time in Paris – which are few in number – he also preferred to talk about them and their progress. In the aforementioned second letter to Feuerbach written in October 1844, he dwelt in some detail on the mood among French proletarians and German craftsmen. Feuerbach's religious criticisms were a success among the working class, and there were even lectures on the subject for hundreds of German craftsmen in Paris, Marx told him.

But above all, his letter was a song of praise to the French proletariat that was not only free of pieties but also aware of its significance for the liberation of humanity. The English working class was also making substantial progress but lacked the culture that characterized their French counterparts. The German craftsmen had come far in the field of theory, but their obstacle was that they were just that – craftsmen, not wage earners.

Marx provided an example of the difference between French and German, but chose nothing from the world of the craftsmen or the workers. The former is from a book by a follower of Charles Fourier, alongside Saint-Simon the most influential of the early French socialists. The author was Édouard de Pompery; in his book, he expounds on Fourier's image of humanity according to which passions not only drive humanity but also give each individual their distinctive character. Passions, not ideas, get people to turn to each other and to choose their lives.

Against this view of humanity, Marx put one of a German, Bruno Bauer. Marx reminded Feuerbach that for many years, Bauer had been his friend but that he had now become increasingly foreign to him. Bauer and the other so-called 'critics' in Berlin did not see themselves as people devoted to criticism, Marx said. In their eyes, they were critics who had the misfortune of also being people.[9]

In these lines to Feuerbach, a writing project about the Young Hegelians can be detected – one which in fact had already begun to take form.

Socialism and Communism

Marx did not make his most important contacts in the salons of Paris but in significantly darker locales. These both shared the idea that society had to be changed completely, but while this topic was the subject of smart conversation at Madame d'Agoult's, it was a matter of life and livelihood in the poorer quarters.

The words 'socialism' and 'communism' were on many lips, though two of the most important advocates of socialism were already dead when Marx arrived in Paris. Saint-Simon had disappeared from the scene in 1825; both his renown and his influence had come late, and largely posthumously. Charles Fourier died in 1837, at a time when his star was also on the rise.

Both are usually packed together as utopian socialists with a third revolutionary – Welshman Robert Owen, the most practically oriented of them, who tried to create a model industry – or rather, a complete little model society where equality and justice would prevail – in New Lanark outside Glasgow.

Marx labelled them 'utopian socialists' in the *Communist Manifesto,* and it has stuck. The fairness of the designation 'utopian' can be questioned. On a small scale, Owen had tried to create something entirely real; he wanted to influence the rest of the world by example of his model. Saint-Simon, as we have seen, spoke about actually existing social phenomena – industry, science, and art – and he was also alert for opportunities for women in the future. At the same time, there was an element of mysticism in him. His most important work was *Le nouveau christianisme* (The New Christianity); it was published in 1825, the year of his death. In it, he sketches out the contours of a worldly Christianity; his ideas could appeal to both the men of practical life and to more romantic souls who dreamed of the 'feminine Messiah' who would redeem the world.

Fourier was the one who best met the original designation of 'utopian', which Thomas More created with his 1516 story of the island of Utopia. Fourier dreamed of small ideal societies – which he called *phalanstères* – whose core consisted of 600 individuals, 300 men and 300 women. The idea was to construct an existence in common with a strict division of labour. The characteristics and interests of each and every person would be used to their advantage, but no one would be stuck in a specific occupation; everyone would be able to switch jobs on a regular basis.

Through the division of labour, each and every person would be dependent on all the others. For this mutuality, Fourier used the term *solidarity*, a word he borrowed from jurisprudence (*solidarité*), where it had to do (and still does) with joint and several liability, or collective responsibility to pay. During the 1840s, the word 'solidarity' became politically fashionable in France and also spread to other countries.[10] But it was not a word that was given space in Marx's vocabulary – not even in the 1860s, when it had become prevalent in the First International.

On the other hand, Marx read Fourier, and made several important personal acquaintances among societal thinkers in Paris. He had already expressed admiration of Pierre-Joseph Proudhon as a newspaperman in Cologne, and now they could both meet face to face. Twenty years later in January 1865, just after Proudhon's death, Marx talked about their meeting in an article. Proudhon had wanted to learn more about Hegel from Marx, and now after the fact Marx was declaring himself responsible for Proudhon's later attempts at adopting Hegel's style. 'In the course of lengthy

debates often lasting all night, I infected him very much to his det-
riment with Hegelianism, which, owing to his lack of German, he
could not study properly.' Marx adds, with his customary caustic
irony, that Karl Grün – a German socialist – continued to speak
about Hegel with Proudhon after Marx left Paris, and that he
'had the advantage over me that he himself understood nothing
of it'.[11]

The result of the lessons was Proudhon's 1846 book *Philosophie
de la misère* (The Philosophy of Poverty), in which the author
attempted to use Hegel's dialectic in his criticism of society. He
sent the book to Marx with an accompanying letter declaring
that he now awaited Marx's 'critical flog' (*férule critique*). When
Marx actually let his paddle fly in his 1847 response, *Misère de
la philosophie* (The Poverty of Philosophy), Proudhon ended the
friendship.[12]

Marx also wrote that Proudhon's debut work, *Qu'est-ce que la
propriété?* (What is Property?) of 1840, remained his best (this was
the one Marx had read when he was still a journalist). Proudhon's
attitude towards Fourier and Saint-Simon was roughly that of
Feuerbach towards Hegel, he says: Feuerbach was less significant
as a philosopher, but nonetheless created an epoch through his
criticism of Hegel's philosophy. In a similar way, Proudhon vanquished his superior predecessors. But his fundamental question
was wrongly put, since property is a historically variable concept.
The property he spoke about was bourgeois property. It is odd to
call it theft, since it is protected by bourgeois right. Proudhon's
weakness, according to Marx, was that he had not sufficiently
burrowed his way into modern economic theory.

Marx here does not take into consideration the fact that
Proudhon did not share his theoretical background. Proudhon
stood out to the world as a worker who wrote – he was a typographer – and it was as such that he had first roused Marx's interest.
But Proudhon himself was no propertyless proletarian; rather, he
identified himself with small businessmen. Small businessmen and
small farmers, who worked to acquire what they owned, were
protected in his ideal society whereas the large owners – those
who could live off the toil of others – would pass into history.
It was *their* property that he famously called theft (though the

phrase had been coined before the French Revolution) – theft from the little people, theft from the commons.

Proudhon was critical of all centralized power because it protected the propertied classes with its state apparatus and its laws. According to Mikhail Bakunin, who is extraordinarily competent in the subject, Proudhon was the first to call himself an anarchist, in 1840 in connection with *What Is Property?*

Bakunin was, incidentally, another important acquaintance Marx made in Paris. Bakunin, the Russian nobleman who loved revolutions and hated everything to do with the state, remained an admirer of Marx's intellectual capacity long after they had parted ways. In a manuscript from 1871, he recalls that he and Marx became friends in Paris, and that Marx was by far superior to Bakunin himself in acumen and knowledge. 'Although younger than I was, [he was] already an atheist, an erudite materialist, and a well-reasoned socialist,' he wrote. It was no close relationship, he added. Moreover, they were both far too different. Bakunin remembered that Marx called him 'a sentimental idealist and he was right; I called him faithless, conceited, and treacherous, and I also was right.'[13]

The young Marx hardly drew any lessons from Bakunin, but the Russian's passionate social engagement certainly made an impression on him.

Wilhelm Weitling

An important part of the company Marx kept in Paris consisted of revolutionary Germans living in the city. This took place in meetings arranged by an organization called *Bund der Gerechten* (League of the Just).

The *Bund der Gerechten* had been called *Bund der Geächteten* (League of the Outlaws) in the beginning, but the German tailor and writer Wilhelm Weitling had pushed through the name change in 1836. Weitling had a more radical agenda than earlier iterations of the league. A political revolution was not enough to create a good society, he declared. It would also require a social upheaval that completely transformed property relations.

In 1839, the League of the Just had taken part in a failed attempt at a coup against the prevailing order in France. The leader of the coup was Louis Blanqui, a French socialist who claimed that a group of closely-knit revolutionaries would be able to seize power and bring along the great majority of the people in its revolutionary enterprise. Their tactic was called *putschism* after the German word *Putsch*, which means 'coup'. The 1839 attempt failed. After the defeat, Weitling left for London, which was intended to be the association's new headquarters. But their activities there were rather lacklustre, while those in Paris at the time of Marx's debut in society were flourishing.[14]

Police spies have given us the names of the meeting places that Marx and his newfound friends frequented: Café Scherger, Café Schiewer, Restaurant Schreiber, and so on. Picture the scene: shabby places run by German emigrants, overflowing with master craftsmen and more bookish types with soft hands. In the midst of the gathering, cleverly disguised as a member of the working class, there is a police spy dispatched by the Ministry of the Interior, tasked with reporting what he observed to the Prussian ambassador. The spy's reports have been preserved, and give us a vivid picture of this side of Parisian life at the time.

The revolutionaries' activities soon became more extensive, and a larger locale was needed for their meetings. The police spy now reported that the League of the Just met every week at a wine merchant's on Avenue de Vincennes. Sometimes thirty participants gathered; often it was between 100 and 200. The police spy took pity on all these journeymen who allowed themselves to be seduced by a few schemers. He concluded his report of 1 February 1845: 'I write to you in great urgency so that Marx, Herwegh, A. Weill and Börnstein will not be able to continue to drag these young men down into misfortune.'[15]

Only a few weeks earlier, on 16 January, Marx had been forced to leave Paris for Brussels. The report showed that he was already playing a leading role in the League of the Just. It was his name that the spy mentioned first in the string of dangerous seducers of the people. Such were the ravages of Marx in life: Wherever he turned up, he made himself known. While still very young, he became a central figure among the Young Hegelians. Within a short time, he had developed into a leading journalist. Now he stood out as a particularly dangerous revolutionary.

In all these roles, he enjoyed these successes as a novice. When he came to Paris, communism was a movement that he had regarded unenthusiastically from a distance. In a letter to Arnold Ruge in September 1843, when he was just about to leave Germany, he claimed that it was a 'dogmatic abstraction'.[16] In Paris, he would become a central figure in that dogmatic abstraction.

There were two persons who above all introduced him to what communism, at best, could be. One was Moses Hess, the man who admired him so tremendously back in his time as an editor in Cologne, and the other was Wilhelm Weitling, the tailor and writer who had been forced to leave Paris when Marx arrived. Hess was above all a theoretician who had adopted socialist and communist doctrines earlier than Marx. There are signs indicating that the owners of *Rheinische Zeitung* made Marx – and not Hess, who was six years older – editor of the newspaper because they regarded Hess as entirely too radical.[17]

Like Marx, Hess had a Jewish background, but his parents did not convert, and Hess had had a strict religious upbringing. While Marx, by all appearances, remained irreligious in a rather unproblematic way, Hess preferred to describe even completely worldly events in religious terms. Inspired by seventeenth-century philosopher Baruch Spinoza, who spoke of 'God *or* the world', Hess expressed himself during an important period of his life in purely pantheistic terms: the universe is God. In his ideal society, this divine reality would appear in all its glory. Earlier than Marx, he developed ideas on humanity's *Entfremdung* – its alienation – and he would obviously inspire his friend here. But his ideas always had religious depths that were lacking in Marx. Despite the fact that Hess, like many others, spoke of religion as the opium of the people, he equally sought something holy in the social community that would replace a world dependent on religion.

Hess called the programme for the radical change of society that he advocated both socialism and communism. His view of the relationship between them is indicated in a letter he wrote to Marx in July 1844. It is characterized by great optimism, although it starts off with a warning that Marx should be careful about setting foot on Prussian territory. According to newspaper information, an arrest order was ready for execution. Radical forces were nevertheless rapidly gaining ground in Germany, Hess assured him. The *Deutsch-Französische Jahrbücher* was enjoying great success, although the censor was doing everything to stop it. New socialists were turning up everywhere. 'Soon, all of educated Germany will be socialist – radically socialist, in fact; I mean communist.'[18]

Hess thus sees chiefly a difference of degree between socialism and communism. There is nothing indicating that Marx would have thought anything else at the time. It was also in accordance with the prevalent linguistic usage. In fact, there is yet another nuance in meaning: communism was more proletarian in its orientation. It attracted workers and craftsmen rather than armchair radicals.

As regards the other source of inspiration, Wilhelm Weitling, it was on the contrary Marx who was most impressed from the start. It was the same sort of admiration he had felt for Proudhon: both were advocates of the working people in whom Marx had begun to set such great hopes.

Weitling had an entirely different background than Marx or Hess. His mother was a maidservant, and his father a French officer in Napoleon's army in Germany who had soon disappeared from his mother's life. Weitling grew up in great poverty and trained as a tailor. He just barely supported himself while becoming engrossed in his studies, and gradually began to write. It was his second book – *Garantien der Harmonie und Freiheit*, published in 1842 – that so impressed Marx. We must go into it in depth somewhat because it says a lot about the communism Marx was now definitively growing closer to.

It is a book that contains multitudes – it could be said an entire outlook on the world and society. 'Progress is a natural law,' Weitling declared by way of introduction, and then paints a picture of an idyllic proto-society that had to be burst asunder by the contradictions created through 'the origin of all evils': property. This is Rousseau's picture of development. But Weitling's ideal society is not Rousseau's; he sketched out the contours of a good, equitable, and just world that now lay within reach. The influence of both Saint-Simon and Fourier is evident here. Science and technology are given key roles, and Weitling even adopts Saint-Simon's idea of the guide to a better world as a second Messiah, 'greater than the first'. Fourier's ideal that everyone should be trained in a practical occupation and, moreover, should have the opportunity to switch between various employments also became Weitling's, though he did not conceive of any self-sustaining small societies or *phalanstères* as the basic political units. Even Fourier's way of talking about highly peaceful and comradely associations such as armies is found in Weitling. School armies, for example, occupy an important place in his society. Like so many other radicals at that time – especially Fourier – Weitling was an ardent supporter of women's liberation.

Freedom of the press, and even freedom of choice – which are impossible as long as money rules – prevail in this future society.

Weitling spoke relatively little about the revolution he nevertheless saw as necessary in order to be able to create this good society. Most important here is the distinction he made between a political and a social revolution – a distinction that became crucial for Marx. In Germany, Weitling said, it was more difficult to carry out a political revolution than a social one. Both, however, were wholly possible. He said nothing about whether or not he imagined the upheavals to be violent.

What is surprising is that he was open to the possibility of a people's monarch at the head of this good society of the future. A contemporary reader could also wonder at the fact that he mentions Louis von Hessberg among his models. Hessberg is entirely forgotten today, but a moment's research shows that he was a high-ranking officer and nobleman who, despite his position, proposed the establishment of 'God's kingdom on earth' with such things as community of property. This scandal forced him to leave his posts. It is only thanks to Weitling's appreciation that posterity still remembers him.[19]

But was this appreciation not odd? Hessberg's inspiration was obviously Christian, and his dream was to re-establish a primitive Christian community. He inserted himself into a tradition stretching back to the Middle Ages, culminating in the German Peasant

Wars of the sixteenth century and the most far-reaching radicals
of the seventeenth-century English Revolution. Swedish literary
historian Kurt Aspelin called this tradition *utopian mysticism*. In
it, the future appears in the chiaroscuro of dreams, and prim calculations are united with ecstasy.[20]

Was it not odd that Weitling could appreciate a present-day
advocate of this tradition? No, it was not. Even at that time, the
inspiration of primitive Christianity was strong among revolutionaries. Marx was a newcomer to the group, and through his
unhesitating atheism he belonged to a minority among them.
Obviously, this circumstance did not alter his enthusiasm for
Weitling. He expressed this above all in an article in a German-
language newspaper in Paris called *Vorwärts* (Forward).

Vorwärts, the Weavers' Uprising, and Ruge

The original task of *Vorwärts* was to provide news about the
arts, the sciences, and social life in Paris. The successful Franco-
German opera composer Giacomo Meyerbeer was responsible for
the funding, and its editor-in-chief was fairly reactionary. It was
thus no left-wing organ – quite the contrary – but the left had the
initiative among German emigrants, and with it pulled the newspaper in their direction with their delight in debate.

A weavers' uprising in Silesia in 1844 became the subject of
lively attention in the newspaper. Heinrich Heine published a
magnificent poem on the subject. It has the refrain 'We weave, we
weave' and deals with how weavers wove a triple curse into the
burial shroud they were working on: a curse on God, who proved
himself deaf and blind to their prayers; a curse on the king, who
protected the rich and squeezed out the last penny from the poor
only to have them shot like dogs; and a curse over the fraudulent fatherland where lies and atrocities reigned and the stench
of corpses had begun to spread. It is for this fatherland that the
shroud is intended!

Heine sent the poem to Marx, requesting publication. He also
attached another poem touching on a theme that had belonged
to the repertoire of social criticism ever since the carnivals of the

Middle Ages and had a special place in Marx's critical disputes: the world turned upside down. His poem begins: 'The world is topsy-turvy turn'd,/We walk feet upwards in it'.[21] Fifty thousand copies of the poem about the weavers were also distributed as flyers in Silesia. It is not surprising that it was forbidden by the Prussian authorities. An agitator in Berlin, who nevertheless recited it, was thrown into prison.

The revolt in Silesia was not the first of its kind, but it attracted greater attention than earlier similar incidents. The 1840s were a period crisscrossed by new revolutionary ideas, and at the same time by increasing repression, particularly in Prussia. As far as the weavers were concerned, their wages had been drastically reduced. Competition with incipient industrial production in Great Britain was beginning to be felt. Textile products became cheaper, but the necessities of life did not. Many factory owners, moreover, acted ruthlessly towards people living at or under the limits of starvation. The revolt became even more pointed through socialist and communist ideas having begun to spread among German workers. The revolt itself, which brought many weavers with it and led to a number of violent conflicts, came to a quick end when the authorities in Breslau called in the military, who struck down all resistance with great brutality. Eleven people, including a woman, were shot and killed; twenty-four were seriously wounded. Many were put into prisons or fortresses. Others were sentenced to flogging.

The weavers' uprising remained an important reference point in German workers' history. In 1893, Gerhart Hauptman's great drama *Die Weber* (The Weavers) premièred in Berlin. It represented something completely new in German theatre. Here, the common people took the stage and were not, as otherwise was the case, relegated to the peripheral role of servants. Hauptmann's drama, for its part, provided immediate inspiration to a long series of magnificent, gripping lithographs by Käthe Kollwitz.[22]

In the 1840s, the period of the revolt, the bloody days in Silesia led to a heated debate within and outside Prussia about what these disturbances were due to. The most common explanation was summarized in the word 'pauperism' (from the Latin *pauper*, 'poor'). Pauperism was talked about around Europe; both high-born and low, left and right, took part in the conversation – which easily became heated. One conviction that most shared was based on the fact that the age – with its ever more intense trade, its growing industry, and its more rapid communications – was creating a new type of poverty, more dangerous than the traditional kind because it gave rise to continuing impoverishment in large groups of the population. A smouldering dissatisfaction that could turn into open revolt followed on its heels.[23]

Conservative forces in Prussia, with King Friedrich Wilhelm IV at their head, asserted that old-fashioned Christian charity would reduce the tensions and make it so that the Silesian weavers' revolt would be the last of its kind. Liberal forces in the country imagined some form of social reforms that could counteract pauperism.

Of course, the Germans in Paris followed the revolt and its consequences with boundless excitement. Arnold Ruge, with whom Marx had recently collaborated, quickly published an article in *Vorwärts* in which he played down what happened in Silesia to some extent. He justified it with the fact that the king had declared himself not very alarmed and instead aimed his fulminations at the country's zealous supporters of reform. Ruge signed the article 'A Prussian', which could have given rise to the misperception that it was Marx – a Prussian subject – and not Ruge, a native of Saxony, who wrote it. But Marx was of an entirely different opinion than Ruge and thought that what had happened in Silesia was a magnificent event that would have consequences in the future.

It is not at all strange that the king was more worried about the liberals than the workers, Marx wrote in his response. It was not the king the workers had turned against, but the bourgeoisie. An aristocrat like the king could not but abhor the bourgeoisie. The workers were far too distant to worry him.

In the same way, an orthodox Catholic is more hostile towards an orthodox Protestant than an atheist, Marx continued. For a legitimist like the Prussian king, the liberals were a worse enemy than the communists.

He thus uncovered an important aspect of the dynamic in various kinds of differences of opinion. It is the close neighbour who is the most hated opponent, while those on the other end of the scale of opinion were not perceived as competitors.[24] The idea of *la petite différence* – the small difference between opinions and orientations that, seen from outside, lie very close to each other – most recently goes back to Sigmund Freud's 1932 book *Das Unbehagen in der Kultur* (Civilization and Its Discontents), and is used more often in psychology and religious research than as regards political ideologies.[25]

Now there is no one who runs the risk of confusing the ideals of Friedrich Wilhelm IV and the German liberals. But the differences are, if anything, relative. King and liberals were on the same political field, whereas the communists were hopelessly outside the discussion. Marx himself would soon become a tireless and unrelenting guard concerning the social theory he had worked out. But as a novice, he was still open to many variants of communism and socialism. On the other hand, Ruge's standpoint – which must be characterized as liberal populist – was entirely foreign to him. He and Ruge would never be able to publish a joint periodical again. There would be only one issue of *Deutsch-Französische Jahrbücher*.

Marx developed his polemic in his customary way, which took up quite a lot of space. He followed his opponent's text, argument for argument, and often offered up detailed quotations. He then tore these arguments to bits, one by one. Ruge took up pauperism, the subject of the day in Prussia. Marx reminded him that England was 'the *country of pauperism*': the word 'pauperism' had come from there. Impoverishment was universal among workers in England, and not only partial as it was in Germany. It played a central role in English political economy, and impoverishment there appeared as an unfortunate but inevitable result of modern industrial development.

Marx's article makes its way through the polemical thicket to its crucial point: that pauperism cannot be remedied only with political measures; a social upheaval is additionally required. In his article, Ruge asserted that the weavers who revolted had a limited horizon. Marx indignantly responded that this was completely wrong. The weavers' revolt had a more '*theoretical* and *conscious* character' than similar events in France and England. He referred to the popular *Weberlied* ('song of the weavers', not to be confused with Heine's poem), the text of which clearly expresses the contradiction between the proletariat and private property.

Marx pointed to Wilhelm Weitling as the most striking example of German consciousness. His writings are genius, Marx wrote. In their theoretical aspects, they often exceed even Proudhon, however inferior they were in their execution. The bourgeoisie had nothing to put up against a book like *Garantien*. Marx spoke about 'this *vehement* and brilliant literary debut of the German workers'. He continued by repeating Weitling's assertion that there were good possibilities in Germany for a social revolution, but worse for a political one. The latter was namely the affair of the bourgeoisie, the former that of the proletariat. It was not abnormal for Germany to be equally as politically backward as it was philosophically advanced. On the contrary, it was a necessity. 'A philosophical people can find its corresponding practice only in socialism, hence it is only in the *proletariat* that it can find the dynamic element of its emancipation.'[26]

That last sentence is noteworthy for several reasons. On the one hand, it is clear that Marx had not yet distinguished between socialism and communism. Perhaps, like Hess, he saw communism as a pure cultivation of socialism, but here nothing of that interpretation is discernible. He speaks simply of 'socialism'. On the other, he expressed an idea that had been common among German intellectuals all the way back to the beginning of the nineteenth century and still was among the Young Hegelians: namely that the Germans were a particularly philosophical people. He would not express himself in this manner later on.

Weitling was among the readers of *Vorwärts* and wrote a cheerful letter from London in which he repaid Marx's appreciation. 'We are friends,' he declared optimistically, and hoped that their correspondence would continue.[27] It is unknown whether Marx ever responded; no other letters between the two have been preserved. There was much else taking up Marx's time when he received the letter. The most important of them was already discernible in his articles in *Vorwärts*: economic theories had entered into his sphere of interests. Previously, they had been below his horizon. Soon, they would dominate his field of view.

This encounter with economics was brought about by a single person: Friedrich Engels.

Friedrich Engels

The names of Marx and Engels are often mentioned in the same breath. Marx always comes first; he is the central figure who, in the heroic pictures of the Soviet era, is often portrayed sitting while Engels stood somewhat discreetly beside him. This was also the way they were immortalized in bronze in the mid-1980s, in what was called the Marx-Engels-Platz in Berlin during the GDR era. (Today, the location is called Schloss-Platz; the statues have been moved.)

In Soviet and East German literature, Marx and Engels are often portrayed as some kind of kindred souls, agreed in all essentials and fighting for the same thing: the victory of communism. They are also portrayed this way in the authoritative foreword to the entire *Marx-Engels-Gesamtausgabe* with which the Institute for Marxism–Leninism in the Soviet Union and the GDR introduced the first volume in 1975. Their names are repeated like a mantra: 'Marx and Engels … Marx and Engels …' They have a central place in the history of revolutionary thought, it is said; they were giants of learning and at the same time champions of a new society, they vanquished idealism in philosophy and created a firm materialist basis for dialectical thought, and so on.

At the same time, there were authors outside the Soviet sphere of influence who painted the opposite picture. Engels never understood Marx's theory, but interpreted it in an absurd direction. But there are also more well-balanced portrayals such as Tristram Hunt's 2009 book *Marx's General: The Revolutionary Life of Friedrich Engels*. The only major problem with it is that Hunt exaggerates Engels's importance for Marx.[28] We will illustrate the relationship between Marx and Engels in more detail in a later chapter. For now, only their initial meeting and the start of their collaboration is of concern.

Even in outward appearance, they both were different. Marx was so dark-skinned that his children called him 'the Moor'; on the other hand, Engels was blond – a Nordic type, in fact – tall, slim, and vigorous, and moreover a skilled fencer, rider, and dancer. Marx was shorter, without being short, had an enormous head and a powerful chest with stouter legs.

Both had grown up in affluent homes. Engels's father, also named Friedrich, was a well-to-do partner in the firm Ermen & Engels, which he ran with the Dutch brothers Godfrey and Peter Ermen. The elder Friedrich was a brilliant entrepreneur who focused his activities on cotton, and opened factories both at home in Barmen and in Salford, the junior twin city of Manchester.

The Engels family was strictly religious – Lutherans with a Pietistic orientation. Fervent piety was to be united with strict fulfilment of duty. Earthly successes meant that God was on your side. Life was a grimly serious business.

But the younger Friedrich did not want to follow in these foot-steps. He developed his own interests and an independent will. He did remarkably well in high school, but before finishing, his father decided he had learned enough of dry theory. It was now time he learned what it meant to work in commerce and industry. He had to acquaint himself with the secrets of cotton manufacture and travel around England with his father. After that, he was sent to the office in Bremen to get some idea of international business. The younger Friedrich was already open to new, radical ideas, and it only got worse when he chose to train as an artillery officer in Berlin. There he learned military tactics and strategy, something he took pleasure in throughout his life. He became a military expert, earning the nickname 'The General' from Jenny and Karl's youngest daughter Eleanor. The name stuck.

But what is more important is that in Berlin, he joined the circle of Young Hegelians, as Marx had done earlier. We have already encountered Engels as a Young Hegelian of the radical type. Society had to be changed – not through business or industry, but through thought.

Marx and Engels met for the first time in 1842. Engels had finished his military training, and on the way home he visited the editors of *Rheinische Zeitung*. Under the name Friedrich Oswald, he had already published a number of minor essays, including on Schelling's lectures in Berlin. Now he was ready for new journal-istic adventures.

The encounter, as Engels would remember long afterwards, was a chilly one.[29] Marx still had a bit of the Young Hegelian notions but was already on the way towards new horizons. Engels still had the glow of the proselytizer. It was Moses Hess whom Engels hit it off with instead. Everything indicates that it was Hess who got Engels interested in communism, and soon to see himself as a communist, too.

But now Engels would use the situation to his advantage. His father sent him to Manchester to work for the firm. It was, to say the least, an instructive period. Apart from his work, Engels managed to both carry out intensive studies in the new economic theories, and survey the social relations that industrialism brought in its train.

The Manchester he came to was a remarkable city. It was 'the cradle of the Industrial Revolution', as it is called in the tourist brochures. During the 1830s and 1840s, it was an exceptionally creative environment. The famous Manchester liberals who created modern *laissez-faire* liberalism dominated its Chamber of Commerce; Manchester workers created Chartism, the first workers' movement; consumer cooperatives began in nearby Rochester; Engels himself, though also others in Manchester, took the first steps in empirical sociology; and in Salford, the brewer James Prescott Joule was one of the first to discover the principle of energy.[30] It was another kind of creativity than that of Vienna at the turn of the previous century; more down-to-earth but just as fateful.

The first result of Engels's diligent studies was an article he sent to *Deutsch-Französische Jahrbücher*, Marx's and Ruge's journal. The article enjoyed great success; it influenced Marx in particular. We must examine it in a little more detail.

The article was called 'Umrisse zu einer Kritik der National-ökonomie'. It is only an *Umrisse*, a few pen strokes, or – as the English translation goes – 'An Outline of a Critique of Political Economy'. The draft is approximately twenty-five pages, and constitutes at one and the same time a presentation of and a furious reckoning with modern economic theory as created by Adam Smith and further developed by David Ricardo, John Ramsay McCulloch, and others.

It is worth noting that Engels calls the theory 'the liberal one'. The word 'liberal' as a designation of a political concept was rather new at the time; it showed up in 1812. Even later, it became the usual characterization of the economic doctrine that Adam Smith laid the foundation for.[31] For Smith himself, 'liberal' meant generous, and nothing more.

In the same breath, Engels condemned liberal theory as hypocritical. He said that Smith had the same role in economics as Luther had in Christianity.[32] Before Smith, mercantilism ruled with Catholic straightforwardness, but Luther – *alias* Smith – introduced hypocrisy. Smith proved that there was human feeling in the new economic system, and that trade created peace and friendship among the nations. At the same time, he knew very well that the system enslaved people and drove them into the deepest poverty. Riches and poverty lived side by side; since the days of Smith it had only got worse. Families were torn apart by the factories. Workers' children began work at the age of nine, transforming the family home into only a place for room and board. But Smith's followers had become even more hypocritical than their master.

The comparison between economic theories and the development of Christianity contained much of Engels's own personal struggle for liberation. In his house, a strict, introspective Pietist Protestantism reigned. In Engels's eyes, Pietism was the counterpart to Smith's followers like David Ricardo or John R. McCulloch, who had worsened his hypocritical stance.

The reality that the economists' theories dealt with was the daily bread of the Engels family. Even Marx called Smith the Luther of the economists in a text he would soon write. But for him, the comparison did not have the same emotional charge at all.

In the continuation of his 'Outline', Engels discusses the theory of value that stands at the centre for Smith and his followers. In the same breath, he accuses them of ignoring the significance of technological inventions. The forces of production grew through their science and their discoveries, he emphasized. (He still speaks of 'forces of production' (*Produktionskräfte*) and not, as later, of 'productive forces' (*Produktivkräfte*), but the origin is of course Smith's 'productive powers'.)[33]

He emphasizes that it is work itself that was the original capital, but now a definite 'Entzweiung' ('dichotomy' according to the English translation) had emerged between capital and labour that had not only separated them but had also turned them into the antitheses of each other.[34] The word *Entfremdung* ('estrangement' or 'alienation') is conspicuous in its absence despite the fact that it is a word Engels had certainly met in Hegel as well as in Feuerbach and Hess. The 'Outline' had no place for more philosophical vocabulary. In fact, it is only when Engels, in the spirit of Feuerbach, speaks about the *Gattungsbewusstsein* of humanity (its 'species consciousness') that he comes close to philosophy. The ideal is that people work consciously as people, and not as splintered atoms for which the human element (the species being) plays no role.

The comparison between beings without a mutual context and atoms is hackneyed today, but in 1843 it was fresh and new. The atomic theory has roots in antiquity, but remained a mere intellectual curiosity until around 1800 when a poor private teacher in Manchester, John Dalton, gave it its modern form. It is Dalton's image of atoms in a gaseous state, separated from each other, that inspired Engels's description of work in contemporary capitalism.[35]

Factory work was an emblem of this inhuman activity; but it was better represented by speculation on the stock exchange. For Engels, speculation in shares marked 'immorality's culminating point' in which people tried to make a profit from everything, especially the misfortunes of others. This did not mean that everyone who speculated had to be immoral. Competition forced them into it, whatever their personal motives may have been. The alternative was that they would be out-competed and go under.

There was thus something wrong with the system, and not private individuals. In a good society, they would function as actual people, conscious of their humanity. And a society of this kind was the dream of the future! Early on in the article, Engels said that the progress the current system delivered, despite everything, would clear the way for a world that entailed 'the reconciliation of mankind with nature and with itself'. And humanity's forces of production are infinite – something that would then become clear. The deadly competition of today would then be replaced by the peaceful rivalry that Fourier wrote about.[36]

But the road there would be difficult. Stiffening competition
led to constantly recurring crises that cast workers into unemployment and destitution, and ruined many capitalists as well.
And within the crises, the risk always lurked that someone would
knock out all their rivals and create a monopoly on the market,
with all the ruthlessness that entailed.

In the final paragraph, Engels flew the colours for another, even
more important, writing task that now awaited him – dealing
with the factory system and pitilessly revealing 'in detail the despicable immorality of this system, and to expose mercilessly the
economist's hypocrisy which here appears in all its brazenness'.[37]
This would clearly be his later *Condition of the Working Class in
England*.

Engels began writing his article late in 1843 and was finished
with it in January, 1844. He then sent it to Marx and Ruge for the
Jahrbücher. Marx, who in the environment of Paris had already
absorbed a number of new lessons that affected him deeply, must
have realized immediately that Engels's work contained subject
matter that he too had to assimilate. Now economic theory was
the most important of all! He took to the work with his customary energy. He certainly had the article in his hands in January
1844; it came out in print at the end of February, and by April
he was ready to start writing his own work in which economics,
politics, and philosophy would be moulded together.

The project was never completed. A few notebooks remain,
which posterity has chosen to call the *Economic and Philosophic
Manuscripts of 1844*. They are sometimes also spoken of as the
Paris Manuscripts. The text covers approximately 120 printed
sheets.

We do not know what made Marx stop the project at that exact
point. We only know that Engels came to Paris during the summer
of 1844 and stayed there for ten days, during which time Marx
and he became friends. They spent most of those days together,
drinking beer and discussing economics and politics and philosophy. They discovered that they agreed on almost everything and
decided to join forces in a new project where they would settle
accounts with the doctrine they both had once been followers
of: Young Hegelianism. In that radical idealism, they now saw

a danger for the future fate of Germany, namely that idealism blocked the way of real humanism in the spirit of Feuerbach.

It is quite probably that this project, which resulted in a few joint writings, gave Marx a reason to discontinue the work on the *Manuscripts*. Engels should not be blamed for this, however. No one was more eager than he that Marx should finish his criticism of contemporary society. In his letters later on, he would constantly encourage Marx to bring his work to an end. But Marx was constantly finding new books that he first had to read, and new problems he first had to solve.

The *Economic and Philosophic Manuscripts*, which he wrote over a few months in the spring and summer of 1844, were so important both in themselves and for his development, that they receive their own chapter here.

5

The Manuscripts

Belated Renown

The *Economic and Philosophic Manuscripts of 1844* lay with the rest of the papers left by Marx for nearly ninety years. They were finally printed in 1932, in the *Marx-Engels-Gesamtausgabe*. One of the first people to comment on the text was Herbert Marcuse, in an article in the journal *Die Gesellschaft*, in which he drew the basic ideas in the incomplete manuscript into the contest over what constituted the core of Marx's theory.[1] Marcuse was at that time one of the leading representatives of the 'Frankfurt School', which had its centre in the *Institut für Sozialforschung* in Frankfurt. Like his new colleagues, Marcuse distanced himself from the Marxism–Leninism that was being developed in the Soviet Union, the chief task of which was to defend the policies the new country was carrying out. In that context, the central ideas of the *Manuscripts* – such as humanity's essence and alienation – had no place. Those parts of Marx's theories that filtered through were largely limited to what had been passed on by Lenin.

It would be a long time before the *Manuscripts* were published in what after the Second World War was called the Eastern Bloc. In the standard collected works, the *Marx-Engels-Werke* (or MEW), the first thirty-nine volumes had no space for them. Finally, in 1968, they were included in the first of both supplementary volumes (*Ergänzungsbände*) that, at that time, completed the work. By then, the manuscripts had already been in print in countries in the West, and the central idea – alienation – had become the subject of lively, sometimes heated, discussions. The showdown that drew the most attention played out in Poland between the young philosopher Leszek Kołakowski and the then 'chief ideologist' of the Communist Party, Adam Schaff. We will deal with that in more detail in the final chapter.

Several years earlier, the same manuscript had provided arguments against orthodox Marxism–Leninism in Western Europe. People began to speak of a humanistic Marxism in which people, and not the class struggle or the Party, stood at the centre. Roger Garaudy, who throughout his long life would adopt many different points of view, was still a member of the French Communist Party in 1957, when he published a book called *Humanisme marxiste* (Marxist Humanism). Even among non-Marxists, the *Manuscripts* aroused great positive interest. They played a crucial role in Jesuit author Jean-Yves Calvez's 1956 book *La pensée de Karl Marx* (The Thought of Karl Marx), and in particular they contributed to Jean-Paul Sartre beginning to consider himself a Marxist in the late 1950s. The most important result of this new orientation was his substantial 1960 work *Critique de la raison dialectique* (Critique of Dialectical Reason).[2]

In Moscow, the new image of Marx roused vexation. The most influential philosopher there, Teodor Oizerman, published among other things a furious article that was also published in German translation. In it, he branded the 'bourgeois and revisionist "critique" of Marxism' as a 'funhouse mirror'. In 1965 a French Marxist philosopher, Louis Althusser, went on an all-out attack on humanistic Marxism in his book *For Marx*. We will have reason to return to Althusser.[3]

But now, to Marx's work.

A Great Project Is Born

Through the *Economic and Philosophic Manuscripts* we come close to Marx's first, somewhat wary encounter with political economy.[4] Previously, he had only encountered economic theories in a roundabout way – first, perhaps, through Hegel's writings and then through various socialists and communists. Engels, as we already know, was the one who gave him the impulse to start reading Adam Smith, David Ricardo, and James Mill (John Stuart Mill's father) himself. Obviously, Marx had quickly arrived at the insight that he had to get to the sources himself. Moreover, with his considerable self-esteem, he was convinced that he also could achieve something that no one else, not even Engels, could manage.

As he began this new project, he believed that his work on economic theory would be a fairly brief and limited history. In the foreword he attached to the *Manuscripts*, he talked about his newly shelved project, a critique of jurisprudence and political science 'in the form of a critique of the Hegelian philosophy of right'. Uniting the examination of speculation with the review of various more empirical materials proved to be unsuitable, he said. Moreover, he added, an 'aphoristic presentation of this kind … would have given the *impression* of arbitrary systematization'.[5] Hegel made the same kind of reservations in his forewords to *The Phenomenology of Spirit* and *The Science of Logic*, in which he points out that there is a crucial difference between an actual systematic description and one that only loosely puts the results together without accounting for how they were obtained.[6]

Now, Marx had set himself another, possibly higher goal. He intended to publish a series of 'pamphlets' on law, politics, morals, and so on, crowning the project with a work indicating the context among the various parts and carrying out criticism of the speculative treatment thereof – in a genuinely systematic way, one would assume.

The only visible result of these substantial ambitions was the manuscript on political economy. It is difficult to know how economics, in Marx's interpretation, could be put together with 'law, ethics, and politics'. It is not indicated in his letters from that time, or in other writings. In January 1845, Engels was still urging him to quickly finish with his 'political economy book', at a time when Marx had not touched the manuscript for several months. It did not matter whether Marx himself was satisfied with the results, Engels said. Time was fleeting, it was a matter of 'strik[ing] while the iron is hot'.[7] Much later, in March, another of his friends – Georg Jung, whom he had got to know during his time at

Rheinische Zeitung – wrote a letter in which he inquired what had become of 'your work on political economy and politics'. Do not let yourself be distracted by other tasks, Jung encouraged him. 'With your brilliant writing style and the great clarity in your argumentation, you will and must be a success here [in Prussia] and become a star of the first magnitude.'[8]

But no words could persuade Marx. He was already heading in another direction.

In his foreword to the *Manuscripts*, his plans are even grander. He assures the reader that his report is built on solid studies of the literature on the subject, and it is hard for the reader to doubt it. Marx reproduces many long quotes from Smith, Ricardo, and others. But they are not alone in the text. Marx points out that he had also read the works of French and British socialists, and names a few original German contributions as well. First, he calls attention to Weitling's writings, which he had already praised in his article in *Vorwärts*, and points out a few articles that Moses Hess had recently published in *21 Bogen aus der Schweiz* (21 Sheets from Switzerland). One of them was called 'Sozialismus und Kommunismus' (Socialism and Communism); in it, Hess developed the harmonious image of the relationship between socialism and communism that he also expressed in a letter to Marx. Communism was, quite simply, radical socialism. On the other hand, Marx does not mention another article by Hess that he had just been a part of publishing in his and Ruge's *Deutsch-Französisch Jahrbücher*. It is called 'Über das Geldwesen' (On Finances), and according to Hess's foremost biographer Edmund Silberner, it is probable that it had been important for Marx's article 'On the Jewish Question' and also influenced the *Manuscripts* and their treatment of money.[9] But here, Marx's silence is reasonable. There are no obvious similarities between this article by Hess and Marx's thoughts on the significance of money. The only point on which they both agree concerns religion and its relationship to buying and selling.

On the other hand, Marx also mentions Engels's 'Outlines' among his sources of inspiration; it would be strange otherwise. Even Feuerbach's name turned up. But there, it was only a matter of philosophical inspiration. Marx's picture of the world was still characterized by Feuerbach's mixture of humanism and naturalism.

At the end of the foreword, Marx promises a reckoning with Hegel's dialectic. 'In contrast to the *critical theologians* of our days, I have deemed ... a critical discussion of *Hegelian dialectic* a philosophy as a whole – to be absolutely necessary.' By 'critical theologians', he meant Bruno Bauer and his other old friends from Berlin whom he now seemed to see as his main opponents. One question inevitably presents itself: Why is this reckoning so important for Marx in a pamphlet that would concern the criticism of modern political economy? This question cannot even approximately be answered until the contents of the *Manuscripts* have been examined in more detail.

The Struggle Between Worker, Capitalist, and Landowner

Before we go into Marx's text in more detail, there is an important remark to make. Marx speaks throughout of the worker as 'he', never as 'she'. In one sense, he is simply following the grammatical rules of German at the time. Where we, in a later period, would write 'he or she' – or even 'they' – it had long been the rule to simply write 'he'. But Marx's use of language is still odd in light of a few important bits of information he reproduced without commentary. One of the authors he cites in quite a bit of detail is the German Wilhelm Schultz, who in 1843 had just published an ambitious work titled *Die Bewegung der Production* (The Development of Production). In his book, Schultz – who lived a long life in constant opposition to the powers that be – collected a large amount of material on the development of society. The statistical information in particular was useful to Marx. One piece of information he reproduced held that 158,818 men and 196,818 women were working in English spinning mills. Similar conditions prevailed in similar industries in the United States. In wool factories, on the other hand, where the work demanded greater physical strength, men were predominant.[10]

It is odd that Marx did not comment on these numbers. His worker is always a *he*, although the most typical industries of the

Industrial Revolution – and the ones that got the most attention –
were dominated by women. He shared this blindness with many
others of his time, of course, but it is nonetheless a blindness.

In the *Manuscripts*, Marx for the first time describes society as
an arena for conflicts between workers, capitalists, and landowners. He primarily follows in Adam Smith's tracks, but also those
of other, later economists as well. Working wages are determined
by 'the antagonistic struggle between capitalist and worker',
he writes. But the worker 'necessarily' loses in this showdown.
Capitalists gang up, while workers are forbidden to collaborate.
Union struggles are thus still out of sight. Marx did not find it
worthwhile to mention the Chartists' attempt in England; he only
follows in the footsteps of those he cites.

The worker becomes just a commodity. In times of decline, it is
the workers who suffer the most. But not even when the economy
is flourishing can they safely count on better wages. Capitalists
are personally free to take the profit. They can also invest in new
machinery. The labour of the workers thus becomes more and
more machine-like. It becomes '*abstract labour*', Marx says: the
antithesis of the physical and intellectual wealth that he would
now see, following Feuerbach but also ever after, as the hall-
mark of genuine labour. Increasing production can also compel
workers, or deceive them into wearing themselves out in advance
and dying. It is bad for the individuals, but makes room for new
workers.

It is striking how close Marx's text is to Smith's section on
wages in *The Wealth of Nations*. Much of it is pure paraphrase.
Marx painted the same dark, nearly hopeless picture of the lives
of workers as Smith did. Wages normally approach a minimum
under which death by starvation is imminent. Marx was also following closely in Smith's footsteps when he said that prices on
provisions vary more than the wages of labour, and Smith already
called the worker a commodity.

Marx also repeated Smith's assumption that there was a stage
in which all opportunities for growth were exhausted and economic development would thereby reach its absolute maximum.
Even in such a state, the lot of the workers is precarious. Wages

would be as low as possible. Marx spoke of 'static misery'.[11] It was a conviction that Marx would later abandon.

When he got to capital profits, he assiduously cited his political economic authorities, particularly Adam Smith but also David Ricardo and Jean-Baptiste Say. One of those he quoted deviated from the others: the French socialist Constantin Pecqueur. For a time, Pecqueur had followed in Saint-Simon's footsteps, and thereafter counted himself among the followers of Fourier. He did not feel at home in this role, either, and went his own way. He differed from most contemporary French socialists in that he saw industrial development as positive. The error lay in the capitalist system alone. In this he anticipated Marx, who could still quote him with approval in *Capital*. But by the time of the coup of Napoleon III in 1851, Pecqueur had already left both economics and politics behind him. Pecqueur thus differed from the other authors that Marx cited in that he did not speak about the workers' situation as a necessary evil but with the same indignation as Marx himself.

The diversity of quotes in the section on profit is certainly a sign that the pages were less well planned than the previous ones, and are nearly in an excerpt stage. Instead, Marx concentrated on the crucial conclusion that the capitalists' only substantial ambition had to be to maximize profits. The implication: those who did not, fell out of the competition. At the same time, competition is the capitalists' hindrance. This means that larger capital knocks out smaller capital, and that monopoly – with all its negative consequences, especially for the workers – was imminent at the end of the road.[12]

The economists' third fundamental theory (after wages and capital), land rent, is also first presented with a swarm of quotations. But Marx himself soon begins to speak. He argued that the feudal lords – the traditional landowners – were finding it increasingly difficult to resist capital. Greater amounts of land were falling into the capitalists' hands. This had gone especially far in capitalism's homeland, England.

In a few important pages, Marx denies having a misconception that could lie near at hand, namely that he was sorry about the old system disappearing and being replaced with new, cold capitalism. He stressed that, unlike the Romantics, he shed no tears over the development. He was not saying, as they were, that a good and natural system was being replaced by one in which buying and selling was the goal of life. On the contrary, he maintained that by its nature, feudalism was bartering. Of course, the capitalists bartered as well, but they did it in a rational manner. Private property itself had its origins in land ownership, which in and of itself meant that people were subject to a lord. The serfs became 'the adjunct of the land' – at heart a temporary appendage. Even the feudal lords were an adjunct of the land. The inner connection between owner and land was only apparent. That semblance was completely abolished with the capitalization of landed property, something that was happening full-scale in England. There, industry was in the process of conquering the land as well.[13]

Alienated Labour

After the sections on wages of labour, capital, and ground rent, the account changes its character. The texts are more thoroughly worked out, and at times they reach magnificent stylistic heights. We witness an author who is pleased with his devastating irony and rhetorical ability with words.

Now headers are missing entirely. The ones that regularly reappear in various editions originate from the first printed version of 1932. They are of course partially arbitrary, but still created a kind of reasonable order.

The first section, called 'Estranged labour', is the one that has attracted the most attention from posterity.[14] The primary reason is the word 'estrangement' – or 'alienation' – itself, and what that implies. At heart, they have the same meaning, whereas in the German they are matched by two words with clear nuances of meaning: *Entfremdung* and *Entäusserung*. The word *Entfremdung* has to do with 'alien'; *Entäuserrung*, on the other hand, has to do with something 'external', in the sense of selling off or parting with something. The terms are used with no great differentiation in the German tradition, although with the nuance that *Entfremdung* is used more often in relations between people, and *Entäusserung* chiefly in relations between people and things. Both go back to the

Latin *alienatio*, which gave rise to different variations of the word 'alienation' that occurs in modern languages.

The most important thing is to narrow down what Marx meant with these loaded words. As we know, the closest background to the account in the *Manuscripts* was Feuerbach's philosophy, in which concepts like the essence of humanity and its essential forces are central. People have been alienated from their essence; they have become a stranger to themselves and to others. This finds its clearest expression in religion – and in speculative philosophy. In them, people create images such as God or the Absolute as surrogates for the complete humanity that exists in their minds but cannot realize in the society they live in.

An entire generation of young Germans who united philosophical interest with political radicalism were deeply impressed by Feuerbach's thinking for a few years in the 1840s; Marx, Engels, and Hess were only some of them. What Marx wrote in the *Manuscripts* distinguishes itself in the fact that he used philosophical concepts so directly in concrete political economic texts. Hess kept to a more general plane, and as we have seen the word *Entfremdung*, like the rest of the philosophical vocabulary, is missing in Engels's *Outlines*. On the other hand, Marx arranged a direct meeting between the worlds of concepts; he followed the texts on economics in detail and then dissected them with philosophical instruments – several of which come from Feuerbach, and others directly from Hegel.

In fact, we stand before one of the most characteristic features in Marx – not only in his early years, but throughout his life. They can be recognized in his doctoral thesis, where the substantial masses of quotes from Greek philosophers are arranged using Hegel's categories. They continue in his criticism of the proposed law in the Rhenish *Landtag* and in his reckoning with Hegel's philosophy of state and law. Marx was above all a tremendous reader who critically scrutinized what he had read.

In a way, we could speak of an *exegesis* in the literal meaning of the word as commentary or interpretation. But Marx devoted himself almost thoroughly to a sharp, inquisitive *criticism* of what he read. He did not content himself with understanding the text; he also wanted to expose it and reveal its actual content. What is more, in this case, he saw the text as an expression of the reality it depicted – a reality that the text itself was unable to grasp the meaning of.

The section on alienated labour in the *Manuscripts* was a pure example of this method of staying close to the text. In the preceding pages, Marx reproduced numerous long quotations from various authors. Now he could concentrate on summarizing them and revealing their blind spots. In his opinion, the political economists had no explanation for the reality they were depicting. More specifically, he said that they did not *comprehend* it. In German, he used the word *begreifen*. It is an important word in Hegel. It has to do with *concepts*; as always, Hegel is particular about drawing out the literal content of words. To comprehend something is literally to 'grasp it', and thereby have the opportunity to scrutinize it in all its aspects. The concept is the intellect's way of getting a clear idea about reality.[15]

The national economists established the laws of the modern economy, but did not comprehend them. They provide no explanation of the division into labour and capital, capital and ground rent. The only thing that seemed to have put the wheels of the economy in motion are '*greed* and the *war amongst the greedy – competition*'. To clarify the economic context, the economists often looked back to a kind of original condition of humanity before all development began. It is a solution that Marx, with his sense of the historically concrete, found unsustainable. The problem, in that case, is reduced to 'the form of a fact, of an event'.

Instead, Marx saw the solution in what the political economy of the time itself emphasized: the workers become poorer the more they produce, and they themselves become a cheaper commodity the more commodities they produce. It is like religion, Marx said: the more humanity transfers themselves to God, the less they have for their own part.

This transfer, whether it occurs in religion or labour, is what Marx called *alienation*. Alienation has multiple forms. The worker cannot express themselves in their labour, but must see it as forced labour that hunger compels them to. The labour is not their own, but someone else's. They are only freely active in their animal functions: eating, drinking, begetting children – but not in their human ones. Humanity as a 'species being' – people in their specifically human functions – are distinguished by the fact that they are universal and free in their activities. But the worker cannot be that.

People resemble other animals in that they live off of organic nature. But they do it in a more multifaceted way than any other animal. They can make all natural phenomena their objects through the natural sciences and in art. They can also handle them in practice. Marx said that nature is their *'inorganic body'*. The choice of the word 'inorganic' may seem odd to us, because what we can primarily live off of is other organisms. But Marx used the word in a sense that was not uncommon for the time. Whatever serves as food for someone else becomes inorganic in that relationship – that is, it ceases to be an organism itself.

Humanity is bound up with nature, and thereby also with itself, for it is in itself a part of nature. But alienated labour alienates it from itself, and thereby from nature.

Humans produce a world of objects – an *objective world*, something that means they transform parts of nature. A beaver or a bee certainly produces something as well, but only for their immediate physical needs. People also have physical needs, but production is not limited to meeting them. In production, people manifest their freedom by producing more than is necessary for their survival. What is necessary only appears as *provisions* – that is, means for the real, productive lives they live.

But the workers are cut off from this. They are reduced to pure survival. They are not free in their activities. Provisions become not simply means for them, but the entire content of life.

Following Feuerbach, Marx spoke of humanity's *species-life*. The workers are shut off from species-life – a life that provides the individual the opportunity to fully realize their possibilities as a person in community with other people. In similar terminology, the worker cannot realize their *essence* as a human.

The concept of alienation, or estrangement, as it is used in the *Manuscripts* is intimately associated with the concept of *essence* – or, more specifically, human essence. Marx thereby inserted himself into a long tradition that goes back to Ancient Greece, which was given a renewed topicality and partially new content in German philosophy during the first decades of the nineteenth century. Immanuel Kant, for example, held yearly academic lectures on the subject of anthropology. It was still an unsettled field in which he, like many others, took up every subject that had to do with humans' physical and mental capabilities. But it was precisely Kant who, at the end of his life, arrived at the conclusion that the question 'What is man?' was one of the greatest mysteries that philosophy had to grapple with. He himself had become too old and infirm to seriously begin work on this new question, but several of his followers tried to attack it in full force. They spoke of anthropology, but it essentially concerned what would come to be called 'philosophical anthropology' in the twentieth century, in contrast to physical anthropology, which deals with people as biological beings, and social anthropology, which puts their construction of society into focus.

Philosophical anthropology grapples with Kant's question, and it does so through attempting to discover what distinguishes humanity from all other creatures. Early on in Berlin, Marx had come into contact with this tendency through following the lectures of Norwegian natural philosopher Henrik (or Heinrich) Steffens in anthropology – according to the notes, even 'diligently'. Steffens was one of the most zealous advocates of philosophical anthropology, which he saw as the foundation of all the sciences.[16] Any influence he might have had on the young Marx was in any case quickly surpassed by the influence Hegel would come to exert. Anthropology was a smaller part of Hegel's system, wedged into the doctrine of the subjective spirit (humanity) between phenomenology and psychology. Hegel's brief exposé of the human soul had certainly appealed to Marx at one time, but it was far from the author of the *Manuscripts*. The soul is something internal, Hegel said, and this internal requires its external, its physicality. The soul is the subject, the body the predicate. Or, in other words, it is the soul that is the starting point, and the body only something required for the soul to be able to act and react in a world of bodies.

Marx's anthropology is of the Feuerbachian type, but nevertheless has its own distinctive character. The sensuous, or empirical, is the starting point. People are bodies equipped with the senses. They are also thinking beings, but it is not thinking that comes first; it is the senses. Both the senses and thinking are necessary conditions for their activities. Humans are, from beginning to end, active beings. Their lives are a continuous interaction between activity and passivity. They act, and with their actions they change their reality – not only their own, but that of others as well. They are dependent to the same extent on what others do. '[J]ust as society itself produces *man as man*, so is society *produced* by him.' This dialectic is the condition for their possibility of being an individual and a social being at one and the same time. In fact, they are only individuals through being social beings and only social beings through being individuals. It is in and through community with others that they can distinguish themselves.

Like Feuerbach, Marx followed in Hegel's footsteps in this conviction. In the tradition that Hobbes and Locke inaugurated back in the seventeenth century, the individual came first. Society was built on an agreement between individuals who in principle could break out of that community at any time in the event that society did not provide them with what they had a right to expect.

This societal ontology, which from the beginning of the nineteenth century was called 'liberal', stood in sharp contrast to a much older conception, according to which people in their original condition were social. Aristotle characterized humans as social beings – a *zōon politikon*, or political animal, as the common, slightly brutalizing translation goes.

In that aspect, Hegel was an enthusiastic follower of Aristotle, and here Marx followed in the footsteps of his first great master. It is only in community with others that a person can become themselves, he also argued. Even when they are working alone – Marx provides the solitary researcher as an example – their entire activity is imbued with the fact that they are social beings. The labour of others is the condition for their own. What they achieve becomes useful and a delight for others.

What is more, it is only through others that they can become an individual. 'Man's individual and species-life are not *different*,' he wrote. It is society that gives the individual access to nature, through the labour and knowledge of others. It is through society that they can be their own distinctive person.

It is important to distinguish Marx's characteristic *individualism*, so unlike the faceless collectivism that characterized the Soviet Union and Maoist China. Humans are not fully fledged individuals right from the start; they *become* – or, rather, *can become* – individuals. The worker, deprived of humanity, is denied this, just as the capitalist is (as we shall soon see).

Private Property and Communism

The immediate obstacle to people being able to realize their inherent possibilities in a highly developed society is private property.[17] Private property attains its perfection with capitalism, but it does not start with capitalism; it is also found in feudalism. Marx once again denies the suspicion that he had any love for the feudal system. In an eruption of linguistic delight, he imitates how feudal lords and capitalists slandered each other. The feudal lord

> depicts his adversary as a sly, hawking, carping, deceitful, greedy, mercenary, rebellious, heartless and spiritless person who is estranged from the community and freely trades it away, who breeds, nourishes and cherishes competition, and with it pauperism, crime, and the dissolution of all social bonds, and extorting, pimping, servile, smooth, flattering, fleecing, dried-up *rogue* without honour, principles, poetry, substance, or anything else.

Movable or personal property, on the other hand,

> points to the miracles of industry and progress. It is the child of modern times, whose legitimate, native-born son it is. It pities its adversary as a simpleton, *unenlightened* about his own nature (and in this it is completely right), who wants to replace moral capital and free labour by brute, immoral violence and serfdom. It depicts him as a Don Quixote, who under the guise of *bluntness, respectability*, the *general interest*, and *stability*, conceals incapacity for progress, greedy self-indulgence, selfishness, sectional interest, and evil intent; it pours cold water on his reminiscences, his poetry, and his romanticism by a historical and sarcastic enumeration of the baseness, cruelty, degradation, prostitution, infamy, anarchy and rebellion, of which romantic castles were the workshops.

It is a festive pyrotechnic display of words.

According to Marx, private property is the great evil, regardless of whether it wears feudal or capitalist clothes. The great counterforce of the time against private property was communism.[18] But communism appears first in a raw, immature shape. It is, as we remember, what Marx said earlier on the verge of departing for Paris, and Moses Hess had developed a more detailed argument along the same line.[19]

But here, Marx concentrated on a particular point in immature communism – the idea that women would also be the common property of men. Marx said that this thought involved a denial of the *personality* of humans. 'Personality' is not a common word in his vocabulary, but it has its evident proximity to a significantly more central concept – namely, the individual. Personality is the distinctive character in a fully developed individual. The intimate relationship between men and women regresses to a purely brutish sexual relation in which all women are seen and treated as objects of lust held in common. In fact, Marx said, the relation between the sexes reflected 'the entire world of culture and civilization'.

He also perceives another, somewhat higher but still immature communism. It could be democratic or despotic in nature, but still primarily political; its goal was the abolition of the state but it maintained private property.

It is only a third kind of communism that Marx stood behind. To describe it, he took up the very key of Hegel's philosophy itself, with its magnificent but hard-to-grasp dialectic: *Aufhebung*. The word is almost impossible to translate into English or French in any adequate fashion. In French, Gwendoline Jarczyk and Pierre-Jean Labarrière made up an entirely new word, *sursumer*, to cover the multiplicity of meanings found in the German that Hegel consciously made use of.[20] In English, *aufheben* is usually rendered as 'sublate', an uncommon word. The *Collected Works*, on the other hand, uses the word 'transcendence', which does not adequately capture its content.

Marx, with his supreme mastery of Hegel's conceptual apparatus, naturally uses the word *Aufhebung*, fully conscious of its triple meaning. The communism he swore allegiance to had as a goal a '*positive* Aufhebung des *Privateigentums* als *menschlicher*

Selbstentfremdung und darum als wirkliche *Aneignung* des *menschlichen* Wesens'. The *Collected Works* translates this as: 'the *positive* transcendence of *private property* as *human self-estrangement*, and therefore as the real *appropriation* of the *human* essence by and for man'. Only the word *aufheben* makes Marx's meaning clear: it is not quite simply a question of abolition. The things that historical development up until then had borne with it would remain in place, but on a higher plane. 'Private property' literally means that the public was *dispossessed* of property (from the Latin *privo*, 'I rob'), but this dispossession had been the precondition for the entire process of progress. Now, Marx argued, the time was ripe to realize the possibilities that each person has in their essence. Finally, they would become the social beings they had the internal resources for. The conflicts between humanity and nature, and between people, would be abolished, and humanity would achieve a perfected humanism that at the same time was a perfected naturalism. The contradiction between humanity's existence and their essence would be abolished; that is, their actual existence would not be in glaring opposition to their inherent possibilities. Nor would their need to affirm themselves and their abilities stand in opposition to the results of their labour.

These are sweeping formulations about a good society, but no concrete information about what the road there would look like. The pages on ideal communism are a typical expression of what, a few years later, would be called 'utopian socialism' in the *Communist Manifesto*. They are only philosophical, but more sophisticated than most other, similar depictions of the future.

The method of equating humanism with naturalism, of course, indicates the influence from Feuerbach. But behind Feuerbach, Spinoza can also be glimpsed. The formula 'God or nature' inspired Marx, as it did Hess. If God is only another name for humanity *as it could be*, then the step between humanism and naturalism is a short one. But that idea also leads him, as we shall see, to quite risky conclusions.[21]

Of particular interest is the idea that humanity should appropriate (*aneignen*) its essence. In German, this is the same *eigen* as in *Eigentum* (property, or possessions). Both have a fascinating origin. To possess something and to appropriate something means making it your own. The modern conception of property began with John Locke. For him, sovereignty over one's own body is the foundation and starting point of all property. From this also follows the right both to one's own thoughts and to the product of one's own labour. Locke seemed unaware of the paradox that lay in the fact that he also counted the labour that 'my servant' performed in the property of the free ego.[22]

With that, Locke glossed over a still dormant but soon to be explosive contradiction between masters and their servants. If the master has the right to the products of his labour, the servants should reasonably also have the rights to theirs too. But how would they both share? Or is there a possibility of sublating the entire conflict?

A century and a half later, the battle lines had been drawn and Marx had joined those who stood on the side of the servants and the workers. But he did not see the solution in all property simply changing owners and going to those who performed the labour. Instead, the category of ownership would be transformed.

People have to live off nature, and through their work they transform the products of nature for their own consumption in an ever more artful fashion. But who should have power over what was thus created? Through private property, certain people appropriated this power to themselves. Others became dependent on them and were compelled to work for them for compensation that was barely sufficient for their own survival.

It could be said that both the private owners and those who work for them must *assimilate* the products of nature. But the assimilation occurs under very different conditions. A fundamental inequality prevailed, which hinders both parties. The assimilation that Marx saw in a happier future applied to the whole of the human essence. People would thus be able to realize all their inherent capabilities. They would become comprehensively active, fully social beings in collaboration with other social beings. Instead of having exclusive access to certain property, they would thus assimilate what nature and society offer, but they could thereby also access themselves and their fellow human beings.

It is striking how Marx, who constructed his reasoning with examples from economic theory, largely left economics out on these pages. Instead, he paints a picture of a kind of *homo universalis*, a universal human not far from the Renaissance ideal. While private property limits humanity, in a society where this is sublated they can assimilate their 'comprehensive essence in a comprehensive manner'. All their ways of relating to reality through 'seeing, hearing, smelling, fasting, feeling, thinking, observing, experiencing, wanting, acting, loving' could then reach their full potential. Private property has made us 'so stupid and one-sided that an object is only *ours* when we have it – when it exists for us as capital, or when it is directly possessed, eaten, drunk, worn, inhabited, etc.'. Real life is only seen as provisions, whereas the life of private property – labour and capital – appears as the actual. The real senses have been displaced by 'the sense of *having*'.[23]

Each of us still carries the development that humanity has gone through. 'The *forming* of the five senses is a labour of the entire history of the world down to the present,' Marx wrote. Someone eating cooked food with a knife and fork experiences something different that someone who tears off raw meat and devours it. The person weighed down with sorrows or worn out from all their labour cannot enjoy a play like a person who is rested and open to impressions. Narrow interests are also limiting. A merchant dealing in precious stones can only have a sense of their economic value, but not for their aesthetic value – that is, their beauty.

Another particularly interesting example he provides concerns music. It is only music that 'awakens in man the sense of music'. But to an unmusical ear, even the most beautiful music has *no* meaning. In fact, it does not even exist as an object for such an ear, 'because my object can only be the confirmation of one of my essential powers'. The object only has meaning for me 'as far as *my* senses reach'.

Marx rarely talked about music. But he did so in a few extremely central, although incomplete, texts. The *Manuscripts* were the first of them. He did not speak about any particular music, either regarding genre or the work of an individual composer. While he often mentioned particular authors – everyone from Aeschylus to Balzac – he only spoke about music in general. By all appearances, it was in Paris that he encountered the most sophisticated music of his life. As we have seen, it was quite possible that he heard Chopin and Liszt – two of history's most legendary piano virtuosi – at Madame d'Agoult's salons. But we know nothing of his reactions. In the many depictions of him from friends and acquaintances that are preserved there is no talk of music in his life; on the other hand, there is much about his tremendous literary reading and the role that drama, poetry, and novels played for him.

Music was not nearly as easily accessible as it is today. Perhaps this was a reason that he was not as concrete as when he talked about literature. This does not mean that references were lacking: Mozart, for example, appears numerous times in his articles and correspondence.[24]

But Marx was particular about linking historical development not only to art, but to human activity in general. The history of industry, he said is 'the *open* book of *man's essential powers*, the perceptibly existing human *psychology*.'[25] The word 'industry' here should not be understood in the current everyday meaning of the word, as companies in which various objects are produced with the help of more or less advanced modern technology. Marx used the word in its original Latin – and in his time, still common – meaning of human diligence and initiative as expressed in general practical activities. But, at the same time, he emphasized that it was '*ordinary essential industry*' he had in mind – that is, manufacture as regards material products.

The use of the word 'psychology' can also easily lead our thoughts astray. Psychology was not yet a highly specialized scientific discipline, but simply a subdivision of philosophy in which people tried, in thought, to get a clear idea of different mental phenomena and their distinctive character. The psychologists, Marx said, had only placed their subject in relation to 'an external relation of history' and not to the essence of humanity. They had not understood alienation, but only talked about humanity in general and in sweeping terms.

But in the objects that people had produced during different periods, we have '*sensuous, alien, useful objects*' in which humanity's '*objectified essential powers*' appear to us, although in the form of alienation.[26] There is much to notice in these lines. First, it indicates that Marx here saw all production up to that point as alienated. Alienation did not begin with capitalism, or even with feudalism. It has been the companion of humanity ever since the beginning. He did not, as is often asserted, have any notion of an Edenic primitive condition.

Secondly, it is important to pause here at the word 'objectification' (*Vergegenständlichung*). It is a central idea in the Hegelian tradition, accented by Feuerbach, that in and through the results of its work humanity creates something that is found within them as a possibility or a natural ability and is thereby expressed in the things they produce. The phrase 'essential powers' itself contains the important word 'power', with the meaning 'that which produces or accomplishes something'. In production, humanity creates objects that are the expression of themselves. As we have seen, being active is part of humanity's essence. Their activities express what they bear within themselves.

Thirdly, it is therefore important to note that Marx emphasized the crucial significance of *material* production. It is easier to see the results of labour as an expression of a person's innermost essence as regards intellectual activity, and art in particular. We imagine that we encounter Beethoven's stormy emotional life in his music, or Dagerman's anguish in his novels, or Picasso's profound rashness in his art. It is also easy to detect a conscious intent in the labour of a skilled craftsman. But in machine-made products? In mass-produced artefacts?

Did Marx wish to say that alienation made it impossible for industrial workers to objectify themselves in the products of their labour? Alienation seems to be universal; no one escapes its curse. Nevertheless, wage workers seem to be particularly affected by it; it is their lot that Marx dwells upon. The *Manuscripts* provide no clear answer to the question. Marx would come back to it thirteen years later, in the *Grundrisse*.

At the same time, the assertion remains that it is in humanity's material production that their essential forces are expressed most clearly. Marx wanted to achieve a paradigm shift. It is neither in art nor in philosophy that we above all can discern what is human. It is in all the useful objects produced – everything from the simplest clay pots, and tools for hunting and agriculture, to steam engines and rotary presses (or, in our contemporary perspective, the most advanced electronics or biotechnology). In short, it is the history of technology that best reveals what kind of beings humans are. Their active essence is most clearly indicated here – their characteristic as working and producing beings. In it, they also prove themselves to be social at heart: they do not work only for themselves, but for everyone else. Clay pots or hand-mills did not only have significance for just a few, but for the development of the entire human race.

Marx emphasized that the history of technology was interwoven with that of the natural sciences. Through technology, the natural sciences reshaped the entire lives of people and their relationship to nature. But philosophy had not succeeded in integrating the natural sciences into it. 'Their momentary unity was only a *chimerical illusion*.'[27] With this, Marx was obviously alluding to Romantic natural philosophy as created by Schelling in the 1790s, which lived on for a few decades. Even Hegel indulged in this fantastic illusion, although in a somewhat divergent version.

Marx's reasoning here is read as indicating that he now wanted to achieve a unification of this kind, not only in the imagination but in a more tangible fashion. It would mean that philosophy would at one and the same time be realized and sublated, interpreted in the common history of technology and of the natural sciences as a key to the question of the essence of humanity.

It was an ambition that led him into far-reaching reasoning about creation and about God. There were still several years to go until Darwin's *The Origin of Species* in 1859, and the idea of species development was not held in great repute. But the new geology had made creation theory unlikely, Marx argued contentedly; had his manuscript come to the attention of his contemporary readers, they would likely have known that he was thinking of Charles Lyell's 1830 book *Principles of Geology*, according to which the forces impacting the surface of the Earth had to have existed for a very long period. Of course, it was so far still more difficult to prove with biological evolution, and Marx felt himself compelled to take refuge in an old theory that had just begun to lose its credibility when he began writing the *Manuscripts*: the doctrine of spontaneous generation (*generatio aequivoca*). According to this theory, life could arise spontaneously out of inorganic material. But with the rapid development of the microscope and the contemporary development of modern cell theory, such ideas had begun to appear outmoded.

Even more feeble was his reasoning when he explained how humanity had come to be. We see an infinite succession of generations without end. It raises the question of whether there should not be a first beginning to this succession. But no, Marx said; that question was an abstraction. Through it, people abstract from humanity itself, just as with nature, and they imagine something independent of them both before the beginning of time.

Moreover, Marx emphasized that 'for the socialist man', the history of the world was a creation of human labour. It is through their labour that nature exists for them. These lines have made several readers of Marx – chief among them Alfred Schmidt – question whether Marx in general assumed a nature outside of humanity and their labour. In its time, Schmidt's 1962 book *Der Begriff der Natur in der Lehre von Marx* (The Concept of Nature in Marx) played an important role in the criticism of the dialectic of nature that Engels developed during the 1860s and 1870s, which later became a fundamental part of Marxism–Leninism.[28]

It is, however, risky to draw general conclusions about Marx's interpretation based on these somewhat sophistic lines in the *Manuscripts*. Only fifteen years later, when he encountered Darwin's theory of natural selection, did he return to questions of this type – and then from entirely different starting points. He betrays no doubts about the independent existence of nature, either in his earlier doctoral thesis or in his later works. Nature preceded humanity. But through its labour, humanity transforms nature.

Needs, Division of Labour, and Money

Marx emphasized that humanity's needs are not fixed. It is always possible to expand them and to create new ones, as it is possible to reduce them to a bare level of subsistence. What decides which needs a person can develop or decrease is their level of wealth. Refined desires can be brought out among those who can afford to satisfy them, but an almost brutish lifestyle is forced on the workers. Even sunlight can be denied them. 'A dwelling in the *light*, which Prometheus in Aeschylus designated as one of the greatest boons, by means of which he made the savage into a human being, ceases to exist for the worker.'[29]

It is the division of labour that, according to Adam Smith and other economists, makes labour more productive and thereby creates greater wealth. The division of labour is not for those whose labour is cut up into ever smaller areas, but for the capitalist. Nor does it serve all of humanity; it only favours a few. It has become a tool of egoism.

Through division of labour, the activities of an individual become increasingly impoverished, which means that everyone affected gets farther and farther from the full wealth of humanity's essence. The division of labour also increases the difference between the talents of different people. It makes the individual increasingly dependent on the labour of others; since it favours capitalism, it also drives development towards concentration and ultimately monopolies.

The power of money in society constantly increases. With its help, everything can be purchased and all human shortcomings can be compensated. The ugly can purchase love, the lame can purchase the muscle power of horses, and the uneducated can purchase an ostensible education. It means nothing if 'I am bad, dishonest, unscrupulous, stupid', for 'money is honoured, and hence its possessor'. But the entire compensatory power of money, looked at more deeply, is still illusory. Money cannot be exchanged for love, only love for love. However much money someone has to purchase art, literature, or musical experiences, it does not help: 'If you want to enjoy art, you must be an artistically cultivated person.'

In this text, Marx got help from the expressive power of literature through generous quotes from Goethe's *Faust* and Shakespeare's *Timon of Athens*. In *Faust*, it is a question of the strength obtained by owning six stallions: 'I tear along, a sporting lord,/ As if their legs belonged to me.' From Shakespeare's play, he chose the charged scene in which the once-rich but now destitute

Timon, hunting for edible roots out in the wilderness, finds a chest of gold instead. He curses his bad luck – he wanted roots, not riches. He knows all too well that money seems to make evil good, stupidity wise, cowardice brave, and baseness noble. But he wants to avoid being caught in its curse yet again. Instead, he wants to live an honest life on his own strength, and thus says no to the gold.[30] In just a few pages, Marx thus managed to cite three of the authors he had the highest opinion of: Aeschylus, Shakespeare, and Goethe. In short, he mobilizes another kind of riches – cultural riches – than the kind money automatically gives access to.

For Marx, money constituted the very culmination of alienation. Through it, I can exchange and transform everything that is a part of what is human; I can unite the irreconcilable and replace what I might lack in my own equipment. I can develop the most prodigious needs. Those who have no money also have needs, of course, but they are 'a mere thing of imagination', Marx said.[31] (Readers of Strindberg may recall *The Red Room*, in which the dead-broke Sellén and Olle Montanus try to satisfy their hunger by reading about cabbage rolls in a cookbook.) If I need to travel but have no money, I need to repress that need. If I am gifted but poor, I am not in reality suited for studies, but with a fortune I can earn my degrees even if I lack talent. Money is a means to realize desires that actually lie beyond the reasonable, but its absence makes the most reasonable goal completely unattainable.

And Finally, Hegel …

In his foreword, Marx starts by pointing out that he was thinking of concluding his work with a critical review of Hegel's dialectic. Such a critique exists, but it is as incomplete as most of the *Manuscripts*.[32]

The contemporary German philosophers, with Bruno Bauer at their head, had forgotten to take a position on Hegel's dialectic despite claiming to be critics, Marx asserted. The only exception was Feuerbach, who demonstrated that philosophy had the same roots as religion, and that the relationship between human and human also had to be the foundation for every good theory.

In Hegel, everything took place in thought. Even sensuous entities, like religion and the state, are intellectual phenomena. The greatness in his system lies in his view of the creative process as a succession of negations in which what is achieved is continuously sublated and at the same time lifted to a higher stage. He thereby ascribes a key role to labour, and defines humanity as a result of its own activities.

In his view on labour, Hegel agreed with the modern political economists, Marx said. They also see the positive side of labour, but are blind to the negative. But the only labour Hegel recognizes is spiritual (or, to use contemporary language, intellectual). When a person of flesh and blood creates objects that are alien to him, however, it is not the activity that is the active subject but the person himself. Hegel did not start from reality, but from thinking about reality.

Marx did not yet see himself as a materialist. Both materialism and its opposite, idealism, differ from humanistic naturalism in the spirit of Feuerbach, which at that time Marx was an adherent of. In fact, the contradiction between them is sublated in this observation, which is superior to both.

On the one hand, humanity is subject to the forces of nature like all other living beings. On the other hand, through its knowledge, humanity consists of beings that can change their lot. In their thinking, according to Marx, humans are still doomed to make use of formal categories of thought that are ultimately a sign of their alienation. It is Hegel's merit that he showed both this and that the categories inevitably had to pass into each other in a dialectical process. But he had really shown how impossible his own system was. It was the Absolute Idea that, in Hegel's system, constituted the culmination of development. But did he not say that all concepts, and thereby even his own, had to be abolished and to make room for something else in an eternal process of change? Hegel thus abolished himself, thereby revealing against his will that abstract thinking, regarded in its isolation, was nothing. With that, he paved the way for Feuerbach.

And so end the *Manuscripts*. In a substantial respect, Marx still agreed with the Young Hegelian criticism that he himself once directed against Hegel: dialectical development could never come to a halt, either at the Absolute or at the existing Prussian state. Everything was subject to the law of changes.

But, at the same time, inspired by Feuerbach, he argued that he had overcome his previous standpoint. If so, how did it relate to humanistic naturalism? Did this not also have to pass into the continuous succession of categories? And what about communism? Was it not depicted in the *Manuscripts* as the stable future of humanity? Was that not, too, insufficiently dialectical?

These are unanswered questions. Marx, in the spirit of Hegel, would probably see them as meaningless. We can never lift ourselves above the historical situation we live in. The possibility of communism becomes apparent in the time we live in, but beyond this possibility we cannot distinguish any more distant future. And humanistic naturalism is the development that philosophy has arrived at. It is meaningless to speculate about knowledge that we do not yet have. The insights of the future lie beyond our horizons.

An Important Stage in Marx's Development

The *Manuscripts* are a remarkable work that contain some of the most brilliant pages Marx ever wrote, but also long quotes and an account of Hegel that only someone who is already versed in his philosophy can fully follow. We can also see the first impression of his encounter with modern political economics, and Adam Smith in particular. The quotes, the paraphrases, and the summary conclusions are the result of a brief, intense period of reading. Smith and James Mill are quoted in French; the originals were perhaps unavailable in Paris and, in any case, French was nearly a second mother tongue for Marx while English still seemed quite exotic. But the little that is reproduced from Ricardo is still in English.

Marx had not yet managed to form his own interpretation of economic questions. He made a point of emphasizing that he was following closely in the footsteps of the specialists – often word for word, in fact. He reproduced their thesis that it was labour that gives a commodity its value. He followed them in the conviction that development would nevertheless only make the workers' situation even worse and push their wages further down towards the minimum. In short, he wholly accepted the dominant theory of impoverishment and Ricardo's famous 'iron law of wages' that a forgetful posterity often blames Marx for, even though he abandoned it after 1848.

His own original contribution in the *Manuscript* consisted of his setting this brutal reality against an idea of what a very expressive human life would be. Without going into more detail, he also argued that technological and scientific development had now gone so far that a life of that kind, purely as regards resources, lay within reach. But a system hostile to people does not force just the workers into a life that is wretched in every way. It also puts their opponents, the capitalists, in a situation where they cannot develop their humanity either. All their attention is directed towards saving their own skin in competition with other capitalists, resisting the workers' demands, surviving recurring crises and keeping their machinery on a level with technological development. People are, by nature, active and social beings, Marx said. Neither worker nor capitalist has the opportunity to realize this in the prevailing situation.

The *Manuscripts*, on the one hand, paint a bright picture of the essence of humanity and the possibilities of the time, and on the other hand a dark picture of its realities. The contrast brings Marx to see the overthrow of existing conditions as posing few practical problems. The French revolutions of 1789 and 1830 were political revolutions, but what was now required by extension was a social transformation in which people finally liberate themselves from the bondage of private property. Marx had nothing to say about violence, barricades, or military adventures. The *Manuscripts* are perhaps his most optimistic writings.

But it could be said that he painted a rare image of what people can be and painfully contrasted it with the kind of life the workers are forced to live. More briefly, but just as starkly, he observed the barrenness of the existence of the capitalists.

We have to remember that Marx's picture of humanity forms the antithesis of the one that predominated in political economics, and by and large in the liberal tradition in general. There, people were lazy at heart and work had to be organized so that it forced the person performing the work into diligence. The small carrot of wages and the powerful whip of discipline had to exist so that a person would not sink into the swamp of indolence.

According to liberal economists, people were not social at heart, either. They voluntarily allowed themselves to become members of society and remain there because they find particular advantages through the protection of their own persons and their property. Marx's human blooms only in community with others. But Marx is not alone in his interpretation. The active and social person has a central place in the philosophy of Hegel, and behind him is a tradition that reaches all the way back to Ancient Greece. The ideal of the *vita activa*, which Hannah Arendt wrote about in her famous book of 1958, has a long and rich tradition.[33]

And finally: Why does Marx feel compelled to take up Hegel in the *Manuscripts*? In the foreword, he himself declared that the reason was because the Hegelian dialectic still held a strong position in Germany. But there was also another reason indicated by the text itself, which has to do with what Marx now seemed to have arrived at. Marx was still following in Feuerbach's footsteps, and Feuerbach had asserted that philosophy – particularly Hegel's – related to people's reality in the same way as religion does. Behind the ideal greatness that in religion is called God and in philosophy the Absolute actually hides humanity *as it could be* in an ideal society. Now Marx placed political economy in the same scheme. The national economists and Hegel were in agreement on one point: labour is the driving force in history and society. But neither Hegel nor the national economists could see the negative side of labour, because they did not begin from the point of view of a person performing the work but from an abstract idea. The political economists' view of labour can thus be inserted into Feuerbach's scheme alongside the God of religion and the Absolute Idea of philosophy.

This new insight prepared the ground for an in-depth study of economic theories and the reality that they both revealed and concealed. But Marx let that study wait for a time yet. Instead, it was Hegel's radical pupils who became the subject of his next great writing project.

He laid the *Manuscripts* aside, incomplete.

6

The Years of Ruptures

After Marx abandoned his work on the *Manuscripts*, he completed three larger works in rapid succession, two of which found publishers and thus a circle of readers. In the first, *The Holy Family*, Engels made a smaller contribution, while his role in the second – *The German Ideology* – was equal to Marx's. On the other hand, the third – *The Poverty of Philosophy* – was exclusively Marx's work.

These three works are our focus here. But as always, the author's own life forms an important background to what he achieved on the path of writing. The years between 1844 and 1847 were turbulent ones in Marx's life. He was deported from Paris early in 1845, the city he loved most, and was forced to take refuge in Brussels, which lay some distance away from the centre of events. The deportation hit him hard, and with all certainty contributed to the harder polemical tone that characterized his writings in Brussels. His political standpoint also became more clean-cut and pushed him into feuds with people he had previously praised.

The Holy Family

When Friedrich Engels came to Paris at the end of August 1844, Marx was still working full-time on the *Manuscripts*. The visit from the man who had inspired him to pounce on political economic literature also got him to set aside his work. A new joint writing project took form over the ten days Engels stayed in Paris, and both new friends set immediately about their self-imposed task.

The joint plan concerned a clever little pamphlet. Engels had already written his share – a little over fifteen pages – during his time in Paris. But, for Marx, the writing project grew, and it occupied him well into November. He had then reached more than 200 pages, and the pamphlet had become a book. It would be called *Kritik der kritischen Kritik: gegen Bruno Bauer und Konsorten* (Critique of Critical Criticism. Against Bruno Bauer and Company).[1] But the publishers, Joseph Rütten and Zacharias Löwenthal, found the title abstract and not a very easy seller; in a letter to Marx, Löwenthal suggested the book be rechristened *Die heilige Familie* (The Holy Family).[2] And so it was. What had previously been the main title became the subtitle.

The change alarmed Engels. He was at home in Barmen-Wuppertal, among his strictly religious family, and now both the blasphemous title and his own name were shown on a book cover that anyone could see in the bookstore. He already found it odd that his name stood alongside Marx's – even first, according to alphabetical order. His own contribution had been quite modest.[3]

Later readers could agree with him on the latter point. In essence, it is Marx's book. Engels contributed a few short sections, kept in somewhat the same style as Marx's but significantly tamer.

For the new work, Marx had the use of his intensive economic studies. When, for example, he answered the criticism of Proudhon as it was formulated in *Allgemeine Literatur-Zeitung*, he interspersed bits of text that are easily recognizable from the *Manuscripts*. But this, and similar sections, do not carry the account forward. Marx only demonstrated his newfound knowledge that was already miles superior to that of his opponents.

As a whole, on the other hand, the text is marked by tireless energy and sparkling humour in its attacks on his old friends among the Young Hegelians. The parodical device is pervasive and carried out with great consistency. Bruno Bauer and the others appeared on a metaphysical stage on which the Last Judgement is immediately at hand. This device, of course, has its background in the fact that Bauer was a theologian, although with negative overtones as time went on. Only a few years earlier, as we have seen, he had published a pamphlet called *The Trumpet of the Last Judgement*, and in general his texts were full of Biblical allusions. The direct target of attack for Marx and Engels was the afore-mentioned monthly periodical with the engaging title *Allgemeine Literatur-Zeitung* – a venerable name borne by an earlier German periodical that was influential in its time. Bauer and his fellow thinkers in the group that now called itself *Die Freie* (The Free) published it between December 1843 and October 1844. It cultivated what Bauer called 'pure criticism' in contrast to other, clearly more sullied criticism that was flourishing at the time. Marx forced the expression to parodic heights by calling the activity 'critical criticism'.

With particular ardour, Marx objected to the negative, and often condescending, declarations 'Die Freien' were scattering about regarding the workers and what they called 'the masses' despite calling themselves socialists. Edgar Bauer, Bruno's younger brother, argued that the workers who had united in England and France had shortcomings in their thinking. Marx responded that these workers could not argue away their degradation in practice through pure thought. On the contrary, they were experiencing the painful difference between '*being* and *thinking*, between *consciousness* and *life*'.[4] They did not stop being wage workers through any theories. Bauer's idealism constituted the difference between his socialism and that of the workers.

When Edgar Bauer asserted that Proudhon had not thought through his attitude towards society, Marx snorted with contempt before such conceit. He was no less contemptuous of Bruno Bauer's criticism of the masses. Bauer saw the masses as the real enemies of Spirit. Marx's retort was that people 'must know the studiousness, the craving for knowledge, the moral energy and the unceasing urge for development of the French and English workers to be able to form an idea of the *human* nobility of this movement'.[5] Implied: Bauer did not know, while Marx himself did (though as regards the English, only through Engels).

Bruno Bauer was concerned about the chasm that separated him from 'the crowd'. Pure criticism aimed at feeling and knowing everything. But how could he convey his insights to the ignorant?

It was there he saw his great and difficult task. Full of sarcasm, Marx distanced himself from these concerns.[6]

In his periodical, Bauer had attacked Marx's article on the Jewish question. Marx replied that Bauer could not see the difference between political and human emancipation. It was now, as we know, a crucial difference for Marx. Political liberation concerned people's relationship to state power; human liberation their relationship to their labour, to each other and ultimately to their own egos.[7]

Marx also took the time to polemicize against Bauer's view of history. Bauer had spoken of 'ideas that produced the French Revolution', and Marx responded: 'Ideas *cannot carry out anything* at all.' For that, people who could realize what they desired in practice were required. Here, Marx drew out the revolution's most radical advocates from the shadows: people like François-Noël Babeuf and others. They were people and movements who had become important for him when, in Paris, he studied an impressive amount of literature on the French Revolution. He regarded the revolutionaries who stood furthest to the left as the forerunners of communism.[8]

Bauer saw each individual in society as an atom, alone in its orbit. Marx replied that this was an idea that an egoistic individual could use to make themselves feel more important. But in fact it was 'a *need*, a *necessity*' that drove people together.[9] The reader may recognize the insight from the *Manuscripts* that a person must be a social being before she can become an individual.

Marx also entered into a battle on the history of philosophy. But there, in *The Holy Family*, he took up a different attitude than he usually did. Following Feuerbach, he sees radical empiricism (or sensualism) as the very basis of the materialist tradition. Francis Bacon was its forefather and John Locke was an important person in the tradition, whereas Hobbes was a more dubious figure who made geometry out of reality and thereby developed materialism into a 'misanthropy'. Materialism was civilized with the thinkers of the French enlightenment; it took form and became eloquent.

In a direct polemic with Bauer, Marx banishes Spinoza from the history of materialism. This was something new, and possibly his understanding became more incisive in the heat of battle. He evidently wanted to place maximum distance between himself and not only 'The Free' but also Hegel and his historical writings. It also made it possible for him to emphasize that French and British socialists and communists were carrying on the tradition from Bacon and d'Holbach. Humanism and materialism ran together in them (in the *Manuscripts*, Marx had spoken about humanism and naturalism; the difference is unimportant).[10]

The Bauer brothers were the most important target of attack in *The Holy Family*, but Marx had his eye in particular on one of their companions: 'Herr Szeliga', who was actually named Franz Zychlin von Zychlinski and was not only a Young Hegelian but a Prussian officer. In the most crushing manner, Marx summarized Herr Szeliga's way of writing: 'His art is not that of disclosing what is hidden, but to hide what is disclosed.' Szeliga's particular sin was that he held the novels of Eugène Sue in high regard, and that he seemed to see important truths in them about contemporary society.[11] Marx, on the other hand, is contemptuous of Sue's sentimental depictions of the metropolitan slums in *Mystères de Paris*. Marx therefore attacked an article by Szeliga on the hero in Sue, named Rudolph von Gerolstein. The polemic runs over a long chapter that is rather impenetrable to a modern reader.[12] Only after that comes the final chapter, with a much more distinct depiction of 'the Critical Last Judgement', in which the conditions from Revelations are joined together with a bombastic statement taken directly from *Allgemeine Literatur-Zeitung* on the contemporary era as the age of decision. The medieval hymn *Dies irae* (Day of Wrath) sounds, and the sign of the Bauer brothers (*Bauer* means 'farmer' in German) is shown, together with the French words of wisdom 'With the oxen paired together, *Ploughing* goes much better!'.

And now the world ought to come to an end, but in a 'Historical Epilogue' Marx stated that it was not the world that disappeared, but *Allgemeine Literatur-Zeitung*.[13]

The Holy Family is the first book by Marx (as well as by Engels) that went into print. It was no brilliant debut. It contains witticisms and biting irony, but it is long-winded in places and entirely too comprehensive in relation to its relatively limited subject.

Even Engels, the co-author, was frightened at the format; Georg Jung, their friend from Cologne, let Marx know in a letter that the many enumerations of inessentials were tiring. At the same time, Jung sweetened the bitter assessment with an admission that the criticism of the Young Hegelians was a reward for the reader.[14]

The question that above all has to be asked is why Marx found it so important to write all those pages about the Bauer brothers and Szeliga. The purely psychological explanation that it concerned a kind of escapism – it was easier to settle accounts with old friends from his youth whose arguments he had mastered to perfection than to complete a work that touched on new and difficult themes – is insufficient.

There must have been more objective reasons as well. Something made Marx see it as necessary to put Young Hegelianism behind him once and for all. It soon also turned out that not even the more than 200 pages he devoted to the subject were enough; he was ready to throw himself into a new, even lengthier work on the same subject.

That work began when the scene of Marx's life completely changed. That change must be accounted for before the question of what pushed Marx to yet another work on the Young Hegelians can even approximately be answered.

A Painful Farewell and a New Life

After proposals from Prussia, the French government under the leadership of Guizot decided to deport Marx from France. The decision came as a complete surprise to Marx. In the beginning, he took the deportation order lightly. Perhaps he could still remain? But when he realized that it was serious, he became deeply depressed. The Belgian capital of Brussels was the only reasonable place that now stood open for him – but what was Brussels compared to Paris? He had really loved the lively, multifarious environment in Paris, where he could freely move both among the salons and the secret political societies that stood farthest to the left on the political scale. He had made many new friends in Paris – everyone from Heinrich Heine to French socialists and communists. His working energy had been great; he had produced a large manuscript and nearly an entire book, at the same time as he devoted himself to exhaustive studies in economics and history. Moreover, he had had time for political meetings, nightly conversations and the odd evening in the salons of Madame d'Agoult.

Now all this would disappear before his eyes.

Brussels was not just much smaller than Paris. The cultural and intellectual environment was also significantly poorer. The city had become the capital of the new kingdom of Belgium only fifteen years before, after a revolution that began following a performance of Daniel-François-Esprit Auber's rather new opera *The Mute Girl of Portici* at the La Monnaie theatre. The opera dealt with independence, and the Belgians burned for independence from the Dutch. The uprising quickly succeeded. A king was brought in from the extremely small German principality of Saxe-Coburg and crowned Léopold I.

Most in Brussels still spoke Dutch, a language that neither Karl nor Jenny had command of. One comfort for the family was that they were not alone in their situation. There were already numerous refugees and guest workers there, in particular German ones – a good breeding ground for radical political thinking. In addition, Brussels had the advantage of lying centrally between the metropolises of Europe. Karl would soon discover that it was excellently suited for building networks.

But when he left Paris, he saw nothing but wretchedness in his banishment. His melancholy was so great when he hastily set off that his travelling companion and friend, Heinrich Bürgers, tried to cheer him up with happy songs while they were both seated in the stagecoach for Brussels. We do not know if he succeeded.

For Jenny Marx, her spouse's deportation meant even more acute problems. She was the one who had to dispose of the family's small amount of property left behind in Paris in order to produce a little bit of cash. She was pregnant again, this time with their daughter Laura; by her side she had Jennychen, still an infant. In a letter to Karl, written in French, she described her endless and fruitless troubles. But she also talked about the friends who surrounded her: Heine, Bakunin, and in addition the poet and revolutionary Georg Herwegh. Not a word of complaint was

directed at Karl; all problems are blamed on the infamous governments personified by Guizot and Alexander von Humboldt,
the Prussian minister in Paris (more famous for being a natural
scientist and explorer).[15]

But Jenny and Jennychen would come to Brussels soon enough,
and it was there that Laura was born. It was also in Brussels that a
woman named Helene Demuth would make her entrance into the
lives of the family Marx. Jenny's mother had sent her over from
Trier, well aware of all the hardships her daughter was encoun-
tering in her new daily life, particularly as the help she had had
in Paris could not follow them to Brussels. Demuth would soon
become the family's right hand, skilfully piloting them through all
the trivial but painful problems that waited in the times to come.
She also became a friend to the family, taking part in their joys
and sorrows. She stayed patiently at her post for as long as Jenny
and Karl lived.[16]

For her part, Jenny had developed an ability that was invaluable for her spouse. She was long the only one able to decipher
his singular handwriting and was the one who copied it all out
for him over nearly the entire remainder of her life. She was no
passive copyist but became his closest partner in discussion, better
informed of her spouse's work than even Engels.

In the beginning of their time in Brussels, Engels kept Karl
informed on what was happening in Barmen-Wuppertal. The
picture he conveyed was a twofold one. On the one hand, his
letters dealt with the great successes he met with in his home
district with his communist propaganda. He was completely
euphoric over the stream of interested people: soon there would
be a hundred attending. He did not, however, mention the composition of his audience: it was the citizenry who were taking seats
on the premises, not proletarians. His optimism at the future was
not tarnished by that fact. He expressed the same kind of euphoria that Marx did during his time in Paris. The future was turning
out to be splendid: 'Wuppertal communism is *une verité*'.

But the meetings would soon come to the attention of the
authorities, and they were forbidden without further ado. The
success story ended just as hastily as it had begun.[17]

Engels's letters also had another theme: the fury his father was developing over his son's radical aberrations. I'm living a real dog's life, Friedrich complained. The old man can't distinguish between liberalism and communism, but he's furious. Both are equally revolutionary in his eyes. The most important thing Engels achieved at that time was the great, nearly sociological investigation *The Condition of the Working Class in England* (in the original German, *Die Lage der arbeitenden Klasse in England*). In it, he depicted the hard, dirty, and precarious lives the new industrial proletariat was being forced to live in northwestern England and southern Scotland, in a manner that was simultaneously lucid and minutely accurate. In its way, it is a pathbreaking work; as a whole, it is the best book of which Engels was the sole author. He was still only twenty-five years old.

The Condition also played an important role for Marx. The empiricism in it was crucial, especially for his great work on capitalism that was now constantly in progress.

Engels would soon enough come to Brussels in person, thereby inaugurating a few years of intensive collaboration. Even Moses Hess joined the little colony. For a time, they all lived in three adjoining houses on Rue d'Alliance in Brussels.

But the neighbourliness was not entirely good. Both Engels and Hess lived together with their lovers. Engels had Mary Burns from Manchester with him, and Hess had Sibylle Pesch, who – according to stubborn rumours – he had met in a bordello. Jenny Marx would come to hate Mary Burns intensely – certainly not because she was a factory worker, but because according to Jenny she was blunt and a gossip. Things were better with the cheerful Sibylle Pesch.

It was inevitable that Friedrich and Karl, but indirectly also Moses, would be drawn into the conflict. We best know the nature of the discord through a letter from Heinrich Bürgers that has been preserved (the same Bürgers who accompanied Marx to Brussels but was now in Cologne). The letter was written at the end of February 1846, when Marx had been living in Brussels for just over a year. Evidently, Marx had given Bürgers a careful account of what had happened in a letter that is now lost, and Bürgers repeated and commented only on what his friend had told him. Engels had complained that Marx was too bound to his family, and gave Jenny the blame for it. If Jenny had not been there, Karl would have admitted the advantages of untethered relations, Engels was to have said. Nor had Hess been without blame. Bürgers asserted that Engels had a 'shallow nature', while Hess did not understand the problems of daily life and therefore endured his friend's stupidities without grumbling. In fact, Marx had criticized not only Engels's moral superficiality but also his intellectual limitations. Bürgers wrote: 'Your judgment of Engels's intellectual condition surprised me less than his other exploits. Distancing himself from philosophy and speculation has much less its ground in his insights about their essence than it has in the trouble they would involve for his scarcely persevering intellect.' It was only possible to defend oneself against such an attitude with 'the exorcism of contempt'. Engels had to get a clear idea that 'he could go no further with his style, just as little as Hess could with his apparently profound meditations'.[18]

Another of Marx's loyal friends, the doctor Roland Daniels, had clearly also received a similarly indignant letter at the same time. Daniels's letter was in the same style as Bürgers's. Engels is called 'the tall fellow', which is a coarse allusion to his military past. 'The tall fellows' was the popular name for the Prussian king's special guard. Another sobriquet that also surely originated with Marx and occurs in Daniels's letter is 'l'ami des prolétaires' (friend of the proletarians), who had to wear such fine clothes because contemporary society was so wretched. Daniels said that the unphilosophical Engels was no good for a criticism of philosophy. Hess also came in for his share of scorn. He was called a 'kitchen sponge', sucking up everything in its way – a rather unfair term, considering that Hess actually also inspired Marx, and not just the other way around.[19]

Marx must have been deeply wounded when he wrote those words to some of his most loyal friends. We do not know for certain what caused his wrath towards Hess, other than that Hess seems to have echoed Engels's complaint about Jenny. Karl's all-consuming love for his wife could not be criticized, just as little as could his bonds to his family. For his part, Engels could not tolerate his relationship with Mary Burns being subjected to reproach, or Mary being treated with contempt.

These emotional storms broke at a time when Marx and Engels found themselves in the middle of their work on the tremendous manuscript known to posterity as *The German Ideology*. Work on it began in September 1845 and continued until the next summer. The assessments of Engels's unphilosophical nature are particularly surprising, considering that philosophy plays such a large role in *The German Ideology*. It is tempting to imagine internal feuds between the both of them while they were writing. But, here, the source material runs out on us. We know only that the most important target of attack for the work, Max Stirner's 1844 book *Der Einzige und sein Eigentum* (The Ego and His Own), was judged differently by the both of them from the beginning. When he was still in Germany, Engels had written a rather enthusiastic letter to Marx about the book, which had just been published. Stirner was the most talented of the Young Hegelians, he wrote. But it was also easy to show that his 'egoistic man is bound to become communist out of sheer egoism'. Now it was for us to build further upon him by turning his intellectual construction upside down. In his now-lost response, Marx evidently painted a significantly more negative picture of what Stirner had achieved, and Engels quickly yielded and confessed that he himself had been mistakenly carried away during his reading of the book.[20]

Barely six months later, in September 1845, they both began their work in which Stirner's book played the main role. Moses Hess was also brought into the project at the beginning and wrote a shorter text, most of which has been lost. It did not take long before he was set aside. His name shows up in the manuscript, and then in anything but flattering terms. What he achieved in theory was 'quite vague and mystical', and he himself was a half-educated man among other half-educated men.[21] But Engels and Marx continued untiringly side by side, despite the fact that one of them, in the middle of their work, could accuse the other of being unphilosophical. Something other than lifestyle and depth of thought must have been – and remained – the grounds for their collaboration.

Right at the beginning of their time in Brussels, during the summer of 1845, they both took a trip to England, specifically Manchester. It was Marx's first visit to the country where he would spend half his life. For the first time he could see, with his own eyes, contemporary capitalism in full bloom and experience the enormous vitality and human misery of a purely industrial city. It was a reality in which Engels moved like a fish through water. Through his excellent survey of this in *The Condition of the Working Class in England*, he had a better overview than perhaps anyone else. In such an environment, he had to serve as a guide and introducer for his travelling companion. In addition, the language was completely natural to him, whereas for Marx English was a reading language in which he was less fluent than in French, Italian, or Spanish (or Latin or Greek...). In 1844, Marx was still getting his excerpts on most British economists from French translations, while he readily excelled in quotes from Dante and Cervantes in the original. In this, he was a typical educated continental European of his time. Engels's knowledge profile was different; he had gone into commerce, knew how an industry worked from the inside, and knew the environment of the factory and the factory worker like the back of his hand. The most important woman in his life worked in a spinning mill.

But if the trip had significance for their joint project – how was it that it would, once again, concern German philosophy and not the world that spread itself out before their eyes in London and Manchester? The question *The Holy Family* had already roused had to be posed with even greater clarity before *The German Ideology*. Why did Marx (and Engels) go in for these projects? Why did Marx not write further in his work on economics and politics, which Engels recently so eagerly encouraged him to complete and evidently was so important to him himself? Moreover, one of the aims of the England trip was that he would collect literature for precisely that work.[22]

Before it is possible to answer these questions, we must look more closely at the new text that grew out of their joint labours.

The German Ideology

The title *The German Ideology* was not chosen by Marx and Engels for the enormous manuscript they left behind.[23] It is the creation of the editors of the first complete publication in 1932. It is apt, since the expression 'German ideology' occurs in numerous places in the text. In addition, it turns up in a notice concerning the work which Marx published in *Trierische Zeitung* on 9 April 1847.

The authors had the idea of publishing the manuscript in two volumes: the first would be a comprehensive study of the Young Hegelians; and the second, significantly shorter volume would be an attack on the group that appeared under the designation 'true socialism'.

In the present-day printed editions of the work, the important section on Feuerbach – which in certain editions is also called an introduction – comes after a brief foreword. The section was in fact written last, in the autumn of 1846. It is, as Michael Heinrich points out, also purely objectively the result of the work and not a starting point for it.[24] It is therefore reasonable to go into this section by way of a conclusion.

The German Ideology is the most comprehensive evidence of a sweeping change in their views on history, society, and politics that both Marx and Engels underwent during 1845 and 1846. The changes are the ones that garner the most attention in the whole of the literature on Marx. In Soviet and East German schoolbooks and handbooks, it was seen as the most decisive step towards the understanding that Marxism–Leninism would much later adopt as correct, true, and scientific. The French philosopher Louis Althusser, a major Marx scholar in the 1960s and 1970s, maintained that during 1845 Marx had made a great new discovery: he had seen a new continent that he called History. Between the 'young Marx' – who, following Feuerbach, had spoken of humanity's essence and of alienation – and the mature, real Marx whose work culminated in *Capital*, there was a decisive difference. The Marx of alienation was still imprisoned in the speculative mist of German idealism; the Marx of *The German Ideology* was on the path towards creating a new science.[25]

Other interpreters have asserted, on the contrary, that substantial features of Marx's theory can already be found in the *Manuscripts* and that the theory of alienation constitutes an indispensable and often neglected element of this theory. Joachim Israel, István Mészáros, and Bertell Ollman can be cited among

the influential advocates of this interpretation. An original variation can be found in the Japanese economic historian Takahisa
Oishi, who in his book *The Unknown Marx* (2001) argues that
Marx's great economic project is moulded in one piece and that
its substantial elements are already found in the *Manuscripts*. In
Oishi's perspective, *The German Ideology* does not represent anything decisively new, whereas Marx's great settling of accounts
with Proudhon in *The Poverty of Philosophy*, on the other hand,
is given a key role.[26]

Michael Heinrich, on the other hand, has embraced the opposite standpoint that there is a clear break in Marx's development
– several, in fact, of which this was the first. Heinrich concedes
that even much later, Marx used the word *Entfremdung* – alienation – but argues that it was no longer a question of alienation
from the essence of humanity.[27] This is a problem that will occupy
us later on.

Doubtless, *The German Ideology* is something new in relation
to *The Holy Family*. As regards Marx, we can easily see that the
change had already begun before the summer of 1845 – that is,
right after he came to Brussels. The proof can be found in the
famous *Theses on Feuerbach* that he wrote early in 1845. They
are part of a notebook Marx kept between 1844 and 1847; they
were published by Engels more than forty years later in 1888 as
an appendix to Engels's own work, *Ludwig Feuerbach and the
End of Classical German Philosophy*. Engels did not doubt that
these *Theses* (the designation is his own) signified the rupture
in Marx's development, and thereby indirectly in his own. He
expressed himself a trifle bombastically: they were certainly
'hurriedly scribbled down for later elaboration, absolutely not
intended for publication, but invaluable as the first document in
which is deposited the brilliant germ of the new world outlook'.

Engels was essentially right. With these eleven short, more or
less aphoristic statements, Marx had taken a decisive step. In
the first thesis, he said that the error in all materialism so far,
Feuerbach's included, was that it had only perceived reality as an
object for a way of thinking, and not as '*sensuous human activity,
practice*'. The materialists said that people were the result of circumstances and of upbringing, but forgot that 'circumstances are

changed by men and that the educator must himself be educated'. In short, people are both active and passive in this process, an idea that Marx would express many times in the years to come.

In another thesis, he asserted that Feuerbach, with his emphasis on sensualism, forgot that this sensualism consisted of *'practical, human-sensuous activity'*; with that, Marx was ready for the decisive blow against the foundation of Feuerbach's outlook that had recently also been his own: against the talk of the uniform essence of humanity. This essence was perceived only in the abstract, as something that existed within the individual; Marx said, 'In its reality, it is the ensemble of the social relations.' Feuerbach, with his abstract concept, was forced to ignore history. But 'all social life is essentially practical'. The mystery of the theory is solved in human practice and in the insights into it.

Marx saw materialism up to that point as an expression for bourgeois thinking. The thinking materialist appears as an indifferent observer of a reality that at heart is constant. But it is human activity that creates the world around us.

With that criticism, Marx has prepared the way for the final thesis, which has become by far the best known: 'The philosophers have only *interpreted* the world in various ways; the point is to *change* it.'[28]

There are two concepts in this little document that particularly stand out: *praxis* and *history*.

Praxis, with its derivation 'practical', has its origins in classical Greek, where it has to do with action in its broadest sense. It takes on special content in Aristotle, who distinguished between three different human faculties for knowledge: *theory*, *practice*, and *technique*. Theory, with the original meaning of seeing or scrutinizing, is the passive consideration of reality – more precisely that part of it, according to Aristotle, that we cannot influence: Nature and its laws. Technique, from the Greek *téchnē*, means the human ability to produce various kinds of objects through handicraft and art, whereas practice – *práxis* – has to do with relationships between people and thereby contains ethics with its subdivisions of politics and economics.

The distinction between praxis and technique, however, was difficult to uphold in the traditions from Greek antiquity. Even during the Middle Ages, they both often became blurred, and even more so during the seventeenth century and later. Kant, who was so careful with distinctions, tried to classify *practical* as simply an ethical concept. According to him, practical actions were either good or evil, and they were therefore performed only out of duty and not because they led to desired consequences of various kinds. When, on the other hand, insight was required into how something functioned, the actions according to Kant were technical-practical. It is an interesting hybrid form, which shows that not even for so scrupulous a person as Kant was it possible to make a sharp distinction between practical and technical. It was as if modern reality itself had created a transitional zone between ethics and technique.

With Hegel, this transition zone spread out, and in general he did not distinguish between praxis and technique. Humanity's practical relationship with Nature was its 'technical activity'. In the foreword to his 1811 work *Wissenschaft der Logik* (*Science of Logic*), Hegel spoke of a 'Geist des Praktischen', a spirit of the practical that encompasses all forms of natural and intellectual life. The difference between what Kant called the technical-practical and the practical was, in principle, obliterated.

Marx went a step further. The field of theory also became blurred with the technical-practical. Theory, which in Kant and Hegel had been a screened-off field, lost its independence. It appeared as an expression of human action. His encounters with down-to-earth British and French economic literature had certainly contributed to this new orientation. In it, the difference between theoretical and practical was partially erased.[29]

The boundaries of the concept of *praxis* itself are difficult to draw, and controversial. Is praxis only that kind of action that transforms human reality? Or is it all human activity, however routine, that through its enormous collective weight changes their conditions over the long term? Back in the *Manuscripts*, Marx pointed out that Hegel's idea of labour was a permanent part of his thinking. In Hegel, it was actually a question of labour in its broadest sense. The earlier idea that only physical labours were to be designated as labour ('to work by the sweat of one's brow') was on the point of giving way. The old nobility by birth had been contemptuous of work; on the contrary, the rising citizenry embraced it but perceived it in its broader sense. They especially counted their own toil on negotiations, business, and accounts as part of it. The activities of technicians and inventors, and gradually also that of scientists, were of obvious significance for industry and the new agriculture as well; the boundary was thereby crossed. By extension, all purposeful, reasonably strenuous human activity could be designated as labour.[30]

Labour and praxis evidently lie close to each other in Marx's usage. But the question of the boundaries for praxis had not been answered in and through the brief, hastily written notes on the path away from Feuerbach's philosophy. On the other hand, it is clear that he put focus on the praxis that changes or simply revolutionizes humanity's reality.

The other central concept, history, does not of course appear here as a term, but this brief document is permeated by its presence. The essentials deal with processes, new circumstances, and creative actions. This historical interest is not new in Marx's life; it has, however, been given not only another more central role, but another main emphasis as well. Previously, it was the history of thinking that had a crucial role in Marx's writings. It is a history that he learned a lot about early on, and which he also would come to master throughout his life. But that concerns only the world of ideas; in the theses on Feuerbach, it is history in a broader and more varied sense that is the centre of his attention. Purely concretely, it was a result of an intensive reading in the French Revolution above all but also, through the economic literature, in more general economic and social history. Here, the relative order of ideas of the Hegelian history of thought, in which ideas encounter other ideas and of philosophers who learn from each other or struggle against each other, does not prevail. Instead, a chaotic multiplicity dominates in which everything can seem important and common people are part of creating history.

At the same time, this kaleidoscopic multifarious history is a history of change – development, in fact – just as much as the history of philosophy is. However multifarious and however mixed up with small coincidences it may be, at the same time it

seems to display a pattern or an aim, even if it is difficult to sub-
stantiate its major features in the small details. If you are satisfied
with the lives and work of the kings of philosophy, or the kings of
music, or the kings of industry, or of even ordinary kings, then the
task becomes that much easier. The field to be investigated there
is limited, and the teeming world that lies outside the circle of the
select few is perceived mostly as unstructured noise.

It is the history of the multiplicity that Marx wants to bring in
focus. It is there that real change occurs, and it is also there that
every person can appear both as marked by circumstances they
cannot prevail over, and as active and creative. The educators are
themselves educated, but as educators they nevertheless achieve
something new.

It is important to remember that Marx wrote his theses long before
he and Engels began their work on *The German Ideology*. For
a present-day observer, the theses form a matrix for the greater
work. From that matrix, many of the fundamental ideas in the
larger manuscript could be developed.

The *Theses* did not entail anything completely new at all in the
development of their author. In *The Holy Family*, we can note
how, in his polemic, he scoffs at the Bauer brothers' way of speaking disparagingly about the masses. Instead he calls attention to
the individual workers, their diligence in studying, and their consciousness. Society cannot be divided up into the elite and the
masses, where the elite go on ahead and the masses trudge after
them. It has been made clear to him that even the philosopher
must count on many actors – a varied mass, in fact.

As nearly always with Marx when new insights or theories
were concerned, the *Theses* had already been foreshadowed. Their
author had previously simply not gone through the full consequences of what he already thought. Perhaps it was the brutal
deportation to Brussels that unleashed a series of insights that
would guide him from that moment on. The doctrine of an invariable human essence appeared in that flash of inspiration as an
unnecessary, cumbersome fiction.

He jotted down these new thoughts into his notebook. But it
was still just a small draft. It was in order to expunge the remaining

questions that, six months later, he was prepared to devote all his time to a demanding collaboration with Engels.

For his part, Engels had in his own way already described society as a multiplicity that was difficult to take stock of. In his book about the working class in England, he did not presuppose an essence common to all people living their broken lives in the shadow of industry. He had simply not thought through what the things he had so convincingly portrayed meant for his general outlook that had recently been marked by the influence from Feuerbach. He was thus a few steps behind Marx. The positive reaction to Stirner's thinking that he expressed in his letter to Marx testifies to this. Stirner had given him an insight that he previously lacked.

Stirner's book was also the main subject of *The German Ideology*. The section on Feuerbach, written last but placed first, covers approximately sixty printed pages. The chapter on Bruno Bauer, which follows, is only one-third as long. The entire concluding second part on 'true socialism' is a total of ninety pages – but the Stirner polemic, the central section, required more than 330! It is no wonder that many later interpreters saw this as a sign that both authors – Marx in particular – had lost all sense of proportion in an attempt to paper over the significance Stirner's book had had for them.

Were they correct in their criticism? That remains to be seen.

The chapter on Bruno Bauer forms a direct continuation of the polemic in *The Holy Family*. After Bauer and the other representatives of 'The Free' were forced to shut down their periodical, they found refuge in *Wigand's Vierteljahrsschrift*. There, Bruno Bauer polemicized against Feuerbach and Stirner as well as against Marx and Engels. Even Hess came in for his share.

Bauer held fast to his Young Hegelian convictions. Two key phrases in Hegel – *consciousness of self* and *substance* – were still at the centre of his philosophy. According to Hegel, substance – or, in simpler terms, objective reality – was pervaded by consciousness of self, that is, by the thinking and acting subject. Bauer radicalized this thinking to the point that consciousness of self was given the dominant role. From that position, he accused

Feuerbach of thoroughly being the prisoner of substance. In short, he was a materialist – and, moreover, a communist. He embraces sensualism, which Bauer interpreted in moralistic terms and associated with sin. For his part, Stirner – according to Bauer – did not come up to the mark because he embraced pure egoism. Both he and Feuerbach were dogmatics.

The authors of *The Holy Family* also got a response to their criticism of Bauer. Marx and Engels noted that he attacked their book although he thoroughly dwelled upon a review of it – a review that on top of it all abounded with misperceptions. Bauer singled out 1842 as a great year, as liberalism occupied the seat of honour and was embraced by the philosophers. As we remember, Marx was part of that crowd, but according to Bauer he now had taken to worship of 'common sense'.

Marx and Engels were annoyed by Bauer's assertion that Moses Hess had achieved something Marx and Engels were unable to, namely criticizing Stirner's book. Marx and Engels dismissed this; the accusation was unjust since they had written *The Holy Family* before Stirner's book came out. Bauer tried to show that Hess's key concept was taken directly from Hegel, and he added the accusation even Marx and Engels were latent Hegelians. Marx and Engels indignantly repudiated the assertion.[31]

It is clear that the pages on Bauer in *The Holy Family* were written as a matter of routine. More important for the authors was the enormous section on Stirner, so we must first acquaint ourselves somewhat with him.

Max Stirner and His Book

Max Stirner was a pseudonym; he was actually named Johann Caspar Schmidt. He was twelve years older than Marx, and he had been a member of the Doctors' Club that had played such a great role for both Marx and Engels. When the club adopted the name '*Die Freien*' (The Free), he was still part of it. He earned his living through occupations such as teaching at a girls' school; *The Ego and His Own* was his only significant work and a book that immediately created a big sensation.[32] After a short while, it sank into obscurity, but has since come under discussion again and again, above all in anarchist circles where Stirner is regarded as a predecessor alongside Bakunin and Proudhon. He himself lived in ever deeper destitution and died penniless in his fifties. But his book has survived him.

The two thinkers that Stirner primarily braced against and distances himself from are Bruno Bauer and Ludwig Feuerbach – more precisely, their image of humanity. His starting point was two aphoristically incisive statements from them. Feuerbach: *'Man is to man the supreme being.'* Bauer: *'Man has just been discovered.'* Stirner adds, drily: 'Then let us take a more careful look at this supreme being and this new discovery.'

Stirner proceeds carefully in his 450-page book. He started with the rudiments of human life: the child's path towards adulthood, and finally aging and death. After that he a conducts a historical survey of how this life was regarded during different eras: antiquity, in Christianity, and in more modern times. Philosophical idealism was in focus: it also dominated the immediate intellectual environment during his adult life. The text here is full of extraordinary anti-Semitic flourishes that not only concern the religion of the Jews but Jews as people as well. He spoke disparagingly of 'Jews of the true metal' and declared that he did not count on having them among his readers. We have no idea how Marx reacted to these very lines. As we know, he himself spoke poorly of the Jewish religion and Jewish business activities, but he was undoubtedly a 'Jew of the true metal' in Stirner's meaning.[33]

According to Stirner, pure idealism led to a world of phantoms. Religion made us into fools and clowns; not even Feuerbach, who called himself a materialist, avoided the curse of this world of phantoms. He renounces gods and other great persons, but morals kept their hold on him. He may have let subject and predicate switch places, but when instead of 'God is love' he said 'Love is divine', it meant that he submitted to love.[34]

In his own way, Stirner joined the intellectual development of humanity with the then rather new racial doctrine developed by the biologist Johann Friedrich Blumenbach a few decades earlier. According to Stirner, before Christianity there reigned 'negroidity', when people related their success to physical events such as the flight of birds, or thunder and lightning. Then everyone became Mongols, when the spiritual became crucial in their lives. Only Stirner could show humanity into the higher, Caucasian stage, when the individual sees herself and her own actions as the only possible guarantee of an independent and thereby perfect life. This person could say, using a famous Goethe quote: 'Nun hab' ich mein' Sach' auf Nichts gestellt.' That is: I rely on nothing or no one apart from myself.[35]

In their reckoning with Stirner, Marx and Engels poked fun at these constant trisections. He reminded them of Schelling, who always used to stuff reality into an enormous abstract construction. But they added that an echo of Hegel could also be felt. Reality was schematized according to a constantly recurring pattern.[36]

It is easy to agree with this criticism. Nevertheless, *Der Einzige und sein Eigentum* is above all a book marked by life and energy. Topic after topic is dealt with in rapid succession; there is not much that does not become the subject of Stirner's treatment. Even later posterity can understand why so many – Engels among them as well – were impressed. But Marx, as we have seen, was not captivated and brought his co-author along into his antipathy. In *The German Ideology*, Stirner was not given an ounce of praise.

One part of the polemic is aimed directly at the author of the book. For example, Marx and Engels said that abstract thinking becomes a welcome expedient for a schoolteacher living a hard, morose life in which the horizon was limited to a few districts in Berlin.[37]

Stirner was otherwise seldom called by his pen name. The entire chapter devoted to him is called 'Saint Max'; part of the polemical fiction is that 'The Free' are actually a kind of group of learned church elders. Other more folksy names for him were Jacques le Bonhomme and Sancho. On the contrary, with names like that, their adversary was ascribed a kind of boorish loutishness. Jacques le Bonhomme was the French nobility's contemptuous term for a member of the underclass, and Sancho is the ordinary, limited voice of would-be wisdom in Cervantes's *Don Quixote*.

The latter, moreover, was a novel that was cited assiduously – in Spanish! – in *The German Ideology*.

But, at the same time, this device meant that the main point was easily hidden away. This has certainly contributed to the fact that so many interpreters of Marx exhaustedly put aside the section on Stirner before they managed to reflect on the entire mass of text, thereby missing its points. Even Franz Mehring, the most loyal of his interpreters, found the account of Bauer and Stirner tiring and long-winded. Francis Wheen, less patient when he has no funny anecdotes to relate, argues that 300 unreadable pages are devoted to Stirner's nonsense. Jonathan Sperber, who would rather dwell on *life* than *letters*, speaks about the 'bizarre length' of the chapter, arguing that the account slipped 'completely out of hand'. But, at the same time, he points out that Stirner's reckoning with Feuerbach's theses on the species-being of humanity had a positive significance for them. On the latter point Tristram Hunt, Engels's latest biographer, goes further and asserts that he and Marx both stood in intellectual debt to Stirner and tried to hide it with their excessive polemics. As proof, Hunt cites several lines from the aforementioned letter that Engels wrote to Marx when he had just read Stirner. We must take our starting point from the ego, the individual of flesh and blood, he wrote. Much earlier, in 1975, Paul Thomas had shown that the length of the Stirner chapter was justified, since it meant a decisive step in Marx's and Engels's development. At the same time, Thomas certainly exaggerated the positive influence Stirner had had, at least concerning Marx.[38]

It is possible that Hunt is correct as regards Engels, but he is not about Marx. In his now-lost response, Marx must have dismissed Engels's enthusiasm, and we do not need to doubt the reason. It was not *the* individual man, the ego, that would be the starting point; instead, it was the diversity of concrete people marked by their varied circumstances. That was the idea animating the polemic against Stirner in *The German Ideology*.

Right at the beginning of their account, Marx and Engels attack Stirner for not taking the individual's physical and social life into consideration, thereby consistently ignoring historical epochs, nationalities, and classes. The consequence was that he perceived the image of the world and society that was typical of the class that was closest to normal for him. He would need to rouse himself out of his schoolmaster's world and see how it related to an office boy, an English factory worker, or a young American, to say nothing of a Kyrgyz.

In this remark lies the main idea of what would later be called the materialist conception of history. The philosophers since Kant had devoted themselves to searching for the ultimate theoretical conditions for our convictions and values. But that was not enough, Marx and Engels now said. We have to relate our own ideas, just like those of others, to the circumstances under which they arose and are constantly reaffirmed in our everyday life. Otherwise, we are caught up in the ideology that is closest to us.

The same critical requirements bring the authors to object to Stirner's way of making all of history the history of philosophy (something that characterized many of their own early works). In his view of humanity's relation to nature, he had no sense of the significance of industry and the natural sciences, but devoted himself to mere fantasies.[39] In his view of political outlooks, he was equally lost. The liberalism he spoke of was typically German. While the French bourgeoisie made a revolution and the English created industry and subjugated India, the Germans had only arrived at Kant's 'good will', which was a true expression of the impotence and wretchedness of the bourgeois class. But now it nonetheless began to awaken, and in its demands for protective duties and a constitution, it would soon be as far along as the French were in 1789. Stirner, unaware of this process, thought that it was the citizen, *le citoyen*, who came before the bourgeoisie – *le bourgeois* – when in fact it was quite the reverse.[40]

As regards economic relations, it was even worse. Stirner thought ill of money and its rule, and wanted to do away with it. He did not realize that it was necessarily a consequence of certain conditions of production and distribution. Stirner wanted to liberate the workers and their labour. The authors of *The German Ideology* objected that labour was already free and that it therefore was 'not a matter of freeing it but abolishing it'.[41]

Here, Marx again uses the word *aufheben* ('sublate', not 'abolish'), and again, this is worth particular attention. It is, as we have seen, the keyword in the Hegelian dialectic: something disappears, but at the same time is lifted up to a higher level. Work is not to be abolished; it is to be given new content.

Hegel's dialectic did not disappear from Marx's and Engels's horizon. It was idealism (which at the time was often simply called philosophy) that they abandoned. In a fit of boisterousness, they formulated an aphorism about this exact thing: 'Philosophy and the study of the actual world have the same relation to one another as onanism and sexual love.'[42]

They attacked not only Stirner, but also Feuerbach. Feuerbach showed that religion was actually just a phase, but neither he nor Stirner asked themselves why humanity had to form these false religious notions. Nevertheless, the question itself should pave the way for an empirical study of actual conditions. The authors pointed out both of Marx's articles, 'Introduction to a Criticism of the Hegelian Philosophy of Right' and 'On the Jewish Question', in which there is at least an insinuation in the right direction.[43]

That last remark shows that they wanted to see a certain continuity in their own development. There is, perhaps, something in this: Marx, at least, was already talking about the real foundation of religious faith in his criticism of Hegel but he was then still a good follower of Feuerbach in the field of philosophy.

Now, both Marx and Engels considered themselves as having *sublated* philosophy, just as they dreamed that labour someday would be sublated. Their goal was thus not to obliterate philosophy but to raise it to a higher stage in which it would, at the same time, be permeated with and give order and clarity to the tremendous world of experiences that Stirner and Feuerbach and many others had stood on its head. In this upside-down world, it was ideas that seemed to have an independent shape through language. The authors saw the reason for this error in the division of labour itself. The German philosopher was a petty bourgeois and saw his activity in thought as separated from the noise and multifariousness of life. At the same time, he imagined that it was ideas, such as his own and those of others like him, that governed the world.[44]

Marx and Engels's criticism here is not fully carried out. Why is it precisely a petty bourgeois intellectual who is so devoted to

philosophical idealism? His position evidently limits his outlook –
but why must it pave the way for idealism in particular?

The question naturally leads further to another: what is the
situation in France, Great Britain, and other countries? Evidently
it was a question that Marx and Engels were not quite finished
with. For example: in their foreword to the entire manuscript,
they wrote that people always had erroneous ideas about themselves. They were governed by products of their brains about God
or about a normal person (that is, a nature common to all people).
They thus believed in the rule of ideas, something that also applied
to Young Hegelian philosophy. Now, Marx and Engels would
reveal that these philosophers were sheep in wolves' clothing.

In a continuation of the foreword that they later struck out,
they said that the Germans' ideology did not differ from that of
other people's. They also saw themselves ruled by ideas. We do
not know why this continuation found no favour with its authors.
It squares with what was said previously – all people had up until
then been ruled by the products of their thoughts – but it is possible that the term 'German ideology' itself had all too clearly come
into conflict with what was stated in the text itself. There was no
doubt that the German ideology that was under the magnifying
glass differed from a French and British world of ideas that was
more rooted in reality. To take one striking example: when Marx
and Engels determined the connection between both of the parts
their work encompassed, they contrasted the real social movements in France and England, and German trends of thought. The
bourgeoisie in France and Great Britain formed a dominant social
and political force, whereas liberalism in Germany – which the
Young Hegelians belonged to – stopped at words. 'True socialism'
in Germany took the same attitude to actual proletarian movements in the other countries.

Here, the German ideology appeared as something for itself.[45]
But before we can go further, we must scrutinize the word 'ideology' – a newcomer in their prose – more closely.

The word 'ideology' had only had a brief history when Marx
and Engels began using it. Its originator was a Frenchman named
Antoine Destutt de Tracy, and he presented it in a speech on

21 April 1796. At the time, the French Revolution had reached a turning point. The left had been beaten back, and with it the demands for the people's immediate participation and involvement in the affairs of the country. Another way would now be chosen, which would lead more quickly to the goal: the best society. The philosopher Destutt de Tracy wanted to do his part with his 'ideology'. According to him, *ideology* was the sum of all knowledge. More precisely, it was on the one hand the principles for how to arrive at certain knowledge, and on the other a compendium of this knowledge. No longer would development be governed by the capricious variety of opinions. This was certain knowledge.

Destutt de Tracy gained a number of devoted followers who were called ideologues. But their success would be brief. In Napoleon's seizure of power, they gained a powerful critic. The pragmatic new ruler saw Destutt's system as the height of ridiculous rigidity of principle and intellectual fanaticism. His negative view of the term has stuck. It is still found in dictionaries and encyclopedias.[46]

But the word had greater success in Germany. There, it could be said that, while the French had made a revolution and the English established industries, the Germans had created another, and ultimately sharper, weapon: ideology. It was another way of saying that while the Germans could not compare with the French in military bravado, or with the English in trade and industry, for Germans the road that stood open was that of knowledge and education. Such thoughts lay behind the great reform of the educational system that had Wilhelm von Humboldt as its most important architect.

But the advocates of German ideology belonged to a somewhat later generation. Two of them might have been important for Marx and Engels: Friedrich Rohmer and Alexander Jung. Rohmer, a Swiss philosopher and politician, shows up in passing in *The German Ideology*.[47] It is less likely that he was the one responsible for the direct inspiration. More likely, it was Jung. Jung was a literary historian and journalist, and Engels had been in a polemic with him as far back as 1842. At that time Engels wrote under the pseudonym Friedrich Oswald, and in one reckoning Jung called

him 'little Oswald', by which he certainly did not mean his opponent's height, but probably his age: twenty-two years. At the time,
Jung was forty-three and Engels still a fervent Young Hegelian,
annoyed that Jung called Hegel an intellectual inspiration for the
literary trend called *Das junge Deutschland* (Young Germany).

In *The German Ideology* it is Young Hegelianism in particular
that is under fire. But it is likely that it was Jung that inspired
Engels – and through him Marx as well – to use the word 'ideology'. The difference is only that, while Jung saw ideology as
the German's chief asset, in Marx's and Engels's eyes it was on
the contrary the thing that alienated humanity from reality. From
Heine, who was present throughout *The German Ideology*, a
quote is reproduced in the same spirit: the land belonged to the
French and the Russians, and the sea to the British, but to us
Germans belongs 'the airy kingdom of dreams'.[48]

After *The German Ideology*, Marx seldom used the word
'ideology', while it is more frequent in Engels's works. Marx
does so above all in the famous and oft-quoted foreword to *A
Contribution to the Critique of Political Economy* from 1859. But
the word 'ideology' is in focus in Marx's and Engels's great manuscript. According to them, ideologies are closely bound up with
division of labour. A person is marked by what she does. What
she is able to do determines her perspective of herself, society, and
ultimately all of reality. Ideologies live off their bearers' narrowness of outlook.

Marx and Engels did not mince words. With indignation, they
saw that Max Stirner did not have any problems with a society
in which different people were completely reduced to different
kinds of activities. While communist propaganda argued that
even workers should develop their natural abilities all around and
thereby also their natural abilities for thinking, Stirner objected
that each individual could free themselves within their own sphere,
without such efforts. For Marx and Engels, it is the same as saying
that the worker, like all others with narrow working tasks, should
continue living a restricted life. But only when individuals can
realize all their intrinsic capacities will we have reached a reasonable goal, they object.[49]

It is the same utopia expressed in a more drastic and memorable way in the chapter on Feuerbach, in which the authors depict a society that 'makes it possible for me to do one thing today and another tomorrow; to hunt in the morning, fish in the afternoon, rear cattle in the evening, criticize after dinner, just as I have a mind, without ever becoming hunter, fisherman, shepherd, or critic'. The word 'critic' places us among German philosophers, but the ideal is above all that of Charles Fourier, who most consistently and successfully cultivated the dream of the variation of labour.[50]

To Stirner, such ideas were deeply alien. According to him, it was on their own that people could reach the innermost extraordinary qualities. Liberation, in other words, is an individual project and not a societal one.

He pointed out the artistic or scientific genius who alone could complete their musical compositions or painter's sketches. But he had no luck with his examples, Marx and Engels said. Mozart was one of his geniuses, but it was not Mozart himself who completed his *Requiem*. (The example is truly not a good one: Mozart could not complete his work because he died; had he not done so, Franz Xavier Süssmayr would have not had anything to do with the work.) Marx draws the conclusion that even artistic labour in contemporary society is subject to the law of division of labour. The greater the demand, the larger the selection of works. The interest in vaudeville and novels in Paris had driven along a growing host of vaudevillians and novelists. And within science, for example, astronomers had begun cooperating on developing their observations further.[51]

Stirner's thoughts on the unique qualities of genius can be found in the other, more comprehensive section of *Der Einzige und sein Eigentum*. It is called simply '*Ich*' (Ego), and its parts are called '*Die Eigenheit*' (The Ownness), '*Der Eigner*' (The Owner), and '*Der Einzige*' (The Unique One). Crucial for this triad, such as it is, that Stirner sticks blindly to the linguistic connection between Own and Owner. He was not the first to do so. John Locke, as we have already seen, was the pioneer in a long development that also included the author of the *Manuscripts*. Stirner, in contrast to Locke and Marx, was not primarily interested in economic categories. He had the state in his sights, and the state was his enemy in everything (something that made him of interest to anarchists). 'The State always has the sole purpose: to limit, tame, subordinate, the individual,' he said. In his eyes, the state was supreme, something that Marx and Engels did not agree with at all. The state owns factories and everything else in the country, Stirner argued; the factory owners were only borrowing and managing them.[52] It was the same kind of delusion that the clownish and reactionary Prussian king Friedrich Wilhelm IV was cultivating, said Marx and Engels. The king thought he was supreme – but economically, his kingdom was weak in comparison with England, and there was nothing he himself could do anything about it.[53]

Uniquely enough, Stirner called communism – the idea that property should be made common – social liberalism. It was the same struggle against egoism that was found in Christianity, he explained. He received the reply that communism did not demand that individuals sacrifice themselves. On the contrary, it safeguarded their total development. It preached no morals. It did not, for example, say that people should love each other. Communists 'knew on the contrary that egoism, just like sacrifice, was a necessary form of self-confirmation'.

In the eyes of his critics, Stirner had the loose relationship of the idealist to the hard realities of existence. He was asking for a better means of exchange than money and did not understand how money was rooted in the society he lived in. In a bourgeois manner, he thought that each and every person bore the blame for their own financial worries.

Stirner embraced the person who did not submit to any external system, and the only social community he found commendable was the loosely composed association (der Verein). Whereas society consumes you, you yourself consume an association of this kind. The association is a true community, because in it you can be yourself. The state and society, on the other hand, are false.[54] Marx and Engels suspected that hearsay from Paris had reached him about Fourier's small societies (the phalanstères), but that he did not understand that Fourier required a total transformation of society in order to realize his ideals. Stirner's associations, rather, were the result of the arbitrariness of a few individuals.

~

The patient reader of the long chapter on Stirner's book will gradually find its meaning. It is a broad reckoning with the most significant work that was produced by the New Hegelian school that both Marx and Engels had once belonged to. In an entirely different manner than in *The Holy Family*, they were given opportunities in their chapter on Stirner to develop their own views on society and humanity. They clarified for themselves – and certainly for others as well – where they stood on almost all questions that were of significance for them.

First and foremost, they could develop in full scale their materialist understanding in contrast to Stirner's idealist one. On point after point, they could bring out the messy, inflexible foundation of society and place it in contrast to Stirner's ideas that so much could be made subject to the individual's arbitrariness. They could develop their view on the relationship between the state and capitalist economy, and they could even touch upon how the division of labour within art and science related to the one within society in general.

It is understandable, but not excusable, that so many who write books on Marx or Engels are not capable of the task of reading the section on Stirner in *The German Ideology*.

The reckoning with the advocates of the tendency that dubbed itself 'true socialism' was of another kind. Here, Marx and Engels came close to the interpretations that they themselves had quite recently advocated. Moses Hess also participated in their writing project at the beginning and many 'true socialists' held up Hess as their model.

Marx and Engels did not attempt to gloss over the fact that they themselves had recently been close to the interpretations they were now castigating. The 'true socialists' were a typically German phenomena, they said; their audience was not proletarians but petty bourgeois, and their current standpoint was a necessary transitional stage before they could go further. Perhaps they had already done so, after having written the works being criticized here.

Moreover, Marx and Engels declared that they had nothing personal against the authors being attacked. Their works were only the necessary products of a country that had fallen behind in development.[55]

But all the same, the polemics that followed were mercilessly sharp. The 'true socialists' usually held up German science in contrast to the 'crude empiricism' of other countries. Their own socialism was claimed to be so much more advanced than the communism of the French. Their communism was 'raw', one of them said – the same criticism that Marx levelled a few years earlier. Marx and Engels now make ironical remarks about the expression, and again have a quote from Heine at the ready: 'Die Deutsche öffnet den Mund weit:/ Die Liebe sei nicht zu *roh*,/ sie schadet sonst die Gesundheit' ('With gaping jaws the German cries:/ Too *crude* love must not be/ or you'll get an infirmity.')[56] In Heine, it is certainly not any German who was speaking but a churchwarden, but with that clarification the point would not have been driven home.

The sharpest and most detailed criticism is directed at Karl Grün, a person who had long been close to them and whom Marx had come across in Trier, Cologne, and Paris. He was the one who succeeded Marx as Proudhon's teacher, and it is easy to see how they both followed somewhat parallel paths up until the mid-1840s. In his biography of Marx, Jonathan Sperber is actually of the opinion that the attack in *The German Ideology* is conditioned by rivalry and pure quarrelsomeness. But, once again, it shows that Sperber has not read the text that carefully. The chapter reveals, namely, that Grün's knowledge of French socialism and communism was fragmentary. With an exactitude that would have suited an old-fashioned and merciless faculty opponent, Marx compares Grün's quotes and other assessments with what Saint-Simon, Fourier, Cabet, and Proudhon actually said. Page by page, it is revealed that Grün leans on second-hand sources – and sometimes not even that – and still pretends to have deep first-hand knowledge. His general assessments were also shallow and ignorant.[57]

What does it say now, other than that Marx – and perhaps also Engels – knew more than Grün about contemporary French radicalism?

It indicates something that was, and remained, extremely central for Marx: his requirement for scholarly scientific exactitude and comprehensive reading. It was his strength, but would also become his fate. He read copiously and took careful, detailed notes on what he read. He was a one-man university, and was scornful and ruthless towards those who wanted to skate by more easily. But it also meant that he found it notoriously difficult to complete his larger works. It went better with shorter articles, as it did when – like here – he could collaborate with Engels, who found it easier to bring his writings to a close.

The approximately sixty pages that form the chapter on Feuerbach are a summary, but also a way for the authors of getting their bearings. It is the most known and the most read section of *The German Ideology* – often the only one read. Some of its more sloganistic formulations are often reproduced, such as 'The ideas of the ruling class are in every epoch the ruling ideas,' or 'In direct contrast to German philosophy, which descends from heaven to earth, here it is a matter of ascending from earth to heaven.' But it is only the context and the whole that gives the chapter its significance.[58]

Feuerbach actually played a relatively insignificant role in the chapter; the most that was said about him constituted repetitions of what Marx had already established in his *Theses*: Feuerbach had been satisfied with sensuous objects and ignored sensuous *activity*, and he did not realize that it was not only a matter of interpreting the world but of changing it as well.

The essential thing about the chapter, which also takes up almost the entire text, is a clarification and a summary of a view of history and society that Marx (and Engels as well) would thereafter adhere to in all essentials. But the analysis of capitalist society is still extremely rudimentary, and the view of the relationship between theory and empiricism is far less developed and sophisticated than it would be some decades later.

A crucial idea in *The German Ideology* is that it is production that makes a person a person. Production distinguishes humanity from the animals. The production of ideas is interlaced with material production, and can only provisionally be distinguished from it.

In Germany, an understanding of history predominated where, on the contrary, ideas were seen as the conductors of history. In

England and France, the same attitude also set the tone, at least as far as political history was concerned. But there, the first steps had nonetheless been taken towards giving history a more solid foundation as regards trade and industry. Evidently, they were alluding to the economists here – the same economists who had played such a crucial role for both Engels's and Marx's new orientation. The difference was that the economists had not intended to – or even had enough knowledge to – provide a total picture of history.

Before Marx and Engels went on to draw up the guidelines for their own view of history, they attached a warning that has all too seldom been noted. 'These abstractions in themselves, divorced from real history, have no value whatsoever', they stressed. It is only when grappling with putting the material into order – 'whether a past epoch or a present' – that the real difficulties begin. The general principles can only provide guidance before the actual work begins.[59] Once again, we glimpse the implacable rigour that was so typical of Marx, which he observed both in himself and in others.

There are four 'abstractions':

1. People must create conditions for their material lives themselves: food and drink, clothing and housing;
2. Once those have been satisfied, new needs are created that require new productive forces in a continuing spiral;
3. People must procreate, and increasing production creates space for a growing population; and
4. Production requires constantly increased collaboration between people, and this collaboration itself becomes a productive force.[60]

It is not a question of any chronological order; these are simply four necessary conditions for the development of humanity. The point is that only according to these four conditions do we arrive at the fact that humans also have consciousness. The German philosophers' favourite category, Spirit, is inseparable from matter from the very beginning. Spirit is also directly linked to language, without which no intellectual communication or development is possible. Consciousness, in other words, is a social product.

The division of labour also influences people's way of thinking, and this is the ultimate condition for a phenomenon that Marx had not previously spoken about: the class struggle. In every hitherto existing society, the ruling class has not only directed production, but has also been responsible for the ruling consciousness. What appears as normal and natural to think and believe in a society, in other words, agreed with what the ruling class thinks and believes.

One sentence in the introduction deserves particular attention. As in the *Manuscripts*, it is said that in and through the division of labour, people feel like strangers in their work. This is what Marx called *estrangement*, or *alienation*. But now he wrote the word in quotation marks, and italicized it with the comment: 'to use a term which will be comprehensible to the philosophers'.[61]

How should this now be interpreted? It is clear that the authors were distancing themselves from a word that was so closely associated with the idea of the essence of humanity. But it was even more important to realize that the phenomenon itself that the word represents was equally as important and central as it had ever been in the *Manuscripts*.

Larger parts of the text consist of a thorough history lesson on the Middle Ages and the beginning of the new era, with hurried associations with contemporary conditions. Trade and manufacture are dealt with in detail. It is a text that shows how important historical concreteness was, for Marx in particular. But we have no reason to dwell upon this.

The German Ideology never came out in print during its authors' lifetimes. They made many attempts to convince various publishers. The one who came closest to publishing it was Carl Friedrich Julius Leske, who lived in Darmstadt and who had already paid an advance for Marx's outline of a book on economics and politics. Leske inquired about the work but received a response from Marx that he had postponed it and first completed 'a polemical piece against German philosophy and *German socialism up to the present*'. This was necessary 'in order to prepare the public for the viewpoint adopted in my Economy, which is diametrically opposed to German scholarship past and present'.[62] Leske proved to be reluctant. The Prussian authorities were monitoring him scrupulously, and he therefore asked Marx to look for another publisher.

Marx, and Engels in particular, made more attempts to find a publisher, but their efforts were in vain. Marx would soon be consumed by another writing project that he successfully brought to a close without going overboard. Engels was more stubborn in his attempt to convince publishers, but he too was forced to quit.

More than a decade later, Marx noted that he and Engels had given up in the hunt for publishers. He added, with a gentle smile, that 'we abandoned the manuscript to the gnawing criticism of the mice all the more willingly, since we had achieved our main purpose – self-clarification'.[63]

This was justified. With *The German Ideology*, both Marx and Engels had arrived at an understanding of the principles for what would later be called their materialist conception of history. But there is more to be said about the work – things that only become clear with posterity.

The Hard Edges of Polemics

Early on, Marx had shown himself to be argumentative. In his doctoral thesis, he vehemently attacked those who thought differently. The young journalist had a sharp pen, and in *The Holy Family* he was merciless against his former fellow Young Hegelians.

But when he and Engels wrote *The German Ideology*, something new had come into both their lives. Engels was living a financially insecure life. He was dependent upon his father, despite the deep mutual discord. He was roaming between his home districts in Germany, Paris, and Brussels, with detours to Manchester. He had not been as at home as Marx in the French metropolis. He lived an erotically dissolute life that involved not only pleasure, but also hard emotional blows.

For Marx, the situation was even more precarious. He had settled down in Paris, happy to live his life in the midst of what he saw both as a new intellectual home and a centre for political and cultural development in Europe. He had absorbed everything novel that met him there, with tireless energy. His financial situation was, as always, precarious, but he could greet tomorrow with the hopes of something better. Life with Jenny and their little daughter was full of causes for rejoicing.

With the deportation, he was thrown off track. Everything in his life became even more limited, more shabby. He no longer had a large, multifarious social life, and he was forced to experience the complete degradation of the deportation. The passing quarrels between him and Engels certainly had their basis not only in sexual morals, but also in the fact that both were easily irritated in their new environment.

But more important were the consequences that the disappointments had for Marx's actions in both a political and theoretical context. He became even more polemical than before, and above all he attacked perceptions that had recently been his own with remarkable ardour. In Paris – in fact, even back in Bad Kreuznach – he had embraced most of what he saw as the revolutionary left with sympathy. Like many others at the time, he drew no sharp boundaries between socialism and communism.

He regarded the workers and journeyman craftsmen who formulated their radical opinions in writing with particular warmth. Fully admiring, he dove into the writings of Pierre-Joseph Proudhon, the former typesetter. He was even more effusive, as we have seen, in his initial assessments of tailor Wilhelm Weitling.

One could perhaps talk about the uncritical enthusiasm that easily affects the learned academic when he has just become an enthusiastic socialist. Everything seems attractive; everything is promising. Gradually, his ability to discriminate sharpened and his assessments were marked by greater critical moderation.

But one can also speak of the openness and tolerance that the feeling of progress and positive outlooks provide. Marx felt he was living and working in the right environment, and he received appreciation – and high expectations, in fact – from many quarters.

But the happiness would be of short duration. He was hastily forced out from the centre to the periphery, where he had to construct his own, far more limited centre. In his letters and writings, he did not display the same enthusiasm as he had in Paris. His polemics often took on a tone of bitterness.

His reckoning with Weitling was much discussed. Its objective basis was in actual, and important, differences of opinion. But the mercilessness in Marx's attack was unexpected. Let us observe the background to this clash more closely. Marx and Engels had created an International Communist Correspondence Committee in Brussels.[64] The committee was an attempt to link up the various centres of the still rather modest revolutionary movement: Paris and London, but also New York City and a few places in Germany and Switzerland. Most correspondents were German refugees or emigrants, who in their letters – conveyed through the well-developed postal system of the time – supplied the others with what was happening in their respective locations. Brussels would serve as a hub and Marx would be its dominant voice. The committee would thereby contribute to breaking his enforced isolation and make him as central as he had ever been in Paris. But something had changed in Marx's attitude: he distinguished between friends and enemies in the radical left movement in a new, sharper way. Engels did likewise: likely they both egged each other on, even if Marx – as always – was the dominant party in their collaboration. Marx wrote the first preserved letter in the name of the committee, while Engels added a few brief lines, as did the third initiator, Belgian communist Philippe-Charles Gigot. (Gigot was part of Marx's close circle of acquaintances in Brussels; by all appearances, he shared Marx's opinions loyally.)[65]

This first letter is an example of the newer, harder attitude. It was directed at Proudhon, in the context an important name in every respect. Marx encouraged him to become a hub in the work of the Correspondence Committee. In a special postscript, Marx warned Proudhon about Karl Grün, who was described as a charlatan who trafficked in modern ideas. *The German Ideology* indicates why Marx disliked Grün so intensely. Grün had not read the writings he had definite opinions on, and, in Marx's eyes, such things were unforgivable.

But the step from there to making the repudiation of Grün into a main question for the new committee was a large one. Grün was, of course, intellectually insignificant and, moreover, pretended to have knowledge he did not possess. But why brand him for that reason? Nor is the explanation sufficient that Grün, with his so-called 'true socialism', stood politically a good distance from

Marx. Marx knew quite well that Proudhon did not agree with him either on crucial points, and it was still to Proudhon that he now turned.

Proudhon's response to the letter breathed surprise over Marx's unforgiving attitude. Evidently, he did not recognize his friend from the many joint meetings in Paris. He said that he found the idea of a Correspondence Committee splendid. But he did not want to take part in it if it was to become a tool for a new dogmatism. Do not become a new Martin Luther! he exclaimed. Luther had settled accounts with all Catholic orthodoxy, but soon created his own. You, my dear philosopher, cannot make this classic German mistake again. Let us instead together give the world an example of scholarly tolerance and good polemics. We cannot become apostles for a new religion – 'the religion of logic, the religion of reason' – simply because we are among the leadership of a new movement.[66]

That last remark is important. Proudhon saw both himself and Marx as leading figures. But he did not want to know about any joint excommunication of anyone who had to write in order to provide for his wife and children.

Marx evidently drew the conclusion that he and Proudhon could no longer collaborate. He did not even respond to the letter. Or, rather, his response came in the form of a book that will be dealt with soon.

The campaign against Grün continued. Now it was Engels who became the most active in the controversy. In contrast to Marx, he could work in Paris, where Grün was also staying, and where both socialism and communism had their natural centre.

From Paris, Engels sent reports to the committee alongside private, franker letters to Marx.[67] The campaign against Grün was a main issue there right from the beginning; nor did Weitling escape disparaging judgements. Grün was accused of plagiarism, and Weitling of having written his main work, *Garantien*, with the help of other, more knowledgeable persons. Even Hess was treated roughly in the correspondence, as was Feuerbach. In his private letters, Engels also described his erotic escapades with wonderful French women, and gave an account of new setbacks in his attempts to find a publisher for *The German Ideology*.

The letters showed that Engels wanted to carry out a hard and merciless campaign just as much as Marx did. Even supporters could express concern over what they saw as unnecessary quarrelsomeness. Would it not have been better to concentrate on their opponents in common instead? What would they win in this 'mutual causticness', asked August Hermann Ewerbeck, one of Marx's faithful correspondents.[68]

But Marx and Engels had made up their minds. The Correspondence Committee would become an organization of struggle within the incipient workers' movement, tasked with not only directing polemics outwards against the aristocracy and bourgeoisie but also inwards against socialists and communists of other opinions. Success in these ambitions was not a given. No unity prevailed within the groups now being linked together.

One crucial issue concerned how communists and socialists should act in the event of a future revolution in Prussia and other German states. Marx had arrived at the conclusion that proletarians could not seize power before the bourgeoisie had first transformed the old feudal society the way it had done in England and France. In England, the transformation had started with the various revolutionary upheavals in the 1600s; in France, in 1789. The Germans had not yet managed to get that far, but were now ready. Only after that could the working class seize power. Until then, it was a question of supporting the struggle of the bourgeoisie. The first goal was to establish democracy with universal voting rights, and civil rights and freedoms.

But there were many who held other interpretations. They saw the opportunity for a more rapid seizure of power. Their hopes were a child of the utopian 1840s, where Marx had recently felt at home. Some believed that the transition to an entirely new and just society would occur rather peacefully. The majority of the people would quite simply realize the superior advantages of a system in which opportunities in life were divided fairly, and they would therefore resolve to change the prevailing circumstances. Others propagandized for a violent revolution in which a smaller group would actively bring the masses along with it in a total transformation of society.

Wilhelm Weitling was among the latter, and he held a strong position both in Paris and in London, where he was living in exile at the time. As we saw earlier, he laced his political theses with Christian messianism but that made him no less militant. He dreamed of assembling a large army with which he would liberate the oppressed in his old homeland.

For these plans, he believed he could obtain a majority among the members of the Correspondence Committee, and it was with that intent that he set out for Brussels. The meeting was held on 11 May 1846, and became turbulent. We know about the course of events from an eyewitness description. The Russian Pavel Vasilyevich Annenkov – who would later become known as one of Russia's foremost literary critics – was a friend of Marx during their time in Brussels. Both shared an interest in economics, politics, and especially literature (Pushkin was one of Marx's favourite writers, and in the 1850s Annenkov would become the first to publish a critical edition of Pushkin's writings).

According to Annenkov's account, some of the committee's members were seated around a small table.[69] Marx took his place at one of the narrow ends 'with a pen in his hand and his leonine head bent over a sheaf of paper' while Engels, 'tall and upright', gave an introductory address. In the middle of the speech Marx interrupted him, sprung up from his seat and addressed himself directly to Weitling. 'Tell us, Weitling – you who have raised such a racket in Germany with your preaching: on what basis do you justify your activity and what do you intend to base it on in the future?' When Weitling answered in evasive terms, Marx struck his fist on the table with all his might and roared: 'Ignorance has never helped anyone!'

With that, the break was complete. Weitling was, of course, deeply offended by the attack. Here he, the former tailor, had been accused of ignorance by a man with a doctorate. A person claiming to be central to a movement acting in the cause of the workers could not speak disparagingly to an autodidact. But the effusively positive evaluation of Weitling's efforts a few years earlier had been replaced by an equally complete belittlement of his capacities.[70] Naturally, it can also be said that Marx was essentially right. Weitling's military plans were completely unrealistic. But this fact does not excuse the vehemence of Marx's attack or his disparaging judgement.

The Correspondence Committee's meeting not only saw the quarrel between Marx and Weitling. It was also decided, entirely in the same spirit, that a strong condemnation would also be aimed at the *Volks-Tribun* (People's Tribune) newspaper, published in New York for the rapidly growing German-language minority there. Only Weitling voted against the resolution; the other six members supported it (one of whom was Marx's brother-in-law and former classmate Edgar von Westphalen). The editor of the paper, Hermann Kriege – who was a part of the committee – was ordered to publish a succession of articles Marx and Engels had written that were devastatingly critical of what Kriege himself had written. Kriege was part of the group of 'true socialists' who united the hope for a rapid transformation of society with a doctrine of love, more or less tinged with Christianity, that had a clear eschatological element: the End Times were near, and soon the Kingdom of Heaven would be realized on earth. The condemning articles were done in Marx's usual polemical style that Engels also appropriated. Scornful quotes were mixed with powerful condemnations. Communism had become 'love-sick' in *Volks-Tribun*; the paper was blowing 'metaphysical trumpetings' and Kriege himself posed as a prophet and apostle of love. This device had been well honed since *The Holy Family*. Their opponent was depicted as a quasi-religious cheat who lacked all deeper insights into society and its development.[71]

Marx and Engels not only gained enemies for their new, hard line, but also a number of enthusiastic adherents. Some of them were in their immediate proximity in Brussels. The most important of them was Wilhelm Wolff, called 'Lupus', who would come to be the closest to them of all. In contrast to Marx and Engels, Wolff had painful personal experiences of the mercilessness of class society. His parents were smallholders in Silesia; in practice, serfs subordinate to a harsh landowner. Despite opposition from above, Wolff succeeded in studying and at long last becoming a private teacher. Latin and Greek were his specialities; here, Marx and he could meet in a lifelong interest in the classics.

But Wolff's path continued to be thorny. For several years, he was imprisoned in a fortress during the so-called 'persecution of demagogues' that was mainly directed against radical students and academics during the 1820s and 1830s. He came to Brussels fleeing a Prussian prison sentence, and soon became an important member of the Correspondence Committee. He had something that both Marx and Engels were in great need of after settling accounts with Weitling: an ideal combination of lower-class background, solid and multifarious knowledge, and a good ability to express himself in writing. He remained a loyal supporter until his death in 1864. Engels wrote a series of articles extolling him in the 1870s; they were also included in the edition of Wolff's collected works that Franz Mehring published in 1909 on the 100th anniversary of his birth.[72]

One of Wolff's works lives on indirectly, in the history of literature. He was the one who wrote the account of the weavers' uprising in Silesia, his home province, that Gerhart Hauptmann built his drama *Die Weber* on.

Another name that should be mentioned is that of Georg Weerth. Weerth was born in 1822 and was still a young man when he turned up in Brussels. He was the son of a priest, but, when his father became ill, Georg could not continue his studies and went into commerce. Cotton became his speciality. Through his occupation, he learned French and English, and supplemented his education with diverse university lectures. He entered literary circles and was encouraged in his writing. For a period, he worked in England, where he got to know Engels personally. He had already become a communist by the time he turned up in Brussels, and distinguished himself as the foremost poet of the new movement. For Marx, who so bitterly missed the literary social life of Paris, having him close by was a comfort.

The remainder of Weerth's short life was turbulent. Like Wolff, he was extremely active in the revolution of 1848–9, thrown into prison for his writings, and came out a crushed man who abandoned both poetry and politics. He sought refuge in the Caribbean for new business there, and died in Cuba at the age of thirty-four. On his tombstone in Havana, it says he was a close friend and fellow thinker of Marx and Engels.[73]

Through people such as Weerth and Wolff, Marx and Engels built a small community for their activities. Weerth, who was constantly travelling for his profession, became especially useful because with his personal warmth, he could keep the spirit alive among sympathizers in other towns.

The Correspondence Committee could thereby also better serve its ultimate purpose, namely to imbue the *Bund der Gerechten* with Marx and Engels's ideas and to make the organization ripe for their type of communism.

How this succeeded is the subject of the next chapter. But before we get that far, we must stop to consider a work that Marx was writing at the time – because in the middle of all the turbulence, he managed to develop his critique of society and of economics a great deal further in Brussels.

The book is called *Misère de la philosophie* (The Poverty of Philosophy) and it was written in French.

The Poverty of Philosophy

Pavel Annenkov, the Russian who reported, wide-eyed, Marx's fit of rage against Weitling in 1846, wrote a letter to Marx from Paris six months later, on 1 November. Annenkov had just read Proudhon's 1846 book *Philosophie de la misère* (The Philosophy of Poverty), and he was of two minds. Of course, he saw that the book contained a great deal of dross about God, about Providence, and about the contradiction between intellect and matter. But the economic portion of the book was rich in interest. Never before had Annenkov seen, in black and white, how civilization could not abandon what had been won through the division of labour, machinery, competition, and so on. But, when it came to the disadvantages of the system, which Proudhon also convincingly pointed out, the remedy he proposed was again one of his own old dogmas. Annenkov could not follow him there, and therefore he now asked Marx for guidance.

He concluded the letter with a long and eloquent farewell of the type possible only in French. It concerned Jenny Marx, who had received him – a foreigner whose only merit was 'loving and respecting you, Monsieur Marx' – with such hospitality.[74]

Marx did not respond before the end of December. At first, he had had difficulty getting hold of the book, and now he had still only managed to skim it. His response was as might be expected, he said – but that response was ten pages long and already provided the outline of the reckoning he would soon publish in book form.[75] The manuscript of the book, entirely in French, was begun at the same time as the response to Annenkov and was completed in early April. Marx thus was not disturbed by his otherwise quite inhibiting demands for perfection. Perhaps it was the polemic which now – as it did both previously and later – made it easier for him to bring it to a close. As we have seen, where personal reckonings were concerned he was quick to send his manuscript to print.

But, in content and substance, *The Poverty of Philosophy* is a more serious work than both *The Holy Family* and *The German Ideology*. What Marx had won through his previous account with German idealist philosophy was a kind of philosophically imprinted method, and he used it now both in his criticism of Proudhon and of the economic theory in general. Even in the letter to Annenkov, certain main points can be divined. Society, Marx said, is the result of people's '*actions réciproques*' (their reciprocal actions). Different societies had different forms; these forms could not be freely chosen, but the former presupposes the latter. Productive forces constitute '*la base de toute leur histoire*' (the basis for their entire history).

The latter is an interpretation he would come to modify later on in his life.

In *The Poverty of Philosophy*, Marx follows Proudhon's work closely. After a brief, ironic foreword there follows an initial chapter on 'a scientific discovery' and a second on 'the metaphysics of political economy'. The tone is sharply polemical, and sometimes condescending. It is a text that must have wounded the victim of the attack.

Proudhon evidently had great ambitions with his *Philosophie de la misère*. On the one hand, he claimed that he was bringing an original economic theory. On the other, above all, he wanted to develop a method under inspiration from German idealist philosophy, in particular Hegel.[76]

Marx completely rejects the results that Proudhon had achieved. Not a word of praise escaped his lips. It was a frontal attack.[77]

Marx mobilizes both his enormous and rapidly growing reading and his great analytical ability to interpret complicated texts. He could show that Proudhon's bright hopes of a speedy transition to a society without injustices and poverty had already been proposed by several authors in England, chief among them John Francis Bray with his 1839 *Labour's wrongs and labour's remedy*. Bray had the same idea as Proudhon that a condition of equality, decency, and contentment was within reach if only people would make full use of the resources that contemporary development offered. With a few simple arrangements, people would be able to switch work efforts fairly.

Marx objected that Bray's societal ideal was only 'the reflection of the actual world' and asserted that 'therefore it is totally impossible to reconstitute society on the basis of what is only an embellished shadow of it'.[78] Marx's metaphors in these lines deserve to be remembered: base, shadow, and reflection are all here. Optical images were and remained important for Marx. And we will return to the word 'base'.

A metaphor that faces an entirely different direction is 'Robinson', after Daniel Defoe's 1719 novel *Robinson Crusoe*, in which the shipwrecked Robinson builds up a rudimentary civilization step by step on a deserted island. Proudhon, like many leading economists, was trying to make large, complex contexts intelligible by bringing them down to the individual level. As individuals functioned in their everyday context, so also in principle did all of society. Without further ado, he adds a 'collaborator' to the solitary person Proudhon first introduced. Marx likens the trick to Defoe's. In order for Robinson to be able to complete his societal project, he also needs another person; conveniently, an ideal servant – christened Friday – appears.[79]

According to Marx, we must always presuppose society. Without society, there are no individuals; consequently, no people either. People live in structures they take over from previous generations, and to which they change through their own activity.

Even at a somewhat higher level, Marx opposed what we could call Proudhon's reductionism. Based on the division of labour in the factory, Proudhon could side with the division of labour in the whole of society. Marx objected that it was the affair of management to divide labour in the factory, while competition pushed forward degrees and types of specialization in society at large.[80]

Another important difference between Proudhon and Marx concerned the view of the interaction between production and need. According to Proudhon, they both condition each other; he seemed to assume that there was a natural tendency towards an increase both of production and of human need. Marx, on the other hand, asserted that it was collective production that changed the conditions for human life. People produce something new that would not have existed without their work. New and growing needs are the result of more diversified production. Needs, in other words, are a dependent variable, according to Marx; on the other hand, production is an independent variable.

No product is useful in and of itself except that it is useful for a consumer, he said. Consumer stands against producer. Consumers always have to be convinced that they need what is being produced. If supply and demand are not at all in balance, the result will be shortage or surplus.[81]

Proudhon asserted that producers and consumers were free in their activity. No, Marx said. As long as the producers are subject to the division of labour, they are compelled to sell. In the same way, consumers are bound to their means and their needs. A worker who buys potatoes and a mistress who buys lace can imagine that they are free, but are acting only in accordance with their social position.

Proudhon claimed he was making an original contribution to economic theory. Marx found that the results were merely a number of abstractions of small explanatory value, and plays off a long line of British and French economists against him. He placed special importance on the contributions of David Ricardo. Proudhon polemicized against Ricardo, calling him a cynic. Of course, Ricardo was cynical, Marx said – cynical and clear. The costs of buildings and machines were no different from the expenses for the workers. It was a cynicism that lay in the thing itself, and not the words. Proudhon tried to get away from the mercilessness of capitalist production with dreams about a 'revolutionary theory' of proletarian emancipation. In fact, he had only stopped at the formula for 'the present enslavement of the worker'.[82]

Out of Ricardo's theories, Proudhon seemed to draw his own conclusions that the present society was heading towards increasing equality. This was due to a fundamental mistake, Marx said. He was confusing the value of the labour required to produce a given object and the value of that same labour on the market. In short, he did not see the difference between the use value and the exchange value of the labour. For example: if a given amount of grain costs two working days instead of one, this did not mean that the amount of nutrition doubled – on the other hand, the amount of labour did.

Proudhon's confusion also occurs in Adam Smith, Marx said. On the other hand, Ricardo was entirely consistent. *The Poverty of Philosophy* testifies eloquently that Marx had devoted an in-depth study to Ricardo since the days of the *Manuscripts*.

Proudhon let slip that labour was something vague. Marx objected: 'Labour is not a vague thing; it is always some definite labour, it is never labour in general that is sold and bought.' But when it is sold and bought, it itself is a commodity. Marx argued that Proudhon was seized with uncertainty in the face of this double essence and sacrificed the basis of his entire theoretical construction: labour time as the yardstick of value. 'And for the sake of life to lose the reasons for living!' Marx added derisively, with a quote from the poet Juvenal reproduced in the purest Latin.[83]

Marx's text is scarcely intended for a proletarian reading group. But his criticism shows that he had arrived at a distinction that only several years later he would put into his own words: the one between concrete and abstract labour. In capitalist society, abstract labour is sold per hour against wages. Concrete labour is the production of a definite product, whether it is a piece of cloth or a machine part.

Proudhon's view of society is optimistic. Just under the surface of injustices and workers' poverty, the possibilities of an equal and just society open up. Marx is not as optimistic: the antagonism between worker and capitalist characterizes society and is inevitable until the day the workers rebel.

Both are agreed on one point: technological development is an awesome force that transforms humanity's living conditions from the bottom up. But the consequences they draw diverge. Marx emphasized that the anarchic relations under capitalism have irrational consequences. Machines make it easier to produce luxuries than commodities necessary for life. He chose a topical example: hard alcohol was threatening to supersede wine and beer. Governments were fighting against pure spirits, 'the European opium', but ultimately it would be the economy that decided the matter.[84] Marx's example shows that he was marked by the conditions in areas where wine and beer traditionally had the dominant position but were now facing stiffer competition from distilled drinks; in countries such as Sweden and Russia that typically drank schnapps and vodka, the same changes were not taking place.

But the example itself does not need to be examined in detail. The important thing is the critique. Increased productivity did not mean, as Proudhon thought, that things would automatically get better for everyone and that what was necessary for the lives of the poor would automatically become cheaper. There were no economic mechanisms that would result in the use values and exchange values of the products meeting. On the contrary, luxuries or items that were dangerous to health could very well be profitable. What generates profit is produced, whether it favours everyone or only a few and regardless of whether it helps or harms the consumer.

The division of labour is another area in which Proudhon and Marx had the same fundamental assessment but held opposing interpretations of contemporary development. Both argued that narrow working tasks means that individuals were limited in their development in an unfortunate way. But according to Proudhon, mechanical development meant that everyone would at last be able to be active in a way that would do their inherent possibilities justice.

Marx pointed out that on the contrary, the machines in England had meant an even stricter division of labour. He clarified: it was typical of modern society that it 'engenders specialities, specialists, and with them craft-idiocy'. At the same time, it was wrong to see the machines as conductors of economic development. 'The machines are as little an economic category as the oxen that draw the plough.' They are both simply a productive force. On the other hand, the factory – which is built on the use of machines – is 'a social production relation, an economic category'.[85]

Once again, we see how his reckoning with Proudhon led Marx to distinctions and clarifications that were previously missing in his texts. Here, for the first time, the term 'social relations of production' turns up. In *The German Ideology*, he and Engels had made use of the broader and more indeterminate word *Verkehr*, which if anything corresponds to 'traffic' or 'communication'. 'Social relations of production' (*rapports socials de production*) is much clearer: it concerns how owners, workers, and work equipment relate to each other in production.

It is worth recalling that the word *Verhältnis* in Hegel's logic has a particular meaning, different from the related word *Beziehung*. *Beziehung* denotes any relationship at all, however temporary (for example, the one between the blossoming meadowsweet that is just now in my field of vision and white house to its right). *Verhältnis*, on the other hand, refers to a fixed context that changes as soon as one of its parts changes. A living body with the organs necessary for life is a good example; the relationship between parent and child is another. The parts in a *Verhältnis* condition and mark each other; they are part of what, in the language of logic, is called an 'internal relation'.[86]

Marx distanced himself from Hegel's conception of the world. But these foundations of the Hegelian conceptual apparatus were crucial for his arguments.

His reasoning involved machines being able to take on another meaning in another type of society. Through their standing in a factory owned and governed by a factory owner and served by a number of workers, they take on a particular content; they are part of a definite system. They are a part of a capitalist context that, according to Marx, is characterized by its anarchy.

He thus said here, clearly, that machines as such – regardless of the context they are used in – are not an economic category.

He gives them no designation other than forces of production. We could say that they belonged to the field of technology; in that case, an important conclusion would be that technology and economics are not indissolubly linked together. It is, in fact, a necessary consequence of the conviction that development in capitalism prepares the ground for catastrophe and opens the way towards an entirely different type of society.

To describe the development of both technology and the economy, Marx had to broaden his reading. He referred not only to a growing number of economists and showed not only a renewed and in-depth reading of Ricardo's great 1817 work *Principles of Political Economy and Taxation*. He also cited in detail works by Charles Babbage and Andrew Ure. Both were important conquests and reminders of the intellectual strength that distinguished Marx from most other theoreticians. He was willing to incessantly incorporate new areas into his work and never hesitated to make the effort to learn something new.

These were important new territories he was surveying. Babbage was an outstanding mathematician who was convinced that his subject would play a crucial role in technological and industrial development. He devoted himself to organizing the previously rather anarchic British sciences, and for posterity he became famous for his ideas on an analytical machine – one of the most important forerunners of the modern computer. Babbage's work was taken on by people such as Ada Lovelace, another British mathematician and the daughter of the poet Lord Byron. The Swedish polymath Georg Scheutz, who was the first to construct a machine in the spirit of Babbage, also joined the group.

It was, however, not these ideas that attracted Marx but Babbage's 1832 work *On the Economy of Machinery and Manufactures*. Economics was thus a major subject for him, but observed with a different eye and from a different direction than the usual one. In present-day terms, it could be said that Babbage was trying to establish relations between technology and business economics; this would become important for Marx.[87] In *The Poverty of Philosophy*, Marx faces Babbage's definition of the concept of a machine. If the division of labour is reduced to the management of a simple tool, and if all these tools are set in motion by a single motor, then we are talking about a machine, Babbage said.[88] Marx would continue to ruminate over what characterized a machine for a long time.

The other new conquest, Andrew Ure, had trained as a doctor, became famous as a chemist and would take great interest in contemporary technological development. By travelling around among various industries, he acquired an overview that he accounted for in works like his 1835 book *Philosophy of Manufactures*. It was a work that played a large role for Marx both here and later, although at the same time he had an ironic perspective of Ure's praises of the modern workplace. In *The Poverty of Philosophy*, he could refute Proudhon's idea that mechanization would reduce the division of labour through long quotes from *Philosophy of Manufactures*.[89]

Marx's increasing interest in the interaction between the natural sciences and technology also comes out in another section of *The Poverty of Philosophy*. Speaking of the fertility of the soil, Marx pointed out that it could now be improved chemically. Agricultural chemistry had thereby come into his field of vision.[90] It would come to interest him ever after.

Marx asserted throughout that Proudhon overestimated humanity's possibility of influencing fundamental social development through subjective decisions. Proudhon hinted, for example, that the system of manufacture could have arisen through a kind of peaceable agreement, while according to Marx it was a natural result of development.[91]

In his polemical zeal, Marx exaggerated his opponent's idealism. He asserted, for example, that Proudhon believed that it was kings and dukes and others in power who turned gold and silver into money by their own efforts, whereas in fact they were subject to 'economic relations' (once again, *Verhältnisse* in German – that is, firmly entwined relations). It was not money that was stamped; it was the weight of the coins.[92]

Even more exaggerated is the statement that Proudhon saw competition as a consequence of economists' theories. But Marx's comparison is telling: asserting that economists' theories push forth competition is like asserting that circulation of the blood is a consequence of Harvey's discovery of 1628. Once again, then, a way of comparing the context of society with the conformity of nature to law.[93]

The difference between Proudhon's and Marx's opinions is substantial in another, more down-to-earth area: the importance of trade unions. Proudhon was sceptical of such associations. In his opinion, they disturbed development towards increasing equality in society, which was a consequence of industrial development. The trade unions' weapon was the strike, and their goal was wage increases. But the effect of wage increases, from beginning to end, was price increases.

Marx noted that Proudhon was just as damning towards workers uniting – or entering into 'coalitions' – as the leading political economists, with Ricardo at their head. The reason was not quite the same: Ricardo argued that such associations disturbed the steady pace of industry, whereas Proudhon was occupied with the determination of prices. But the opposition was the same.

Marx was of a different opinion. There is no self-evident connection between wages and prices. Higher wages had decreasing profits as an immediate effect. Machines were replacing human workers to an increasing extent, and machines received no wages. Strikes and higher wages forced technological development, since over the long term it would become cheaper for factory owners to mechanize their production. This was a consequence Marx did not at all find negative – quite the contrary. The development of productive forces was the precondition for another type of society.

Marx had previously placed his chief hopes in development in France. England – or, rather, Great Britain – had only come second. But now he emphasized the British example. The trade unions there had expanded rapidly and efficiently. Since 1845, there had been a National Association of United Trades with 80,000 members. He also pointed out that the union movement had arisen at the same time as the Chartists were taking up the political struggle.

This was an early example of how he saw trade unions and political actions as two sides of the same workers' movement. He himself could only participate in political work, but here it was the trade union side whose importance he emphasized. It was no prospect of a reformist path with gradual improvements of the workers' situation that he held out. The trade union actions had developed into a 'veritable civil war' and were preparing the way for the coming battle, he said. Thus, revolution!

It is easy to see in hindsight that his ideas about the development of the early British workers' movement quickly came to naught. Chartism lost its significance, and the early national union organization was left rather powerless after the great ideological change that took place around 1850. It was formally dissolved in 1861.

But the pages about trade unions and strikes that conclude *The Poverty of Philosophy* are important ones. Marx gives the final word to George Sand, his friend from Paris, who in her 1843 historical novel *Jean Ziska* exclaims: 'Combat or death; bloody struggle or extinction. It is thus that the question is inexorably put.' (Jean Ziska was actually named Jan Žižka z Trocnova a Kalicha and led the rebellious troops in the Hussite Wars in Bohemia, which lasted from 1419 to 1436. The Hussite Wars were both an important part of the pre-Luther Reformation, and a stage in a popular Czech liberation struggle against German supremacy.) These words, which reflected the rebellious moods among many intellectuals in Paris of the 1840s, also gave voice to Marx's view of social development in 1847.[94]

The Poverty of Philosophy has become known above all for its reckoning with Proudhon's Hegelianism. It is correct that Marx aimed withering criticism at Proudhon's attempt to create a philosophy of society with its starting point in Hegel's dialectic. The criticism was otherwise not unfounded; the dialectical play Proudhon was chiefly interested in was that between positive and negative sides in various economic categories. It is not necessary to go to Hegel to find inspiration for this double meaning. On the other hand, he did not take up the interesting aspects of the dialectic.

But in his critique of superficial Hegelianism, Marx went no further than he had in *The Holy Family*, or – with Engels's support – in *The German Ideology*. *The Poverty of Philosophy* is important chiefly because it testifies to the fact that Marx had gone further in his thinking on society, and in particular in his handling of economists' theories. He had not only broadened his reading. He also clarified his distinction between concrete and abstract labour, and between productive forces and what he now called 'relations of production'. He had developed a distinct view of the importance of union organizations.

At the same time, the book represents an extreme in his writings. He forcefully and unreservedly established his convictions – both new and a few years older – in a way that he rarely did before or after. His voice was more solitary than before; the recently so-admired Proudhon was brusquely dismissed and Weitling already revealed as an ignorant chatterbox. The proletarians no longer had their own spokesperson; now it was only Marx who, with the support of Engels, could point out the path to the future.

And the future? The future was blood and struggle and revolution. Only beyond that could something else be glimpsed. An unexpected light, like through a door ajar, enters Marx's text: 'a future society, in which class antagonism will have ceased, in which there will no longer be any classes'. It is no longer exchange value that rules, but use value.[95]

They are four lines in a text of more than 120 pages.

In another, more tangible sense *The Poverty of Philosophy* also meant something new and extreme in Marx's writings: it was written in French and thus intended for a circle of readers Marx saw as setting the tone for the questions the book dealt with. If it were only spread widely, its success would be assured.

But its impact was limited. Both Engels and Marx certainly thought that it sold decently – Engels reported ninety-six copies after a few weeks – but it did not rouse any debate to speak of. To rouse interest, Engels visited Louis Blanc, one of the leading socialists in Paris. Engels assured him that Marx was the leader for 'our party' which was 'the most advanced section of German democracy', and that the book about Proudhon was to be regarded as the programme of the party. Blanc declared himself interested, but when Engels returned to him a few months later, it turned out that he had only managed to leaf through Marx's book and that he saw that Proudhon had been '*assez vivement attaqué*' (quite vigorously attacked) in it. He did not have the time to write a review, but offered to have Engels do it instead: his report would be published in the periodical *La Réforme* – something Engels declined.[96]

Other matters besides *The Poverty of Philosophy* and its fate had already occupied both Marx's and Engels's attention. Time hurried on; the year 1848, a memorable year in history – of Europe and these two men – loomed on the horizon.

Theory and Practice

The *Manuscripts*, for all their incompleteness, are a captivating work. Where Marx calls on himself to speak, they are stylistically brilliant; the image of humanity he draws is part of the great humanistic tradition from Ancient Greece and Renaissance Italy. Marx succeeded in formulating a classic, and yet also modern, ideal of humanity in the merciless epoch of early industrialism.

What Marx wrote in the years that followed had sharper edges. He had not abandoned his ideas about what a person *could be*, but the outlooks for a better future only gleam in passing in texts that are otherwise marked by sharp polemic, merciless reckoning, and heartless satire. In *The Holy Family*, *The German Ideology*, and *The Poverty of Philosophy*, the targets of attack come closer and closer to Marx's own standpoints, as he had more or less recently formulated them. First the Young Hegelians were castigated, then also the 'true socialists', and finally Proudhon, who was still spoken of in the warmest terms in *The Holy Family*. He did not condescend to give Weitling, so recently admired, even a mention in the work, only a scolding face to face. Something clearly had happened.

We have already touched upon one reason for the change: the purely personal. Marx experienced the deportation from France as a deep outrage. In addition, the exile to Brussels made his financial situation more difficult. For example, he was forced to write a begging letter to his Russian friend Annenkov.[97]

But there were also other reasons. Marx was not alone in calling himself sometimes a socialist and sometimes a communist from the beginning. He found himself in a large and growing circle of especially young women and men who wanted to work for a new, better, more equal and more just society. The apex of culture in the salons, and the journeymen and workers of the dark cellars seemed united in the hope of being able to fundamentally change a society where either avarice (as in France) or stale prejudice (as in Prussia) reigned. There were various opinions on how the change itself would come about, but that was not in focus. In the *Manuscripts*, it was not a question of political revolution, only social upheaval.

But the question of the transition to another society inevitably became decisive as soon as their enthusiasm was channelled into various associations and organizations of struggle. Marx was not alone in creating a sharply outlined picture of these issues in the years up to 1848.

Many among them who had recently stood out as his fellow thinkers developed a political outlook that they called 'true socialism'. Its representatives were mostly those close to the author of the *Manuscripts*; this applied in particular to Moses Hess, intellectually the sharpest among them. But by degrees they developed a markedly more optimistic view of the social upheaval Marx felt they were working for. They argued that the new society they sought could be helped forth by the social, cultural, and political development that itself was already in progress. In particular, if people were enlightened about its character, they would be so moved that they would work to realize it.

Proudhon was no 'true socialist' – they were mainly Germans – but he was also hopeful about the possibilities of abolishing poverty and injustices in a peaceful way. It was not only Marx's annoyance over Proudhon's sharply unsympathetic response to the letter in which Karl Grün was painted as a charlatan that fuelled the rage in *The Poverty of Philosophy*. There were more objective reasons.

Weitling, on the other hand, was a revolutionary but had a different understanding of strategy than Marx. Weitling asserted that a broad popular uprising was a realistic possibility in Prussia and the other German states as well. Marx, on the other hand, argued that a bourgeois revolution – such as the French Revolution in 1789 – was a necessary condition for the proletariat to seize power. Whereas Weitling was ready to march off with an army of journeymen and industrial workers, Marx advocated a more cautious approach. A popular army could easily be put down by professional Prussian soldiers. Nor were the necessary political institutions in place. Weitling's way would result in chaos.

Both the bright hopes of a peaceful path to an equitable society and Weitling's more violent strategy – sweetened with a dollop of Christian messianism – won many adherents. The path that Marx identified seemed both longer and more strenuous. It also required more thought to fully understand it, lined as it was by rather abstract reasoning about the difference between political and social conditions and the possibilities of democracy. Convincing organized revolutionaries about the correctness of this strategy became important.

How they succeeded is an important question in the next chapter. But before that, the question must be asked: why did Marx choose the path of violent revolution? The importance of Engels cannot be understated. In contrast to nearly all other socialists and communists at the time, he had direct occupational experience of the businesses of the time, seen from the side of the owners. He knew that the world of the factory would scarcely be conquered with Weitling's tactic of surprise; nor could he be convinced by the thoughts that the current society could be transformed from a class society to an egalitarian republic in a peaceful way. The political institutions with military and police power at their head would not voluntarily let something like that happen.

But Marx could have also drawn similar conclusions on his own. Moreover, both his intensive study of economic theory and his rapidly increasing reading in modern history – with an emphasis on French history – contributed. It should also be added that he still made use of central categories from Hegel's dialectic, particularly *Aufhebung* – sublation – which coloured his ideas about what a coming revolution could be. Current society would be overthrown to make room for a new one, but in this new society what was valuable in the former society would be preserved and at the same time raised to a new level.

Thus there were not only personal reasons for his polemical outbreak. It was only their ardour that can be explained by his increasingly precarious living conditions.

7

The *Manifesto* and the Revolutions

The Struggle for Influence

With his increasingly polemical writings, Marx seemed to have put himself into a difficult position in the political and ideological left wing. He heatedly opposed Weitling's proposals for an immediate popular uprising. But he just as unhesitatingly distanced himself from the optimistic conviction that united Proudhon and his followers with those who claimed to be the only true socialists. According to them, the opportunities for a peaceful transition to a just world would soon reveal themselves. It was only a question of spreading this insight to the oppressed.

Marx met this hopefulness with contempt. Without struggle and conflict, the lords of today would also be the lords of tomorrow, he held. But the rancour in Marx's reckoning with both the advocates of immediate action and those of the peaceful transition roused a certain degree of consternation. When Marx contacted Heinrich Otto Lüning, a doctor and journalist living in Switzerland, Lüning expressed delight with the contact but also objected to the quarrelsome tone in Marx's writings. 'You attack everything that deviates from your opinions in any way,' he wrote, and asked, 'Why use a cudgel when you are working in the same direction, more or less …?'[1] Even close friends of Marx such as Heinrich Bürgers expressed concern over Marx's style of writing. Bürgers's concern was less over the tone in the polemics than it was over the degree of difficulty. There was a point at which our ideas diverged, he acknowledged in a long letter. Marx assumed he had his readers on his side. But Bürgers doubted that was so. It was certainly good to assume that people know more than they actually do. But in *The Poverty of Philosophy* it was a matter of knowledge that was entirely foreign to most. You then become entirely incomprehensible in their eyes, Bürgers said. Not even in France does your work on Proudhon make the impression it should; in Germany, the level of readers and critics was unacceptably low. Here it was not a matter of opponents who were equal in merit; they had to be created first.[2]

We do not know how Marx reacted to letters like this. He could at least have been happy that his campaigns were received with satisfaction in one direction: London. That support would turn out to be important, even crucial, for Marx's (and Engels's) most-read text: the *Communist Manifesto*.

Right after the dramatic break with Weitling on 6 June 1846, Marx received a long letter from friends in London. It was signed by a long series of names, but the pen had been wielded by the verbally most driven of them – Carl (or Karl; the spelling varies, but he himself signed with a C) Schapper. Alongside Joseph Moll – another of the letter's signers – he was the one who would also play the most important role in preparing the way for the *Manifesto*. Let us linger on him and Moll a moment.

Carl Schapper was the son of a priest from Alsace. As a young student, he became involved in a democratic movement – something that was strictly illegal. He was arrested, and spent a part of his youth in different prisons. Constantly involved in revolutionary movements, he was deported from country after country and finally took refuge in the most tolerant one at the time: Great Britain. In London, he became involved with the League of the Just, with Weitling.

Joseph Moll came from impoverished circumstances, was apprenticed to a watchmaker, and like many others set out on his journeyman's travels across Europe. He also devoted himself to political activities that the authorities in various countries found punishable; he too ended up in London and there got involved in the same way as Schapper.

In the letter to Marx, Schapper told him about Weitling's reactions to the heated meeting in Brussels. Schapper had been frightened at first. He thought that Marx and Engels wanted to establish a kind of 'aristocracy of the learned' (*Gelehrten-Aristocratie*) that would govern the people from a divinely elevated position. But after the performance, Marx must have written a letter to Schapper in which he gave his version of what had been dealt with. The letter no longer exists, but it must have convinced Schapper that Weitling's account was misleading. Schapper called his friends and fellow thinkers together, who were unanimous that they should establish a correspondence committee of the same kind that Marx had taken the initiative on in Brussels.[3]

It turned out to be an important step. While Moll and Schapper were pushing Weitling aside as a quarrelsome dictator of opinions who loathed all scientific literature, the path towards lively contact with Marx and the small group in Brussels was opening up.

The letter is interesting because it also provides a quite vivid picture of the activities being conducted in London. Schapper said that he and his friends had started an association for educating workers. It had approximately 250 members, and met three times a week. Certain Tuesday evenings were devoted in part to a book by Friedrich Feuerbach (Ludwig's younger brother) on the religion of the future, which was being discussed and scrutinized paragraph by paragraph.[4] The other Tuesdays were devoted to lectures and discussions, for example on raising children in a future society. On Saturday evenings they contented themselves with lighter activities such as song, music, and readings, as well as lectures on good newspaper articles. On Sundays, subjects such as ancient and recent history were treated; lately ancient history – that is, antiquity and the Middle Ages – had covered Lycurgus, the more or less mythical lawgiver in Greece, while recent history dealt with the Reformation of the sixteenth century. But geography, astronomy, and other educational subjects were also part of the Sunday diversions. Another theme that had been up for discussion was the relationship between workers and bourgeoisie, for example the relation between workers and bosses.

Besides these three evenings, there were also meetings with the city's radical French minority to get acquainted with their ideas about communism (which were a little too republican in Schapper's eyes). Every two weeks, they got to know their English fellow thinkers – among them George Julian Harney, one of the most famous Chartists, was held in particular esteem.

But that was not all. On Wednesdays there was singing instruction, on Thursdays they practised linguistic proficiency and drawing, and on Fridays there was dancing. That is, they had programmes throughout the week. In addition to that, there was a library of approximately 500 volumes, and there were hopes of soon being able to move into larger premises. The association did not have only German members. Apart from the 140 Germans there were forty Scandinavians, twenty Hungarians, and even Russians and Italians.

In a new letter, which again is a response to a letter from Marx that has been lost, Schapper and two other signers emphasized that the association's activities were seasonal. In the spring, there were plenty of job opportunities, and many people came to London from the rest of Europe; in July, they left the city to seek their fortune in other quarters. For the tailors, the situation was miserable; they had no place else to go and were forced to remain in London without work. That was why the educational society had helped them and rented a few cheap apartments where those who were hard up could stay for a minimal sum of money. Their need for education was not forgotten despite all their distress: they were given a book that one of them could read from aloud, and which then would be the starting point for discussions in the entire group.

Other members with better prospects for occupations had travelled home – a number of places, including Gothenburg, are mentioned in the letter. The association had also received additional outside contributions: a professor had come from Paris and a student from Heidelberg, and moreover a certain Baron Ribbentrop. The professor was especially useful; he knew a lot about Feuerbach.[5] The account concluded in an appeal to infuse more life into the League of the Just. 'We must have a conference this very year, in 1846!' he wrote. Only in London could it be held undisturbed. More well-to-do communists could help poorer ones with travel money.

The primary goal of this lively educational association was to get more people politically active. Schapper and his friends were convinced that knowledge was the best path towards meaningful political action. *Aufklärung* – enlightenment – was his watchword. 'When the intellectual revolution – which has now begun – is completed, the physical one will come by itself,' he wrote optimistically in the first of the two letters.

It was a standpoint that Marx at the time must have seen as entirely too idealistic. But neither difference of opinion nor the association members' intensive study of Friedrich Feuerbach – who, in all essentials, was following in his brother's footsteps – influenced his attitude towards the activities in London. He must have realized that this was the big chance for him to achieve the influence he had been seeking. On the whole, Great Britain in general – and London in particular – began to take up greater space in his consciousness. In that spirit, he also contacted one of the leading Chartists – the previously mentioned George Julian Harney. Marx's letter has been lost, but not Harney's response. Harney took Marx's side completely in the conflict with Weitling, and it was also clear that he saw himself as a communist.[6]

But it was Schapper and the other German communists who would play the crucial role. For their part, they realized that Marx would be able to promote their cause better than anyone else. How eager they were is shown by the fact that in January 1847, Joseph Moll travelled to Brussels with authorization from his comrades to negotiate linking Marx and Engels even more closely to the League of the Just.[7] We know nothing of the meeting itself, but from the continued developments we can infer that it must have been successful.

In June 1847, a conference in London for the League of the Just was actually arranged.[8] Marx did not participate, of course, but Engels – who also represented his friend – did. It was decided that the organization would change its name to *Bund der Kommunisten* (The Communist League) and – after Schapper's suggestion – adopted the slogan 'Proletarians of all countries, unite!' More important was the idea that they had to gather around a joint, fairly detailed programme. It ripened over the year, and in October the London circle – which could now title itself *Zentralbehörde des Bundes der Kommunisten* (Central Committee of the Communist League) – sent a letter to Brussels in which the Correspondence Committee was encouraged to send a delegate to the second congress, which was to be held in London a few months later. They also explained that there was a special wish that Marx would come – they would try to subsidise the costs for his trip and subsistence.[9]

There is an important little comment. It was Marx, and no one else – not even Engels – who could put the Communist League into order. There was no doubt that Marx was the leading theoretician, and moreover he was considered to have greater ability to gather people around his line than Engels, who – in words from sympathizers in Cologne – easily caused problems through his 'arrogance and vanity'.[10]

According to the group in London, confusion prevailed in the Communist League. Weitling's followers continued to cause difficulties, many members in Paris had been expelled, and in Switzerland (according to Schapper) 'all hell had broken loose'. The section there was led by a 'horribly confused and narrow-minded person, a Swede by the name of Oebom' who was distinguished by 'his limitless hate for all men of learning'. This person had, moreover, the audacity to propose himself as the editor of the league's new newspaper although he could not write a single sentence correctly in German.[11]

Briefly put, the business of the London communists was to convince Marx to travel to the congress for the purpose of creating order in the League. And Marx was convinced. Both he and Engels came to London and participated in the deliberations that were held between 29 November and 8 December 1847. It was there they were tasked with working out what would become the *Manifesto*.

We will remember that earlier that same year, Engels had explained to Louis Blanc that *The Poverty of Philosophy* was to be regarded as the programme for the most radical German social democracy. This is not a surprising statement. The severely polemical tone that distinguished what Marx and Engels had written and said during their time in Brussels was part of the attempt to mark off a definite political understanding. In *The Poverty of Philosophy*, Marx summarized his theory of society in a sharp and explanatory fashion, and a political programme of action can also be glimpsed there.

But something more easily accessible and cogent was needed. Members and sympathizers had to be assembled under a few clear slogans. Scatterbrained people like Oebom and pious swindlers like Weitling had to be made to toe the line, and the boundaries with 'true socialists', Proudhonists, Weitlingians and their followers had to be clearly drawn.

Before we go into greater detail on how the *Manifesto* developed and what it gradually became, we must get a clearer picture of what kind of people the *Manifesto* would convince, assemble, and keep at a distance all at the same time. Where did they belong, in the class society of the 1840s?

Wandering Journeymen, Intellectuals, and a Few Industrial Workers

Industrial workers were the greatest social innovation of the nineteenth century. In the 1840s, they were still found primarily in only a few areas, the most important being in Great Britain but their population was growing in Belgium and France. In the many large and small German states, on the other hand, they were few and far between. Schleswig was an early exception, and industrial development was at least underway in the Rhine provinces.

But, on the whole, the industrial worker was rare in comparison with agricultural workers and smallholders. Among those that did exist, the largest group originally came from the countryside. The lands simply could not provide for the growing population there. The alternatives became emigration to America or work in some factory. The typical industrial worker was a starving ex-agricultural proletarian, forced into the darkness and noise of the factories and housed in the cramped, unsanitary slums that were springing up in the shadow of the factories. It is not odd that faced with their new existence, industrial workers – both women and men – were gripped by a violent longing for the earth, light, and air. Their utopia was not a future high-tech just society, but their own bit of land on which they could just sufficiently provide for themselves and their families. In early documents, above all from Chartism in Britain, the most common dream of the future is of one's own little patch to cultivate.

But there was another, numerically smaller but still influential group among industrial workers – former journeyman craftsmen. Both the former journeymen and those craftsmen who were still working constituted a crucial element in the movement that Marx was now on his way to gaining great influence over. There are several reasons for their central position. One was that many of them risked losing their jobs through industrialization. The skill of craftsmen was making a poor showing against new machines that could perform the same tasks more quickly and more cheaply.

At the beginning of this process, many textile workers in England responded by smashing knitting machines and automatic looms which could be run without a long apprenticeship, and thereby for lower wages. Their activity was particularly wide-spread during the 1810s; those involved were called Luddites, after a more-or-less mythical figure called General (or King) Ludd, who like Robin Hood was said to live in Sherwood Forest.

There was symbolic power in smashing machines, but as a method of struggle the venture was futile. Individual companies and their owners were affected, but the machines could be found in other quarters and new ones were being made in an ever-steadier stream. Technology that made production cheaper could not be stopped with sledgehammers.

More important was the fact that many journeyman craftsmen began to see the development from a broader perspective, realizing that long-term cooperation could better improve their own situation, as well as that of others being oppressed, than could actions aimed only at restoring a system that had been altered forever.

In the mid-nineteenth century, many of Europe's journey-men were both worldly and hungry for knowledge. They had no schools of learning or universities under their belts, but they had something else that only few students at the time possessed: great international experience. They made themselves at home in the great metropolises of Europe, with Paris and London at the head; they learned foreign languages (as we have seen, lectures were held in German, English, and French in London's workers' educational association) and they constituted the great majority of radical, more or less revolutionary clubs founded chiefly in the 1840s. Both lectures and the reading of books and newspapers played a crucial role there.

Journeymen came wandering from all corners of Europe; we have already seen how great the international diffusion in London had been. Often it was pure necessity that drove them, but not even in London could most of them get anything but seasonal work. It is easy to understand that their situation, which was gradually worsening, made them receptive to revolutionary ideas. But they were no longer tempted to actions where they could spontaneously give vent to their fury, instead choosing the longer and more arduous path through joint deliberation and study.

Considering the diversity of journeymen, is it not curious that it was the industrial worker who was the focus for Marx and many others of his kind? No; we have to understand that first of all, Marx was not talking about the present but about *the future that awaited with rapid industrialization*. Dimensions of this industrialization could be anticipated in Great Britain, but with greater difficulty in France and even less so in the German states. The journeymen flocking into the seditious clubs were convinced – and with good reason – that the hard, monotonous life at the machines was their own future, or at least that of their children.

But it was not only journeymen who participated in the many radical deliberations in the 1840s on the world that had just begun to take shape. Quite a few of them had university degrees. Perhaps, like Schapper, they had early on joined forbidden clubs and not only been expelled from university but thrown into prison as well. Several of them worked as journalists in radical newspapers that were constantly threatened by censorship. For them, writing was natural, and that qualification made them important for the dissemination of ideas.

One large group participating in the discussions was doctors. We have already had glimpses of some of them: Roland Daniels and Heinrich Otto Lüning. But there were countless others, and their presence is not as surprising as it may seem today. On the one hand, doctors did not yet have their social status to safeguard – they would obtain that in the twentieth century. On the other hand, and above all, many of them who stood far to the left were active among the people who were the worst off in society. Government doctors were already playing an important role in charting the special misery that industrialism created. We have already met James Philips Kay in Manchester; others followed after him, writing reports on the underside of society. A great many of them were not satisfied with analyses, but wanted to fundamentally change the society of the time.[12]

Marx was an odd character in this company, with his doctoral degree and his erudition. It cannot be said that he ever blended in among his new fellow thinkers. He remained for them the one who would say what everyone had been waiting to hear, and provide the final theory. It was a role he gladly took on.

Engels, in his way, was even more odd in the context – the son of a factory owner with his own experiences of what it meant to run a company and act as a capitalist. While Marx could always be affected by the antipathy of the self-taught manual labourers for the well read, Engels's position was even more uncomfortable. He was a member of the upper class who sided with the workers – but how far could the unemployed journeyman or the impoverished factory worker trust him?

We have already seen that neither Marx nor Engels were particularly tactful in their efforts, despite their backgrounds, to play leading roles in the struggle for the cause of the oppressed classes. Nevertheless, they succeeded marvellously. They were the ones tasked with writing the manifesto of the communist party. How could that happen?

This is one of the questions we must bring with us into the next section. But there are others that are even more important: Why a manifesto? Why was this manifesto given the form and content it had?

A Catechism Becomes a Manifesto

Marx and Engels had gained a crucial point of support in London. But they had also successfully worked to strengthen their position in Brussels, which, for the time being, was where Marx could be active. The Correspondence Committee was not the only important project. Radical forces had started a newspaper in town: the *Deutscher-Brüsseler-Zeitung*. However, its founder and early editor, Adelbert von Bornstedt, was neither a follower of theirs nor a friend. Bornstedt was a Prussian officer who left his position early on and set out into the world. After some time in Brazil, he came to Paris, where he moved in the same radical circles as Marx and Engels. Like Marx, he was deported from France and also took refuge in Brussels. Once there, he started his newspaper.

He gave free rein to a sharp criticism of Engels, but he also allowed both Marx and Engels to submit a contribution in response. Engels defended himself bravely against an attack from Karl Heinzen, a German writer who spent a large part of his life in the United States and who regarded himself as a socialist rather than a communist. Heinzen attacked a sensitive point: he called Engels a turncoat who had recently become communist, while Heinzen himself held fast to his earlier position. Engels responded furiously, but it was Marx who dealt the real death blow to their impudent, self-satisfied opponent. He wrote a long series of articles in a style that had become typical for him as a journalist. He generously scattered fragments of his learning, citing Shakespeare, Goethe and Ariosto (in the Italian) and went to war against Heinzen's ignorance. Heinzen had declared that he knew nothing of philosophy and that for him, Hegel was 'indigestible'. Marx objected sternly: '*Ignorance* is generally considered a fault. We are accustomed to regard it as a *negative* quantity. Let us observe how the magic wand of the philistine as critic converts a minus quantity of intelligence into a plus quantity of morality.'

Marx saw Heinzen as a narrow-minded moralist who was satisfied with demanding that people of all types should be decent and good, and did not care at all about fundamental questions concerning property or labour.[13] Both Marx and Engels became regular contributors to *Deutsche-Brüsseler-Zeitung*, and at the end of the paper's brief existence – it was shut down in early 1848 – had crucial influence over it. Once again, it had become apparent how Marx (assisted by Engels) could fight his way forward to a central position in a project that at the beginning was not even his.

Marx also helped create another (though short-lived) arena that was given the name *Demokratische Gesellschaft zur Einigung und Verbrüderung aller Völker* (Democratic Society for Unity and Brotherhood of All Peoples). He was elected its vice-president on 15 November 1847; the president was a Belgian with a political past. The intent was to unite various groupings into a joint organization of struggle that strove for a democratic society with equal and universal voting rights and a parliament that possessed ultimate power. It was entirely in accordance with Marx's strategy for countries that, in his opinion, first had to undergo a bourgeois revolution. Here, he could unite his forces with people who stood quite far away from his communism.

He did not conceal his own opinions, however. In early January 1848, he held a lecture in French on the question of free trade: *Discours sur la question du libre-échange*. The background was the major struggle in Great Britain over protective duties on grain. These duties were attacked by the 'Anti-Corn Law League', a broad liberal association in which the 'Manchester liberals' (or Manchester School, as they were known, with Richard Cobden and John Bright at their head) played a leading role. Manchester liberalism was largely similar to the neoliberalism of our time that follows in Milton Friedman's footsteps. Not only did they preach the blessings of free trade, they also recommended maximum deregulation of the economy. As regards their ideas about free importation of grain, they brought forward the fact that the workers would thereby have cheaper bread to eat as a crucial argument. But Bright and his fellow thinkers were no friends of the workers, Marx pointed out. They had frenetically resisted the law on a ten-hour working day.

Marx declared that he himself embraced no protective duties, seeing them instead as a necessary stage in the development of a country. Great Britain had now managed to get past that stage, while protectionism was inevitable, for example, for the German states on their path towards industrialization. It was also an economic necessity that cheaper bread would entail lower wages. Economic forces bring wage reductions when the costs of keeping the workers alive fall. The arguments from David Ricardo and other economists reverberate in Marx's reasoning. But the most interesting thing about his lecture is that he set liberalism and democracy against each other quite clearly. The freedom that the Manchester liberals preached was not the freedom of individuals in relation to other individuals. It entailed only the 'freedom of Capital to crush the worker'. Democracy entailed something entirely different: the path towards the liberation of all.

According to the records that have been preserved, the lecture was met with enthusiasm from the large number of attendees. It was also published as a pamphlet, which was translated into several languages, including German, and enjoyed a certain degree of success.[14] But it was also one of the democratic association's last shows of force. The wave of unrest that swept over Europe in 1848 overshadowed their activities. It was dissolved the following year, by which time Marx had left Brussels.

Marx's most important task at that time was undoubtedly writing the programme for the Communist League. A few attempts had already been made in that direction when Marx was called in to the work. Engels had written a draft of around twenty pages on his own: 'The Principles of Communism'. But there would be no final version without Marx's contributions. It was precisely for the sake of this matter that he received the urgent request to come to London in person. Everyone was agreed that he was the one who had to complete the project. Engels also thought so, and there is nothing to indicate that Marx himself held any other opinion.

But Engels's draft would form the basis for the final text. It had the form of a traditional catechism, with questions and responses like 'What is communism?' and 'Will it be possible to bring about the abolition of private property by peaceful methods?' The programmes of many radical groups had looked like this for a great many decades. As late as 1884, the Swedish playwright August Strindberg could write *A Small Catechism for the Underclass*. The Swedish historian of ideas Adrian Velicu has shown how secular catechisms flooded the market during the French Revolution.[15] The form had obvious advantages: it was clear and simple, and it was well known to generations of women and men who had been primed with various Christian catechisms. For Engels, with his strict religious upbringing, it was certainly a particular delight to use it for purposes other than Christian edification.

At the same time, the long series of questions and responses sounded both stiff and repetitive. Engels himself realized these limitations. In a letter to Marx, in which he enclosed his draft, he proposed that the final version should not be a catechism, but that the thing (*das Ding*) should be called a manifesto instead. The reason he gave was that historical development needed to be taken up, and it would be difficult to keep to such a rigid form. Nor was he satisfied with what he himself had achieved. The result was 'quite unsuitable', he said bitterly.[16]

It is entirely too harsh a judgement. As always, Engels had written a clear and lucid text that flowed elegantly and naturally. On the other hand, it is not at all on the level of the final *Manifesto*. Comparing Engels's 'Principles' with the final text, both in form and content, is of some interest.

There was actually also another reason to speak of a 'manifesto' – a reason Marx and Engels themselves gave in the preface to a new German edition published in 1872. The Communist League had been a secret organization, but it would now no longer be so. It was time to *manifest* – to make clear what the organization stood for.[17]

Linguistically speaking, the *Manifest der kommunistischen Partei* (Manifesto of the Communist Party) bears the stamp of Marx in all essentials. Engels was also prepared to ascribe the fundamental ideas to Marx – they belonged 'solely and exclusively to Marx', he wrote in the preface to the 1883 German edition.[18] This is certainly an exaggeration. On the other hand, the wording is not Engels's. The only person who could have influenced this is Jenny Marx. This is at least what her biographer Ulrich Teusch wants to have us believe; a few lines in the only preserved manuscript are unmistakably written in her handwriting.[19]

But it is still without a doubt Karl who was responsible for most of the wording. What is most striking is the impact of the incomparable art of his writing in the small introductory preface and in the first section, 'Bourgeois and Proletarians'. Marx reaches stylistic heights there that Engels never even came close to, where neither the complicated diversity of the textual references nor the gravity of the precision of terms weighed down what he wrote. We have already encountered his lines about the opium of the masses and what a lack of money does to a person; other such pearls await us in coming chapters.

The best pages in the *Manifesto* are unsurpassed in their kind; rarely, if ever, has anyone written so brilliantly on societal issues. The very first sentence has attained iconic status: 'A spectre is haunting Europe – the spectre of Communism.' (The background is the panicked alarm of the contemporary European regimes at communist conspiracies; dangerous secret societies were suspected in every nook and cranny.) The memorable sentences follow in quick succession. Despite their being quoted *ad nauseam* and having served as fodder for countless book titles, they have never lost their radiance. Like all classical texts, they have also preserved their topicality. It is still possible to recognize our own time in the most well-known paragraph:

> The bourgeoisie, wherever it has got the upper hand, has put an end to all feudal, patriarchal, idyllic relations. It has pitilessly torn asunder the motley feudal ties that bound man to his 'natural superiors', and has left remaining no other nexus between man and man than naked self-interest, than callous 'cash payment'. It has drowned the most heavenly ecstasies of religious fervour, of chivalrous enthusiasm, of philistine sentimentalism, in the icy water of egotistical calculation. It has resolved personal worth into exchange value, and in place of the numberless indefeasible chartered freedoms, has set up that single, unconscionable freedom – Free Trade. In one word, for exploitation, veiled by religious and political illusions, it has substituted naked, shameless, direct, brutal exploitation.

Or stop a moment before the sentence 'All that is solid melts into air, all that is holy is profaned, and man is at last compelled to face with sober senses, his real conditions of life, and his relations with his kind.' We still live in this world.[20]

But this also says that the promises for the future that the *Manifesto* contains never came true. Russia's October Revolution never came close to what Marx pointed out in advance, and its results now belong entirely to the past. The Chinese analogue was at least equally as far from the prototype of 1848, and the more than sixty-year dictatorship there has been alloyed with an equally implacable capitalism. In today's China, Marx's words about the solid melting into air and the holy being profaned are just as applicable as they are in most refined capitalist countries.

But with this, we are already well into the content of the *Manifesto*. Let us stay here. It is striking that the *Manifesto*, with its just over thirty pages of text, contains so much more than Engels's 'Principles' does in seventeen. This is due in part to the fact that the *Manifesto* discards the catechism's responses to questions such as 'In what way does the proletarian differ from the slave? From the serf?' and so on, which take up a lot of space. Tellingly enough, Engels provided no answer to a question that he nonetheless asked regarding the difference between the proletarian and the craftsman; the question may simply have been too sensitive, considering that craftsmen made up the majority of the text's immediate recipients.

Such matters were settled in the *Manifesto* with a few terse formulations. The question of the relationship of the craftsman to the industrial worker is given a response in one sentence, which also provides information on a range of other societal classes. It speaks of 'the lower middle class, the small manufacturer, the artisan, the peasant', all of which are now on the path to sinking down into the proletariat because their capital is too little to cope with the competition from modern industry.[21]

The *Manifesto* portrays contemporary society as an enormous centrifuge. From its violent movements, some are pushed upward, becoming members of the ruling class: the capitalists – or, in another word, the bourgeoisie. Many more are on the way down, more quickly or more slowly; farmers, craftsmen, merchants – all are gradually proletarianized. They seek to preserve their position in vain; they become reactionary.

The implacable path downwards that most are compelled to take is widely shared. Nor are the well educated spared. Once they were surrounded by respect, but now the bourgeoisie has 'converted the physician, the lawyer, the priest, the poet, the man of science, into its paid wage labourers'.[22]

The phrase 'wage labourer' rouses wonder: are the doctors and the others becoming proletarians? Are all wage labourers simply workers – the doctor and the dean, the lawyer and the novelist? The reader finds no answer. This is not that strange. The *Manifesto* depicts ongoing development but is always hurrying on ahead in the direction of what awaits in a nearer or more remote future. The perspective in time is undetermined. The tense is at once the present and the future.

The same thing thereby also applies to the revolution that stands in focus further on in the *Manifesto*. It seems that the bourgeoisie's fateful hour could strike tomorrow, but the text can equally readily be interpreted so that the great upheaval will only take place in a more far-off future when society has been transformed even more radically. The workers join together in this process, and they struggle to keep their wages up. Here and there, it leads to riots. 'Now and then the workers are victorious, but only for a time.' In the long run, their situation continuously worsens.

The authors of the *Manifesto* are still adherents of 'the iron law of wages'. There is nothing strange about this; the doctrine was entirely predominant at the time, especially among economists. Only later would Marx – and following him, Engels – abandon it.[23]

The important thing about the workers joining together is instead that their combined forces increase, the more people are pushed down into proletarian impoverishment from development. Even their intellectual capacity is improved when people who previously found themselves higher up on the class ladder are forced to tumble down. The fact that a small part of the ruling class joins the revolutionary workers is also an advantage (and Engels must be counted among this minority).

But the working class not only grows – it is also feminized. This fact, about which Marx only gave intimations in a few figures without notes in the *Manifesto*, is given a few lines of attention here. It says that men's labour 'is superseded' by women's because labour through machinery no longer requires great bodily strength. Gender and age have become inessential in general, and women and children cost less (though it is unclear why women do). 'All are instruments of labour.'[24]

The second chapter of the *Manifesto*, 'Proletarians and Communists', is shorter than the first one and contains a number of interesting points. It observes, for example, that communism does not abolish property in general, only 'bourgeois property' – ownership of the means of production such as machinery, purchased labour, and so on. But, on the other hand, this property tends to push out all others to become the only kind. The distinction between *Eigentum* and *Aneignung* that Marx made in other texts does not appear here; perhaps it was regarded as far too subtle for a party programme. In any case, the point is that capital is not a personal, but a 'social power'. The capitalists do not appear as concrete individuals but as bearers of the impersonal power that both supports and permeates the society where capitalism reigns.[25]

In the *Manifesto*'s day, communists were accused of their battle against private property also being a battle against the family. Of course, the authors responded, the bourgeois family must be abolished. Only among the bourgeoisie was it fully developed. The proletarians were forced to break up their families, and prostitution was rampant in contemporary society.[26]

Engels's 'Principles' are much more illustrative on that point. Engels said that the relation between the sexes would become completely private and would only be the business of those it immediately concerned. Women would no longer be dependent on men, nor would children be dependent on their parents. The accusation that communists would bring women to be owned in common is levelled against bourgeois society, in which prostitution was flourishing.[27]

The reason for the *Manifesto*'s more evasive statements can only be the subject of speculation. We know that Engels and Marx had different views on marriage in the age in which they lived. Is that why the answers are so vague in the text Marx was responsible for? Perhaps so. But we know nothing for certain.

On the other hand, both the original and the final *Manifesto* are equally unambiguous as regards upbringing and education: they will become a common affair. The accusation that communism would destroy eternal values such as freedom and justice is emphatically dismissed. The coming upheaval would cast off 'certain common forms, or general ideas, which cannot completely vanish except with the total disappearance of class antagonisms'.[28] But this statement also lacks clarity, and above all gives rise to a number of questions. Even after the revolution, people will be conscious beings – but what will then fill their consciousness? We are given no information about it.

Another question is even more pressing: *What are the ideas that engage those opposing contemporary society? Where do they get their ideas and ideals from?* They are obviously borne by a passion that has its roots in the distant past. Ideas of resistance turned against the reigning power can be traced back for millennia. No one knew that better than Marx himself, whose lifelong ideal was Prometheus, defier of the gods.

What will remain of this after the revolution? Would Prometheus and the eternal spirit of revolt he stood for lose their urgency? Would Aeschylus, Shakespeare, and Goethe sink into an indifferent past? Would Balzac's depictions of a cynical social apparatus that bred careerists and losers become only a curiosity?

In other texts both before and later, Marx made use of Hegel's key concept of *Aufhebung* – sublation – which meant that something was both abolished and raised to a higher level. In that case, the best of the inherited culture would certainly lose its earlier, class-based meanings but at the same time be refined and deepened.

Perhaps Marx had found these thoughts entirely too complicated for a text that was supposed to be read and understood by everyone. But the consequence was that society after the revolution only appeared as a total contrast to the world Marx and Engels were living in. It was otherwise featureless. Everything would be good, yes – but how?

The unsurpassed depiction in the first chapter of capitalist society is succeeded by a second chapter that produces more questions than answers. Greater clarity only makes an appearance with a ten-point programme on what the communist party wanted to achieve. The list, which modifies but in all essentials agrees with its counterpart in Engels's 'Principles', contains everything from the expropriation of landed property, equal obligation for everyone to work, and the centralization of the transport system in the hands of the state to free public education of all children and strongly progressive taxation. On a few points, the enumeration of the *Manifesto* diverges from the one Engels stood for. It is perhaps telling that Engels was satisfied with heavy taxation of inheritances, whereas the final version – the one Marx wrote – simply demands that the right of inheritance be abolished. Engels's idea for a large palace where residence and work would be combined, and industry and agriculture meet, also disappeared.[29]

But all these measures, whether in the one version or the other, are simply steps on the road towards a future society – the one only described through a series of negations: it is classless, without exploitation and without the kind of morals born out of the rule of one class over all the others. Medieval philosophy spoke of a *via negativa*, a road to knowledge that ran through negations. Marx and Engels embarked upon the same road, but in an entirely different area.

One reason for their reticence on the society of the future is the fear of fancifully depicted utopias that were prevalent at the time, which both Marx and Engels had been attracted to not so long ago. That fear, which at the same time contained a great fascination, found expression in the third chapter of the *Manifesto*, which deals with various kinds of socialist and communist literature. There was a model here in Engels as well, but in comparison the difference with the final version in the *Manifesto* is great. Equally as strong as the first chapter, it bears the obvious stamp of Marx's singular style of writing with its coruscating details.[30]

The description begins with the one furthest from the *Manifesto*'s own standpoint, namely what is here called 'Feudal Socialism'. In this variant, capitalism is criticized for having broken feudal social bonds and also for having called forth a revolutionary proletariat. There are crucial similarities between this kind of socialism and Christianity, and Marx is not surprised: 'Has not Christianity declaimed against private property, against marriage, against the state? Has it not preached in place of these, charity and poverty, celibacy and mortification of the flesh, monastic life and Mother Church? Christian Socialism is but the holy water with which the priest consecrates the heart-burning of the aristocrat.'[31]

'Petty-Bourgeois Socialism' is treated with greater sympathy, even identifying a hero: the Swiss political economist and historian Jean Charles Léonard de Sismondi. Sismondi, who was born in 1773 and died in 1842, belonged to a different generation than Marx. He had been influenced by Adam Smith, but objected to the passion of Smith and other economists for constant growth. Humanity, not production, should be at the centre. The current system bred constant crises and created poverty for the many in society. Sismondi's ideal was, rather, a system in which smallholders and petty bourgeois could live a good, secure, and relatively equal life.[32]

In the following section, Marx and Engels drew nearer to themselves, or rather their own development. The subject is 'German, or "True", Socialism'. This, the authors said, was the inevitable result when German philosophers and scholars met French socialist and communist literature. France had undergone the bourgeois revolution that the Germans still had before them, which is why the Germans would devote themselves to 'interests of Human Nature, of Man in general, who belongs to no class, has no reality, who exists only in the misty realm of philosophical fantasy'.[33]

The criticism is ruthless. But Marx, with good reason, had to count himself among the Germans who had begun their wanderings towards socialism and communism with ideas about the essence of humanity and its alienation. The chief expression for this entire stigmatized literary genre is and remains the *Manuscripts*. The world did not yet know about them.

Proudhon, once the object of Marx's admiration, was dismissed under the heading of 'Conservative, or Bourgeois Socialism'. Once again, it was his book on the philosophy of poverty that was being pilloried. Proudhon's dream, Marx says, was a bourgeoisie without the proletariat. It is a crushing judgement, but not a fair one. Proudhon's ideal society was a society in which no one lived in misery or was subjected to oppression.[34]

More positive is the description of 'Critical-Utopian Socialism and Communism'. Of all the sections in the chapter, this is the one that likely had the greatest influence. It was through this section that the term 'utopian socialism' became a natural component of the political vocabulary. Saint-Simon, Owen, and Fourier have been branded with this term. They were utopians. They built castles in the air.

The reader who has only this idea about them will certainly be surprised that the picture being painted here has such praise. The early socialist and communist systems certainly belonged to a time when the proletariat was still in an immature stage of its development. The path to liberation lay in the darkness. Fourier and the others were not prepared to pursue any politics – least of all anything revolutionary – but were inspired instead to various experiments with miniature societies that were doomed to fail.

But this kind of socialism or communism was not only utopian. It was critical as well. The word *critical* has a central place in Marx's vocabulary, as it had during his entire Young Hegelian period, and in other respects in the entire tradition from Kant. Being critical did not mean simply being negative. Someone developing criticism in Marx's meaning illuminates an object or a phenomenon so that its anatomy and method of functioning are exposed. Critical analysis thereby opens the path for a programme of action.

The *Manifesto* says that authors in the tradition of Saint-Simon and Fourier 'attack every principle of existing society' and that they thereby 'are full of the most valuable materials for the enlightenment of the working class'. What they say about the future society, on the other hand, is to be regarded as pure utopianism – for example that the antithesis between town and country is to be abolished, that the institution of the family is to be dissolved, and that the state alone will administer production.[35]

There is much to say about this brief text. As regards the elements pointed out as purely utopian, their counterparts can be glimpsed in several texts by both Marx and Engels – in fact, even in other parts of the *Manifesto* (at least concerning marriage). The utopianism in them must be attributed to the lack of concrete ideas about how all these new things would be realized. The authors of the *Manifesto* pointed out in particular that the critical utopians had had no idea of the crucial significance of the class struggle.

It is also worth noting that the nuanced assessment of the critical utopians had no counterpart in Engels's 'Principles'. It was Marx's point of view that found expression in these pages. Only he could also write a sentence like this: 'They still dream of experimental realisation of their social Utopias, of founding isolated "phalan-stères", of establishing "Home Colonies", of setting up "Little Icaria" – duodecimo editions of the New Jerusalem ...' This lingering dream turned the followers of Fourier and the others into reactionaries who turned their backs on the rapid development of recent years, instead dreaming of the time when their teachers lived and worked.

These crushing formulations appear all the more acerbic knowing that the 1840s saw an unprecedented number of small-scale social experiments. Many people, particularly in France, dreamed of realizing Étienne Cabet's ideal society of Icaria. *Phalanstères* sprang up in many quarters, especially in the New World. Owen's ideal society, New Lanark, still stood in Scotland and inspired many. The second- and third-generation followers of 'the Critical-Utopian Socialists and Communists' were real competitors of the communist movement that Marx and Engels were part of constructing.

These movements are the subject of the very last pages of the *Manifesto*. The authors mention developments in a series of different countries. The account is quite succinct, and the main attention is directed towards Germany because 'that country [was] on the eve of a bourgeois revolution'. That revolution is particularly significant because it would take place at a higher level of development than the analogous upheavals in seventeenth-century England and eighteenth-century France. The proletariat had already managed to go farther than the workers in both of the other times and places.

There and everywhere, the communists wanted to make common cause with other democratic forces. But they did not conceal their goal: a society that could only be created 'by the forcible overthrow of all existing social conditions'. The proletarians had nothing to lose but their chains. They had 'a world to win'. That is why they had to unite, wherever on earth they were located.[36]

The Time of Revolts

The *Manifesto* was published in late February 1848. Its triumphal march did not begin immediately. Quite the opposite – the pamphlet long remained largely unnoticed. Only decades later did it become an important introduction, not only to Marx's view of society and political programmes but also to socialism and communism in general.

But a series of translations of the pamphlet were published during its first few years. Marx and Engels spoke proudly of them in the preface to the new German edition, published in 1872. The enumeration concluded with information about a Danish translation.[37] But that was a mistake – the translation was Swedish and done by Pär Götrek, an eccentric bookseller who early on introduced socialist and communist ideas to Sweden. It is possible that he had help from a few journeymen with experiences from the rebellious metropolises of the Continent. The translation had the placid title *Kommunismens röst* (The Voice of Communism), and it replaced the militant 'Working men of all countries...' in the original with the somewhat more stylish but still deeply controversial motto 'Folks röst är Guds röst' (The voice of the people is the voice of God). These words had tradition on their side, at least; ultimately, they go back to Hesiod, the oldest named Greek poet, who in his *Works and Days* asserted that even the speech of common people is divine in its way.[38]

The first English translation appeared in 1850. It was done by Helen Macfarlane, a Scottish Chartist, journalist, and philosopher, and was published in four parts in George Julian Harney's newspaper *Red Republican*. Macfarlane had a splendid knowledge of German philosophy, especially as regards Hegel. Marx esteemed her highly and was indignant when she was treated poorly by Harney. She was 'the only collaborator on his insignificant little rag who really has any ideas. On his rag, a *rara avis*.' Macfarlane's translation is lively and imaginative. In her version, the famous first line runs: 'A frightful hobgoblin stalks throughout Europe. We are haunted by a ghost, the ghost of Communism.'[39]

But in the year 1848, it was rather quiet regarding the *Manifesto*. Nor did Marx have time to reflect particularly much on the pamphlet that had just come out into print. It so happened that revolution – the revolution he had just written of in advance – broke out in Paris as the *Manifesto* was leaving the printing presses. The events in Paris came as no great surprise. The year 1847 had been a difficult one in Europe, with crises in all major branches of industry and financial troubles. The convulsions actually began in Italy, but there it was a question of liberation from foreign powers. In Sicily they wanted to get rid of the Spanish, and in Lombardy the Austrians.

Nonetheless it was Paris that everyone expected to revolt; it was the capital of the European revolutionaries. It had been clear for some time that something was brewing. Oppositional forces had arranged a long series of mass meetings masqueraded as banquets; dissatisfaction with the current regime, with Louis Philippe – the 'Pear King' – at its head, was great and well articulated.

When the government forbid a banquet planned for 21 February, unrest grew rapidly; barricades were raised and street battles were fought, and after only a few days – on the 24th – Guizot, the head of government, gave the battle up for lost. The king fled across the Channel to Great Britain. Alphonse de Lamartine, a Romantic poet and also an experienced diplomat and dedicated liberal, proclaimed the Second Republic the day after. The provisional government now formed was made up of a motley collection of men from right to left, united only by certain ideals about freedoms and rights – something that found expression in a number of important reforms, for example the introduction of freedom of the press and abolition of slavery in the colonies.[40]

Marx, of course, was full of enthusiasm for the revolution. He wrote a congratulatory letter to Paris on behalf of the democratic association, at the same time asking permission to travel to the new France.[41] A few days later, on 1 March 1848, he had the pleasure of receiving a letter from Ferdinand Flocon, one of the members in the new provisional government, welcoming him to Paris. It was a great turn of events, and Jenny Marx was even more delighted, if that can be imagined. Much later, in her grand but incomplete memoirs from 1865, 'Short Sketch of an Eventful Life', she could depict this feeling of triumph: 'Paris again lay open to us. And where else could we recover our spirits than under the

rising sun of the new revolution? We had to go there, simply had
to!' *Dorthin, hiess es, dorthin*, as it was in the original German,
sounds even more jubilant.[42]

But Brussels would not let either Jenny or Karl go without
harassment. Its leaders feared Belgium would also see its own
1848. The same wave of changes that brought Louis Philippe
to power in France in 1830 had made Belgium independent and
Léopold I its king. Would Belgian rebels now create a republic
like the French one, thereby destroying the right-wing bourgeois
regime? Faced with such prospects, Karl Marx – with his rapidly
growing revolutionary network – was a dangerous figure. To top
it all off, he had received a part of the inheritance from his father
and, according to him, he had immediately donated the money
to the movement he himself was now leading. So he was thrown
into prison, and the same fate befell Jenny. Jenny depicted the
familiar course of events: Late one evening, two men broke into
the Marx family's residence and took Karl away. Jenny sought
help among her acquaintances but was also arrested and thrown
into a dark cell among beggars and prostitutes. The next morning,
she was interrogated for two hours before she was released. Karl
was also released on the promise to leave the country within
twenty-four hours.

Karl described what he himself, Jenny, and others had to endure
while the memory of the events was still fresh. He had been treated
roughly; even worse, his friend Wilhelm Wolff had taken a fist to
the eye, was spat on in the face, kicked, and severely humiliated.
In an article in the Parisian newspaper *La Réforme*, Marx was
particularly indignant over what Jenny had to endure. Her only
crime, he explained, consisted of the fact that 'although belonging
to the Prussian aristocracy, she shares the democratic opinions of
her husband'.[43]

In Paris, however, the family's happiness was short-lived. The
French example inspired Germans to place demands on their government. A wave of rebellions had begun on 27 February with
the 'Mannheim Popular Assembly' (*die Mannheimer Volksver-
sammlung*) where the crucial *March Demands* were set. Their gist
was freedom of the press and the establishment of a popular army
instead of the career army that was completely controlled by the

kings and princes of the various states. An all-German parliament was also called to begin functioning immediately. The demands were quickly accepted in state after state, but the traditional rulers were not willing to give up their positions of power; the inevitable result was a revolution. Almost immediately it was called the 'March Revolution', and it naturally roused great hopes among the many German exiles in Paris and other cities. A large group wanted to take immediate action in the spirit of Wilhelm Weitling, in the hopes of stirring the masses to a mighty popular rebellion. Marx, like Engels, adopted a completely negative attitude towards this type of spontaneous, half-military action. His conviction that the German states still had to undergo a bourgeois revolution first, expressed so starkly in the *Manifesto*, was not shaken by these dramatic events.

On the other hand, Adelbert von Bornstedt, the editor of the German paper in Brussels, believed that immediate action would result in a socialist society. Georg Herwegh, one of the oddest figures in the German left movement of the time, had the same idea. A few words need to be said about him.

Herwegh, a year older than Marx, had had early success as a poet, and just as early on had been forced to flee to Switzerland to escape charges of rebellious thinking and actions. He had his first contact with Marx as a contributor to *Rheinische Zeitung*, and Marx thought highly of him at the beginning. But Herwegh was open to many kinds of influences; the Russian anarchist Bakunin soon became one of his teachers. The idea of quick, resolute rebellious actions took root in his world of ideas.

When the March Revolution broke out, he did not hesitate to join, placing himself at the head of a popular but militarily unschooled army that consisted largely of people who had lost their jobs during the crisis. It was not difficult to predict that the adventure would end in complete defeat. 'The German Democratic Legion' lost its first and only battle against career soldiers from Württemberg. The Legion dispersed, Herwegh sought refuge in Switzerland, having had enough of military adventures. But he did not lose his ability to move along the outer edges of this innovative history. He became friends with a number of the great minds of the century: Herzen and Turgenev the writers, Wagner the composer, and Semper the architect. Later, he would play a role in the prehistory of the German Social Democratic Party. The whole time, he continued to write his sometimes inflammatory, sometimes bombastic poems and songs. The most known of them was *Das Bundeslied*, the Song of the League, which was quickly banned but still became one of the central songs of the German workers' movement.[44]

Von Bornstedt, his closest friend in the popular campaign, was not as lucky. He ended up in prison, and despite soon being released, never recovered and died in 1851.

Marx did not expose himself to these kinds of dangers. It was not with firearms that this desk-bound family man fought, but with words. True to habit, he devoted himself to organizational work as soon as he got to Paris. With him, the Communist League established its new centre there, and he also started a German Workers' Club.

During the month of March, the revolution spread to both Vienna and Budapest. On 18 March, barricades were raised in Berlin. Marx was convinced that central Europe was faced with its delayed bourgeois revolution. Together with Engels, he wrote a text titled 'Demands of the Communist Party in Germany'. The idea was that the communists would also make themselves heard among the various tendencies fighting for democracy. Many of the demands agree with those imposed by other revolutionaries. Germany would be a united republic, universal suffrage would be introduced, a popular army would replace the career armies, elected representatives would receive fair pay and legal aid would be free of charge. Other demands were more far-reaching: the banks and transport system should be nationalized, and the right of inheritance limited. (Still only limited – it was Engels's, not Marx's, line that was victorious.) The list of demands was disseminated as a flyer and also printed in several German newspapers.[45]

But Marx was still trying to influence the Germans from afar. It would not long remain so. At the end of March, he received a letter from his good friend Weerth that encouraged him to leave for Cologne. A new newspaper was in the offing there, and Marx would be crucial to its fate. Communists were unpopular in the Rhineland, Weerth explained.[46]

He neglected to mention that their enemies were found not only among conservatives and cautious liberals. There were many adherents of the 'true socialists', whom Marx and Engels had so vehemently fought against, especially among journeymen, workers, and others far down on the social ladder. They did not want to hear about the detour through bourgeois democracy that Marx recommended. The goal – a society without poverty and injustice – lay within reach for those who dared.

The leader in this opinion was Andreas Gottschalk, a butcher's son from Düsseldorf who had the opportunity to pursue academic studies in both classic philology and medicine. He became a doctor, and like many other radical young Germans became a government doctor with great insight into destitution and human suffering. In the *Rheinische Zeitung* period, he found himself on the periphery of the editorial staff. It was not Marx, however, but Moses Hess who made the strongest impression on him. In Gottschalk's eyes, Marx was a 'learned sun god' who devoted 'only a scientific, doctrinaire interest to the misery of the workers and the hunger of the poor'.[47] A sun god is elevated over everything earthly. Like Amon-Ra or Phoebus Apollo, he watches the strivings of humanity from a distance.

Gottschalk had been very successful in organizing workers and journeymen in Cologne. It was 'true socialism', not communism, that stood out as the radical popular opposition there. Weerth was convinced that Marx could change the situation, not only for the sake of communism but for the revolution.

Marx did not require a great deal of pressing. He and Engels soon set off across the border. By 11 April, they were in Cologne. Preparations for the new publication were in full swing. Once Marx was on site, he naturally took over the leadership. There were still many in the region – even some bourgeois – who remembered his contributions to *Rheinische Zeitung* a few years earlier with delight. The new newspaper now being founded was naturally named *Neue Rheinische Zeitung*.

Funding was, of course, a constant problem. Engels took a trip to his hometown to get moneyed families to contribute, but it was in vain. There was not much coming in from Cologne or its neighbouring cities, either. But Marx as editor-in-chief received a decent

salary – the best he would ever get. It was not certain that the
entire amount could be paid out each month, but it was enough
for the family to reasonably get by. During their time in Cologne,
the worst financial problems were lifted from Karl's – and especially Jenny's – shoulders (it was she, not he, who managed the
family's finances).

Marx would soon also create an alternative organization to
Gottschalk's great *Kölner Arbeiterverein*. It would be called the
Demokratische Gesellschaft and following Marx, would be a coalition among various democratic forces, not just those furthest to
the left. There was no direct conflict between the two associations.
Quite the opposite: even though differences of opinion remained,
they would ultimately unite.

But now we are hurrying ahead of events. The most important
thing for Marx was the newspaper. Like Engels, he began feverish
journalistic activity as soon as *Neue Rheinische Zeitung* started
publication. Engels primarily monitored events in other quarters
of Europe, while Marx preferred to keep to the political problems
of the revolution in the German states.

The Impotence of Parliament and Freedom of the Press

The revolutionaries had succeeded in winning a relatively far-
reaching freedom of the press, which Marx – true to habit – would
make use of to its breaking point. Equally as important was the
German parliament – the *Nationalversammlung* – that began
meeting in May, in Frankfurt am Main. There, 809 members representing the various states – and ideally, the various classes as
well – met. But not much would come of it later. The great majority of the representatives were drawn from the growing layer of
the population that would distinguish Germany over the course
of the nineteenth century: its large and influential educated middle
class, the *Bildungsbürgertum*. Ninety-five percent of the members
had high school degrees, and more than two-thirds had taken an
academic degree. Of these, more than half were lawyers. A striking
number were state employees: judges, professors, and the like. A
satirical poem that spread in radical circles ran: 'Three times one

hundred lawyers – O Fatherland, you have been betrayed / Three times one hundred professors – O Fatherland, you are lost.'[48]

The chief task of the parliament was to create a constitution; the country was not only to become a political unit, but a constitutional monarchy as well. But the work was strenuous and the demands many. However sociologically homogeneous the members were, they represented opinions ranging from the conservative right to the radical left. The biggest problem was the assembly's own status. It was unclear how it stood legally in relation to kings, princes, and governments, as well as to the individual states they represented. The more radical members recommended a truly revolutionary solution: they should simply seize power and push through the new constitution on their own. But a more cautious majority recommended an agreement with the powers already established.

This idea of a possible, peaceful, and successful compromise was sometimes called *die Vereinbarungstheorie* – a hope that it would be possible to bring the desires of the assembly into line with those of the traditional powers. In *Neue Rheinische Zeitung*, the idea became the subject of a sweeping polemic.

Other important issues also had to be dealt with. The biggest one, after the constitution, concerned which previous states would be incorporated into the new German community. Two solutions crystallized. In one – the 'greater German' solution – the entire Habsburg empire would become part of the new Germany. (There was also a somewhat more modest variant of this, in which only those parts of the Habsburg empire where German was the predominant language would be incorporated, and Hungary and the Slavic parts would be left out.) The 'lesser German' solution involved Prussia and the other states in the central, northern, and western parts constituting Germany, while the large Austrian kingdom in the southeast would continue on its own way.

The National Assembly did not come to a decision, and none would come until 1871 when Berlin then became the capital under Wilhelm I, the Kaiser of the German Reich. The lesser German proposal was victorious. The dream of a greater Germany did not die, however – Adolf Hitler was pursuing it when he first annexed

Austria, and then the Sudetenland. But the history of greater
Germany, as we know, was a brief one.

The *Neue Rheinische Zeitung* began publication on 1 June 1848
(the first issue actually came out the day before). The editor-in-
chief had a staff that was close to him personally: not only Engels,
but also Georg Weerth, Heinrich Bürgers, Wilhelm Wolff, and a
few others. There was no risk that the newspaper would speak
with a forked tongue.

Marx edited his staff with a heavy hand, but the corrections
concerned form and not content. In the second issue of the newspaper, he thoroughly remoulded an article on 'The Democratic
Party' that Bürgers had written.[49] *Neue Rheinische Zeitung*
counted itself among the democratic camp; the slogan under its
masthead was 'Organ der Demokratie' (Organ of Democracy).
But the article described how the victorious democrats had been
cheated by the bourgeoisie, who created an undemocratic electoral law, thereby thwarting the radical opposition in the National
Assembly. It was becoming clear how difficult it would be to create
the great democratic coalition Marx had dreamed of.

In the beginning, Engels wrote the most articles about the
hardships of the National Assembly, while Marx attacked those
who attempted to reconcile the monarchy's claims to power with
the actions of the new parliament. Ludolf Camphausen was the
Minister-President after the March Revolution, and as such had a
delicate role to play. He was a well-known figure in Cologne, one
of the city's great tradesmen and bankers. He was indeed a *bourgeois* in the style of the new era, and invested significant capital
into railroads and steamer traffic. As a politician, he hoped that
the royal power and the National Assembly could unite over a
constitution that gave the parliament decisive power. Marx found
fault with such naiveté and compared German developments
with those of France in 1789. The revolutionaries should not be
satisfied with tranquil reforms, he pointed out. He was neither
surprised nor saddened when Camphausen had to leave his post.[50]
But it was no better with new Minister-Presidents; if anything,
they grew ever closer to royal power and the state bureaucracy.
Marx had his eye in particular on David Hansemann, minister

of finance under Camphausen and then in several other govern-ments. For Hansemann, Marx quoted Heine: 'Der Henker steht vor der Türe' (The hangman stands at the door). Hansemann's proposals for press laws would mean that Prussian civil servants could sleep soundly in future. Slander of state servants would be especially punishable.[51]

In another article, the author makes an assault on the press laws Hansemann wanted to implement. A quote from Mozart and Lorenzo da Ponte's *The Marriage of Figaro* ('If you are after the amusement...') garnishes an article concerning Marx's friend in London, Carl Schapper. Schapper had returned to Germany after the March revolution and placed his energies at the service of the newspaper, but he was now being threatened with deportation with the curious justification that he was not German.[52]

Marx described a development further and further from the original ideals of the March Revolution in the appointment of the minister Pfuel. Ernst Heinrich Adolf Pfuel was a sixty-nine-year-old Prussian general, and the monarchy's – not parliament's – man. Speaking about him, Marx quoted Falstaff in Shakespeare's *Henry IV*: '*Lord, Lord, how subject we old men are to the vice of lying!*' It could not get worse. 'The Pfuel Government can only be followed by a *Government of Revolution*.'[53]

But it did. When Pfuel resigned in November 1848, he was succeeded by another general: Friedrich Wilhelm, Graf von Brandenburg. It was not possible to get any closer to the king himself, Friedrich Wilhelm IV, than that. Brandenburg was the son of Friedrich Wilhelm II from a morganatic marriage, and thus Friedrich Wilhelm IV's own uncle.

Marx hailed the new government with a bitter article titled 'Counter-Revolution in Berlin'. Everything that had been achieved now lay devastated. Those who stood behind Brandenburg had hoped to share the plunder, but they would only get gra-tuities – and blows. The liberal bourgeoisie would gladly have changed the feudal monarchy into a bourgeois one, but they did not succeed. Brandenburg answered their half-revolution with a counterrevolution. Marx now encouraged everyone who con-tinued to hold fast to the demands for democracy to refuse to pay taxes.[54]

With the Brandenburg government, Prussia would take an unsympathetic – in fact hostile – attitude towards the National Assembly in Frankfurt. It refused the demands for German political unity, free and general elections, and extensive freedom of the press. The revolution was thus unmade, and the situation that prevailed in the German states before March 1848, with Prussia at their head, would be recreated.

Neue Rheinische Zeitung now became increasingly militant. On 15 November 1848, Marx published a special edition of the newspaper with a fiery article in which Brandenburg, in bold text, was charged with high treason for ignoring the National Assembly. The call to evade taxes was repeated. It was a matter of starving the enemy out. Citizens were encouraged instead to send money to a committee in Berlin that was working for democracy.[55]

The highest Prussian power in the Rhine province, Franz August Eichmann, issued a formal prohibition on tax evasion. Marx fearlessly responded that Eichmann was merely the henchman of the Brandenburg government, and the charge of high treason therefore also applied to him.

But Eichmann received support from a completely different direction. In the official newspaper, *Preussischer Staats-Anzeiger*, eighty professors from Berlin and Halle objected to the call for tax evasion. Among the signatories were big names such as Jacob and Wilhelm Grimm, the linguistic researchers and fairy tale collectors, and August Boeckh, the great specialist of antiquity. But *Neue Rheinische Zeitung* was not impressed. In an article that – judging by the style – Marx himself wrote, these learned men were castigated as men with the nature of lackeys, more subservient than Russia's serfs and worshipers of the Dalai Lama. But how could they behave otherwise? Without taxes, 'the privileged erudition' would go bankrupt.[56]

Marx acted with the conviction of being completely right in relation to the Prussian powers. In his opinion, the March Revolution opened up the way for a democratic society in which the lords in Berlin had to be pushed aside. He saw, of course, that most revolutionaries were more cautious in their claims. But again, he supported himself with a historic example that lay near at hand: the French Revolution of 1789. Then, the revolutionaries did not seek to reconcile parliament and royal power; royal power had to yield. The German revolution risked becoming 'a parody' of the great French example, Marx said.[57]

The error lay in the idea that it could be possible to unite the claims of royal power and the central bureaucracy with the National Assembly's demand for the people's decisive influence. This *Vereinbarungstheorie* seemed absurd and repellent to Marx.

It is doubtful whether he knew that to the north, Sweden had established in its 1809 constitution that the king would 'rule the kingdom alone' and that 'all power emanates from the people' at the same time. This peculiarity gave rise to confusion – and even recurring crises – over a long period, but under this arrangement Sweden could nonetheless ultimately develop into a political democracy that lasted until 1974, when the country got a new, less contradictory, constitution.

Marx did not like such compromises, and he was convinced that the revolutionaries in Germany had to take all power in order to create a new society, as they once did in France. In an imposing series of articles on the crisis and counterrevolution, he maintained that it was impossible to treat the crown and the constituent assembly as parties with equal rights. The result would inevitably be that the revolutionaries lose the initiative to their opponents. It was the people who, through their representatives, would create the new order. They had to appropriate all political power. For the first time, the word 'dictatorship' appears in Marx's vocabulary. Here, as later, he used it in the Roman sense, which was the only meaning it had at the time. The Roman Senate could elect a dictator when the country was in danger. The appointment only lasted six months. Only with Julius Caesar did this system change, when Caesar made himself dictator for life.

It was not the Rome of the Caesars, but of the Republic, that Marx had in mind when he spoke about dictatorship. Nor was it an individual dictator he spoke about, but the National Assembly in its entirety. Only the Assembly could create a new order – a democracy. With the old order, embodied by the Prussian king, there could be no compromise. Marx maintained: 'Every provisional political set-up following a revolution requires a dictatorship, and an energetic dictatorship at that.' *Neue Rheinische*

Zeitung had already reproached the first Minister-President, Camphausen, for not having smashed the remnants of the old institutions, losing himself instead in 'constitutional dreaming'. During that time, their opponents – the bureaucracy and the army – strengthened their positions, and now it was they who laid down the terms. In this development, Marx saw the bourgeoisie as the great deserter. They had wished for an agreement with the crown on a peaceful path. But a popular movement had been preparing the way for a revolution. The bourgeoisie, having attained the pinnacle of society, still wanted to come to an agreement with the royal power. They felt no solidarity with the proletarians, as the English bourgeois class had in 1648 and the French in 1789. The developments underway pointed to the definitive victory of the crown – the king, the generals, and the civil servants – and the bourgeoisie had paved the way.[58]

Marx spoke about the ever deeper degradation of the German-speaking states in a process where the bourgeoisie believed they could ally with the traditional apparatus of power but were increasingly pushed aside. He quoted John Milton's great epic, *Paradise Lost*: 'beneath the lowest deep a lower still'.[59]

The gradual radicalization of *Neue Rheinische Zeitung* was in the first place not a question of Marx and his contributors changing their understanding of the society they wished for. On the other hand, developments had clearly shown that the cautious strategy Marx had recommended from the beginning was untenable. The leading liberals of the National Assembly would rather compromise with the royal power and the state bureaucracy than with the far left. The price was that the royal power strengthened its position step by step. *Neue Rheinische Zeitung* radicalized concurrently, taking a more militant line.

But these developments were also accelerated by the course of events in France. On 23 June 1848, a rebellion broke out among journeymen and workers in Paris. New barricades were raised, now against the conservative-liberal government that had come to power after the parliamentary elections. Violent street battles ended in a total, bloody defeat for the men of the rebellion: 5,000 were killed, 11,000 imprisoned.

Marx and his editorial staff wrote profusely on what had

happened in Paris. Engels was particularly voluble, speaking about a pure workers' uprising. Marx was behind an authoritative article he dubbed 'The June Revolution'. The workers in Paris were beaten but not conquered, he assured readers. But the brutal violence that triumphed had dispersed all illusions that the February Revolution had awakened. Now there was no longer the possibility of mutual understanding; a civil war threatened.[60]

Marx saw the developments in Paris as paradigmatic. What happened in the German-speaking areas was a pale copy of the French example. The uprising was also beaten back with the consent of the bourgeoisie. The sacrifices were just not as great; nor was the spirit of rebellion in the German states as strong.

But even in Berlin, in Vienna, in Dresden, and especially the Hungarian city of Budapest, there had been violent outbursts. In the Saxon city of Dresden, the young composer Richard Wagner was among those who raised the flag of rebellion; in the struggle, he became friends with a significantly more persistent revolutionary: Mikhail Bakunin.[61]

During all these events, Marx spent most of his time at the editorial offices in Cologne. But he sometimes went on trips in service of the revolution. In late August and early September 1848, he was in Berlin and then Vienna to build his network of contacts among democratic organizations. In Vienna, he held two lectures. One dealt with the role of the proletariat in the revolution, the other on wage labour and capital. He had spoken on the latter theme in Brussels, and he inserted the manuscript as a short series of articles into his newspaper.

The radicalization of *Neue Rheinische Zeitung*, purely from a business perspective, was a success. Circulation skyrocketed, and at last reached 4,000 copies. That may not sound like much today, but it was in 1849. In the end, the newspaper became one of the most read in the German-speaking states.

This radicalization went hand in hand with an increasingly heated defence of freedom of the press. Marx and his editorial staff made use of every occasion to stress the importance of the right of newspapers, in principle, to express any opinion whatsoever. This had also been Marx's understanding several years earlier, when he led *Rheinische Zeitung*. Back then, he had state censorship to struggle against. This was abolished after the March Revolution, but it was replaced with press legislation that was gradually made more stringent. Marx – often in Engels's company – was often compelled to defend himself in court. They were capable and successful; Marx was a splendid pettifogger who had the benefit of legal studies from his university years, and the arguments were printed in *Neue Rheinische Zeitung*.

The charges against the newspaper changed, but it was its outspokenness that was a thorn in the side of those monitoring observance of the press laws. Dealings with the court began almost immediately – only a month after the newspaper began publication – and they continued throughout the rest of its brief history.

The first charge entailed *Neue Rheinische Zeitung* having insulted a prosecutor named Zweiffel and some policemen. The case was as follows: according to the newspaper, Friedrich Anneke, a newspaper editor, and Andreas Gottschalk, the government doctor who both competed with and collaborated with Marx, had been treated particularly brutally when they were arrested. Public prosecutor Friedrich Franz Karl Hecker protested against the newspaper's accusations, and Marx responded. The case was not taken further.[62]

But new charges accumulated. Hecker distinguished himself as an angry opponent and an ardent defender of the new order that had been provisionally established. He singled out Marx as a dangerous type in the press as well, writing that Marx must be constituted a traitor. The word 'constitute' roused Marx's vociferous derision.

In early February 1849, both Marx and Engels were forced to defend themselves before the court against charges of slandering the authorities in their newspaper. Their pleas were reproduced word for word in *Neue Rheinische Zeitung*. Marx's contribution in particular is brilliant, supported in equal parts by humour, irony, and legal quibbles. Engels's contribution is in his usual style: straightforward, bordering on blunt. The result was as desired: the newspaper and its editors were acquitted. Marx was equally fortunate a few days later, when he appeared again before the bar – now for the call to tax evasion.[63]

But developments in the German states, above all in Prussia, moved inexorably towards an editorial line such as *Neue Rheinische Zeitung*'s becoming impossible. The attacks against Marx were increasing, and becoming more serious. On 19 May, he defended himself against charges of having attempted to rouse contempt of the government, to encourage subversive activity, and finally to inaugurate 'the social republic'. The assertions, as we have seen, were not unfounded, but Marx emphatically repudiated them. The reader could easily suspect that he was poking fun at the authorities: what other than contempt did he show for Brandenburg, and did he not embrace the rebellions that flared up during the years of revolution? And was not 'the social republic' his goal – a republic in which not only political, but also social and economic relations were transformed? A few months earlier, he had declared that *Neue Rheinische Zeitung* would not celebrate the anniversary of the March Revolution, but it would celebrate 25 June. He probably meant 23 June; it was then one year since the more left-oriented and proletarian rebellion had broken out in Paris.[64]

On 19 May the editors had nonetheless given up; Marx's objections to the charges would come out in the paper's very last issue, printed on red paper. In the same issue, there is a notice in which the editors warned the workers in Cologne against rebelling. The events in Elberfeld showed that the bourgeoisie was prepared to send them to their deaths.[65]

One of the members of the editorial staff, Friedrich Engels, had direct experience of what had happened in Elberfeld, having been there.[66] Marx followed the many phases of the revolution, chiefly from the editorial offices in Cologne. Engels, with his military education and his eagerness to fight, was not satisfied with that. He participated in various more or less military demonstrations that forced him to flee from Germany, first to Belgium (where he was not welcome) and then to Switzerland. As soon as the opportunity presented itself, he set off again for Prussia – more specifically, his childhood haunts: Elberfeld, the sister city of Wuppertal and Barmen (both Barmen and Elberfeld are now districts in Wuppertal). There, the rebels had turned against the increasingly reactionary superior Prussian forces. He reported himself from the barricades in *Neue Rheinische Zeitung*. With a box of bullets, he had gone from Cologne to Elberfeld, where the rebels immediately entrusted him with the task of leading the work on fortifying the barricades. He also organized companies of combat engineers, and explained when asked directly that he would only devote himself to military actions and not to any form of political activity. But Elberfeld's bourgeoisie was not reassured by that. They feared that Engels would declare a red republic at any time, and encouraged him to leave the city. Those who had hoped for battle protested, but Engels found that he might as well return to Cologne – by all appearances, without any of his bullets having been put to use against the enemy.

It was these experiences that lay behind the call to the workers of Cologne to keep calm. The bourgeoisie would side with Prussian military power in the event of war.

During the years of revolution, Engels's parents had followed their son's actions with alarm. In October 1848, his mother wrote him a resigned letter. Engels was in Geneva just then, and was in sore need of money from home. Reluctantly, his father supported him with a tidy sum, furious over his son's errors that brought shame to him and his company. His mother was deeply distressed. Her son had horrible opinions, and he was doing poorly. Worst of all: she had found out from her husband, who had been to Cologne, that 'your good friends, Marx etc. are all sitting in peace and quiet in Cologne, writing *Neue Rheinische Zeitung*' and that they 'now did not want you back as a contributor'. In my honest opinion, Mrs Engels said, they were 'all villains who used you as long as they could make use of your money, and then terminate their acquaintance'.

Engels must have responded that this was a complete mistake, that Marx and the others supported him wholeheartedly, and that he was staying in Geneva on the newspaper's behalf. (All Engels's letters home have been lost, in all probability destroyed so that his transgressions would not be known to posterity.) His mother replied that if it were as her son asserted, then on the contrary she would like to thank Marx.[67]

It got even worse, of course, when in the final stages of the revolution, Engels prepared himself to organize street battles in his own hometown. No letters are preserved that could describe his parents' dismay; on the other hand, there is a great variety of anecdotes, one of which has father and son meeting on either side of the barricades. It is not particularly likely, and even without this story the drama is still quite real. The elder Engels was part of the ruling class in the Wuppertal area that ordered Friedrich Engels the younger to leave the city immediately.

Marx experienced no similar family drama. His father was long dead, and his mother seems not to have asked much about his political activity.

Above all, Marx wrote about topical issues. But at least from time to time, he enlightened his circle of readers on the relations beyond and below the current of violent events. In the midst of the stream of news, he printed parts of a lecture titled 'Wage-Labour and Capital' that he had held in 1847 for the German Workers' Association in Brussels. The account would be elementary so that it would be comprehensible to workers, he promised.

He actually kept away from terms and references that required extensive prior knowledge. The foundation stones are more or less directly taken from the introductory pages of the *Manuscripts*, but they now emphasize very strongly how competition between businesses pushes forward more effective machinery and greater division of labour. The consequence is that capital grows, and competition for job opportunities stiffens among workers.

Marx emphasized that not only capital and working conditions, but also needs themselves, are determined by the society we live in. What is produced must be sold, and with more and newer types of products, people's habits must be updated, too. If a palace is built among normal houses, the houses suddenly look like cottages. Marx implies that the magnificent new house aroused desires for larger residences among those who until recently were satisfied. But he does not complete this line of argument.

The main thing for him – as it was in the *Manuscripts* and as it was for Adam Smith and David Ricardo – was that competition always pushes wages down. New machines are being developed all the time. The capitalist who is first with more efficient equipment gets temporary satisfaction from it. Soon, his competitors will have caught up with him, and the rat race continues.

Marx also paints a depressing image of industrial work to an audience predominated by journeymen fearful of being forced into the factories. Proficiency at work means less and less, he said, and competition for the most loathsome jobs is hardest.[68]

The series concludes with a 'To be continued'. But this sequel never followed, and probably had not been written. Nor do we know anything about the relationship between the article series in Neue Rheinische Zeitung and the lecture he held once in Brussels. The newspaper text was later published separately several times, including in 1891 with a long preface by Engels. Because the text was intended just for a rather unschooled audience, it has been used regularly for propaganda purposes. Engels announced, with a certain degree of pride, that the 1891 edition had been printed in 10,000 copies.[69]

Nonetheless, the text on several points contradicted conclusions that Marx later came to. The thesis that workers' wages must always tend downward was gradually abandoned, and he avoided the distinction between abstract and concrete labour, probably for pedagogical reasons. He had not yet arrived at the theory of surplus value. 'Wage-Labour and Capital' provides a simple summary of Marx's standpoint in 1849, but is still a good bit away from what he arrived at when he again took hold of economic subject matter after the revolutionary years.

Retreats

When Neue Rheinische Zeitung shut down, Marx and Engels moved to Baden and Pfalz. Revolutionaries there were still offering a degree of resistance. The martial Engels fearlessly entered into the battles, while Marx stayed in the background.

In the end, the struggle was futile. In early June, Marx returned alone to Paris, where a new hope of continuing the revolution had been ignited, sending his family to live with Jenny's mother in Trier. Jenny was full of apprehension over Karl's fate – apprehension that intensified when the news came that an attempted rebellion had been put down on 13 June. And as if that were not enough, a cholera epidemic struck the city (an epidemic that also broke out in German cities; in Cologne, it brought Andreas Gottschalk, the government doctor and revolutionary, to an early grave). The dread Jenny expressed in a letter to Lina Schöler, a friend of the family and a teacher in Cologne, is understandable. Up to now, her 'dear Karl' had escaped all dangers, and however the problems accumulated, he was constantly full of good spirits and hope. But what could have happened to him during the days of violence and epidemic in Paris? On 29 June, the date of the letter, his fate was still unknown in Trier.

The uncertainty would soon be dispersed; Karl was safe and sound, and also wanted the family to come to Paris. Jenny was not slow in complying with the invitation. In a new letter to Schöler, she said that she and the children had arrived 'cheerful, and safe and sound'. Paris was once again a shining metropolis, coaches with glittering footmen were again rolling along the streets, and the children could not get enough of all the splendour surrounding them.[70]

Only a few days later, Jenny received a letter from Engels, who had taken refuge in the town of Vevey in Switzerland. He spoke in detail about his military exploits, also praising his comrades' bravery – occasionally reaching foolhardiness – but was full of concern over how it had been going for Karl. There were rumours that he had been imprisoned in Paris.

Karl himself was able to reassure his friend in a response. He had his entire family with him. But the French government wanted to banish him to the notorious swamplands of Morbihan in Brittany, a district where malaria and other plagues were still rife. He had appealed the decision and was waiting on a conclusion. If Jenny were not pregnant, he would gladly have left Paris.[71]

As always, he was feverishly active despite his precarious situation. He was investigating opportunities to publish pamphlets in Germany, among them one with his own text about wage labour and capital that had only partially been printed in *Neue Rheinische Zeitung*. In the same letter, he expressed a paradoxical optimism. 'However fatal our personal relationship may seem at the moment, I am still among the content,' he wrote. 'Things are developing very well, and the Waterloo that official democracy experienced is to be regarded as a victory. The governments, out of God's mercy, are taking over the task of wreaking our vengeance upon the bourgeoisie and of punishing them.'

He also played down the defeat in an article in the newspaper *Der Volksfreund* (The Friend of the People) about the dramatic events in Paris of 13 June. The opportunities for the left had only been frittered away by imprudent leaders who had been entirely too sure of their victory. On the other hand, he put his own situation in focus in an open letter to the Parisian newspaper *La Presse*, in which he declared that the Prussian government had not, as *La Presse* had reported, banned *Neue Rheinische Zeitung* – something it lacked legal cover to do. It had, however, made further publication impossible by exiling Marx. He had now come to Paris, not as a refugee but to collect material 'for my work on the history of political economy, which I had already begun five years earlier'.

In fact, his situation in France was more awkward than he made out here. He was, however, not depressed. Yet on 17 August 1849, he wrote a long letter to Engels; in the energetic final point (written in French) he asked his friend what they both should do now. They needed a new writing project, he said, and wondered what ideas Engels had.

Six days later, the final judgement came: he was to be banished to the malarial districts in Brittany. It was the same as a death sentence, he wrote in a new letter to Engels. 'So I am leaving France.' He received no passport to Switzerland, 'hence I must go to London'. Engels also had to set out for there immediately, he stressed. In Switzerland he could do nothing, and the Prussians would have a double reason to shoot him. He would be safe in London.

And even more triumphantly: 'Besides, in London there is a *positive* prospect of my being able to start a German newspaper.' And finally, pleading: 'I confidently count on you not to leave me in the lurch.'

Engels did not. In a letter to George Julian Harney – the Chartist we have already met – he announced that he was leaving Geneva on board the schooner *Cornish Diamond* and counted on being in London by mid-November.[72]

The years that followed in London were the hardest in the life of the Marx family. We must now describe them. But first, a summary of the years of revolution.

With Words as Weapons

In Brussels, Marx had developed a kind of cheerless aggressiveness. Contacts with his fellow thinkers in London put him in lighter spirits. The best pages of the *Communist Manifesto* – which, in its final version, is his own work – breathes a magnificent energy and delight in language; never has the dynamic of capitalism been better depicted.

On the other hand, the *Manifesto* contains nothing new as regards a view of history and society. The author's relationship to the various radial tendencies of the time is also unchanged, as is the strategy in the face of future upheavals. It is the linguistic force and the direct, inspirational popular address that distinguishes the *Manifesto* from the polemical pamphlet against Proudhon. The only thing that could surprise a person who let themselves be hypnotized by the label 'utopian socialism' is the appreciation shown to Fourier and Saint-Simon: they had their day, to be sure, but they were pioneers of a careful critical analysis of society.

The actual tense of the text is consciously doubled. The present is being depicted, but also a future in which capitalism has developed even further, in which the proletarianization of an increasing number of groups in society has gone even deeper and in which the class struggle has thereby sharpened. The journeyman craftsmen, which constituted the majority of those immediately greeted by the message of the *Manifesto*, could not only recognize their own current situation there, but also see how their path implacably led to industrial work – as long as a revolution did not intercede. Doctors, teachers, and other intellectual groups would also realize that their futures are dark, and that it was a question of their siding with communism. Even capitalists who were less successful in constantly stiffening competition with other capitalists would be proletarianized. Better, then, to anticipate the development!

It is easy to read a far-reaching historical determinism from these statements. The development is predetermined, and moves inexorably towards revolution and a new classless society.

But this conclusion – constantly drawn anew by readers of Marx – is a hasty one. First, the principle that Marx and Engels developed in *The German Ideology* and later repeated many times should be remembered: namely that general guidelines for how society ought to be studied cannot be used as a diagram according to which history can be put in order. What is actually occurring emerges out of a swarm of details that are not on a timetable. This principle also applies, of course, to the present and to the future.

Second, the *Manifesto* is propaganda that simultaneously is to convince the reader and urge them to action. In texts of this type, it is not possible to introduce reservations or to get wrapped up in historical and philosophical arguments. The *Manifesto* meets the requirements that apply to all party programmes. A picture of societal development is provided and a number of assessments of what a life fit for human beings entails lie encapsulated in the text. For those who are overcome by the argumentation, the path to the concluding standards of action lies open. In the *Manifesto*, these standards are summarized in the exhortation of the final words: 'Workers of all countries...' This is the most important message of the work. The thesis that the proletarians of tomorrow will be many more than those of today broadens the circle of direct recipients.

The *Manifesto* would gradually become the most important gateway into Marx's world of ideas. This was of great importance for its dissemination, but also for its simplification and vulgarization. For readers of the *Manifesto*, development seemed bound by fate and the final words were perceived less as a call to action than as a promise that would be fulfilled on its own.

When this little pamphlet first met the world, it ended up overshadowed by the revolution that broke out at roughly the same time. Marx did not grieve over it. Quite the opposite; the dramatic events filled him with an appetite for action, putting him in a good fighting mood. It was as if the life he had been forced to leave a few years earlier had opened up to him again. First, he got to return to Paris, the city he so bitterly missed; then he took a further few steps into his past and got the opportunity to again manage a newspaper in Cologne. It again turned out that he could be brilliantly productive when he was writing short pieces. The succession of newspaper articles that he produced during this brief period as editor-in-chief for *Neue Rheinische Zeitung* is impressive, and despite his productivity most are stylistically sparkling – and bitingly venomous towards everyone in power.

Two themes dominated his journalism. One is the same as in the old *Rheinische Zeitung*: the freedom of the press. Back then, he defied censorship daily; now he was defying the press laws, and almost all persons in authority.

The other main theme concerned the hope, cherished by many, that the new parliament would reach a fair agreement with royal power and its state apparatus, thereby achieving a constitutional monarchy. Like Engels, Marx from the very start was critical of this idea – hostile, in fact. The word 'dictatorship' turns up in Marx's vocabulary for the first time here, and its content is crystal clear: the parliament had to seize *all* power and dictate the conditions for the future Germany. If the king and his ministers were to be part of the deliberations, they would soon seize the entire initiative.

In his struggle against this political development, Marx did not hold back. He encourages his readers to evade taxes, and he charged the Brandenburg government with high treason. In contrast to Engels, Marx was not the kind to set out on military adventures. Words were his weapon, and he hurled them fearlessly at whoever he chose. His struggle was impossible in the long run, but even in defeat he still saw opportunities for future victories. When he was forced to leave not just Germany, but France as well, he was still hopeful.

This may seem paradoxical. He had hoped for a broad alliance against kings and princes, but the liberals' mistrust towards communists and socialists was greater than their reluctance towards the men of the old system. The choice was not entirely surprising: Marx made no secret of the fact that he saw such a coalition only as a stage on the road towards a communist seizure of power. The

German liberals cherished great hopes of being able to influence royal power in their own direction. Those hopes came to naught, and Marx's reaction was not discouragement but rather a new passion for struggle. Now he knew the lie of the land!

He took this optimism with him to London. He could not imagine that Europe was facing a thorough ideological change after the revolutions – a change that would not be to his advantage, or to the advantage of his political programme.

8

Difficult Times, Difficult Losses

Ideological Change

Marx grew to manhood in the shadow of the Great French Revolution, which lasted from 1789 to 1794. The revolution did not only entail political upheavals, it paved the way for Napoleon and the violent reaction that followed the Battle of Waterloo, and gave us the metre and the kilogramme. The French Revolution also became the background against which nearly all European thinking on society, all political ideals, and most ideas about development, progress, or degeneration took place for more than a half-century.

With a few exceptions, the political ideologies we talk about today are reactions to the French Revolution. Conservatism is usually derived from the Irish philosopher and politician Edmund Burke's 1790 book *Reflections on the Revolution in France*,[1] and the name itself was fixed in the French newspaper *Le Conservateur*. The paper began publication in 1818, and its best-known contributor was the French poet and diplomat François-René de Chateaubriand. 'Liberal' and 'liberalism' made their debut as designations of a political ideology in Spain in 1812, where a grouping that called themselves *los liberales* played a crucial role for the constitution in Cadiz. Their success was brief, but the term spread quickly.

Socialism and communism became political ideologies a few decades later, still with the French Revolution as the most important historical reference. It is scarcely different with anarchism, to which Pierre-Joseph Proudhon gave the name in 1840. Even this took its colours from what happened in 1789 and the years after.

The purely *reactionary* ideology, which wanted to recreate the society that was shattered during the years going forward from 1789, also belongs to this group. Reactionaries – those people pushing purely backwards – were strong in France after the fall of Napoleon; they have of course turned up again and again in later periods and other countries, even if it was not precisely the pre-revolutionary French state but some other imagined paradise from the past that they were dreaming about.

Only fascism and Nazism are children of a later period – to be precise, the late nineteenth and early twentieth century when nationalist mass movements began to take shape. Marx did not live to see their first great demonstration, which took place in France in 1889. At the time, a coup d'état was very close at hand. Its figurehead was general Boulanger, a pathetic figure who wanted revenge for the defeat in the Franco-German war of 1870–71. The ideology only emerged fully with Mussolini and Hitler.

The French Revolution also determined a great deal of Marx's political horizon. Through his father, Heinrich Marx, he had got a positive image of what it meant early on, especially for the personal liberation that Heinrich himself had experienced. When Karl's own political interests had been awakened, the French Revolution was one of the areas he studied the most assiduously. For him as well, it provided a paradigm for future revolutions. He applied its various forms – and especially its party designations – to the current course of events. Marx took the inspiration for his idea on the divided revolution – bourgeois and political first, then proletarian and social – from it.

The revolutions in Europe during 1848 and 1849, in his eyes, were continuations of the upheavals sixty years earlier. Europe had developed, technology had made new conquests, and industrialism was establishing itself more and more firmly with two new, rapidly expanding social classes: industrial capitalists and industrial workers. When a relatively calm situation once again settled upon Europe at the end of 1849, Marx – like many others – thought it was only the calm before the real storm.

That is not at all what was to come. Politics stabilized, a new kingdom took shape in France, and reaction prevailed in the German states. Marx's brother-in-law in Prussia, Ferdinand von Westphalen, became minister of the interior and thereby had a hand in the country's domestic order. Consistent and unyielding, he made life difficult for anyone with anything to do with communists and socialists. The revolutionaries who succeeded in fleeing to London were closely monitored by Prussian police spies, and von Westphalen also tried to persuade the British government to deport at least a few of them. Marx and Engels protested in a few brief articles in English, one of them in *The Spectator*, a magazine with a long-established conservative tradition. They passionately repudiated the charges that they and their fellow thinkers were taking part in a conspiracy against Friedrich Wilhelm IV. There had actually been an attempt on the king's life shortly before, but the guilty party was not only mentally disturbed but additionally a man on the extreme right.[2]

But enough about that. By and large, the revolutions had ended in fiasco. It was only in Denmark that something new materialized for good. Royal absolutism came to an end there, and the country gained a constitution.

During the early 1850s, Marx became much more alone in his thinking than he had been in the 1840s. The circle closest to him had already been thinning out. Engels remained, of course, and Wilhelm Wolff joined the London group in 1851 after a period in Switzerland. Joseph Moll, another of Marx's closest friends, had – like Engels – taken part in the battles in Baden. On 28 June 1849, he was killed during an action in Rosenfels, not far from Freiburg. It was a hard blow for his friends. Carl Schapper, who had been of such great importance for Marx's position in the Communist League, soon openly rebelled against him.

Others among those closest to Marx ended up in Prussian prisons in 1851 and stayed there for a year and a half before any sentence was pronounced. Their crime consisted of trying to continue their activities within the *Bund der Kommunisten* even after the defeat of the revolution. The two among them whom Marx knew best were the inseparable friends Heinrich Bürgers and Roland Daniels. Bürgers was sentenced to six years in a military fortress. When he was finally released in 1858, he had given up his sympathies for the workers' movement and instead became active in the liberal *Deutsche Fortschrittspartei* (the German Progress Party), ending his days as a member of parliament. Daniels did not recover from his time in prison, dying only a few years after his release.

Marx wrote a pamphlet about the trials. It was called *Revelations Concerning the Communist Trial in Cologne* and was published anonymously in 1853. The German edition, printed in Switzerland, fell into the hands of the police; the work enjoyed greater success in the United States. In his usual way, Marx took the part of a skilled lawyer, although he himself was not permitted to appear before the bar. He showed how the charges were based to a great extent on falsified documents, misconceptions, and misinterpretations. He dwelt on the fact that an unsigned letter had been ascribed to him. 'No one who has ever read a single line by Marx could possibly attribute to him the authorship of this melodramatic accompanying line,' he wrote. In other regards, he pinned a number of lies to Wilhelm Stieber, the head of Prussia's 'political police'; the biggest was that he had done more favours for the democratic movement in Prussia than anyone else.

The accused were all declared by the prosecutor to have belonged to 'Marx's party'. This in itself was considered criminal. If nothing else, the documents show the heights of dread that the the figure of Marx had assumed in Prussia.[3]

It was not only the trial in Cologne that depleted the group around Marx. As we have seen, Georg Weerth – one of his most esteemed friends – emigrated to Cuba, where he gave up both political agitation and writing. Another American emigrant who on the other hand continued his political activity was Joseph Weydemeyer. Weydemeyer was born the same year as Marx, and had military training. He did not retreat an inch from his earlier ideals, but established himself as a radical journalist in the United States. Over the years, he became deeply rooted in his new homeland, taking part as a lieutenant colonel in the American Civil War before succumbing a few years later during one of the many cholera epidemics of the nineteenth century. Throughout his life, he remained an important correspondent for both Jenny and Karl.

But the distance between Europe and America was difficult to bridge.

The change that made Marx even more alone in his thoughts and actions was more extensive than these names suggest. It concerned not only the group of sympathizers who died, gave up, or emigrated to faraway lands, but ideological changes of a dimension that can be compared with those of the French Revolution of 1789 (or the years around 1980 in our own time).

After 1789, violent social upheavals stood out as a fairly natural result of modern social development. It was an outlook that filled many with hope, and others with fear or aversion. The July Revolution of 1830 and the February Revolution of 1848 seemed to confirm this tendency. The latter in particular – anticipated in the thoughts of so many, and which spread over Europe so quickly – strengthened these convictions.

But the rebellion resulted in the opposite of what the revolutionaries intended. A new emperor came to power in France, insignificant in comparison to the first, and a man who only safeguarded his own power and honour. In Prussia, the king and his government came out of the battle strengthened, and the same applied to other German-dominated states. Reactionary Russia, with its despotic tsar, Nicholas I, strengthened its position on the continent, and Great Britain – the last refuge in Europe for revolutionaries – became even more vigilant against its own threats. In the revolutionary year of 1848, Chartism had experienced its last great period of growth. The activists – who again quickly increased in number – were optimistic, but the keepers of order were on their guard and every attempt at rebellion was smothered in its cradle. In addition, many Chartists were hesitant with regard to the more downright socialist slogans.[4]

After the wave of revolutions, the front against all social change was stronger than ever, both in Great Britain and across Europe. It was a change that not only dashed many hopes. It also opened the path to a new way of thinking – or, rather, it brought ideas that had recently been repressed to the foreground. Views on social development – in fact, on change in general – were transformed. The conviction that most processes require dramatic breaks was overshadowed by its opposite: the idea of continuity.[5]

Central players in this shift were both politically active and outstanding scientists. The German doctor, archaeologist, and politician Rudolf Virchow – who was three years younger than Marx – was certainly the most important of them. As a doctor he was innovative, one of the foremost of the nineteenth century. For him, the real political alarm clock was the 1847 typhus epidemic in Upper Silesia, a few years after the great weavers' uprising. Despite the deaths of 16,000 people, the government authorities merely shrugged their shoulders. The reason for the deaths of so many was nonetheless patently obvious: poverty and wretched hygienic conditions. Like many other young doctors, Virchow drew the conclusion that society had to be fundamentally changed. He hailed the 1848 revolution with joy, and eagerly involved himself in it. His foremost biographer, Constantin Goschler, even asserts that he was close to the young Marx. He probably means the Marx of the *Manuscripts* rather than the Marx who stood behind the *Manifesto*. In a letter Virchow wrote to his father, which Goschler quotes, he explained that he was not a communist: communism was madness to the extent that it strove to realize its ideals in one stroke. On the other hand, he was a socialist. It was a socialist system that he wanted to see with the revolution.

It is natural that he had primarily social and medical aspects in mind in the society he wanted to fight for. And it remained so even after the revolution. But now he believed more in a slower, more gradual development towards a more just order of things. That is why, like Heinrich Bürgers, he got involved in the Progress Party, became a member of parliament, and represented a nationally-minded reformism in numerous parliamentary debates. The dominant figure of the conservative bloc, Otto Bismarck, soon become his chief opponent. At one point, the exchange of opinions became so intense that Bismarck challenged Virchow to a duel. As the challenged, it was Virchow's business to choose the weapon, and his proposal got Bismarck to back down immediately: the duellists would choose between two sausages, one of which would be filled with a deadly poison.

Enemies or no, Virchow and Bismarck were united in a belief

in evolutionary processes. Revolutions were a bad thing. The idea of continuity also influenced Virchow's scientific convictions. Cellular pathology was his great contribution to medicine. In it, he built on the relatively new theory that all living creatures consisted of cells, and he launched the theory that illnesses had their basis in harmful cellular changes. He would come to emphasize the gradual more and more in the process of an illness. Even his archaeological studies were characterized by the same fundamental pattern of thought.[6]

It is particularly interesting to see which theories in evolutionary biology dominated before and after the middle of the nineteenth century. The 'catastrophe theory' occupied the seat of honour for a long time. Its chief representatives were the French biologist Georges Cuvier, who maintained that the fossils of extinct species indicated earlier catastrophes that annihilated various life forms again and again. It is telling that Cuvier, in the title of his central work on the subject, spoke of these changes as *révolutions*. This word, as we have already seen, designated courses that were constantly repeated – such as the path of the planets around the sun, according to Copernicus – but from the mid-eighteenth century had been given entirely different content, namely the one we use now. Marx belonged to a generation that had also begun to talk about social revolutions. The term 'industrial revolution' had already begun to be used.[7]

In the middle of the nineteenth century, the idea of revolutions was overshadowed more and more by its opposite: the idea of slow, continuous processes. Charles Darwin and his 1859 book *The Origin of Species* became the symbol of this ideological displacement. According to him, species changed step by step through natural and sexual selection. One foundation for his theory was the geological work of Charles Lyell, according to which the same forces had acted on the surface of the Earth throughout its entire history. Lyell presented this 'uniformitarianism' in his 1830 book *Principles of Geology*, but it was only with Darwin that this line of thought became known to a greater public.

Darwin also sought support for his thesis in an economist named Thomas Robert Malthus, whose population theory became crucial for Darwin's conviction that each species produced such a large amount of offspring that not all individuals would survive. It is an interesting detail that the first edition of Malthus's 1798 work, *An Essay on the Principle of Population*, was a polemical pamphlet against on the one hand the 'father of anarchism', the Englishman William Godwin, and on the other hand one of the French Revolution's most brilliant spokesmen, Jean Antoine de Condorcet. Both recommended violent upheavals. Malthus, on the contrary, emphasized continuity. The development of a population would always remain such that those in the worst position would perish. There was, simply, never enough food for everyone who was born.

Darwin generalized a demographic theory to apply it to every living thing. He himself was extremely reluctant to draw just any conclusion regarding people and their world from his thesis on natural selection. But he took important support for his argument from social theory.[8]

The ideological changes around 1850 did not, of course, mean that ways of thinking that had recently been dominant disappeared, and that an opposite way of thinking that previously had had no representatives was suddenly alone in the arena. Our examples show that there had already been ideas about continuity in the late eighteenth and early nineteenth centuries, and that the idea of drastic upheavals did not disappear after the failed revolutions of 1848–49. Rather, it is that the one kind of thinking seemed more and more *natural* during the one epoch, while on the contrary its opposite had to raise more and more arguments in its defence.

Nowadays, it is often said that one discourse has been replaced by another. For my part, I prefer to speak about ideological changes. The new, dominant way of thinking is related to the unsuccessful revolutions. But, at the same time, the interaction between the various courses of events is extremely subtle and complicated. There is no direct connection between what happened in Paris, Berlin, and Vienna in 1848 and 1849 and the enormous response to Darwin's *Origin of Species* a decade later. Darwin himself was certainly not influenced significantly, if at all. On the other hand, the public responded to the decisive outside events of the period. Expectations about the future had changed. It became easier to think in long, continuous processes of development than in drastic social changes. Even the accent in ordinary people's view of nature shifted as a result. So it was in Great Britain as well, where a potent hope – or vision of horror – during the 1840s was that the Chartists would seize power.

Marx fought bravely against these shifts in thinking. But he could not remain uninfluenced by them, either. At the same time, during the 1850s he experienced a difficult – horrible, in fact – period in his private life. The burden was nonetheless greatest for Jenny. It is therefore natural that she, rather than her husband, come into focus over the following pages.

Poverty and Death

Jenny von Westphalen was born a baroness, but as Jenny Marx she lived a life of poverty, occasionally bordering on pure destitution. The worst years were the early ones in London, and a real improvement in the situation came only in 1864 when she and her family moved into their own, rather spacious house. Hitherto, that had been far beyond the borders of possibility. But the change did not mean that their financial problems were over and done with. Karl lived beyond his means even as a student and he did so throughout his life, even when age began to weigh him down. But from the mid-1860s, their money woes moved on to a higher level, so to speak. It was no longer a question of bread and potatoes, but of gowns for their daughters.

Moreover, few could equal Jenny in generosity and hospitality. After the defeat in 1849, German refugees flocked to London. Many were as bitterly poor as the Marx family; others had it even worse. One of the youngest who sought refuge in Great Britain was named Wilhelm Liebknecht, a student of languages who had become a revolutionary and who would at length become one of the most important leaders of German social democracy. He was quickly sucked into the magic circle around Jenny and Karl Marx. Karl would remain his political model throughout his life, and he would always describe Jenny with great warmth, admiration, and gratitude. Without her generosity, he would scarcely have survived the poverty of his refugee years, he wrote. Ulrich Teusch, who wrote the finest and most well-balanced biography of Jenny, points out that she became a mother figure for Wilhelm, who lost his mother early in life. Women long remained foreign to me, he admitted in his autobiography. 'And here I found a beautiful, noble-minded, high-spirited woman who in a half-sisterly, half-motherly way took care of the friendless fighter for liberty, driven ashore on the banks of the Thames,' he wrote. 'She was to me the ideal of a woman, and she is the ideal even now.'[9]

Jenny's care for the young Liebknecht is that much more impressive as she daily had to fight hard to get food on the table. She was, of course, not alone in that fight. Helene Demuth, the family's self-effacing maid, stood unflinchingly by her side. She was the one who handled practical matters, made purchases, cooked the food, did the laundry, fixed and mended. But Jenny was the one who chiefly tried to keep the host of creditors in check. The baker, the butcher, the greengrocer, and many others kept knocking more persistently and more threateningly on the door. It was the master of the house – or, more correctly, of the narrow hovel – they were looking for, but he was often not at home. Gradually, he had found the only temple he ever worshipped: the British Museum, a place where he could sate his unique hunger for reading. There he sat, safely anchored during periods when his family – and he himself – were somewhat healthy and his own clothes presentable enough that he could show himself among society. His tattered coat became legendary, and when in the 1860s he allowed himself to be photographed in an elegant topcoat, there were friends who expressed their happy surprise.[10]

But he also often worked at home, under intolerable conditions. Jenny did everything so that he could nonetheless further his great work – what would become *Capital*. In the spring of 1850, the plans to finally complete this project that had already occupied him for a great many years had awakened again. Jenny was in agreement with the plan and supported it wholeheartedly. In fact, she took an active part in it, as she did with everything else her husband wrote. She was not only his secretary, but discussed his texts knowledgeably. It was work she perceived as a comfort during those heavy years. She wrote in her memoirs: 'The hours I sat in Karl's little room making fair copy of his texts were among the happiest in my life.'[11]

Karl's income always remained too little to cover the costs of the household. During their first years in London, when Engels was also trying to support himself as a freelance writer, there was no help to be had even from their friend, whose own economic situation had also started to become precarious. Engels's father, the elder Friedrich, was becoming more and more reluctant to help his wayward son with more money. Finally, the younger Friedrich had to make the best of a bad job and set out for Manchester to work in the family company, Ermen & Engels. At first, the father had no faith in his son's ability – or, rather, desire – to make a real effort. But he was mistaken. The younger Friedrich discovered early on that their business partner, Ermen, was cheating the Engels family out of their rightful share of the company's profits. He thus finally proved to his father that he could be a capable force. His position was assured.[12]

But his wages were relatively insignificant. Nevertheless, he tried to share it with the Marx family. It was important help – in fact, the deliverance from pure destitution. Gradually the allowance became bigger, but nonetheless it remained insufficient – at least up until 1864.

We have gripping testimony of what Jenny had to endure in a letter she sent to Engels in early 1853. It was, she wrote, 'a hateful task' to write to him about money; he had already helped them entirely too often. But now the situation was intolerable. She had written to many of her acquaintances, including her mother-in-law and her sister. She had not received a single response, and now her hopes – as they often were – were set on Engels. Could he send something? The baker was threatening to stop the delivery of bread.[13]

But Karl was not living an easy life, either. To the same Engels, he wrote in September 1852: 'My wife is ill. Little Jenny is ill. Lenchen [Demuth] has some sort of nervous fever. I could not and I cannot call a doctor because I have no money to buy medicine. For the last 8–10 days I have been feeding my family solely on bread and potatoes, but whether I shall be able to get hold of any today is doubtful.'[14]

There is an eyewitness description from the same period that heavily underlines the poverty in the Marx household. It is written by a German police spy who had wormed his way into the hovel on Dean Street (Marx had been monitored by police spies ever since the first years in Paris). The narrative is so frightful that it is difficult to believe its veracity. A thick layer of dust lay on the furniture; diapers with the customary contents lay strewn over the chairs, and Marx himself was wearing unwashed underclothes. It is highly improbable that Helene Demuth would have let the dust collect in drifts, or that she would not have scrubbed even the most tattered underwear clean. Was our friend the spy, with his racy description, trying to say that Karl Marx would soon be a closed chapter and thus not much to worry about?[15] But those who love anecdotes about Marx's life of course hold this description in high regard.

Poverty was not the only issue; the entire family was affected by various painful illnesses. They lived in an unhealthy apartment on an unsanitary street – the dark, stinking Dean Street in Soho. Overcrowding made the situation even worse. Six, seven, and at one point eight people lived in two rooms. The toilet was located in the back yard. The hygiene problems were terrible.

It is understandable why Jenny was not only affected by physical illnesses. The desperate situation made her constantly anxious, and periodically deeply unhappy. Everyday life was difficult to endure, and her burden became too heavy. It so happened that she sought out more long-term relief in the situation, but was unsuccessful. She talks about it in a letter to Karl, written in August 1851. The text breathes despair, but there is also a streak of bitter humour. Jenny was a masterful writer of letters, even under the heaviest of circumstances.

She had taken a trip to see Karl's relatives in the Netherlands, the Philipses. The journey was a terrible one, with seasickness and other hardships, and once at her destination she only met one of the less influential members of the family, a certain Fritz. Fritz did not know who Jenny was, but once informed of it he embraced her. The conversation that followed dealt with revolutions and communism – the theme of the day – and Fritz also encouraged the Marx family to emigrate to the United States. So far, the conversation had been pleasant, but when Jenny turned to the reason for her journey – namely money – Fritz's tone changed. He complained about bad business and wretched financial prospects. He could not relinquish a single penny to his relatives.

Jenny then gave up and set out for her simple bed for the night, exhausted and dissolved in tears. The entire journey had been in vain. '*Zerrissen*' – tattered – and plagued by mortal dread, she set off for home. Certainly you, Karl, would have had much better success! she exclaimed.[16]

That last sigh of course raises the question why it was not actually Karl who made the trip. The Philipses were his relatives, not Jenny's. Did he think that his charming wife would make his rich kinfolk more generous? Or did he feel that his journalistic, political, and scientific work bound him to London? We do not know.

The dreary lot of the Marx family in London was not only poverty and illness, but death as well. The family had grown just before their move. Apart from the older daughters, Jennychen and Laura, there was also a little boy, Edgar (named after his uncle), who had been born in Brussels. He had been part of the revolutions in both Paris and Cologne in his young life, and now he was a child refugee in the poorer districts of London. In the midst of all the sorrow he was a constant source of joy, a little humourist and a rogue. In her gloomy begging letter to Engels in the spring of 1853, Jenny wrote how her six-year-old son fooled the baker who had come to call in his debts with Karl. 'Is Mr Marx at home?' the baker asked, and the boy quickly answered in the local dialect: 'No, he ain't upstairs.' The baker left, cross, and Edgar quickly scampered up to his beloved Moor (as everyone in the family, and some even outside it, called Karl) and told of his successful efforts.

When Jenny arrived in London, she was expecting yet another child. A boy was born on 5 November 1849, less than two months after the strenuous journey from Paris. 5 November is an eventful day in England's history. On 5 November 1605, the conspiracy Guy Fawkes became a symbol for was exposed – the plot to blow up King James I and the entire House of Lords. Fawkes was a zealous Catholic who ardently wished that his faith would once again become the official religion of the country. He was thus far from one of Marx's fellow thinkers. But Marx was attracted by his rebellious spirit and named his newborn son Heinrich Guido – Heinrich after his grandfather, Guido after the given name Guy Fawkes used when he fought on the side of Spain in the Dutch Revolt.

The little boy was given the nickname Föxchen ('the little fox' in Germanized English) and his father also called him *der Pulververschwörer* ('the Gunpowder Plotter'). But the boy was not healthy; he seemed to constantly be hovering between life and death. Above all, he suffered from intense convulsions. He died a little over a year old.

Marx was beside himself with despair. The only one he could turn to was Engels, who was now in Manchester. 'Just a line or two to let you know that our little gunpowder plotter, *Föxchen*, *died* at ten o'clock this morning', he wrote in a letter. 'Suddenly, from one of the convulsions he had often had. A few minutes before, he was still laughing and joking. The thing happened quite unexpectedly. You can imagine what it is like here. Your absence at this particular moment makes us feel very lonely.' He asked Engels to write a few words of comfort to Jenny. His friend did so, and Marx was very grateful. Jenny received the little comfort she could in this terrible situation. She had nursed the child at the risk of her own life. Marx exclaimed: 'And on top of this, the thought that the poor child was a victim of bourgeois *misère* ...' Marx was convinced that Heinrich Guido would have survived if his parents had had enough money for a doctor's care and medicine.[17]

At the time of her little boy's death, Jenny was pregnant again. Her daughter Franziska was born on 14 March 1851. She was also a sickly child. In the spring of 1852, she suffered a severe attack of bronchitis. Jenny wrote in a letter: 'For three days, the poor child battled death. She suffered horribly. Her small, lifeless body rested in the little room; we all went out of the room into the street, and when night fell we made our beds on the floor; our three surviving children lay with us and we cried over the little angel who rested, cold and white as chalk, next to us.'[18] The scene is a gripping one: the family joined together in the face of this bottomless misfortune. But it was not always like this, as we soon shall see.

1852 was a horrible year, with all its sorrow and the torments of poverty. Jenny, who was brought up with the paraphernalia of German Christmas, was compelled to celebrate the holiday without the least bit of decoration or presents for the children. The following year, at least, was better at times. At the end of the year they could afford both presents and decoration, and she was wholeheartedly delighted with the children and certainly with Karl. It seemed to be brightening a bit on the horizon. But the hardest blow was still to come.

In the spring of 1855, eight-year-old Edgar fell seriously ill. Karl was supposed to travel to Manchester but stayed at home, beside himself with worry. Jenny broke down. 'For the last week emotional stress has made my wife more ill than ever before,' Marx wrote to Engels. 'As for myself, though my heart is bleeding and my head afire, I must, of course, maintain my composure.'

On 6 April 1855, the boy died in his father's arms. It was an even harsher blow than the deaths of both the other children. An eight-year-old is already a fully fledged personality, and Edgar – nicknamed *Musch*, 'the fly', or even Colonel Musch – was, according to all testimony, an incredibly charming boy: affectionate, happy, and moreover brilliantly gifted. The mourning for him became difficult to endure for the surviving members of his family – his sisters and parents. Jenny and Karl, who knew that life in nineteenth-century Europe was easier for men than for women, had placed great hopes in little Musch – and now he was dead.

Jenny wrote in her memoirs that the day of Musch's death was the most painful one of her life. 'He was the love of my life, as he was for almost everyone who gazed into his beautiful, sunny face.' He was also 'my dear Karl's complete pride, joy, and hope'. The boy had loved his father to the same extent, she continued, and during his illness constantly wanted 'Charley' by his side. The latter hardly left the boy during the weeks his suffering lasted. Jenny herself could not endure the sorrow; it was entirely too difficult for her to bear.

Wilhelm Liebknecht bore witness to Karl's sorrow at the funeral.

Lessner, Pfänder, Lochner, Conrad Schramm, the red Wolff and I rode together – in the same wagon as Marx – he sat there silently, with his head in his hands. I stroked his forehead: Moor, you have your wife, your girls, and us – and we all think so much of you! 'You can't give me my boy back,' he moaned, and we rode silently on to the graveyard in Tottenham Court Road.

Liebknecht also said that when the casket was lowered into the ground, Marx was so forlorn that his friends were afraid he would rush down into the depths after it.

Marx expressed his feelings in a letter to Engels. 'I've already had my share of bad luck but only now do I know what real unhappiness is.'[19]

But at the time of Musch's death, Jenny was already at the beginning of a new pregnancy, and in January 1855 she gave birth to a girl. This was little Eleanor. Like her brother, she was uniquely gifted – the most brilliant of the surviving children. But she did not have Musch's bright temperament. Her life was lined with troubles and sorrows, not all of which can be put down to external circumstances.

But she was healthy, and she became the family's little darling. She developed into a tomboy, says Jacques Attali, and her own father shared that opinion. 'My father used to say that I was more like a boy than a girl,' she wrote in a letter. Her father went even further. 'Tussy *is* me,' he could say. He concentrated his hopes in her. It is not strange that he was particular about her education, especially literary – fiction from Aeschylus to Balzac were and remained one of his favourite fields, which he also initiated her into.[20]

Jenny gave birth to another daughter, but the child died almost immediately after birth. The circumstances around the event were so terrible that Marx did not wish to go into the details in a letter to Engels; they were not suitable for writing down.[21]

Jenny and Karl had now lost four children. Their losses would mark the remainder of their lives. The joyfulness they were able to express throughout their lives would always have a dark background of sorrow and loss.

~

It is not surprising that Jenny's and Karl's dream in common of a better, more just society was often overshadowed by all their personal sorrows and troubles. Jenny, who bore the heaviest burden, was periodically gripped by what in the language of our time we would call depression. Reality became so hard that she lost herself in passivity. She simply had had enough. Her sorrows also taxed her physical health. The numerous pregnancies likewise wore her out. What is striking, however, is not that she sometimes lost her spirits and her strength; it is everything she accomplished despite all the difficulties.

Certain of her letters to Karl are almost unbearably gloomy. In June 1852, when he was in Manchester, she went through all the horrors she had to endure, finally exclaiming: 'My head is about to explode. For eight days I have gathered all my strength; now I can do no more.' And finally: 'The lady [that is, she herself] is becoming very repulsive, and rightly so.'[22]

But still, everything was not darkness. Even during these gloomy years, the family went on Sunday outings marked by high spirits and practical jokes. Much later, they still brightened up Wilhelm Liebknecht's memories. 'A Sunday in Hampstead Heath was the greatest delight for us. The children spoke of it the entire week, and even we adults rejoiced in it. The trip itself was a party.' Helene, who they called Lenchen, bore the picnic basket on her arm. The main attraction was a thick joint of veal she had prepared for the hungry group. Liebknecht continued: 'In the wild moorlands of Hampstead Heath we ate and drank exhaustively, and we read and talked politics while the children played and romped.' On the way home, they sang patriotic songs like *O Strassburg, o Strassburg, du wunderschöne Stadt*. But above all, Karl and Jenny recited entire scenes from one of Shakespeare's dramas from memory.[23]

No sorrows pervaded these excursions. The family permitted themselves to burst out in joy. Both Jenny and Karl knew that the joint of veal was entirely too expensive for them, and that in a few days the butcher would be standing – by turns pleading and threatening – at their door. But what did that matter while fortune smiled? Jenny's life during these years was thus marked not only by troubles and sorrows, but also by joy, even happiness.

Much the same could be said about her husband. His temperament was just of another kind, more choleric and expansive. In
his letters to Engels, he could have intense outbursts over what the
hardships their marriage had cost both him and his wife. During
their years in Brussels, when domestic bliss was uninterrupted, he
was shocked at Engels's erotic escapades and the contempt for
marriage that accompanied it. But during the 1850s in particular,
he could complain numerous times about the variety of horrors
that family life entailed when their resources were constantly
running short. He could, for example, give a lively description
of how he hunted around London in vain in the hopes of pro-
curing some money, thereby losing both work time and power
of thought, at the same time as Jenny – hounded by constant
worries – was breaking down in nervous troubles.[24] Engels tried
to comfort him and his wife through his constant remittances,
and moreover with an encouraging word or two. But their troubles eased only temporarily. The Marx family would soon be in a
jam again.

Even in the 1860s, when the financial situation had improved,
he could express himself dramatically over the torments of family
life. He did so above all in a letter to Paul Lafargue, his future son-
in-law, who was already longing for Laura's hand in 1866. Marx
wrote that he had sacrificed himself for the revolutionary struggle
and never regretted it – quite the opposite. He would do the same
again if he had to live his life over. He would only do one thing
differently: he would never have got married. And so comes a
sentence that is aimed directly at Lafargue: 'As far as it lies within
my power, I wish to save my daughter from the reefs on which her
mother's life was wrecked.'[25] Here it is not his own unhappiness
he has in mind, but Jenny's. The marriage had destroyed her life.
The girls would not meet the same fate.

His power turned out to be highly limited on this point. Lafargue
soon became an esteemed son-in-law.

But the darkness in Marx's life was not solid – far from it.
Suddenly everything was once again joy, ecstasy, and great love. In
the summer of 1856, when Jenny was visiting her mother in Trier
and Karl was visiting Engels in Manchester, Karl wrote a letter
to Jenny where he maintained that happiness could be perceived

most clearly when people lived apart for brief periods. The little things of daily life then gave way, and people could see what they really had. The true, enormous proportions of love stood out. Karl told Jenny how he kissed her picture with the same passion the pious kissed their icons. Her portrait did not do her any justice, of course; 'your dear, lovely, kissable, *dolce* countenance' was not reflected there. But it nonetheless depicted her![26]

In another, oft-quoted letter from 1863, it was Karl who found himself in the couple's mutual birthplace. His mother had at last died, and he could collect the inheritance he had been longing for. He therefore had reason to feel a certain degree of optimism before the family's financial future. But that could not be the only reason for his outburst of joy over the fact that Jenny was his sweetheart. Every day, he said in a letter to her, he made a pilgrimage to the house on Römerstrasse because 'it reminded me of the happiest days of my youth and had harboured my greatest treasure'. He was delighted that people asked him left and right how the woman who had once been 'the most beautiful girl in Trier' was doing, and he asked himself if anyone could experience anything more pleasing than the thought that this belle of the ball was now his beloved?[27]

Karl and Jenny could also be exuberantly happy together. Their youngest daughter, Eleanor, talked about how her parents could burst out in uncontrollable laughter until tears ran down their faces. Sometimes it was inappropriate to laugh so unrestrainedly, and at those times they dared not even look at each other, certain that the merest glance would provoke hilarity as uncontrollable as it was inappropriate.[28] Eleanor had a tendency to idealize her parents' marriage. But there is no reason to doubt this sharply outlined image of mutual, exuberant delight.

The entire Marx family had got accustomed to living under burdensome financial conditions. When the situation eased temporarily, it roused great joy. For many years, the head of the family was compelled to wear a tattered overcoat. At length, he got money enough to buy a new, elegant topcoat, and he then took the opportunity to also be photographed. Both older daughters, Jennychen and Laura, burst out in wild enthusiasm over the new creation and praised his sober, elegant appearance.[29]

It is clear that Jenny's and Karl's marriage and family life contained both happiness and adversity, radiant light and gloomy darkness. Above all, it was characterized from beginning to end by a unique intensity of feeling.

So far, most of it seemed obvious and clear. But there was an additional side where the essentials are hidden in darkness – something important, and by the standards of the day extremely shameful.

In June 1851, Lenchen Demuth, the indispensable housekeeper, gave birth to a strong and healthy baby boy. He was named Frederick, and would be called Freddy. His given name is the English variant of Friedrich, and everyone around them – including Jenny's and Karl's children – were told that it was Engels's child. Engels was still a man known for his loose love life, and a further affair would not affect his image. But most of the information points to the fact that Karl Marx was the actual father.

There is clear testimony indicating this. There is a letter from Louise Freyberger, an Austrian social democrat who had previously been married to Karl Kautsky, the greatest ideologue of Marxism after Engels. Louise now had a new husband, and together with him she kept house for Engels during his last years. Freyberger said in a letter that Engels, on his deathbed, succeeded in convincing Eleanor Marx that her father, and not Engels, was the father of Freddy Demuth.

Objections can be raised to the letter. What has been preserved is a typed copy made a year later. The typed copy gives the text a degree of protected anonymity, and its contents can be read as part of the campaign of hate and slander against Marx that has been conducted with greater or lesser vehemence since the 1840s, and continues today. Incidentally, Marx mentioned this campaign in a letter to Engels in August 1851, at the time when Freddy was only a few months old. In it, he brought out not his own suffering, but Jenny's. She was becoming worn out by all the problems of daily life – and on top of this, terrible slander as well!

But was it really the rumours about Freddy's parentage that was the concern here? Around the same time, Marx wrote a brief, unpublished text titled 'Skizzen über die deutsche kleinbürgerliche Emigration in London im Sommer 1851' (Sketches of German petty-bourgeois emigration of London in the summer of 1851). These emigrants, he wrote, were distinguished by their unreasoning hatred of Marx (the text obviously was to be published anonymously). Among the assertions, it was mentioned above all that Marx, brother-in-law of Ferdinand von Westphalen, the new Prussian minister of the interior, was a spy charged with providing information on other emigrants. This is assuredly the rumour that hurt Jenny so deeply; Ferdinand was her half-brother.

Somewhat stronger evidence that Marx was *also* referring to the rumours of who was father to Freddy is a letter he wrote a few days later in which he spoke about a mystery in which Engels was also involved, which had given the matter a somewhat tragicomic turn. Just as he was writing this, he was interrupted and stated that the matter could wait until he himself came up to Manchester and could take it up face to face.

If the insinuations really concerned the issue of Freddy's parentage, and if Engels were in the know about Marx's actions, such a statement would have seemed comic, even ridiculous. But Engels did not betray himself with any indication that he found Marx ludicrous.[30]

There are thus certain arguments against the assumption that the rumours were true. But they still seem rather weak, and Louise Freyberger is not the only one who indicated Marx's paternity. It is of course not true, as is sometimes asserted, that Jenny was travelling at the time of conception. She was not; both she and Karl, the children, and Lenchen were crowded into the little apartment at the end of August and beginning of September 1850. If Karl were the father, he and Lenchen must have met somewhere else – but where? Or did Marx creep into her bed 'late at night', as Sperber has proposed?[31]

One possible indication is that after Franziska's birth in late March 1851 (barely two months before Freddy's!), Jenny did not become pregnant for several years. This could be interpreted as a punishment for her husband's infidelity. But could her precarious health, alongside the family's wretched finances, not be reason enough for mutual caution?[32]

A weightier argument is that Clara Zetkin, the leading German social democrat and the mother of International Women's Day, asserted that her friend Eleanor Marx called Freddy her half-brother. Other documents indicate that several leading social democrats were in the know on the matter, as was possibly Freddy Demuth himself. Or were he and the others also victims of the gossip that had plagued Karl and Jenny ever since the early 1850s?[33]

But the strongest argument for Karl Marx's paternity still remains. In 1896, the year after Engels's death, Eleanor Marx wrote a letter to her sister Laura that Marx had proved his greatness as a politician and a thinker – but not as a human being. What besides the paternity of Freddy, kept in secret, could she have been referring to? What else could have so fundamentally changed her image of her father? Note that she wrote the letter a short time after Engels's death, when according to Freyberger's letter she should have been let in on the family secret.[34]

Purely psychologically speaking, it is difficult to understand how Marx could have acted indifferently – distantly, in fact – to a boy who might have been his own. Towards the children that were demonstrably his, he showed a fatherliness that was unusual for the times. His relationship with his son Edgar (Musch) is telling enough. Jennychen was the apple of her father's eye, and even Laura was the subject of his constant care. His love for Eleanor was inexhaustible.

Little Freddy, on the other hand, was immediately placed with foster parents. How could Marx have done that to his own son? Could he have so totally disinherited his own son – the only one not to die in childhood – just to keep up his family façade? Could he have denied Freddy the kind of knowledge that was so precious and dear to his own self? It is difficult to understand.

And how could the child's mother permit such a thing? To all appearances, she had no choice; she shared the hard lot of countless other maidservants of having to sacrifice an immense amount for the family she served. Helene Demuth saw her son often, of course, but he seldom was found in the Marx household.

Jenny Marx could certainly have imposed her definite conditions for how the matter would be handled. Karl would outwardly have nothing to do with the boy. The world would believe that Engels was the father. Only she and Karl and Lenchen (and Engels) would know how things really stood. Their own children would be kept out of it, as would the often hostile world around them. But the indifference Marx showed the boy can neither be explained nor forgiven by this.

The person who has provided the most well-considered account of the subject is Rachel Holmes, in her great 2014 biography *Eleanor Marx*. The pieces that point to Marx's paternity are carefully put together there. Even Lenchen Demuth receives a reasonable portion of the attention. She was not just the one who handled the family's last line of defence against pure destitution. She was a beloved and respected member of the family, a good friend to Jenny, a comforting asset for the children, and – especially – a fairly irreverent comrade to the head of the family with whom she gladly played chess and often beat. This is a possible background to the relationship between them becoming more intimate.[35]

And yet: Lenchen was among the many women of the age (and, perhaps, of all ages) who never had space for their own lives. She continued to serve the Marxes, husband and wife, for as long as they lived. When they both died, she managed Engels's household as well.

In summary, it is easy to say that in his view of women – and especially of those who were closest to him – Marx was a child of his time. But this also means that in his view of equality, he was far less advanced than his friend Engels, to say nothing of another contemporary: the liberal philosopher and political economist John Stuart Mill, author of the 1869 book *The Subjection of Women*.

Karl Marx's daily life was often hard and brimming with troubles. But it was still Jenny Marx who bore the heaviest burden. Like many other contemporary women, she bore a long series of children – the last when she was over forty (an age that today does not need to entail any risks, but which did to a great extent in the 1850s; at that time, in fact, every birth regardless of the mother's age was life-threatening). It was she who first had to tackle the daily problems – everything from the children's illnesses to the creditors constantly knocking on the door. This taxed her mental powers heavily. Karl had his scientific and journalistic work. For her, putting his writings into presentable and readable condition was one of the greatest causes for joy. A brilliant, first-rate stylist, like many other women of the time she had to otherwise be satisfied with letter-writing. It was there she could give her talents free rein.

We know that she accepted the lot of women in the age she lived in before her marriage to Karl, even if it was with regret. She bravely defended her fiancé against the criticism of her relatives. Life with Karl later became harder and more bitter than she ever could have imagined. It weighed heavily on her, but she endured it. It was a heroic achievement.

9

Journalist on Two Continents

Work, Despite Everything

Daily life in the slum quarters of London was hard. Nonetheless, Marx tirelessly continued his activities on many fronts. Only a few months after his arrival, he started his life's project again – the project that had occupied him ever since 1844 and would be the backbone of his work up until his death. 'Here you have to study matters' (*Hier muss studiert werden*), he exclaimed in a letter to Joseph Weydemeyer on 4 February 1850.[1] But it would be several years before the great project yielded anything besides further contributions to the increasingly bloated pile of excerpts.

There was also much else that occupied Marx and demanded more immediate efforts than the grand unified theory of society. He once again took up the work of the Communist League and its central committee. He helped organize the efforts to resettle the large group escaping the repression in the German states. He joined London's 'Educational Society', soon offering his services there and lecturing both on economic theory and on the fundamental ideas in the *Manifesto*.

There were attempts to unite all radical forces in the mixed (to say the least) community of people who had been stranded in London. The refugee committee was called social democratic because it was to both help and unite those who had demonstrably taken part in the revolution and now needed relief. The phrase 'social democracy' began showing up here and there, and people even spoke of 'a social democratic party' even though it would be long before this party actually established itself as a mass movement. The purpose was obviously to include not only organized communists, but other radical forces as well.[2]

As we will remember, during the years of revolution Marx had had the ambition for an even broader radical coalition in which faith in democracy would constitute the principle of unity. This was the main line he pursued in *Neue Rheinische Zeitung*. But it soon proved difficult to preserve the line of mutual understanding. Many of those with democratic goals believed that a compromise with royal power would be possible. Marx found this hope preposterous and abandoned the line of compromise. His newspaper reaped numerous successes at the same time as popular rebellions flared up in several places. With the defeat of the revolution, a new attempt at a broader coalition began. But even this time, the united front was soon broken up.

Marx was not the first to sound the call to battle. Back in the late fall of 1849, the Marx family's doctor, Louis Bauer, had been part of founding a *Demokratischer Verein* (Democratic Association), which was a direct competitor to the Educational Society Marx was devoting his energies to. Furious, Marx wrote a letter to Bauer in which he declared that the latter's attack on Marx's colleagues and friends made all personal relations impossible. Marx wanted only a bill for the services Bauer had provided to him and his family as a doctor. After that it was 'thanks, and farewell'.[3]

He appeared even more furious in a letter to another London emigrant, Eduard von Müller-Tellering, a lawyer who had previously contributed to *Neue Rheinische Zeitung* but had never been a supporter of Marx, despite holding Marx's writings in high esteem. He did not belong to Marx's group, but felt he was 'opening a new world that we have before us,' he wrote in a letter in the fall of 1849. But once in London, he ventured to criticize Engels, and accused Marx in a letter of striving for the role of 'democratic Dalai Lama and the possessor of the future'. Marx's letter to him outwardly bears witness to a boiling rage. His handwriting was even more cryptic than otherwise, and he crossed out a part of what was written with thick lines. He concludes the letter by declaring that von Müller-Tellering had acted wisely in not turning up at a meeting the evening before. 'You knew what was to be expected from a confrontation with me.'⁴

The strife would soon come closer to Marx himself. But now it was not an issue of leadership; it was an issue of whether the radicals, with the communists at their head, would go immediately on the attack against the counterrevolution that was now triumphant. In a way, it was a repetition – though on a smaller scale – of Georg Herwegh and others' direct but doomed war of aggression against Prussia early on in the revolution of 1848. Now it was August Willich who placed himself at the head of the men of immediate action.

Willich had a remarkable life. Having lost his father early on, he was brought up in the home of the famous theologian Friedrich Schleiermacher. But he embarked upon a military career, not a theological one, and he climbed the ranks to lieutenant before his radical opinions made it impossible to serve any longer in the Prussian army. On the other hand, he was given a prominent place in the revolutionary battles, particularly in Baden. Engels was directly subordinate to him there. As a refugee in London, Willich wanted to continue his military adventures. He did not receive much of a hearing for his plans, instead just barely earning a living as a carpenter; after several years, disappointed with Europe, he emigrated to the United States. He had his great breakthrough there in the Civil War; his efforts gained him attention and he again climbed the ranks to brigadier general. But he also continued with his grand ideas; he was among the pioneers of Hegelianism in the United States. When in 1870 he returned briefly to Prussia, he was not accepted into the victorious army, and instead defended his doctoral thesis in philosophy at the age of sixty at the University of Berlin.⁵

This remarkable man rebelled against Marx and Engels in the Communist League; as if that were not enough, he recruited Carl Schapper – one of the most important contributors to the League and now a zealous supporter of immediate revolutionary actions – to his side. There were intense disputes, and Conrad Schramm, one of Marx's most faithful followers, even challenged Willich to a duel. Marx and Engels tried to prevent the spectacle, but in vain. The combatants set off for Brussels, where duels were still permitted. It was a foregone conclusion: Willich was a trained military man, his opponent a businessman and private teacher. But Schramm was only lightly wounded – whether from luck or Willich's competence has been left unsaid. Their friends were relieved. Schramm was known for his excitable temperament. 'He was the Percy Hotspur of our party,' Marx wrote after his premature death from tuberculosis. This was a comment typical of Marx. Shakespeare's characters (in this case from *Henry IV*) constantly populated his world of ideas.

Both Marx and Engels also had lively temperaments and pushed through the expulsions of Willich and Schramm from the association – in contravention of its regulations.[6] But why were they both now so hostile to the idea of initiating a new rebellion? The answer is already clear from their actions during 1848–49. Once a worker's rebellion had broken out, they supported it wholeheartedly. But they considered it futile, and fundamentally incorrect, for a leading group – however revolutionary the party they were in – to try to start an insurrection. The liberation of the working class must be the act of the working class itself, as they maintained in the *Communist Manifesto*.

This is a long way from Lenin's notion of a party elite bringing the masses with them. It is not the professional revolutionaries who would start a revolution. But on the other hand, the manner of excluding those who hold different opinions can be seen as the start of a bad tradition.

The *Neue Rheinische Zeitung* as Periodical

It was through enlightenment, not military actions, that Marx, like Engels, wanted to influence the working class. This is why the press became such an important channel for them both. Their first great project in London was a continuation, in journal form, of *Neue Rheinische Zeitung*, now with the subheading *Politisch-ökonomische Revue*. For nearly a year starting in the late fall of 1849, this was Marx's and Engels's primary effort. When Marx started the project, however, he believed that it would soon be interrupted by a new, bigger revolution. 'A world conflagration will intervene,' he wrote confidently to Joseph Weydemeyer.[7] But the world conflagration failed to take place and other, more trivial things caused the journal's downfall.

Neue Rheinische Zeitung had been a brilliant success in Cologne, particularly after Marx gave up the idea of a broader democratic coalition. It turned out to be significantly more difficult, after the guns fell silent, to raise similar enthusiasm among potential readers. In addition, it was now a thick journal with long articles. Marx was aware that the new *Revue* would lose the opportunities of a newspaper to comment on current events. He comforted himself with the fact that on the other hand, it would gain analytical depth.

Their journal would contribute to providing for both Marx and his family, and Engels. This required a great stock of subscribers, and additionally a number of individual issues sold.

The diligence of the editors was exemplary. The first issue came out on 6 March, and the last on 29 November. They both had written a large part of the content themselves.[8]

But by 29 November, Engels had already given up. In Manchester, he was going to acquire the fixed income that would not only provide for him, but also in part for the growing Marx family. At the same time, the decision meant a defeat. For a few years, he and Marx had stood side by side, though Marx was the leader in both their own eyes and those of the world around them. Now they were going their separate ways. It was Marx who would write the heavy, epoch-making tomes, with the great work of social theory that would become *Capital* in the centre. Engels would earn his daily bread in the family company, supporting the Marx family with what was left over. The time and energy not required by his ordinary work could be devoted to the Great Cause.

The journal had not been the success they expected. The difficulties emerge with painful lucidity in the substantial correspondence the project gave rise to. Marx sent a long series of letters, above all to fellow thinkers stationed at various locations in the German states. But the responses were rather discouraging. There was not as much interest as they had expected. Weydemeyer, still in Frankfurt, did not have much of anything positive to report, or money from sales to send. He observed bitterly that even the workers in Frankfurt had become petty bourgeois.

But the difficulties did not stop there. Distribution was poor; subscribers were not getting their issues. Finally, even the editors were handing in their manuscripts late.[9]

In short, it was a project that gave neither Marx nor Engels any income or any new influence among those in Germany whose revolutionary convictions could be strengthened and deepened.

The contents of the journal were considerably more solid than its influence, to say nothing of its finances. Both Marx and Engels started by summarizing what had actually happened during the revolutions that had just taken place. Engels wrote on the struggle for a new constitution, and Marx's first major contribution was a long text on the class struggles in France during the last revolution: 'The Class Struggles in France, 1848 to 1850'. It is the first work – and one of few – in which Marx provided a picture of all social classes in a society of the time and of their mutual battles and compromises. We must therefore stop a moment before this text, which is barely a hundred pages long.

Marx began with an assurance that the result of the revolution was not due to the revolutionaries themselves but to the fact that the development of society had not managed to go far enough. But the tragicomic result was a counterrevolution. Now it was a question of getting to know the true face of the counterrevolution in more detail.

The masters after the July Revolution of 1830 were not the entire bourgeoisie but only sectors of them: the bankers, the kings of the stock exchange, and other similar groups with rapidly growing fortunes – in short what was called the 'finance aristocracy', in contrast to the old aristocracy that was soon to be left behind. This finance aristocracy was made of the people who had flourished in the 'fabulously rapid enrichment' of the years Guizot and Louis Philippe were in power.

An observer from our time, seemingly so distant from France of the 1830s and 1840s, would suddenly feel at home. In the world of the 2010s it is also the bankers, the kings of the stock exchange, and their ilk who have ultimate power in their hands. Politicians are at their beck and call, as Guizot once was, and the smallest ripple on the surface of the stock market rouses their consternation – or their delight. We are living in a modified July monarchy.

But the real July monarchy fell in February 1848. The provisional government that was first formed at the time constituted a compromise between various classes. The bourgeoisie was in the majority, but there were also petty bourgeois; even the workers were allowed to be part, in a (small) corner with Louis Blanc as their chief representative. But the mutual understanding could not last long, and moreover the various social perspectives and interests were too different – incompatible, in fact.

The role of the industrial proletariat was, as Marx pointed out, rather insignificant in France. Simply put, industry had not managed to go far enough in its development. The workers disappeared behind all the petty bourgeoisie and farmers, and were sucked into the general talk of brotherhood. Under that word, brotherhood (*la fraternité*) – that old slogan from the French Revolution of 1789 – everyone could be united in a 'pleasant dissociation from class antagonisms', a 'sentimental reconciliation of class interests', and people dreamily believed they could rise above the class struggle.

But concrete political actions always favoured someone and were unfair to someone else. The state needed money, but a tax increase primarily affected the farmers. To defend itself against discontent, the Republic created a 'garde mobile' that consisted of what Marx called the 'lumpenproletariat', which meant everything from career criminals to people with unspecified occupations. The temperature rose. The workers – journeymen and others who were imbued with radical thinking, it should be said – gathered on the Champ de Mars. The rumour spread that they were armed, and the regular army was called in. But the general election was a success for the left, and the antagonisms soon hardened. The bourgeoisie could no longer tolerate the advances of the left; in Marx's interpretation, they forced the June rebellion, which ended in a bloody massacre. He saw one cause of the left's defeat in the lack of planning and leadership.

The February Revolution was the beautiful revolution, and the June Revolution was the ugly one, he said. In the long run, the bourgeoisie could not stay on good terms with the petty bourgeoisie, but got into constant conflicts. Moreover, the interests of the shop owners or journeyman craftsmen were far too different to those of the factory owners, the big merchants, and the bankers. The former thought they had a trump card in their hand through their parliamentary situation. But they never got any equivalent power. In the election of September 1848, both Louis Bonaparte – the future Napoleon III – and the chemist François-Vincent Raspail, a radical leftist (Marx called him a communist) who had just been sentenced to a long term of imprisonment for the sake of his opinions, were both elected as representatives.

The revolution swerved to the left. It was now that a new human right was proclaimed by the revolutionary left. To those which had already been established during the revolutionary years of 1789 to 1794, the *right to work* was added. It was a social right, if anything, and as such was something new. Marx had always had a sceptical attitude towards declarations of rights, which in his opinion easily became empty rhetoric in a class society. But, he added, behind the demand for the right to work lay another, larger, demand: power over capital, and thereby the appropriation (*Aneignung*) of the means of production. Another programmatic point was progressive taxation – but, Marx said, progressive taxation was fully compatible with a bourgeois political system. It was even the most cherished alternative of the petty bourgeoisie.

Marx must have been arguing that the radical demand for the right to work was being watered down by the other demand – higher taxes for those who earned or owned more. (On the other hand, progressive taxation was also a demand in the *Manifesto*.) The right to work was shrunk in its parliamentary treatment to a right to relief. In a historical perspective, this radical demand is still the most important contribution the revolution of 1848–49 left to the future.

In all the developments that followed, a tug-of-war dominated between parliament on the one hand and Louis Bonaparte, who after many strange turns – but with a large majority – had been elected President of the Republic, on the other.

Election reforms deprived a large part of the impoverished male population of the right to vote for a time. The consequences were that parliament came to be dominated by petty and big bourgeois forces who considered themselves as standing for law and order (women were still excluded entirely). 'The party of Order' again favoured the finance aristocracy, as well as the industrial bourgeoisie and the large landowners – groups that could agree on common politics in relation to the other classes. Many urban citizens with more modest economic conditions also adopted the demands of the bourgeoisie in the hope of being able to improve their own situation.

But 'the party of Order' had a powerful opponent in Louis Bonaparte. The president knew he was a man of the people. Above all, he had the farmers on his side; the freeholders constituted the great majority – two-thirds, Marx claimed – of the population of France. When the majority of parliament voted through a tax on wine, their discontent reached boiling point.

When Marx was writing his article, the struggle for power was in full swing. He did not yet know its outcome. He was only trying to find fixed points in an unceasing flow of current events.

There are a few elements on the class struggle in the article that deserve mention. Marx compared France with Great Britain, pointing out that the stock exchange aristocracy in the latter was the subject of sharp, effective attacks from the leaders of industry, naming once again Richard Cobden and John Bright, the most colourful among the Manchester liberals, whose clarity and consistency he most reluctantly admired. The schism was due to the fact that Great Britain was a country that had managed to go farther in its capitalist development, he pointed out. Implicitly understood was that the representatives of productive capital had a stronger position.[10]

It is also worth noting that his conviction that the revolutions were natural features of this historical development remained unshaken. More than that: they drove history forward. Or, as he said with a typical metaphor that would be repeated among many of his more militant followers: *'Revolutions are the locomotives of history.'*[11] It was a conviction built on the experiences of 1789, 1830, and 1848. Rebellions that knocked sitting regimes out of the saddle were inevitable features of the development of modern society.

One term that, on the other hand, was given a new and much more important role in the article on the class struggles in France was *interests*. But it would be scrutinized in connection with another work: Marx's real test of strength from the early 1850s, namely *The Eighteenth Brumaire of Louis Bonaparte*. Before this comes up for discussion, something must be said about the concluding texts in *Neue Rheinische Zeitung*. These are made up of reviews of newly published literature that Marx and Engels wrote, more or less together. They are often rather detailed examinations of books, with a shifting character – everything from a two-volume work on religion in the new era to François Guizot's attempt to explain why England had succeeded with its revolution in the seventeenth century, but not France with its corresponding political revolutions much later. Guizot had himself become the leading politician after the July Revolution of 1830, but he had no more than anyone else managed to create a stable constitutional monarchy of the British type.

It is hardly surprising that Marx and Engels found Guizot's explanations insufficient. Guizot only had an eye for the political game, and saw in Great Britain a congenial interplay between Whigs and Tories, liberals and conservatives. He did not see that the political stability had its foundations in a great alliance between the bourgeoisie and the large landowners, and above all he did not see the dramatic developments that occurred in society while the governments shifted. The manufacturers had developed to the degree that they burst their own frames asunder and made a place for industry that through steam machinery had become 'gigantic factories'. A successful bourgeoisie had conquered the world market. But the development had also created a rapidly growing proletariat that threatened the peaceful game of governmental power that Guizot praised so lyrically. In France, on the other hand, the bourgeois class had had enough problems to cope with after the revolutions that they themselves had more or less been the architects of, but had time and again slipped out of their hands.[12]

The review is one example of materialist historical writing as Marx and Engels imagined it. But the example has its limitations. Guizot chose them, not his critics. A crucial part – perhaps *the* crucial part, in fact – of the journal was to have been a 'Review' in which neither books nor the February Revolution would be debated, but where the crucial events of the recent period would be scrutinized. Certain parts of the text that were to cover the first months of 1850 were certainly written by Marx, even if the author's name is missing. Only he, and not Engels, could have come up with the idea of comparing the ambition of the Prussian king Wilhelm Friedrich IV to fortify his sovereign power with the Greek poem *Batrachomyomachia* (The Battle between the Frogs and the Mice), a ruthless and comical parody of classic depictions of war in the style of the *Iliad* that was composed sometime between 500 and 300 BCE.[13] But it is neither Germany, nor Austria, Russia, Turkey, England, or France that made the deepest impression on the author of the article but the United States – more specifically, the discovery of gold in California. This was more important than the February Revolution – in fact, it was said, perhaps even more important than the discovery of America itself. Eighteen months after the discovery there was already a railroad, a major highway, and a canal in the state. Trade changed direction, and San Francisco developed as a new centre of world trade. A long coast – one of the most beautiful and fertile in the world – would contribute further to rapid development. World trade would soon get a new centre in California, and American traffic would soon not only be heading eastward to Europe but westward as well. People of all types would gather in this new earthly paradise, from Yankees to Chinese, from Blacks to Indians to Malays, from creole and mestizo to European, and the most recalcitrant peoples would be pulled into world trade, Marx maintained.

It is a sure prophecy of the time when the Pacific Ocean would become more important for trade than the Atlantic. Above all, it is a spectacular picture of the *globalization* that the forgetful 1980s gladly saw as something entirely new.

Marx also maintained (more or less without support from Engels) that Europe's only possibility of holding its own in stiffening competition was a social revolution that transformed the relations of production in such a way that they could interact with modern productive forces. On the other hand, nothing was said about the need for a similar revolution in the United States. But was the United States of the 1850s not a country where capitalism reigned? Certainly it was.[14]

The reviews that followed do not have the same powerful content. What is interesting, however, is an appreciative and critical report of Thomas Carlyle's recent *Latter-Day Pamphlets* (published in 1850). Carlyle attacked contemporary society from a conservative position, but there are elements in his criticism reminiscent of those Marx and Engels formulated. The book was praised for that reason, but was criticized for its author's veneration of the Middle Ages.[15]

One powerful contribution in the double issue of the journal dated May–October 1850 is Engels's more than eighty-page article on the German Peasant Wars of the sixteenth century. It may seem like an odd deviation from the orientation on the contemporary era that characterizes everything else in the journal. But at the beginning and the end, Engels connected with the current situation. Even Germany has a revolutionary tradition, he said by way of introduction, and he concluded by assuring his readers that the final defeat of the peasant wars would not be repeated in nineteenth-century Europe: the future beyond the rebellion was bright.[16]

In the concluding issue of the journal, it was noted that the project was nearing its end; it had not become what Marx and Engels had hoped. Somewhat discouraged, they printed parts of the *Communist Manifesto*, and in the extensive 'Review' on the events from May to October 1850 they were compelled in the introduction to observe that revolutionary forces everywhere had been pushed back. The overview went on to deal with railroad construction and the accompanying speculation on the stock exchange, the potato blight of the 1840s, and problems with raw materials in the cotton industry where Engels was soon to serve. But the United States and its rapid development soon came into focus again, and the growing significance of the Pacific Ocean for trade and shipping was emphasized as it had been before. More, however, dealt with the disintegration of the Chartist movement in Great Britain and on the tug-of-war in France between Louis Bonaparte and parliament. The entire article was an attempt to catch the period in flight. The text has a journalistic drift, but lacks structure. It would be Marx's and Engels's last contribution to the journal, which went to its grave with this text.[17]

A Little Masterpiece That Brought in 'Less than Nothing'

A few years ago, one of the leading German newspapers of our time, *Die Zeit*, selected the hundred greatest literary works of world history. Thomas Mann's *Buddenbrooks* is there, as is Heinrich Mann's *Der Undertan* (The Loyal Subject) and Alfred Döblin's *Berlin Alexanderplatz*. August Strindberg's *Miss Julie* is among those selected, but the list also contains a surprise: Marx's *The Eighteenth Brumaire of Louis Bonaparte*.

Of course, Marx's book is a masterpiece. The first pages in particular are among those in Marx's works that are never to be forgotten, on a level with the very best he wrote. It belongs to the tradition of world literature.

The book (or booklet) came into being over an astoundingly brief period. Marx began the work in December 1851 and was finished in March 1852. The year that had passed since *Neue Rheinische Zeitung* was shut down had been full of problems, of which familial and financial were far from the only ones. The schisms within the still young and limited German workers' movement had deepened. Among those who were still active in German territory, Marx had good support for his tactic of waiting for a spontaneous proletarian uprising before the *Bund der Kommunisten* would go into action. In October 1850, Hermann Wilhelm Haupt wrote from Hamburg that their opponents, Willich and Schapper, did not stand a chance. Opinion was unanimous in Hamburg, likewise in Frankfurt and Wiesbaden. The zealous supporters of revolution in London were asses if they thought they could get any support in Germany.[18]

In London, on the other hand, where the German refugees were like dogs fighting over a bone, the polemics continued tirelessly, and both Marx and Engels devoted a seemingly unreasonable attention to the conflicts. The communists quarrelled internally, and outside their circles there were other refugees who were

socialists, more indeterminate democrats, republicans, or something else, and the differences in opinion gave rise to endless
controversies. Marx and Engels took part wholeheartedly. As
we know, Marx had been subjected to shameful slander among
these people, but neither he nor Engels were slow to give as good
as they got. Marx wrote the brief, unpublished text mentioned
earlier, 'Skizzen über die deutsche kleinbürgerliche Emigration in
London im Sommer 1851' (Sketches of German petty-bourgeois
emigration of London in the summer of 1851) in which some
of his most detested opponents, Arnold Ruge among them, were
castigated. But that was just the beginning. He and Engels soon
pulled themselves together for a joint attack on all their opponents in the pamphlet *The Great Men of the Exile*.

A great deal of work lay behind it, consisting of an intense collection of material in which Jenny Marx also took part – as did
Ernst Dronke, who at that point was one of Marx's and Engels's
loyal followers (but would soon give up both communism and
political activity and become a tradesman). The pamphlet was
sent by courier to Germany where it was to be printed, but the
courier was a police spy and delivered it to the police authority
in Prussia instead. It was never printed during Marx's or Engels's
lifetime, and no great damage was done with it. It is a text partly
in the same style as *The Holy Family* or *The German Ideology*,
but it does not have the same intellectual scope. There is only one
phrase that really stands out, and it is certainly Marx's creation:
'character mask'. The inspiration came from a satirical poem by
Heinrich Heine, in which someone was said to lack talent but was
still a character (*kein Talent, doch ein Character*). Briefly put, he
could play the game without understanding what it was about.
The phrase 'character mask' itself, however, provides further
and more interesting associations with classical Greek drama
and its masks. The word would return in Marx's later production, and that with a crucial significance for his fundamental
theory.[19]

It is not Marx, however, who inspired those who use the phrase
'character mask' in current English. On the Internet, a character mask is a mask portraying a politician or other celebrity, like
Barack Obama or Michael Jackson.

But enough about that. The manuscript on the great men in exile came into being in a great hurry in May and June 1852. A lot had already happened by then. The Communist League had dissolved, and a visible organizational boundary had thereby been erased between Marx and Engels on the one side and men such as Ruge and his ilk on the other.

The death blow for the League was dealt, as we have already seen, by Prussia and through the trials of communists in Cologne. When its most important representatives in the German states were locked up in houses of correction, the organization no longer meaningfully existed.

It is easy to see how quickly the mood shifted. In March 1850, Marx and Engels had written an optimistic address in the name of the League. The predictions in the *Manifesto* had come true to the letter. The death of Joseph Moll was a hard blow, it is true, but now it was only a matter of waiting for the proletariat to rise under its own power, or also for the Holy Alliance to attack 'the revolutionary Babylon'. Faced with these prospects, the workers had to arm themselves, and Marx and Engels even hoped for an alliance between the proletariat and the lumpenproletariat – the same lumpenproletariat that had been castigated in the *Manifesto* and other writings.

The optimism in those pages did not have much support in reality. No rebellions shook 'the revolutionary Babylon'. The trials of communists in Cologne did not arouse the protests of the masses, only their fear.[20]

As always, the dark clouds got Marx to take up his pen. The most important result is his book about Napoleon III's path to power. It was his friend Joseph Weydemeyer who let the text fill an entire booklet of the newly founded journal *Die Revolution*. Weydemeyer had, prudently enough, left Germany and moved to the United States, and it was there he published his journal. Obviously, Jenny and Karl had hoped for a certain financial dividend for such an excellent text. But no, it brought in '*weniger als nichts*' – less than nothing, Jenny wrote. In general, the little book remained a black sheep of the family. Even in a letter from 1869 to her sister Jenny, Laura complained that there would be no French translation, despite its continued topicality.[21]

Only posterity has been able to appreciate the work according to its merits.

The Eighteenth Brumaire of Louis Bonaparte[22] contains not only a vivid portrayal of the course of events that ultimately made it possible for Napoleon's nephew to become emperor after a coup. It also contains fundamentally important arguments that cast light on Marx's view of history; in the first pages in particular, Marx formulates a few brilliant aphorisms that often appear in collections of familiar quotations.

We will begin with the bit of French history between 1848 and 1850. Marx had already depicted the start of this process in his article on the class struggles in France. But he was then compelled to bring it to an end in the middle of a flow of events whose continued direction lay hidden. Now, his depiction reached the definitive end of the revolution, when an entirely different history began: that of the Second Empire.

In the classical style, Marx divides the course of events into three parts. First, a prologue. The ruling finance aristocracy of the July monarchy was to be overthrown, but the rebellion soon took on greater proportions. The common folk mounted the barricades, demanding more than a political revolution: social conditions must also be transformed. But during the second phase, the leaders of the new bourgeois republic tried to stop developments that threatened their own position. This led to open rebellion, which cost many lives.

Marx provided a split (to say the least) image of the efforts of the proletariat. On the one hand, they raised demands that were nothing more than 'utopian nonsense' (*utopische Flausen*); on the other, the June uprising was 'the most colossal event in the history of European civil wars'.[23] The bourgeoisie won, and stabilized their power. The proletariat was forced back onto the revolutionary stage (Marx gladly used metaphors from the theatre in the presence of dramatic events), and their ever more questionable leaders devoted themselves to diverse experiments marked by the conviction that the desired changes to society would occur 'in private fashion' through anticapitalist banks, workers' associations, and so on. It was Pierre-Joseph Proudhon and his followers that, without naming names, Marx was criticizing. In Marx's opinion, the social revolution cannot be realized through gradual measures that undermine the power of the capitalists. This can only happen in open battle. The bourgeois republic means pure class despotism.

The third period, which ended with the coup of 18 Brumaire (2 December), was characterized by the power struggle between parliament and the popularly elected president, Louis Bonaparte, whom Marx had already depicted in his article on the class struggles. Legislation and taxation was in the hands of parliament; the majority of the people (the farmers) embraced the president, and the latter also succeeded in winning the loose elements of society – its outcasts, the lumpenproletariat – by providing them with food, wine, and weapons. When Bonaparte's term as president was nearing its end and he could not be re-elected according to the constitution, he staged a coup d'état, entrenching himself at the top of a substantial imperial bureaucracy and a loyal army. The choice of date for the coup was not at random. 18 Brumaire was, according to the French Revolutionary calendar, the day in 1804 when the first Napoleon crowned himself emperor, and also the day a year later when he won his most famous victory: the Battle of the Three Emperors at Austerlitz.

The interest and strength of Marx's writing is not in the depiction of this series of events. It is brisk and skilful, but also arbitrary. The important thing is what he says about social classes, on the difference between saying and doing, on the history that marks people's thinking and language, on historical patterns that are repeated, and especially on people's freedom and lack of freedom.

First, class. The freeholding farmers did not constitute a class, Marx said. Their conditions are homogeneous, it is true, and they are all affected by the same kinds of taxes. But they live and work independently of each other and constitute only a 'vast mass'. Neither division of labour nor technological development based on contemporary science affects their labour yet. No one can really represent them; they exist one by one. Of course, there are revolutionary farmers, but they have been defeated. Conservative farmers are the ones Napoleon III could support himself on. It certainly looks like the new emperor's state constituted its own independent power, but it has its essential support among the farmers.[24]

The different layers of the bourgeoisie, on the other hand, are a class like the petty bourgeoisie and the workers. The French workers may have bad leaders, but they nonetheless constitute a class. The petty bourgeoisie believe themselves to be above class interests, but of course they are not. The stock exchange aristocracy, productive capitalists, and large landowners may often fight against each other; in the parliament of the revolutionary period they formed a common front against the president, who was on his way to making himself emperor.

It is clear that Marx's classes are not complete, closed entities as they are in a contemporary statistical overview of various occupational categories. It is not generally the term *class* that is in focus for him; it is, as French philosopher Louis Althusser pointed out, the *class struggle*. In other words, it is not the anatomy of society that occupies Marx, but its conflicts.[25]

Here, there is a particular problem with the groups we would call intellectual – the people tasked with creating, developing, or conveying knowledge, values, and programmes of action. All democratic representatives are not shop owners, Marx pointed out. On the contrary, with their education and their positions as intellectuals, they may be far from them. But they will not cross the boundaries of the material interests of their class. The background, of course, is that many leading figures in various parties do not have their occupational experience in the various core activities of their parties but could be teachers, lawyers, doctors, authors, or journalists. How could they see society from the perspective of the petty or big bourgeois? And how could Karl Marx, with his lawyer's education and his doctorate in philosophy, assume the standpoint of the waged labourers?

The statement just expressed – that all intellectuals in politics are nevertheless limited by the class interests they represent – does not provide a satisfactory answer to the question. It is further brought to a head by the fact that many intellectuals, especially at that time, maintained that their opinions had the sanction of science. Marx himself was one of them. He claimed to be an innovative scientist. Questions of this kind will occupy us in due course. They are crucial for understanding Marx's perceptions of society. But in *The Eighteenth Brumaire of Louis Bonaparte* they are still open, without answers.

Another term that plays a central role in the same book is *interest*. Marx said: 'And as in private life one differentiates between what a man thinks and says of himself and what he really is and does, so in historical struggles one must still more distinguish the language and the imaginary aspirations of parties from their real organism and real interests, their conception of themselves from their reality.'[26]

The expression 'real organism' may seem strange today, but in the mid-nineteenth century it was not. The real organism was the party as it *was*, not as it wanted to *appear*. Through this quote, we come back to the most fundamental figure in Marx's world of ideas ever since his early youth: the opposition between heaven and earth, head and feet, form and content – what through various turns of history would come to be cemented in the more rigid pair of base and superstructure in the textbooks. But here, as in the article on the class struggles, the term *interest* stands out. It is never again as important in Marx's writing as it is in both these works.

The root is in two Latin words, *inter* and *esse*, 'between' and '(to) be'. But *interest* is no classical Latin term. Marx came into contact with it chiefly through British philosophy. It is both a central psychological, perhaps even anthropological, term, and a narrower economic term having to do with dividends earned against a loan or investment. From the start, interest is the amount a capitalist pays to a landowner or property owner to be allowed to produce goods in a fixed location, perhaps in buildings that are not even their own. With the development of the stock exchange, the word *interest* gains additional content; speculation picks up momentum.

The psychological term has a certain relationship with the idea of *homo oeconomicus*, 'economic man', who knows exactly what favours them or is to their disadvantage. The unbiased person can navigate through existence in a way that, given the circumstances, makes their life better than if they had been guided by prejudices of various kinds. On a political plane, this means that if people's interests become generally accepted in decision-making associations, they will also correspond to the prevailing interests in society.

Marx was not unaffected by this discussion when he was writing his articles in the early 1850s. But the content was entirely different. Interest is set against conscious ideas, whatever those may be. Interest has nothing to do with what people 'think and say' but with what they *are* and what they *do*. Phrases and fancies may not be mixed together with real interests.

The meaning is not uncomplicated. It conflicts with its daily use in sentences like 'foreign languages and picking mushrooms are my main interests'. Rather, Marx is referring to the social forces operating under the surface on which our consciousness moves. It is not strange that the word in this sense fades away in Marx's later writings and is replaced by other, more sophisticated ways of describing the play between conscious ideas and driving forces in society. But the content has stuck in common perceptions of Marx's theories, which is perhaps why his writings on the eighteenth Brumaire are so widely read.

Interest in the economic sense, as dividends earned, also plays a role in Marx's writings, his later ones in particular. But there, it is embedded in his more central categories such as capital and surplus value.[27]

It is not the comments on interest that made *The Eighteenth Brumaire of Louis Bonaparte* so admired. It is rather the very first pages of the work, which contain a chain of sentences that are often quoted. First is the reference to Hegel, who said 'somewhere' that history always repeats itself. But Marx interjects that Hegel forgot to point out that the original course of events takes the form of a tragedy, to later be repeated as farce. Robespierre of the 1790s had his counterpart in Louis Blanc of the 1840s, and instead of the uncle came the nephew (that is, Napoleon III had to shoulder the role of Napoleon I).[28]

But more interesting is what Marx immediately thereafter says about history. People make their own history, but they do not freely do so; they do so under immediately given circumstances. The past sets the framework for them. 'The tradition of all the dead generations weighs like a nightmare on the brain of the living.' These lines are an interesting example of the often abused term *dialectics*. So much is settled in advance, but people are nevertheless creative. Marx was not, as is often asserted, determinist. On the other hand, he occupied himself intensely with what limited human action.

The leading actors of history also themselves contributed to bringing the past to life. Luther dressed up as St Paul. The French Revolution of 1789 mirrored the Roman Republic, and Napoleon imperial Rome. The revolution of 1848 tried to follow in the footsteps of 1789. 'In like manner a beginner who has learnt a new language always translates it back into his mother tongue,' Marx said. Only someone who can move freely in the new language can create something independently.

The comparison also applies to the social revolution that Marx hoped would soon break out. It was preceded by a series of bourgeois revolutions; the first was Oliver Cromwell's in England in the mid-seventeenth century. The bourgeoisie in itself was unheroic but still needed heroism, sacrifice, terror and civil war to reach its goal. All revolutions bring the dead to life in order to endow their own battles with heroism. What happened in France between 1848 and 1851 meant that an entire people found itself transported to a past epoch.

But it had to be different with the nineteenth-century social revolution! It 'cannot draw its poetry from the past, but only from the future', Marx said. It must let the dead bury their dead, and reach out to its own content. In other words, it should not dress up in the clothes of older times (their forms) but concentrate on what is the core of its task.[29]

A social revolution is precisely a matter of content, that is, the material basis of society, while strictly political revolutions necessarily concentrate on form, which is politics. The line of thought is not difficult to understand, but it still raises questions that we had previously skirted. What did Marx mean about poetry in that quote? It can scarcely be the poetry he loved so much, from the ancient Greeks to Heinrich Heine. Rather, this poetry is the phrases and opinions that previous revolutionaries took from the past, whether it be Ancient Roman heroes or Robespierre or

Napoleon I. As he often did, Marx depicted the future that he desired only in negative terms. The coming revolution will *not* be like the previous ones. It will *not* dig into the past. On the contrary, it will meet the future without being guided by ancient ideas.

Marx's work was published in a second German edition in 1869. In the preface, he observed that initial distribution of the book in Germany had been insignificant. In 1869, on the other hand, there was great interest in it.

Marx compared his *Eighteenth Brumaire* with two other books on the same dramatic period: Victor Hugo's *Napoléon le petit* (The Little Napoleon) and Pierre-Joseph Proudhon's *La révolution sociale démontrée par le coup d'état du 2 décembre* (The Social Revolution Illuminated Through the Coup of 2 December), both of which were published in 1852, the same year as Marx's work. Hugo, who Marx never held in particular regard, explained the course of events entirely with the person of Louis Napoleon himself. He turned up 'like a bolt from the blue', Marx said. But in that case, wouldn't the main character of the book be great, and not little, if he could produce so much on his own initiative?

For his part, Proudhon tried to see the coup as the result of historical development, but in his zeal to be an objective historian turned the retinue of putschists into heroes. Marx emphasized how the class struggle in France lifted up the bizarre Louis Bonaparte as the final solution to an otherwise unsolvable dilemma.

He did not revise the work. If he had, it would have lost its distinctive colouring, he claimed.[30]

Conquering the World with a Pen

A large, important part of Marx's journalism is composed of the articles he published in the *New York Daily Tribune*. The background is an interesting one. The paper's managing editor, Charles Anderson Dana, took a trip around Europe in the late 1840s. In revolutionary Paris, he ran into Karl Marx, who made a strong impression on him through his uncompromising radicalism and his enormous wealth of knowledge. The idea of linking Marx to the *Daily Tribune* had stirred back then, but could not be realized immediately since Marx soon became occupied with his own newspaper in Cologne. When Marx arrived in London, destitute and in desperate need of money, it became that much more important for him to establish close contact with the newspaper on the other side of the Atlantic. The platform Dana and his editor-in-chief, Horace Greeley, could offer him was not just any platform: the paper was successful, respected, and had a broad circulation, especially among the lower classes of society.

The *Daily Tribune* was as serious as it was radical, founded and managed by Horace Greeley. Greeley was a socialist, primarily a follower of Charles Fourier, and he conducted an involved struggle for workers and others forced to live on the margins of the economy. Back in the 1830s, he had emerged as one of the most important moulders of opinion against slavery.

Charles A. Dana, long his right-hand man, had more direct experience of the socialist experiment. For five years, he had lived and worked in a small utopian society of which there were so many at the time. It was called Brook Farm, located in Massachusetts. Fourier was its guiding light, and its founder, George Ripley, at length became the literary editor at the *Daily Tribune* and thus a colleague of Dana's. Brook Farm had come to nothing by then, by all appearances because the participants had not sufficiently mastered the art of either managing a farm or carrying out production on an industrial scale.

Dana made for revolutionary Europe instead. There he met not only Marx, but also encountered the future Napoleon III. It is striking how much he agrees with Marx in his description of this remarkable man. Dana saw from his spectator's seat how the future ruler captured everyone's attention in parliament although he was an ordinary man with an unbecoming moustache and marked by a life of dissipation.

It is not odd that Marx felt at home in the New York paper and that Dana, responsible for reporting from Europe, so generously prepared a place for his articles. And Marx was assiduous. Only the American Civil War put a stop to his collaboration. Strangely enough, the interruption coincided with Dana being fired from the paper in 1862, for reasons that are shrouded in mystery. For the *Daily Tribune*, it meant a setback, but Dana himself had a splendid career. He first became assistant secretary of war in Abraham Lincoln's cabinet, and after the war he took over another New York paper, the *Sun*, which under his management achieved wide circulation and great influence.[31]

But we are here concerned with Marx. Ostensibly, Marx's debut in the paper was back in October 1851. But despite Marx being indicated as the author, it was Engels who wrote the debut articles dealing with revolution and counterrevolution in Germany. Marx was busy with something else at the time, nor had his own English reached the level that it was good enough for newspaper prose (in Sperber's words, it always remained 'noticeably Teutonic').[32]

After that, Marx became that much more assiduous. Despite his poverty and despite the sorrows, he wrote a copious number of articles for the *Daily Tribune*. They are so many that, compiled into books, they extend over several thousand pages and constitute an important part – predominant, in fact – of the mass of text he sent to print. Posterity has forgotten that he stood out as a journalist in his time. After the revolutions in the late 1840s, it was not Europeans but Americans who got to acquaint themselves with the art of his writing. He himself saw the United States as an increasingly important recipient of radical ideas. Many Europeans had escaped the wave of counterrevolutions to the other side of the Atlantic. But above all, the United States was undergoing dramatically rapid industrial and economic development. It should have been a good breeding ground for radical ideas.

The *Daily Tribune* was thus an important forum, and not just an insufficient though necessary contribution to supporting Marx's family.

But, despite everything, he also published a number of articles in Europe. At irregular intervals, he submitted contributions to the Chartist organ *The People's Paper*, and in 1855 he devoted his main energies to a new radical German paper, *Neue Oder-Zeitung*, which in due course, however, was quickly banned by the authorities. In the early 1860s, he wrote a number of articles in *Die Presse*, a Viennese newspaper that opinion-wise suited him poorly and at times refused to publish what he had written.

(*Die Presse*, which began publication in the revolutionary year of 1848, is otherwise still around, despite various interruptions to its publication.)

Marx wrote his articles in a period when technology was developing rapidly in both the United States and Europe. Rotary presses, it is true, were not in practical use until the mid-1860s. But the telegraph was already playing a major role in the dissemination of news. It was already in use in Europe and in North America, and news thereby spread rapidly over an ever greater portion of both continents. The idea of an enormous Atlantic cable linking the United States and Great Britain had been raised back in 1851 at the Great Exhibition in London, and a few years later Cyrus W. Field, an American as rich as he was enthusiastic, decided to invest much of his fortune into the project. Field was a paper mill owner, and the development of the press was economically important to him.

In 1858, it seemed as if a connection had been successfully set up, and Queen Victoria sent a telegram to the American president James Buchanan praising God for the wonders of technology. But the cable soon fell quiet, and new attempts could not be made until after the American Civil War. A functional cable was laid only in 1865.[33]

By then, Marx had stopped writing for the *Daily Tribune*. During his time as a contributor, his texts had to be shipped across the Atlantic by steamer. He always dated his articles, which is why it is easy to see that it took at least 14 days before they were published. The news served to readers on the East Coast was thus not completely fresh. But, by the standards of the time, the distribution of news across the ocean was still fast.

Marx's standpoint was from London, and it can be seen in everything he wrote. The British press, the British Parliament, and the British governments – in particular their prime ministers – remain at the centre of his reporting. The British workers' movement was also important, as are strikes and lockouts in an industry that constantly swung between boom and bust.

But the British outlook also guaranteed that the perspective would never be narrowly national. The Empire – as time went on, the biggest the world had ever seen – was under construction.

India was subjected to British domination, and China was forced into a dependency through widespread opium addiction. Marx wrote so many articles on both countries that there are special collections of them. *Marx on China* thus constitutes a separate volume, as does *Karl Marx on India*.[34]

Between 1853 and 1856, the Crimean War was raging, in which a coalition of France, Great Britain, and the Ottoman Empire defeated Russia. 'The Turkish Question' is of course a recurring theme in Marx's articles. (Where purely military questions were concerned, Engels stepped in.) War and the risks of war were generally central themes in Marx's reporting. The war between France and Austria in 1859 received its share of attention, but this applied even more to the American Civil War.

Moreover, Marx provided many glimpses of what was happening in the German states, in France, in Denmark, and in several other European countries. His articles were often an audacious potpourri of various subjects. One article could have a headline such as 'The Russian Humbug – Gladstone's Failure – Sir Charles Wood's East Indian Reforms' and another 'Advertisement Duty – Russian Movements – Denmark – The United States in Europe'. But sometimes he concentrated on one subject, for example 'The Worker Question'.[35]

His reporting could sometimes be rather impersonal, sequences of events and statements that could have been made from starting points entirely other than his own. In short, he appeared as a competent and objective news journalist. But the typical Marxist convictions often shine through, and he even more frequently sets what he talks about in the context that his theories and political programme represent. He knew that the *New York Daily Tribune* was a radical newspaper and that Charles Anderson Dana had recommended precisely him so that he would voice his unmistakable opinions about what was happening in the world. Marx would not otherwise have agreed to anything else; he had an unwavering *courage de son opinion*, the courage to stand for his opinion even in the most inconvenient context.

A common feature in his articles, as with what he wrote previously and would write later, is the conviction that technological development drives humanity forward, despite the sacrifices it cost. He could recount how many horsepower were now driving British industry.[36] Statistics, with their exact figures, filled him with evident satisfaction; with their help, one can measure the rapidity of development and its potential failings.

The telegraph, with its increasingly rapid flow of information, found an admirer in him. He found the conservative *The Times* excessively ridiculous when it questioned the reliability of the 'mendacious wire' of the new era, so unlike the messages by letter or oral information of previous epochs.[37] *The Times* otherwise was among the constant subjects of his venomous attacks, as was British conservatism on the whole. The same applies to the even more extravagant Prussian right wing. In one article, he mentioned his own brother-in-law with disapproval: 'The Minister von Westphalen represents the ultra-Prussian aristocracy.'[38]

The loathing for the Russia of the tsars was even greater and partially rubbed off onto his attitude towards Denmark. With a certain degree of Russian assistance, Denmark had gone to war with Prussia (which had just been shaken by revolution) and won a victory that was confirmed through the peace at Malmö in 1848. Marx returned several times to the deceitful little country. He does not spare a word for the fact that Denmark got its first constitution in 1849. On the other hand, he depicts with relish some reactionary critics of that constitution, including the famous Nikolai Frederik Severin Grundtvig, who predicted the prompt downfall of the country when it so shamefully broke with its ancient tradition of royal absolutism.[39]

While he castigated all conservative regimes, he expressed his admiration for Great Britain. This was the country where the revolution of modern society first took place. But it was admiration that flourished best at a distance. In an article on *The Times*'s denunciation of radical refugees, he quotes its assessment of his lot: 'Their punishment is exile in its harshest form', and wryly concurs, 'As to the last point, *The Times* is right; England is a lovely country to live out of.' With a sigh, he quoted Dante, another writer forced into unhappy exile: 'How salt the bread of others.'[40]

Despite the bitter taste, he welcomed every measure that hastened development into the modern age. This was the explanation for him expressing himself positively towards those who held the most immediately opposing views, the Manchester liberals with Bright and Cobden at their head. He supported them in their untiring battle against the British right wing. In Marx's opinion, free trade expedited the classless society.

At the same time, he observed bitterly that the same representatives of the Manchester School opposed every proposal for improving workers' conditions. In fact, his tone against the party of the factory owners became even harsher, the more union questions came to dominate his reporting.

The Workers and Their Opportunities

In the 1850s and early 1860s, Marx's own political activities were negligible. This did not mean that his interest in the great social questions or the situation and possible future of the working class had disappeared. It is only that he saw no other opportunities to influence the situation himself than through his pen. The liberation of the working class was and would remain the achievement of the working class itself.

He could express himself strikingly optimistically, for example in an article on Chartism in the *New York Daily Tribune*, in which he asserted that the crucial step would be the implementation of general and equal voting rights. The working class would thus not win victory with barricades and live ammunition but thanks to its superior numerical strength. The British were generally not naturally suited for revolutions but rather for reforms, he pointed out. Through their reform work, the Manchester liberals undermined the power of the old landowners; they were therefore carrying out the necessary work for future social upheavals.

In these memorable articles, Marx spoke about revolutions without any violence whatsoever. The political revolution would be carried out with the ballot box, and the social revolution would also take place through the increasingly crucial role of the workers in production. The article actually dealt with the Chartists, who Marx called 'the politically active portion of the British *working class*'. If Chartism could be brought completely back to life and

organized in a better way, it would perform great deeds on the
ground it had prepared. Here, as in many later articles, he cites
Ernest Jones, a Chartist leader himself with anything but a proletarian background – he had a distinguished ancestry and a good
education – but an unwavering sympathy for the cause of the
industrial workers. Jones had spent hard time in prison in 1848–49
when the authorities in Great Britain tried to prevent the troubles
on the Continent from spreading across the English Channel, but
during the 1850s he could again freely publish newspapers and
give speeches.[41]

Marx also expressed optimism and great delight at the plans for
a special workers' parliament. When it actually met in Manchester
in March 1854, he did not mince words, characterizing the gathering as a decisive sign that a new epoch of world history was
breaking.

The background to the parliament was a wave of strikes that
broke out in Great Britain in the early 1850s, which Marx carefully reported on in the *Daily Tribune*. The idea was raised that the
workers had to join their forces in order to assert their demands
against the capitalists with greater success. The optimists – to
whom Ernest Jones also belonged – imagined that the union and
the political struggles would be united as a result of such a parliament. It was with that expectation that Marx wrote about the
event in the New York newspaper. In the initial article, he pointed
out that the delegates did not sit by the grace of any state or other
authority. They directly represented all branches of the British
labour market. Their most important task was to organize the
working class into a functioning unity.

Marx could also proudly announce that 'Dr Marx' had unanimously been elected an honorary member of the parliament. It is
true that he had to share the honour with Louis Blanc and Martin
Nadaud, two French socialists who were not among his favourites. But he was flattered, he wrote in a letter to the parliament
which was published in the Chartists' *The People's Paper*. The
parliament had great tasks before it. Nowhere had the despotism
of capitalism gone so far as in Great Britain. On the Continent,
there were still large classes of farmers and craftsmen. In England,
they were on the way to disappearing.

But the working class in Great Britain was also the most competent. By creating modern large-scale industry, they had laid a firm foundation for another society. 'The labouring classes have conquered nature; they have now to conquer man.' Much of the letter turned up again in an article in the *New York Daily Tribune*. But in it he also reproduced a programme of action that had been drawn up by the committee that had taken the initiative for the parliament. The most important proposal was the creation of special funds that would help workers who were striking, locked out, or wrongfully terminated. Quite simply, it concerned an early version of strike funds.[42]

From a trade union perspective, the parliament was a success. Politically, on the other hand, it was tantamount to a disappointment. Most of the delegates were not interested in a broad political coalition. They wanted to concentrate on the immediate issue: the right to struggle for working conditions and wages.

Marx's optimism over the development was not broken by this setback. He had faith in the inner dynamic of the development, seen for example in a speech that he held in 1856 for the fourth anniversary of the *People's Paper*. The speech was reproduced in the same newspaper and expressed the confidence in the future that was so typical of him. Steam, electricity, and spinning machines were more dangerous revolutionaries than bourgeois rebels like Raspail and Blanqui. 'In our days, everything seems to be pregnant with its contrary,' he declared. Machines were replacing labour – and labour was still getting more burdensome and more tiring. Riches were creating destitution. Humanity was learning to master nature – but was being compelled to submit to other people. Even the light of science seemed able only to shine against the dark background of ignorance. All our successes meant that we were replacing material forces with intelligent life, but at the same time we were dulling human life. The contradiction between modern industry and science on the one hand and the misery and degeneration of social relations on the other was obvious. But circumstances would change. English workers were 'the first-born sons of modern industry' (sons, not daughters, despite the countless women who worked, above all in the cotton industry). It was their task to lead the great liberation that was at hand.

The contrast between the sharply outlined description of the times and the vague promises of future development are striking.[43] This example of eloquence, however, is rare in Marx's newspaper articles from the 1850s and 1860s. More frequently, he wrote about the concrete conditions in the factories. He then had great use of the reports that factory inspectors, appointed by the British Parliament, published once every six months. He commented on the results in a series of articles. They tell us much about the 'social anatomy' of Great Britain and reveal how vampires feed on 'the life-blood of the young working generation', he declared in 1857. And it was actually a grotesque reality presented here, with death, mutilation, lost eyes, and horrible burns.

The safety measures that the inspectors recommended roused the indignant protests of the factory owners. Their operations would not break even with such comprehensive regulations, they declared. They ardently conveyed this opinion through their representatives in Parliament. Ridiculous battles between landowners and manufacturers – combatants who, in Marx's opinion, were united in their contempt for the people – took place there. But the moral bravery of the factory inspectors was worth all admiration, he said.[44]

In a new report from the factory inspectors in 1860, Marx found particular interest in an account that one of the deputy inspectors gave of a pioneering operation in Rochdale. Rochdale is known to history as the actual birthplace of the consumers' cooperative, in which the weavers joined together in a shop where they themselves were the owners through their shares, thereby having democratic influence over it. Posterity has found it easier to forget that producers' cooperatives also gained a foothold there, and it is this audacious operation that deputy inspector Patrick (his first name is unknown) talked about. A cotton factory had been in operation since the end of the 1840s; it was owned cooperatively, and most of the owners were workers. Other similar industries had also grown up in the vicinity. Marx said that Patrick's information is valuable, but at the same time expressed a fear that the operation would be swept away during the next industrial crisis. On the other hand, he avoided any deeper commentary. Did he not see the producers' cooperative as an opportunity to strengthen the power and freedom of the workers? We cannot judge this from these statements.[45]

Industrial workers not only had to live under constant risk of accident and endure unreasonably long working days. Pure destitution threatened them in times of crisis, and not only then. During booms, riches were created for the few and continued poverty for the many. On top of it all, workers – like other poor people – were threatened by the deteriorating quality of basic foodstuffs. Marx devoted special attention to bread, and he was not the only one to do so. Parliament became concerned over the hazardous, strange, or nutrient-poor additives that were mixed into foodstuffs in order to stretch them further and thereby increase the profits for the producers, and subjected them to the investigative gaze of socially critical scientists. When Marx returned to the topic a few years later, he relied upon *Adulteration Detected*, the impressive 1861 book by doctor and nutrition specialist Arthur Hill Hassall.

In an article in the *New York Daily Tribune*, Marx touched upon the adulterations, but above all complained about the wretched hygiene of the bakeries. Spider webs, insects, and other things that were more or less dangerous to health ended up in the dough. He imagined a future where giant bakeries with the highest mechanical standards provided people with bread.[46] It was a dream that was nearly realized a few decades after the Second World War, but the bread produced was neither tasty nor nutritious. Since then the path has partially swung back towards small bakeries, which, one hopes, are now rid of spiderwebs and insects ...

Marx saw all issues that had to do with the status of the working class in the light of the class struggle. Their immediate opponents where the factory owners. It therefore irritated him – as it did many others – that the most visible spokesmen for the factory owners, Richard Cobden, John Bright, and their ilk, so readily spoke in the name of the entire people when they turned against the traditional upper class. In an 1855 article in *Neue Oder-Zeitung*, Marx spoke about a meeting in London that attracted a large audience chiefly of workers. But the speakers who appeared were no workers, and they praised the middle class to which they themselves belonged and which in their opinion should take over the responsibility of government in the name of the entire people. This speech roused lively protests, and order was only restored when Chartist leader Ernest Jones stepped forward and declared that the people really should not ally with Bright and Cobden, who had so vigorously opposed all humane factory laws. Marx commented that universal suffrage would one day be pushed through and contribute to changing society. Then, of course, the real people would attain decisive influence.[47]

Political and Economic Crises

In an article about a political crisis in Great Britain, Marx complained that the press devoted much more space to the political game in Parliament then to the ups and downs of the economy. It was an observation completely in agreement with his basic understanding of society. On the other hand, it is striking that Marx the journalist did not deviate from this pattern he found reprehensible. Of course, he devoted many articles to industrial, trade, and financial crises. But in many more, he dwelt upon debates in both the House of Commons and the House of Lords, as well as to the constantly recurring political crises. The leading politicians of the time were the subject of many of his commentaries. The names of quite a few still have a certain aura: Benjamin Disraeli, William Ewart Gladstone, and of course the aforementioned Cobden and Bright.

The 1850s were a highly volatile, not to say turbulent, period in British politics. The Empire was growing, war was raging, and new conflicts constantly seemed imminent. The contradictions between the traditional aristocracy and the bourgeoisie were sharpening, at the same time as discontent among workers and other lower classes was perceived as a distant but threatening noise in Parliament.

Henry Temple, third Viscount Palmerston – commonly called Lord Palmerston – occupied a unique position in Marx's reporting. He was born in 1784 and was thus a man well on in years in the 1850s and early 1860s. His career had been exceptionally long: he made his debut in the House of Commons in 1807 when Napoleon I was the subject of the day in British politics.

Over the decades he found himself close to the centre of power, finally crowning his career in 1855 with the position of prime minister.

In 1853 when Palmerston was home secretary, Marx wrote a long series of articles with the collective title 'Lord Palmerston'. The articles were intended both for the Chartists' *The People's Paper* and for the *New York Daily Tribune*, but only certain articles ran in the latter. This series would soon come out as a pamphlet, and it enjoyed a certain degree of success.

Marx always had an ironic perspective on Palmerston: he was not a statesman equal to his tasks, but he was a clever actor for any role, Marx said. He harboured no great plans, but got himself entangled in trifles. He was not worthy of any great opponents, but he always knew instead how he could choose insignificant people for his duels. When it proved opportune, he became a supporter of the Whig Party, which soon made him foreign secretary. He was contemptuous of the people: the common man had no rights. But he was pleased to appear as a benefactor.[48]

This series of articles is highly retrospective. Palmerston's exploits during the 1830s and 1840s are put under the magnifying glass. In many later articles, Marx castigated the prime minister's more current efforts. In 1855 when *Neue Oder-Zeitung* was Marx's main newspaper, he again devoted several articles to the British statesman. He reported the rumour that Palmerston was a Russian spy and therefore little inclined to inflict a decisive defeat on the Russians in the Crimean War. But he countered with another rumour – that the same man belonged to a secret society in Italy. In another article, he reads the physiognomy of the entire British ruling class from Palmerston's conduct.[49]

Briefly put, Marx had no high opinion of Palmerston. There were, however, even greater nobodies than he. One such nobody, the subject of Marx's particular contempt, was Lord Aberdeen (or, with his official title, George Hamilton-Gordon, fourth Earl of Aberdeen). Lord Aberdeen was prime minister as England entered the Crimean War. Marx excels in virulence when describing how the Earl presented the declaration of war in Parliament. Ostensibly, Marx introduced his article with something completely irrelevant. The French, he wrote, could not understand

Shakespeare's greatness because he so freely combines the sublime with the low, the grisly with the ridiculous, and the heroic with the burlesque. But there were limits to the contrasts: Shakespeare had never let a jester deliver the prologue to a heroic drama. This had just taken place in the British Parliament. Lord Aberdeen had performed the role of the jester brilliantly when he gave official confirmation that the country was at war with Russia. Only a farce could follow such an introduction, Marx sighed.[50]

On the other hand, he harboured great admiration for another British politician of the time: Benjamin Disraeli. Ideologically, the distance from the conservative Disraeli was even greater, but Marx also had an eye for intellectual acuity and quality among those who held opposing opinions. He returned time after time to Disraeli's merits, usually in contrast to Palmerston's arbitrary mediocrity. His praise was never greater than in 1858, when he described how Disraeli, now chancellor of the exchequer, submitted his budget to Parliament. He praised the clarity of the analysis, the simplicity of the proposal, and the dexterity – judgements he never would have squandered on Palmerston or Aberdeen, or for that matter Gladstone.[51]

Those who say that Marx hurled abuse at Jews in a kind of self-hate are building on a fragile foundation. It is true that he often pointed out that people he did not like for some reason were Jews. But he thought highly of Disraeli, the only British prime minister ever of Jewish ancestry, despite the fact that he was conservative. Marx did not say a word about his family background.

The 1850s, like the early 1860s, were a turbulent time in British politics. But these were also the years when the economy was flung between boom and bust, great profits and crises. Marx was deeply engaged with these dramatic changes. But like other newspaper writers, he devoted less space to them in his journalism. Only now and then did he comment on the signs of dramatic declines, supporting his statements with statistics. Cotton production was collapsing, and other branches of industry were following, he wrote in 1855, adding that when the working class experienced the decline, it would come to life again after a few years of passivity.[52]

But the real crisis only came in 1857. It was an important one in Marx's life. In its shadow, he wrote the substantial manuscript that goes under the name *Grundrisse*, which is not only a preparatory work for *Capital* but is an important work in itself. He also devoted a few newspaper articles to the dramatic course of events. He described the collapse on the Hamburg stock exchange, which had repercussions in Sweden, Norway, and Denmark. London was not unaffected.[53] Similar convulsions in France also came into focus.[54]

Marx's fascination for the course of events was bound up with his conviction that a deep economic crisis would trigger a new revolution. So it had been in 1789, 1830, and 1848; so it would also be in the future. Previously, Great Britain had succeeded in resisting the atmosphere of rebellion, but it would not be so the next time, he declared in one of his articles on the subject. He added that even Russia had been shaken: serfdom was being questioned there (it was finally abolished in 1861).[55]

But the crisis of 1857–58 blew over without a revolution. This did not mean that Marx became less attentive to the oscillations of the market. So, for example, the readers of *Die Presse* were informed in 1861 that the American Civil War was threatening British industry because imports of cotton, an important raw material, were about to be choked off.[56] Nevertheless, there were other aspects of the war that above all occupied Marx the journalist.

London and the World

Paris may have been the capital of the nineteenth century, in Walter Benjamin's sense: the agenda for most cultural issues was set there. As regards economic and political power, however, no metropolis could compare with London. This became increasingly clear in particular during the decades that Marx and his family lived in the city. Many of the leading politicians, with Lord Palmerston at their head, may have cut a poor figure on the international arena. Behind their often clumsy words, however, there was a force as regards industrial resources, worldwide communications, and money with which no glittering Continental rhetoric could compare.

This power was the reason that Marx and many others were surprised by the rather feeble efforts of Great Britain during the Crimean War. It was also the reason that the rule over India and the subjection of China were seen as a confirmation of British efficiency and ruthlessness.

As we have seen, the Crimean War – which from the start was called the 'Russian War' – was an important (in fact, long dominant) topic in Marx's journalism. It was now a question of looking at this war from a broader perspective than that of the British Parliament.

Most of what Marx wrote on the subject is commentary. He brings in his own sources – often directly from the sultan's foremost advocate in London, David Urquhart, a well-informed but deeply reactionary journalist and politician. In the literature, it is sometimes suggested that he was close to Urquhart, but the only thing that united him and his informer was their loathing of Tsarist Russia. It is true that Urquhart appreciated Marx's articles and had contacted him personally – in fact, Urquhart even got him to write a few articles for his own newspapers. But Marx did that chiefly for the money, and broke off contact when he did not receive compensation he considered reasonable.[57]

Marx took pains to counteract the image of the Ottoman Empire as exotic beyond measure in contrast to the completely normal Great Britain. In his eyes, Islam was neither stranger nor more oppressive than Christianity. When Richard Cobden of the Manchester School warned against alliance with the 'fanatical Muslims', Marx pointed out that Cobden nevertheless could have directed his accusatory glance towards his own country, where the Church had a firm grip on state power.[58]

In another article, he reported on all the obstacles the Grand Mufti had put in the way of an alliance with Christian states. In the next breath, he talked about how Christian churches fought tooth and nail over the sole right to the Holy Sepulchre in Jerusalem. Marx obviously wanted to strike a balance. Religions always had their breeding grounds in the shortcomings of society. People everywhere sought relief from a harsh reality through the soporific drugs of religion. Religious leaders built their position of power on pious dreams of a better existence in the name of one or another tendency of faith.[59]

But at the end of 1854, another topic besides the Crimean War captured Marx's attention: Spain. In Western Europe, Spain was almost as exotic as Turkey, he said. He had equipped himself well to make the country less foreign, at least for American readers. He had learned Spanish so well that he not only read fluently, but according to Spanish acquaintances could eventually speak it admirably, although he had problems with pronunciation.

In Spain, a power struggle between the keepers of tradition and the modernizers had been raging for decades. Marx was fascinated by the battles and contrasted Spain's development with that of France. In France, they had made a revolution in three days, and then that was enough. In Spain, they had been holding out for three years, and were prepared for new clashes a decade later. Storm clouds were once again gathering on the horizon.

Marx wrote eleven articles on the topic for the *New York Daily Tribune*. Eight of them were published; two have been lost, and only a few fragments of one have been preserved. Perhaps the editorial staff found there was too much Spanish history. Marx provided a proper history lesson in which the focus was primarily on the years around 1812, when the Spanish liberated themselves from Napoleon's rule and the typical contradiction between reactionaries and modernizers was established. Marx pointed out that the latter were the first in the world to designate themselves liberals, and that the name then spread to other countries. It is an assertion that still holds true.[60]

But Marx also followed developments in more distant countries, above all India and China, from his British outpost. He started there, as he otherwise did, from the conviction that the contemporary period was a stage in a long process of advance. This idea found expression in a few sweeping judgements in his most talked-about – one could say notorious, or at least deeply controversial – article on British rule in India. India had succumbed to many conquerors, he pointed out. But the British were the first to carry the country up to a higher level of development through telegraphs – and soon also railroads and steamer traffic.

This reorganization entailed immense suffering for the people, but was still a necessary step forward. The bourgeois civilization pushing through the changes was certainly shamelessly hypo-critical. The British were seeking new fortunes in far-off lands, although they made a show of being driven by nobler intents.[61]

Marx's attitude towards India and its brutal modernization has long been controversial. Edward Said, the Palestinian-American literary scholar and critic of modern society, saw him as a represen-tative of Western Orientalism. In one India article, Marx quoted Goethe's *West-Eastern Divan*, the great poem on Eastern poetry in its meeting with its Western counterpart; in Said's opinion, he thereby revealed himself to be a Romantic in his view of the East. Said even argued that 'Marx's theoretical socio-economic views become submerged' in the prevalent image of India.

The latter may seem excessive: in Marx the telegraphs, rail-roads, and steamers still have the last word. The quote from Goethe deals with the pleasure that could shoot forth out of the suffering that had consumed 'myriads of young souls'. No doubt it is the victims of civilization he was talking about, regardless of whether they were in Great Britain, India, or China?[62]

It is otherwise telling that it is Goethe, one of his literary favor-ites, that Marx refers to. But he did not study Persian or Arabic, as Goethe did, and despite his first-rate knowledge of classical Greek, he was not tempted, as many others in the Europe of his time were, to learn the most cherished language of the Orientalists: Sanskrit. His frame of reference remained Western; he had deeper knowledge of the path from Homer to Goethe. He approached India more from the outside, though he was roused by the hunger for knowledge that was typical of him.

Said's picture has been questioned by Aijaz Ahmad, an Indian literary scholar and political commentator, who in his article 'Marx on India: A Clarification' emphasized that India in 1853 was an entirely new topic for Marx and that what he said was not characterized by the deep insights that were otherwise character-istic of much of what he wrote (it is worth noting, for example, that Marx repeated Hegel's peculiar statement that India was a country without a history). Ahmad also calls attention to an oft-forgotten sentence in one of Marx's articles in which his views on the blessings of civilization appear more clearly than elsewhere. He said there that the Indians would not themselves enjoy the fruits of everything the British were now scattering about in their country until the working class had seized power in Great Britain, or until the Indians themselves had become strong enough to cast off the British yoke. The subjugated people were thus weighed down under the same yoke as the industrial workers in far-off Great Britain.[63]

This was the conviction that got Marx to entertain certain hopes for the Sepoy uprising that broke out in India in 1857 and continued through 1858. Sepoy was the name given to Indian soldiers serving in the British Army. They were used rather ruthlessly in the procession of British wars and conquests in Asia and had no opportunities to make a career in the army. In addition, they saw their home districts in northern India taxed even more harshly. The spark that set off the rebellion was the rumour that the ammunition they had been issued was greased with beef and pork fat, in the provocative indifference for various Indian taboos that generally distinguished British rule in the country. The rebellion called for major British efforts before it could be put down.

Marx wrote a few articles on the insurrection. His position was obviously a split one. The English conquerors could equip the country with modern technology that was necessary for the real liberation of the people. The Sepoy warriors had succeeded in besieging Delhi, it is true, but they lacked leaders and their dream was of a pre-modern India.

In another article, Marx reproduced what had been reported chiefly in British newspapers about the atrocities that the rebels had committed against Englishmen. Marx agreed that the outrages were appalling, but at the same time pointed out that the British conquerors had maimed, raped, and killed both Indians and Chinese with the same frenzy. The Indians were thus not exotic creatures equipped with a particular Oriental cruelty. The British and other rulers only imagined that their own indifference to the suffering of others was more justified; they were good Christians.[64]

China was also an important topic of Marx's articles. In the first one dealing with the country he took up Hegel, although without mentioning the philosopher's name; he hid it behind the circumlocution 'a most profound yet fantastic speculator on the principles which govern the movements of Humanity'. This philosopher had upheld the thesis on the unity of opposites. Marx found examples of this unity in the relationship between Great Britain and China. In China the 'Taiping Rebellion', inspired by a doctrine that had one of its roots in Christianity, was underway. The rebellion – or revolution, as Marx said – started from below; its spread would have been unthinkable without the farmers' growing discontent.

The name of the movement, incidentally, meant 'complete equality'. There were leaders in it who did not at all live up to the ideal, and spent their days in luxury and affluence. But the goal was to create a more modern China. The British chose to back the other side, that of tradition and empire. The rebellion was put down only in 1864. It is probably the bloodiest war in history, even if the calculations of the number of dead are extremely vague. It is estimated that between 20 and 70 million people lost their lives.

Marx did not go into a description of the background of the rebellion or previous events in his article from 1853, but above all provided an idea of how the world had come to constitute an intimately connected unity in which its antitheses were forced together. In this global perspective, the Taiping Rebellion constituted a step direction of modernity; an anti-feudal striving for freedom was the leading element. Stephen R. Platt, a contemporary historian who wrote a monograph on the great drama in China, agrees with him. When the British supported imperial power, they consciously chose the side of Chinese passivity and foreign dependency. With the help of opium, the people would keep calm. The British could ship their profits home.[65]

Opium addiction is a theme by itself in Marx's journalism. He even wrote a history in article form on the trade in this dangerous drug. As for China, he believed the reason it could be so oppressed by foreigners was that it itself was a fossil. This fossilized society had also called forth its internal enemy, the rebellious masses who under the slogan 'Taiping' – complete equality – went on the attack against their masters and also indirectly against the foreign invaders. Marx in no way idealized the popular violence but connected it with the severe poverty. People lived on looting and were then satisfied with crumbs. For the ordinary Taiping soldier, 'a human head means no more than a head of cabbage'.

Nevertheless, Marx spoke of 'the revolutionary army' and pointed out that its core consisted of regular troops that had developed into experienced partisans. But the great mass of warriors were smallholders and moreover lived rootless existences. Once a city had been conquered, it was carte blanche for the soldiers to rape women and girls for three days.

He concluded: Taiping was obviously the devil personified as the Chinese imagination pictured him. But it was also only in China that this devil was possible. His prerequisite was a petrified social life.

For the first time, it could be said that Marx here portrays a far-off country in exotic colours; unlike in the case of India, he does not relate the violence of the rebellious troops to the corresponding violence of the foreign masters.[66] At the same time, he emphasized in his previous reporting how dependent on China Great Britain had become. Thanks to the uprising, prices on a range of goods would rise in London. That is to say, both countries were entwined with firm global ties.

When Marx wrote about the treaty on mutual trade relations that the British and the Chinese signed in 1858, his article became the subject of a dispute with Charles Dana. Marx vented his wrath in a letter to Engels in December 1858. Dana had printed his earlier articles about China as anonymous editorials without complimenting Marx at all for his efforts. But when this article was published, it was said to be written by an 'occasional correspondent'; moreover, Dana had the audacity to polemicize with it. Marx had established that the Chinese had legalized the import of opium and probably also the cultivation of the dangerous poppy in China through the treaty. Now he was experiencing the triumph of members of the British government drawing the same conclusions he had.

Marx was and remained an enemy of colonialism, particularly British colonialism. His fundamental attitude appeared most clearly in an article he wrote in 1857 about an attempt by the English to win dominion over Persia. His picture of British actions was extremely dark. He spoke with disgust about the cunning and ruthless tricks of British diplomacy in Asia, sparing no colour in depicting the repulsive behaviour of the intruders.[67]

The image of Marx's views on European – particularly British – colonialism changes markedly if one is not satisfied with a single quotation out of context from one of his many articles on India. Marx was no Orientalist in Said's meaning, and he did not believe in what Rudyard Kipling would later call 'the white man's burden' with the task of raising other races up to the heights of civilization. He never wavered in his belief in the positive significance of the railroads, the telegraph, and steam power. But he viewed the situation of the colonized peoples with the same eyes that he viewed the working class of the industrialized countries. They paid for the blessings of civilization with sweat and toil without themselves being allowed to take part in them.

He did not believe that the Taiping or Sepoy rebellions would lead to any real liberation. Something like that presupposed far-reaching industrialization. But this industrialization was not bound to Europe and North America out of necessity. People in far-flung corners of the world were no less suited to it than, for example, the British.

The United States and the World

The American Civil War of 1861–65 also threw a long shadow over Europe. Slavery had gradually come to be regarded as its most decisive issue. The Northern states fought to abolish this inhumane system; the Southern states wanted to keep it.

Long before the war, slavery had led to political controversies of the first order. The idea of equal freedom and rights for everyone obviously conflicted with the system according to which certain people were the owners of other people and could therefore freely use (and abuse) them. In the United States, the Founding Fathers could shut their eyes to this consequence; several of them – with Thomas Jefferson at their head – themselves held slaves. In the French Revolution, the most radical groups gave prominence to the absurdity of slavery; the idea that everyone, regardless of race or even gender, should enjoy the same rights and freedoms including the vote gained a number of zealous advocates. But when former Black slaves in the French colony of Haiti made a revolution, France under Napoleon I responded by attempting to crush the rebellion. He did not succeed; the French were compelled to leave the island and a free republic was proclaimed. In its new constitution, the equality of the races was particularly emphasized.[68]

During the first decade of the nineteenth century, the slave trade was banned in many countries including Great Britain and the United States. The question was whether the states could really guarantee that no trade was occurring. New slaves were constantly being offered for sale on the market. There was a suspicion that, despite the ban, ships under the flag of the United States were transporting people under customarily inhumane conditions over the Atlantic. The question, raised by the Bishop of Oxford, turned up in the British Parliament and Marx reported on it in an 1858 article for the *New York Daily Tribune*. The government dismissed it: searching vessels under the American flag was out of the question since it would lead to open conflict and perhaps war. There was, moreover, the conjecture that the supply of new slaves was being guaranteed by Spanish ships that were also supplying Central and South America with new blood through 'the infamous traffic', as Marx wrote.[69]

When Abraham Lincoln was elected president of the United States in 1860, eleven of the thirty-four American states seceded from the union and formed what they called the Confederacy. The formation of this new state was the immediate cause of the war, which began on 12 April 1861. The Confederacy was fighting for its independence, the Union to restore the country as it had been before the secession; but the issue of slavery had always been important and gradually stood out as the dominant one. The secessionists won a series of military victories in the beginning, but in the long run the Northern states – usually called the Union – would win by force of its superior economic and industrial strength.

Marx's sympathies were always on the side of the North. This was fully apparent in the articles he managed to publish in the *New York Daily Tribune* before the war put obstacles in the path of his further contributions. He reported indignantly on the reactions in the British government – led by Palmerston – and in the British press. Palmerston paid lip service to the abolition of slavery, but in reality the North was causing concerns for him as well as *The Times* and other newspapers. The struggle of the Southern states for the freedom to enslave other people was met with deep understanding, Marx said, while the genuine desire of the Northern states to oppose slavery was questioned. Harriet Beecher Stowe, author of the famous 1852 novel *Uncle Tom's Cabin*, also played an important role in the British debate. In an open letter to the Earl of Shaftesbury, she pointed out slavery as the real cause of the war, thereby compelling many leading British to show their hands.[70]

But officially, Great Britain was neutral in the conflict. Slavery, of course, had no advocates in the government or in Parliament. But in his inauguration speech, Lincoln declared that the states that already allowed slavery would be permitted to keep it during his administration. From that, the British government concluded that the slave issue played no role in the Civil War. Palmerston and his ministers even leaned towards the opinion that the Southern states had the right to leave the Union.

The Southern states saw their chance, in particular as they concluded that British industry was completely dependent on cotton imports from the American South, and in that certainty they sent two negotiators to London – both die-hard advocates of slavery. They travelled on a British vessel, the *Trent*, and from that they believed that they would be able to break the marine embargo that the Northern states had imposed. But the vessel was boarded despite its British flag. The event roused enormous indignation, and Palmerston seemed to be leaning towards the opinion that the boarding was reason enough for the British to go to war with the Northern states.[71]

Marx wrote in detail about the *Trent* affair, just as he also otherwise covered the Civil War. But only one of his articles on the *Trent* affair managed to be published in the *New York Daily Tribune* before his contract came up and he became a contributor to *Die Presse* instead. In his eyes, leading politicians and leading British newspapers were playing a complete double game. Even

if they were opponents of slavery and the slave trade they nevertheless supported the political association of the slave owners.
In Marx's opinion, the Civil War was from the very beginning a
question of Black liberation, and the British who questioned that
were prevaricators who were chiefly guarding their own economic
interests. He related with pride that those primarily affected by
the rapidly decreasing cotton imports, the workers in Lancashire,
never wavered in their support for the United States. In a few
articles in *Die Presse*, he even argued that the *Trent* affair had
developed into a conflict between the English government and the
English people.[72]

Marx's view of the United States was marked to a great degree
by the positive encounter with Charles A. Dana and by his good
experiences of the newspaper that Dana gave him the opportunity to write for. Add to that how a number of his friends and
comrades-in-arms, with Joseph Weydemeyer at their head, carved
out an existence in the new country and it is understandable that
his image of America was rather bright. There were opportunities
not only for technological and economic development, but for a
more just society as well.

His image of Europe after the revolutions was significantly
darker. Great Britain inspired a certain hope, but the class struggle there was also more bare and raw than anywhere else. France
under Napoleon III was the object of his particular loathing.
Not much new in relation to *The Eighteenth Brumaire of Louis
Bonaparte* emerged in the many articles where he touched upon
French development under the new emperor.

He followed the war between France and Austria in 1859 with
a perspective of antipathy. Both regimes were odious to him but
he still seems to have endured the reactions in Vienna more easily.
The French cause might have seemed good – it was Italy's freedom
from the Habsburg Empire that was at stake. But the false popu-
larity of the French emperor was so repugnant in Marx's eyes that
he was unable to express any joy over French successes. In addition, the maxim that no one can fundamentally liberate anyone
else applied. The freedom of Italy must be the Italians' own affair.

From the very beginning, Marx casts suspicion on Napoleon's

reasons to go to war. The emperor had been the object of an assassination attempt perpetrated by Italians; in Marx's opinion, he should have perceived that as a warning. In his adventurous life before his promotion, he had been a member of a secret Italian organization with the unification of the country as its goal. The assassination attempt was a signal: be faithful to the promises you made in the society, or we will kill you!

It was a long time, however, before the struggles broke out. Most still hoped for peace, but Marx insisted defiantly: there would be war.[73]

And there was war. The Austrians' setbacks triggered ominous moods in Vienna. A scapegoat was needed and the Jewish minority was selected, as they often were. Jews were being assaulted in the streets, Marx said. The war ended quickly, and Austria was compelled to hand over parts of its former Italian territory. But, Marx wondered, had Italy actually won anything? The Habsburgs kept their western border and therefore still had the key to northern Italy.[74]

In the eyes of many, Napoleon III now stood at the height of his career. France had staked more during the Crimean War than Great Britain, and had won the decisive battle. Now the powerful Habsburg double monarchy had also been beaten. Who would be the next victim? Was it possibly Great Britain's turn? Rumours buzzed in London. Or was it Prussia, rapidly becoming ever stronger?

Marx reproduced the rumours of war with great seriousness. He was still just as negatively disposed towards the battle-happy emperor. He reproduced with enthusiasm Giuseppe Mazzini's rhetorically brilliant reckoning with Napoleon. Mazzini, the creator of *La Giovine Italia*, was otherwise not a man Marx regarded highly. But this text, in Marx's opinion, lacked almost entirely 'that false sublimity, puffy grandeur, verbosity, and prophetic mysticism' that otherwise marred his writings. Here the author spoke directly to the point, and he succeeded in completely reviewing what a humbug the French emperor was.

Marx's own loathing was no less than Mazzini's. But why was he so furious? One main reason, of course, is that Napoleon was the one who put a stop to the French Revolution that Marx attached such great hopes to. But the fact that in the presidential election that brought him to power, the emperor became a man of the people – especially the farmers – also played a role. He claimed to be able to solve the problems of modern poverty, or pauperism. Back in the 1840s, the decade of the utopias, he asserted in his pamphlet *Extinction du paupérisme* (The Extinction of Pauperism) that he possessed the answer to the question of how pauperism could be remedied. He even considered himself a kind of socialist; Marx's contempt for his alleged ideology was at least as vivid as his contempt for Karl Grün's or Arnold Ruge's.[75]

Europe of the 1850s did, however, offer certain bright spots. While France was being oppressed by its usurper, Prussia had got rid of the king whose intolerant regime put a stop to Marx's career both as an academic and as an editor-in-chief: Friedrich Wilhelm IV. In several articles, Marx reported on the rumours that the king had been seized by delusions; among other things, he believed he was a fish ready for the frying pan. The official historiography speaks of a stroke; however the matter stood, Friedrich Wilhelm handed over power to his brother Wilhelm, the future Wilhelm I, in the late 1850s. Marx followed carefully what was now happening, and could tell his American audience that the mood had changed fantastically in only two months. The tyranny of Friedrich Wilhelm IV was gone; his brother, with a much softer hand, remained. And freedom was expanding! Marx swore that Berlin was now the most revolutionary city in Europe alongside Palermo and Vienna. He was thinking, of course, of Garibaldi's rebellion in southern Italy and of the seething discontent in the capital of the Habsburg Empire after the defeat against France. In Berlin, the feeling of relief after their former oppression had given people the courage to imagine a completely different society.[76]

The situation gradually calmed down in Vienna and Berlin, and the new Italian state of 1871 was the result of an entirely different development than what Garibaldi (and perhaps even Marx) had imagined: a cautious regime that placed the king atop its hierarchy.

But the gaze of Marx the journalist swept restlessly over Europe, registering sometimes hopeful, sometimes discouraging signs. Even the undeveloped Nordic countries sometimes captured his attention. In an 1857 article, he called attention to the Swedish Crown

Prince – the future Carl XV – and his 'resolute and energetic character'. He could very well create a Scandinavian union, thereby preparing the ground for a new conflict over Schleswig-Holstein.

The reason for these lofty thoughts about the Swedish Crown Prince are partially obscure. During the Crimean War, the Crown Prince had worked for Sweden to enter in on the side of France and Great Britain against Russia, but his plans did not gain a hearing. His dreams of a new Greater Sweden were not realistic; he soon also calmed down and was satisfied with more immediate causes for rejoicing such as women, parties, and hunting trips.[77]

Marx devoted a certain degree of interest in Sweden and House Bernadotte in another context as well. In *The New American Cyclopaedia*, which Charles A. Dana and his newspaper colleague George Ripley published, Marx contributed a few articles and Engels even more. It fell to Marx to write about Jean-Baptiste Bernadotte and the strange career that brought him to Sweden. Engels had already informed him in a letter about Bernadotte's military achievements, and especially emphasized the earlier indications of independence in relation to Napoleon.

In his article, Marx also gives an account of all the strange turns around the Swedes' choice of Bernadotte for king, and their hopes that the French marshal would reconquer Finland from the Russians. They were astonished to discover that he would rather choose a union with Norway and conclude a peace treaty with the Russians. But the Norwegians proved to be more independent than he thought, and despite his resistance created Europe's most democratic constitution. Stockholm was actually too small for Karl Johan, and after the July Revolution of 1830 he hoped to be offered the French royal crown. But nothing came of it and he had to stay in the Nordic countries.

Marx summed up: Sweden had nothing to thank Karl Johan for. If the nation had recovered from earlier misery and misfortune, it was only due to their own energy and a long period of peace.[78]

Marx would devote particular attention to the issue of Ireland's independence. In their letters, he and Engels could throw out sneering assessments about the Irish (as they did about many other people). But when it came down to it, Marx and his friends unswervingly supported the demand for Irish independence from

England. Full of hope, they also followed the Irish workers' struggle for freedom and human dignity. In one article, Marx could
rejoice at the fact that Irish influence in the British Parliament was
great and a thorn in the side of both aristocrats and Manchester
liberals; in another he could depict with warmth the funeral of
an Irish worker and Chartist leader active in London, Feargus
Edward O'Connor.[79]

Nonetheless, the Irish issues were overshadowed by much else
in Marx's journalism. He had the entire world as his newsbeat;
the wars and acute crises were always the focus of his attention.
After 1864, Marx's newspaper-writing rapidly became more and
more sporadic, confined mainly to brief petitions and protests,
often in the name of the International.

Over three periods, Marx would devote a large and crucial portion
of his time to writing articles in newspapers and journals. Both of
the initial periods took place in the 1840s, when he first managed
Rheinische Zeitung and later the *Neue Rheinische Zeitung*. The
last period extended from 1851 to 1864. Marx no longer wrote
as editor-in-chief but as a correspondent. On the other hand, his
articles circulated over two continents; most of what he submitted
was also published.

It is easy to see the many articles of the third period as bread-
and-butter writing, and they have often been treated as such in
the literature. But this is ill-advised indifference. In a different
way than the letters – and the highly private letters to Engels in
particular – the articles are carefully prepared and intended to
influence a larger readership. Studied carefully, they also turn out
to form a necessary background to Marx's printed or incomplete
larger works from the period after the revolutions of 1848–49.
A number of patterns that would otherwise remain obscure, for
example Marx's views on imperialism, emerge in full clarity.[80]

With a solid background in the articles, it is easier to go further
on to Marx's great social theoretical project, which would gradually be given the name *Capital*. This is exactly what we shall now
do. But first we shall review the great preparatory work that goes
by the name *Grundrisse*.

10

The Most Intensive Effort

The *Grundrisse*

Ever since the *Grundrisse* became generally known among readers of Marx in the 1950s, the text has been the subject of contradictory interpretations and assessments. It was written in the late 1850s, first in a kind of euphoria of revolutionary expectations, and as time went on, under increasing discouragement and sickness.

Thematically, the *Grundrisse* is broader than anything else Marx left behind. He opens with both a distant past and an imagined future. Complex philosophical concepts share space with pure arithmetical exercises. In a sense, the text is a bridge between the *Economic and Philosophic Manuscripts* of the 1840s and Volume I of *Capital* from the 1860s.

Arguments about the place of the *Grundrisse* in Marx's works diverge widely. Those who wish to fish out a fixed and clearly outlined theory, either in the name of orthodoxy or for present-day scientific development, tend to underestimate the *Grundrisse*. Those who would rather seek inspiration for a free, radical illumination of capitalist society up through the early twenty-first century often tie together the loose threads in the *Grundrisse*.

A New Joy and a Sick Liver

On 8 December 1857 Jenny wrote a letter to their close friend
Conrad Schramm. In it, she touches upon the current economic
crisis, noting with satisfaction that 'the rotten old structure is
crashing and tumbling down'. A similar precariousness was also
noticeable in the Marx family's own finances. Karl could not
write more than one article a week, against two previously, for the
New York Daily Tribune. But Karl was nevertheless in the best of
moods. 'He has recovered all his wonted facility and capacity for
work, as well as his liveliness and buoyancy of a spirit long since
blighted by great sorrow, the loss of our beloved child'.[1]

That same day, Karl informed his friend Engels: 'I am working
like mad all night and every night collating my economic studies
so that I at least get the outlines *(Grundrisse)* clear before the
déluge'. In a letter to Ferdinand Lassalle a few weeks later, he used
the word *Grundzüge* in German (which also translates to 'outlines' in English), and somewhat later he wrote to Engels about
his 'principles'. But the content was the same; he was finally going
to present the essentials of his great social theory.

Over the months that followed, the tone in his letters became less
and less triumphant. He wrote to Lassalle at the end of February
that it was a great deal of drudgery to summarize many years'
study, particularly if one was not master over one's own time.
Only his nights were free, and then he suffered from constant
recurrences of liver disease.

Marx's liver was a recurring theme in his letters. It is certainly
impossible to establish what his suffering was actually due to,
based only on scattered statements in letters. In Marx's time, pains
in the abdominal region were almost automatically blamed on the
liver. Perhaps the cause of his poor health was significantly more
trivial. The enormous tension and the unreasonable working
hours scarcely aided his health.[2]

He was, in short, not feeling well, and the mass of text his night
work resulted in became too much for him. One theme quickly
led to another, which in turn opened the way to a further problem
that immediately demanded a solution. In the same breath as he
asked the big questions about the dynamic of society, he grappled

with a number of calculations in which certain connections would be evident with mathematical exactness.

He grasped at everything, sensing that he risked losing the thread. In a way, it came to pass. He would never be finished with the *Grundrisse*. He regarded the endlessly growing pile of notebooks with increasing dissatisfaction. He could not even find his way in his own notes, he complained to Engels at the end of May 1858. 'The damnable part of it is that my manuscript (which in print would amount to a hefty volume) is a real hotchpotch, much of it intended for much later sections.'

Ultimately, he was seized by aversion to what he had written. In November 1858, he wrote to Lassalle that the task was exceptionally important – 'an important view of social relations is scientifically expounded for the first time'. The content was ready, but not the form. And the results so far had been ruined by a style marked by a sick liver.

By that time, Marx had already decided to narrow down his project. He was occupied with an initial instalment of a planned series in which the form would be as austere as it had been undisciplined in the *Grundrisse*. The result was his 1859 work, *A Contribution to the Critique of Political Economy*. There, most of what was allowed to take up space in the larger manuscript was kept out. The instalment was at least the beginning of what eight years later would become the first volume of *Capital*.

Independent Work or Preparatory?

It would be a long time before Marx's great manuscript – which went not only by the name *Grundrisse* but sometimes was also called *Rohentwurf* (rough draft) – became known to the world. Not even Engels had paid it any regard; it was chiefly the still incomplete portions of *Capital* that he devoted himself to trying to get ready for print after Marx had died. Karl Kautsky – who wanted very much to finish Engels's work – had the introduction that belonged to the *Grundrisse* project printed only in 1903, in the German Social Democratic theoretical journal *Die Neue Zeit*. The editing was not particularly careful, but the text roused great interest among those who wanted to delve deeper into Marx's thinking. The Austrian Max Adler, the foremost theoretician of what was called 'Austro-Marxism', attached great importance to the introduction, as did the Hungarian philosopher Georg Lukács in his epoch-making 1923 work, *History and Class Consciousness*.[3] It continued like this throughout the twentieth century up to today. A more reliable edition of the entire manuscript was published between 1939 and 1941. But, in the shadow of the war, it was little read. Only the new edition of 1953, with the title *Grundrisse der Kritik der politischen Ökonomie* (Outline of a Critique of Political Economy), published in Berlin and soon also in Frankfurt and Vienna, attracted greater attention, becoming part of the renaissance of the 'young Marx' – the Marx of the *Manuscripts* – that played a big role in the oppositional Marxism aimed at party orthodoxy and oppression within the Soviet Empire. Marx spoke about alienation in the *Grundrisse* as well. Moreover, he opened up broader prospects than in the more focused *Capital*.[4]

Antonio Negri, the Italian philosopher and activist, published the book *Marx oltre Marx* (Marx Beyond Marx) in 1979; in it, he maintained that the *Grundrisse* was marked by the fact that it had come into existence in a revolutionary situation. Marx wrote it at the same time as he was following the current crisis, step by step, with endless excitement. Theory and practice came closer to each other there than in any other of Marx's works, Negri argued. The *Grundrisse* was thus not primarily a stage on the road towards *Capital*, but rather a deed in words.[5]

A particular *Grundrisse* line, in which the openness and freedom in the great work tempts readers to audacious present-day applications, can perhaps be distinguished in the modern reception of Marx. In the 2000s, Negri and the American Michael Hardt published a trilogy that attracted a great deal of attention – a bold attempt at finding the keys to unlocking the present: *Empire*, *Multitude* and *Commonwealth*, with a concluding *Declaration*. Despite all his differences, the Slovenian intellectual Slavoj Žižek also belongs to the same tendency. It is the open spirit of the *Grundrisse*, rather than the strict logic of *Capital*, that characterizes his work, as it does Hardt's and Negri's.

The American literary scholar Fredric Jameson is also among those who handle Marx rather freely. Incidentally, one of his students, Thomas M. Kemple, wrote an original book in which the *Grundrisse* is treated rather as a work of fiction – the work of an innovative author.[6]

But the *Grundrisse* is naturally also a preparatory work for *Capital*. The first person to investigate – and with great accuracy – how Marx's project of social criticism developed through his work on the *Grundrisse* was Roman Rosdolsky, a Ukrainian historian and economist, who collected his results in his major 1955 work, *Zur Entstehungsgeschichte des Marxschen* Kapital (The Making of Marx's *Capital*). In it, he showed how in a number of drafts Marx played with the idea of what the intended work would contain, and how much of it was later realized in the three volumes of *Capital*.

There are two main questions that can then be asked, as well as about other later investigations of the same type. Both: What is there in the *Grundrisse* that is not found in *Capital*? And: How far did Marx manage to get in the *Grundrisse* with the work that gradually resulted in *Capital*? Which central concepts had already been worked out by the late 1850s, what exists in more rudimentary form, and what is missing entirely?[7]

The first question is the starting point not only for Negri's, Hardt's, and Žižek's free application of Marxist perspectives to the problems of the age we live in. It has also driven more modest investigators of the incomplete manuscript. The *Grundrisse* is a work that has often been commented upon, even if it is in the shadow of *Capital*.

It was the second type of question that dominated Soviet and East German Marx research, as it did interpretations on the topic that were more directly loyal to the Party. The critical edition of the *Grundrisse* in the *Marx-Engels-Gesamtausgabe* was introduced with a long preface in which the crucial question was how far along the path to *Capital* Marx had travelled during 1857 and 1858. It was then that he realized the nature of labour in capitalism, and it was then that he recognized that the *commodity* is the crucial point in the economy itself, it is said.

Quite simply, a teleological process is depicted in which the goal was the definitive theory Marx developed in *Capital*. The process had begun with Marx's and Engels's earliest writings on the economy from the 1840s, and only reached its goal with Engels's final edit of the third volume of *Capital*. It did not stop there, in fact; it continued with Lenin all the way forward in the history of the Soviet Union and actually existing socialism. This continuation, however, is not clearly delineated in the *Marx-Engels-Gesamtausgabe*, whereas its outlines are that much sharper in the *Marx-Engels-Werke* from a few decades earlier. There, the introductions are signed by the Communist Party of the Soviet Union, which carefully impressed Lenin's interpretation on the reader. It is like reading classic Lutheran theology: the words of the Bible take on the interpretation that the great reformer gave them.[8]

Even in such an undogmatic account as Michael Heinrich's *Die Wissenschaft vom Wert*, the *Grundrisse* stands out primarily as a stage on the road to *Capital*. But here it is no longer a question of teleological development. On the contrary, Heinrich emphasizes that it is not at all certain that the changes in Marx's development always entailed improvements. This does not prevent him from seeing in the *Grundrisse* primarily a preliminary work for *Capital*. But he also calls attention to convictions in the *Grundrisse* that disappear in *Capital*. It is chiefly a matter of the idea that capitalism must collapse during a sufficiently deep crisis. In Heinrich's opinion, this fades away in Marx's world of ideas after the crisis of 1857–58.[9]

Seeing the differences and similarities between Marx's great, incomplete work and the text that became the first volume of *Capital* is obviously important. This will also be a theme in the next chapter. But the main emphasis here lies on what is unique to the *Grundrisse* – in brief, what makes it a work that, in all its incompleteness, still stands out as so attractive and inspiring. This applies especially to the oddly incomplete introduction. Through it, one comes inevitably into the strongly Hegel-inspired vocabulary that also marks a number of other parts of the *Grundrisse*. Only a few echoes remain in *Capital*. In the *Grundrisse*, the distance to the *Manuscripts* occasionally seems less than that to *Capital*. The theme of alienation turns up again – in fact, in one place Marx even uses the word *Gattungswesen* (species-being), which otherwise belongs to the period before the *Theses on Feuerbach* and *The German Ideology* and therefore before the great reckoning with the ideas about the essence of humanity.[10]

In stark contrast to these philosophical excursions stands the ambition of working out an exact theory in the most natural scientific sense possible. It turns up several times in the *Grundrisse* and points unambiguously forward, towards *Capital*. Two philosophical ideals therefore stand side by side in the *Grundrisse*: one with roots in the philosophy of Hegel, the other where the exact theories of the age, primarily in physics and chemistry, serve as models. The contradiction is not surprising, considering Marx's intellectual background. What is noteworthy – the thing that requires explanation – is rather how Marx looks back to Hegel during the economic crisis and how he then once again loosens his ties to his old teacher once the crisis has ebbed. This was the same time that he abandoned his magnificent, nearly limitless project. He sets himself a new, significantly more limited task: to write *A Contribution to the Critique of Political Economy* (hereafter *A Contribution*), which we have already encountered. The road from the *Grundrisse* to *A Contribution* is usually described in the literature as a brief and almost natural step towards *Capital* – in fact, just another step. But surely the transition from one project to another is significantly more dramatic? Marx must have fought with himself and decided to feel his way towards a more lucid method of presentation. Now it was to be a series of instalments instead.

The step from the *Grundrisse* to *A Contribution* will be a central theme in this chapter. The comparison between the remarkable introduction to the *Grundrisse* and the influential preface in *A Contribution* will also be important. But the large manuscript also contains other things requiring attention. The dominant chapter in the *Grundrisse*, which deals with capital, never had a counterpart in *A Contribution*. But the chapter deserves its own treatment, especially because it contains themes that are never developed in Marx's later production. A section on what Marx called the Asiatic mode of production has aroused both interest and lively disputes over the last sixty years. In another section, Marx wrestled with the question of how labour can be shaped in a more advanced society than capitalism. Both these themes will conclude this chapter.

A Flow Teeming with Ideas

The *Grundrisse* bears traces of the furious working pace Marx kept during the work. The outline suffers from haste. The presentation is often interrupted by statements saying this or that theme does not belong in this context, or that it must be developed further on. The order bears witness to how quickly and promptly the notes were made, but also to the enormous flow of ideas and knowledge that characterize them. Despite illness, poverty, and the bread-and-butter writing, the period from the summer of 1857 to March 1858 was a time of unremitting innovation. The style may be heavy and clumsy – an immense ordeal for a translator – but this often halting, awkward language supports an enormous load of ideas, and not infrequently the dark forest of words is illuminated by some beautiful aphorism.

The text now reproduced in complete editions – such as in the *Marx-Engels-Gesamtausgabe* and the *Collected Works* – consists of three different parts. First is a brief commentary on two economic theoreticians in the generation after Ricardo: the Frenchman Frédéric Bastiat and the American Henry Charles Carey. The text was written back in July 1857 and its lasting contribution is the term 'vulgar economist'. Carey and Bastiat differed from Smith and Ricardo in that they did not depict capitalist society as riven by conflicts, but on the contrary as a harmonious arena. In Marx's opinion, they thereby avoid any deeper analysis of society and are satisfied with a glossy façade. Marx did not mention the Manchester liberals in the text, but they are kindred spirits who argued that the factory-owning middle class could represent the working class in the conflict-free society of free trade.

An introduction, which in its incomplete form encompasses some twenty pages, also falls outside the text Marx himself named *Grundrisse*. But this introduction, which was written at a breakneck pace at the end of August 1857, sets the tone for much of what follows in the larger manuscript – or, more correctly, the seven notebooks Marx filled with his scrawls – and is naturally always printed together with it.[11]

What follows the introduction is difficult to grasp, it is true, but it still has a basic structure that can be found in a more cultivated form in both *A Contribution* and *Capital*. First is a chapter on money, and then another on capital. They are numbered II and III. The introduction was probably intended as an initial part.

The order within the chapter has the freedom of spontaneity. The chapter on money starts with detailed excerpts from a book on banks by Alfred Darimon, a disciple of Proudhon, and the manuscript concludes with a number of supplements to both chapters. Many digressions occur between them as well, often extremely fascinating but hardly easy to incorporate into the totality for which Marx had been striving.

The 'Introduction' is worth particular attention. It is not only the part of the work that has had the greatest influence on posterity. It is also the closest Marx came to a presentation of his basic method. A few months after he had written the draft for the introduction, in January 1858, he wrote to Engels that he had 'by mere accident' got Hegel's *Logic* in hand. His friend Ferdinand Freiligrath had given it and other works of Hegel's to him as a gift. The books had originally belonged to Bakunin.

There are several volumes of Hegel in the library that Marx left, including the 1841 edition of *The Science of Logic*. It was a work that had been under discussion much earlier in Marx's writings, particularly in the *Manuscripts* but also in *The Poverty of Philosophy*. The copy he had access to around the New Year in 1858, he had probably got two years earlier. It was only in connection with his work on the *Grundrisse* that its contents were brought to the fore for him, when he 'had taken another look' at the book.

In his letter to Engels, Marx wrote: 'If ever the time comes when such work is again possible, I should very much like to write 2 or 3 sheets making accessible to the common reader the *rational* aspect of the method which Hegel not only discovered but also mystified.' Oddly enough, the same idea returned ten years later, in 1868, when he wrote to the German tannery worker and self-taught philosopher Joseph Dietzgen that he intended to write on the dialectic as soon as he had 'cast off the burden of political economy'. The 'true laws of the dialectic' were already in Hegel, and it was only a matter of liberating them from their 'mystical form'.[12]

It is of course impossible to judge how this text, which turned up in his thoughts after such a long interval, could have related to the introduction he had already written in the summer of 1857. There, as in an important part of the *Grundrisse* itself, Hegel is certainly present without being in focus.

Marx never got the time to clarify his relation to the philosophy of Hegel he had developed during the 1850s and 1860s. By and large, we have to be satisfied with the *Grundrisse* and a few sporadic statements in *Capital*. But seen more closely, it is quite a lot.

The 'Introduction' is, from beginning to end, an attempt to explain the difference between the results the classical political economists arrived at and Marx's own. The central section deals with the method of political economy. But Marx also drifts onto Hegel and the Hegelians, despite there being no economists among them who he takes a position on. But Marx had to delimit and determine his method in relation to their philosophical one as well.

In the beginning, he stresses that he is talking only about material production. With that, he comments on the determinations of the materialist conception of history that he and Engels made back in *The German Ideology*. There is a similarity in the wording itself, and this is probably not by accident; when writing the preface to *A Contribution* a few years later, he had the yellowing, decomposing manuscript fresh in his mind, perhaps even in front of him.[13]

In *The German Ideology*, the authors claim to start from real conditions – to be precise, 'definite individuals who are productively active in a definite way enter into these definite social and political relations'. In the *Grundrisse*, Marx writes: 'Individuals producing in a society – hence the socially determined production by individuals is of course the point of departure.'[14]

The essential difference between the statements is that *The German Ideology* was meant as a reckoning with the idealism of the Left Hegelians. The *Grundrisse* turned against the individualism, or atomism, of the liberal economists. The mistake of the Young Hegelians, in Marx's opinion, was that they started from what people imagined about themselves and not from the actual conditions they were living under. The criticism of the liberal economists did not apply to their idealism. It was not their conception of the world that was being attacked, but their economic theory.

The economists started from material circumstances and not, like the idealist philosophers, from ideas. Their mistake lay in the starting point itself. They assumed that the isolated individual – Robinson Crusoe on his island – provided the picture that is easiest to grasp of economic conditions in any society. This recluse, both producer and consumer, obeys the same economic laws as any community, from a tiny village to all of Great Britain.

Marx sees a manifestation of bourgeois individualism in this idea. He admits that the individual in bourgeois society certainly appears as an independent unit, and that the social forms only seem to be the means for the private strivings of the individual. But it is only within a fixed, advanced type of society that the individual can appear as independent. The bourgeois view of history is thus baseless. But why? What is it in the bourgeois economists' approach that leads to absurd results?

For Marx, the answer lies in their way of using scientific abstractions. Abstraction is necessary for every type of scientific work. Certain essential features or phenomena must be sifted out from the extravagance of particulars in empirical material. The incidental must be overcome and the features in common – the connecting, the decisive – must be found. But even these do not show how the various abstractions relate to each other or to the concrete material.

The economists assumed that certain abstractions were always valid – and valid at every level. That is why they were able to move from one type of society to all types, and from society in general to the private individual. But, if certain abstractions were always valid, it had to be possible to isolate the various abstractions from one another and treat them as independent agents running through history, applying to all individual people and groups and to all of society. Conversely, if the relationship among

abstractions shifts from epoch to epoch, or if they generally can be
separated only partially from one another, it will not be possible
to draw lines forward or backward in history with their help.

Economic theoreticians have sought to get rid of this man-
oeuvre in various ways. The great weakness lies in distinguishing
material *production* from *distribution* of the results of production
among various social classes. Ricardo chose to see production
as a given, outside of the actual realm of the economy. The great
issue for that economic theory is then the shifting distribution
among the social classes. Ricardo counted three classes throughout history, precisely those who predominated during the time in
which he lived: landowners, capitalists, and workers. John Stuart
Mill developed a similar line of thought. Production developed
with the necessity of a law of nature, and was thereby not subject
to human will and human calculations. Nature provided the
frameworks within which humanity could move. Distribution, on
the other hand, could be influenced. Production determines the
size of the cake, but people can share the cake among themselves
in various ways.

Mills's determination of the relationship between production
and distribution forms the starting point for Marx's criticism. In
the context, it would have been worthwhile if he had gone into
Mills's 1843 work *System of Logic*, in which he developed his
views on the scientific method and the formation of theory. The
connection with his economic theories is a strong one. But Marx
took no closer notice of this British empiricist philosopher. He
was setting the concrete emanation of this philosophy against his
own scientific theory.

For Marx, Mills's thesis on production was a way of promot-
ing the capitalist method of production to eternal validity. It had
always existed, only in more or less primitive forms, and it would
always exist in increasingly advanced form. On a strictly theoretical economic level, Marx differs from Ricardo and Mill through
his conception that production, just as much as distribution, is
subject to sweeping historical changes. Marx further asserted that
in fact it was production that was crucial for these changes.

But the differences could not be reduced to differences in result;
there were also differences in scientific approach. For Ricardo and

Mill, isolating production and distribution from each other was an obvious condition. In Marx's opinion, production and distribution were mutually dependent variables.

To demonstrate the advantages of his approach, Marx conducts a longer conceptual drill with the main economic categories of production, distribution, exchange, and consumption. Exchange – itself the direct relation between seller and buyer, plays a rather passive role in the argument. Distribution, or allocation, of products among various social classes is that much more central. The crucial thing for Marx is that these categories are constantly interwoven into each other. They can be made independent only temporarily and in the abstract. Even purely logically, they are already bound up: production, for example, is also always consumption (of raw materials), consumption is also always production (of one's own body). In these aspects, there is an immediate identity – as Marx says – between them. But there is also a mediated identity, an indirect relationship between them. Production determines consumption: only what is produced can be consumed. But consumption also determines production – what is not consumed will not be produced, either, in the long run.

Between production and consumption lie distribution and exchange. For that reason, the attempt to isolate distribution already seems futile. Marx also showed how the economists who tested this isolation were compelled to make a number of double determinations, for example of capital, which had to be put in relation both to production and to distribution.

The structure of distribution is in fact determined by the structure of production, Marx said. But this does not mean that distribution is entirely dependent on production. It can be observed, for example, that a form of distribution can historically precede the corresponding form of production (as trade capitalism preceded industrial capitalism). Moreover, distribution is not simply distribution of products; it thus does not begin only where production ends. There is also a distribution of the tools of production, as there is a distribution of members of society among the various kinds of production.

Against the classical liberal political economists, Marx maintained that economic categories could not even conceptually or heuristically be kept apart. Every mode of production constitutes a unique combination of the various categories. The classical political economists were able to assume that capitalism was an eternal form of production because they isolated production from the other basic economic categories. They had thereby been unable to see what was new and unique in various modes of production.[15] But how would the crucial difference between Ricardo's and Mills's approach on the one hand, and Marx's on the other, now be determined?

The Czech philosopher Jindřich Zelený made a respectable attempt back in the 1960s in his book *The Logic of Marx* (which was translated to English in 1980). In it, he sets Ricardo against Marx and draws a number of interesting conclusions from the comparison. Ricardo's analysis of capitalism, in Zelený's opinion, is distinguished by the fact that it differentiates between empirical phenomena and the essence lying behind them, and that this essence is perceived as unchanging. This essence can thereby not undergo any qualitative changes, nor can qualitatively distinct economies (that is, economies with different 'essences') turn up in history. In accordance with this viewpoint, the questions Ricardo could take up strictly are quantitative.

Whereas Ricardo started from 'the fixed essence' – that is, from an abstraction that was to apply to all economic conditions, Marx's starting point was also certainly an abstraction – but as an abstraction perceived as a 'cell', that is the smallest changeable unit in a changing organism. The commodity is this unit he starts from, in the theory developed after the *Grundrisse* and above all in *Capital*. In Zelený's opinion, the commodity could thus be perceived as the cell of the capitalist mode of production.[16]

Zelený's interpretation has fine details, but his attempt to determine how Marx, broadly speaking, differs from Ricardo seems unsuccessful. The image of the cell is not apposite. No biologist in Marx's time tried to determine a species of animal or plant by starting from individual cells. Marx himself could sometimes talk about cells in a biological sense, but he did not construct his argument about basic economic categories on that comparison.

More essential than the analogy itself between commodity and cell is the perspective into which Zelený puts Marx's method.

Zelený emphasizes that Ricardo's idea of the fixed essence belongs in a mechanistic world of ideas. Marx, on the other hand, was working in a more biologically marked tradition – to be precise, in the tradition that sees human, societal, and historical conditions in analogy with biological ones. It is a tradition first of all drawn from Hegel, and from the Romantic natural philosophers with Schelling at their head. In it the organic, the complex, and the changeable in all human processes and events are set off against the attempt to apply the basic principles of Newton's theory in all areas.

Let us examine concretely the significance of the organic model for Marx. First, it can be noted that the immediate biological inspiration in the *Grundrisse* is minimal. Only once does it appear explicitly, when Marx says that pre-capitalist economic systems could only be understood by taking a starting point in the more complex capitalist system, and draws a parallel with comparative anatomy: 'The anatomy of man is a key to the anatomy of the ape.' In the literature on Marx, this statement has given rise to a number of learned commentaries. In reality, it testifies to the fact that Marx was still Romantically inspired in his view of comparative anatomy. For a natural philosopher such as the German Lorenz Oken, it was obvious that humanity in its essence summed up the entire biological hierarchy and that this hierarchy could be understood based on its perfection: the human being. Similar ideas occur in Hegel, who called Spirit the truth of all nature. It was also Romantic natural philosophy that guided empirical research in comparative anatomy for several decades. This inspiration only came to an end when Darwin's theories began to become generally accepted.[17]

It is obvious that this Romantic inspiration had very little to do with the line of reasoning Marx followed in the *Grundrisse*. The idealistic world of conceptions hidden in the anatomical research of the Romantics was no source of inspiration for Marx and his comparisons between more advanced and less advanced systems. The analogy he made is a superficial one.

In *Capital*, the parallels between the natural scientific and social scientific research play a relatively more prominent role; Marx's field of interest had also changed to some extent. But in general, there is no particularly strong emphasis on the organic. As regards Marx's views on biology, the major difference between the *Grundrisse* and *Capital* is that Darwin's *Origin of Species* had been published in 1859. His views on everything living, and in particular their development, had thereby thoroughly changed. But this is a story for later. Let us continue to dwell on the introduction to the *Grundrisse*.

Without a doubt, we can establish that if Marx's ideas of the complex unity derived any real support from the organism model, it was not through biology but through idealistic philosophy. Or, to be precise: if Marx claimed, against the mechanistically inspired conceptions of Ricardo, Mills, and others about the relationship between various economic categories, that there was an organic connection between these categories, we must seek his inspiration not in the development of biological theory but in philosophical speculations about the organic and the inorganic.

Once Marx had marked off his conception against those of Mills and Ricardo, he was eager to also quickly mark it off from Hegel's. After the commentary on the intricate relationship between production and consumption, he added that 'nothing is simpler for a Hegelian than to posit production and consumption as identical'.[18] Further on in the text, he clarifies his own conception on the relationship between the various economic categories – production, distribution, exchange and consumption – thus: they are not 'identical, but that they are all elements of a totality, differences within a unity'.[19]

He holds the concept of totality in common with Hegel against the empirically-minded political economists. But it is the concept of identity that he turns against Hegel. We will soon see what this means. It is clear that his conception of the totality strikes a discordant note with the idea of the organism developed in idealistic philosophy. There, each part is subordinate to the totality; each part serves the purpose of the totality. In this world of ideas, the organism constitutes a single – though constantly changing – harmonious unity. But Hegel's concept of the totality, which consists of much more than the organic even in this wide sense, is also built on a more complex (and complicated) concept of identity than is suggested by the idea that the parts are harmoniously arranged in – or, rather, fused into – the totality. Marx's polemic must be placed in this broader context.

Hegel started from the idea that everything is subject to change, and thereby that everything is part of a restless process of development. In such a process, the totality is formed by parts that are opposed to each other, but these totalities are temporary and are burst asunder, to be superseded by new, more complex totalities. Marx's conception of the growth, establishment, and dissolution of the various relations of production seems to be a very particular application of this idea of development. But Marx was not of the same opinion as Hegel: Hegel had perceived the relationship between the parts in the totality incorrectly and in a speculative fashion, he said.[20]

In his work, Hegel tried to find a simple and uncomplicated starting point that constitutes the beginning of the endless, increasingly complex processes of development. In *The Phenomenology of Spirit* from 1807, in which he followed the path of knowledge, he started from the sensuously immediate; on the other hand, in *The Science of Logic* – published between 1812 and 1816 – he started from the completely indeterminate Being. But no matter what starting point is chosen, something else is always left out. Whatever *Etwas* ('Something') is taken as the subject of the investigation, *ein Anderes* ('an Other') is always ignored. But then this Other becomes a problem, and above all the relationship between the one (the Something) and the Other becomes in principle an insoluble difficulty. Both phenomena must therefore be incorporated into the same totality. But this totality further excludes other phenomena, which in turn must be included. There is still a contradiction between the parts included in the first unity: they do not cease to be a 'Something' and an 'Other' in their union.

This is a description of a theoretical process, a process of knowledge; but Hegel had a fundamentally idealist conception of the universe and asserted that every real development had the same course of events. The path of knowledge is also that of reality. For now, Marx's criticism of Hegel does not apply to his idealism but to the relationship between the parts – the moments – in the totality. We must get a better grip on Hegel's idea before we can understand what it is Marx was criticizing.

The opposing pair of abstract-concrete has a key role in Hegel, as it does in Marx. The simple starting point is always abstract, because it excludes 'the Other'. The unity of 'Something' and 'the Other' is concrete in relation to the moments included: the abstraction means that the concrete is broken down into its component parts. Marx's use of these terms does not differ from Hegel's. In the *Grundrisse*, Marx says: 'The concrete is concrete because it is a synthesis of many determinations, thus a unity of the diverse.' The words are simpler, but the content is much the same.

The difference between Hegel and Marx lies in their views on the relationship between the abstract determinations that are included in the concrete totality. Above all, Hegel uses the word *Reflexion* (reflection). He therefore opens the way for his fundamental conception that there is an agreement between the ideal and the real, idea and reality. In the first place, reflection is a moment in the intellectual process: it is the analysis of a totality, and thus a process of abstraction. But it is not just any analysis. The one moment is regarded in its state of opposition to the other; the totality is kept in mind, but the moments are nonetheless kept separate.

Reflexion does not only have the meaning of 'consideration'; it also designates a phenomenon of light, just as it does in everyday language: mirroring. Hegel makes use of this double meaning. The moment in a totality is broken down not only through a thought process; it also reflects itself and the other moments. It is in this mirroring that the unity of the totality is apparent for reflection.

There is a close connection between reflection and unity in Hegel's thought. The law of identity, $a=a$, constitutes the height of abstraction, and does not help understand any change at all. A reflection that stopped at this purely tautological proposition of identity, Hegel argued, was an 'external' or 'superficial' (*äussere*) one. In a higher form of reflection, they become apparent as separate moments. This 'determining' reflection defines a phenomenon through marking it off from something else; this way, both 'Something' and 'an Other' are already kept within sight.

But identity, like abstraction, is not a phenomenon that applies only to thought processes. The concept of identity is applicable to real objects to the same extent. In a real totality – any totality – the moments included are identical to each other and nonetheless separate.[21] It is this conception of identity that Marx objects to.

Totality, According to Marx

It should be noticed that Hegel, in the above context, was discussing all-encompassing phenomena that are valid everywhere. Marx was occupied with a delimited theory. For Hegel, unity-creating reason raises itself above the various forms of reflection. With his philosophy, he chiefly wanted to solve the great speculative questions that were formulated in the idealistic tradition. He wanted to find the unity between Spirit and Nature. From the beginning, his conceptions of identity were formed in polemics against the 'philosophy of identity' of the Romantics and Schelling in particular, in which the natural and the spiritual fused together in a harmonious unity for philosophical thought.

The totality Marx spoke about was that of material production. This difference is essential. But through confronting his own idea with Hegel's, Marx – despite this limitation – would be faced with methodological and theoretical questions of unlimited scope. In the introduction to the *Grundrisse*, this opposition between the limited and the general is unresolved. He called the central section 'The Method of Political Economy'. But how did it relate to other totalities? The question is left half open. When, six months after having written the introduction, the urge struck to write about the Hegelian method to the whole of its extent (although without completing the attempt), it can be imagined that this relation appeared to him in a much clearer light.

But back in the introduction, he had drawn the key terms from Hegel: words such as 'determination', 'totality', 'moment', and so on were just as unknown or meaningless in the tradition of Smith, Ricardo, and Mill as they had been central to Hegel. When Marx said that the parts in the totality of material production were not identical, he naturally meant identical in the sense of the Hegelian dialectic. Hegel defined 'moment' (that is, moment in a totality) as something that was included in a totality with its opposite – something that was '*ein Reflektiertes*'. The moments in a totality mirror each other. They are subordinate to the higher unity of the totality. The idea that Marx brought out as his own is related to Hegel's down to the details. He asserted the following:

1. One of the moments, production, marks both itself and the other moments (production '*greift über*' itself and the other parts; it dominates the totality, it is all-embracing). 'A definite [mode of] production thus determines a definite [mode of] consumption, distribution, exchange and *definite relations of these definite moments to one another.*'
2. Production is determined '*in its one-sided form*' by the other moments. There is reciprocal action between all the moments.

Marx added that the other moment, reciprocal action, was valid for every organic totality. It is impossible to determine if he was arguing that it was not applicable to the first moment. It can only be said that the traditional idealistic conception of organisms permitted no all-embracing or dominant moment.[22]

Marx clarified his relationship to Hegel through the term 'interaction' itself. According to Hegel, the idea of reciprocal action was a further development of causality ('*a* causes *b*'). When only causality is allowed for, the various quantities are regarded as only external in relation to each other – that is, they are not included in the same totality. Reciprocal action, on the other hand, means that they are no longer isolated from each other.

But merely reciprocal action was no more the constituting factor of a totality for Hegel than it was for Marx. In the first part of his great *System of Philosophy*, Hegel explained that reciprocal action 'stood on the threshold of the concept', that is, not enough to characterize a totality. In that context, he cites an example that is of interest here because it is so concrete it can be compared with what Marx said about his object – namely, material production. It concerns the relationship between the character of a people on the one hand and their legislation on the other. It is a classic problem, founded in the language itself. Words such as 'ethics' and 'morals' have their origins in other words that really signify customs and traditions. But what was the relationship between the both of them now? Keeping to simple causality, we must decide that the one is the cause of the other. Either we say: What people usually do determines what is regarded as good and correct. Or: The prevailing morals determine my actions. Hegel refused both alternatives, maintaining that customs and morals mark each other reciprocally.

It is thus a question of the same type of reciprocal action between moments in a totality that Marx spoke about. But there is one important difference. Marx maintained that there was reciprocal action among four different moments. Hegel generally never spoke about more than two quantities – 'Something' and 'an Other'. As we have already seen, he defined *Verhältnis* as a mutual relation (*Beziehung*) between two sides, and *Verhältnis* is precisely his technical term for the relationship between the moments in a totality, whereas *Beziehung* had no specific meaning in his terminology, signifying relationships in general.

The relationship between 'Something' and 'an Other' in Hegel is the relationship between the positive and its opposite; in general terms, the opposite is no more qualified as an opposite than as just 'an Other'. This means that Hegel's determination of the relationship (*das Verhältnis*) as a relationship between two – and only two – moments was of great significance for his dialectic.[23] But Marx was experimenting with a unity that consisted of four moments. For that reason alone, his concept of totality became considerably much more complicated than Hegel's.

We do not know if this was a conscious departure from Hegel. For Hegel, it was fundamental that there were only two moments in a unity. His logic would simply not allow more. It is a consequence of his particular concept of identity – the one Marx repudiated. Hegel maintained that the mere discovery of reciprocal action between two moments – as in his example between customs and laws – does not permit us to comprehend (get an idea of) the totality in question. With that idea, both moments in a totality are coordinated into a totality. The contradiction between both is sublated, even if temporarily. Both sides in the reciprocal action are perceived as moments in the idea. With that idea, the interaction gains meaning. Hegel's universe is full of meanings; reality is like a book that human reason is able to read.

Since Marx did not find this totality necessary, or even possible to attain, he could incorporate four determinations into the same totality. In other words, he was not looking for the point at which the differences between the moments is dissolved. Instead, he was looking for a dominant or all-embracing moment, a moment that at one and the same time determines the others (and itself) and stands in a relationship of reciprocal action with them.

This analysis in the *Grundrisse* lacks a counterpart in *Capital*. This makes the 'Introduction' exceptionally important. With its help, we can approach a question that will become important in the next chapter: Did Marx tone down the role of production in *Capital*, and instead attach relatively great importance to distribution, and thereby circulation and money?

Economy and Philosophy

Louis Althusser correctly emphasized that the difference between the dialectic of Hegel and of Marx is not only a difference between idealism and materialism, but also a difference in the views on the structure of the dialectic. On the other hand, Althusser's thesis that Marx's theory after the *Theses on Feuerbach* was fundamentally incompatible with Hegel's philosophy is untenable.[24] The dynamic and tension in Marx's relationship to Hegel cannot be captured in such simple terms. It was neither caprice nor chance that drove Marx to once again take Hegel's philosophy in hand in the late 1850s. Faced with the task of finally developing his original social theory, it was important for him to give an account of his own position in relation to both the thinker who once marked him and to the economists who were of topical interest in his time.

He agreed with them all that one should begin with abstractions in the scientific treatment of an object. An older economic theory could start from the extremely complex or concrete – the population of a country, for example – but no real knowledge of the economic contexts could be gained on that path. It was therefore a crucial step when Smith ignored all concrete differences and simply took up labour as the starting point of his doctrine.

But Smith and his followers, once they had found a valid abstraction, committed the mistake of believing that it would be valid in the same way – independent of all other relationships – throughout all of history. When they thus established that labour created all value, they assumed that labour would forever have the same character as it did in capitalist society. The threads could be drawn straight back into history from the present time, and they would always run in the same order among themselves.

Hegel also started out from abstractions. Like Marx (but in contrast to the economists), he did not see this process as a purely formal operation in which the individual was inferred from the general. On the contrary, it was an innovative development where constantly new and varying content enriched the abstractions. The concrete results of an investigation could not be predicted with a set of abstractions.

But Hegel also maintained that reality must be intellectual – or more correctly, ideal – in nature since knowledge could only be attained through an intellectual process. Marx ardently repudiated this. It is true that the path from the abstract to the concrete is taken in thought, at the same time as the concrete is what provides the best knowledge of reality. But this did not mean – as Hegel argued – that the concrete, as a result of scientific work, corresponded to a real development from something abstract to something concrete. The concrete in knowledge is a 'conceptual totality' that cannot be mistaken for the concrete in reality. The development from abstractions to the complex is not, as Hegel asserts, the path of reality. Marx devoted great energy to showing that economic development does not go from simpler to more complicated relationships. In other words, economic history did not proceed in a way that follows the path of developed economic theory from the abstract to the concrete.[25]

In fact, with this demonstration Marx turned against Hegel as well as Smith, Ricardo, Mill, and the other economists. The latter had assumed that capitalist relations would be found throughout all of history – just in simpler and more primitive form the further back in time one looked. Hegel maintained that every development – therefore also historical ones – began with something simple and abstract in the same way as thinking or theory.

But Marx still directed his main attack against Hegel. He was not just an idealist, he did not only see the real as an expression of thinking or the idea. His thinking on identity resulted in the idea of the unity between thought and actuality, the subjective and the objective, idea and reality. The limited criticism of Hegel's conception of identity that Marx previously offered is broadened here to apply to the cardinal thought itself: the identity between theory and its subject. Hegel asserted that every totality is a unity (even if a transitory one) of the elements included. Marx said that this did not apply to the totality of material production. But now the perspective was being widened. He maintained that there was a certain degree of agreement between thinking and reality, but that this agreement could not be comprehended as an identity. Thinking and its objects fundamentally differ.

In his introduction, Marx did not mobilize a materialist conception on this point against Hegelian idealism. We know from other texts that he saw the conception, the theory, or the idea as secondary. Here, he was satisfied with pointing out that knowledge and its objects could not be identified with one another. It is thus misleading both to see the relationship in Hegel's idealistic terms and to believe that knowledge is a reflection of its object.

In the 'Introduction' to the *Grundrisse*, Marx brought his theory on the basic conditions of society face to face with Hegelian methodology. On the other hand, he gave no answer to the question of whether or not what he saw as the best method of economic theory should apply to *all* scientific methods. Hegel ascribed universal validity to his statements on theoretical work. Marx spoke about the method of investigating a very complex and specific piece of reality, namely material production. But in his criticism of Hegel, he made use of terms and expressions that in all likelihood apply to all knowledge.

It seems as though the question of the methodology of *other* sciences had not yet come into his field of vision. That issue, however, lies implicit in what he wrote. If he was speaking about political economy *as if* it applied to all knowledge, this problem would gradually have to confront him. This took place above all in the encounter with the new, revolutionary chemistry and with

Darwin's theory of natural selection. But when he wrote the introduction, it was still an unknown field to him.

At that point in time, it was at least a question of the relationship between two areas of knowledge, the one narrower
and the other wider, and both naturally of equal topical interest
to Marx. The one was material production (political economy
in its narrower sense) and the other was society and history in
general. Unfortunately, Marx did not finish his thoughts. He only
wrote down a few points that provide important suggestions, but
nothing more.

In one of the points, Marx spoke about 'the unequal relationship' (*das unegale Verhältnis*) between the development of
material production and, for example, art.[26] At first, it seems like
a rather banal problem that Marx took up only to protect himself
against various vulgar conceptions that progress in one area –
material production, for example – always meant progress in all
the others. According to such a conception, Greek art would necessarily be inferior to modern art. Marx emphasized that no such
baroque idea followed at all from the belief in the primacy of
material culture.

But there is something more in Marx's assertion than simply the
repudiation of the idea that the degree of development of material
production constitutes the foundation for evaluating all cultural
products. Above all, he was speaking about actual unevenness
in development. This assertion would be set against the idea of
the unique position of material production. It meant that even
though material production determined historical development
in general, this did not mean that all social phenomena were
passively dependent on it.

Marx's standpoint is reminiscent of what Engels wrote to some
young supporters much later, in the early 1890s. This comparison will be made in a later chapter (page 590 below). Marx's
statements are also closely connected with what he said earlier
in the introduction about material production as a totality and
about the relationship between knowledge and its object. In both
cases, it was a question of '*unequal relationship*', in which *one*
moment – production in the totality of material production, material production in society in general, or the object of knowledge

in the process of knowledge – was ascribed a unique position and identified as dominant, but in no way the only crucial or decisive moment. There would thus be a similarity of structure between all the different areas.

In the introduction, Marx was very far away from the ambition Engels would later have of creating a coherent view of all the sciences. In one of the points he did not finish developing at the end of the introduction, he spoke about real (in contrast to ideal) historiography. In another point, he announced his intention to take up the accusations that his interpretation could be characterized as materialist. By all appearances, his response would have started out from a sharp distinction between his own type of materialism and what he called 'naturalist materialism'. By that, he meant the idea that the world of humanity could be investigated with the same fundamental concepts as could the world of nature.

He could then have gone back with advantage to his and Engels's reckoning with Feuerbach in the introduction to *The German Ideology* from 1845 and 1846. But he would not follow up on his intentions. Perhaps he soon forgot them completely. It is striking, for example, that in his reckoning with Karl Vogt in *Herr Vogt* a few years later (1860), he did not mention a word of the fact that this same Vogt was not only a politician, but also one of the foremost representatives of a naturalist materialism. Vogt got involved in the *Materialismusstreit* (materialist controversy) that raged in the 1850s primarily through his 1855 pamphlet *Köhlerglaube und Wissenschaft* (Blind Faith and Science). In it, he granted neither humanity nor art any freedom in relation to the fundamental laws of matter.[27] Marx stood far from him, not only politically but also in his scientific conception of the world.

Internal Discord

Marx polemicized vigorously with Hegel and the Hegelians in his introduction. He not only wished to clarify his own position in relation to an important predecessor with this clear drawing of boundaries. He also wanted to avoid misunderstandings.

Marx's language – and especially his method of argument – are strikingly reminiscent of Hegel in certain parts of the *Grundrisse*. Hegel's texts were constructed around more or less hidden syllogisms. The trisections of both thinking and reality he devoted himself to rather thoroughly, particularly in *The Science of Logic*, reverberate in several places in the *Grundrisse*. Syllogisms still constituted the framework of the logic taught in schools and at university. They had a homogeneous form, and a history that reached all the way back to Aristotle. From two premises, a conclusion of the following type was drawn: All men are mortal – Socrates is a man – Socrates is mortal.[28]

Such logic was purely formal, and thereby valid regardless of the content of the concrete examples. Hegel questioned this strict boundary between form and content. The form also had its content, he maintained. So it was in thought, and so it also was in the reality that at heart was also a world of ideas. New content was added in every conclusion, and the new stood in a relationship full of tension to the original. The processes of thought are like the innovations of reality. The new emerges through contradictions. What was recently achieved is broken down, but not annihilated; it returns on the next level – through the next syllogism – more complicated, with richer content.

The key concept that captures this process is *Aufhebung*, which in German signifies abolition as well as preservation and raising up – the multiplicity of meanings that Hegel was the first to emphasize and recognize. We have encountered this word several times; it also turns up infrequently in Marx, but he sometimes seems to take fright at it.

When he includes the form of the syllogism in the text in the *Grundrisse*, noticeable only to those who are well acquainted with ordinary Hegelian prose, it is both to point out the proximity to – but above all the distance from – Hegel.[29] Marx spoke about the path from production to consumption as a conclusion in which distribution and exchange formed the middle – that is, the mediating link. But Marx's intent was rather to show that it was not enough to see it as 'a proper syllogism'; the relationship between the various links is far more complex: production, as we have seen, is also consumption, consumption is also production,

and so on.[30] With this demonstration, he objected at the same time
to the economists' rigid use of the same concept.

Even after the introduction, Hegelian vocabulary turns up
again and again. It gets most interesting when Marx makes use of
it without accounting for its philosophical origins in more detail
or taking a position on it. This was what happened with the concepts of *form*, *substance*, and *content*. They are certainly much
older than Hegel – form and substance were already fully fledged
in the philosophy of Aristotle, and the concept of content dates
from the Renaissance. But Hegel added something that echoed
in the *Grundrisse*. He subtly develops a double concept of form
that agrees with an everyday use of the word. We do not need to
reproduce this analysis in detail, but an important result is that a
form can be set against both substance and content. Substance is
determined as the formless which is *formed* and is thereby given
unique character, its defined property – that is, it becomes a birch,
a daisy, a cat, or a person. The unity of substance and form is
called content. But if we think more closely about content, we
discover that we are also imagining a form, but another kind of
form, something superficial, perhaps something 'purely formal' or
something that the eye or the ear can pick up without the help of
the intellect. For the sake of simplicity, we can talk about form$_1$
or form$_2$, in which form$_1$ provides clarity about what an object is
while form$_2$ signifies the façade.

Marx uses the terms form, substance, and content numerous
times in the *Grundrisse*, as he does in many other of his works.
Most often, it is to emphasize that the economic analysis ignores
what is being produced, distributed, or sold. It does not matter
which commodities are being produced; the only essential thing
is what value they represent. Marx can also compare the work
to a form that forms the raw material with the help of working
equipment.

In a section that is rather difficult to get through, he differentiates between substance (*Stoff*) and content. The chapter erases
the specific form of the work – that is, its concrete character – and
becomes any labour process 'that takes place within its substance
and forms its content'. Or, in other words: the particular work
processes its typical raw materials and produces its particular

products, however meaningless this specificity may be in the narrow economic analysis.

What is most interesting, however, is another section in which he talks about the role of labour in creating value. Boards do not become a table and iron does not become a cylinder in the same way that an acorn becomes an oak. But through labour, the boards and the iron are still given life. The labour that has already been put into them (both boards and iron have been produced) ceases to be 'a dead, external, in different form' and becomes 'an element of living labour'. Labour thus forms its products, and thereby corresponds to the power of growth in the acorn.

This line of argument constitutes an example of the Hegelian distinction between form$_1$ and form$_2$. But Marx is not satisfied with this dry distinction, and the next moment becomes lyrical: 'Labour is the living, form-giving fire; it is the transience of things, their temporality, as the process of their formation by living time.' The boards, which were once sawn, and the iron, which was once cast, come to an end in the new labour process that transforms them into the table and the cylinder.[31] This is how Marx could write when, alone in the night and in a great hurry, he tried to summarize his enormous project.

Even when it concerned what was and would remain a main problem for Marx – the dynamic nature of capital – he some-times connected with his philosophical teacher in the *Grundrisse*. Syllogisms are again glimpsed in one place, but this time it is their extremes and not their middle term. The extremes are capital on the one hand, and labour on the other. They meet in the labour process, but as strangers. Something new still arises from the labour process: a greater value. It is thus not a question of an eternal repetition, a circle, in which machinery and raw materi-als, through labour, restore the production that was consumed through consumption. No; the process leads to increasing results. It is, Marx said, a spiral – an increasing curve.[32]

The spiral is one of Hegel's favourite metaphors for develop-ment. But in the *Grundrisse*, Marx also tries to express the same conviction in a clearer, more formalized fashion. He has not yet reached the simple expression in capital for the increase of commodities: P – V – P' – V' – P", in which P signifies money used for commodity production, V, which can be sold against a greater sum of money, P', which makes greater commodity production, V', possible, and so on. But he is already on the way in the *Grundrisse*, without, however, being able to symbolize the increase; he can only represent the circulation, the repetition as P – V – V – P.[33]

Faced with this dilemma, he sought a way out in pure mathematical exactness. He had found the secret behind capitalist production: a *surplus value* is created as a result. The worker receives only compensation for a part of what was created in the labour process. The rest becomes an increase in value that the capitalist can freely make use of. Marx first tried to clarify this process using arithmetic. He was not satisfied with the result, with some reason. The calculations led nowhere, and in his hurry he not infrequently miscalculated. Further on in the manuscript, he tried to sharpen his implements via simple algebra, and now it concerned such things as the circulation of capital – that is, the phenomenon that would later be the topic of the second volume of *Capital*.[34]

It is without doubt another scientific ideal than the one that marked his attitude towards Hegel that he tried to realize here. He was not satisfied with reasoning, but wanted to show what his theory revealed with the exactness of figures. The striving for exactness, as well as for conceptual simplicity and clarity, soon took the upper hand in the work that followed after the *Grundrisse* and will also be treated there. One could even speak of an inner conflict in his great project, and it is now high time to examine this conflict closely.

A More Manageable Project?

The *Grundrisse* contains so many subtle arguments that it is easy to get caught in its unique details and forget its great task: to clarify the peculiar nature and the dynamic of capitalism – and its fragility. Marx was writing in a race with an economic crisis that he long believed would result in a total collapse. Only when the crisis subsided did he realize that the great manuscript he had produced was entirely too formless to be presented to a readership, even in edited form.

It was in this situation that he sought advice from his friend Engels. On 2 April 1858 he wrote a long letter in which he not only complained about his wretched health which made it nearly impossible for him to work. He also talked about the plans for his continued work with his great social theory. The whole would cover six topics, he said, namely 1. Capital, 2. Landed Property, 3. Wage Labour, 4. State, 5. International Trade, and 6. World Market. It is interesting to compare this plan with what he had already sketched out in the introduction to the *Grundrisse*. His plan there was significantly more abstract. Point one would deal with the general determinations that were common to all societies, and after that he would set about the structure of bourgeois society. The third concerned the very 'epitome' of bourgeois society (*Zusammenfassung*) in the form of the state and also the nonproductive classes, circulation, the credit system, and other things he did not specify in greater detail. After that, international conditions and the international division of labour would be dealt with. The final section would deal with 'World Market and Crises', in part the same topic as in the plan of 1858. But there was still one important difference. The crises were set off as a particular topic. They had certainly not lost their role a year later. But the road from crisis to revolution was no longer as short or as obvious.[35]

Between the plan from August 1857 and the plan from April 1858 lay the work on the *Grundrisse*, and also a series of newspaper articles in which the effects of the crisis were illuminated from various aspects. It was important that capital had now gained decisive significance in the plan. Instead of the more or less historical and philosophical topic that was announced in 1857 – perhaps intended as a further development of the discussion about production, distribution, and so on – the specific dynamic of contemporary society now came into focus. The changes can be seen as a result of the intensive work of the intervening months, in which capital had become precisely the crucial topic. But it was also a narrowing and a sharpening of the tremendous task Marx had made up his mind to do.

One important practical circumstance had also arisen. In March 1858 Marx had agreed with the publisher Franz Duncker in Berlin to publish his great criticism in instalments. He still believed that it would be child's play to sort out what he needed for the entire work from the *Grundrisse* material. But he was mistaken. The freedom that the *Grundrisse* radiated would now be disciplined – perhaps to excess.

In the above-mentioned letter to Engels with the new plan, Marx also accounted in greater detail for how he intended to make use of his study. In the first instalment he would deal with '*Capital in General*', and after that deal with competition, credit, and share capital by turns. Share capital was the consummate form of capital, on the threshold to communism. But it also contained a number of internal contradictions.

Before grappling with capital, however, he had to deal with its conditions: value and money. Only after that came the main topic of the instalment. But, Marx wrote to Engels, as regards that topic I need your opinion first.

It is a remarkable letter. It is easy to imagine the background: Marx had awoken from an inspired intoxication. The words had flowed over the paper, sometimes heavy and clumsy, but not infrequently packed with meaning – brilliant, in fact. The crisis had subsided, the hour of uprising had not struck, and Marx, worn out from work and sick, had to try to develop what could be of value for another, slower period from his massive manuscripts.

Engels's reaction to the letter was mixed. It was 'a very abstract abstract indeed', and he found it difficult to follow a number of the dialectical transitions. He excused himself by saying that he was unused to that kind of reasoning, now that he was compelled to occupy himself with mere earthly affairs. But with these words, he implied that most potential readers of Marx's future work would encounter the same problems he had.[36]

It would be several weeks before Marx responded. His illness had become so severe that he had become unable to write. He was compelled to dictate his articles for the *New York Daily Tribune* to Jenny. His liver problems were worse than ever; it was the price for all the late hours. The illness could not have come at a more inconvenient time. Now it was simply a question of working![37]

Karl Marx as a student, c. 1840

The house in Trier where Marx was born

An anonymous lithograph from 1851 depicts the women workers of a cotton
factory while capturing none of the noise and dirt of the environment.

A. Carse, Berlin University featuring equestrian statue
of Frederick the Great, 1850, lithograph

Jakob Schlesinger, portrait of Georg Wilhelm
Friedrich Hegel (1770–1831), 1831, oil
on canvas, Alte Nationalgalerie

August Weger, portrait of Ludwig Andreas von
Feuerbach (1804–72), c. 1860–70, lithograph

Portrait of Bruno Bauer (1809–82), photo by Philip Graff, 1860

Cartoon of Max Stirner
(1806–56) by Friedrich Engels,
c. 1841, ink on paper

Arnold Ruge (1802–80),
1880, wood engraving

A young Jenny von Westphalen (later Marx, 1814–81), 1830

Karl Marx and Jenny Longuet (née Marx, 1844–83), c. 1864

Paul Lafargue (1842–1911), Laura Marx's husband, 1871

Jenny and Laura Marx, c. 1840–50

Eleanor Marx, youngest daughter of Karl
and Jenny Marx (1855–98), c. 1875

Helene Demuth (1820–90), who kept house for
the Marx family for many years, 1870

E. Capiro, *Karl Marx and Engels in the Printing House of the* Neue Rheinische Zeitung, 1849, oil on canvas

Barricade at the corner of boulevards Voltaire and Richard-Lenoir during the Paris Commune, photo by Bruno Braquehais, 1871, City of Paris Historical Library

Karl Marx as editor of the *Neue Rheinische Zeitung*, c. 1848

Political cartoon by Jean Jaurès showing Karl Marx as Prometheus chained to a printing press while the eagle of Prussian censorship rips out his liver; created after the forced closure of the *Rheinische Zeitung*, 1843, lithograph

Gustav A. Köttgen, portrait of Moses Hess (1812–75),
1846, oil on canvas, Cologne City Museum

A photograph of Friedrich Engels
in his twenties, date unknown

Adolph von Menzel, *Public Funeral of the Victims of the March Revolution in Berlin*, 1848, oil on canvas

Edward Walford Cassell, *The South Front of the British Museum*, c. 1880, lithograph

KARL MARX

PARIS

ÉDITEURS, MAURICE LACHATRE ET CIE

38, BOULEVARD DE SÉBASTOPOL. 38

Title page from a French edition of *Capital*, c. 1920

Mikhail Bakunin (1814–76), photo by Nadar, c. 1860

Pierre-Joseph Proudhon (1809–65), photo by Nadar, 1862

Friedrich Engels, 1891

Last known photograph of Karl Marx, 1882

Karl Marx's grave at Highgate Cemetery, photo by Jon Bennett, 2007

Engels responded that Marx could at least travel to Manchester, and Marx agreed to the adventure because he had got somewhat better. In addition, Engels promised to guarantee his travel costs.

The weeks Marx spent in Manchester would restore his health. He went out riding with Engels every day, and had withdrawal symptoms when he returned to London. Engels had been a skilled rider since his youth. In a letter of thanks, Marx wrote apologetically that it was his own misfortune that he was always compelled to break off his exercises on horseback as soon as he had begun finding pleasure in it – that is, achieving an elementary level of skill. It must have been a priceless sight when they both set out for the surroundings of Manchester: the one in good form in the saddle like a cavalryman, the other more like a sack of hay.

During the time in Manchester, they naturally also spoke about the writing Marx would grapple with as soon as he returned home. In fact, he could not completely abstain from the pen. Sorting out something that could be presented to the public from the kitchen sink of the *Grundrisse* was urgent.[38]

Having returned to London, he drew up an index that would help him find his way through all the notebooks full of scribblings that constituted the *Grundrisse*.[39] It certainly worked. But the little amount of writing he later completed differed fundamentally from the matrix. The flow of associations had been toned down, and the diversity of topics had been replaced by a dry, logical consistency. Corresponding to the 'Introduction', as difficult to read as it was profound, was a brief, pithy preface to *A Contribution*, the simplicity and clarity of which played a large role in its success. The significance of the preface for the most widespread interpretations of Marx is so overwhelming we must pause to consider these brief pages in depth.

Base and Superstructure

The preface is four pages long and has a clear, simple construction. First, Marx indicates the plan for the entire critical work, which the published text was only the first instalment of; it was otherwise the same plan that he set out in the letter to Engels. Capital would be dealt with in the first section, and Part One deals only with the conditions for capital – that is, the commodity and money. The reader is given the impression that the remainder of the work lies ready to be sent to print.

Marx also explains that he did not intend to publish the 'Introduction' that he had already written in connection with his work on the *Grundrisse*. He found it inconvenient, 'on further consideration', to anticipate results that first needed to be substantiated. The reader who followed him would travel the path from the simple up to the general.[40]

Why had he not felt the same suspicion of far-reaching philosophical commentary when he sat down to write the 'Introduction'? Why did he allow himself to be captivated by theoretical problems that were fascinating but difficult to penetrate in August 1857, while in January 1859 he found the same problems impossible to treat except after long, more down-to-earth exposition?

The explanations lie close at hand in external circumstances. The introduction was written on the cusp of a rapid social transformation. The fundamental mood was cheerful: no problem was too big to take hold of. The preface came to be in a more dismal time, when everything had returned to order after the crisis and Marx himself was sick and worn out. In addition came Engels's reaction to a significantly more easily strained plan – 'a very abstract abstract'.

But there were also internal reasons. Marx's attitude towards these types of great philosophical questions that the 'Introduction' raises had long been split. He was both fascinated by and entertained suspicions towards them. It is no coincidence that the *Grundrisse*, as we shall see, has topics reminiscent of the *Manuscripts*; first of all alienation but also far-reaching theories about humanity, history, and even the future. In *A Contribution*, he was more ascetic in his choice of topics.

In the preface, he described in a few lines his own intellectual development, his studies where law was to have been the main subject but soon had to make way for philosophy and history, his experiences as a journalist, and his encounter with socialist and communist ideas in Paris. He spoke about his acquaintance with

Engels and their common intention to reckon with Left Hegelian philosophy in the large manuscript that posterity – but not Marx's own time – knows under the name *The German Ideology*.

It is the standpoints from *The German Ideology* that remain in the brief, constantly quoted declaration that Marx made about his scientific method of working. This declaration often serves as a summary of his entire theory – without exception in Soviet and Soviet-inspired descriptions, and is worth quoting here:

> The general conclusion at which I arrived and which, once reached, became the guiding principle of my studies can be summarized as follows. In the social production of their existence, men inevitably enter into definite relations, which are independent of their will, namely relations of production appropriate to a given stage in the development of their material forces of production.

The passage also appears in the study by British philosopher Gerald A. Cohen, *Karl Marx's Theory of History: A Defence*. Cohen reproduces the central parts of the preface as a model for his account, which at the same time is an impassioned defence and a meticulous illumination of Marx's arguments. He asserts that Marx provides a functional explanation of the relationship between base and superstructure. In order to explain his interpretation, he draws a concrete example from *Capital*, in which Marx says that Protestantism, 'by changing almost all their traditional holidays into workdays', was important for the emergence of capitalism. In Cohen's opinion, this meant not only that the new religion had this effect, but above all that through this effect, it contributed to the explanation of the emergence of capitalism.[41] It is certainly an important clarification, but still does not cover the entire problem area that Marx dealt with. The error does not lie in Cohen's interpretation of Marx's preface, but in that the preface is entirely too simple and conventional to be interpreted as a summary of Marx's entire work.

It is important that Marx himself obviously did not have these ambitions with his declaration, either. He said explicitly that it was a thread (*Leitfaden*) for his studies. This term is important: the classically trained author thinks of the ball of yarn Ariadne

gave Theseus as an aid to finding his way back out of the labyrinth once the Minotaur had been defeated.

Marx left a thread behind him when he entered into the confusion of paths that human society represents. Concrete reality
forms such a confusing diversity that it cannot be made comprehensible without strict scientific studies. With the help of the
thread, he would find his way back.[42]

A thread is not a map. The thread is a heuristic principle in the
most literal sense of the word: it helps someone find a way out of
a dilemma. The word can be compared with a similar reservation
in *The German Ideology*: guidelines do not provide a schedule
according to which history can be arranged. The concrete study of
reality always remains; the result is not given from the beginning.
But a guide is needed.

The guide Marx provided in his preface is robust enough.
People enter into fixed relations of production that are independent of their will but a condition of their lives. The relations of
production correspond to a fixed level in the development of the
forces of production. A given economic structure is the *base* on
which society rests. People's consciousness is determined by the
actual material circumstances under which they live. But these
circumstances change. At a certain level, the forces of production come into conflict with the relations of production; people
can achieve things with their skills, their technology, and their
knowledge that are incompatible with the prevailing power over
production. The conflict is inevitable, and eventually the productive forces burst the limits set by the prevailing order. As a result,
the enormous superstructure of political and legal institutions, as
well as religious, artistic, and philosophical relations – or what
Marx summed up as *ideological forms* – is transformed.

There is much to be said about these lines. The metaphorical
pair of base and superstructure is defined here. 'Base' is no newcomer; for example, the word occurred a couple of times in the
Grundrisse. But here it has been given its complement – superstructure – and the building is finished, a permanent structure that after
Marx's time has occasioned much more confusion than clarity.
Dogmatism of all kinds has taken the simple analogy with a house
as its starting point, and nothing has been simpler for opponents

of everything Marx stood for than to interpret the metaphor narrowly and literally. This preface not only opened *A Contribution*, but also the entire motley tradition called Marxism.[43]

As we have already seen, early on in his development Marx was eager to emphasize his predilection for the stable and the robust through various images. He differentiated between earth and heaven, head and feet – in short, between more and less earthly conditions. Base and superstructure belong to the same family of expressions, but lend themselves more easily to dogmatic deadlocks: society becomes a building.

For his part, Marx is chiefly interested in the methodological difference between studying the play between relations of production and productive forces on the one hand, and political and legal institutions as well as human ideas on the other. An upheaval in the former can be observed with the exactness of the natural sciences, he said. This is not possible with the latter. But it is in politics, in art, and in thinking that people become aware of the conflicts that they are inevitably drawn into. It is there as well that they fight one another – with weapon in hand, or with words. Both ideas and feuds change with the base – sometimes more slowly, sometimes more rapidly.

In Marx's own writings there is no clear boundary between the study of the fundamental conflicts and ideological forms. Material production is in focus in *A Contribution*, as it is in *Capital*, but in his purely polemical writings – as in his journalism – political complications, theories, and other subjects that must be considered part of the superstructure predominate.

There is a further problem with the superstructure that neither Marx nor anyone who wishes to anchor ideas and conceptions in concrete circumstances can escape. Does scientifically well-founded knowledge not become relative in this case? Is what we designate as true only true in relation to a given historical situation? What position did Marx himself speak from?

One thing is certain: Marx was not a relativist. Valid knowledge may have its basis in a definite historical conjuncture. Its validity is tested in other ways. In *Capital*, he would make his position perfectly clear.

Value and Money

There is more to be said about the relationship between the *Grundrisse* and *A Contribution*. The only instalment of *A Contribution* that Marx completed contains nothing more than the preliminaries to the promised work. The reader would reap their rewards only in the next instalment, with a better understanding of the age they lived in. *A Contribution* can only be regarded as a model for *Capital* in a limited sense. The opening scene is identical: bourgeois society appears as an 'immense accumulation of commodities'. But, from there on, the text is more barren, lacking the perspective-widening concreteness that characterizes *Capital*.

The fundamental relations, however, are nailed down with a steady hand in *A Contribution*. The commodity as commodity has nothing to do with its concrete content. An ounce of gold can have the same value as a ton of iron or twenty lengths of silk. Value is determined by the labour time required on average to produce the commodity. In short, an abstraction is made from the concrete commodity, but this abstraction is not the product of ideas; it belongs in the real everyday world. The labour of the individual does not remain separate but is immediately incorporated into a wider social context of value exchange.[44]

The object of one of the most brilliant sections of *Capital* – commodity fetishism – is already under discussion here but only briefly, and it is easy to overlook. It is said that the labour that produces (exchange) value makes the relationship between people appear distorted, as a relationship between things. Another important thought also flickers by. Use value – that is, the usability a commodity has – is not created through labour alone; it has its basis in the material nature provides. It is only exchange value that is entirely dependent on labour time. A length of linen does not satisfy the same needs as a half pound of tea, but the exchange value can be just as great.

The chapter on the commodity ends with an overview of previous theories on the subject. Criticism of political economy for Marx was never simply a criticism of actual conditions, but also of the ideas about them. With this collected history of economic thought, he refers to a particular manuscript that was published in an incomplete state long after his death as *Theorien über den Mehrwert* (Theories of Surplus Value). The brief sketch he provided in the middle of his account in *A Contribution* contains some interesting details such as the fact that James Steuart – the Scotsman Hegel was deeply influenced by – spoke about alienation in connection with industry, or that Benjamin Franklin, the American Enlightener and inventor of the lightning conductor, was the first to posit the idea that the value of commodities was determined by the labour put into it.[45]

The second chapter dominates the first instalment, and deals with money. It has counterparts in both the *Grundrisse* and in the first volume of *Capital*; even a brief comparison among the three can open up certain perspectives. In both *A Contribution* and *Capital*, the commodity has been broken out as its own, introductory chapter. Marx left a more chaotic, open account rich in associations and instead presented a text that had been cleaned up and strictly constructed. In the postscript to the second edition of *Capital*, he made a sharp distinction between the methods of research and of presentation. The researcher operates in a diversity of details that is difficult to grasp, where it is a matter of finding connections. These connections then govern the final presentation itself, which can easily give an impression of 'a mere *a priori* construction'.[46]

Nowhere is this step from the diversity of research work to an almost ascetic method of presentation clearer than from the *Grundrisse* to *A Contribution*. The *Grundrisse* is marked by sudden changes, dizzying views, and genius flashes of wit. With the first instalment of his great criticism, on the other hand, he showed that he assumed a patient reader who gladly awaited the grand perspective of society in the coming instalment. The reader of the *Grundrisse* has a journey that is more entertaining but not as certain.

The chapter on money in the *Grundrisse* is full of exciting digressions, not infrequently bracketed by parentheses. Marx could scatter brilliant thoughts about in a few inspiring pages. Universally developed individuals are not the products of nature, but of history, he stressed. It is not nature, but people themselves who created the circumstances that compel them under definite relations of production. Liberation must also be a human deed. At earlier levels of society, private individuals could appear as more comprehensively developed than today, due to the fact that material conditions were not as complex back then. Today, people are locked up in their narrow roles, but the longing to return was a romantic whim, as much as it was a bourgeois illusion that people will have to live forever under the lack of freedom that reigns today. Liberation must mean that all people become masters of their own circumstances, thereby developing fully.

And, he added in a new set of parentheses: A comparison can be made here with the relationship of the individual to science. He does not develop the idea; it remains open to our own further interpretations. These words probably point forward to his conclusion further on in the manuscript that satisfactory labour must have a scientific character (see below, page 392).

But he is soon ready for a third set of parentheses, and he has changed subjects. It now concerned money, the main theme of the chapter. Comparing it to blood is incorrect, he said. It is the word 'circulation' that gives rise to this absurd comparison. It was equally wrong to see money as a kind of language. Ideas cannot be separated from language, he said, implying the continuation 'like commodities can be separated from money'. In short, there is a temporary relationship between commodity and money whereas language constitutes the solid anchorage of every idea. However, in the next breath he remembers how beautifully Shakespeare showed how money places completely different things on an equal footing. As in the *Manuscripts*, he certainly had *Timon of Athens* in mind (see above, p. 155).[47]

Sometimes the presentation calms down, the multitude of associations thins out, and the main argument about money in its various present-day functions is carried further. But the difference with *A Contribution* is still enormous. In the *Grundrisse*, we can acquaint ourselves with Marx's flow of associations in its full breadth; he does not brush aside thoughts that do not carry the account forward, and his image of humanity and society develops. If the *Grundrisse* is like a primeval forest where everything can grow freely, *A Contribution* resembles more a French garden. The

Grundrisse is an adventure in reading, *A Contribution* is a walk among a number of well-groomed concepts.

But *A Contribution* also provides some interesting glimpses of other concerns. In his newspaper articles, Marx had provided several lively descriptions of the phenomenon of globalization, and in *A Contribution* he did so again brilliantly. 'The busiest streets of London are crowded with shops whose showcases display all the riches of the world. Indian shawls, American revolvers, Chinese porcelain, Persian corsets, furs from Russia and spices from the tropics, but all of these worldly things bear odious, white paper labels with Arabic numerals and then laconic symbols £. s. d.', he wrote.[48] It was a world that Charles Baudelaire saw developing in the new, wide, straight boulevards in Paris, and that Emile Zola would write a famous novel about fourteen years later in 1883 – *Au bonheur des dames* (The Ladies' Paradise).

Equally as striking is Marx's image of people who see mere riches as the highest aim in life. They are the martyrs of exchange value, holy ascetics who live on their pillars of precious metals.[49]

But the text soon returns to its normal dry objectivity. A problem that would come to occupy Marx throughout his life turns up in the text. A commodity has a value that, according to his theory, is determined by the amount of labour put into it. But the commodity also has a price. How does one go from value to price? In *A Contribution*, he makes it easy for himself as regards what is known as the transformation problem. The commodity is the standard, the value is the gauge. It is a statement that may seem plausible. A metre is a standard, and the length of something can be determined with the help of a metre stick. If the comparison is to hold, price is only one way of checking the value. But it is not so simple: price varies even when the value does not. Marx knew that, of course, but he did not show it in *A Contribution*.[50]

The Chapter on Capital

It is easy to misunderstand the relation between money and capital in Marx. Money has existed since antiquity, but according to Marx, capital is a modern phenomenon. Did he not sketch out a historical development from something simpler – money – to something more complex – capital – when he took up the one and then the other in the *Grundrisse*, in the plans for *A Contribution*, and in *Capital*?

No, this is not so. He was not unaware of the previous history of money, but the money he was interested in here is money in a system where capitalism already exists and increasingly dominates both the economy and society in general. This can already be seen from the historical digressions in *A Contribution*. They never go further back than the epoch of merchant capital, which in the history of economic thought first left its mark towards the end of the seventeenth century. But more important is that the substantial treatment of money itself prepares the investigation of capital. Capital assumes money. The greater the power of capital, the more things become commodities. Money is invested in production in order to become commodities that can be sold for money, which in turn can be invested in the production of new commodities. The dynamic of capitalism is inseparable from money. But not all money is included in this creative circulation. A portion of it is placed in lockboxes, and as long as it stays there it is withdrawn from circulation.

As we have seen, it was the intention that the first instalment of *A Contribution* would come out at the same time as the second, on capital. Capital had been the subject of by far the largest part of the *Grundrisse*, and the topic thus seemed well prepared there. But, once Marx had sent off the manuscript for the first instalment to Duncker in Berlin – Engels had to pay for the postage – there was nothing more. It is true that in a letter to Engels in February 1859, he stated that he was working on the second instalment.[51] But, if so, it was more an intention than actual writing. Soon after that he felt compelled to take on an entirely different task, namely to answer an opponent who spared no effort to smear his reputation: Karl Vogt. For eighteen months, he let his main work lie to instead write the 300-page pamphlet *Herr Vogt*, the last in a series of his violent polemical writings and the only one that came out in book form without Engels's assistance. We will briefly take up the content later, but here we are concerned with the *Grundrisse* and *A Contribution*.

A Contribution was a torso, if even that. Without the analysis of capital, the point remained unclear for most readers. Engels bravely tried to rouse interest in the instalment with a review in the journal *Das Volk*. The review was to have been in three parts, but the third was never written. It was disastrous. The first part dealt exclusively with the conception of history that Marx had developed in the preface to his work, and the second also touched upon preliminaries – namely, Marx's way of developing a rational scientific method from the philosophy of Hegel. The reader was given no idea of what the main text of the book dealt with.[52]

A Contribution aroused no enthusiasm even among their most faithful followers. Wilhelm Liebknecht, otherwise a devoted admirer, wrote in a letter to a friend that no book had disappointed him as much as this one.[53] It is easy to understand why. He had expected an answer the great questions about society and got only a few introductory analyses about money.

The *Grundrisse* contains so much more, but the manuscript long remained unknown to the world. There, Marx laid important foundation stones for his economic theory, and in the chapter on capital, developed perspectives that he never had the occasion to return to. It is this latter aspect that will now come under discussion.

Marx often opened important perspectives on society and history in a few short lines. The free exchange of exchange values was 'the real productive basis of all *equality* and *freedom*'. It is thus in commerce not inhibited by privileges and other restrictions that the highest bourgeois ideal has its necessary foundation. Perceived as pure ideas and ideals, they are only this base at 'a higher level'.[54] How this metaphor, this higher level, is to be perceived in greater detail remains unclear, except that there is a relationship of dependency. Marx's historical digression is clearer: Freedom and equality were certainly being spoken of back in antiquity. But the freemen of antiquity had their freedom at the price of other people's direct forced labour. In bourgeois society, the worker is formally free. It is better to be free than a slave, and yet the freedom of the worker under capitalism is illusory. The choice is between barely scraping by at the machines or pure starvation. Even equality remains illusory. The difference in power and influence are entirely too large.

In light of this, he attacks the conviction of Proudhon and other socialists that material production in itself is good. The relationships between people are destroyed by money and capital, Proudhon said. If these powers can be held in check, both freedom and equality would flourish. Marx angrily dismisses this: production and distribution – all of society, in fact – constitutes a totality. Both capital and wage labour are inevitably parts of the capitalist totality.[55]

Marx uses the word 'power' relatively infrequently, but his fundamental social theory deals with power relations in society to a great degree. There is a memorable formulation in the *Grundrisse* in which he turns his venom against David Ricardo, who maintained that capital only strove for more wealth. No, Marx said; the goal was to 'command' – that is, to rule over as much value and as much objectified labour as possible. In short, economic power was the main issue.[56]

This observation is a result of the conviction that production does inevitably appear as an interaction between things, but that ultimately deals with relationships between people. With aphoristic incisiveness, he wrote: 'Society does not consist of individuals, but expresses the sum of the relationships and conditions in which these individuals stand to one another.'[57] This is an interesting sentence, in which he attempts to capture the dynamic in society. Physics speaks of field theories, in which the starting point is neither atoms nor smaller particles but the dynamic interaction between them. Marx, it could be said, embraced a field theory of society.

Society Beyond Capitalism

One of the most famous sections in the *Grundrisse* deals with the forms of production and property that preceded capitalism.[58] What Marx called the Asiatic mode of production has in particular attracted attention and debate.

The immediate reason for the interest cannot be sought in

Marx's own text, but in the Marxist orthodoxy that developed chiefly during the Stalin epoch. According to this, development and all societies follows a fixed schedule. First came a primitive proto-society, then a slave society of the Greek and Roman type, and after that a feudal system from which the capitalist system sprouted forth. Faced with the simple theory of stages, a particularly Asiatic mode of production appeared as an inconvenient exception or even an alternative road to capitalism.

Ideas that China – and India in particular – fundamentally differed from most European states had turned up in the 1850s in Marx's and Engels's newspaper articles and correspondence. But the idea's presence in the *Grundrisse* signified something entirely different. It could not be blamed on any temporary deviations; it constituted an integrated part of an ambitious work.

Heated discussions broke out about pre-revolutionary China not having been a feudal society, as had previously been said. In fact, how did it relate in general to what was sometimes called the Third World, the lands beyond Europe, the United States, and the Soviet Union?

The debate acquired new overtones when, in 1957, German historian Karl A. Wittfogel published his work *Die orientalische Despotie* (Oriental Despotism). Wittfogel was a peculiar man; he began as a communist but gradually developed into the exact opposite. In the United States, where he emigrated, he even took part in Senator Joseph McCarthy's campaign of persecution against 'un-American activities'. In his book, Wittfogel maintained that both the Soviet Union and the newly communist China were contemporary examples of Oriental despotism. But he also carried out a rather ambitious survey of Marx's theories on the Asiatic mode of production.

After Wittfogel's book, a few more level-headed voices also made themselves heard. Back in 1964, Eric Hobsbawm authored an elegant and illustrative introduction to the first English translation of the *Grundrisse*, in which he concentrated on the question of the Asiatic mode of production. The preface can be found in the updated 2011 version of his great book, *How to Change the World*. In 1969, Italian political scientist Gianni Sofri published *Il modo di produzione asiatico*, which not only meritoriously summarized the ongoing discussion but also – and above all – went through the Marxist text and the historical background to it.[59]

A new angle on the question of the Asiatic mode of production emerged with the Marxist and feminist Gayatri Chakravorty Spivak. Marx and Wittfogel, Hobsbawm and Sofri had regarded the Asiatic mode of production from a European point of view. Spivak's starting point was Asia – India, to be precise – at the same time as she also analysed British, French, and North American culture at the highest level. Marx came into her life early, and the *Grundrisse* has remained his text that she recommends above all to everyone who wants to know more about Marx.

She herself has consistently depicted reality in a perspective from below. The peoples of the colonies, women, and proletarians have been the subject of others' expositions, but are there reasons to listen to their own voices? Can the subaltern, the subordinate, speak in general? Spivak tries to listen.

Spivak is usually considered to be part of the tendency called post-colonialism, which has played an important role in the intellectual and scientific debate from at least the 1990s and onwards. Several of its leading representatives have a free, anything but uncritical yet devoted relationship to Marx. The *Grundrisse* – especially the section on pre-capitalist forms of production and property – has played a special role.[60]

Now it is time to look at this text more closely. It is barely forty pages long and rather freely organized. Marx distinguishes a number of different social forms, the primary common element of which is that they are pre-capitalist. On the other hand, he does not sketch out a one-way line of development through a number of stages. This notion – which Marxist orthodoxy long recommended – has no support in the *Grundrisse*, while it has been easier for them to reproduce a sentence in the preface to *A Contribution*: 'In broad outline, the Asiatic, ancient, feudal and modern bourgeois modes of production may be designated as epochs marking progress in the economic development of society.' But is he really talking about a chronological order? Of those mentioned, capitalism obviously comes last, but what about the others? The far more detailed presentation in the *Grundrisse* provides no conception, for example, of the Asiatic mode of production passing into either an ancient or a feudal mode. The focus lies entirely on the relation to capitalism. His images of humanity's early development are vague; he has not yet familiarized himself with the new social anthropology.

Nor is he on the hunt for a strict classification of pre-capitalist societies. That would be the timetable of history that he otherwise had warned about time and time again. He could speak about a Germanic form of society – and even a Slavic – in passing. But they are, if anything, elements in a typology.

Humanity's first great decisive step entailed becoming farmers. There was no private property yet; it would not arise until the cities began to flourish and then also to obtain power over the lands by force. But different forms of society could arise from this town–country relationship, depending on a number of external circumstances.

It is crucial that Marx sees this entire course of events from the point of view of 'the working (producing) subject'. Whereas his first great teacher, Hegel, began from the top and spoke about Asiatic despotism – a term that also provided the title for Wittfogel's book – Marx started with those who were directly involved in material production. It was, he said, really only a tautology that human lives had always been dependent on material production (implied: whatever we do, we are dependent upon the bare necessities of life and strive for more). This is the starting point he would arrive at in his introduction.[61]

In this process, there is always a more or less obvious dynamic, a development of productive forces and thereby an expansion that sooner or later leads to conflicts among neighbours, and perhaps subjugation or colonization.

This is how Marx distinguished a particularly Asiatic mode of production. He not infrequently also used the term 'Indian', but neither Indian nor Asiatic have any fixed and limited geographic meaning. One crucial factor is the need for great collective efforts in order to ensure production, particularly in the form of irrigation works of various kinds. In this way, ancient Egypt as well as Peru also qualify for the designation.[62]

Large projects of this type provided living space for a number of small producers; high above them dozed the autocrat and his bureaucracy. The ruler was formally owner of everything of value in the country, but in reality the farmers provided for themselves and their progeny with what the earth produced. Above all, this required that they relinquish certain mandatory tributes to the despot. The mode of production lacked an inner dynamic to a great extent, Marx said.[63] It is the same thought he expressed in his most famous article on India in the *New York Daily Tribune*, the one in which he said that British colonization was required for the country to be modernized.

There are two clear main themes in the section on the various pre-capitalist societies. The first is property in its various forms. Marx arrived at the conclusion that the original tribally-based forms of property have their foundation in peoples' relationships with each other and nature, something that was the result of their special mode of working. European forms of production such as slavery and serfdom meant that the worker appeared as a natural condition for the entire society's – and thereby free individuals' – production.

It is the development of productive forces – that is, the development of people's skills and knowledge, and thereby technology in the broadest sense of the word – that sooner or later dissolve the various modes of production (as regards the Asiatic mode of production, as we have seen, the dissolution must be pushed through by foreign invaders). Productive forces are dynamic, whereas the relations that regulate production are on the contrary conservative. Or, in other words: the ruling class wants to preserve the established relations of power, but the prevailing social structure that is the condition for their power increasingly becomes an obstacle for the development of production that takes place through the labour of the workers.

In the section on pre-capitalist societies, the latter form of expression with its perspective of class struggle would make way for the more impersonal terms 'productive forces', 'relations of production' and 'forms of production'. The structure, in other words, is emphasized at the cost of the actors.

As Hobsbawm points out, the various forms of production that Marx spoke about (or in certain cases only suggested) are not without problems.[64] Was there, for example, anything in ancient society that inevitably led to a feudal system? Ancient society preserved its stability through enslaving people that had been conquered in war, and at the same time letting foreigners handle trade and handicrafts. In this way, the free citizens ensured their supremacy. But, in the long run, it did not succeed, and a new form of society gradually developed. But why precisely feudalism?

Even the term 'feudalism' itself in Marx's text is troubling, Hobsbawm said. It is difficult because he says so little about the form in question. He does not discuss the inner tensions, and is equally quiet about serfdom as he had previously been on ancient slavery. The crucial difference between both of them therefore does not emerge: the serf, but not the slave, is an economically independent producer.

Hobsbawm's criticism shows how completely crucial is Marx's own warning against historical schematism. It was a warning that unfortunately resounded unheard when Marxist orthodoxy took form a few decades after his death.

The other dominant question in the section on pre-capitalist forms of production and property concerns the transition to capitalism. This had been prepared earlier in the text, it is in general *the* historical question that occupied the author of the *Grundrisse* more than any other.

Marx stressed with great emphasis that the conditions for the domination of capital are not an integral moment in capital itself. They 'belong to the *history of its formation* but by no means to its *contemporary* history', he said. One such condition is that the serfs free themselves from their serfdom and pour into the cities. They have thereby emancipated themselves from the bonds that formerly shackled them to the earth, but they are also without their own provision and their ability to work is their only asset.[65] In order not to be cast into starvation, a future capitalist is required who is ready with capital large enough to keep the workers alive during the labour process. In this way, capital conquers its 'eternal right to the fruit of other men's labour'.[66]

There is nothing in Marx's text that says that feudalism is the only possible condition for capitalism. What is required is the free worker and the capitalist with their assets. It is the *relation* between them that is decisive. As we have seen, the German word *Verhältnis* signifies the parts in a totality in which no part can be replaced without a totality being dissolved. It is therefore, as Marx talks about, a *Produktionsverhältnis*, a relation of production. Surely, he also observes the freeman and the slave in ancient society, or the lord and the serf in feudalism, in the same way. But he does not emphasize this at all as strongly as when capitalism is concerned. It is capitalism that finds itself the focus of his constant attention.

This does not mean that what he said about previous societies lacks significance. On the contrary, he promised a more detailed analysis of landed property and its development in the work that the *Grundrisse* was to result in. This was certainly the planned part on ground rent and the work that ultimately shrank down to one single instalment.[67]

Among the most remarkable things about the *Grundrisse* is that there Marx betrays something of his thoughts about the nature of work in the society of the future. He does not say much; actually only a few pithy lines are involved, but it is still a lot in comparison with his other texts.

The theme is work as sacrifice and as self-realization. He objects to the bourgeois economists from Smith to Senior, who see work as the same kind of burden throughout all of history. Only at rest can a person experience freedom and happiness. Such is their image of humanity: by nature, we are not active beings, naturally fitted for great efforts.

Marx was and remained the advocate of another view of humanity. Back in the *Manuscripts* he had sketched out an image of humanity as fundamentally both social *and* active. In the *Grundrisse,* the image returns, but now without the wrapping of the thinking about essence. On the other hand, the word 'alienation' remains, even if not as frequent.

Smith and his followers imagine not only that human production requires capital from start to finish. They also believe that bourgeois economists are the same as human beings that existed long ago, and that they would continue to exist for as long as the human race endures. They would always shun labour. The eternal indolence of the land of Cockaigne was an absurd utopia during the Middle Ages and it would remain so in the world of tomorrow. But its attraction would always remain just as great for Smith's and Ricardo's human being.

In Marx's opinion, people's relation to work changes with the variation in the modes of production. Before capitalism, toil at the washtub or behind the plough was an external compulsion for the overwhelming majority: someone was commanding them. As a result of capitalism, the worker became formally free to work or to loaf about. But destitution forced them onto the factory floor. And the future?

Fourier was mistaken when he asserted that work in a good society becomes a pure pleasure that could be performed under noisy cheerfulness, Marx said. He himself struck a different tone in one of his very finest aphorisms: 'Really free work, e.g. the composition of music, is also the most damnably difficult, demanding the most intensive effort.'

The word 'compose' deserves particular attention. In English, as in German (*komponieren*) it has the basic meaning of creating music, and Marx was of course not unaware of this. The profession of composer appears to many as the freest of all; it was certainly also like that for him. But the word can also have a broader meaning, referring to the work of creating order and the large amount of material where such an order is not given but requires both reflection and ingenuity. (The qualifier 'of music' is in addition to the English translation.)

It was the kind of activity with which Marx was extremely familiar. He knew everything about both seriousness and toil. There was a fundamental freedom in the choice of projects – the exact freedom that neither the slave nor the wage labourer would ever experience during their working hours. But once the choice had been made, it required all the energy and care that could be raised.

Marx's brief sentence could stand as a model for all serious artistic, intellectual, and scientific work. But it is primarily not his own situation, and that of those like him, that Marx had in mind. In the next sentence, it turns out that it is material production of the future that he was speaking about. The sentence is long and rather complicated, and can well be quoted in its entirety:

> Work involved in material production can achieve this character only if (1) its social character is posited; (2) it is of a scientific character and simultaneously general [in its application], and not the exertion of the worker as a natural force drilled in a particular way, but as a subject, which appears in the production process not in a merely natural, spontaneous form, but as an activity controlling all natural forces.[68]

Both elements in Marx's image of humanity are thereby provided for. Work is social. People are not isolated from one another in and through production; they collaborate. Work is also scientific. Marx had recently pointed out that the modern wage worker did not understand the scientific principles that governed the machines of industry. But this distinction between brain and hand had to be overcome

Work must also become general. Marx had come back to a question that occupied him greatly during the 1840s: the division of labour. In the *Manuscripts*, he saw the division of labour as the radical evil that maimed people. In *The German Ideology*, he and Engels dreamed of an existence in which people could switch between various activities.

The brief lines in the *Grundrisse* did not mean that people would become free at any time to choose between a number of different pleasant occupations. The tone had been set by the sentence about the seriousness and the effort that characterized the activity once the choice of work task had been made.

But what, then, is general labour? It must be work in which the person doing the work is in command of all the moments required, and thereby has the opportunity to govern and develop the machines that production requires. It is thus not the activity of a jack-of-all-trades but rather of the universally knowledgeable specialist. From these scanty lines of Marx, it is easy to become attached to the image of an extremely advanced production in which technology and science live in symbiosis. Activities of this kind are encountered today in both medicinal research and advanced programming.

We do not know his own concrete ideas. He did not paint a vivid utopia. He did not even make any general predictions; he only indicated the conditions for free labour within material production (which, in his opinion, sets the limits for all other activity). He said nothing about how all the people who do not have a place in this advanced industry are to occupy themselves.

Nonetheless there is a remarkable brightness around these few lines. He compares good work with both art and science, he gives away how he views his own research work, and he gives an idea of what human freedom is: the project that absorbs everything else, in close collaboration with other people.

He spoke not of the many small freedoms of choice in capitalist society, but the choices of decisive importance and existential proportions.

The Great Matrix

Of all the finished and unfinished works of Marx, the *Grundrisse* is the most complete, claimed British scholar David McLellan in his introduction to a British selection of the works. Another translator, the American Martin Nicolaus, calls it Marx's 'unpolished masterpiece'.[69]

The unrestrained character of the text has made it popular among postmodernists. One of them, Thomas M. Kemple, concentrated in part on Marx the *author* in his 1995 book *Reading Marx Writing*. He emphasizes, with reason, Marx's interest in fiction – Balzac in particular – but in the final chapter he goes further and finds a grandiose erotic and aesthetic utopia in Marx's works in general. It can be questioned whether his interpretation has textual support.[70]

The *Grundrisse* is a work that continuously inspires (and even entices) readers to entirely too audacious wanderings far from Marx's intentions. On the one hand, the work is the result of a tremendous creative rush; on the other hand, it is unfinished with many loose threads and marked in long sections by the down-heartedness that replaced the initial enthusiasm.

When Marx gave up the project, he sought to arrive at a clearer and stricter form in *A Contribution*. But, after the preliminaries, new tasks intervened. It was often like this for Marx: something else always came up. Nine years lay between the *Grundrisse* and the first volume of *Capital*. During those years, he managed to do a lot – but only a smaller part of what he had mentioned in advance in his great manuscript.

Despite its unfinished state, the *Grundrisse* is an important work. In it, the outlines emerged of the entire project that Marx never managed to complete. The self-criticism that otherwise was so typical for Marx sometimes had to give way to the momentary flash of wit. Among these flashes of wit there are also pearls of wisdom that we have every reason to make use of. They are scattered everywhere, from the quick sketches of the introduction to the remarkable ones about the strict internal conditions of free labour.

The *Grundrisse* points forward to *Capital*, but also contains much else that bears witness to Marx's entire multifarious world of ideas. It is both a preparatory work and a work in itself.

11

The Unfinished Masterpiece

The *Grundrisse* is a crucial stage in the great project that a few years later would be given the name *Capital*. *Capital* is not a finished work. Marx did not even bring the first volume – the only one he sent to print – to a conclusion. He reworked it for every new edition, and at the end of his life he was ready to tear the text up again. *Capital* is otherwise a number of manuscripts, often in several versions, and various even more incomplete drafts and rough outlines – quite a few of them in the form of letters to friends and acquaintances.

Summarizing *Capital* is the greatest challenge for anyone writing about Marx. The attempt that follows here begins with a few glimpses into the life Marx was living when he was working on his great project. After that, it concerns the external history of the work: how the first volume was completed, printed, and edited time and again, and how its sequel remained a series of fragments.

What was nevertheless written constitutes a grand attempt at capturing an entire society in its dynamic development. Marx weaves an intricate net of concepts in order to succeed in his purpose, and it is this network that is scrutinized closely in the following section. *Capital* also has its own history of interpretations, which starts with Engels and continues on up to the present – in fact, it has been given renewed intensity in our time. A special section deals with this history, and in particular with the interpretative alternatives that today seem the most fruitful.

A number of problems that a reader of *Capital* will encounter are dealt with individually in the second half of the chapter.

This concerns both what I call the metaconcept of the 'form and content' type with which Marx constructed *Capital*, and also the connection he sees between ideas about society and the world on the one hand and fundamental social relations on the other. One important theme is his sometimes misdirected striving to provide his account with a kind of natural scientific exactness. It was an ambition that could come into conflict with his method of constructing his conceptual apparatus. Another question I ask concerns the extent to which his general view of history influences the specific theory he develops in *Capital*. Finally, I illustrate how his concept of class goes no further than a few suggestions in *Capital*, probably because he encountered unexpected problems at the prospect of joining empiricism with theory.

When Marx finally saw the end of the work on the first volume approaching, he remembered Honoré de Balzac's story 'The Unknown Masterpiece'. He clearly recognized himself in the main character, the painter Frenhofer. As we shall see, the parallel says much about his own hopes and fears before *Capital*.

New Trials

The first volume of *Capital* was published in 1867. For Marx and those close to him, it was a great relief. Marx had never been able to work undisturbed on his big project. In the early 1860s, he was still plagued with serious financial troubles. They became worse after losing his income from the *New York Daily Tribune* thanks to the American Civil War. Things went so far that he sought a position at a railroad office. But nothing came of it; his handwriting was entirely too illegible.[1]

He now had to harass Engels all the more intensely with constant new appeals for financial assistance. On at least one occasion, he was so occupied with his own quandaries that he appeared thoroughly heartless to his friend. This was when Mary Burns, Engels's live-in partner for many years, died unexpectedly at the age of forty-one. 'I simply can't convey what I feel,' Engels wrote to Marx in January 1863. 'The poor girl loved me with all her heart.'

Marx's reaction was strangely indifferent. The news surprised him as much as it dismayed him, he wrote. 'She was so good-natured, witty and closely attached to you.'

That was all. In the next sentence, he declared that he certainly also had problems. The attempt to raise money in France and Germany had been unsuccessful, and now the family had no credit with either the butcher or the baker. They were behind on the rent, and the children needed clothes – in brief, there was no end to the misery. At the end of the letter, he tried to mitigate the effects of his words by admitting that he was horribly egotistical. He would rather have seen his own mother die than Mary!

Engels was upset and put off his response for a few days. In it, he admitted that the cool reaction had been very disagreeable to him. His philistine acquaintances had shown him greater sympathy and friendship than his closest friend! A penitent Marx explained that his wife and children could attest that he had become as upset at the news of her death as when any of the members of his own family had died. But before he had written his response, the troubles of daily life had overwhelmed him and rubbed off onto the letter. He had wanted to take back his words as soon as he sent them.[2]

Engels was satisfied with that, and their correspondence returned to its customary order in which economic theory, politics, and daily problems and reasons to rejoice were given their fair share.

Marx had wished for his mother's death instead of Mary Burns's, and in November 1863 the seventy-three-year-old woman actually died. The inheritance she left behind meant palpable economic relief; six months later, in May 1864, another death occurred that Marx really had not been looking forward to but which further improved the family's situation. Wilhelm Wolff, his friend of many years, died after a painful illness, and when the will was read it turned out that the revolutionary teacher had bequeathed the greater part of his small fortune to Marx. Suddenly, they were in the money. His gratitude was of course great; he dedicated the first volume of *Capital* to Wolff with the words 'my unforgettable friend Wilhelm Wolff, intrepid, faithful, noble protagonist of the proletariat'.[3] (The intent was that the second part, which would consist of what posterity knows as Volumes II and III, would be dedicated to Jenny Marx, but nothing came of that as Marx never completed the sequel.)

The money chiefly went towards the purchase of a house and a more respectably bourgeois lifestyle. Marx, however, never abandoned his habit of living beyond his means. But his troubles were on another level; destitution was no longer at the door.

Now instead it was his health that tormented him the most. His ailing liver, which had bothered him as soon as he started grappling with his great scientific project, was now accompanied by an even more serious complaint – a skin disease that gave rise to an endless succession of large, pus-filled, painful carbuncles that sometimes prevented him from sitting, sometimes from standing, and occasionally became so bad that he had to lie in bed, unable to work. Jonathan Sperber conjectures that he likely was suffering from the autoimmune disease *Hidradenitis suppurativa*, which is still difficult to treat today. Arsenic was used as a remedy in the 1860s, with the risks that such a cure entailed.[4]

But it was not only private circumstances that made Marx's road to the finished work longer and more difficult. Just when he was at the point of completing the second instalment of *A Contribution to the Critique of Political Economy*, he was subjected to the furious attack from Karl Vogt that we have already touched on. His entire political activity was maligned, and he thus saw himself compelled to devote his entire attention to politics in the narrower sense and not social theory. The result was a text of another kind than the *Grundrisse* or *A Contribution*. *Herr Vogt* can rather be seen as a belated continuance of the *Eighteenth Brumaire*.

A few years later still, he entered into politics again, and this time with full strength. Now it was a question of organizing the working class across national borders. Marx soon found himself in the midst of events – ideologically, in fact, he set the tone in constructing what posterity would know simply as the First International. His political activities will be the focus of a future chapter; both *Herr Vogt* and the International will be dealt with there, as well as Marx's relationship with the Paris Commune of 1871. But for the immediate future, our object is the story of the genesis of *Capital*.

The Long Road to Volume I

Marx's economic writings began in Paris in 1844 with the *Economic and Philosophic Manuscripts*. Back then, he believed that he would soon be finished with his basic theory of society. But the years of revolution intervened, and he set to work again on his great project only in 1850, when the family had established itself in London. In many ways, the work took a new direction at that time. On the one hand, Marx got a great deal more material to work with through the British Museum. On the other, he engaged his predecessors – David Ricardo in particular – in a new, critical way. He questioned Ricardo's fundamental theses, including his theory of money, and in that way set out on his own path as an economic theoretician as well.[5]

As usual, he thought he would be able to finish his great project soon. He wrote to Engels in 1851: 'I am so far advanced that I will have finished with the economic stuff in 5 weeks' time. *Et cela fait*, I shall complete the political economy at home and apply myself to another branch of learning at the museum.' Sixteen years later, he announced to the same man: 'So this week the whole vile business will be over.'[6] And this time it really would be!

The *Grundrisse* and *A Contribution* had been crucial stages on the road to the first volume. But he was still far from the goal. He continued reading copious amounts of literature on the subject that in some way could be of significance for his great social theory. But that was not enough: he constantly developed his theory, step by step constructing the finely branched conceptual apparatus with which he tried to capture the essentials of the society he lived in.

It was at this point that he arrived at the conclusion that his life's work should be named *Capital*, with *A Critique of Political Economy* as the subheading. He announced the new title in December 1862 in an interesting letter to his friend in Hannover, the doctor Ludwig Kugelmann. The letter gives the impression that he was practically finished with the work, which he saw as a more comprehensive continuation of *A Contribution*. He would clarify 'what Englishmen call "the Principles of Political Economy"', thus in brief (once again) the essential features of

the theory. He hoped that not only he himself, but others as well
would be able to build further on this foundation.[7]

But he could not finish the work this time, either. In fact, Marx
had written an enormous manuscript of approximately 2,400
printed pages, in which an important part was not intended at all
for the volume he had promised. This part is known to posterity as
Theories of Surplus Value and was first published by Karl Kautsky
between 1905 and 1910 in a state that aroused a great deal of criticism for its inaccuracies. This large amount of working material,
including *Theories of Surplus Value*, is available today in a critical
version in the *Marx-Engels-Gesamtausgabe*.[8]

But none of this was still ready for print; nor was the considerable pile of manuscripts that was the result of Marx's work between
1863 and 1865. There are preparatory works for all three volumes
comprising *Capital*, but also a lecture in English: 'Value, Price, and
Profit', which he held for the leadership of the International.

He now had a clear picture of the totality he had been striving
for. In the summer of 1865, he wrote to Engels that the advantage of his work was that it constituted 'an artistic whole'. The
entire manuscript therefore had to be ready before he sent it off
to the publisher. It was dialectically structured, which was why
he could not do as the Brothers Grimm did with their *Deutsches
Wörterbuch* and send it off instalment by instalment.[9]

He had come a long way from the idea that led him, six years
earlier, to publish the first instalment of *A Contribution*. Now
everything had to be made ready for print at the same time, both
for the reader's sake and also his own, since every part was going
to be connected with every other part.

He was obviously talking here about all of *Capital*, which he
had now done the preparatory work for. Only three chapters
remained and then everything would be ready, he said. The final
volume – 'the historical-literary one' – was not part of the same
totality and had been easy to complete, since all the questions had
been answered in the three previous volumes.[10]

As we know, Marx's hopes were not fulfilled. Only the first
volume came out during his lifetime. His idea about the totality
deserves to be examined more closely, but, before that, a sketch of
the continued work on *Capital* is needed.

On New Year's Day 1866, Marx began working on the text that would finally go to print the following year. But despite all the preparatory work, the path to completion remained an arduous one. His health did not hold out. By February, he said in a letter to Engels that he could work like a man possessed as long as he was free from the usual liver troubles. But now, instead, he had suffered an attack of that odious skin disease. He was still so weak that he could not manage to grapple with the purely theoretical parts, but had only expanded a section on the working day.

Nonetheless, he thought that he would soon be finished not only with the first part, but the second as well. So as not to tire the reader out, he was thinking of having the second part – which would in fact correspond to what is now divided between Volumes II and III – published three months after Volume I.

His health continued to disrupt his peace and quiet. If it was not the carbuncles plaguing him, it was his liver; and if it was not his liver, it was toothache and neck pain. In July, he nevertheless believed that Volume I would be ready for print in August, and in November he saw completion as only a week away.[11] But it was not until April 1867 that he went in person to the publisher, Otto Meissner in Hamburg, to deliver the entire manuscript. Meissner wanted Marx to stay in the area for the sake of editing, so he set out for the Kugelmann family home in Hannover where he stayed for a few weeks.[12] But finally he was forced back to London, and now Engels assisted him with the editing. Engels found parts of the text difficult to understand, and encouraged Marx to make them more easily accessible as far as they would permit. But the acuity was commendable, he assured Marx. For his part, Marx could pester Engels up through the final edit with questions regarding the latter's purely practical insights as a 'manufacturer'.[13]

Engels could not only provide him with information on these matters, he also realized what the work that was now reaching its partial completion had cost his friend. 'Forever resisting completion, it was driving you physically, mentally and financially to the ground,' he wrote.[14]

In September 1867, the bulky tome of the first volume was finally ready. But new problems now awaited. How would the work get the attention it deserved? Engels wrote a steady stream of reviews: nine in all, eight for German newspapers and the ninth for the British *Fortnightly Review* – which, however, refused publication. Engels's ability to vary his texts is admirable. One of the reports ended up in *Elberfelder Zeitung*, a local paper for the town in whose vicinity he was born and where he had stood on the barricades nearly twenty years earlier. In it, he emphasized that Marx's work laid the scientific ground for socialism. The daily press could not judge the science, he said; here science itself must have the last word. But he also joked about how long it had taken before Volume I was finished – and much still remained.

Another interesting review was written for *Rheinische Zeitung*, which however did not print it. Here, he called *Capital* the Bible of the new Social Democratic Party. It rose far above ordinary social democratic publications, he declared, and despite the first forty pages being difficult with all their dialectics the book was easy to understand and marked by 'the author's sarcastic manner of writing which spares no one'.[15]

The rejected report for *Fortnightly Review* is above all an outline of Marx's book, and is both quite long and quite dry. It is not likely that it would have attracted many English-speaking readers to *Capital* if it had been published.[16]

Despite the pains of Engels and other followers, the work on distribution went rather sluggishly. A number of negative reviews also appeared. The most important of them was the one published by Eugen Dühring, a senior lecturer in philosophy in Berlin and a social democrat.[17] It was a fateful event; without it, Engels would never have written *Anti-Dühring* a few years later. It would also affect Marx, however condescendingly he would express himself about the review in his correspondence. Dühring had misunderstood a great deal, he wrote to Engels. Above all, Dühring was afraid, he wrote to Kugelmann. But in a later letter to Kugelmann, he was upset over Dühring bundling him together with Hegel – Hegel was an idealist; Marx, on the other hand, was a materialist.[18] It would soon appear that Dühring's statement had hit him hard. In a moment, we will see how this became evident.

Otherwise there was silence and indifference around *Capital*, which bothered both Marx and Engels. The foremost exception was the interest that some Russians showed in Marx's work. Crucially, a young Russian, twenty-five-year-old Nikolai Danielson, contacted Marx about a translation. Marx was enthusiastic. He had certainly not placed hopes for speedy social changes in Russia, but the positive interest that not only Danielson but a number of his countrymen showed him gradually gave him new ideas. He immediately began teaching himself Russian, and after six months of intensive study he had got so far that he could make excerpts of Russian-language literature.[19] He himself asserted that texts in Russian were necessary for him to be able to complete the manuscript of Volume III that had lain dormant since 1864. But this was surely not the only reason.

An acquaintance of Danielson's, German Lopatin, was the first to grapple with a translation. But it was Danielson who, together with his friend Nikolai Lyubavin, completed the project. The book was published in Russia on 27 March, 1872. The censors let the book through with the words: 'Although the political convictions of the author are completely socialist and the book is socialist through and through, it is certainly not a book accessible to everyone; what is more, its style is strictly mathematical and scientific...' The reassuring final point reads: 'Few people in Russia will read it. Even fewer will understand it.'[20]

The book quickly sold 900 copies. It was no grand success, but nonetheless it was a good reception. Marx's Russian adventures had begun. Danielson had wanted to translate the second volume together with the first, but Marx blocked that. In October 1868, he wrote that it would not be possible – it would be perhaps six months before it was completed, since he first had to wait for a series of important statistical information to be published in France, the United States, and Great Britain. In other respects, the first volume constituted a totality in itself, he added.[21]

The work on what is today Volume II did not take six months, but the rest of Marx's life. He wrote a number of new versions that Engels had to make up his mind about when, after Marx's death, he was going to publish the work.

Nor did the first volume give its author any peace. A new edition in the original German had to come out, and that required a great deal of work. Marx was not satisfied with the earlier results, and readers had informed him of the unnecessary difficulties that met those interested. He carried out an exhaustive revision, which we can now follow in detail through the critical edition of the *Marx-Engels-Gesamtausgabe*. Among other things, he worked out an outline that is far more easy to grasp. The formerly six chapters became twenty-five. In an afterword to the second edition, he wrote that the central section on *value* 'has been carried out with greater scientific strictness', and that this strictness was certainly something he had been striving for in the entire work.[22]

The new edition was published in nine instalments from the summer of 1872 to the summer of 1873. At that time, a French translation was already on the way, done by Joseph Roy. Marx was satisfied with Roy's work at the beginning, but he gradually became increasingly critical. It was too literal, and Marx therefore had to make the text more French in places where the original German shone through. The corrections cost him more work than if he had carried out the entire work himself, he said; the entire text had to be reshaped. Ultimately, his own changes became so sweeping that the title page of the final translation, published in 1875, said that it was a 'Traduction de M. J. Roy, entièrement révisée par l'auteur' (Translation by Mr. J. Roy, completely revised by the author). In fact, Marx had not been satisfied with rewriting the text, but also made changes and supplements to the second edition of the German original. The remarkable thing is that the French translation is the last version of *Capital* that Marx himself prepared for printing. Everything published later was marked to a greater or lesser extent by Engels's editing. In those editions, incidentally, Engels did not include all the additions and changes Marx made to the French version.[23]

Considering the constant reworkings of the first volume, it is no wonder that Marx had difficulties finding enough time to complete the sequel. Political work also demanded plenty of time. Add to that his health being unstable; in fact, he aged markedly during the 1870s – entirely too early by today's standards, but hardly by those of the time (if anything, Engels with his good health and his well-maintained physique was among the exceptions).

None of the many different versions of the text for the second volume that Marx left behind met his strict requirements for a print-ready manuscript. (The third volume remained in the state he left it in 1865). In addition, he always felt compelled to enter deeply into his widely differing areas of knowledge. He read literature in subjects such as agrarian chemistry, interested in what the constantly expanding productivity of the time meant for the environment, and he tried to improve his mathematics in the hope of being able to bring his theory to greater heights. Stacks of new excerpts joined the older ones. The fourth section of the *Marx-Engels-Gesamtausgabe* contains such excerpts, as well as short paragraphs and notes in the margin, most in Marx's hand and significantly fewer in Engels's. Once the work was completed, it was thirty-two thick volumes all in all, with an equal number of volumes of commentary and indexes. Marx was, and remained, the master of the unfinished work.

The Structure of *Capital*

Capital is indisputably Marx's most discussed piece of writing. Engels's reviews of Volume I were the first attempts at leading readers by the hand into the great work. Since then, the streams of interpretations, popularizations, and rebuttals has continued without interruption. After the fall of the Soviet Union in 1991, the literature concerning *Capital* changed its character. Now, there is no longer any accepted orthodox tradition to take a position on. Its echoes can certainly still be felt, but they no longer have a state or an army to lean on.

After the global economic crisis of 2008, *Capital* has become as topical as it had rarely been before. Marx has found a large new audience, and a long series of commentators have come to their assistance with all kinds of introductions and interpretations. Old and new problems and points of conflict have become urgent, and are discussed with both acuity and passion. The grizzled veterans of reading Marx have met the enthusiastic newcomers who never needed to take a position on the orthodoxy once dictated from Moscow. They were quite simply too young for the question when the Berlin Wall came down. Many of them had not even been born.

In the next section, we will get more closely acquainted with this 'new reading of Marx' (*neue Marx-Lektüre*), as it is called in Germany.[24] But before that, Marx's original texts must be presented so that at least their construction is explained. A survey of this kind can never be completely uncontroversial; there is disagreement on several fundamental points where *Capital* is concerned. Different authors also place different stresses. Often, the governing question is: What is still topical – still opens perspectives – today? The hopelessly out of date must also have a place in a historical account.

What follows first is a summary account of the main content of the three volumes, and after that a survey of the central conceptual apparatus.

When Marx was writing the *Grundrisse*, he had in mind a work in six different parts. In the mid-1860s, as we have seen, there were only four parts that had crossed his mind – the first three of which would constitute 'an artistic whole'. These three parts, in order, would deal with the production process, the process of circulation, and finally the total process of capital. He himself said that the construction was dialectical. It is easy to see that he was moving from the abstract to the increasingly concrete.

First, production, which capital acquired power over and thereby directs. One condition is a developed monetary system. The owners of capital invest their money in the production of commodities that can be sold at a profit, which can then largely be invested in new and expanding production. They take into service people who, unlike the slaves or serfs of previous epochs, are not bound to a certain master but free to choose the occupation that makes it possible for them to survive. Thus arises the working class, which like the industrial capitalists is a new phenomenon in history. Capitalist and worker have opposing goals: the capitalist wants to squeeze out as much work as possible at as low a price as possible; the worker strives for the opposite. The resulting struggle over the working day and wages for labour is an unmistakable feature of capitalism.

Capitalism is a dynamic economy in which each capitalist must invest in more efficient technology just to remain in competition. When the capitalists as a collective draw down their investments, the system ends up in crisis. When it flourishes, new and larger capital accumulates. The original accumulation, which made capitalism possible at all, took place in an earlier society in which the conflict-filled relationship between capitalist and free worker had not yet been established.

In the second volume of *Capital*, circulation is in focus. Once a commodity has been produced, it must go out onto the market to meet its potential buyers. This entails additional costs for the capitalist. Intermediaries responsible for transport and sales must have their compensation, the necessary bookkeeping is not free, and so on. Only when the capitalist has sold their commodities at a price exceeding the costs they had for production have they reached their goal. Now the cycle can begin again: with the money the commodities sold brought in, the worker can be hired anew, raw materials procured, and new commodities produced – preferably more than were recently thrown out onto the market. And so it continues, round after round, for as long as capitalism remains.

In the third volume, the entire process – both production and distribution – are dealt with. The concreteness is greater than in both the previous volumes, and thus also the proximity to empiricism. Profit and interest, shares and banks are the central themes. The theme of class turns up only in the very last chapter, and that in a fragmentary account. The reader is reminded that the third volume was built on a relatively early and unfinished manuscript that Engels was forced to complete.

In principle, *Capital* begins in the same way as *A Contribution* from 1859: with the question of how wealth 'presents itself' (*erscheint*) in a society in which the capitalist mode of production prevails. The answer is also the same: with 'an immense accumulation of commodities'. It is thus this quantity of varied commodities that we first catch sight of when we search for clarity in the question of what capitalism is. Other modes of production also had commodities that were bought and sold. But these commodities did not have the same dominant role at all as they do in capitalism.

Commodities have two different factors, Marx said: use value and exchange value. Once again, the classical distinction from Aristotle comes into favour. Use value is the *quality* of the commodity, Marx said. It informs us *how* the desirable object is constructed. It has to do with benefit, with usefulness. A commodity is acquired because it is needed, whether it be iron, paper, food, or luxury articles.

Exchange value, on the other hand, is *quantitative*, and thus answers questions such as 'How many?' or 'How much?' Exchange value makes commodities with completely different properties comparable. A kilogramme of coffee is worth as much as so much ground beef, or so many apples. Where exchange value is concerned, the physical properties of the commodities are completely ignored. The incomparable becomes comparable.

Marx was not satisfied with talking about exchange value. When use values are ignored, it is the *value* that appears in the exchange values, he said. In other words, exchange value is what we can immediately observe, value is what we can infer from it.

The distinction between exchange value and value may seem like an evasion, and a few words of explanation are therefore required. It is that much more important, as we can then figure out how Marx generally constructed many of his concepts. Exchange values are surface phenomena; values lie under them. The relationship, which Marx only fully elucidates in the second edition of *Capital*, has its foundation in the classical distinction between essence and phenomenon.[25]

It is important that the essence Marx spoke about is *changeable*. He has thus not relapsed into the ideas of his youth, according to which it is possible, for example, to speak about an unchanging human essence. What he was talking about here is a rapidly changeable surface (exchange value) and a more slow-moving, underlying essence (value). The central thing is the word 'appear' (or, in German, *erscheint*, 'shines through, becomes visible'). We already encountered it in the first sentence of *Capital* on the wealth of society appearing as commodities. Here, it is thus a question of the relationship between the exchange value a commodity has, and its value. Exchange value is immediately empirically accessible. We discover value only after an analysis. The distinction has significance for the interpretation of certain central – and controversial – parts of the whole of *Capital*.

There is another central pair of concepts that have a certain degree of similarity with the previous pair without being exactly the same; namely, form and substance (or form and content). This is found throughout all of *Capital* and is applied even in the initial pages to the relationship between exchange value and use value: use value is the material content, exchange value the social form. Often, the form signifies the immediately observable, and substance (or content) the part that must be uncovered. But it is not so here. Value is what the exchange value expresses, and the sensuous (or intellectual, if any) properties of a commodity constitute the basis of its use. A kilogramme of bananas can be exchanged for a given amount of bread, a book for so much cloth. If I have no bananas but I have bread, I can exchange the one for the other; if I have cloth but nothing to read, my clothless neighbour can get my cloth by giving me a book I want to read.

The important thing in this exact relation of form and substance lies in the determination of the social against the material. Exchange is a social relation; use value is linked to the specific properties of the commodity. We part with what we do not need in favour of getting something else that satisfies a need within us.

But there is something that unites all the commodities we exchange: they cost labour. Something that has not done so – the air we breathe, for example – is no commodity. Through labour, all the specific objects we can get in exchange because we covet them are created. The work that produces them is equally as specific as the commodities themselves. The carpenter makes a table, the tailor sews a coat, the programmer compiles a specific programme. But there is still something we can compare, and that is what Marx called labour *power*. The worker is *not* their labour power, but they can *sell* it to someone who can pay a wage so as to do business with the commodities produced – that is, a capitalist. But the worker always sells their labour power against time, and it is time that determines the compensation.

Different kinds of work can be differently productive, depending on which tools – machines and the like – are on offer. Using a concept of Adam Smith's – *productive force* (which can also occur in the plural, *productive forces*), Marx narrows down this productivity as follows: 'This productiveness is determined by various circumstances, amongst others by the average amount of skill of the workmen, the state of science, and the degree of its practical application, the social organisation of production, the extent and capabilities of the means of production, and by physical conditions.'

This determination shows that Marx takes various kinds of factors into account. The word 'average' is important; Marx was not talking about the exceptions, the particularly unskilled or the particularly outstanding workers, production taking place with out-of-date technology or with tools so advanced that they have not yet become prevalent in the industry. Nor was he talking about the clumsy or extremely efficient co-operative organizations. There, as wherever the entire scope of the means of production are concerned, competition compels an equalization. The productive forces are continually being developed under capitalism. Everyone must keep up – or be eliminated. But the more production increases, the more the labour time necessary for production decreases.[26]

The distinction between concrete and abstract labour plays a key role in the construction of Marx's conceptual apparatus in *Capital*. Concrete labour has a use value. Through it, concrete products – whether bread, bananas, books, or coats – are manufactured for the market. Abstract labour, on the other hand, is exchangeable; it has an exchange value that involves a cost for the capitalist and wages for the worker. As always, the exchange values are comparable. The many stages of labour that are required to produce a loaf of bread cannot be compared with the assuredly equally as many stages that differentiate the idea for a book from a book in the bookshop. But the compensation the baker receives for their labour can be compared with the compensation for the printer (or publisher's reader, or author).

Through its exchangeability, abstract labour is a commodity among other commodities in capitalism – that is, something that is bought and sold. One hour's labour can be worth the same as a certain number of litres of milk.

All commodities can thus be exchanged for all other commodities in fixed proportions. Marx was talking about equivalent forms. Completely different objects are worth the same as each other in fixed proportions. Three apples = one cup of coffee = eight caramel candies = a bus trip across London. Everything can in turn be put on an equal footing with so many minutes of net income for a certain kind of work.

This may seem trivial. But Marx had the researcher's ability to be surprised at the most obvious relationships. How could a fixed use value be made equal to all other, equally specific use values? Apples and railroad trips – to say nothing of a worker's labour time – are completely different in their natures. In contrast to use values, exchange values have nothing to do with nature, but with society.

There is reason to remember the opposition of nature and society. It is crucial for Marx's entire theoretical construction. A number of concepts – we do not have to note all of them here – can be deduced from it. Money can be deduced from the exchange-ability of commodities. Pure barter would be unspeakably difficult to manage. A perhaps wants what B is selling, but A does not have exactly what B needs. B then has to go to C, who has the desired object on offer, but C in turn has to go hunting for someone that can meet their needs. The results would be complete chaos.

The solution is a commodity that can be exchanged for all other commodities: the money commodity. The material form the money commodity takes is unimportant. In Marx's time, both coins made of precious metals and paper notes were in circulation. Today, the money form also takes many other, more abstract shapes, but nothing substantial has changed.

Marx is thus ready for one of the most important sections in *Capital*: the one where he introduces the concept of commodity fetishism. In Marx's time, the word 'fetish' was associated with a form of religious faith that belonged among what were called primitive peoples. These 'savages' regarded many objects as animate, and equipped with magic powers.

It was therefore provocative when Marx claimed that the society regarded as the most advanced – capitalist society – was characterized by the same kind of ideas. Fetishism here applied to commodities. Outwardly, a commodity seems like a completely trivial thing. But if it is analysed, it turns out that it is 'abounding in metaphysical subtleties and theological niceties', Marx said. A table is made of wood, but as soon as it is to be sold it becomes 'something transcending' (a not entirely satisfactory translation;

Marx says a 'sensuously supersensual thing' – something contradictory in itself). In relation to other commodities, it no longer stands on firm ground, but on its head. This has nothing to do with its use value, but instead the commodity form itself.

The peculiar character of the commodity form is in turn due to commodity-producing labour. Specific labour – of the baker or the machinist – becomes a commodity as a result of the fact that its value becomes comparable to all other specific labour. Why is this so? The secret lies in labour time, which makes itself felt in commodity value with the power of a natural law. The relationship is valid without anyone needing to be aware of it.

Commodity fetishism is not something timeless, but is the result of the capitalist mode of production. Bourgeois economists do not realize this; they search for timeless categories instead. They vary the story of Robinson Crusoe in different ways, but always so that the social character of a commodity remains the same. But think about the Middle Ages, Marx said. Everyone was dependent on everyone else back then – serfs and landowners, laymen and priests. Under capitalism, the worker is free to sell their labour power – or to starve; the capitalist free to purchase labour – or to go without commodities to sell and thereby no longer a capitalist.

Commodity fetishism makes itself felt in all relations of exchange. People there appear only as representatives of commodities, and not as concrete persons. Their will seems to have passed into the thing. In relation to each other, they array themselves in their character masks as capitalists, workers, or something else.[27]

In a society like this, money becomes the bonding agent among commodities, and through them also among people. The seller of a commodity receives money from the purchaser, and the money can then be exchanged for other commodities. Marx lays out the formula $C - M - C$, in which C stands for commodity and M for money. It is a simple circulation. Money flows constantly onwards towards new acts of purchase. It is a monotonous repetition, Marx said. One person sells linen cloth and purchases a Bible. The seller of the Bible uses his money for whisky. So the money flows on; human actors seem lifeless in comparison with the transactions they are involved in.[28]

Money is a necessary condition for the formation of capital. Capital always emerges first as money. So it was historically: through accumulated fortunes, trade, or usury, capital at one point could assert itself in relation to landed property. And so it would remain: capital takes form again and again as money – money that makes commodity production possible and which, once the commodities are sold, becomes money again. Capital circulates and, in that way, is similar to ordinary, simple commodity circulation. But the *form* is different. Simple commodity circulation is static; the sum of money put into the purchase of commodities is the same as the one the seller gets in their hand: $M–C–M$. But capital must be dynamic in order to survive as capital. The form becomes $M–C–M'$, where M' means more money. Profit, in other words, is the point of capitalist production: this profit cannot only, or chiefly, serve for the maintenance or luxury consumption of the owner of the capital, for in that case, the owner of the capital would be knocked out of competition with other, more thrifty owners of capital who invest their surplus into expanded production: $M–C–M'–C'$, which in turn is intended to generate even more money (M''), which makes even greater production of commodities possible, and so on.

Where does this surplus value come from? Marx is in no doubt about the answer: from the labour that the worker performs. The only commodity the worker has to offer is their own labour power, and the capitalist buys this labour power for a certain time and against a certain compensation that will cover the worker's immediate needs. But the value of the labour the worker performs is greater than the compensation. The worker makes *surplus value*, Marx said, and this surplus labour provides the *surplus value* which in the formula is represented by M'', more money.

The capitalist has a constant hunger for increasing surplus value. This has nothing to do with any personal qualities, but is part of his character mask as a capitalist. Without this hunger, he will of course disappear from the scene. The hunger in turn makes him constantly want to extend the working day of the workers. But this has its inevitable limits, the day has twenty-four hours, and of these each person must have time to recuperate (a period that in early capitalism was pushed down to an inhuman minimum).

This limit forces the capitalist to look for another way, namely
to increase the productive power of labour. Productive power is
complex, as we have already seen, but it seems possible to lim-
itlessly develop a significant factor: technology. Capitalism has
put its inventions into the system. Researchers and technologists
are necessary for great and constantly accelerating technological
development. Thanks to technological development, more and
more can be produced in an increasingly shorter time.

Marx also makes an important distinction between constant
and variable capital. On the one hand, the capitalist must invest
their money in raw materials, machines, and other equipment. On
the other hand, workers who are willing to sell their labour power
at a certain price are required. Raw materials and machines do not
change their value (or the magnitude of their value, as Marx says)
during the production process itself, but remain constant. Labour
power, on the other hand, creates a value that exceeds the costs
for it, thereby creating surplus value. In other words, it is variable.

The relationship between constant and variable capital, that is,
the ratio between them (or c/v, with the symbols Marx used) plays
a crucial role for his view of the development of capitalism. It is
only in Volume III that he developed his idea in full.

It has already become clear that Marx placed special emphasis on two closely associated areas: the length of the working
day and the development of machinery. Each received their own
comprehensive chapter – 10 and 15 – which differ from the rest
of the account in their detailed empirical data. Marx had use of
his extensive studies of documents, official and otherwise, and
in the chapter on the length of the working day an interesting
picture emerges of a tug-of-war between capitalists and workers
in which the outcome does not seem decided, in particular as state
power can go in and (to the dismay of the capitalists) legislate
on the maximum legal length of the working day, as it can for
the conditions for women's and children's work. Each such limitation intensifies the capitalists' efforts to develop more efficient
machinery that increases productivity, thereby compensating for
the reduction in pure working time.

Marx was not satisfied with giving a fluent account, rich in
detail, about both the modern history of technology and its

consequences for the workers. He began with a definition, still often cited, of what a machine is. A machine has three parts, he declared. The first he called *die Bewegungsmaschine*, that is, 'the motor mechanism' that can either create its own movement, such as a steam engine, or draw it from some other source, for example water, as a waterwheel does. The second part required is a 'transmitting mechanism' that conveys, regulates, and perhaps converts the movement through driving shafts, gears, and so on. Finally comes 'the tool or working machine' which performs the tasks that the totality is intended for: it spins, it knits, it cuts, it glues together – the possibilities are endless.[29]

The machine does not have the limitations of the human organism. It also makes labour power relatively cheaper, since it increases productivity. In this way the limitations of the working day are compensated for. But as soon as a given piece of equipment has become standard in the industry, it is important for every capitalist to install even more powerful machinery. The race goes on.

Even before Marx got into the development of machinery, he introduced the concept of relative surplus value. One part of the worker's labour time is equivalent to their wages, while another part provides surplus value for the capitalist. The time required for wages becomes shorter with more efficient machinery. More surplus value can thereby be created over a longer time. In other words, surplus value is related to technological development; in short, it is relative.

The basic formula of capital, $M - C - M' - C' - M''$ indicates a continual increase in the amount of both money and commodities. Surplus value is transformed again and again into new capital, and capital increases both for the successful individual capitalist (the less successful one is constantly threatened by elimination) and for society in general. Briefly put, capitalism grows; it *accumulates*. Marx spoke about the development of capitalism as a process of accumulation.

Capital is accumulated through labour. Technological development makes the labour more efficient, and the workers can produce more. But at the same time this means that fewer workers can accomplish just as much production as previously. The workforce can decrease, which means that variable capital becomes less. A growing number of people are without work and form what Marx called a reserve army, which is constantly prepared to step in as soon as work opportunities present themselves. This means there is a relative overpopulation, forced to take the work on offer regardless of the conditions. For capital, this is an excellent situation; wages can be pushed down through unemployment. Many workers are compelled to go from job to job in positions that are at most temporary. Others drag themselves along as agricultural proletarians, defenceless against ruthless owners. Still others are forced into unproductive occupations, chiefly as servants in aristocratic or bourgeois families.

Well-functioning capitalism offers more and more commodities on the market. But the process cannot continue forever. One day, a surfeit sets in, the commodities are not sold; the money people have to purchase with is no longer enough. In brief, there are too many commodities and not enough money; prices drop and it costs everyone. The crisis has become a fact.

According to Marx, periodic crises are inevitable in capitalism. If the crisis is to be surmounted, production and consumption must meet again but now at a lower level than before the crisis. And so, a new cycle begins again; production and consumption increased to a certain, unpredictable level ...

So far, Marx has followed the capitalist system as it is in working order. But the question also arises of how it first became possible. For this, both original capital and a sufficient number of people who are no longer bound to any master but free to sell their labour power are required. Here, Marx could largely put together what he had already investigated in the *Grundrisse*: merchant capital and usury, the discovery of precious metals in America, and people who were driven out of their tenancies on the land and herded into the cities without other opportunities to survive than to pounce upon the jobs that were offered.

Once Marx had opened the view back to the time before the genesis of industrial capitalism, he could also play with the idea of the time *after* it. He could not say *which* crisis would knock down the system. He only knew that the end would come 'with the inexorability of a law of Nature'. 'It is the negation of the negation.'

'Individual property' would thereby be restored, but on the basis of 'the acquisitions of the capitalist era'.[30] We will have reason to return to these words.

The first volume of *Capital* is a comprehensive and ingenious construction of concepts. The second volume seems significantly simpler in comparison. The title itself offers the greatest problem: 'The Process of Circulation of Capital'. Marx himself had declared in 1864 that the production process, regarded as a totality, comprises one point of the process of production and circulation. 'Production' thus signifies a part of the totality on the one hand, and the totality itself on the other. It is in principle the same idea found in the incomplete 'Introduction' to the *Grundrisse*. Even here, its purpose is surely to emphasize the unique position of production. It is with production that everything begins anew, he said in the earlier text.[31]

At the same time, circulation would be given ever greater significance in Marxist theory through money having assumed a role that it did not yet have in the *Grundrisse*, where it could be completely separated from value.

In Volume II, Marx carefully surveys the entire circulation of the commodity, which contains a number of important transformations. The journey begins with the capitalist's purchase of machines and raw materials, and ends with their selling the commodities that production resulted in. The money invested in the first moment will be reaped with interest in the last; anything else is a failure.

From the point of view of circulation, production is a black box, the workings of which are mysterious: money seems to become more money through the market's own dynamic. Money differs from other money only through its quantity; in the flow of money and commodities, the latter only appear as bearers of a certain value that can be expressed in money. At the same time, commodities are concrete things with fixed use values.

The concept of circulation means an unceasing flow. If the flow is interrupted in any of its moments, circulation ceases. The capitalist who does not invest their money in new production accumulates wealth instead. If production itself does not start, the

means of production are of no use; if the commodities produced
lie unsold, crisis threatens.

Transport of commodities and people must be consumed in the
same moment as they are produced. A train trip cannot be put
into storage. Production is the transfer itself of commodities and
people, and consumption is the journey. This is how it is in general
where services are concerned.

Seen from the point of view that the circulation of commodities
provides us, the transport of commodities is only one moment
necessary in what Marx called total circulation. This circulation
begins with the money that the capitalist invests and ends with
the money they earn on the commodities they sold. It thus encompasses both circulation and production. Once the circulation has
been concluded, a new one immediately begins.

So far, we have seen money – that is, money capital – as the
starting point of circulation. But we can just as easily start from
productive capital, thereby taking our starting point in production – or for that matter start from commodity capital, with the
path of the commodities. Marx developed the three possibilities
with almost scholastic exactitude. The point is that different economic theories placed the main emphasis on one kind of capital or
another – the mercantilists on money, Quesnay and the Physiocrats
on commodities, and the classical economists (Ricardo, Smith, and
their followers) on production. But wherever they begin, industrial capital runs through all three stages. Marx found it suitable,
however, to distinguish between the circulation of money capital
(which he called Form I) and the circulation of productive capital
(which he called Form II).

The time that both production and circulation require has
particular significance. The more quickly both processes go,
the more quickly the value of the capital invested can increase.
But the increase itself comes almost solely from production; the
only exception is transport, which is necessary so that commodities find their consumers. Others involved in the process, such
as advertising executives and salesmen, perform no productive
work. This does not prevent their efforts from being necessary.
Marx made a clear distinction between productivity and benefit.
All conscious human activity may be beneficial, but only a small

part of it is productive – that is, it contributes to increasing value.

Marx called the total of production and circulation time *turnover time*, and he was interested in how many turnovers a given amount of capital could manage to go through in a year. But here it is important to distinguish between *fixed* and *circulating* capital. Tools and machinery necessary for production do not circulate; the only change they undergo after they have been put to work is a more or less slow wearing out. They can sometimes be replaced in advance, for example if newer, more efficient machinery has come out on the market. In production, on the other hand, raw materials are consumed – as is labour power – and must thus be completely replaced. Simply put, they are variable.

In the continuation of Volume II, Marx studied the relationship between production, circulation, and time in more detail, and he devoted great attention to the ideas and theories of his predecessors. As he did in the first volume, he concluded with the problem of accumulation. An important distinction, which he did not introduce into the more abstract Volume I, is the one between production of means of production and production of consumer commodities. Production of machines, for example, serves to make other production possible and more efficient. Marx spoke of this as *Department I*, while production intended for consumption became *Department II*. Commodities from Department I are necessary for production in Department II, and the costs within the different departments must therefore be assessed differently. Marx experimented with a number of calculation examples that we do not need to go into. The main thing is that whatever department we are in, the owner of capital cannot devote all their profit to their own consumption but must reinvest a substantial portion in order to assert themselves in competition with other capitalists.

The Volume II that Engels put together after Marx's death is a compilation from a number of different manuscripts that Marx had worked out – most of them after Volume I had been published. We cannot get a clear idea of why Marx was never satisfied with any of these versions, but constantly began new ones. Obviously, as Engels said in the foreword, his failing health played a role. But his health still didn't prevent him from writing these versions and, moreover, from going deep into comprehensive studies of the literature in a number of different subjects.[32]

One of the versions – the fourth – was even edited for print but clearly was still not good enough; it was outbid by newer versions. Marx obviously wrestled a lot with his calculation examples, which he always hoped would show more than they actually did. The final version naturally bore the mark of Engels; this applies to an even greater degree to Volume III, which is built on a single, large, but unfinished manuscript by Marx. The manuscript is one example among many of Marx's enormous productivity during the early 1860s. He wrote thousands of pages, all of which were left open for later revisions. The manuscript Engels primarily had to go on contains approximately 900 printed pages. This substantial mass of text, which Marx left to its fate in December 1865, was in no way ready for print; it gave Engels a great deal of work before, towards the end of his life in 1894, he was able to complete the edition. Since 1992, Marx's own manuscript has existed in a model critical edition, and it is thus now an important task of research to see what Engels's editing meant for the final result. A great deal of literature has developed in which these differences are analysed. The evaluations of Engels's influence change, but there is great unanimity that it had been crucial for posterity's views of Volume III and thus all of *Capital*.

We will return to the problem of the relationship between the worlds of Marx's and Engels's ideas. For now, it is important to remember that the original of the third volume came to be before the first was ready for print, nor is the former completely in step with the latter.

According to Marx's own declaration, Volume III of *Capital* would 'locate and describe the concrete forms which grow out of the *movements of capital as a whole*'.[33] In order to manage this task, Marx first made an important distinction between *surplus value* and *profit*. As we will remember, surplus value is the value conveyed to the product through the worker only receiving wages for a certain portion of their labour time. As soon as we talk about profit, we are regarding the matter more from the capitalist's point of view. For them, profit is the difference between what was invested in machines, raw materials, and labour power, and what they bring in from the sale of their commodities. It appears as though it was capital, and not labour, that generated profit. In Marx's opinion, it is the same error of judgement as seeing workers' wages as compensation for the entire labour time.

Now there is also another difference between surplus value and profit: profit, but not surplus value, is calculated in dollars and cents. Profit has a price, but value does not. We are thus faced with what is known as the *transformation problem*, which has led to many controversies among interpreters of Marx; we will also return to this in a moment. In Volume III, Marx tried to solve it himself but came to the conclusion that the method selected did not work. He put it aside rather casually with the words: 'Our present analysis does not necessitate a closer examination of this point.'[34] Posterity has not been as unconcerned about the issue.

It is from the concept of profit that Marx developed his law of the tendency of the rate of profit to fall. Essentially, this law says that the ratio between profit and capital invested falls over time. When Marx overshadowed all his predecessors and the age he lived in, it is easy to believe that this is a thesis that was original to him. This is not so. Most economists from Smith forward embraced it, but their explanations varied. Marx was original in finding the cause, as he described it, in 'the nature (*Wesen*) of the capitalist mode of production'.[35] His line of thought is simple and clear. Capitalism is dependent on the unceasing development of labour power. But at the same time, this development means that the value of fixed capital increases. Dead labour, which has passed into the machines, grows at the expense of new, living labour. Calling constant capital c and variable capital v, the ratio c/v thus increases. Profit will constitute an increasingly smaller portion of the capital its owner commands.

Marx also entered upon more concrete economic relationships that play a crucial role for capitalism. Interest belongs here. It is certainly ancient, but it is no longer just a speciality for profiteers. Even ordinary workers take out loans, and the interests they have to pay can be of use for capital. Certain capitalists specialize in loaning out portions of their wealth to other capitalists, who invest the money in production. Marx distinguishes between *money capitalists* and *industrial capitalists*. The money of the money capitalists seems to grow by itself through interest. Interest-bearing capital, Marx said, is thereby the 'most external and most fetish-like form' of capital.[36] Its formula is $M–M'$: money that yields more money. The money seems to be given life; it is equipped with its own inner power. This organic increase, in Marx's opinion, is an illusion that capitalism inevitably creates. (We can observe today that the illusion remains. Money in an account seems to grow under its own power.)

According to Marx, the banks take on ever greater significance in capitalism, and especially through them credits of various kinds as well. Marx also spoke about *fictitious capital*, by which he meant stocks and shares. He certainly would also have counted options and other derivatives as part of that, if he had only lived to experience them.

One important theme in Volume III is the recurring *crises* of capitalism. Through its constantly increasing productivity, the system is constantly threatened by overproduction. No previous society could have been stricken with an overabundance of commodities. Capitalism can. It happens again and again.

We will remember that the crisis of the late 1850s filled Marx with hopes of speedy social change. The disappointment he experienced when nothing of what he imagined happened meant that he toned down the significance of crises. He developed no theory of crises in Volume III, but still emphatically asserted that crises constitute an inescapable ingredient of the capitalist mode of production. Aggregate production gradually and inevitably becomes greater than the consumption that people can manage. The crisis means that value is destroyed and many people – primarily the workers – suffer greatly. But on the other side of the crisis, production and consumption will meet again, a new cycle of development begins, and productivity again increases up until the next crisis. From inside the system, it is impossible to determine when the increase of production leads to increased sales, and thereby increased wealth, or when it yields overproduction. The individual capitalist always has to invest in producing more and selling more, and the illusion that new crises are impossible re-emerges. It is still so now, at the beginning of the twenty-first century.

Marx's hopes that an economic crisis would pave the way for a revolution have been toned down in *Capital*. There is no obvious path from the crisis to a new society. Change can only be the work of the working class, and it is not at all certain that the working class will be ready when the crisis breaks out. Marx did not say this directly, but this is the conclusion that can be drawn from how his words changed from the time he wrote the *Grundrisse*.

At the end of Volume III, he returned to a theme that played a large role in Volume I – namely, the ideas that are inevitably generated by the capitalist mode of production. Modern society may have liberated itself from diverse traditional religious ideas, but their counterparts exist in people's relationships with the coldest economic conditions. Marx spoke about superstitions that only the scientific gaze is able to penetrate, which find expression in what he called the 'Trinity Formula' – in which the appropriate parts of the Godhead were capital, landed property, and labour power. They provide income to their respective owners, and for the observer they thus seem to also create value to an equivalent extent. But this is not so, and the basis for this error lies in the fact that the character of labour under capitalism does not emerge for the observer. The worker appears as free as the capitalist and the landowner. But this freedom is illusory, since the worker is compelled to sell their labour power for their survival. Nor does it become clear that the worker sells only their labour power, and that the capitalist in return pays for only a part of what was created through labour power. A part of the surplus value created goes to the landowner, while the capitalist keeps the rest for themselves – and above all for future investments in new production.[37]

The very last chapter in the work is only a torso, if that. The subject – the social classes – is central enough, but it is interesting to note that while the class struggle appeared before all other concepts in the *Manifesto*, as the actual driving force of society, Marx put off its systematic treatment until the end in *Capital* – so late, in fact, that he did not even manage to bring his argument to its point. This of course does not mean that classes had negligible significance for him. His Trinity Formula deals with exactly those three classes that his predecessor David Ricardo had already pointed out as involved in an irreconcilable struggle. Rather, the essential thing is that Marx's last words on the class struggle were never spoken in his main scientific work.

The Interpreters

The first interpreter of *Capital* was of course Friedrich Engels, and his significance for the reception of the work was that much greater, as he brought two of the volumes to some kind of conclusion. The extent to which he accomplished his friend's intentions is one of the most controversial questions in the substantial literature on Marx. In the next chapter, the relationship between the two men will be examined more systematically. Until then, only a few short points will be adduced.

Engels never expressed himself as subtly as Marx; he always wrote more simply and in a more straightforward manner. That simplicity, as Hobsbawm points out in his 2011 book *How to Change the World*, also implied a vulgarization.[38] Others have spoken about pure misinterpretation.

What Marx called dialectics was always inseparable from his method of presentation. The very beginning of Volume I – on the commodity and money – is a prime example. Engels sighed over the degree of difficulty in the account. He himself always wrote *about* the dialectic, and did not employ it in his own presentation.

There is also a difference of nuance between their views on capitalism. Marx treated developed capitalism chiefly as a *system* that functioned when all the essential bits – capitalists, free wage labourers, and so on – were in place. Historical changes such as the development of productive forces and the concentration of capital were consequences of the system itself. In his analyses of capitalism, Engels gave more place to broad historical overviews.

Let us be satisfied with these points for the time being. The essential thing is that Engels not only completed *Capital* but also, through his own works – *Anti-Dühring* (1877) and *The Origin of the Family, Private Property, and the State* (1884) – would leave an imprint on the general notion, especially among social democrats and socialists of the time, of Marx's theory of capitalism. People read and were influenced by Engels first of all, whereas

Capital stood out as an entirely too demanding work, suited more for academics than workers hungry for reading. Engels's presentations were not only simpler. Analyses of value and capital were added into a huge framework of historical development in which all signs pointed to socialism and communism. The sympathetic reader could feel a sense of secure hopefulness at the prospect of the future.

Engels would long dominate the interpretation of *Capital*. His line was continued by Karl Kautsky, who developed a kind of orthodoxy that could be condensed into catechism-like works. But further development also took place after 1900, and that directly on the basis of *Capital*. Also to the point is that what generally came to be called Marxism became popular especially among young academics, at the same time as the German Social Democratic Party was enjoying great electoral success. Success breeds resistance, and Marx's economic theories – officially embraced as the very centre of social democratic theory – became the subject of heavy-handed scrutiny. Chief among the critics was the Austrian economist Eugen Böhm-Bawerk, who belonged to the 'neoclassical' tendency that maintained – as against Ricardo and the other classicists – that prices are not related to the value created by labour but exclusively obey the law of supply and demand (an idea that is still completely dominant among economists today). Böhm-Bawerk addressed himself directly to Marx, who had created an alternative to the classical theory.[39]

Another Austrian, Rudolf Hilferding, appeared in Marx's defence. Hilferding, who began his career as a paediatrician but soon went over to economics and politics, played an important role in both the Austrian and the German workers' movements. But above all, he was the author of the 1910 book *Finance Capital*, which was an audacious attempt at simultaneously updating and modernizing Marx's theory in *Capital*. According to Hilferding, development had left the stage Marx had depicted in which individual capitalists found themselves in life-or-death competition with each other. Instead, large monopolies had developed – companies that in turn had become increasingly dependent on the banks, which had taken a dominant role in the economy. In brief, finance capital and industrial capital had grown together.

In this economy, the capitalists had become dependent on the state, which with its forces could promote the export of capital that had become necessary once the large monopolies had saturated the domestic market. It could be said that Hilferding depicted very well the period of enormous concentration of wealth that characterized the period before the First World War, which had no equal until the dawn of the twenty-first century.[40]

Hilferding's analysis also became influential in the workers' movement of the time. Weightiest was the contribution Rosa Luxemburg made through her 1913 book *Die Akkumulation des Kapitals* (The Accumulation of Capital). Luxemburg, who was from Poland but would make her most important contributions in Germany, was especially interested in what Marx called 'primitive accumulation'. Something like this had also gone on outside of capitalism, but as a result of colonialism these pre-capitalist societies were integrated into the new world economy, which was becoming increasingly dependent on the exploitation of people and natural resources in other parts of the world.

Luxemburg criticized Marx for treating capitalism as a closed system. Against that, she maintained that capitalism could only survive as long as it had non-capitalist surroundings to expand into.[41]

The Russian revolutionary Vladimir Ilyich Lenin went further along Hilferding's and Luxemburg's line while at the same time disputing their conclusions; in his 1916 book *Imperialism, the Highest Stage of Capitalism*, he declared that contemporary developments would inevitably result in a revolution and a new type of society.

Through the Bolshevik seizure of power in 1917 in Russia, he seemed to have confirmed his thesis. Now socialism would be built; no sacrifice was too big for this task. Luxemburg was among the sharpest critics of the dictatorship of opinion that Lenin and his closest collaborators exercised. 'Freedom is always and exclusively freedom for the one who thinks differently,' she declared.[42]

Luxemburg can be said to have been correct on another point in relation to Lenin and his followers: in the future society Marx sketched out, there is a market of goods and not a completely regulated planned economy. But the market is equal, in contrast to the kind that characterized capitalist society.

The decades after 1917 are not marked by any audacious interpretations or further developments of *Capital*. When Stalin, after Lenin's death, created what he called Marxism–Leninism, Marx (or, rather, Marx via Engels) was overshadowed by Lenin, and gradually also by Stalin himself. There were new issues on the agenda, especially how a socialist economy could be constructed, and the capitalist system stood out chiefly as the foreign Other that could be dismissed with a few stereotypical phrases.

There were individual thinkers outside the Soviet Union who wanted to work in the spirit of Marx instead of following the directives from Moscow. For Hungarian philosopher Georg Lukács, who wrote the important 1923 work *Geschichte und Klassenbewusstsein* (translated in 1967 as *History and Class Consciousness*), there was a particular concept in *Capital* that stood at the centre: reification. This was concerned with commodity fetishism, according to which it is people who appear as things in capitalism.[43] (Lukács met violent criticism from Moscow for his unorthodox book, and soon fell back in line.)

The influential Frankfurt School, with Max Horkheimer and Theodor W. Adorno as prominent figures, were implacable critics of both the Soviet Union and capitalism. They further developed a central concept in the tradition from Marx, namely *critique* in the sense it occurs in the subtitle of *Capital*: *A Critique of Political Economy*. In general, *Capital* played an important role as a source of inspiration and a model. But Horkheimer, Adorno, and their colleagues were less interested in political economy in the narrow sense than they were in a broader critique of society and culture, according to which people in capitalism had become easy victims of totalitarian ideologies. In countries where dictatorship had not been victorious, the inhabitants had on the other hand become passive consumers of a soulless culture. The foundation of these defects could be found in capitalism itself.[44]

Marx's critique of economics also had a number of direct followers, particularly from the 1930s onwards. One prominent example of this tendency is the American economist Paul Sweezy, who played a crucial role for decades in the Marxist-oriented

journal *Monthly Review*. Together with Paul A. Baran, an
American of Russian extraction, he wrote the influential 1966
book *Monopoly Capital*, in which the authors could be said to
have brought forward arguments not only from Marx but from
Hilferding and Luxemburg as well. Thanks to capital accumulation, it becomes more and more difficult for the capitalists to
make profitable investments. The economy threatens to stagnate
when companies in monopoly positions draw down production in
order to avoid overproduction.[45]

The book on monopoly capital came out at a time when Marx
and Marxism were again attracting many readers and interpreters.
Whereas *Capital* had been overshadowed by later interpretations
for decades, the work was now being put into focus. Competing
readings fought for attention. French philosopher Louis Althusser
and a group around him published a collection of analyses in
1966 under the title *Lire le Capital* (Reading Capital).[46]

Althusser and his collaborators had an extremely firm idea
about Marx's development. The author of the *Manuscripts* was
a young philosopher who wrote texts in the style of the times in
which he tried to lay bare the essence of humanity. But a short
time later, he was awakened to new, crucial insights that he
expressed in the *Theses on Feuerbach* and *The German Ideology*.
There, as Althusser says, he discovered 'the continent of history'.
Only there does the Marx who would later write *Capital* emerge.
The basis of his theories was the conviction that material circumstances govern history: the class struggle – that is, the struggle
for power over production and the results of production – is the
motor of history. Under capitalism, the class struggle assumes its
particular character with wage labourers and capitalists as the
major antagonists.

Thus the materialist conception of history stands at the centre,
and it is based on this that *Capital* should also be interpreted;
namely, as a book about an epoch with its unique features.[47]

Althusser's interpretations were subjected to harsh criticism
by a number of young readers of Marx on the Continent. West
German philosophers Hans Georg Backhaus and Helmut Reichelt
were some of the most important, and the Danish historian of
ideas Hans-Jørgen Schanz was part of the tendency, at least at

the beginning.[48] A common designation of their interpretation is 'capital-logic' or the 'capital-logic school', but in Germany they prefer to speak of *die neue Marx-Lektüre*, 'the new Marx reading' (or Marx interpretation); this is certainly a more suitable name. Capital-logic is only the designation for what Marx himself called the expansive nature of capital. The essentially new thing with this loosely put together tendency is the method of reading both *Capital* and the *Grundrisse* in detail without being guided by the traditions of interpretation based on Engels, which continued with additional simplifications and later additions in 'Soviet Marxism'. What was crucial was both the almost ascetic strictness in the reading of Marx's texts and the firm idea that Marx's theory of capital had no substantial connection with his materialist view of history in general.

There is already a rapidly growing body of literature on this new reading. Ingo Elbe has produced a summary, as comprehensive as it is energetic, in his 2010 book *Marx im Westen*. The 2011 omnibus *Kapital & Kritik* provides a series of longer articles that are examples of the approach.[49] One of its pioneers, Hans Georg Backhaus, provided his version of the path to a new understanding of Marx in his 1997 book *Dialektik der Wertform*. In an introductory text, he talks about his own development as well as that of his closest collaborators. Important impulses came from the Frankfurt School, but the specialization in certain texts of Marx awakened during the encounter with the first edition of *Capital* from 1867. The second edition, as we have seen, is partially a popularization of the first, and by going back to a succession of texts and letters Backhaus can show how after the *Grundrisse* Marx strove to make his theory more accessible to more readers.

In the *Grundrisse*, therefore, the outlines of the real, original theory that Marx – supported by Engels – gradually watered down can be detected. It got worse when Engels later misinterpreted the theory by placing an equals sign between 'simple circulation' and 'simple commodity production'. With that, he erased the boundary between distribution and production that was so important for Marx.

The essential part of the original theory that remains even in later editions of *Capital*, according to Backhaus, is commodity fetishism. On the one hand, the commodity is something real and concrete; on the other, an abstraction that is ascribed an exchange value. The fundamental economic categories are twofold all along. This duplication continues in the distinction between value and exchange value. Exchange value is the visible, expressed in price. Value, like surplus value, is something fundamental that only thought can show the necessity of.

Backhaus thus makes Marx more of a philosopher than an economist in the narrow sense. Readers can themselves draw the conclusion that Marx, in and through his simplifications, is merely placed before certain insoluble dilemmas. Backhaus does not even mention the transformation problem. On the other hand, he admits in his survey of the new Marx reading that as an older man, he can see difficulties with his and Reichelt's interpretation of Marx.[50]

Michael Heinrich, who we have encountered several times, also sees himself as a representative of the 'new Marx reading'. But his background is different, as are his interpretations to a considerable extent. Whereas Backhaus and Reichelt had their main schooling in Frankfurt am Main, Heinrich was from Berlin and was associated early on with the journal *Prokla* (a contraction of *Probleme des Klassenkampfs*, Problems of the Class Struggle) where he still has a dominant position. Otherwise, the central figure of *Prokla* has long been Elmar Altvater, a political scientist and critic of capitalism who, moreover, was one of the founders of *Die Grünen*, the German Green Party. Heinrich himself is a mathematician and political scientist.[51]

Unlike Backhaus, Heinrich does not regard the second edition of Volume I of *Capital* as a superficial version of a scientific project whose real outlines can be seen in earlier versions of the text. In a direct polemic with Backhaus and Reichelt, he points out that what Marx wrote after the *Grundrisse* consisted not only of popularizations but clarifications as well. On the other hand, he sees the many different versions of the text as a link in a great, unfinished project that in his opinion had its start in 1850, after the revolutions, when Marx set about his new project on the critique of economics once more. It is this project that, according to

Heinrich, constitutes the most important turning point in Marx's development and not, as Althusser states, the introduction of the materialist conception of history. The critique of economics that Marx developed before the revolutions was coloured by speculations about the essence of humanity.

In Heinrich's opinion, Marx remained fundamentally ambivalent towards his new project. It is not only the concept of alienation that turns up here and there in his later writings. His relationship to his predecessors in economic theory is also ambiguous. On the one hand, he continued in their line, presenting yet another variation of their theory; on the other, his project constituted a critique of the social conditions for the type of theory that Smith and Ricardo developed, as did later economists following them. According to Heinrich, it is the latter that constitutes the important and valuable thing in the project, while Marx's own variation of the theory is interspersed throughout the entire effort. The subtitle to Heinrich's most important work, *Die Wissenschaft vom Wert* (The Science of Value), indicates the ambivalence in Marx's attempt: 'The Marxist critique of political economy between scientific revolution and classical tradition.' In other words, Marx was an innovator in the theory who did not fully realize the consequences of what he had done.

According to Heinrich, Marx had developed a theory that was not empirical in the sense that it generalized what was sensuously evident. In that case, Marx asserted, we should be satisfied with the merely apparent, as for example John Stuart Mill, Nassau W. Senior, and others were. Instead, Marx created a particular theoretical level at which the inner coherence in capitalist society would be laid bare. Its historical character would also become evident here. Heinrich does not mention the term 'hypothetical deductive theory' – that is, a theory that generates certain general hypotheses that can directly or indirectly be tested on empirical material. Theories like this are commonly accepted in the modern natural sciences, but this is surely not the type of theoretical construction Heinrich has in mind. Rather, he refers to the strict conceptual construction that characterizes *Capital*, in which the view is opened at times to a fluent empiricism, for example in the chapters on the working day and on the development of machinery. Only through theory do we know why there must inevitably be a struggle on the length of the working day and why capitalism, equally inevitably, must strive for increasing productive force. Only through theory can we thus interpret empiricism.[52]

Heinrich is otherwise best known for having developed a *monetary* interpretation of Marx's theory. On that point he comes close to Backhaus, who asserts that 'as regards simple circulation, the Marxist theory of value is essentially a theory of money'.[53] Heinrich goes further, however, and draws support from the most astute of the GDR's Marx specialists, Peter Ruben (typically enough a *persona non grata* in his homeland), who in 1977 pointed out that Backhaus seemed to ignore that value cannot exist outside the 'form of appearance' of the commodities – that is, 'their actual sensuous existence'.[54] Heinrich is of the opinion that Marx himself put obstacles in the way of the development of his theory through immediately perceiving money as an actual commodity, thereby linking it to its historical genesis. The essential thing, however, is the conventionally determined symbol of value that can take any form whatsoever. *Something* has value attached to it, regardless of what that something is (today we often encounter it as a few digits on a bank statement). Products of labour are neither commodities nor objects of value if they are regarded in isolation. Only through commodities being related to money can the connection between different individual labours be established, Heinrich says.[55]

The interpretations by Backhaus, Reichelt, and Heinrich may seem complicated. I believe that what they say can be more easily understood if the philosophical background to Marx's conceptual construction is examined. But, before we do that (and thereby distance ourselves from both Heinrich's and Backhaus's modes of expression), we have to take a look at some other traditions of interpretation.

Robert Kurz, another German philosopher, was an original author who vigorously attacked anyone and everyone who interpreted Marx. His last book, published posthumously in 2012, was called *Geld ohne Wert* (Money without Value). There, as previously, he asserted that many of these people were continuing in a tradition from orthodox Eastern Bloc Marxism by talking about labour and about class struggle in an antiquated manner. Heinrich, on the other hand, was in Kurz's opinion a postmodernist Marx interpreter.

The concept of crisis stood in the centre of Kurz's own analysis. Inspired chiefly by Roswitha Scholz, he emphasized that the patriarchal element in capitalism – and here he warned about the development the world was now going through – could result in an endless catastrophe and not at all in peaceable socialism.[56] Another subject of Kurz's attacks was Wolfgang Fritz Haug, a German philosopher who became known for things such as being the publisher of *Das Argument* and of the enormous anthology *Historisch-kritisches Wörterbuch des Marxismus* (Historical-Critical Dictionary of Marxism), which began publication in 1994.[57] Haug, who has also authored a long series of books, is one of those who unhesitatingly asserts that there was not only a structural dimension, but also a historical one, in *Capital*. It is in this spirit that, over the last few years, he has begun dealing with what he calls 'high-tech' capitalism, the latest phase in the development that Marx only saw the beginning of.

Haug is also part of the growing group of specialists who have published detailed instructions on how *Capital* should be read. Over the last few years, this species of literature has increased drastically. Michael Heinrich is one of its most assiduous contributors; a shorter version of this pedagogical work exists in English under the title *An Introduction to the Three Volumes of Karl Marx's* Capital (2004); a more comprehensive, as yet unfinished version exists in German. A Swedish professor of cultural studies, Johan Fornäs, has authored a book of great merit called simply *Capitalism: A Companion Guide to Marx's Economy Critique* (2013). Two renowned American specialists, cultural geographer David Harvey and literary historian Fredric Jameson, have also written similar guides. Moreover, Harvey has put out lectures on the subject on the Internet.

The English-language commentary already shows that 'the new Marx reading' has also made its entry into the Anglo-Saxon world. There is also other, less pedagogically arranged literature that bears witness to this. One example is Andrew Kliman's 2007 book, *Reclaiming Marx's 'Capital'*. We will return to this.[58]

Now, it is time to tackle a few important and controversial themes; here, I will also take my own position.

Essence and Appearance; Form and Content; Surface and Depth

In the substantial current literature about *Capital*, it is striking that many authors avoid exploring the devices according to which Marx created a dominant part of his conceptual apparatus, above all through categories such as 'essence' and 'appearance' (*Wesen* and *Erscheinung*) and the related 'form' and 'content' (*Form* and *Inhalt*). Even 'surface' (*Oberfläche*) can be considered as part of the same category, though its counterpart 'depth' is only implied.

But there are exceptions, of course. Backhaus is among those who point out that the thinking around essence, like other tools of classical philosophy, is central to Marx. The same applies to older Marx specialists from the Soviet era. But a greater or lesser dose of Leninism is thrown into the bargain, especially a firmly rooted conviction that Engels thoroughly understood Marx's intentions and developed them further in his own work. This is the price that has to be paid for becoming acquainted with, for example, Jindřich Zelený's works, which we have done in the previous chapter. One of the most thorough analyses of *Capital* is of the same type: the work of Russian philosopher Mark Rozental, translated in 1957 into German as *Die dialektische Methode der politischen Ökonomie von Karl Marx*. It is a solid work, certainly the best on *Capital* from the Soviet school, and the author did not conceal the fact that the concept of 'essence' has a fundamental role in Marx.[59]

The timidity of many other interpreters is likely due to the fact that the thinking about essence had become so unwieldy because it was associated with Marx's early and soon abandoned ideas about the essence of humanity. This timidity is also discernible in the face of Marx's later use of terms such as 'alienation' (or more precisely, of both the related German terms *Entfremdung* and *Entäusserung*). To choose a single example: Heinrich asserts that when the word *Entfremdung* turns up in *Capital*, it should not be interpreted in any literal sense but in the same spirit as when

Marx and Engels laughed the word off in *The German Ideology* by using it so that the 'philosophers' would grasp what they were saying.[60]

But what Marx said about alienation in both the *Grundrisse* and *Capital* was completely serious. It is obvious that he was not using it in the same way he had in the *Manuscripts*. He now had another understanding of what humanity was, and what it could be.

His definitive reckoning with the image of humanity in the *Manuscripts* came in the sixth of the eleven *Theses on Feuerbach*, in which he said that the essence of humanity was not an abstraction residing in each individual person, but 'the ensemble of social relations' (*das Ensemble der gesellschaftlichen Verhältnisse*).

Marx's choice of words is important. He did *not* assert that humanity did *not* have an essence. He said that this essence changes along with changes in society. The thinking around essence remains, also where humanity is concerned. But the essence of humanity is not stable; it was not the same in the thirteenth century as it was in the eighteenth (or the twenty-first).[61]

It is obvious that Marx in future would not try to interpret the essence of humanity, since it would become an unutterably lengthy affair. It would be much more fruitful to analyse society in its various aspects. People are social beings marked by their different roles in one type of society or another.

But the rather passive word 'ensemble' does not capture the dynamic in Marx's idea of humanity's interaction with society. Marx did not only talk about how we bear the mark of the external circumstances under which we live. He also talked about the *possibilities* that these circumstances opened up for us under certain definite conditions. The most beautiful example we have is, perhaps, from his journalism. He wrote about how the Indians' *possibilities* for a modern life were being opened up by the British conquest of their country, but how these possibilities were closed off in the same moment by the oppression the new masters were committing. He drew a parallel with the lot of the workers in Great Britain. With their hands, the workers were creating the wealth of the age, which was nevertheless entrusted not to them but their masters.

This form of thinking was a recurrent one, from at least the *Theses on Feuerbach* forward. People are *alienated* from the possibilities that society opens up. The good life lay in full view of the proletariat, who were nonetheless compelled to live in poverty. Only in a radically different society could the prosperity that had been created be entrusted to everyone.

Humanity changes with society. But there is a danger in overemphasizing its variability. Marx did not run that risk, especially not after his encounter with Darwin's theories. We will return to this in the next chapter.

It was not the essence of humanity that interested Marx in *Capital*. It was commodities, money, productive forces, capital, and much else of a more mundane character. But some of the central vocabulary of classical philosophy was put to use in their treatment. Essence and appearance, form and content, surface and depth can be seen as a kind of metaconcept in the abundantly rich world of concepts in *Capital*. The ordinary concepts can be related to one another using these metaconcepts, often in an ingenious way.

The reader has already encountered the greatest challenges in the introductory chapters. Marx was aware of the difficulties: 'Every beginning is difficult, holds in all science', he said in the beginning of the foreword.[62] Capitalism appears in an enormous accumulation of commodities. But these commodities turn out to be more mysterious than their appearance hints at. To attract buyers, they must have a use value that is dependent upon their concrete properties. This use value has nothing to do with their exchange value. Use value divides them – a coat is not an iron – but exchange value makes them comparable. Exchange value has nothing to do with their nature; society is entirely its arena. The boundary between nature and society is crucial in *Capital*. It is hidden away in spontaneous observations, but it can still be seen: society becomes second nature.

The distinction between exchange value and *value* is only made fully clear in the second edition. The relationship is less clear in the first edition, whereas the significance becomes evident from the *Ergänzungen und Veränderungen* (Supplements and Changes) to the first volume of *Capital* that Marx worked on between December 1871 and January 1872.[63] In the completed edition, Marx emphasized that exchange value, also called the value form, is the value's *Erscheinungsform* (form of appearance). Value is thus the *essence* of exchange value. It can also be called its *content*.

Why were these terminological subtleties now so important for Marx? The answer is rather simple: from exchange value, we cannot infer the secret behind the increase in value that occurs in production. Exchange value lies on the surface; it is immediately visible. If we are satisfied with that, we end up with the idea that what the capitalist invested of fixed and variable capital – raw materials, machines, and workers' wages – has increased under its own power. But the increase in value, according to Marx, lies completely in the labour that the workers performed when they sold their labour power to the capitalist.

Value is thus the essence, exchange value the form of appearance. Or, in other words: value is the content, exchange value the form. But when we put the matter into words, we catch a difference between both pairs of concepts. The essence itself does not have an essence, whereas the content can very well be the form of another content. Or the same content can also have two different forms: value also has use value as a form of existence (a use value – a coat, for example – can be a 'mode of existence of value').[64]

There is no peculiarity in the Marxian conceptual apparatus; this relativity belongs to the ancient logic of the concept of form and content. Clarifying this requires a brief excursion into the fascinating history of these concepts.

Marx himself invited us on such a trip by citing Aristotle (also in Greek, for safety's sake) in his text.[65] Aristotle was the one who codified the terms 'form' and 'substance'. His word for substance is *hylē*, a word that means wood or timber, and he indicates the relativity of the pair of concepts with the word itself. Wood that is cut down can be the substance for sawn boards, which in turn become the substance (or material, as we say) for a table. Aristotle used the same pair of concepts for most areas of knowledge: the acorn is the substance, the fully grown tree is the form; the body is the substance and the soul its form; the uneducated man is the substance, and the educated man its form. With Aristotle, the form is the goal of a process. It did not need to be so in later traditions, and absolutely was not so in Marx.

Only during the Renaissance, some 600 years ago, did *content* turn up as another paired concept to form. It spread the same way over many areas, and not infrequently would interact with substance. It is like this to a great degree in Marx. In *Capital*, he spoke more often about content than substance but he always had the word 'substance' at the ready as a synonym, showing that he had not abandoned his fundamental conviction that capitalist society had its roots in concrete, earthly relationships.[66]

Let us return to our example. The content of exchange value is value, which also has use value as (another) form – that is, what makes a commodity desirable to a buyer. But use value also has a content comprised of its various physical (and in certain cases also intellectual) properties. A slice of bread is desirable because it has material properties that both provide nutrition and taste good. A novel often attracts buyers more often for the sake of its aesthetic qualities than for its external assets.

Even labour has its use and exchange values. The use value is the concrete labour necessary to transform raw materials, using machines, into products that can be offered on the market. The exchange value is the power that the worker sells to the capitalist against a fixed working time. Labour has a twin nature, Marx said, and he himself was the first 'to examine critically this twofold nature of the labour contained in commodities'. Concrete labour produces concrete products: the weaver weaves cloth, the metal-worker joins machine parts. Labour in its abstract form – labour power – is a commodity that the worker sells to the capitalist against a certain amount of compensation. This compensation is in turn exchangeable for other commodities: loaves of bread, clothing, or whatever is offered on the market.

Money is the general bonding agent between commodities. It does not matter what external forms they have; when Heinrich asserts that Marx perceived money as an actual commodity, it is possible that his criticism affects certain statements in *Capital* but hardly the central one, in which Marx does things like erupt in a quote from Revelation (in Latin!) where these important words are found: 'no man might buy or sell, save he that had the mark, or the name of the beast, or the number of his name'. Here, it is thus the symbol of value that is the only thing of decisive importance in business. In the Latin text, suitably enough, the word 'character' turns up, and Marx has a convenient opportunity to talk once again about character masks and go into commodity fetishism. In the exchange of commodities, people exist for each other only as representatives of the commodity. They are nothing more than 'the personifications of the economic relations that exist between them'.[67]

Here it becomes clear that money is only a form that can have any material content at all: gold or silver, paper notes, or – as it does today – numbers on a bank statement. Naturally, Marx knows that money also has a history; but this history has no significance in the conceptual construction of *Capital*.

In this construction, form has a distinct similarity with *surface*. The form is visible, or has been made visible through analysis; it is therefore accessible to the observer. In fact, surface figures even earlier – namely in the very first lines of *Capital*: the commodity is 'an object outside us, a thing'.[68] Immediately thereafter it says that exchange value 'presents itself' (*erscheint*) as a quantitative relation. 'To appear' means precisely to be visible on the surface. At the beginning of the section on commodity fetishism, Marx said that at first glance the commodity seems to be a trivial thing, but that analysis shows that it is full of subtle points and theological subtleties.

The concept of surface adds nothing new to the concepts of essence and appearance, or to the concepts of form, content, and substance. It only brings home the way Marx worked in *Capital*. The starting point is empirical material, which in turn is to be broken down and its secrets revealed. Empirical work meets theoretical.

Natural and Supernatural; Freedom and Equality

When Marx quotes Revelation in the middle of his presentation on the nature of money, it is not a temporary outburst of humour. On the contrary, the quote slides into a stream of Biblical or generally religious allusions that characterize the whole of *Capital* (as they did most other writings by Marx). The very first pages, as we have just seen, talk about theological subtleties concerning commodities, and a few dozen pages further on it says that the value of a commodity is something 'übernatürlich', actually 'supernatural' but toned down in the English translation to 'non-natural'.[69] This turns out immediately to be the same thing as 'something purely social', and the reader easily gets the impression that Marx was only playing with the word 'supernatural'. But he was being serious! The contradiction between nature and society is crucial. Use value is anchored in nature, or more precisely in the concrete properties of the object of use. This is not so with value. Value has its only origin in interpersonal relationships (where the one between capitalist and worker, who respectively buy and sell the commodity of labour power, is the decisive one).

People's ideas also shoot forth out of interpersonal relationships. Nature as such provides no basis for religious or magical ideas. Society is their breeding ground. In one spot, Marx describes the transformation of commodities into money as a transubstantiation.[70] The word is central in theological contexts, designating the transformation of the host and the wine into the body and blood of Christ in communion.

The specific superstition of capitalism is commodity fetishism. It is not a set of false ideas that can be corrected with a sufficient dose of enlightenment. It is a result of the way itself in which value is created in capitalism. The value form has nothing to do with the physical properties of the commodity. To find their counterpart, we have to look in 'the mist-enveloped regions of the religious world'. The human brain's own creations appear as 'independent beings'. The religious reflection of the actual world can only disappear if people enter into rational relationships with each other and with nature, Marx said.

All this is only further development of lines of thought Marx had been following since the early 1840s. It is important to remember that they are central throughout the whole of *Capital*. In Volume III, they culminate in the 'Trinity Formula' of capital, land, and labour. The text in which this formula is developed – Chapter 48 of 52 – is partially in draft form and was put together later by Engels. But the main theses there tally completely with the lines of thought on commodity fetishism from Volume I. Capital 'is not a thing, but rather a definite social production relation', Marx assured us.[71] This thereby applies once again to the difference between nature and society. The means of production are definite objects; they consist of machines and raw materials and as such are no more capital than gold and silver are in themselves money. But in the same way as metals (or slips of paper or numbers in an account) are transformed into money, so are raw materials transformed into capital. Nature is transformed into the supernatural – that is, the social.

Land in itself creates no value, however fertile it is. Only through labour does it generate such products as can be sold on a market. Nor does labour produce any value outside society, however useful it may be. Society, in short, is the arena in which the trinity of capital, land, and labour emerge. Each of the three are historically determined. Their interaction and conflicts are bound up with a particular mode of production in a particular type of society: capitalism. Land and labour have a much older history, but appeared then in entirely different forms.

Humanity under capitalism is still not free. The forces of production have certainly developed splendidly, but necessity still governs it. As he did so many times, Marx held out the prospect of another society: a 'realm of freedom' that certainly assumed necessity but which still freed humanity from subjection under the dictates of other people.[72] The reader is not allowed further details; the *Grundrisse* has more to give on this point.

Marx showed clearly how religious or pseudo-religious fantasies flourish under capitalism. But highly respectable ideas such as freedom and equality can also develop there. He had already taken up the basis of bourgeois freedom in the *Grundrisse*, but now he completed the picture. Purchases and sales in the sphere of circulation are 'in fact a very Eden of the innate rights of man'. 'Freedom, Equality, Property, and Bentham' reigned supreme there.[73] Jeremy Bentham, the English philosopher, here represents the entire sphere of ideas, even if for Marx himself it might have been more apt to associate it with the French Revolution. But Bentham was certainly quoted more often in the circles where capitalism is defended and where for every person it was only a question of looking after themselves.

The ideals in question, according to Marx, shoot forth out of the formal freedom and equality that prevails between those buying or selling a commodity, whether it be clothing, machinery, or labour power. Both buyer and seller are free to reject the offer; they seem completely equal before the commodity, and they bargain over a property that can legitimately migrate from the one to the other. The problem is that the defenders of these ideals in bourgeois society ignore the conditions in production. Neither freedom nor equality prevail there, and the worker is robbed of every property in their labour.

Marx's analysis did not mean that he denied the ideals of freedom, equality, or justice. But he maintained that they could not be realized unless it was in a completely different type of society than a capitalist one.

Striving for Exactitude

So far, we have examined Marx's method of using a conceptual apparatus from classical philosophy. It was without doubt central and important for him. Marx's historical and philosophical depth of vision is impressive; he knew his Aristotle and other ancient philosophers well. As always, Hegel made up his closest background, but the relationship with him was ambivalent. Hegel's dialectic was important, Marx argued, but the idealism it was interwoven with was untenable. The airiness of philosophy is unusable where the real world is concerned; Hegel was standing on his head, and it was a question of turning him right side up. In the first edition of *Capital*, this right-side-up Hegel is often present, or at least suggested. The construction of many conceptual investigations was obviously inspired by him. But in the afterword to the second edition, Marx inserted a reservation. Hegel mystified, and I objected to that almost thirty years ago, he pointed out. But today, in an educated Germany full of mediocre epigones, Hegel was being treated like 'a dead dog', he continued. Thus, in the first edition, Marx 'openly avowed myself the pupil of that mighty thinker, and even here and there, in the chapter on the theory of value, coquetted with the modes of expression peculiar to him'.[74] In the French translation, these portions of the afterword have been left out, because Marx did not find them of interest on the other side of the Rhine. In other editions down to our time, however, the entire text has been included.

We have already seen that Marx was upset by Dühring's review, in which the author of *Capital* was painted as a pure Hegelian. He was in fact the opposite of Hegel. But the criticism nonetheless meant that Marx toned down the Hegelian elements in his analysis of the commodity and money. This also involved popularizing the content. The main point still remains: *Capital* without Hegel was unthinkable.

But Hegel is never alone. Marx also had other important sources of inspiration. Adam Smith and David Ricardo scarcely need to be mentioned in this context; it is their theories he both assumed and cudgelled in his critique. On the other hand, it is necessary to call attention to the ideals he sought in the various natural sciences. There was a tension that occasionally intensified into opposition between his philosophical inspiration and his striving after the exactitude he admired in the physics and chemistry of his time. To this must be added Charles Darwin's 1859 book, *The Origin of Species*, which he read early on.

He expressed this ideal back in the famous foreword to *A Contribution* with the view that the upheaval of the base could be observed with 'the precision of natural science'.[75] An ambition of this kind would have been completely foreign to Hegel, and it also meant something new in Marx's life.

The words are not repeated in *Capital*, but this does not mean they were no longer of interest to him. His imagery already bore elements of his fascination for the natural sciences of his time. Metaphors such as 'crystal' and 'cell' are legion, and one of the leading chemists of his day, Justus von Liebig, is assiduously cited. Marx's interest in Liebig chiefly concerned agrarian chemistry and soil exhaustion in nature, but he was certainly also impressed by the precision with which chemists could analyse complex processes. Also to the point is that, via Engels, he came into personal contact with one of the era's great figures in

organic chemistry: Carl Schorlemmer, a German socialist living in
Manchester. Schorlemmer's direct – and above all indirect – influence on him and Engels will be dealt with in the next chapter. The
same applies to Darwin's influence.

Here, it is a question of how the striving after 'the precision of
natural science' marked his own presentation. He happily worked
with simple mathematical expressions. The most obvious example
concerns the concepts of *surplus labour* and *surplus value*. The
starting point is the length of the working day, and he asks how
many hours of labour cover the capitalist's costs for wages. Since
the capitalist must make a profit in order to continue as a capitalist, the formula $M–C–M'$ (as we have seen) applies, where
M' means 'more money'. The question is then how much of the
working day does the worker have to work in order to create the
value corresponding to their own wages.

A misunderstanding immediately presents itself here. Researchers who were worse than Marx are actually guilty of it. In *Capital*,
there is a very funny section called 'Senior's "Last Hour"'. This
was Nassau William Senior, who, considering the question of
shortening the working day hinted that surplus value was created
at the end of the day, so therefore that hour was necessary. Marx
was full of sarcasm for such a faux pas. The worker, of course,
works up their wages – as they do the capitalists' surplus value –
throughout the entire working day.[76]

The example Marx deals with is entirely hypothetical. The day
has twenty-four hours. If we start from a twelve-hour working
day, perhaps only six hours are needed for the worker to create
the value that covers the capitalist's expenses. Over the remaining
six hours, the worker thus creates surplus value for the capitalist.
The capitalist's ambition is to increase working time and reduce
wages, but there is a limit to what is possible so that the worker
can survive. The status quo threatens, and that means ruin for
the capitalist. The productive forces must therefore constantly
increase, and the relative costs for wages thereby decrease; more
can be produced in a shorter time. Marx illustrated the process
with more fictitious examples concerning what this increase
means for necessary work time. One important concept is the *rate
of surplus value*, or the relationship between *constant* capital,

which the capitalist invests in raw materials and machinery, and *variable* capital, which the workers' wages require. With the increase in the productive forces, according to Marx, this ratio has a tendency to fall – that is, the share that represents above all more advanced machinery increases in relation to the share that goes towards wages.[77]

At last, Marx had arrived at what he called a law. This involves the amount of surplus value produced being equal to the variable capital multiplied by the rate of surplus value.[78] It sounds abstract at first glance, but the meaning is simply that this amount corresponds to the number of workers whose labour power the capitalist purchases multiplied by the degree of exploitation the individual worker is subjected to. The idea that the specific case – the specific workplace, the specific business – can be inferred from this law is reasonable, but it assumes not only devoting time to thought experiments of the kind Marx had done previously in *Capital* but also being able to work with exact numerical values for the degree of exploitation. Marx also seems to have assumed this when, on the same page, he said that variable capital is to be expressed in money; as we know, money is always a quantity.

We therefore seem to be faced with the notorious transformation problem: how to go from value to money. The problem arises through Marx speaking here about laws, and obviously meaning 'law' in the sense that occurs in the natural sciences. A law of this kind assumes that the variables in the predication of the law can be quantified.

It is, as we will remember in the third volume, as if Marx attempted to solve the transformation problem but immediately admits that he failed. The origin of the problem itself is interesting: from the beginning, Marx criticized Ricardo for confusing labour value with production prices, and the very concept of the *transformation problem* has its origins in this critique. But he would thus come to work on it himself, although only in passing. In the ninth chapter, he grappled with the task. At first, he seemed full of confidence: he presented a solution, but after a number of pages he said that it was not valid and satisfied himself by observing that 'the cost price of a commodity is always smaller than its value'.[79]

Marx's own original text, which Engels revised and in this case also shortened, shows more clearly than Engels's version how Marx tested various hypothetical arguments in a manner reminiscent of natural scientists. He clearly marked the hypothetical level by breaking in with another argument that began 'In der Wirklichkeit...' (In reality...).[80]

We have already encountered Marx's way of concluding fruitless investigations with the sentence: 'Our present analysis does not necessitate a closer examination of this point.' The meaning must be that it would be meaningful to look for a solution in a completely different investigation. Here, at least, Marx did not think (when he was writing his enormous manuscript in a terrific hurry) that the problem in itself was insoluble or meaningless.

The transformation problem has given rise to many controversies. The Polish-Russian economist Ladislaus von Bortkiewicz criticized Marx's unfinished efforts as early as 1907. He maintained that the error was due to the foundations of Marx's theory themselves. Namely, that Marx saw the various economic factors united in a causal chain in which the preceding moments marked the following (machinery and labour power are purchased for money, set into movement, and result in products that become commodities that are sold and yield more money), whereas, for his part, Bortkiewicz concurred with the marginalism that he above all associated with Léon Walras. According to this, the various factors mutually condition one another.

In addition, Bortkiewicz regarded values and prices as two entirely different systems, and it was therefore a mistake by Marx to generally ask the question of their relationship to each other. Value has to do with production costs, whereas price is ultimately determined by supply and demand on the market.[81]

Bortkiewicz wanted to show that Marx's theory was fundamentally untenable, and it may therefore seem surprising that many adherents of Marx concurred with his critique. This applies, for example, to one of the most influential Marxist economists in the West – the aforementioned Paul Sweezy, who maintained that Bortkiewicz had provided a crucial defence of Marx's doctrine of labour value. He also maintained that Marx's theories thereby became compatible with modern economics, created by Walras and others, in which the question of supply and demand – and not the amount of labour – determines the price of commodities.[82]

Even Heinrich, in *Die Wissenschaft vom Wert*, expresses his great appreciation for Bortkiewicz's efforts and – more precisely – enters upon the use the latter makes of Marx's trisection in the second volume of *Capital* between means of production, wages, and luxury goods. Bortkiewicz created a system of three equations from this. But the system has four unknowns: the rate of profit, as well as the three already mentioned. This opens the way for a fourth equation in which it can be assumed that the sum total of prices is equal to the sum total of values. Other economists have expanded the system into an arbitrary number of spheres of production, and with that, Heinrich says, the transformation problem finally seems to have been solved.[83]

But what consequences does this solution have? Does it mean that the analysis of capital can be developed? Does it open the way for new insights? On this, Heinrich says nothing.

Another leading Marx interpreter of today, the aforementioned American economist Andrew Kliman, has a completely different interpretation strategy concerning Marx's text. Kliman limits himself largely to the three volumes of *Capital* as they exist in traditional standard editions. He is of the opinion that anyone who maintains that Marx was really trying to solve the transformation problem in the third volume but failed is betraying the chief duty of the good interpreter (the 'principle of rationality'), according to which finding the most favourable interpretation of a complex text is important.[84]

Heinrich, on the other hand, sees *Capital* as only a great unfinished project with a number of sometimes contradictory attempts. There is thus no *one* final text for people today to go back to, not even for Volume I in the condition it is found in the French translation. In December 1881, near the end of his life, Marx was ready to break the text up again. In a letter to his Russian translator, Danielson, he wrote that he wanted to 'change the book in the way I should have done at present'. Only his fragile health prevented him. Whereas Kliman and the chiefly US school that he is the most renowned representative of are thus building a theory for the present that is ultimately based on Marx's *Capital*, Heinrich sets himself and others an even more demanding task: to further develop the unfinished Marxian research programme in a way that it can capture the capitalism of our time.[85]

It can be added that Kliman and Heinrich do not seem to have concerned themselves with each other's interpretations. Kliman's book is equally as absent from Heinrich's *Die Wissenschaft vom Wert* as Heinrich's books are in Kliman's *Reclaiming Marx's 'Capital'*.

The interpretation that Kliman represents is called the *Temporal Single-System Interpretation*, or TSSI; it aims chiefly at demonstrating the logical consistency in Marx's theses on the tendency of the rate of profit to fall and on transformation. Their chosen main opponent is still Bortkiewicz's solution and the critique associated with it that implies Marx's theoretical construction is contradictory on one important point. But Bortkiewicz has also become the spokesman for the great majority of economists who are not Marxists (and, as we have seen, even for a number who *are*) and agree that there are internal contradictions in Marx's presentation.

TSSI has two main components that even its designation hints at. For the first, its advocates maintain that investment and starting price can vary over time, and normally do. In Marx's formula, $P–V–P'$, the relationship between P and P' is not as obvious as it may seem. In general, Kliman and his fellow thinkers object to the ambition of mathematizing Marx's theory more than Marx did. Marx developed a dynamic theory, they point out, whereas equilibrium is the precondition for the mathematics that prevailing economic theory works with. Heinrich, who himself has a background in mathematics, can criticize the equilibrium models but not the mathematical usage as such.

Second, Kliman maintains that values and prices constitute a single system, whereas Bortkiewicz on the other hand sees them as separate. In plain language, this means that Kliman believes that both values and prices are expressed in money.

There is thus a point here where Heinrich and Kliman approach each other. For both, as for most of the present-day Marx interpreters, money has a key role in *Capital*. Heinrich just goes a step further and develops a purely monetary theory. According to this, value does not belong to the individual commodity; only price does. Money appears exclusively at the societal level, and not in production itself.

It is uncertain whether Kliman wishes to go that far. For him, the essential thing is that Marx's theory is logically consistent. According to Heinrich, on the other hand, the transformation problem is not just a figment of the imagination with some interpreters; Marx really made an attempt at solving it, saw that he failed, and moved on after that. After Marx's death, Engels tried to find new solutions but he also failed, though without himself admitting his failings.

This is also the interpretation that appears most plausible to me. But I would like to add that the transformation problem can be explained to a decisive extent from Marx's ambitions of achieving a natural scientific exactitude. On the purely conceptual level, it seems given that the distinction between value and exchange value – so important for Marx in the second edition of *Capital* – deals with the relationship between surface or form; that is, between exchange value, expressed in money, and value, which is an intellectual construction necessary for the insight into the role of labour in capitalist development. Marx himself expressed the matter clearly and distinctly in *Capital* when he said that value had its form 'only in the shape of money'.[86] But he was not satisfied with this purely theoretical operation; he also wanted to see it expressed with 'the precision of natural science'. That ambition led him astray at times.

Historical Development in *Capital*

For decades, readers have battled over the relationship between historical materialism and the fundamental theory of *Capital*. The 'new Marx reading' has largely wanted to get rid of the idea that *Capital* lies embedded in a general theory of human development. Marx's more far-reaching statements – phrased most simply and clearly in *A Contribution* – on the relationship between humanity's actual existence and its ideas and ideals have only a superficial connection with the specific theory he was busy developing, the most elaborate result of which is the first volume of *Capital*.[87]

This severe, nearly ascetic, standpoint becomes comprehensible in light of the conventional view of history that became a dogma in the Soviet Union and Eastern Europe. There were eminent – even brilliant – historians there, but they were always compelled in their works to pay at least lip service to a system of assertions that only had a vague connection with what Marx himself said on the subject. Most had been developed after him.

But the repudiation of historical materialism is not problem-free. The dominant idea seems to be that the core of Marx's project on *Capital* has nothing to do with any form of philosophy of history. More than that, in fact: if an aspect of development is brought into the theory, it loses its acuity and its definite area of application. This applies both to ideas about pre-capitalist development and to ideas about different, more or less advanced stages within capitalism.

As regards the latter point, it is easy to find support for the ascetic standpoint in central portions of Marx's texts. Back in the *Grundrisse*, as we have seen, he emphasized the difference between the capitalist system and the circumstances under which it arose. He was not as explicit in *Capital*, but the difference constitutes a condition for much of his argumentation. So, for example, he contrasted technological development in a capitalist society with what had occurred earlier in history. This is particularly evident in the immense chapter on 'Machinery and Modern Industry'. In it, he emphasized that technological innovations since the eighteenth century are not the result of any isolated individual events but are part of the inevitable striving of capital to increase the productive power of labour. The more the machine produces, the cheaper – relatively – labour power becomes. This is why everyone who is to have a chance in competition has to put their trust in technological reorganizations.

It is also clear that Marx saw the epoch often called merchant capitalism as a condition for the actual (industrial) capitalism his theory dealt with. Certain portions of the wealth that were part of the primitive accumulation of capital were created thanks to the faraway trade that was made possible through Europeans' combined procession of business, plunder, and conquest both eastward and westward. Another source was pure usury, in which unjustified interest rates meant that wealth could be piled up and then put to use for early industrialization.[88]

Only when both of the two decisive classes of capitalism – the capitalists, who wish to increase their assets through production, and the free workers, who are compelled to sell their labour power for their survival – are found on the social stage, only then does Marx's theory of capital become valid.

But the question of the role of history in *Capital* is not finally answered with this. A theory always has assumptions that are not part of the theory itself. This concerns themes that are usually dealt with in introductions or only act as tacit assumptions. (External conditions of this kind are, incidentally, a logical necessity. A theory never stands entirely on its own, however exact it may be. According to Gödel's theory, nothing of the sort is possible, even in arithmetic.[89])

Marx commented explicitly on the further assumptions of his theory of capital in a long note at the beginning of the chapter on the development of machinery under capitalism. It is a very important note, perhaps the most important in the entire book. He pointed out there that a 'critical history of technology' was missing, which coming from him meant that a history would be needed in which technological innovations are related to material production in a scientifically satisfactory manner. He compares with Darwin, who in *The Origin of Species* was interested in how the organs in plants and animals developed in an endless adaptation to changing environments. The comparison is striking, but also very typical of the time: like his contemporaries, Marx saw biological evolution as a process of advancement that had similarities to the technological development of the age.

But the note contains more. From the comparison between biology and technology, Marx's thoughts move to the eighteenth-century Italian thinker Giambattista Vico, who in his work from 1725, *Scienza nuova* (The New Science), argued that it was easier for humanity to understand history than nature because they themselves were the creators of history and not, on the contrary, nature. Technology, Marx said, reveals the active relationship of

humanity to nature. Social conditions and the ideas that humanity recreates the world and themselves also proceed from this. It
is easier to bring out the worldly core from these ideas through
analysis than it is to go the opposite way, from material production to the ideas. But the latter way is 'the only materialistic, and
therefore the only scientific one'. This materialism differs from the
'abstract materialism of natural science', which ignores human
history.[90]

The latter comment will be central in the next chapter. Here,
what the note says about Marx's view of history in general and
under capitalism in particular is important. One thing is clear:
Marx kept the general conception of history that appeared back
in *The German Ideology*. As far as I know, there is no one who
has denied this, either; the controversial issue instead is what
significance these general, sweeping theses have for the theories
of capital that Marx developed (and modified) over a number
of years.

First, it can be shown clearly that Marx made no direct der-
ivations from his general conception to the specific theory. The
relationship between production and circulation, between constant and variable capital, or between concrete and abstract
labour has no necessary connection with the theses on the relationship between humanity's mode of production and its ideas.
On the other hand, it can be asked whether the latter has any
heuristic significance – that is, if they guided Marx in any way in
his work on *Capital*.

The response is 'no' where the more specific development of
concepts in Marx after the *Grundrisse* is concerned. A certain
shift of accent from the sphere of production to the sphere of
circulation can be spoken of, naturally without production losing
its significance as the starting point for the economic analysis. But
money is given a more prominent and dynamic role in the total
process of capital. In the *Grundrisse*, Marx could still deal with
value and money separately from each other, but in the manuscript he worked out a few years later – which would come to be
called *Theorien über den Mehrwert* (Theories of Surplus Value) –
this no longer appears possible. Value can only be expressed in
money; money is the appearance of value, its form.[91]

Marx's thoughts on the relationship between existence and ideas played no role for this shift. But, as the long note we recently examined shows, they are still important for the author of *Capital*. There is an excess of examples of how he made use of religious allusions and metaphors; they are not just ornamentation but serve to emphasize how the capitalist mode of production itself promotes certain kinds of ideas. Even more explicit is the analysis of how ideas about freedom, equality, and property arise out of the relationship between capitalist and free worker. The general conception of history is important here.

The next question is inevitably how central this analysis is for an understanding of Marx, and the answer may be twofold: for the specific theory of *Capital* it plays no role, but it is important for Marx's assessment of the totality of the time and society he lived in. It is especially of crucial significance for his political analysis.

There is one inflammatory subject that still remains to be taken up regarding the development of capitalism. As we have seen, certain interpreters such as Wolfgang Fritz Haug claim that Marx also captures the development of capitalism – that is, its various stages – as a result of his theory. Many others who are part of the traditions from Marx discern a particular, contemporary phase they call late capitalism. This is a term that is more than a hundred years old, and it was given the meaning of 'the last stage of capitalism' (before its ruin) sometime in the 1930s. From the 1950s onwards, on the other hand, it became more the designation of development after the Second World War with a strongly developed welfare state. The word was used in this way by the Trotskyist Ernest Mandel and by the representatives of critical theory, for example Habermas. After the tide turned around 1980 and classical capitalism quickly gained ground, the term again became less common, and many who wanted to give the period that began thereafter a particular name have, like Haug, preferred to talk about 'high-tech capitalism' or something similar.

An even more popular term for the new epoch is postmodernism. The word is ambiguous, to say the least, as it can stand in opposition to both aesthetic modernism (Baudelaire, Picasso, Schönberg, and so on) and to modernity in the sense of the entire enormous process of transformation the world has undergone over the last few centuries in which capitalism – cast with the expansion of trade, industrialization, urbanization, and much else – constitutes the very centre. It is chiefly in the latter sense that the word has direct bearing on the debate having to do with the inheritance from Marx. A key role is played here by the American literary scholar Fredric Jameson who, in the title of his 1992 book *Postmodernism, or, the Cultural Logic of Late Capitalism*, directly attempts to revive the term 'late capitalism'. He sees no break in the development of capitalism itself, but places the new in the sphere of culture. However influential Jameson's book may have been, it has not meant that the idea of late capitalism as an unbroken development – at least after the Second World War – has been vitalized. Today, a good bit into the twenty-first century, the epochal designation 'postmodernism' also obviously finds itself on the wane.[92]

It is naturally uncontroversial to state that society has undergone a tremendous change since Marx wrote *Capital*. Rather, the debate concerns whether the fundamental theoretical assumptions Marx made must be changed in any radical way in order to be able to cast light on a later phase in his development. Have electronics and biotechnology meant that the theory of capital must be recast in some way?

In one sense, the answer must be no: over the last few decades, we have only witnessed yet another great step in the development of productive forces. Money has become even more abstract thanks to computers, but its role is in principle the same. Marx himself discerned a stage of manufacture in capitalism, with its beginnings back in the mid-sixteenth century. The craftsmen soon lost their former specialities, just as they did their own tools. So developed the system whose essential elements were not changed through the mechanization of industry.

Stages in the development of capitalism that Marx never got to experience have not changed the exact relationships that represent the elementary building blocks in his theory of capital. It is another thing if *Capital* is seen – as Heinrich does – as an unfinished project that it is now important to bring forward into our own time. But Heinrich gives us no detailed information about what this means.

Back in *The German Ideology*, Marx and Engels pointed out that the general guidelines they provided for how society was to be studied could not be used as a timetable according to which history could be put in order. What is actually occurring emerges out of a swarm of details. Only when this swarm has been overcome can the real description of history begin. A pattern emerges, and the more this pattern is concretized, the more complete the picture becomes.

It is naturally this concretization that Marx was striving for in his project on *Capital*. What he said about the place of religion, the origin of liberal ideals, and much more has a place in this concretization, even if these phenomena have not been defined; nor *can* they certainly be defined as well as the concept of productive forces or the relationship between abstract labour and value.

Humanity and Classes

Labour is primarily a process between humanity and nature, Marx says. To describe how intimate the relationship is, he used a term he drew from contemporary physiology and organic chemistry: through labour, humanity 'arranges, regulates, and controls' its *metabolism (Stoffwechsel)* with nature.[93] This metaphor could possibly be seen as an example of how Marx can sometimes naturalize humanity's reality – that is, express himself as if the boundary between humanity and (the rest of) nature had been erased.[94] In the French translation, Marx inserted a note: not about the word 'metabolism' – which disappeared without further ado from his French text – but about the 'process' in the compound term 'labour process' (*procès de travail*). By that, he said, he meant 'a development regarded in the totality of its real conditions', pointing out that the meaning, separate from the one found in jurisprudence ('lawsuit' or 'trial'), had in French become common in physics, chemistry, and even metaphysics. It would gradually become completely natural, he assured the reader.[95]

Marx meant what he said literally: in relation to nature, humanity is one natural force among others. With its 'arms and legs, head[s] and hands', it shapes nature according to its needs and thereby also changes itself. We are again reminded of the sharp boundary Marx drew between labour as a force of nature (the sphere of use values, of concrete labour) and work as a social phenomenon (the sphere of exchange values, of abstract labour).

Immediately afterwards, he was ready to demonstrate the crucial difference between humans' and animals' ways of working upon nature. His example is rightly famous. A bee, he said, can build the most perfectly shaped cells that an architect could never even come close to. But even the most wretched architect differs from the cleverest bee in that they build a house in their thoughts before they build it in stone. Construction work is a conscious activity in which each stage is anticipated in thought.

François Mitterrand published a book in 1978 – a few years before being elected president of France – called *L'abeille et l'architecte* (The Bee and the Architect).[96] At that time, it was still important for a socialist to show they knew their Marx, and Mitterrand not only succeeded at that but also extracted an elegant piece of rhetoric about his own audacious political programme from the parable. (By the time he became president, he had shed his skin and become less a social architect than a building contractor for state monuments.)

The similarities between the bee and the architect say something essential about Marx's image of humanity. Consciousness may always be marked by the society in which a person lives. It is through constantly setting goals and plans that they differ from other living beings. In their work, they are a force of nature – but a force of nature that in contrast to all other forces of nature knows what they are aiming for.

A question nevertheless presents itself. Did Marx see labour only as a transaction between humanity and nature? How did he view the activities of lawyers, doctors, researchers, or teachers? Of course, he viewed such occupations as labour. In his letters, he often described how hard he was working, or complained about illnesses and other concerns putting obstacles in the way of his work. Only two examples among many possible ones: I 'am working like mad all night', he wrote in a letter to Engels in 1857.[97] More than eight years later, he wrote to him again that a new outbreak of carbuncles involved an 'interruption in my work'.[98]

Marx lived in a time when the word 'labour' itself had been given an expanded meaning, from having signified only physical work to also encompass intellectual and artistic activities. Hegel was among those who enthusiastically adopted this meaning; as we will remember, Marx asserted back in the *Manuscripts* that Hegel's commentary on labour were the most praiseworthy things in his philosophy (see above, p. 157).

But in the theory that Marx developed in *Capital*, it is only labour that has to do directly with material production that is up for discussion. At the same time, he emphasized the significance of science and technology for the development of the productive forces. In this context, this activity does not itself appear as work, but only an activity that makes labour power cheaper.

Marx happens to approach the question of what research is in this context. This becomes clearest in a commentary in *Theories of Surplus Value*. Thomas Hobbes, the seventeenth-century English philosopher, is up for discussion, and Marx comments that according to Hobbes '*science*, not *performative labour*, is the mother of the arts'. The word 'arts' here has its classical meaning of handicrafts, but Marx certainly meant physical work in general.[99]

It is tempting to draw the conclusion from Marx's statement that research, in his opinion, is *non-performative labour*. Research, Marx implies, is an activity that is similar to work but does not result in any products of labour to be offered on the market. This line of thought is easiest to follow in the field of technology. The person with the research task of improving or renovating the technology used, for example in industry, recreates the labour processes – not in order to produce commodities, but to arrive at how production itself can be improved. Research in the natural sciences that is less oriented on production can also be of significance for future technological breakthroughs, and even a medical student who sets themselves the goal of improving people's health contributes to the development of productive forces. If looked at carefully, every scientific activity can have this effect.

But, Marx said, where scientific reorganization, like all non-manual labour (*geistige Arbeit*), is concerned, the costs of reproduction are not at all as high as for their production. He takes Newton's binomial theorem as an example. It cost great effort to develop it, but today a student at school can learn it in an hour, Marx said.

The interesting thing, of course, is that Marx in general talked about '*geistige Arbeit*' which can also include artistic activity. In his analysis of labour in *Capital*, it is only labour that is of use in material production that Marx is interested in. At least in English industry – the one he actually investigated – academically trained engineers still had no role. It was in Germanic culture, including German-speaking Switzerland, that this sort of engineer first turned up.[100] What would Marx have said about their significance for material culture? Did they also have productive work in the sense of *Capital*? Did they sell their labour power, like the workers?

These were questions Marx was not confronted with, and we can only speculate about his answers. As we have just seen, when clarifying how human activity differs from that of animals, he mentioned the architect (*der Baumeister*, which can also be translated as 'master builder'; the distinction was fluid in Marx's time). In all likelihood, he must have had human labour in quite general terms in mind, and not the labour he would later talk about in the chapter on labour time – that is, what the capitalist buys against time for a certain amount of compensation.

Marx was not talking only about humanity in general terms. We have already encountered his concept of the character mask several times. In our time, this would be seen as a concept in social psychology. It describes how inhabiting a certain role in society leaves its mark on a person. They become only a living representative of certain economic relations. The capitalist gets a 'soul of capital'. What they are like in private life, or more precisely when they are not buying labour power or selling commodities, is of no significance. Marx dramatizes the text; he puts himself in the worker's place and says to the capitalist: 'You may be a model citizen, perhaps a member of the Society for the Prevention of Cruelty to Animals and in the odour of sanctity to boot; but the thing that you represent face to face with me has no heart in its breast.'[101]

What Marx said here is a powerful argument against everyone who claims that capitalists are particularly greedy people. The personal qualities of the capitalists have no significance for how they act in their role as capitalists. They may be greedy or generous, but they will not survive as capitalists if they do not minimize their costs and maximize their profits.

Marx said nothing more detailed about how the worker is marked by their role, but we know this from much of what he wrote in other quarters, from the *Manuscripts* to his later statements on political questions. Workers differ among themselves, but are similar in that they must give up their formal freedom and sell their labour power for as high a price as possible. Their subordinate position leaves its mark as soon as they are compelled to take on the role of workers.

In the *Communist Manifesto*, Marx (and Engels) held out the prospect of development towards a society of two classes in which there would be workers and capitalists, and beyond that only small remnants of other occupational groups. In *Capital*, he provides another, richer image of the time he lived in and the future that awaited. The concept of *reserve army* is now central.[102] With the development of productive forces, fewer workers can perform more and more work, while others are sent off to unemployment or forced into other occupations. Most often this concerns unproductive activities such as maids, servants, or footmen for the aristocracy and the middle class. Marx reproduces figures from the 1861 census carried out in Great Britain. Out of somewhat more than 20 million inhabitants, just over 1 million were agricultural workers, and approximately 642,000 worked in the cotton and wool industry as against 565,000 in the mines. The metal industry employed close to 400,000, while 'the servant class' – working in the homes of the finer folk – encompassed no less than 1,208,648 persons. It is clear that Marx was arguing that many of them had been forced out of an industry that no longer needed them.

He also pointed out that technological developments created entirely new categories of labour. Telegraphy, photography,

railroads and gas works occupied a large number of people. The
population also contained other groups: apart from children
and housewives there was also what Marx called 'the 'ideological' classes' – that is, those tasked with upholding and protecting
certain ideas about people, society, and the world: the government, priests, lawyers and members of the armed forces.

It was the number of 'domestic slaves' that above all surprised
Marx. They were more than the industrial workers, and he sighed:
'What a splendid result of the capitalist exploitation of machinery!'[103] On the other hand, he did not talk about the character
masks these people wore in their work. There is no reason to
suppose that on this point he would deviate from what he was
saying about the capitalist. In their work, a person's personality
bears the mark of the requirements the activity places (we should
recall that the word 'person' originally meant 'mask').

The few pages on the various population groups of Great Britain
indicate that Marx's concept of class had become significantly more
complex than it had been in the time of the *Manifesto*. We have
already observed that he never got to the subject of classes, even
in the third volume (the one that remained a manuscript from the
1864–65 working period that Engels later tried to complete). He
wrote barely a page but then immediately concluded his project.
There could naturally be external reasons for the interruption, but
there were probably also objective reasons for the text not being
longer. When this was written, Marx – to all appearances – was
already familiar with the British population statistics from 1861.
In the text, he nevertheless began by establishing the thesis he
had found in Ricardo, namely that there were three main classes
in capitalism: free workers, capitalists, and landowners. But not
even in England, the most modern of societies, did these classes
appear in pure form; there were various grey areas between them.
He defiantly continued, saying that this played no role here; there
was an obvious tendency towards converting more and more
work into wage labour and more and more means of production
into capital. Moreover, landed property was separating more and
more from both capital and labour.

But, he asked in the next breath, what constitutes a class? We
see that the members of a class each have their definite source of

income: wages, profit, or interest. This, however, is not enough. In that case, doctors and civil servants – for example – would also constitute classes. In addition, workers, capitalists, and landowners could also be split up into different interest groups through the division of labour.

Just when he had piled up a number of difficulties, he left off. It is an educated guess that he was not sure how he would go further. After 902 pages, he put the enormous manuscript aside and never seriously took it up again.[104]

The concept of class is not given the space in the *Capital* project that should reasonably be its due. On the other hand, Marx devotes proper attention to it in his political activities, as we shall see.

Marx ascribed no prominent role to the issues of schooling and education in *Capital*. In the chapter on the development of machinery, he provided shocking examples of how labour in industries, mines, and agriculture undermine the workers' health and make even the most elementary schooling impossible. He noted with a certain degree of satisfaction that factory legislation at least made certain demands – though modest ones – as regards hygiene, safety, and the acquisition of knowledge. Children who worked would be allowed to acquire certain fundamental insights and skills at the workplace itself.[105]

It may seem surprising that Marx did not in principle have anything against a system that involved children over a certain age combining schooling and work. He quoted with a certain amount of approval a statement by Nassau W. Senior, whom he otherwise mocked and dismissed as a vulgar economist. The children of the middle and upper classes spent an unreasonable amount of time at their desks, Senior said. Much of their time, health, and energy was thereby wasted. Better with a more even division between work and education! Marx calls attention above all to Robert Owen, the founder of New Lanark outside Glasgow and – according to the vocabulary of the *Manifesto* – one of the utopian socialists. According to Marx, Owen had observed that the factory system had laid 'the germ of the education of the future, an education that will, in the case of every child over a given age, combine productive labour with instruction and gymnastics, not only as one of the methods of adding to the efficiency of production, but as the only method of producing fully developed human beings'.

A few pages later on in the text, Marx spoke of a future – whether it was near at hand or far off, he left unsaid – in which the working class had seized power and saw to it that theoretical and practical vocational training characterized the schools. He thereby professed himself an adherent of the polytechnic idea that had had a prominent place among radicals of various kinds, from liberals to communists, since at least the French Revolution. He shares the opinion also that became prevalent during a large part of the twentieth century that school was an institution that over the long term could transform society and reduce or eliminate class differences.[106]

He said nothing about his own very thorough theoretical education. He was certainly of the opinion that substantial parts of it could also be incorporated into the schooling of the future. But we do not know how he imagined the matter in more detail.

The Unknown Masterpiece

In February 1867, it was clear that Marx would finally be finished with the first volume of *Capital*, and he had good hopes that the second would soon follow. On 25 February, he wrote a letter to Engels. It had to be short, he explained. The landlord was visiting, and before him Marx had to play the role of the ruined businessman Mercadet in Balzac's comedy – a man who was always trying to convince his creditors that he would pay his debts as soon as the mysterious Monsieur Godeau finally turned up.

'À propos Balzac,' Marx continued, there were two of his stories Engels had to read: *Le Chef-d'œuvre inconnu* and *Melmoth réconcilié*. They were two masterpieces, 'full of the most delightful irony' (*voller köstlicher Ironien*), Marx assured his friend.[107]

We do not know if Engels followed the suggestion. He was no lover of Balzac, and in general not a great reader of literature like his friend. Many who later wrote about Marx, on the other hand, have noticed these short lines, and we will not deviate from this tradition here. Attention is usually paid exclusively to *Le Chef-d'œuvre inconnu* (The Unknown Masterpiece), while the other story, *Melmoth réconcilé* (Melmoth Reconciled) is left aside. But this one also deserves a moment's reflection, even if its contents do not open themselves to equally exciting interpretations as 'The Unknown Masterpiece'.

'Melmoth Reconciled' can be seen as a parody of that type of fantastic story that was popular during the Romantic period. It deals with a materialistic time: the period after 1815 when the 'principle of honour' was replaced by the 'principle of money'. The main character is named Castanier, and he has followed this exact development in his life. But he has spent all his money on a prostitute and has ended up insolvent. A strange Englishman turns up to his rescue: Melmoth, who is the Devil himself ('the bearer of light' – that is, Lucifer). Castanier sells him his soul, but soon discovers that the limitless ability to enrich himself that he has thereby acquired drives him to the 'horrible melancholy of the almighty' that only God and the Devil can endure. Full of gloom he sets off for the Stock Exchange, the holy site of the money men, and there he succeeds in selling his curse off to another man weighed down with debts, who soon experiences the same melancholy and passes the diabolical baton on. Finally, it ends up with a priest.

Marx's fascination with this story is easy to understand. Balzac was painting a picture of capitalism. The capitalists live their lives at the Stock Exchange in a pact with the Devil, equipped with petrified character masks.

Forming associations between Goethe's *Faust*, another of Marx's literary favourites, and Balzac's story is reasonable. Faust also sells his soul to the Devil, and also becomes a hard-boiled exploiter by the end of the second act. But he does not let his curse pass further on to others; he dies with it. He is saved from the torments of Hell at the moment of his death simply for the sake of his constant striving.

'The Unknown Masterpiece' has an entirely different resonance for Marx. At its centre stands a purely invented character, the great painter Frenhofer. Around him, Balzac grouped a few well-known persons from the history of art – among them Nicolas Poussin, who here appears as a young man eager to learn the secrets of the profession. Frenhofer is the great master, ruthless in his criticism of others but above all of his own work. For ten years, he has been working on his great masterpiece without letting anyone else see it. The solution comes when he is permitted to use Poussin's wonderfully beautiful fiancée as a nude model. It is a great sacrifice both for her and for Poussin. Their love feels tarnished, and comes to an end.

But the painting is finished. Now, Frenhofer can proudly show the results to his friends. It is a shock for them. They see a jumble of colours. It is possible only to clearly discern a foot. Faced with their reaction, Frenhofer breaks down. That night, he dies.

His goal had been to present movement in a picture. Even the best works of art were unable to do so, but he wanted to be the first to succeed. His friends and admirers believed that he had failed.[108]

Many commentators have noted that Balzac, with his imagination, anticipated modernist art, in which movement in a two-dimensional image had been an important goal for many leading artists. One only need think of Marcel Duchamp's 1912 work *Nude Descending a Staircase*, or works by Umberto Boccioni, in which the rapid tempo of modernity is captured in a way that cartoonists later took over.

Marx's enthusiasm for the story had to do with his own attempts through *Capital* to develop a theory that captures the movement in capitalist development. It is an ambition that separates him from most other economists, who instead worked with various types of equilibrium theories. But now, with the first complete results of his many years of toil, he was seized by doubt. Had he, like Frenhofer, only succeeded in achieving a confusion of colours? Would his closest critics also turn their gaze away from his work in consternation?

According to his son-in-law, Paul Lafargue, Marx willingly compared himself to Frenhofer. The reference in the quick lines to Engels was thus not just a moment's inspiration. In the literature on Marx, his fascination for 'The Unknown Masterpiece' has often been pointed out. Opinion is undivided that in Frenhofer, Marx saw an image of his own struggle to create a theory that captures the dynamic in the development of capitalism. There is something gripping in the worry he expressed in and through the comparison. He knew he was creating a masterpiece. But would the world realize this, and admit it?[109]

There is an important difference between the works of Frenhofer and Marx. Frenhofer was finished with his work before he died. Marx was not. He was not satisfied even with the first volume – the one he still saw as finished in 1867 – but was constantly prepared to make revisions; he was planning the last one during his final years.

What is there to say, then, about his unfinished masterpiece?

His anxiety is understandable. Engels and other friends had let him know that his earlier texts on value and money were difficult to understand, bordering on incomprehensible. *Capital* is no easier, and moreover a bulkier volume.

But he also harboured another worry that lay deeper. Had he really succeeded in capturing the movement, the violent force in capitalist society? Had he convincingly demonstrated how the interaction between capital and free labour inexorably led to greater efficiency and increased production – and crises? Was it clear how the formal freedom of the worker to sell their labour power bears its own inner compulsion? Were his theses on commodity fetishism and character masks convincing? Had he succeeded in clarifying how the bourgeois ideas on freedom, equality, and justice grew out of the labour market's own dynamic?

In the first tremendous pages of the *Manifesto*, he had succeeded in describing how capitalism destroyed and renewed everything. But there, it was still a matter of just a description. With *Capital*, he would lay bare in a scientifically convincing manner how this process of destruction and renewal came to be, and how it constantly had to be driven further until the day – when was left unsaid – when capitalism's most important product, the workers, would have enough of their lack of freedom and cast off the yoke.

He expressed his worry in comparing himself with Frenhofer, the old master who year after year struggled with his masterpiece but ultimately lived to see that not even his greatest admirers saw anything but a jumble in his painting. Balzac's character says a great deal about form and movement that Marx could very well have agreed with. But he was probably most deeply struck by the following words from the old master: 'After all, in fact, entirely too much knowledge, like entirely too great ignorance, results in a negation. I have no faith in my work!' That is: an overabundance of knowledge can, like the absence of every insight, place obstacles in the way of a convincing presentation.

Marx, constantly immersed in new books that complicated the image of the society he lived in, had difficulties not only in bringing his presentation to an end but also in setting out the decisive results of his research without letting them be buried under the tremendous profusion of the fruits of his reading.

Frenhofer died, grieved, after what he saw as his failure. But posterity could see that he had in fact anticipated the art of a later time. Marx's *Capital* did not have many contemporary readers. Most did not even notice the work. Others found it entirely too difficult to understand. One thing is certain: there are today many more people who are not only reading his great works but also seem to understand the essential features of its content – and its greatness.

12

Twin Souls or a Tragic Mistake?

Anyone who wants a picture of Marx needs to take a position on Engels. The two of them were the closest of friends for several decades. They wrote a few early works more or less jointly. In abundant correspondence, year after year, they exchanged ideas on society, politics, science, and life. There were fewer letters after 1870, when Engels moved from Manchester to London. But then they could meet face to face more often. The intellectual and emotional exchange ought to have been enriched, but posterity – obliged to use words on paper – can only follow the course of events indirectly though impressions in the things they wrote down during the London years they spent in common.

As we know, there were also more prosaic bonds between them. Without Engels's constant subsidies, Marx would not have been able to provide for himself and his family. Neither of them wasted many words on this aspect of their relationship. It became a matter of course for Engels to send his friend money week after week. Marx was like a nestling who constantly needed more.

It is difficult to say what this financial dependence did for their relationship. Their views on capitalism played a role, of course. It was profits from Engels's capitalist operation that Marx was living off. Their common goal was a society without such private profits. But what did the incessant need for money mean on a more personal level? Did Marx feel coerced into a kind of gratitude? Did he, the inveterate critic, become careful before reading what Engels wrote?

That last question inevitably presents itself in the face of Marx's

reactions to Engels's first independent post-1840s work, his 1878
book *Anti-Dühring*. It is both a defence of *Capital* and a tract
on science and reality in quite general terms. What did he think
of the defence, and how did he view the text? The few reactions
that posterity can acquaint itself with are rather uninteresting.
But many have had quite definite ideas about how it *should* or
must have been. Their views differ widely. According to the one
extreme, Marx and Engels were like twin souls; according to the
other, Engels made a 'tragic mistake' when he tried to make Marx's
theory accessible to many while at the same time wrapping it up
in a comprehensive philosophy.[1]

Here, it is not a question of the one extreme or the other. Marx
and Engels were two very different people who collaborated for
many years, and thereby also influenced each other. Marx played
first fiddle, Engels explained, and he himself said he was satisfied
with playing second.[2] Their division of labour was definitively
established when Engels gave up the attempt at supporting himself
by his pen and went off to Manchester to work in the family
company of Ermen & Engels. In practice, this meant that, for
most of the 1850s, he could manage neither any political nor any
scientific activity to an appreciable extent. He only barely kept
the journalist alive through the articles in the *New York Daily
Tribune* he wrote on Marx's behalf. But they dealt primarily with
current economics – that is, what he was occupying himself with
every day of the week. When in 1859 he wrote the manuscript for
a review of Marx's *A Contribution*, he asked the author himself to
correct the text. 'Through lack of practice I have grown so unused
to this sort of writing that your wife will be greatly tickled by my
awkwardness,' he sighed. 'If you can knock it into shape, do so.'[3]

Incidentally, it was right at the end of the 1850s that Engels
began taking sporadic notes on a subject to which he would gradually devote great energy but which Marx would only touch on
in passing: the conception of the world that could be furnished in
connection with current scientific development. In *Anti-Dühring*,
Engels excelled in far-reaching ideas of that type, but he would
never complete the greater project that occupied him up until
Marx's death – the result of which posterity only got to read in the
1920s under the title *The Dialectics of Nature*.[4] After 1883, his

main task became bringing the second and third parts of *Capital* to a successful close. In addition, he had to take over first fiddle in the rapidly growing international workers' movement. But he also managed to write a shorter work titled *Ludwig Feuerbach and the End of Classical German Philosophy*, which was published in 1886.

We will return to all this later. But to put the issue of the relationship between Marx the author and Engels the author into some sort of order, we will have to start with a few more basic circumstances. We will begin with mathematics. Towards the end of his life, Marx worked assiduously on mathematical manuscripts. Engels expressed his enthusiasm over the results, but by all appearances was not as fascinated by the subject. His notes in *Anti-Dühring*, at least, are more dutiful. After that, there is a question of the interest that both men devoted to technology and the natural sciences in particular, areas that in accordance with their views of society and of history are of crucial significance for historical development. Further on, we will have to see how this interest is expressed in their work. A number of important themes will thereby have to come into focus. One of them concerns what similarities Marx on the one hand and Engels on the other found among the natural scientific theories they encountered and the theory of capital that Marx in particular was trying to develop. The concept of *dialectical law* will be in focus here. Organic chemistry provided Marx with the material for a law of this kind. The representative of chemistry in the lives of Marx and Engels is named Carl Schorlemmer, a major scientist and a striking individual.

Darwin's theory of natural selection was just as important for the Marxist conception of the world. But Marx also took up certain ecological problems. In addition, a new subject came up that would occupy him over his final years, and which Engels afterwards would work at in his own way: social anthropology.

Both Marx and Engels thus tried to get a clear idea of development within a broad range of fields. The question, ultimately, is: How did all this new knowledge relate to the theory of capitalism that Marx was in the process of developing? Could *Capital* claim a central spot in the world of late nineteenth-century science? If so, what did its scientific value consist of? Did this scientific value risk being lost when Engels tried to make it the fixed core of a philosophy that resembled a conception of the world?

Both Marx and Engels tried – in somewhat different ways – to understand and interpret the world in many of its aspects. But how did this intensive activity fit with their ambition to also *change* the world? The question naturally leads to the next chapter, which deals with political activity in the International and beyond.

Mathematics

Mathematics was a recurrent problem in the construction of Marx's theory. He made a number of quantitative calculations and worked up a large amount of statistical material. When he was working on the manuscript that would later be called the *Grundrisse*, he was tormented by a number of miscalculations and tried to find a better way through making use of algebra instead (see above, p. 370).

In *Capital*, he contented himself with the thesis that economic crises could not be predicted – a claim that holds true even today, after an infinite amount of mathematizing within economic theory. But, however correct the statement was, Marx nonetheless dreamed of surmounting this obstacle to the knowable. He talked about his hopes in a letter to Engels at the end of May 1873. Engels was on a short visit to Manchester (he was now living in London), visiting people such as their friends Carl Schorlemmer and Samuel Moore. Moore had a solid education in mathematics, and Marx plied him with questions on the mathematics of a potential crisis. These are thoughts I have long gone over again and again by myself, Marx wrote in his letter. But Moore considered the problem to be unsolvable, or at least impossible to treat for the time being. Marx had hoped that a regularity could be read in the zigzag movements of prices, interest rates, and the like. But no, Moore assured him, it was impossible to mathematically determine 'the principal laws governing crises' – at least as long as a number of factors were unknown. Marx wrote in his letter that he had decided to 'give it up for the time being'.[5]

On the other hand, he obstinately continued to improve himself in mathematics. He had begun this back in 1859, and his efforts had intensified over the last few decades – in fact, during the last few years of his life. It is impossible to read from the excerpts whether he was ultimately aiming for the solution of the crisis question. It could be said, at least, that in that case he had a long way to go. The path from the type of differential equations he was occupying himself with to the mathematics of economic crises seems quite far.

His work consisted of both excerpts from above all English textbooks, and a number of his own comments. Only in 1968 was the entire material published in both the original German and in a Russian translation by the Russian mathematician S. A. Yanovskaya. A German edition, in which the excerpts were cut out, was published in 1974. The publisher, Wolfgang Endemann, also wrote a foreword and a long introduction. Endemann asserted, as against Yanovskaya, that Marx's notes only aimed at further developing the great project of *Capital*. Through mathematics, Marx hoped to reach 'inner connections that would barely be conceivable without mathematical language', he said.[6]

But above all, Marx's notes contain a number of ideas on dialectical connections within differential calculations. He sees a negation of the negation in the very starting point of the zero of calculus signifying the 'absolute smallest' – a nothing that nonetheless 'leads to real results'. The line of thought is simple. Zero signifies a nothing that nonetheless turns out to be something, namely the instantaneous change.[7]

The basic problem for Marx was the relationship between mathematics and reality, and it was his hope, through more advanced mathematics, to be able to capture deeper aspects of an economic development that was changing and difficult to survey. The equations themselves were 'only a symbolic indication of operations that had to be carried out'.[8] This is an enigmatic expression: what, besides operations, are being carried out when the mathematical symbols are being used? But, with these words, Marx surely wanted to emphasize the close connection between calculus itself and the processes it was to demonstrate. He could hardly have intended anything else when he spoke about the contents of the equations. He complained that contemporary mathematicians were not interested in this aspect, while those who had discovered differential calculus – Marx uses just that word, 'discovered' – made the differential symbol itself the starting point of calculus. He had Isaac Newton in mind, who never forgot that with his new method of calculation he had reached aspects of reality, primarily instantaneous movement, which previously had resulted in paradoxes of the 'Achilles and the tortoise' type.

According to this paradox, attributed to the Greek philosopher Zeno of Elea, Achilles would never catch up to the tortoise despite running ten times as fast. When Achilles had run a hundred metres, the tortoise had managed to crawl ten, but when Achilles had run those ten metres, the tortoise was still a metre ahead. After that metre, the tortoise would have crawled a decimetre, and so forth. With his 'fluxions' (his term for derivatives), Newton overcame such problems mathematically; Leibniz did the same thing on his own with the nomenclature still used today. Marx, reasonably, devoted particular attention to this historical development. It is easier to learn something new by seeking its historical roots, when the problem to be solved was still relatively simple.[9] He never had any opportunity to make serious use of his new insights in his work on *Capital*. If, in the end, it was 'the principal laws governing crises' he wanted to get at, it would have required him to thoroughly revise what would become the third volume of *Capital* in Engels's edition; Marx had not worked on that since 1864. The reality he wanted to capture was entirely too chaotic.

His studies in mathematics nonetheless certainly gave him a certain amount of pleasure. He seemed to imagine more effective ways of capturing a constantly changing societal reality. In a sense, he anticipated the later mathematization of the subject of economics. But he of course cherished other hopes than those who still dominate neoclassical economic theory.

Engels had not had any particular access to Marx's manuscripts and excerpts while he was alive. When he went through what

Marx left behind, it surprised him that the text on dialectics Marx had talked so much about was not there.[10] The condition in which the continuation of *Capital* found itself it was also an unpleasant surprise for him. We do not know if he had any awareness before Marx's death of the existence of excerpts in social anthropology that would later form the starting point for his own book on the same subject.

On the other hand, Marx at least let him read a part of the mathematical manuscripts. We know this from a letter Engels wrote to Marx in August 1881. The letter is full of appreciation and agreement. He was even of the opinion that Marx had realized something that mathematicians usually denied. It seemed not to concern any shocking innovations, just a way of understanding the nomenclature.[11] Marx did not react to the praise; his subsequent letter dealt with entirely different concerns.

By all appearances, Engels was not influenced any more deeply by Marx's notes. What he stated on the subject in *Anti-Dühring* lay five years back in time, and even the notes and drafts for *The Dialectics of Nature* had come into being earlier. In *Anti-Dühring*, he asserted that mathematics has its origins in the practical needs of humanity despite it developing into an exact system, and in *The Dialectics of Nature* he stressed that the number 0 was not devoid of content, but on the contrary found itself at the centre of the entire sequence of numbers.[12] The statement appears extremely trivial but could lead to the most extraordinary consequences when *The Dialectics of Nature* became an important part of Marxist–Leninist orthodoxy. One such consequence occurred when the regime of Mao Zedong was going to create a new centre of power after taking over in 1949. One idea was to locate this centre outside the old city. But Mao and his advisor Chen Gan came to the conclusion that the old city would then be competing with the new one. They found support in Engels, who said that the zero point in relation to both positive and negative numbers 'is the point on which they are all dependent, and by which they are all determined'. Conclusion: the zero point of the emperor's power had to be razed and a new zero point created.[13]

Encounter with the Natural Sciences

Engels had been forced to give up his successful high school studies early to go into commerce. A few years later he underwent a year's training as an officer in Berlin, where he also came into contact with the radical currents of thought blossoming in the city's young universities.

Marx finished both high school and university. He ground away at the classical languages and was forced to cram in a bit of jurisprudence, but above all philosophy – in its wide-embracing version of the time – became the centre of his studies. His doctoral thesis in classical Greek philosophy testified not only to his ability to handle Greek texts, but also to his interest in natural philosophy in a broad sense, regarding the smallest component parts of matter and the necessity or randomness of the course of nature.

There has been a bit of fuss made about the fact that, back in high school, he had teachers who were close to some of the men behind the breakthroughs in natural science of the time, and that in Berlin he heard lectures by the polymath natural philosopher Heinrich (or Henrik) Steffens and one of the men behind the breakthrough of modern geography, Carl Ritter.[14] In the long letter to his father in 1837, he wrote that he was also studying 'natural science, and history'.[15] We know nothing about how deeply he was influenced by these studies. On the other hand, we know that early on, he displayed the interest in technological innovations that would follow him throughout life. His fiancée, Jenny von Westphalen, jokingly called him a 'dear little man of the railways'.[16] This means of transportation, at the time absolutely new, roused a burning interest in him. In general, he was convinced early on that the lives and labour of people were on the verge of being fundamentally changed by an entire suite of technological innovations.

When, in the mid-1840s, he and Engels came to the conclusion that 'industry' – that is, humanity's adaptation of nature through various kinds of technology – was the most dynamic power in historical development, both of them were well prepared to understand it. This applied in particular to Engels, who during his time in Manchester could not only see how the factories drastically transformed all of society, but also came into contact with the daily life of capitalism from the perspective of the factory owners. It was also he – not Marx – who first engaged the new economic theories of the Manchester School.

But Marx contributed to their collaborative effort with all of his intellectual acuity, his broad education, and especially his enormous appetite for reading. The difference between him and Engels cannot be perceived if their different ways of reading are not taken into consideration. Engels also read a great deal, even though other duties long divided up his time. But he was not a devourer of books like Marx, and above all he did not regularly compose detailed excerpts. Marx obviously most often had the ambition to fundamentally *learn* what he read, with a view to using it for future writing. All his notebooks, which became an increasingly bulky collection over the years, also served as a reference library. Marks in the margins show that Marx returned to his excerpts, and it was from them that he poured out the myriad of notes that flow through *Capital*.

His endless reading and composition of excerpts sometimes appear to be an escape from the demands of completing the great project he had outlined back in the 1840s. *Capital* would be his *magnum opus* in every respect, and for the sake of perfection no expense would be spared. Its composition had to be made artistic; above all, no gaps in knowledge could be left open. At the end of his life, the demands for all-round knowledge became increasingly and heroically unreasonable. Aged and sick, he continued more hectically than ever to throw himself into new worlds of knowledge, whether it was mathematics, chemistry, or social anthropology.

In his private life, the sorrows accumulated. Jenny, who was such a great part of his life, fell ill with an incurable cancer and died in December 1881. It was a horrible blow for him, and it became even worse when his oldest daughter Jenny – his beloved Jennychen – was struck with the same illness and died a few months before her father.

But Karl Marx continued reading and taking notes as if he himself were immortal. He did not even interrupt his studies during his late recreational trips to Algeria and southern France, which he did on the advice of his new friend, the biologist Ray Lankester. Right up to his death, he was on the path towards new knowledge. Fittingly, he died sitting at his writing desk.

Engels's notes are far more sparse. They testify more infrequently to his wanting to learn a subject from the bottom up. It was after *Anti-Dühring* that he above all composed a few really ambitious excerpts in physics, obviously to get a solid foundation for the planned work on dialectics that remained unfinished. There are two contemporary works that he primarily delved into: William Thomson and Peter Guthrie Tait's 1867 work *Treatise on Natural Philosophy* and Gustav Wiedemann's two-volume *Die Lehre vom Galvanismus und Elektromagnetismus* from 1874. In *The Dialectics of Nature*, electricity is the subject of by far the most comprehensive and ambitious section, some fifty pages long.[17]

With electricity in particular, Marx and Engels expressed a strong interest in both the practical and the theoretical sides. Early on, Marx had been preoccupied with its significance for material production. In the middle of the revolutionary tumult at the end of the 1840s, he was captivated by the work of German scientist Gustav Kirchhoff, who showed that circuits were of the same nature as electrostatic phenomena. The possibility of transmission of power across distances could thereby be imagined, something that would be equally as revolutionary as steam power. Marx was enthusiastic.[18]

During the first dark years in London, he also experienced the highest point of capitalism up to that point: the famous 1851 world exhibition, where the Crystal Palace became a contemporary unifying symbol for a dazzling modernity that was either promising or frightening depending on one's outlook. The exhibition also turned up in passing in Marx's and Engels's correspondence. Engels had to go there on behalf of his job, and Marx visited the exhibition because the world of commodities there appeared more clearly than anywhere else: commodity fetishism took concrete form in front of his eyes before it became a central concept in his theory. Nor could he avoid being fascinated by the remarkable machines that were on public view there: steam locomotives that could reach a dizzying 100 kilometres per hour, and printing presses with theretofore unseen capacities. Even prototypes for electric motors and dynamos, both of which promised a grand future, could be observed.[19]

Electricity continued to fascinate him. During the last years of his life, he devoted a particularly intensive interest to it. An 1881 exhibition of electricity in Paris was followed by another in Munich in 1882; both had lively commentary by him and Engels. Above all, they stayed with the electro-technician Marcel Deprez, who had – fittingly enough – succeeded in transporting electricity from Miesbach to Munich, a distance of forty-three kilometres. Marx was eager to know more, and in the letter to Engels was annoyed at his son-in-law Charles Longuet for not having sent him the information about the new breakthrough that he had requested. Clearly, he was trying to acquaint himself with the theoretical background to Deprez's achievements.[20] He composed excerpts from an entirely new work by Deprez's colleague Edouard Hospitalier: *La physique moderne: les principales applications de electricité* (The Modern Applications of Electricity) from 1882. His notes are nowhere near as detailed as those for chemistry, but Marx's copy of the work shows that he had carefully read through it, underlining and commenting briefly on many parts. He did not get very far in making the excerpt; his death put an end to it.[21]

Engels was equally fascinated by the long-imagined opportunities now being realized. In a letter to Eduard Bernstein – a young German Social Democrat who we will be talking about later – he did not mince his words. The transmission of power that Deprez had demonstrated would 'free industry for good from virtually all local limitations'. It 'makes possible the harnessing of even the most remote hydraulic power', and over the long term it would erase the differences between town and country. Productive forces would soon grow beyond the control of the bourgeoisie.

Marx and Engels were seeing the beginning of the second Industrial Revolution. Electricity would play a crucial role there, alongside a range of specialities within chemistry such as agrarian chemistry and petrochemistry.[22]

Agrarian chemistry became a central field of study for Marx during the 1850s and 1860s. In particular, he studied the great German chemist Justus von Liebig carefully. He would sometimes mention the latter's colleague, Christian Friedrich Schönbein, in the same breath. This took place when he was working with ground rent, the large field of study that David Ricardo had placed at the centre of economic theory. With all due respect to Ricardo and his colleagues, 'the new agrarian chemistry in Germany, especially Liebig and Schönbein, is more important than all the economists put together', he exclaimed in a letter to Engels in 1866. One week later, in an entirely euphoric epistle, while speaking of these same chemists and their achievements, he burst out in English: 'I feel proud of the Germans. It is our duty to emancipate this "deep" people.'[23]

This outburst must be viewed in light of what he just said about his own soon to be completed work, *Capital*. Despite certain weaknesses in the details it is a triumph for German science, he assured Engels; in fact, the results belonged to the German nation, which is that much more gratifying because that nation was otherwise the stupidest under the sun. He had, perhaps, never expressed his ambivalence for the German people more clearly.

But back to chemistry. He pointed out the significance of Schönbein in his letter, but the man's name was given no place in *Capital*. Another author whom he had read and been influenced by to a certain degree without citing him in *Capital* was the Bavarian agronomist Carl Fraas. Unstable development leads to wasteland, he wrote to Engels regarding Fraas's 1842 work *Klima und Pflanzenwelt in der Zeit* (Climate and the Plant World); he did not only have capitalism in mind, but also ancient Mesopotamia, Persia, and Greece.[24] But the book that above all roused his interest was Liebig's 1840 work *Die organische Chemie in ihrer Anwendung auf Agricultur und Physiologie* (Organic Chemistry in its Application to Agriculture and Physiology). Marx was not alone in appreciating the book; it was published in numerous editions and translated into many languages. Earlier on, Liebig had established himself as one of the great pioneers in the new speciality of organic chemistry, and he also made a name for himself for his practical efforts in a number of fields, from the first sleeping pill to bouillon cubes.[25]

Most saw in Liebig's work on the chemistry of agriculture grand promises of a future when no one would have to starve thanks to a judicious use of artificial fertilizer. But Marx belonged to the minority that also saw something else in it. Increasing ruthless exploitation threatened to deplete the soil over the long term. 'To have developed from the point of view of natural science, the negative, i. e. destructive side of modern agriculture, is one of Liebig's immortal merits,' he wrote in a note in *Capital*. He also reproduces a few striking figures on how, in a number of European states, height and capacity among soldiers decreased from the end of the 1700s to the 1830s, something that according to Liebig (and Marx) would be a sign of impaired nutritional intake. On the other hand, he was not satisfied with certain other elements in the German chemist's account, for example how he presented contemporary economic theory.[26]

But the essential thing is that Marx took arguments in Liebig to mean that capitalization of agriculture, which he seemed to see, would entail increasing depletion of the soil. More than that, in fact: it would create a growing gap between humanity and nature.

In the third volume of *Capital* – which Marx wrote the manuscript to back in 1864 – important references to Liebig are found. Supported in part by Liebig, Marx speaks there of an 'irreparable break' (*unheilbarer Riss*) between nature and society, which is created through fewer and fewer people pursuing increasingly industrialized agriculture while more and more people are drawn to the industries of the cities. In his treatment, Engels made rearrangements in the text and moved the expression 'irreparable break' to a later context, where the reader gets the impression that it is the transition itself from small-scale to large-scale agriculture that creates the growing gap.[27]

Engels also struck out a number of Marx's references to Liebig, which blunted the acuity to a certain extent. The distance that capitalism creates between humanity and nature plays a large role in the first volume of *Capital*. The power of the soil to grow is ruined, and this ruination is spread over national borders through commerce. In this way, large-scale industry and industrial agriculture aid each other.

The person who above all has the honour of centring Marx's alarm in the face of the destruction of nature is American author John Bellamy Foster, through his book *Marx's Ecology*. But Foster

does not escape the danger of presenting Marx as a champion of
the environment, or at least an ecologically conscious person in
the modern sense.[28] This was not the case. Marx found support in
Liebig for his thesis that over the long term, capitalism was devastating in all respects – including where the production of food
was concerned. But he also imagined that the society that would
replace capitalism could also restore the balance between humanity and nature in agriculture. The growing gap between town and
country would then be filled in a way that many utopian socialists
and communists had previously imagined. The countryside would
no more sink back into its old narrowness of outlook than the
industries would be localized to growing megalopolises.

The pessimistic conclusions that Marx – in glaring contrast to
most of his contemporaries – drew from Liebig's book are thus
not unconditional. In *another* society, agriculture would not drain
nature of its resources, just as industry would not devastate the
air, the water, and the soil. All the blessings of technology would
then be bestowed on both humanity and nature. The 'irreparable break' he spoke about is thus only irreparable in a capitalist
society.

A present-day reader must remember that Marx lived in a
time the environmental impact of production was insignificant in
comparison with that of the early twenty-first century. Locally, it
could be devastating – industry's contamination of the local environment was frightening, and large areas of land were devastated
by injudicious agriculture – but it affected the entire atmosphere
of the Earth and its water resources only marginally. Like any of
his contemporaries, Marx could little imagine the development of
production that has taken place over the last 150 years.

As has been pointed out, the word Marx used throughout when
portraying the relationship between humanity and nature was
'Stoffwechsel' – that is, metabolism. The idea that man lives in
symbiosis with nature had been a natural one for him since his
youth. He had encountered it among his Romantically inspired
teachers, with Heinrich Steffens at their head, and in the
Manuscripts, nature is called humanity's 'inorganic body'. But
the concept of *metabolism* is more precise and advanced. It had

spread out among German biologists in the 1830s, and had its big breakthrough thanks to Liebig's 1840 book *Tierchemie* (Animal Chemistry). Humanity's manner of assimilating various nutrients could be studied at a certain level of detail there.[29]

But Marx used the concept in a broader sense. He included everything that had to do with humanity's adaptation of nature, both in agriculture and industry, in humanity's metabolism with nature. Humanity lives on nature, but through its work and its production it also changes nature. Sometimes, as in capitalism, humans do this in a way that is harmful to both nature and to themselves. But the idea of a possible healthy relationship between humanity and nature was important to Marx.

In the previous chapter, we saw how Marx argued in *Capital* that the theoretical apparatus concerning society in nature that we have constructed expressed the altered relationship between both. He derived the entire world of religious ideas, including commodity fetishism, from this fundamental disharmony.[30]

It is therefore entirely natural that both technology and the natural sciences played a central role for him. But his interest was not always of the same type. Sometimes it is practical to a great degree; so, for example, when he wrote the long chapter on machinery in *Capital* or when he composed excerpts on the development of technology. The excerpts, unfortunately, have been lost. Marx wrote about them in a letter to Engels in 1863, and Georg Lukács was able to read them in Moscow in the 1920s.[31] But sometimes his interest concerns more vague theoretical topics. For him, chemistry was not just a discipline that had achieved the most striking results in both industry and agriculture. It also entailed an adventure into the world of theory, and adventure that could lead him along remarkable paths that in due course would turn out to be fraught with momentous consequences. No one played a greater role in this conviction than Carl Schorlemmer.

Carl Schorlemmer

Carl Schorlemmer was an internationally acknowledged specialist in organic chemistry. He was also a member of both the First

International and the German Social Democratic Party. Next to Marx, he was Engels's closest friend. He also played an important role for Marx, but has strangely been forgotten. In three of the latest great Marx biographies – by Attali, Sperber, and Stedman Jones – he is not even mentioned. Nor does Foster, who none-theless dwells much upon the significance of chemistry for both Marx and Engels, speak about him.[32] If anything, this indicates selective dealings with the sources. Schorlemmer's name occurs frequently in Marx's and Engels's correspondence, just as he is mentioned a number of times in their writings. Only a very few of Schorlemmer's own letters are preserved. In the obituary he wrote for his friend in 1892, Engels declared that they both exchanged many ideas by letter on 'the sciences and party affairs'.[33] But it was also Engels who went through all the papers Schorlemmer left behind. For some reason, he must have destroyed what he wrote to his friend, just as he destroyed nearly all the letters he himself received. What remains is only one letter from Engels in a manuscript on the history of chemistry, and a few letters from Schorlemmer. In addition, there are seven brief messages from Schorlemmer to Marx.[34]

It is not much, considering how important he was in the lives of both Marx and of Engels. In addition, this life played out within the borders of three extraordinarily dynamic fields: organic chemistry, the prevailing fashionable science of the time; social-ism, embodied in both of its principal leaders; and the external environment that 'the cradle of the Industrial Revolution', the Manchester area, represented.

We also know relatively little of Schorlemmer's life before he came to Manchester. He was born in Darmstadt in 1834 and received a scanty education. Like many chemists of the time, he learned the basics of the subject as an apprentice pharmacist. He is said to have attended lectures on the history of chemistry in Heidelberg without enrolling at the University. In the spring of 1859, he had the great luck to get work in the most celebrated of all chemical laboratories at the time – the one that Justus von Liebig had constructed in Giessen. Once there, he was soon invited to come to Manchester to be the personal assistant of English chemist Henry Enfield Roscoe. Roscoe's move of bringing on a rather unlearned apprentice pharmacist was a consequence of his respect for German chemistry. Like most of the more prominent British chemists of the time, he himself had been educated in Germany. Now it was a question of constructing the theoretical basis for a chemical industry in Great Britain. This is why Owen's College – the educational institution that later became Manchester University – came to Manchester. Roscoe's own speciality was inorganic chemistry. Schorlemmer would soon master organic chemistry.

In Manchester, there was a large German colony that flourished up until the outbreak of the First World War in 1914. The men created a meeting place in the Schiller-Anstalt, in which Engels was an important member. Schorlemmer also went there, and made Engels's acquaintance. Engels mentioned his name in a letter from 1865.[35] Soon, the both of them would be close friends.

Both of the men who had the most to do with Schorlemmer, Roscoe and Engels, provide entirely different pictures of him. Roscoe wrote in an obituary of his friend: 'He was of a retiring, most modest and unassuming disposition.' Oddly enough, Roscoe – who himself was politically active as a liberal – maintained that he did not know much about Schorlemmer's socialist opinions.[36] Engels and Marx were much better informed about their friend's political involvement; in addition, they had a standing nickname for him: Jollymayer. It meant that Schorlemmer was a jolly fellow. If anything, it became clear when happiness left the sick and prematurely aging Schorlemmer.[37]

Schorlemmer and Engels saw a lot of each other; Marx and his family were also drawn in to their social life. When Engels moved to London in 1870, the chemist often came to visit. They both went on holiday trips together. Schorlemmer also followed Engels to the United States, as did Eleanor Marx and her lover Edward Aveling. On his own, he visited Paul and Laura Lafargue in Paris.[38]

Schorlemmer the chemist first made a name for himself through his experiments. But gradually, he moved more and more of his activities from the laboratory to the writing desk. Together with Roscoe, he became a leading textbook author in chemistry in the late nineteenth and early twentieth centuries. The magnificent three-volume work, *Ausfürliches Lehrbuch der Chemie* (A Treatise on Chemistry, 1877–84), was published in many editions and translations, including English. Writing a comprehensive handbook in the subject such as chemistry was not, unlike today, a pedagogical task. It was a question of creating a synthesis of many fields that had not yet been joined. According to Roscoe, Schorlemmer was the one who bore the heaviest burden in the work.[39]

Schorlemmer conducted his most important experiments back in the 1860s. We have reason to dwell upon what in Schorlemmer's time were called paraffins, from the Latin *parum affinis*, 'little related'; today we speak of alkanes. This concerns simple hydrocarbons, or the compounds constructed according to the formula C_nH_{2n+2} – that is, methane (CH_4), ethane (C_2H_6), and so on.

Schorlemmer's discoveries have a direct connection with the great controversy over the electrochemical theory of Jöns Jakob Berzelius – the theory that radicals in organic chemistry corresponded to the elements in inorganic chemistry. They were, so to speak, the fixed building blocks whose electrical charge determined how they could be combined with other substances. Schorlemmer was able to add a piece of the puzzle to the new molecular theory, in which the radical could be defined in relation to the molecule. The radical was a 'remnant' of the molecule.

Schorlemmer encountered resistance from adherents of the older theory of radicals. Edward Frankland, who was regarded as a leading chemist in the 1860s, persistently defended it. He took his starting point in certain problems concerning hydrocarbon radicals. With support from the available empirical data, he maintained that there were two homologous series: the radicals (methyl, ethyl, propyl, and so on), on the one hand, and on the other the family of methanes, or hydrides (methyl hydride, ethyl hydride, and so on).

It was here that Schorlemmer made his contribution. He showed that methyl and ethyl hydride were identical and traced both of them back to ethane (C_2H_6). He could thus assume that there was only a single series, and the hydrides could go all the way. In a long series of reports to the Royal Society – which he would soon join – he continued to show his results concerning the simple hydrocarbons. He could show that Frankland was wrong when he maintained that radicals and hydrides would have different boiling points.[40]

This was important for the foundations of organic chemistry, but it also had massive practical significance. Knowledge of the boiling points within the methane series would later be of significance for the oil industry. Refinement of rock oil, or petroleum, is based on knowledge of the different boiling points of the hydrocarbons. The earlier members in the methane series are in gas form at normal room temperature, but the more complex compounds concerned, the higher the boiling point.

Obviously, Schorlemmer could not predict the enormous significance of oil in the future. At the end of the nineteenth century, it was still an unreasonable thought that it would take up the fight against coal; only the automobile industry changed the picture. Oil had certainly been extracted in small quantities for a long time, but it was only in 1859 – in Pennsylvania – that real development got its start. The export of kerosene to Europe began in 1861. By 1862, Schorlemmer had analysed 'amerikanisches Steinöl' (American rock oil – that is, petroleum). This seems to be the way by which he got into the problem of hydrocarbons. His interest continued. He was the one who synthesized octane, so important in oil.[41]

In our context, the crucial question is how Schorlemmer, with his research – which he later summarized in his textbooks on chemistry – influenced Marx and Engels. This, of course, he did. Having an outstanding chemist in their circle of acquaintances was of great significance for the both of them. As we know, Engels wrote more about the natural sciences than Marx did; above all he was eager to draw conclusions that could support what he saw as a scientific worldview. But it was Marx who first made use of the results of Schorlemmer's research to strengthen his own line of argument.

Quantity Turns into Quality

While Marx was working on the final version of the first volume of *Capital*, he also found time to attend the popular lectures held by the German chemist August Wilhelm von Hofmann in London. He talked about them in a letter to Engels. He was not impressed by the lecturer, who nevertheless seems to have given him new ideas. Namely, he inserted a note in the proof sheets in which he compares the transition from handicraft to manufacture with the new chemical theory of molecules. He would not mention Hofmann, he told Engels; on the other hand, he would mention the three French chemists Auguste Laurent, Charles-Frédéric Gerhardt, and Charles Adolph Wurtz. The latter was 'the *real man*', he added. Engels did not react appreciably to the statement that the same kind of relationship of laws could be found in chemistry and in history. He only said that Schorlemmer said that Wurtz was a popularizer and that apart from Gerhardt, the German chemist Friedrich August Kekulé von Stradonitz was the one who had developed the theory concerning molecules. Incidentally, Schorlemmer was going to send Marx a book that had the correct information on the development of molecular theory.[42]

Marx took the correction only in part; in the brief note that remained unchanged through both German editions and the French translation, only Laurent and Gerhardt are mentioned.

But the significant thing is not the note, it is what Marx said in the text. He said that in history, as well as in chemistry, 'is shown the correctness of the law discovered by Hegel (in his *Logic*), that merely quantitative differences beyond a certain point pass into qualitative changes'.

It is correct that Hegel, in his great *Science of Logic*, wrote a lot about quality and in particular quantity; a large part of the first volume consists of different determinations of the concept of *quantity*, and at the end of the same volume quantity and quality are put in relation to each other. The increase of a quantity can yield a new quality.

But it would never have occurred to Hegel to call this a law. For him, a law in science was '*etwas Ruhende*' – something quiescent – whereas the dialectic deals with the constant changeability and development of reality. By speaking of laws, Marx introduces a concept that belongs to the modern natural sciences but not at all in the philosophy of Hegel. We have already seen that in other places in *Capital* as well, Marx speaks about laws in a way that lures him into quantitative calculations of a risky nature.[43]

The concept of 'law' in science is already ambiguous. On the one hand, we have laws that apply when certain conditions exist. Chemical reactions are of this type. Ammonia and sulfuric acid form ammonium sulphate within a given temperature interval. If ammonium sulphate is heated up to over 280°C, ammonia and sulfuric acid are re-created.

Laws of development are of an entirely different type. The second law of thermodynamics – which involves nature tending towards increased entropy – was known in Marx's time. Heat can never completely be transformed into movement. This applies to both steam engines and human muscles. One popular metaphor that is easy to misunderstand is 'heat death'. One does not die from heat; it is heat that dies.

It was German physicist Rudolf Clausius who first formulated the second law of thermodynamics; he was also the one who later introduced the concept of entropy, which is the measure of how much heat energy cannot be transformed into kinetic energy. Marx did not react with any intensity to the second law of thermodynamics, but Engels did so much more eagerly. Like Marx, he had studied the principle of energy (first called the law of conservation of energy) that William Robert Grove proposed in his 1846 book *Correlation of Physical Forces*. Grove, a judge and physicist, is today chiefly known as the father of the fuel cell, but his work on how forces transformed into each other was very influential. Marx read the books more by accident, whereas Engels was more deeply influenced by it. He saw it as a brilliant example of a materialism that did not assume that all forces could be reduced to mechanical movement. As he understood the energy principle, it involved matter in movement under quantitatively determined conditions passing from one form of movement into another. It was always a question of attraction and repulsion, but in different forms. Engels wrote: 'Mechanical motion of masses passes into heat, into electricity, into magnetism; heat and electricity pass into chemical decomposition; chemical combination in turn again develops heat and electricity and, by means of the latter, magnetism; and finally heat and electricity produce once more mechanical movement of masses.' These words are found in the important section of *The Dialectics of Nature* that he called '*Grundformen der Bewegung*' (Basic Forms of Motion), written in 1880–81.[44]

This harmonious image of a number of forces that are quantitatively related to each other but qualitatively different had now been disrupted by Clausius's calculation of the inevitable heat loss. Back in 1869, Engels complained in a letter to Marx about the new idea running rampant in Germany that 'the world is becoming steadily colder'. The theory of heat death had its popular breakthrough with the lecture *Über den zweiten Hauptsatz der mechanischen Wärmetheorie* (On the Second Law of Thermodynamics) that Clausius held in 1867 at the Natural Research Society in Frankfurt am Main, which was later published in a separate pamphlet. Engels heard about it directly through Schorlemmer, who had taken part in the meeting, and was shocked.[45] In some of the notes that posterity has collected in *The Dialectics of Nature*, he continued his somewhat bizarre polemic. Obviously, it was not only the idea concerning the content of the principle of energy that riled him, but also the deathblow to the idea of the eternity of the universe that he, like many other materialists, embraced.

Gradually, the name of Clausius stopped being like a red rag to a bull for him. Quite the contrary, he referred with respect to Clausius's chief work from 1876, *Die mechanische Wärmetheorie* (The Mechanical Theory of Heat). Most likely, he realized that the second law of thermodynamics was a great development, and that in his world of ideas it could thereby be compared with Darwin's theory of biological evolution and Marx's theory of historical development.[46]

But back to Marx and the parallel between the transition from handicraft to manufacture, and the relationship between, for example, the various compounds in the alkane series such as methane (CH_4), ethane (C_2H_6), and so on. At first, the parallel seems strange. Marx maintained that handicraft became manufacture when the number of employees reached a certain level that made the typical forms of work in handicraft, with masters, journeymen, and apprentices impossible. In its place, a form of production develops in which the division of labour is important and natural.

The relationship between the different hydrocarbon compounds in a series such as the alkanes is of an entirely different type. Methane does not develop into ethane. Only through analysis can the striking regularity in the atomic setup be found. One carbon atom binds four hydrogen atoms, two carbon atoms six, and so on. These purely quantitative similarities are not matched by any similarity as regards properties. On the contrary, the substances in the series are strikingly different; that is why they were previously called paraffins.

What, then, was the connection Marx saw between hydrocarbons and the path from handicraft to manufacture? Obviously this: that a certain increase in quantity (in the one case, the number of employees, in the other the number of atoms) leads to something qualitatively new. The similarity does not lie in the processes (no process can be spoken of as regards the hydrocarbons). Nor is there similarity between any theories. The similarity that can be spoken about concerns a phenomenon, examples of which can be found in many areas of reality. In connection with changes in temperature, the substances can transition from solid form to liquid, and from liquid to gas. People assembled for a common task behave differently if they are only five than if they are twenty – or 10,000. When one type of air pollution reaches a certain limit, it has catastrophic consequences. As the popular phrase goes: It is the last straw that breaks the camel's back.

Hegel saw the transition from quantity to quality as a regularity to dialectical thinking – in brief, what Hegel called logic. It is actually a line of thought that is a consequence of his idealism. Reality is, in essence, thinking. But Marx was not an idealist. What is it, then, that he concurs with when he cites Hegel? Does he mean something that has its basis in material reality? Or can we talk about quantity passing over into quality only at the theoretical level? In the first case, it would concern a kind of super-law that would apply in principle to all areas of reality. But the question of why reality agrees with this law would have different answers in different areas. The relationship between the different hydrocarbons included in the alkane series is of a different type than the one prevalent among different groups of people, work communities, or projects.

If validity is limited to the theoretical level, we come significantly closer to Hegel's own ideas, with the substantial difference that this theoretical level – for a materialist such as Marx – only deals with our method of organizing knowledge and not with the reality the knowledge is about. We could say that theories in all areas must reckon with limits of different types. A handicraft company may not grow over a given level in order to preserve handicraft production. One carbon atom in the alkane series can only be combined with four hydrogen atoms. Two carbon atoms are inevitably combined with six, three with eight, and so on.

John Bellamy Foster opened the way for a third possibility, namely that Marx was following in the footsteps of Immanuel Kant. In his 1790 work *Critique of Judgment*, Kant dealt with humanity's way of experiencing functionality in their world. He deals with two areas, separate today but often brought together in Kant's time – even more so under the following Romantic era: art and organisms. It is said of both that they are so functional, regarded as totalities, that we inevitably imagine them as created by some intelligent being. As regards a work of art, this is in fact so – but living creatures? Within the horizon of human experiences, there is no organizer of the living. Creatures are born and develop according to a fixed pattern; in their bodies, there are numerous processes taking place that interlock in an artistic manner. We have no right to imagine an independent creator – we have the right to imagine that we better understand how organisms function if we look for the functional within them. This is a *regulative* idea, Kant says. It regulates our thinking, but does not lead us to any certain conclusions of the type that science advances.

Foster, of course, is very familiar with the fact that Marx asked no questions about organisms and their method of function. But he maintains that the dialectical method he seems to see in Marx is a more radical alternative to Kant's way of thinking. 'Dialectical reasoning can thus be viewed as a necessary element of our cognition, arising from the *emergent, transitory character of reality as we perceive it*,' Foster says.[47]

The concept of *emergence* plays a key role in many different scientific and philosophical contexts; it means that a more complex structure arises from a less complex one. Relatively simple patterns can give rise to more complicated ones. This applies to both inorganic and organic nature, as well as to society. Meteorology talks about how small changes in the weather can trigger hurricanes. At one point, life arose from complex organic compounds – a splendid example of emergence. The human species, with its large brain, its singularly useful hands, and its larynx placed so low that it can pronounce vowels, involves something crucially new in the development of species. And the history of humanity and its societies is full of examples of similar leaps. A range of circumstances are joined together and give rise to something new. Marx spoke about the transition from handicraft to manufacture. In the *Grundrisse*, he made a bigger move and spoke about relationships that constituted the preconditions for capitalism without being an element of it. Here, capitalism stands out in an eminent sense as an example of an emergent phenomenon. There is nothing mysterious in its origin. But it entails something qualitatively new.

Foster thus has an important point when he introduces the concept of *emergence* into the context. It is much more apposite than the concept of *limit* that we recently examined. But Foster is definitely wrong when he introduces Kant into the line of argument, thereby limiting the scope of Marx's idea. Marx did not talk about reality 'as we perceive it', but about reality quite simply as what we gain admission to through observing it, and above all through working on it.

This does not mean – as is often said in the tradition after Marx – that human knowledge is a reflection of reality. Marx has a few explanatory lines to say about this in the postscript to the second edition of *Capital*, which we previously dwelt upon. In research, the whole material is assimilated in its diversity, which is hard to grasp. There is no obvious order in this mass of material; this order is only created in the description. The dynamic in the material is 'ideally' reflected in what may appear as an *a priori* construction, Marx said. There is thus no question of any reflection of reality, nor of reality as we imagine it. It is the result of an aggregate process of work and description – a production, if you will.[48]

The concept of *emergence* also helps us to realize that the example that Marx gave in his note about quantities passing into qualities is entirely misleading. The transition from handicraft to manufacture is a fine example of emergence – but the hydrocarbon series in chemistry is definitely not. The alkanes may all be constructed according to the formula C_nH_{2n+2}, but there is no process that leads from methane to ethane, and so on. There, a conformity to law applies that says that one carbon atom binds four hydrogen atoms, but two carbon atoms bind six hydrogen atoms. So it always remains – it is 'something quiescent', something stable, as Hegel said.

Marx's mistake can be explained by the enthusiasm that all the new knowledge of chemistry roused in him: Hofmann's lectures, his acquaintance with Schorlemmer, and much else in a time and environment where many more than just the specialists wanted to acquaint themselves with the new advances of chemistry and the natural sciences in general. As we have seen, Engels did not react appreciably when Marx wrote to him that he was going to compare a historical course of events with the chemists' new theory about molecules. Marx did not develop the consequences of the concept of *dialectical law* he thereby introduced, nor would he ever do so. For his part, Marx never returned to his innovation. He did not even use the word 'law' when he spoke about the negation of the negation (p. 416 above) at the end of *Capital*. But his little note about the laws in chemistry and history had repercussions that no one could have imagined. We will now cast a glance over this history.

Anti-Dühring

On 30 May 1873, Engels wrote a dramatic letter to Marx. 'This morning in bed the following dialectical points about the natural sciences came into my head,' he wrote. The letter was clearly hasty. Marx and he would meet again soon enough. Karl was on a temporary visit to Manchester, and Engels had been living in London for three years.

It is clear that he had not spoken about anything similar under the numerous meetings face to face they had had in London. Marx's response also indicated that he was a bit taken by surprise. He said that he could not say anything definite about his friend's ideas until he had consulted 'the "authorities"'. These authorities were Carl Schorlemmer on the one hand, and on the other Samuel Moore, the lawyer and mathematician we have already encountered who would also at length translate *Capital* to English. While Marx was writing his letter, Schorlemmer conveniently showed up and wrote a few notes in the margins of Engels's letter. They were nothing but agreement: 'Very good, my own view' and 'Quite right!' Engels himself was certainly not uninfluenced by his outstanding chemist friend. But Schorlemmer was obviously not initiated into Engels's new ideas, either. According to Marx's response, he additionally did not want to comment on their more immediate import.[49]

The letter from 1873 meant something new in Engels's life. From that point until Marx's death, the work that posterity would call *The Dialectics of Nature* was at the very centre of his activity. To be sure, since 1858 he had been writing scattered remarks on things that interested him in the natural sciences and in philosophy. But now, a whole big project was taking form for him.

The project was to show how the new natural sciences formed a unity. They formed a hierarchy of different forms of movement. The path ran from the simple to the complex, from mechanics via 'physics proper' and chemistry to biology. Engels did not even need to point out to Marx that he ultimately wanted to find a place in this complex unity for their own theories on human society and its development. It is worth noting that Marx's response to Engels's new ideas was just as indifferent as Engels's response to Marx's ideas on dialectical laws that connected organic chemistry and social theory.

In any case, Engels worked further on his idea. But he would soon be disrupted in his concentration. The reason was Eugen Dühring's vehement attack on *Capital*, which we have touched upon several times and influenced Marx's postscript to the second edition. The attack had not only irritated Marx but also agitated his social democratic sympathizers in Germany. Dühring was a Social Democrat; he lived in Berlin and his influence over fellow party members – in that city in particular – was growing rapidly. Wilhelm Liebknecht, who after his difficult youth in London was now an important man in the party and managed its newspaper *Vorwärts*, wrote to Marx and encouraged him to respond to Dühring's low criticism. But Marx did not have the time; his continued efforts with *Capital* left him no peace.[50] Engels took up the task unwillingly. In the first foreword he wrote to *Anti-Dühring*, which he later discarded and thereby ended up in *The Dialectics of Nature*, he wrote: 'The following work does not by any means owe its origin to an "inner urge". On the contrary, my friend Liebknecht can testify to the great effort it cost him to persuade me to turn the light of criticism on Herr Dühring's newest socialist theory.'[51] The letters between Marx and Engels also testified to the fact that it was after hesitation, and feeling that he had to put aside a more important work – that is, *The Dialectics of Nature* – that Engels took on the task of going after Dühring.

Liebknecht seems to have believed to the very last that it was Marx who should defend himself against Dühring. It was a statement he spread around. Marx got upset and explained that Engels was making a great sacrifice, as this project was forcing him to interrupt 'an incomparably more important piece of work'.[52] The work on *Anti-Dühring* would thus, assumed Engels and Marx, be a parenthesis. In fact, it would change the direction of Engels's philosophical labour.

The Dialectics of Nature consists of a miscellaneous collection of texts. Many of them are only short notices or aphorisms, others are half-length sketches, while others are completely developed chapters. This material is not arranged in chronological order in the printed editions, but most of the texts can be dated. One then finds that what Engels wrote before May 1876, when he began work on *Anti-Dühring*, is limited to nothing but short texts in which Hegel is constantly present. At the beginning of that period, which began with his letter to Marx in 1873 in which he talks about his new ideas, he is occupied in particular with Hegel's *Encyclopedia of the Philosophical Sciences*, published in

1817 and 1830. In it, Hegel puts together a bold compilation of the human knowledge gathered in the various disciplines of philosophy, everything from mathematics and the natural sciences to history. Ernst Haeckel, who was the first to draw philosophical consequences from Darwin's *Origin of Species*, is also often brought up in Engels's notes.

Two lines of thought that are interwoven with each other dominate Engels's early texts, all the way back to the first one from 1858 on Ludwig Büchner.[53] The only thing he ascribes to Hegel is that there are no fixed categories. The new natural science showed that phenomena previously regarded as clearly separate, or even incompatible, flow into and are mixed with each other. In the manuscript on Büchner, Engels makes a distinction between metaphysical and dialectical tendencies; with it, he tries to capture precisely the difference between fixed and fluid categories. Opposites go into each other: reason and consequence, cause and effect, identity and difference, appearance and essence. But the dialectic not only dissolves the concepts. It also shows us that what seems invariable in objective reality passes over into something else and develops into something new. In a note from 1875, it says that there are no 'hard and fast lines'.[54] The examples there are taken from evolutionary biology, which demolishes the idea of unchanging species.

It is important to remember that even in these early notes, Engels spoke of a dialectic of the same (or at least a similar) type in thought and reality. Ultimately, it is the evasive and constantly changing nature of reality that makes it necessary for thinking, and thereby also science, to work with opposite concepts that nevertheless do not exclude each other.[55]

The order of nature is changeable, but all the same there is an order. Such is the second, more specific idea in Engels's early notes. This is what predominated in the letter to Marx from 1873. Everything that exists is matter in movement, but there are different forms of movement. The new natural science could show how the different forms of movement pass into each other. Mechanical movement, heat, electricity, and so on are not thoroughly separate quantities. They are qualitatively separate, but the transition from one quality to another can be quantitatively determined.

Soon enough, he would broaden his examples to biology, and immediately thereafter also to humanity and their societies. When he wrote a small text in rough outline about the dialectic in 1875, he had made room for all of reality. Life was linked to the proteins, and human history was pushed forward through conflicts. The transitions between the various levels of reality go so quickly that the reader can scarcely keep up. The notes were surely made for Engels's own memory and not for other readers.[56]

But *there was still no hint of any dialectical laws*. The dialectical laws first show up when he set about the task of defending Marx's use of the concept in *Capital*. It was a crucial step. The extremely general ideas that support the early, brief notes are given greater certainty in one stroke – namely, the certainty that characterizes all of *Anti-Dühring* and even the majority of the texts that Engels wrote thereafter, which were included in *The Dialectics of Nature*. But what was its price?

Engels wrote *Anti-Dühring* – or, as it is actually called, *Herr Eugen Dührings Umwälzung der Wissenschaft* (Herr Eugen Dühring's Revolution in Science) between September 1876 and June 1878. The text was first published as a long series of articles in the newspaper *Vorwärts* between January 1877 and July 1878, and then as a book in 1879. His correspondence from the time of writing is full of grumbling. Wilhelm Liebknecht is 'that silly ass Wilhelm' who suffered from a shortage of manuscripts for *Vorwärts* and was therefore pushing Engels to write as quickly as possible. In another letter, Engels for once is jealous of Marx: 'You can lie in a warm bed – study Russian agrarian relations in particular and rent in general without anything to interrupt you – but I have to sit on a hard bench, drink cold wine, and all of a sudden drop everything else and break a lance with the tedious Dühring.'[57]

Engels was easily exasperated, but Marx actually also contributed a text to *Anti-Dühring*. He called it 'Randnoten zu Dührings "Kritische Geschichte der Nationalökonomie"' (Margin Notes on Dühring's *Critical History of Political Economy*). It was run in an abridged version in the newspaper, but with various small changes by Engels in the book version.[58] But the whole of it was Engels's, and gradually he also found some greater pleasure in his work. This gave him the opportunity to develop the worldview he had displayed such a desire for even before the work on *Anti-Dühring*.

On the other hand, he could still say in 1879, when the book version came out, that he never again intended to allow himself to be interrupted in more important matters by 'journalistic activities'.[59] Only later, when he had given up hope of ever completing his great work on dialectics, could he speak a little more appreciatively about *Anti-Dühring*. But then the book could also become the gateway to Marx's theories for many active members of the young workers' movement. It would come to leave its mark on what began to be called Marxism around 1890, but what should rather be called Engelsism.[60]

In its way, *Anti-Dühring* is also a clear, easy-to-understand book. There is no equivalence whatsoever to the artistry in the plan in *Capital*. It consists of three parts following an explanatory introduction. First, philosophy, which in full accordance with tradition is divided into natural philosophy and moral philosophy. After that comes political economy, and finally socialism. It is a popular course in Marx's theories wrapped up in the more comprehensive theoretical construction that Engels himself had been putting together for a few years.

But at the end of the philosophy section are a few brief chapters representing something new. The first is called 'Dialectics. Quantity and Quality', and the second 'Dialectics. Negation of the Negation'.[61] In these chapters, Engels replies directly to Dühring's criticism of the brief lines in *Capital* where Marx talks about the law of quantity and quality, as well as of the brief lines about the negation of the negation. Most readers of *Capital* had surely not even noticed these spots in a vast, complex mass of text. But Dühring had, for the simple reason that he had developed his own dialectic to drive Hegel's out. That is why Marx's references to Hegel's connection with the dialectic were like a red flag to a bull for him. He characterized Marx quite simply as a Hegelian, which – as we have seen – enraged Marx. And now it was Engels's task to defend Marx. The matter was thus blown up to proportions other than the ones it had in *Capital*.

Neither Dühring nor Engels made a fuss about Marx, in contrast to Hegel, speaking about a 'law' in connection with quantity and quality. Both took it for granted that he was simply following Hegel. Engels complained about Dühring arguing that Marx saw Hegel's thesis on quantity and quality as a general law, from which every individual case could be inferred through deduction. It is actually the opposite: Marx said that Hegel's law passes the test in the face of both the empirical cases he compares – one from political economy, the other from organic chemistry. This is an important observation. But on the other hand, Dühring's mistake is comprehensible when Marx talks about laws.

Engels also said that Marx was the first to discover this law. Hegel has thus fallen out of the calculation here; Engels himself, with all his ambitions regarding a good natural scientific orientation, grants Marx priority. But in the next step he trumps Marx, talking about the negation of the negation as also a law. Engels describes it as '[a]n extremely general – and for this reason extremely far-reaching and important – law of the development of nature, history, and thought'.[62] As we have seen, the phrase 'law of development' is important. But did Engels really mean that it had the same character as the law of entropy? No, hardly so. What he called the negation of the negation is borne out in a miscellaneous number of contexts – everything from logic and mathematics to history. Engels was aware of its variegated character. The path of the plant from seed to flower with its different stages, for example, did not have a lot to do with integral calculations, he said. We can safely agree with this.

With two dialectical laws, the way lies open for more. When Engels took up the work on *The Dialectics of Nature* again in 1878, he first made a plan for the entire work. The introduction that he wrote before he took up *Anti-Dühring* remains. But an entirely new section came into existence after that: a section on the universal validity of the dialectical laws. Suddenly, these laws have now become *four*. The law of quantity and quality is the first, and it is followed by a law of the unity of opposites. The unity of opposites had been under discussion in *Anti-Dühring* as well, but it had not been pointed out as a dialectical law there. Rather, it had had the status as a dialectical principle superior to everything else. Now, it had been given a co-equal position. The law of the negation of negation is number three, and there is also a fourth law: the 'spiral form of development'.[63]

By all appearances, this fourth law was to capture the tendency of development to repeat previous stages but on another level, an observation that is also found in Hegel. But the law quickly disappeared. When Engels developed the outline plan for a somewhat more detailed text the following year, 1879, it was not included. Three laws remained; they are the laws that have become normative in the tradition that has its beginnings when *The Dialectics of Nature* (first called *Natur und Dialektik*) was printed in 1925.[64] They lived on up to the present day, but above all as long as the Soviet Union existed. They have been repeated in all kinds of handbooks, and expounded in various more or less imaginative ways. Dogmatists have stood up in their defence, but it can safely be said that no one has been drawn to the tradition from Marx, or even Engels, owing to these laws. They have become an extra burden that can only be defended with all sorts of more or less sophistic reasoning.

As we have seen, their position in Marx's writings is extremely fragile. His contribution to them is a single one: a few individual lines in *Capital*. They would certainly have disappeared into the great archive of oblivion if Dühring had not attacked them, and Engels found it important to defend them and then also work further on the concept of 'dialectical law'. But he then had difficulty making up his mind: two laws became four, and then three.

When at the end of his life, Marx was composing careful excerpts of rather advanced textbooks and chemistry, no dialectical laws turn up. He goes carefully through organic chemistry, including the paraffins that were the speciality of Carl Schorlemmer – but not a word about any dialectics in the process. His aim, quite simply, is to understand the context as such – very important for both agriculture and the chemicals industry.

The big question is what attitude Marx took towards *Anti-Dühring*, and in particular the exposition there on the dialectical laws (which were still only two in number). Marx, as we have seen, contributed his own text. But it had nothing to do with the laws. In the foreword to the edition that was published in 1885 – that is, after Marx's death – Engels assures us that 'I read the whole manuscript for him before it was printed'.[65] In all likelihood, Marx was eager to be more closely informed about a publication that dealt with his own theories to such a great degree. But how carefully did he consider the consequences of the dialectical laws? Could he have imagined that they would have served as a basis for the simplest sloganeering?

It is not likely that the concept of *dialectical law* had anything but a highly temporary position in his consciousness. It was the same for Engels. It was not only due to the fact that he was occupied with completing the later portions of *Capital*. He was also concentrating on a smaller publication in which he would summarise his views on philosophy. It was called *Ludwig Feuerbach und der Ausgang der klassischen deutschen Philosophie*, published in 1886 as newspaper articles, and in 1888 as a book (and in English in 1929 as *Ludwig Feuerbach and the End of Classical German Philosophy*).[66] It is surely the best he wrote in the genre, a clear and concentrated presentation of approximately forty pages in which he goes through the thinking of Hegel and Feuerbach, the great natural scientific discoveries during the period in which he himself lived, and finally the theories – inspired by Hegel and Marx – that the new workers' movement were pursuing. But not a word about any dialectical laws! If anywhere, they should have had a place there if they had had any central role in his own philosophy. But the parenthesis is closed; Marx's little deviation no longer needed to be defended against an aggressive lecturer in philosophy from Berlin. Engels could let them disappear into oblivion without regret.

'The Foundation of Our Theory'

Charles Darwin's book *The Origin of Species* came out on 24 November 1859. The first edition sold out almost immediately. Engels was among the lucky few who succeeded in getting hold of a copy, and by 12 December he had written to Marx that the book was 'absolutely splendid'.[67] He saw its significance first in the fact that it made all teleology impossible – that is, all ideas that organisms in some respect are determined for a purpose. Second, that it was the greatest attempt at demonstrating historical development in nature.

The latter meant that Darwin got Engels to change his understanding on an important point. Only a few months previously, in his review of Marx's *Preface to A Contribution to the Critique of Political Economy*, he had established that nature lacked a history.[68] Marx came to the same conclusion when, approximately a year later, he went through *The Origin of Species*. For several weeks, he had been unable to write, since he had been sitting by his wife Jenny's side during the time she was critically ill with smallpox. But he had been able to read a lot by her sickbed, he told Engels, including Darwin's book. Although it was 'developed and accrued English fashion', it was still 'the book which, in the field of natural history, provides the basis for our views'. These were important words. The phrase 'natural history' is, to be sure, a little confusing. Well into the nineteenth century, it was the prevalent term for knowledge that could not be summed up in a few statements of law. Natural philosophy was the opposite; Newton's *Principia* was the very emblem of a natural philosophical tract, while Linnaeus was a typical natural historian. Traditionally, natural history thus had nothing to do with any development in time.[69]

But obviously, it was precisely development in time that Marx had in mind. Humanity had developed from other animal species. Its history is a continuation of a long biological process. Roughly the same viewpoints recur in a letter he wrote to Ferdinand Lassalle a few weeks later. Darwin's publication was 'most important' and 'suits my purpose in that it provides a basis in natural science for the historical class struggle', he wrote, adding: 'One does, of course, have to put up with the clumsy English style of argument.'[70]

Marx's relief, now that he could talk about the biological origins of humanity, is understandable. He had uneasily avoided the question with a rather sophistic line of argument in the *Manuscripts*, and after that he had not even brought it up for discussion. With Darwin, he received a clear and honest response. It is true that in *Origin*, Darwin did not say anything about the genesis of the human species – he did that first in his 1871 book, *The Descent of Man*. But both followers and opponents drew the conclusion that humanity was in the middle of the great process of transformation as soon as *Origin* was published. It would be bizarre for humanity to have remained the same since the dawn of time, while every other living thing had changed.

But Marx complained about Darwin's 'clumsy English style'. This must be the method of presentation itself he was bothered by – the rather artless suite of chapters packed with information, so far from the grand architecture of *Capital*. It was worse with Darwin's enthusiastic references to Thomas Robert Malthus and his theory of overpopulation. Malthus was an important name in Great Britain at the time. His ideas that people – and the underclass in particular – increased more rapidly than food production long remained a fixture in British public debate. Malthus is among those who provided arguments for drastic measures against the poor and the unemployed, at the same time as he was an important target for Chartists and other harsh critics of the prevailing social order. In the liberal environment that Darwin was a part of, Malthus was among the popular topics of conversation. One did not need to read his books in order to get a clear understanding of him. He himself had been dead since 1834, but has name turned up in particular when the social problems of poverty, starvation, and childbirth made themselves felt (Malthus, himself a priest, had recommended sexual restraint as an effective means against overpopulation).

Once Darwin was finally ready to publicize his theory through *The Origin of Species*, Malthus was already being regarded as a bit old-fashioned. But Darwin, who was rather unaffected by the ideas then in fashion, assigned him a place of honour among his inspirers. He called the important third chapter in *Origin* – where the principle of selection itself is established – 'Struggle for Existence', which later in the text is used interchangeably with 'struggle for life', a phrase similar in meaning. He got the idea from the seventh edition of Malthus's 1836 work, *An Essay on the Principle of Population*.[71]

Marx had always been a merciless critic of Malthus, which extended to his traces in Darwin's *Origin*. In a letter to Engels, Marx wrote: 'It is remarkable how Darwin rediscovers, among the beasts and plants, the society of England with its division of labour, competition, opening up of new markets, "inventions" and Malthusian "struggle for existence".' He remembered how Hegel, in *Phenomenology of Spirit*, spoke about bourgeois society as an 'intellectual animal kingdom'. In Darwin, on the contrary, bourgeois society is found in the animal kingdom.[72]

Marx was therefore displeased when Friedrich Albert Lange, a German socialist and neo-Kantian philosopher, presented human history as one long 'struggle for existence' in his 1865 book *Die Arbeiterfrage*. Lange explained that it was his intention to 'derive the worker question from Darwin's principles'. In the same breath, he added that he did not see these principles as inevitable for humanity since they rise above 'the cruel and soulless mechanism through calculating purposefulness'. But they cannot completely liberate themselves from the struggle for existence. Lange saw his own book as an initial imperfect attempt at showing that intellectual as well as economic development can be understood with the same principles as the origin of species – that is, through the struggle for existence.

It never becomes clear where the boundary lies between blind selection and humanity's ability to plan and predict. The main thing was to demonstrate the significance of natural selection for humanity's development. Lange gave the expression 'struggle for existence' a broad interpretation. Even in nature, the struggle concerns not only pure survival but also the *best* conditions governing life. So it is also among humans. The struggle of the workers is primarily a struggle over 'wages'.

The conditions for selection are, naturally, overproduction – of 'the seeds of life' in nature, but of 'talents' in human society. These talents are scattered among the mass of the people, but in a hierarchical society they are never put to use since the leading positions are reserved for 'certain layers'.

According to Lange, a more effective screening of these gifts is required for development in a socialist direction. Capitalism forces the workers to be just that – workers. Their hope lies in a process of moral improvement that can partially eliminate natural necessity. Obviously, the struggle for existence could serve both rational and irrational purposes: both the struggle for justice and for an unjust hierarchical society.[73]

Marx's commentary on Lange's book is thoroughly acid. When he read the second edition from 1870, he wrote to his friend Ludwig Kugelmann that Mr Lange had made a great discovery, namely that all of history can be subordinated to one great law of nature. But this law of nature is nothing more than a phrase – the phrase 'struggle for life' – and its content is Malthus's theory of population, or more correctly overpopulation. Lange did not try to analyse the phrase; he found in it only 'a very rewarding method – for stilted, mock-scientific, highfalutin ignorance and intellectual laziness'.[74]

Marx stressed that Darwin's 'struggle for life' loses its usefulness in the field of history. This was also Engels's view. Selection is crucial for biological evolution, but not for the development of humanity. Long before Marx and Engels had heard the name of Darwin, they explained in *The German Ideology*: 'Men can be distinguished from animals by conscience, by religion or anything else you like. They themselves begin to distinguish themselves from animals as soon as they begin to *produce* their means of subsistence, a step which is conditioned by their physical organization.'[75]

This was a declaration they both stuck to. But, at the time they wrote *The German Ideology*, they still had no biological theory that they could simultaneously assume and contrast their idea with. But Darwin changed the situation drastically. Selection provided a key to the understanding of the development of life on Earth, but with humanity and their conscious production something fundamentally new had come.

But Marx had problems with Darwin's uncritical use of Malthus. It could make Marx himself uncritical in relation to alternative explanations for the development of species. In 1866, when he was finally on the way towards completing the first volume of *Capital*, he happened to read a book by the French polymath Pierre Trémaux, *Origine et transformations de l'homme et des autres êtres* (Origin and Transformation of Man and Other Beings), published in 1865. Trémaux was a prize-winning architect, photographer, and Orientalist who also wrote works on natural science; the book that Marx read is his best known. In it, Trémaux maintained that it was not selection that characterized the various species and their variants, but instead the external environment – the 'soil formations'. His chief interest was in explaining racial differences in this manner: the different human races were formed by various geographical conditions.[76]

Marx became very enthusiastic after reading it. Considering his own basic understanding of history, it may seem surprising that he noted with satisfaction that Trémaux could use his explanatory scheme in a more full and varied manner than Darwin on historical and political conditions. Trémaux had, for example, found the 'natural base' for nationalities. But with that, biology would be muscling in on the field of the social sciences!

Marx's enthusiasm was not to Engels's taste. Engels explained that the fact that Trémaux lacked insight into geology and had no concept of source criticism was reason enough to not take him seriously. His explanation of how white people became Black 'sind zum Kranklachen' (was something one could die laughing at). Marx responded – visibly wounded but nonetheless subdued in his enthusiasm – that whatever faults Trémaux may have had, his basic idea about the influence of the soil was worth taking seriously. But Engels was merciless: the environment is certainly worth taking seriously, but Darwin was already doing that. What Trémaux had arrived at, apart from this scarcely original idea, was pure nonsense.[77]

The discussion was thereby concluded, and Marx seems to have capitulated unconditionally. The disagreement not only testifies to Marx judging Darwin's theory quite highly based on his antipathy towards Malthus, thus becoming uncritical in his hunt for alternatives. It also shows that Engels, in precisely this field, had a more confident assessment than his friend. Up until then, he had also devoted significantly greater attention to the philosophical (or, if you like, ideological) side of the natural sciences. After his university days and until the encounter with Darwin, Marx had largely been occupied with the technical applications.

In *Capital*, Darwin alone ruled the roost. He turns up twice, both times in footnotes. In the first, Marx talks about Darwin's 'epoch-making work' with no reservations whatsoever. He has accepted the correction, an art he was otherwise not very distinguished in.[78]

In fact, his feeling of affinity with Darwin was so great that he sent a copy of the second edition of *Capital* to the great man himself. In the dedication, he described himself as a 'sincere admirer'. Darwin cut open the first pages and observed that it was a 'great work', but at the same time was confused by the German. He wrote back to Marx, thanking him and apologizing that he was not a worthy recipient of the book since he knew so little about political economy. But he understood that Marx, like himself, was working to broaden knowledge and thereby over the long term to 'add to the happiness of mankind'.[79]

Darwin and Marx got no closer to each other. But during his last years, Marx made the acquaintance of Ray Lankester, a gifted follower of Darwin. Despite an age difference of twenty-nine years, Lankester became a close friend to him – so close that he was among the little group at Marx's funeral. Lankester was a first-rate biologist and a sworn enemy of the superstition that blossomed alongside the widespread faith in science during the second half of the nineteenth century. But he was also completely taken by Marx, his knowledge, and his critical disposition. He read *Capital* and wrote an enthusiastic letter to the author of the work. He had obviously also been inspired by Marx's analysis of capitalism. For example, John Bellamy Foster reproduces Lankester's reaction to the sinking of the *Titanic*. It was, he said, one example among many of how impersonal mechanisms drove businesses to put profit before all else – even the lives and safety of people. It was a comment entirely in the spirit of Marx.[80]

One main idea in John Bellamy Foster's *Marx's Ecology* is that Darwin and Marx are the two great materialists of the nineteenth century. It is possible – but, in that case, they are materialists of two highly different types. There is nothing in Darwin of the view of history – and, more precisely, capitalist society – that is at the centre of Marx's interest. It was not by chance that Darwin chose the theses of Malthus on the mechanisms of overpopulation as a model for his theory on natural selection. But the theory does not rise and fall with Malthus; on the contrary, it has only a superficial connection with the theory of that modest pastor. Darwin lived in an intellectual environment that greedily sucked up that type of liberalism whose clearest expression was the 'Manchester School'

with Bright and Cobden at the centre – that is, precisely the ideology that Marx fought so persistently. But personally, Darwin
had very little contact with the hard world where capitalists and
workers dwell. He was privately educated with a private fortune,
and in his view of society he was more an idealist than a materialist. A small patch of this conviction can be seen in his letter of
thanks to Marx: it is through knowledge that the aggregate happiness of humanity increases. The phrase sounds like an echo from
Jeremy Bentham and his thinking.

On the other hand, it can be said without a doubt that Darwin
was of greater importance than anyone else in showing that living
nature developed on its own without intervention from some
metaphysical power. He himself only came to such conclusions
with a certain degree of uneasiness. For Marx, if anything, Darwin
fulfilled a hope. With Darwin's theory, his own view on the history
of humanity gained a foundation. At the same time, he was careful
to separate the development of nature from human production,
which changed both its own circumstances and its environment.
Humanity is and remains one species among many, but it is alone
in changing conditions for itself and other species in a conscious,
planned way.

Human Prehistory

During his final, feverishly active years of life, Marx entered into
a field of knowledge that largely was new to him: social anthropology. As a young man, he had encountered philosophical
anthropology, above all in the form of the Norwegian-German
philosopher Steffens. Hegel later became his guiding star in
anthropology, before Feuerbach took over the role. Once Marx
had pretty well freed himself from Feuerbach as well, anthropology sank out of his consciousness and did not seriously return
until 1880. The new social anthropology he encountered at that
time was something quite different than the thinking of Steffens,
Hegel, and Feuerbach on what was uniquely human. It was now a
primarily empirical discipline that had got some wind beneath its
wings thanks to Darwinism. With the ideas on the development

of species, there also came interest in the earliest history of the human species. This history was now more firmly limited to pure biology. Fossils of a human-like being were found for the first time in 1856, in the Neander valley in the German province of Nordrhein-Westfalen. When Darwin's theory made its triumphal march soon thereafter, the discovery became a rewarding subject of discussion. T. H. Huxley, the indefatigable defender of natural selection, openly declared that humans and 'Neanderthals' originated from the same species of apes.[81]

This was one of the reasons that the earliest history of humanity aroused an increasingly lively interest. People wanted to get as close to the great moment of evolution as possible. As long as one ignored the fundamental discoveries of Gregor Mendel, conceptions of heredity were extremely blurry. It was common to violently exaggerate the speed with which a species changed. For the most daring, it was a question of mere generations. Herbert Spencer imagined he could see a new race of Anglo-Americans being developed, and he awaited the same development among the immigrant Australians.[82]

At the same time, the conviction remained that contemporary societies perceived as primitive in substance resembled the earliest stages of development of civilization. Simply put, humanity's own earliest history was available in the modern age. Marx would also become interested in societies perceived as primordial. But his motives, as far as we know, were different. Above all he was increasingly fascinated by Russia and its distinctive character – something we will come back to in the next chapter.

Marx's ideas on early society were bolstered by the American Lewis H. Morgan, whose 1877 book *Ancient Society* he had read and taken careful notes from. Morgan was an American lawyer, born the same year as Marx, and was one of the first to seriously study the indigenous American peoples. At the centre of *Ancient Society* stood an idea about human progress that is older than Darwin, and had been fully developed by Scottish Enlightenment philosophers back in the eighteenth century. This doctrine says that humans were savages at first, then barbarians, and finally civilized; Morgan refined it further by distinguishing between lower and higher stages of the savage state and barbarism.[83]

This rigid scheme, which assume that all cultures developed along similar lines, constituted the framework for the empirical data that Morgan collected from various Native American cultures. To this, he added information from cultures other than North American ones – many of which had disappeared a long time ago – and he imagined he found similar patterns everywhere. These were ideas that guided many researchers from that era. One only need think of the British anthropologist and religious researcher James George Frazer, whose work *The Golden Bough* first came out as a two-volume edition in 1890. In it, the author sought to show, with almost pedantic precision, how the same religious practices recur from culture to culture as soon as a certain stage of development has been achieved.[84]

Characteristic of Morgan was his ascription of a crucial role for technological progress in the development towards higher stages. It was an important reason for Marx devoting the attention to Morgan that he did. One of Marx's growing number of Russian friends, social scientist Maksim Kovalevsky, cousin to the famous mathematician Sophia (or Sonya) Kovalevskaya, had bought *Ancient History* during a trip to the United States. Kovalevsky himself was an outstanding specialist in the Russian *mir*, or peasant village; he now roused Marx's interest in Morgan's book and loaned it to him. As was his custom, Marx composed comprehensive excerpts before 'the fat boy' got his property back.[85] Marx also took shorter notes from several other books that approached, in various ways, the same subject Morgan was dealing with.

Obviously, he wanted to acquire solid knowledge of societies that were considered to have preceded the breakthrough of private property and the state. But he got no further than the excerpts that Engels later found among the papers he left behind. These were the starting point and the foundation for one of Engels's most widely read books: his 1884 work *The Origin of the Family, Private Property, and the State*. Morgan's significance is emphasized even by the subtitle: 'In the Light of the Researches of Lewis H. Morgan'. In the first sentences of the foreword, Engels stresses that he had taken over the task of writing his book from Marx.[86] The traditional perception has been that it actually was so. Only a more detailed comparison shows that Engels indeed quoted liberally from the excerpts of his deceased friend, but that his work is permeated with his own ideas and unique spirit.

Engels's attitude towards Morgan is without a doubt also more positive than Marx's. The difference can already be seen on the first page of the text (after the foreword). In *Ancient Society*, Morgan wrote that 'mankind are the only beings who may be said to have gained an absolute control over the production of food'.[87] This is a statement that Marx could not feel comfortable with; he protested against it with a vigorous question mark followed by an exclamation point. Engels tried to smooth this over; in his zeal, he quoted Morgan incorrectly. Humanity had *almost* won unconditional dominion, it says in his text. Foster places great importance on Marx's reservations, placing them in connection with his thesis that humanity's exploitation of the soil has entailed a rift in the relationship between humanity and nature.[88]

With his little distortion of the quote, Engels tried to take the sting out of Morgan's resolute formulation. It may seem to be a trifle; Engels was not writing an academic dissertation. But trifles are not isolated – they can fit into a pattern. Engels wanted to interpret Morgan so that the latter could be added to the same tradition as himself and Marx. In the foreword, Engels wrote that Morgan's perception squares with the 'materialist conception of history' that Marx had 'discovered' forty years earlier.

The observation is also interesting for the fact that, by all appearances, this is the first time the expression 'materialist conception of history' occurs in the literature. Marx never used it. It is hardly likely that Marx would have viewed Morgan as an (unconscious) follower. Morgan's emphasis on technological development was extremely appealing to Marx. But he placed an exclamation point after 'ideas' when Morgan spoke about 'the earliest ideas of property'. Nor could Morgan's statement that all 'social and civil institutions' developed from thought appeal to Marx.

This is pointed out by Lawrence Krader, the American ethnologist and anthropologist, who carried out what is without doubt the most thorough investigation of Marx's excerpts from Morgan. Marx himself gave prominence to the significance of the collective in contrast to Morgan, and he maintained that politics is born when one tribe, or *gens*, seizes power over the others. With the *gens*, the 'lamentable religious element' becomes an important point.[89]

We have seen that the boundary between biological development and historical development was important to Marx (apart from the episode with Trémaux). It was not so for Morgan – nor, in fact, for Engels in his book *Origins of the Family*. What is relevant here is that Morgan turned Marx's and Engels's attention to the significance of the *family* in social development. But Engels went a step further than Marx. He not only said that production and reproduction constitute the foundation of historical development. He also said the production and reproduction were of a dual nature.[90] On the one hand it concerns the necessities of life and other things that humanity reproduces; on the other, it concerns the production of new people. He apparently has Marxian support here; he quotes Marx's words in the Morgan commentaries that while families develop, relations of kinship – that is, what constitutes the family – palpably lag behind.[91]

When Engels attributes the production of people to the base of society, a substantial change takes place. According to Marx's foreword to *A Contribution to the Critique of Political Economy*, the base constitutes the relationship between the forces of production and the relations of production. Talking about relations of production in this context offers no difficulties: it is a question of the composition of the family, monogamy, polygamy, and so on. But how did Engels imagine the forces of production? They must be the tools with which people produce children – that is, the genitalia. But, however complex the genitalia may be, the method of functioning is a purely biological matter. They appear as historically constant, and thereby are generally not a historical matter. They have not evolved from time immemorial up to the present day.

Engels simply seems to be allowing biology to invade the field of history. He is tearing up the boundary markers he himself set up in *Anti-Dühring* in an important area. Many, such as Edward Aveling and Karl Kautsky, followed in his footsteps. Aveling's contribution to the confusion is most clearly evident in his 1884 book *The Darwinian Theory* – incidentally, the book that Aveling wanted to dedicate to Darwin, but was told not to. Kautsky's image of the relationship between the theories of Marx and Darwin emerges, for example, in his memoirs *Erinnerungen und Erörterungen*. This book did not affect the age he lived in, however; it was first published in 1960 by his son Benedikt. But, during his years of activity, Kautsky had fed his readership the conviction that Marx's theory and Darwin's fit together like hand in glove.[92]

Engels also devoted himself to a type of psychologizing that was foreign to Marx. For Marx, capitalists are forced to maximize their profits with the same necessity that workers must sell their labour power – the alternative is ruin. It does not matter whether as people they are greedy or generous. So it is generally in every class society. The roles are given. Individual actors could fill them with personal content up to a certain limit. Engels, on the other hand, charges the masters of the first class society with *Habgier* – greed. As Krader points out, this entailed an obvious deviation from Marx. Engels had fallen into an outlook that remained popular up until our own time. Large amounts of wealth or excesses and profit are explained by exceptional greed.[93] Marx was more sophisticated than that.

But there was a central area he often ignored when he talked about society, its history, and its future: women. The notes to Morgan's book, however, constitute an exception. There, he asked himself whether the tales of the great goddesses of Greece did not guard memories from another time when women had a better, freer position.[94] That was all. But the comment testifies to the fact that he assumed that the subjugation of women had to do with the development of class society, and thereby of the state and of politics. At one point, woman had been free and equal, like Athena or Hera. Someday, she would be so again.

It is impossible to determine what Marx would have done if he had worked out a text on the basis of his excerpts. Engels had much more to say in his book. He wrote in detail about sexual life among various species, and then came to humanity. As regards the 'communist household', he established that the woman was the master there. He polemicized heatedly against a conception he traced back to the Enlightenment, that woman was to have been man's slave from the beginning. On the contrary, he said, woman had not only a free but a respected position in the early stages of societal development. Swiss legal historian Johann Jakob Bachofen was of great significance for Engels's idea; his 1861 book *Das Mutterrecht* (Mother Right) made a deep impression on Engels with its thesis that the patriarchy was preceded by an age in which women ruled (a gynaecocracy, as Bachofen called it).⁹⁵

Engels's description has played an important role in the modern history of feminism. This especially applies to one of the great classics in the field, Simone de Beauvoir's 1948 work *Le deuxième sexe* (published in English in 1972 as *The Second Sex*). Beauvoir dismisses what she calls Engels's 'economic monism', but this does not mean that he did not greatly influence her work. As Eva Gothlin showed in her dissertation *Sex and Existence*, early Marx and late Engels were important inspirations for Beauvoir.⁹⁶

Social anthropology became an important concern in Engels's life, while Marx never meant to give it anything but the attention he devoted to a number of other topics he adopted throughout his life, especially during his last years when he also managed to work his way through major works in chemistry, physics, and mathematics. It is not surprising that he would be fascinated by Morgan's theses on early societies with communal ownership. His desire to go deeper into the subject was also intensified by his interest in Russia. This curiosity is also discernible in his excerpts. Morgan's reports on communal ownership that still remained in certain Native American societies got Marx to wonder about how things stood with 'the southern *Slavs*? and also the *Russians* to a certain extent?' in that respect. We know nothing about how Marx intended to use his new insights over the longer term. They could scarcely be inserted as footnotes in the continuation of *Capital*. But was his interest perhaps politically conditioned?

We do not know. On the other hand, we can be sure it would not have been the type of work that Engels created, partially on the basis of Marx's excerpts.

Interpreting the World and Changing It

The *Manifesto* says that the history of all hitherto existing society
has been a history of class struggle. When, in the late 1880s,
Engels published a new edition of the work, he added a footnote.
The statement seemed correct at the time it was made, he said. But
we now know that early society was in no way characterized by
class struggle. It is thus an exception.

Lawrence Krader points out that with that, Engels turned 'a
political act into a learned debate'. It is an interesting observation.
The thesis of ubiquitous class struggle is often interpreted as a
general thesis about history. Engels did so. Krader hints that it was
not so with Marx.[97]

But is it a reasonable interpretation? Is it not a question of historical generalization also for Marx? It is possible. As we know,
he was fond of talking about general laws even when there was
reasonably no such thing. But what consequences would there be
from assuming that every historical course of events is permeated
by class struggle?

First, such a law would be contrary to Marx's (as well as
Engels's) most important meta-historical thesis, namely that
the general guidelines for historical study sketched out in *The
German Ideology* and elsewhere cannot be turned into a timetable according to which history can be arranged. The real picture
of a historical course of events appears only in and through a
detailed study.

Marx devoted attention of this kind only to the capitalist
phase. But we can see that *Capital* does not deal only with class
struggle, either, even if the relationship between capitalists and
workers constitutes the dynamic centre of the account. The conflict between them emerges most clearly in the long chapter on the
working day. But society also consists of classes other than both
the main actors. Take a striking example: scholars of various types
are directly or indirectly influenced by the antagonism between
capital and labour, but the results they arrive at in their research are
not permeated by class struggle. Such an account would conflict
with another of Marx's central convictions, namely that science
understands reality better and better through its development.

In general, it can be questioned whether the thesis that everything is class struggle is consistent with Marx's dialectical method. When it has actually been made absolute, such as in the dogmatic Marxism of Lenin and even more of Stalin, it has been heedlessly combined with the statement that knowledge reflects reality. These are two statements that can only square with each other through a strangely clever solution, according to which the truth (such as it is) emerges for the person who takes the right class standpoint – that is, the proletariat's – which, upon closer inspection, simply becomes that of the communist party elite. The practical consequence is that scientific theories can be treated arbitrarily. For a long time, only the genetic theories of Trofim Lysenko were permitted in the Soviet Union; for a somewhat shorter period, Einstein's theory of relativity was branded as bourgeois and therefore to be condemned.[98]

This was absolutely not Marx's standpoint (nor Engels's, actually). Marx spoke on his own authority only on such things as he regarded as his own field. He did not break the self-evident rules of scientific specialization. When he studied chemistry handbooks, it was to learn something new. He could complain about Darwin's dependency on Malthus, but that was due to the fact that the theories of Malthus directly contradicted his own in the field of the social sciences.

We will stop next at the question of what kind of area of scientific competence Marx claimed, and how these claims fit into the ideas about scientific authority in the time he lived. Finally, we will throw light upon the question of the relationship between statements and norms in Marx. With that we will find a natural transition to the next chapter, which deals with Marx the politician.

Every researcher must have a rather fixed area of competence. Within it, they can speak from their own authority and count on arousing confidence both among their colleagues and among a more or less interested general public. But the area of competence need not be the same as the area of activity. In a hierarchical scientific culture, those at the top have the competence to make statements about things they themselves are not working on. So it was, for example, in the world European universities in the seventeenth century. Theologians could censure well-founded physical theories with the argument that they went against the word of God.

In a specialized scientific culture, the fields of work and of competence tend to coincide. I conduct research on problems in a field in which I have my most solid and deepest knowledge, where I can quickly differentiate between good research and bad. My articles are published in the speciality's own journals, my colleagues reproduce my results, and I count on government authorities and the general public regarding me as an authority within my field.

That is how the placid ideal image of a specialized scientific culture looks. But reality is ordinarily more chaotic and filled with conflict. There are struggles for fields of competence, particularly if there is a lot of research money, or strong and conflicting political and ideological interests there. Who can speak about the continent of Humanity with the greatest authority? Who is worth listening to regarding schools, physical health, or God?

The antagonisms are great, even in the rigidly specialized scientific culture of the early twenty-first century. The scientific world in which Marx moved was not at all as mapped out in detail as today's, but nevertheless it was considerably more specialized than that of the seventeenth century. But conflicts inevitably occurred. In Marx's time, there were still large new areas of knowledge where no specialists had yet established themselves, but where enthusiastic amateurs competed with each other. Social anthropology was one such field.

To come to grips with the problems of specialization we must also grapple with another concept: *professionalization*.[99] They are both often mixed up, but they are not identical. Having a profession entails practising an occupation for which you have a specific education and a diploma accepted by colleagues and government authorities. One does not need to be a specialist for this, nor does a specialist need to have their speciality as their profession. In nineteenth-century Great Britain, many of the greatest scientists were amateurs, professionally speaking. Charles Darwin is the grandest example. He had a flimsy, incomplete university education behind him; he conducted his innovative scientific work against the background of a private fortune. But he did become a specialist.

In the German sciences, speciality and profession coincided far more over the course of the nineteenth century. After the reforms of Wilhelm von Humboldt, the universities had what was up to then a unique position with their demands that professors should not only instruct, but also research. All research at the universities had the rank of science (*Wissenschaft*); the unanimity on this was nearly total. Historians and theologians were quite simply regarded as specialists, and in fact developed specialized research like nowhere else up to that point. But that also meant that those outside the universities, with their scientific professions, found it more difficult to get recognition or attention in general. Marx suffered from that kind of isolation.

In Great Britain, science was nowhere near as boxed in, institutionally speaking. People moved about more freely, in particular in fields that had not yet become accepted specialities. Once again, Darwin is a good example. When he finally ventured to write a book about humanity's biological origins, *The Descent of Man*, he was just as fastidiously self-critical as he usually was, as long as he kept to the domains of biology. But it was different when he got into cultural questions! How, for example, could the origins of religion be explained? Darwin did not go deeply into the subject; he was satisfied with a little anecdote. He is sitting in his garden with his dog. A parasol starts spinning around in the wind. His dog growls. Darwin says that the dog must have believed that there was an invisible power present and concludes: this is how religion must also have arisen among people.

Darwin's dog travelled further in the literature. Herbert Spencer reproduced the anecdote as if it had some form of authority. But scientifically, it did not. On the other hand, it was an example of how a person who is a specialist in a scientific field can roam about with unconstrained amateurishness in another field where they think they will not find any real authorities. If he had been in Germany, he would either have been more careful, or – like his magniloquent follower there, Ernst Haeckel – risen to the role of philosopher with a view over all fields of knowledge. But it is impossible to imagine that the careful Darwin, like Haeckel, would set about the task of solving all the world's problems.[100]

Scientific specialization is thus not a process that takes place uniformly across all areas of knowledge. Nor does it look the same in all countries and environments. Certain specialities can in addition have higher status than others, especially for those in political power but also for a broader public; high-status specialists then gladly invade the domains of the low-status specialists. But even in scientific cultures with limited specialization, questions of the relationships between the various fields of knowledge arise. There may be similarities and methods and theories, tendencies arise that can be followed over large fields of knowledge, and philosophical consequences occur that can perplex, fascinate, and entice people to audacious syntheses.[101]

Many of the great classical philosophers – Thomas Hobbes and Gottfried Wilhelm von Leibniz, for example – tried to assemble all knowledge into one system; during the heyday of German idealism, thinkers tried to add to each other by building comprehensive views of knowledge and the world. When their active period came to an end, a new sort of system-builder turned up – more respectful of the fields of the accepted specialists, but audacious in their parallels between various sciences. Their projects, as grandiose as they were frail, resulted in an overall view of existence and the future, perhaps an ethics, or a replacement for a crumbling religion. French philosopher Auguste Comte, the creator of words such as 'sociology', 'positivism', and 'altruism', was the pioneer for this new type of synthesis; English philosopher Herbert Spencer followed in his footsteps. They were both extremely successful and tempted others to try the same risky path. Ernst Haeckel, whom we have already mentioned, was only one of them. Systems 'have been springing up by the dozen, overnight', Engels wrote in ill humour – and he himself tried in *Anti-Dühring* and *The Dialectics of Nature* to build something that resembled a system.[102]

Marx expressed no clear opinion in the face of this activity. He could test the idea of a similarity between chemistry and history, but no more came of it. His focus lay on the task of creating a sustainable critical theory of capital. To be sure, he also wanted to contribute to changing the world with his work. But he also saw himself as a scientist, who at the end of the foreword to his book could defiantly write: 'Segui il tuo corso, e lascia dir le genti' (Follow your path, and let people talk). He ascribed the quote to Dante, but there is an important difference between what Dante once wrote and what Marx wrote. In Dante's *Divine Comedy*, Virgil says to Dante: 'Follow *my* path...'. But Marx says to himself: 'Follow *your* path...'. People may speak ill of his undertaking, but it did not bother him.[103] He wanted recognition for his effort, and he also wanted to convince economists and historians. We already know that his successes were extremely limited, despite Engels's heroic efforts.

In light of what I have just described, it is easy – entirely apart from the difficulty that reading *Capital* can offer the unprepared – to understand the problem. Marx wrote his work in German, and in Germany the approved sciences were more and more firmly linked to the universities. Marx was an outsider. Political economy had already been established as an academic subject in Germany, although for a long time in combination with other social scientific specialities. The leading representatives were historically oriented, followers of a historicism in Germany that had long set the tone, according to which the real picture of a phenomenon only emerged if it was observed in its development. The German economists were also heavily involved socially and politically, and saw providing for the poor and the unfortunate as the task of the state. That is why they were often called 'lecture-hall socialists', even if politically they were far from the kind of socialism that Marx found himself close to.

The older lecture-hall socialists were already well established as economists when the first edition of *Capital* was published. Foremost was Wilhelm Roscher, whose book *Die Grundlagen der Nationalökonomie* (Principles of Political Economy) was published in 1854 and soon gained a great reputation in his homeland.[104] Marx, with his completely divergent theoretical construction, found it difficult to gain recognition or even attention against such competition.

Among Marx's fellow thinkers, and among politically active people in general, *Capital* – as we have seen – attracted scarce attention in Germany. A small minority – Ludwig Kugelmann, Wilhelm Liebknecht, and a few others – really tried hard to force their way through it, but they all had their own academic back-grounds. For workers in general, *Capital* was a closed book. The latter was surely not a surprise to Marx.

In Great Britain, economics was not yet a profession. The leading economists represented a broad variation of occupations, from bankers to clergymen. So it continued up until the end of the nineteenth century. It was actually only with Alfred Marshall and his generation that British economics was given a natural place in the universities. Marshall even gave the subject a new name: 'political economy' became 'economics', and his *Principles of Economics* from 1890 was long the standard work in the Anglo-Saxon world.[105]

The first people to take in the ideas from *Capital* in Great Britain were not economists, but a handful of men, all of whom had a more or less distinguished social position. We have already men-tioned Ray Lankester, an academic of the highest rank. Another somewhat more questionable character who also engaged Marx's thinking was Henry Hyndman, son of a rich businessman and a graduate of Cambridge. He got his hands on *Capital*, and under its influence wrote *England for All*, published in 1881, which became a great public success. He failed however to mention where he got his ideas from – something that roused both Marx's and Engels's fury. But Hyndman founded his own socialist party, which Eleanor Marx was a member of for a time. The party's successes were limited, especially as a consequence of Hyndman's dictatorial leadership style.[106]

Among those who quickly left the party one above all deserves to be named – the most significant follower of Marx in the nine-teenth century: William Morris. William Morris had the same kind of background as Hyndman: his father was a wealthy busi-nessman, and William studied at Oxford. Early on in his contact with the cultural elite of the time, he developed his ideal of arts and crafts that would counteract the mass production and aes-thetic superficiality of industrialism. He only became a socialist in his fifties and even read *Capital* – a book, however, that according to his own statements cost him a lot of effort and a great deal of confusion. But despite the intellectual obstacles, he became a great admirer of Marx.[107]

It can safely be said that early on Marx gained a certain reputation within British culture, while his influence on academic economics long remained minimal. In France, Marx's early breakthrough was political rather than scientific or cultural. Both his sons-in-law, Charles Longuet and Paul Lafargue, were influential in the incipient French workers' movement. Neither of them had a bent for economic theory, which is why they were not ambassadors for *Capital* either.

It was in France that the words 'Marxist' and 'Marxism' were first used. Lafargue was one of those who claimed the designation, but Jules Guesde was the central figure among the self-identified Marxists in the newly founded *Parti Ouvrier* (Workers' Party). Marx was not impressed by the party's programme, something he made clear to Guesde and Lafargue in a letter addressed to both. He also took up his displeasure in a conversation with Engels. It was then he uttered the words that later became familiar: 'Ce qu'il y a de certain c'est que moi, je ne suis pas marxiste' – (What is certain is that *I* am not a Marxist).[108]

The fundamental ideas in *Capital* played no decisive role for *Parti Ouvrier*. It employed more a rather vulgar materialism, something that even the party's self-characterization as 'the party of the stomach' testifies to.[109]

Capital gained even less of a foothold in the scholarly world in France. French universities did not have a position that could be compared with German universities. Formally, they were dissolved during large parts of the nineteenth century; it was only the faculties, directly subordinate to the Ministry of Education, that were re-established by Napoleon after the revolution. Economic studies scarcely blossomed there, or at *les grandes écoles* such as the École normale supérieure or the École polytechnique. It is telling that the dominant French economist of the late nineteenth century, Léon Walras (the greatest economist of all time according to Joseph Schumpeter, the historiographer of economics above all else),[110] received his professorship in Lausanne in Switzerland. Walras became one of the pioneers of economic marginalism, maintaining that the price of commodities was determined by supply and demand. He thus was not among the converts of Marx.

Marx's cultural influence in France – so great during the twentieth century – was also practically insignificant during the nineteenth, despite the beautiful translation of *Capital* that he himself to a great extent was responsible for.

So far, we have theory, in Marx and in the world around him. But how did theory relate to practice? He had written a heavy but epoch-making work in which he interpreted contemporary capitalist development against a broad historical background. How was this work connected with the ambition to also change the world? To get at this question, a certain philosophical exercise is required.

Capital is a theoretical work. It is thoroughly dominated by statements about reality and its various intricate connections. In just a few sentences, it is established that the capitalist system must tend towards its dissolution. These are not freely evasive theses about a desirable future, but conclusions drawn from a theory that is artfully developed. Formally, apart from the foreword and the postscript, *Capital* contains no strictures of the 'Do this or that!' type – that is, no analogue to the appeal of the *Manifesto*: 'Workers of all countries, unite!'

Nor is there thus any explicit morality. According to Marx, morals are always conditioned by existing social relations, and therefore changeable. The prevailing morals – those that are preached in the schools, the church, and the dominant media – justify the existing relations of power in society. People are raised to see the current order as natural.

The question of whether or not there is an implicit morality in *Capital* – just as in Marx's other works – is an old controversy. When Marx described the situation of the workers, his indignation shone through. It can even be asked whether a certain degree of compassion crept into the description of the compulsion the capitalist experiences.

One person who tries to tackle this question with great energy is the American philosopher Allen W. Wood. In his 2004 book, simply called *Karl Marx*, he makes an important distinction between what he calls *moral* and *non-moral goods*. The former entails that a person should perform certain actions because it is their duty, the latter because these actions satisfy our needs. Marx's thoroughgoing criticism of the moralism of which he accuses Proudhon and many others applies to *moral goods*. Capitalism, according to Marx, can be condemned because it withholds a number of *non-moral goods* from people. It forces them to starve, it enslaves them, and it alienates them.[III]

Woods's distinction is important, but he has no grip on Marx's understanding of alienation from the *Theses on Feuerbach* and *The German Ideology* onwards. As we have already seen, it is no longer a question of alienation from a supra-historical human essence but from the objective possibilities that people have during a certain historical epoch that are denied them through class society. This means that Marx also counts among the non-moral goods a life, satisfactory in all aspects, in which people can realize their potential. That is how we are able to speak about duty or obligation, though in a very fixed sense. It is the duty of people to work for a society in which everyone can realise the opportunities that the level of scientific, technological, and economic development opens for them.

One important theme for Marx is humanity's historical changeability. At the same time, he is acutely aware that there is something that is supra-historically human. After his encounter with Darwin's theory, this insight became particularly salient, and it is discernible in the excerpts from the literature on social anthropology. The very remote social relations up for discussion there still have something important to say to the Europeans of the late nineteenth century.

So far, the picture is clear. But there is still one question that has not been answered. How do the ideas that question the social order the prevailing ideology naturalizes arise? Must it not be a question of a counter-ideology, in which (to use a metaphor from *The German Ideology*) the inverted picture in the *camera obscura* of ideology is turned right side up again? At one point, the bourgeois class debunked the seemingly harmonic ideology of feudalism regarding the natural and timeless mutual relations of the estates. Now the working class was busy doing something similar regarding bourgeois ideology with its theses on liberty, equality, and fraternity. Marx saw himself as having the role that the Enlightenment philosophers of the seventeenth and eighteenth centuries had in the previous upheaval. But the role is only that of an enlightener; the liberation of the working classes is their own work. Marx provides the picture of capitalism and its mechanisms turned right side up. This revelation will provide the workers with tools in their struggle for liberation.

Marx seems to have had no interest in the question of how the prevailing ideology gains its powerful opponent. The counter-ideology must accommodate the crucial components of the prevailing ideology, thereby providing an image of reality, an understanding of a good society, and norms for a successful struggle against the ruling class.

Marx did not make his contemporary counter-ideology explicit. But he was entirely clear that a new order cannot be carried through only with the help of *Capital*. Political activity is also necessary. During the years around 1848, Marx had been intensely politically active. In the 1850s, his activity slackened off considerably. But in the 1860s, just when *Capital* was taking form, a new period of intense activity began. This is what we will now examine. Before that, a brief recapitulation.

Conclusion

Marx and Engels were very different from each other. They were brought together through historical circumstance, and came to be deeply dependent on each other financially, intellectually, and emotionally.

Engels worked nearly twenty years in the firm that his father had helped start. Marx was thus given the opportunity to devote most of his time to *Capital*. His ambitions were so enormous that only certain parts of the project could be completed. What he presented to the world was impressive enough. But its impact was limited because he was so poorly situated in a scientific world. His German was an obstacle in England, and in Germany he was handicapped by the fact that he was not active at a university. *Capital* appeared in French in his own translation, but it would be a long time before the work roused any greater interest. The self-appointed French Marxists did not meet with his approval.

For his part, Engels started working on his own projects in which he would bring together his view of society with a conception of the world based in the natural sciences. The project took another direction when he was compelled to defend *Capital* against Eugen Dühring. A few lines about dialectical laws in *Anti-Dühring*, the origins of which are found in *Capital*, had fateful consequences. Engels laboured over diverse laws of this type for a few years, but then abandoned the whole idea. In orthodox Marxism, on the other hand, the laws were given a strong position in the catechism-like accounts that people within the Soviet Bloc were compelled to read during their education.

Both Engels and Marx had a great interest in what was happening within a number of natural sciences. The energy principle and organic chemistry became important to them, as did biology through Darwin. Darwin's theory of natural selection would form the foundation in natural history for their own social theory, Marx declared.

But Marx and Engels approached the natural sciences in different ways. Engels chiefly wanted material for the construction of his conception of the world. Marx composed detailed excerpts from books that in one way or another would be of significance for his own life's work, constantly in progress. Most likely it was for that purpose that he became interested in the new social anthropologists. From Marx's notes, Engels later wrote a book in his own spirit.

Today, it is easy to see Marx (and Engels, to a lesser extent) as a pure theoretician. This was not at all the case. Politics was and remained important – it was necessary in order to change the world. But the transition from theory to practice was not self-evident. When, in the mid-1860s, Marx once again threw himself with all his might into political life, he could not rely on the *Manifesto* from 1848 to guide him. The world had changed; the political landscape had become different. But his own interpretation of the reality that politics was to influence was also different in many parts. It is easy to ignore this, especially as he allowed new editions and translations of the *Manifesto* to be spread across the world without the text itself being changed. Nevertheless, it was largely with a new agenda that he got into politics.

13

Marx the Politician

Karl Marx kept his roles as social researcher and politician strictly separate. Rarely is this so clear as in a letter he wrote to the English professor of history Edward Spencer Beesly in 1871. Beesly was an acquaintance of his, and additionally a man who published articles on subjects close to Marx's heart. But he was also a positivist in the style of the times – that is, a follower of the doctrines of French philosopher Auguste Comte. In his letter, Marx wrote that he himself 'as a party man' had a thoroughly hostile attitude towards 'Comtism' and that 'as a scholar' (*als Mann der Wissenschaft*) he had a very low opinion of it. Beesly, however, constituted an exception. He depicted the historical turning points in the history of England and France not as a sectarian, but as a 'historian in the best sense'.[1] The position of the opposites is clear: party man or scientist, sectarian or historian. Marx differentiated between research and politics.

That alone is reason enough to examine his more pronounced political work during the 1860s, 70s, and 80s in a chapter by itself. Politics for Marx was not only an emanation or an application of the social theory he was developing in *Capital*. It was, to be sure, deeply influenced by the development of the forces of production and the struggle between capital and labour. But politics is also an arena where people's desires and fears, their ambitions and dreams, their friendship and hate find direct expression. Politics is additionally marked by institutions and factions, traditions and fads.

Marx would play an important political role during several periods in his life. For a long time, it was primarily as a journalist, in his early youth with the *Rheinische Zeitung* and then during the revolutionary years of 1848–49 as the editor-in-chief for *Neue Rheinische Zeitung*. That kind of activity decreased later. It is true that in his articles for the *New York Daily Tribune* he took up political subjects of the greatest immediate interest, but his readers were on the other side of the ocean and entirely too distant for him to directly wish to influence them. The economic crisis of 1856–57 gave him great hopes of a more thorough revolution than the one that broke out in 1848. But nothing happened; by all appearances, this very non-event played an important role in Marx's life. The euphoria from the time of the *Grundrisse* was gone. The clearly more limited work with *Capital* now began. But it had barely managed to get its outlines before Marx broke off to write his thick pamphlet *Herr Vogt*, which was published in December 1860. In a way, this book signifies a low point in his political life. He stood outside all political groups, and was fighting for his own honour.

It is all the more surprising, then, that in 1864, at first hesitatingly and half unwillingly and then with mounting enthusiasm, he got into the work of forming the first International Workingmen's Association. He really did not have the time; the work on *Capital* was in a hectic phase, and Engels up in Manchester was sceptical towards the association. But Marx would soon be the most important inspiration for what posterity would call the First International (which here will simply be called the International). When Engels moved to London in 1870, he too joined the leadership. Marx would get to display characteristics he is not usually associated with, namely the ability to bring conflicting wills into a common project. But it was not the first time he was a forger of compromises; he had been so back when he was editor-in-chief of *Neue Rheinische Zeitung*. In the International, his patience gave out only when the pugnacious Mikhail Bakunin began challenging him on the ideological plane.

The feud between Marx and Bakunin would gradually split the organization. But before that, something happened that Marx did not expect. After the defeat of France by Bismarck's Prussia, an uprising broke out in Paris and the Paris Commune was declared. The intent was to continue along the radical line that the original

Paris Commune had followed, above all between 1792 and 1795. The new Commune held out for two months, and made Marx famous as the brains behind it. He was now beloved and hated across all of Europe. But he did not have any direct relation to the Commune. On the contrary, the Commune posed an important challenge to his political thinking.

Political developments in Germany played a particular role in his life. Ferdinand Lassalle was the first person there to take the initiative for a political party that could be called socialist, but the relationship between Lassalle and Marx was full of contradictions, to say the least. Gradually, another competing party with leaders who stood closer to Marx was formed. In the International, Marx nevertheless tried to keep good relations with both social democratic parties which in 1875, about a year after the dissolution of the International, came together as the single Socialist Workers' Party of Germany (SAPD) at a conference held in the city of Gotha. Marx severely criticized the new party's platform; this criticism became one of his most influential political documents.

In his later years, Marx would become fascinated by political developments in Russia. The 'Russian road' that Teodor Shanin talks about in his 1983 book *Late Marx and the Russian Road*, became a fateful one.[2] It influenced the interpretation of what happened in Russia in 1917.

There are a number of more fundamental questions regarding Marx's efforts as a politician that ultimately must be asked. How did Marx mean his political proclamations to be taken? Did he issue prognoses – that is, did he make predictions about what would happen? Or did they concern rather a normative programme, in which he wrote about what seemed to him to be both a possible and a desirable development?

These are questions we have already touched upon in talking about the *Manifesto*, and now they are important regarding his contribution to the work of the International as well as his commentary on the Paris Commune.

Another complex of questions concerns the political ideals he developed at that time. He often spoke warmly about democracy, above all in the form of a universal right to vote. After an absence of many years, the phrase 'dictatorship of the proletariat' turns up again in his vocabulary in connection with the Paris Commune of 1871. Do democracy and dictatorship not exclude each other? Was Marx developing a more reformist strategy before 1871? Or did he remain a revolutionary straight through?

Herr Vogt

In early February 1860, Marx wrote to Engels that he was going to aim a devastating blow at Carl Vogt. '*The defensive* does not suit our purpose.'³ Engels had no objections in his response, and thus did not advise his friend to stick to his work with *Capital*. On the other hand, his Russian friend Nikolai Ivanovich Sasonov did. Marx reproduced a letter that Sasonov had written to him, advising him instead to continue with the 'admirable work as soon as possible'.⁴ But Marx did not want to hear it. He was firmly resolved to neutralize Vogt and exonerate himself from the accusations directed towards him.

In his time, Carl Vogt was a famous and widely read scientist. But he was also a politician, and as such an opponent of Marx. These were no small matters Vogt had charged Marx with. He maintained that everyone who came into close contact with Herr Doktor Marx sooner or later fell into the clutches of the police. In short, Marx was a police agent.

To posterity, the accusation may seem bizarre. We know that Prussian police spies were on Marx's heels back during his time in Paris. They visited him regularly in London, writing reports about his conditions at home. But they did not know that on the Continent. Vogt was trying to make his accusations plausible above all through the 'Communist trial' in Cologne – the one that Marx had written so vividly about, though anonymously. Was not everyone who got into trouble there closely associated with Marx? And had Marx himself not gone free?

Marx thought about bringing a lawsuit against Vogt, or more precisely against the newspaper the accusations had been reproduced in, the *National-Zeitung* in Berlin. He wrote his petitions according to the rules of the art, but the Prussian court refused to take up his case. It was only then that he wrote his far-too-thick book at breakneck speed.

It is a massive text with many disparate elements. There is a long letter here from the brush maker, polymath, and socialist newspaper editor Johann Philipp Becker who said he knew Vogt personally, but not Marx. Becker unhesitatingly took sides with Marx, expressing his dismay over 'the frivolous and unscrupulous manner in which Vogt has entered the lists on this occasion'.[5]

Marx also provides a small history of the *Bund der Kommunisten*, emphasizing that he had kept out of all political associations since the Bund had dissolved. His only efforts had consisted of holding free lectures in the German Workers' Association in London. On the twentieth anniversary of the Association, the eighty members present had unanimously decided to reject Vogt's slander.[6]

Marx wanted to get his book – or 'pamphlet', as he called it in his correspondence with Engels – out quickly and decided to publish it in London with Albert Petsch, a German publisher in exile. Engels warned in the most resolute terms against hiring an exile publisher; a book like that would go nowhere. But Marx was firm, and *Herr Vogt* joined the ranks of his writings that remained largely unread both in his time and in posterity. As regards *Herr Vogt* in particular, one can scarcely feel sorry about the obscurity. The indignation it expresses is understandable. But nearly 300 pages of rather spontaneous text? Hardly so.[7]

Marx quickly moved on to more productive undertakings. He left *Herr Vogt* behind him. He would reap one triumph from it, however, a decade later. In his book, he had levelled a counter-accusation, claiming that Vogt was a paid agent for Napoleon III. When the emperor fell and his archive was opened, it turned out that a certain 'Vogt' was found on the list of imperial payments. It was almost impossible that the name could refer to anyone other than Carl Vogt.[8]

The International

In the substantial literature on Marx, there are numerous monographs on his political thought and political activity. A well-known example is Israeli political scientist Shlomo Avineri's 1968 work *The Social and Political Thought of Karl Marx*, in which the author asserts that there is a tension in Marx's writings between his conviction about an immediately impending revolution and the better-grounded idea that history is a longer process in which, for example, fully developed free trade is a precondition for the transition to a socialist society.[9]

Doubtless the most well-balanced modern monograph on Marx the politician is Wolfgang Schieder's 1991 work *Karl Marx als Politiker*. In it, Schieder points out that in his time, Marx was chiefly known for his political efforts. Posterity may read him for the sake of *Capital*, the *Grundrisse*, or the youthful *Manuscripts*. That same posterity also tends to see what he did in 1848–49 or in the International as the outflow of his social theories. In the Soviet tradition this was officially so, but the determined opponents of everything he did and stood for also agreed.

In his own time, however, Marx was almost exclusively known as a politician. It is true that his efforts were limited to two periods; Schieder talks about the years 1847–52 and 1864–72. He was nevertheless politically more active than any other political thinker in the nineteenth century.[10]

His most important efforts concerned the International Workingmen's Association. His first reaction to the invitations he received to the constituent assembly was hesitant. In *Herr Vogt*, he had stressed that he had kept himself out of politics for several years. When a Frenchman by the name of Victor Le Lubez encouraged him to participate, he did not react to it. It was only when the English union leader William Randal Cremer contacted him that he yielded. He described the course of events itself in a letter to Engels. Cremer wanted to have a few Germans there. Marx proposed his friend, the tailor Johann Georg Eccarius, but also slipped into the constituent meeting himself 'in a non-speaking capacity'. He knew that this time, significant people were involved in the new project. That is why he could break his 'usual standing rule to decline such invitations'.[11]

Even if Marx had been politically inactive for several years, the idea of a grander project was not unfamiliar at the time. A letter to his old friend, the poet Ferdinand Freiligrath, from 1860 testifies to this. The Communist League was precisely nothing, one association among a hundred others, he said. The aim had to be set on a 'party in the broad historical sense'.[12]

Party formations in the modern European sense did not yet exist at the time (their start in fact took place with various social democratic and socialist parties, but Marx was not directly involved in their creation). What peradventure were called parties had up to then been more or less temporary fighting or collaborative organizations, or quite simply voting communities in decision-making conventions. Often, people spoke about associations rather than parties.

But Marx obviously had something grander in mind in his letter to Freiligrath. The truly historical party is rooted in the class; in comparison with that, the Communist League was only an episode. According to Marx, it is the social development of the class that is the fundamental precondition for it to be able to manifest itself as a political party in a deeper sense. The working class must thus have achieved both sufficient proportions and internal stability before it can support a powerful political party.

This was a magnificent concept of the party. Marx also had to put up with the fact that people often spoke about '*Die Partei Marx*' – the Marx party. The concept was born during the Cologne trials back in 1852, when Marx's closest followers were on trial. It then hung on more as a designation for those who completely embraced his theories than the name of a concrete political party. He often acted in a way that could provide reason for such a term; he distinguished sharply between those who were faithful to him or not.[13]

As we have seen, Marx was careful in his own political activity to point out that the liberation of the working class must be its own work. But with 'the Marx party', the idea that Marx and his followers would direct the struggle for liberation was a natural one. With its careful division of followers and dissenters, he made it easier for such an understanding.

From the beginning, the International was a British and French idea. Napoleon III had given permission for a delegation of French working-class leaders to travel to London to meet a number of union leaders. The French and the British wanted to find a form for lasting and profound collaboration between worker organizations of various types. Representatives from several other countries, most of them refugees in London like Marx, were also important.[14]

The International was thus to be a collaborative body. A Central Committee was formed, consisting of twenty English, ten German, nine French, six Italian, two Polish, and two Swiss workers. Marx was one of the members, and he was also elected to a subcommittee that would propose a manifesto and regulations. The self-evident centre of the work was London, but the annual congresses would be held in other locations.

From the very beginning, Marx was tolerant in his assessment of the men he met in his work with the International. He described the leader of the French delegation, Henri-Louis Tolain, in his letter to Engels as a 'thoroughly nice fellow' (*sehr netter Karl*), and the other French members were also characterized as 'nice'.[15] It is then revealed that Tolain was a follower of Proudhon, whom Marx usually commented so negatively on; even the others stood quite far from Marx in their opinions. Incidentally, Marx was rather unknown – in some cases, forgotten – in France at that time. The British knew more about him but also had other aims than he did; a few were old Chartists, others followers of Owen's ideas regarding an ideal society.

Marx missed several of the programme committee meetings. But when he got to see a proposal he found objectionable, he acted resolutely and invited the key people home for a visit. After a sound mangling that lasted till one o'clock in the morning, they reached an agreement on the rules for the International. After that, Marx wrote an address 'to the working classes' (as they were still called) on his own initiative, trimming down the number of rules. His proposals were accepted, with some interesting and significant amendments. Along with the rules he suggested, Marx's proposals – which came to be called the Inaugural Address – comprise some of the most important political documents in his hand. There is thus good reason to dwell upon them.

The Address

The text Marx presented to his newfound friends is a rhetorical masterwork of barely ten pages. First, the author depicted the contradictory development between 1848 and 1864 – that is, between the years of revolution that were also the moments of the *Manifesto*. What a fantastic development of industry and commerce there had been! The words vibrate with the author's own enthusiasm in the face of the wonders of technology, the enormous feats of machinery, and the ability of world commerce to make neighbours of distant continents.[16]

And all at the same time! At the hub of this development, in Great Britain, countless workers were suffering from destitution. Objective reports testified to poverty, malnutrition, and misery. In 1864, during 'the millennium of free trade', it turned out that craftsmen in London were eating worse than the poorest agricultural workers. For someone preaching 'a fool's paradise' not purely out of self-interest, it was clear that 'no improvement of machinery, no appliance of science to production, no contrivances of communication, no new colonies, no emigration, no opening of markets, no free trade, nor all these things put together, will do away with the miseries of the industrial masses'. Quite the contrary – the development of the productive forces of labour would lead to deepening social rifts.

So far, the picture is unambiguous, and it is the same picture as the one in the *Manifesto*. The overabundance of capitalism was producing the poverty of the workers. Ricardo's iron law of wages applied. But the dialectical turn of the article comes right at this point. A ray of light breaks in: positive things happened between 1848 and 1864! The first was the implementation of the ten-hour workday. The demand met with bitter opposition from the middle class. Marx uses that precise term – 'middle class' – that is, not 'bourgeoisie' as he did in 1848, and not 'capitalist' as he often otherwise did during the 1860s and 1870s. This is certainly not by accident. The term can also include important parts of the petty bourgeoisie, of the smaller tradesman type. The spokesmen for this middle class – Andres Ure, Nassau W. Senior, and others – proclaimed that the ten-hour workday would sound the death-knell of British industry. But now the legislation was in force, and the wheels were spinning faster than ever.

The other positive change that Marx placed even greater importance on was the cooperative movement, which constituted a grand experiment whose value could not be overestimated. If the workers themselves owned and ran their factories, not only slave labour but also wage labour would disappear and be replaced by 'associated labour' where each and every one toiled 'with a willing hand, a ready mind, and a joyous heart'.[17]

But as long as the cooperative movement is reduced to its own forces, it cannot keep step with the formation of private monopolies. Intelligent supervisors had shown this back in the 1850s. To succeed, the movement had to develop on a national scale. But both landowners and capitalists were trying to put obstacles in the path of such a development.

It was therefore the great duty of the working class to conquer political power. The workers had natural strength in their numbers, but the strength only becomes effective if the many individuals collaborate and at the same time are guided by knowledge. Previous experience showed how badly it could go if the 'bond of brotherhood' uniting workers from different countries was held in contempt. Marx concluded with the same slogan as the *Manifesto*: 'Proletarians of all countries, unite!'

There are several things to dwell upon in this text. The importance attached to the union struggle is greater here than in anything else he had written up to that point. The struggle over the length of the working day returns in *Capital*, the first volume of which was first published in 1867. But in the Inaugural Address, its significance is programmatically emphasized. At the same time, he emphasized that it was thanks to the legislation that the shortened working day could be pushed through. This line of thinking returns in regards to the cooperative movement. Only on a national scale would it be able to outdistance privately owned businesses. For that, the workers' collective political activity was required.

One of the keywords of the text is 'association'. The word is a central concept in nineteenth-century political thinking. The opposite was the compulsory communities that individuals were incorporated into, regardless of their wishes. The traditional family was one such; marriage was in principle indissoluble, and children were bound to the parents until the age of adulthood. The idea of the association was also incompatible with the constraint of the guilds, with village communities, and with forced affiliation to the church. Serfdom and slavery constituted the absolute opposites. In the association, both liberals and socialists found a key to a new and better society. The early socialists went further. People should have the right to construct their own societies from the bottom up. Adventurous groups left the Europe of compulsion to build a *phalanstère* in the style of Fourier, or an Icaria as Cabet outlined it, somewhere in America. It should be free to each person to join the collective, or to leave it.

The International itself was an association: the International Workingmen's Association. Free adherence was a fundamental principle. If someone did not feel at home in the organization, they only had to leave it. The principles of military cadres were foreign to it.

And now, Marx had written in the founding document itself that the labour of the future would be organized in accordance with the principle of association. Gone are the individual owners – the capitalists – who purchase labour time from the worker, whose only choice is starvation or toil for someone else's profit. In the cooperative, it is – as the word implies – cooperation that is the essential thing: cooperation among equals.[18]

The text contains nothing more than a faint outline. What is written there can appeal to anarchists to a great degree. The only difference is that Marx says that the association of the workers – and thereby the victory of the producers' cooperative – must occur on a national scale, which is the same thing as saying that the state must be used as a means of force. The difference between Marx's solution and Bakunin's would soon have fateful consequences for the future of the International.

There is yet another element in the Inaugural Address that requires commentary. Marx wrote that the workers could only conquer political power in cooperation with each other, and if they are guided by knowledge. He thus in all likelihood has in mind a social theory that also provides guidelines for political action. This is the very thing he had in readiness, and it is what made him feel he was suited to write the Address. But what is important is that he did *not* say that the workers should be guided by *those who possess knowledge*. He was, as we have seen, very consistent on this point.

At the same time, there is a problem. Marx would be extremely active in the work of the International the whole time. He provided criticism and advice, and was, as always, prone to polemics. He strongly – sometimes ruthlessly – opposed strategies that clearly deviated from his own. The tone and the Inaugural Address, on the other hand, is mild and conciliatory. Here, Marx was not a man of conflict, but of cooperation.

An absence on one point can be noted in his text, just as in his later contributions to the meetings of the International. He used the traditional word 'brotherhood' for international solidarity among workers. This is the old term from the French Revolution – indirectly, in fact, from early Christianity.

The International would otherwise signify the breakthrough of the newer word 'solidarity'. Above all, it was Johann Philipp Becker who was the successful driving force here. Solidarity, he said was 'Brüderlichkeit der Tat' (the brotherhood of action) that should not be confused with the bourgeois 'Brüderlichkeit der Phrasen' (the brotherhood of phrases).[19] It is unlikely that Marx would have anything to object to with the word 'solidarity'. But it would not be part of his normal vocabulary.

Closely linked to the Inaugural Address are the provisional statutes for the International, of which Marx was in all essentials the author. The main ideas are the same as those in the former text. The workers themselves will lead their struggle for liberation. The goal is to abolish class rule. This requires the workers' economic liberation from a subjugation that constitutes the foundation of 'all social misery, mental degradation, and political dependence'. Liberation is neither a local nor a national task, but implies a social transformation that has to embrace all countries. This in turn requires 'concurrence, practical and theoretical, of the most advanced countries'.

Marx also said that the workers' movement had again begun to be a tangible force in the industrial countries of Europe, and arouse both hope and the memory of earlier mistakes. The International Workingmen's Association had assembled in London to fulfil these hopes and to frustrate these fears.

The document concludes with ten points that constitute the actual statutes. In the original proposal that Marx worked up, there were forty such points, but he let the red pencil pass over most of them. It was established that the first conference would be held in Belgium, and that it would be populated by delegates of the workers' associations that had joined in the meantime. Further, it was said that the Central Committee would have its seat in London, serving as a node between the organised workers of various countries, informing itself of their situations, and taking up issues of common interest – including conflicts and controversies. Finally, it was emphasized that although the International served 'fraternal cooperation', the various 'workingmen's societies' that had joined would retain their existing organization.[20]

Marx was satisfied with his efforts, as indicated by the letter to Engels that has already been discussed. His proposals were approved by the subcommittee he was a part of. He acknowledged that he was forced to make certain additions. Before the 10 points, he had to include two sentences on duties and rights, and another about 'truth, morality, and justice'. But, he added reassuringly, 'they are so placed that they can do no harm'.[21]

It is easy to find the sentences Marx referred to. It says that the International and all the associations linked to it fight for truth, justice, and morals both in their mutual relations and in encounters with all other people without regard to skin colour, faith, or nationality. Further on, it is established that rights and obligations hang together; duties are inevitably part of the rights and vice versa.

Marx's aversion to such declarations did not mean that he disliked the ideals expressed in and through them. He maintained, on the other hand, that they were ineffectual in class society, and that additionally they could lead people into a false understanding that freedom had already been won when lofty words of this type were proclaimed as the guiding star of the state without anything being done about the oppression of workers and thus the greatest injustice in society. It is only through a social revolution that justice, which is not only empty talk, can be won.

In his response, Engels expressed his joy over Marx again coming in contact with people of this type. But he was pessimistic regarding the future of the International. It would surely be split 'very soon' between 'those who are bourgeois in the thinking and those who are proletarian' as soon as their positions were clarified, he said. In the German original, he used the pair of opposites 'theoretisch bürgerlich' (theoretically bourgeois) and 'theoretisch proletarisch' (theoretically proletarian).[22]

Marx tried to reassure his friend. The matter was not so complicated when it had to do only with workers. The only 'literary man' (or intellectual, as it might be said today) in the society was the Englishman Peter Fox, a writer and agitator, and he had written an appreciative note about the Address to Marx.

It is obvious that the International had already become a matter very dear to Marx's heart. For the sake of the organization, he was willing to shelve old conflicts. Here he met pupils of Proudhon, whose doctrine he had fought so persistently for many years. Others believed, like Louis Auguste Blanqui, that a revolution could best be realized if a group of enlightened and single-minded revolutionaries carried out a *Putsch* – a coup – in the hopes that the masses would soon follow in revolutionary frenzy. Marx had dismissed Blanqui as 'bourgeois' – a strong word in his mouth (see above, p. 320), but he was now ready to cooperate with the bourgeois adepts. Even more remarkable was that he could get on with Italians who followed in the footsteps of Giuseppe Mazzini and thus the radical nationalistic movement *La Giovine Italia* (Young Italy). Marx could appreciate the Italians' rhetorical ability, but strove for an entirely different type of society than Mazzini. Their personal encounters in London had not turned out well. But now Marx rejoiced over Mazzini's followers signing the texts; his satisfied comment is a hotchpotch sentence typical of his correspondence with Engels: 'Mazzini is rather disgusted, dass seine Leute mitunterzeichnen, mais il faut faire bonne mine à mauvais jeu' (Mazzini is rather disgusted that his people are among the signatories, but one has to grin and bear it).[23]

Value, Price, and Profit

After his initial successes, Marx became a diligent writer in the name of the International. He wrote to Abraham Lincoln with an eloquent assurance of support from the workers in the war against the slave owners; when Lincoln was assassinated, he authored a letter of condolence to Lincoln's successor Andrew Johnson, also promising wholehearted support from the International.[24] He also wrote a number of other, smaller things. But his most important contribution during the first period of the International was a few lectures he held for the other members of the Central Committee.

The background was that another member of the Central Committee, John Weston – a carpenter and follower of legendary socialist Richard Owen – made claims in the *Bee-Hive*, a trade union weekly, that the unions' struggle for pay increases was futile, and was in fact detrimental to the workers' cause. Marx offered to take up the subject in a few lectures. They must have been immensely entertaining. On two occasions, Marx lectured from the manuscript that contains just over seventy pages in the Swedish translation.

But Marx was in his element; it is once more a brilliant text. It is also marked by a mild and conciliatory tone. Weston, the subject of the criticism, is called 'citizen Weston' in the lecture (it is the French revolutionary form of address, *citoyen*, that was still being used in the International) and is treated in an extremely considerate manner.

In many respects, the lecture can be seen as a summary of essential lines of thought in the first volume of *Capital*. The distinction between (concrete) labour and labour power is clearly laid out. Perhaps in consideration of his many British listeners, Marx names Thomas Hobbes as the pioneer of the concept of labour power in an entirely different way than in *Capital*, where the Englishman is only found in a footnote. Marx emphasized the statement that a person is worth the price 'as would be given for the *Use of his Power*'.

In *Capital*, Marx had problems laying out the relationship between exchange value and price. In the second edition, he solved it through a clear distinction between value and exchange value, fixing the latter as equal to price. In the lecture, he manages the same difficulty with the sentence: 'Price, taken by itself, is nothing but the *monetary expression of value*.'

As he did in *Capital*, he got onto the subject of original ('primitive') accumulation. It should actually be called original *expropriation*, he said here. What was actually happening was that the link between the workers and their tools was being severed. It was an idea he had been faithful to ever since the *Manuscripts* twenty years earlier. Profit is the unpaid labour that fattens both the landowner and the capitalist.

Marx views the collective struggle of the workers for pay increases and shorter work times in the light of this fundamental injustice. The workers were only trying to set limits to their exploitation by capital. The other side always has a counter-manoeuvre: shorter work time is met by increased work tempo.

The successful campaign for a ten-hour workday had two conditions. The first was the unceasing resistance of the workers, the other was the legislation (Marx did not even mention Parliament, the institution responsible for the legislation). Trade unions, he continued, work well as resistance against the autocratic ways of capital. But the goal is clear: '*Abolition of the wages system*'.

The presentation concluded without more detailed information on how this goal was to be achieved. Perhaps the reason was that Marx knew that his listeners were divided on the point. But perhaps he considered that he had already said enough on the subject in the Address. He had already achieved what he wanted to with the lecture, namely to outline his own theory and clarify his understanding of the task and significance of the trade unions.[25]

The lecture turns up a few times in the correspondence between Marx and Engels. In an initial letter, Marx wrote that he was struggling with differential calculus but also mentioned Weston's article in the *Bee-Hive*, which had received support from another Englishman on the Central Committee. People were of course waiting for him to respond, Marx said, but for him 'writing more of my book' was more important. That was what Engels wanted to hear. But barely a month later Marx had nonetheless held the first part of the lecture, and the second part was waiting only a few days later. In the first part, he had responded to Weston's 'foolishness' (*Blödsinn*), he said, whereas the second part was a theoretical exposition.

It is striking how differently Marx spoke about Weston in his lecture and in his letter. In the lecture, his tone towards the carpenter was friendly and considerate; in the letter to Engels, Weston's ideas are mentioned only with contempt. But the letters between Marx and Engels are often like that: two rascals nonchalantly throwing insults about.

The most important thing in the letter was something else: 'people' wanted to print his lecture. Marx was hesitant. On the one hand, he would come into contact with people such as John Stuart Mill and Edward Spencer Beesly. On the other hand, the presentation – which was relatively popular – anticipated many of the new things his book contained. Was it advisable to publicize the results of his research this way? He appealed to Engels's more dissociated judgement.[26]

Engels's response was a resolute 'no'. Marx would reap no laurels in a polemic with 'Mr Weston', 'and it would certainly not make a good début in English economic literature'. No, Marx should complete his book – and if he was not finished with it by 1 September, he would owe Engels twelve bottles of wine (this was written on 15 July).[27]

We do not know what happened with the bottles of wine; *Capital*, at least, was not ready by the appointed date. On the other hand, it can be said with certainty that Engels's advice was extraordinarily unwise. Had Marx's lectures been printed, it would have meant an easily accessible introduction to his theories in English. All the willing readers who had difficulty penetrating *Capital* would have avoided the detour through Engels's later writings and would have been able to go to Marx himself. Weston would perhaps have been given a more central role than his ideas in the *Bee-Hive* deserved, but what of it? For a workers' movement, it can hardly be a disadvantage that a carpenter gets attention.

But Engels imagined an entirely different setting for *Capital*. It was a scientific work among scientific works. It should be given an honoured place in the scientific world, reviewed with respect even by its opponents, quoted, castigated, applauded – that is, the way it happened in the German academic world (which was earlier than the English and the French in assuming this modern form).

What Engels did not realize was that this German academic world on principle only reckoned with those who had a professor's chair – preferably at a respected university – or at least were lecturers in a promising academic career. There was a merciless boundary between those who were inside and those who were outside, and Karl Marx found himself irretrievably outside. His academic credentials were worthless in this context.

Marx viewed the matter no differently. *Capital* was to be regarded as a scientific dissertation. The bridge to the common reader would be built later. The bridge-building he himself was busy with in the International could verbally reach the members of the Central Committee, but not the general public – not yet. Marx's daughter Eleanor finally allowed the manuscript of both lectures to be published in 1898.

There is a small note in Marx's letter that deserves a moment's reflection. By publishing the lecture texts, he would come into contact with John Stuart Mill and Edward Spencer Beesly, he wrote. We know that a few years later he actually made Beesly's acquaintance (see above, p. 527). On the other hand, he never did with John Stuart Mill. In his eyes, Beesly was an outstanding historian, despite his positivist points of departure. But Mill? Marx commented negatively – often condescendingly – about Mill as an economist quite consistently. Unlike Smith and Ricardo, Mill did not acknowledge the internal contradictions of capitalism.

But was there something else that tempted Marx into making Mill's acquaintance? Something in Mill's hesitation between capitalism and socialism? Or his ideas on political freedom? Or did Marx simply want Mill to be informed about the theory that supported *Capital*? We will never know.[28]

Bakunin and Marx

In the substantial letter to Engels where Marx reports on his early efforts for the International, he mentioned in passing that he had received a visit from Bakunin. Bakunin was an old acquaintance. The relationship between them had varied, but was mostly tense. Now it sounded entirely different: 'I must say I liked him very much, more so than previously,' Marx wrote.[29]

The sympathies turned out to be short-lived, however. In the battle that would ultimately tear the International to pieces, Marx and Bakunin would be the foremost combatants. Over the years, Marx had been able to put up with the disciples of Proudhon and of Blanqui. He had endured the occasional Chartist or Owenite, and even the occasional follower of Mazzini who was willing to compromise. But with Bakunin in the organization, this was impossible.

Bakunin had lived a singularly dramatic and adventurous life after the revolutionary years of 1848–49. Imprisoned by the Tsar's police, he had been sentenced to death and pardoned, not once but twice. Instead, he was exiled to districts in Siberia that were considered escape-proof. But escape Bakunin did, living on berries and roots, and finding his way at last to the northeast coast of Russia. From there, he took a boat via Japan to the west coast of the United States, crossed the American continent, and turned up in London in 1861.

It is no wonder that he was seen as a hero in many camps, especially among liberals. During a visit to Sweden a large banquet in his honour was arranged in Stockholm, and August Blanche – at that time an extremely celebrated author in the country – gave a captivating speech for him.

Marx did not have much that could compete with Bakunin's adventures. And now the great Russian was ready for new revolutions. He worked untiringly to stir up the people against everything to do with power and authority.[30] Bakunin stayed out of the International for several years. But Marx had his eye on him; the Russian was eager to build up his base of power. '*Mr Bakunin* – in the background of his business – is condescendent enough to wish to take the workers' movement under *Russian* leadership,' Marx wrote in a letter to Engels at the end of 1868. But only a few days later, he received a letter from Bakunin professing his friendship and his support for Marx's fundamental ideas.[31] On that question, however, things were less stable. Bakunin created the *Alliance de la Démocratie Socialiste* (Alliance for Social Democracy) that he linked to the International. Not without reason, Marx perceived the alliance as a Trojan horse with which Bakunin intended to conquer the International from within. To his consternation, one of his warmest promoters in Switzerland, Johann Philipp Becker, also turned out to have a weakness for Bakunin. Simply put, Becker was trying to combine Marx with Bakunin – something that was not easily done. Becker himself soon realized this, and broke with Bakunin.[32]

Marx took action, with the Central Committee in London at his back. This was already his habit; he had become the Central Committee's most important spokesperson. According to Wolfgang Schieder's calculation, Marx wrote more than fifty documents totalling 200 pages over the years up to 1872.

One of the most important official documents by his hand was the decision of the Central Committee on Bakunin's alliance. It said that the Alliance was acting simultaneously outside and inside the International, in a paradoxical manner. It was to have its own Central Committee in Geneva alongside the Central Committee of the International in London. The result would inevitably be a split and factional battles, and internationalism would give ground to nationalism. The adherence of the Alliance to the International was therefore declared null and void.[33]

But Bakunin did not give up so easily. He turned up at the Congress in Basel in 1869. Marx was not there; he did not generally travel to the annual congresses. He did not have enough money, nor did he want to divide his time. Nevertheless, the crucial decisions were made in the Central Committee. He came in person only to the final, dramatic 1872 congress in The Hague in order to fight the decisive battle with Bakunin.

Bakunin had already reaped successes back in Basel. Among other things, he got a majority of the participants to support the demand to abolish the right of inheritance. This was actually what Marx had written back in the *Manifesto*, despite Engels being satisfied with heavy taxation in the proposal (the catechism) that formed the basis for the final text. What was the reason that Marx did not welcome Bakunin's initiative? Inheritance, as we know, had played an important role for his own finances.

In an article in Becker's periodical *Der Vorbote*, which Marx also wrote in the name of the Central Committee, he raised up the question of the right of inheritance to a level of principle. The issue of inheritance was part of the legal superstructure, and could not be regarded as a principal question. By doing so, cause and effect were being confused. As long as the private ownership of the means of production remained, the right of inheritance was a natural consequence. Removing it without doing something about the fundamental conditions of ownership would be ineffective. Until then, people could work for things such as taxation of inheritance.

The article indicates that Marx himself had changed his understanding as his social theory developed from the *Manifesto* to the first volume of *Capital*.[34] But this issue was in no way crucial for the continued fate of the International. It got worse when, during the autumn, Bakunin started attacking the Central Committee in London in a few articles, above all in his own periodical *L'Égalité*. He said that the Central Committee was not meeting the requirements of the statutes to carry out the decisions of the Congress. Marx wrote the Central Committee's response. His words were still marked by the conciliatory spirit that characterized almost everything he had written in the name of the International up to that point. But the response was essentially sharp. There was nothing in the statutes that said that the Central Committee was obligated to engage in polemics with *L'Égalité* or other newspapers. They were only responding to contributions from the regional council in the French-speaking region of Switzerland. But nothing would be publicized from either one side or the other.

Bakunin and his followers were deeply dissatisfied with the dominant role that London, and Great Britain in general, had in the International. Marx responded that the Central Committee was in the happy situation of holding the lever of proletarian revolution in its hand. The English had all the necessary material conditions for a social revolution at their disposal. What was missing was just the ability to see the situation in broad outline (*l'esprit généralisateur*), and revolutionary passion (*la passion révolutionnaire*). It was the business of the Central Committee to help bring out both the one and the other. He went on: our significance is especially vouched for by the leading newspapers in the country that represent the opposite interests, to say nothing of those who support our cause. But to succeed, it is important that we really act as a Central Committee. Diverse other organizations cannot then act as independent units.

Marx accused his opponents of a naïve understanding of the relationship between social and political movements. The statutes said clearly that the main question was the economic liberation of the workers, to which the political movement relates as a means. Unfortunately, the phrase 'as a means' was left out of the French translation, something that had to do with the differences of opinion in the French section.

It can be noted that in the letter, Marx did not respond directly to Bakunin's main accusation that the decision of the Congress on the right of inheritance had not been implemented by the Central Committee. It is easy to conclude that the silence was due to Marx believing that the decision of the Congress was against the International's fundamental thesis on the relationship between social and political conditions. As we know, this is precisely what he had emphasized in the article in *Der Vorbote*.[35]

The conflict between Bakunin and 'the Marx party' entered a new phase when war between France and Prussia broke out in July 1870. At the outbreak of war Marx was unhesitatingly on the side of the Prussians; a Prussian victory would mean the end of the hateful regime of Napoleon III. At the request of the Central Committee, he wrote an initial address in which he spoke for the entire International. Napoleon III – or Louis Bonaparte, as Marx called him throughout – was a sworn enemy of the International, alleging that it was an underground organization with plans to murder the emperor himself. It was a bizarre misjudgement; terror and assassination was not the path the International wanted to take. On the other hand, the organization insistently encouraged its members to vote no in Bonaparte's constant referendums. Bonaparte depended on support from the rural masses in the countryside, and got it. His support was weak in the cities, and weakest in Paris. In the referendum of May 1870 that indirectly opened the way for war with Prussia, five of every six votes were 'yes' to the emperor. But in Paris, 139,538 votes were on his side and 184,236 were against him.[36]

The address that Marx authored as soon as war broke out starts with a quote from the Inaugural Address itself on the significance of international collaboration among workers, especially to counteract war. It is therefore no wonder, he continued, that Louis Bonaparte hated the International and made it the subject of various senseless accusations. The plotting for war now underway was simply an improved version of the coup that brought Bonaparte to power.

For the time being, Prussia was fighting a war of defence. But Prussia was also an accessory to a conspiracy against Louis Bonaparte (this concerned succession to the Spanish throne). And who knew when the Prussians' appetite would be satisfied? If Bismarck turned it into a war of aggression, the workers in Germany would turn against the enterprise.

Finally, Marx – and through him the entire International – held out the prospect of the alliance between workers one day putting an end to all war. A new society would arise, in which peace would prevail and labour would be the common affair of all.[37]

It was this beautiful horizon that the workers' movement worked towards up until the First World War. Marx's address was disseminated in newspapers and flyers in many languages. But in 1914 there were few who remembered the message. Nearly everyone was gripped by the martial frenzy that would cost nine million people their lives.

The Franco-Prussian war was, of course, also discussed in Marx's and Engels's correspondence. Their words there are just as roguishly nonchalant as they usually are. But there was seriousness, and hope as well, under the jargon. Both hoped that Louis Bonaparte would lose quickly. The Prussians were not only militarily stronger; German workers were also superior to the French 'both in theory and organization', Marx said. 'Its predominance over the French on the international stage would also mean the predominance of *our* party over Proudhon's, etc.'[38]

Engels was not in disagreement. But he had a completely different interest in the course of the war itself than his friend did. He had become a real expert in military enterprises through his training and his own experiences, and he published a long series of

articles in the evening newspaper *Pall Mall Gazette* that attracted
a great deal of attention. In them, he could quickly inform his
readers that the plans of Napoleon III to cross the Rhine and then
go carefree all the way to Berlin were entirely unrealistic. It was
instead the German troops who would be able to advance. Engels
admired the German count Moltke and his strategic capability.
According to Engels, the seventy-year-old Moltke was youthfully
energetic and could lead the Germans to a quick victory. By 2
September – just over a month after the outbreak of war – the
French army was crushed at the battle of Sedan. The emperor
was captured, and the French government proclaimed the Third
Republic.

But the war was not finished. A new French army was set on
its feet. This turned out, however, to be just as incapable as the
previous one of effective resistance, and during the autumn and
winter the German troops advanced towards Paris. Engels and
Marx could now see that what had initially seemed as a war
of defence had indeed developed into a large-scale war of conquest. Paris would be opened to the German troops; Alsace and
Lorraine would become Elsass and Lothringen, incorporated into
the new German Reich which – fittingly – would be proclaimed in
Versailles, where King Wilhelm would simultaneously be crowned
Emperor Wilhelm I. In fact, it was above all the arch-conservative
Otto von Bismarck who thus drastically expanded his powers.[39]

Unrest and confusion prevailed in France. The government
capitulated, but parts of the army refused to accept the surrender,
and revolts broke out in several cities.

Marx's attitude towards the events was split. He was definitely
against an anarchistic coup that would lead to spontaneous formation of local governments. He wrote in a letter to Engels only a
few days after the battle of Sedan that one of his faithful followers, Auguste Serraillier, was on the way to Paris to see to it that
the French division of the International did not commit 'all sorts
of follies there in the name of the International'. The plans were
namely to 'bring down the Provisional Government, establish a
commune de Paris' and other similar things.[40]

In the name of the Central Committee, he laid down similar
thoughts in a 'Second Address on the Franco-Prussian War'. It is

a highly complex document of almost ten pages. A longer exposition on the military and strategic consequences of the German
conquest of Alsace and Lorraine was based directly on material
Engels had sent him. A passage on the ideal attitude of the German
workers – peace, and no war of conquest – is certainly his own.
The same applies to the most important parts of the address, on
the French situation. In itself, the provisional government promised nothing good; it was an unsightly mix of followers of the
former royal house of Orléans (which King Louis Philippe had
belonged to) and typical bourgeois Republicans. The working
class had been put into a difficult situation. 'Any attempt at upsetting the new Government in the present crisis, when the enemy is
almost knocking at the doors of Paris, would be a desperate folly.
The French workmen must perform their duties as citizens; but,
at the same time, they must not allow themselves to be deluded by
the national *souvenirs* of 1792.'[41]

1792 was the year of the Paris Commune. Marx's warning,
which the entire Central Committee stood behind, could not have
been more unequivocal: no Paris Commune! But however plain
his words may have been, he was nonetheless more uncertain in
the face of what was actually happening in France. This can be
seen in a letter that he wrote just over a month later to his newfound friend, the positivist historian Edward Spencer Beesly. In it,
Marx said that a revolutionary commune had been proclaimed
in Lyon by a coalition of workers linked to the International
and radical bourgeois republicans. 'But the asses, Bakunin and
Cluseret, arrived at Lyons and spoiled everything. Belonging both
to the "International", they had, unfortunately, influence enough
to misled our friends. The Hotel de Ville was seized – for a short
time – and the most foolish decrees on the *abolition de l'état* and
similar nonsense were issued.' People's sympathies immediately
shifted, and nothing came of the commune.

Marx was describing the events at a distance, and probably
according to information from some of his sympathizers. By all
appearances, the anarchistic elements were stronger from the
beginning than his words hinted at. Incidentally, Bakunin's fellow
thinker Gustave-Paul Cluseret was a battle-scarred military man
with experiences from both Garibaldi's war of liberation in Italy

and the American Civil War. But Marx dismissed him as 'a fool and a coward'.[42]

The main thing in his reaction was nonetheless that he did not condemn the attempt itself to establish a commune, but only the approach. In other words, his attitude was extremely flexible. Before revolutionary communes were established, he warned against them. Once they had been proclaimed, however, he supported them in principle but could criticize their direction. In this light, his reactions to the Paris Commune are understandable.

The Paris Commune of 1871

The history of the Paris Commune is a short one. It was proclaimed on 18 March 1871, and was crushed two months later during *La semaine sanglante* (Bloody Week), from 22–29 May. It aroused loathing and enthusiasm, it had its own song – 'Le temps des cérises' (Cherry Season) – and has been the subject of an enormous amount of literature.[43] The first person to write its history had himself been part of it, and had avoided by a hair's breadth the fate that met at least 20,000 men and women during the horrible massacre in May. His name was Prosper-Olivier Lissagaray and his 1876 book was called *Histoire de la Commune de Paris de 1871* (History of the Paris Commune of 1871). Like many other survivors, Lissagaray fled to London where he came into contact with Marx, who helped him with his book. Even more important was the encounter with Eleanor Marx, the youngest daughter. Prosper-Olivier and Eleanor became a couple, despite Jenny's and Karl's opposition. But their passion withered after a few years, and Eleanor broke off the engagement.

Lissagaray's book on the Commune, on the other hand, has the freshness that eyewitness depictions can provide. It is also built on interviews with others who survived the bloodbath, additionally providing a decent overview over the chaotic course of events.[44]

Only two works from the later literature will be pointed out. The first is a splendid volume for which Jean Bruhat had primary responsibility, but also the help of a number of colleagues. Bruhat was both a historian, educated at the École normale supérieure, and an active communist who broke with the French Communist Party as a result of the May 1968 unrest in Paris. *La Commune de 1871* (The Paris Commune), the second edition of which was published in 1970, is marked by the spirit of the times but is also an ambitious work, with documentation equally as rich as the illustrations. In the eyes of Bruhat and his assistants, the Paris Commune was one revolution in a series of revolutions pointing towards Russia and 1917. Lenin's comments in *State and Revolution* – that the Paris Commune was the first attempt of the proletariat to crush the bourgeois state – are respectfully reproduced.[45]

The second work that should be mentioned is André Zeller's 1969 book *Les hommes de la Commune* (The Men of the Commune). Zeller was one of France's highest military men in 1961, when together with three other generals he staged a coup against President Charles de Gaulle with the intent of keeping Algeria French. The coup was defeated, and Zeller and his colleagues were sentenced to prison. Zeller was freed in 1966, and then devoted himself to completing an extremely knowledgeable 450-page book on the Commune.

It could be expected that his understanding would be the direct opposite of Bruhat's, and that he would thus see the Commune as a lower-class uprising directed against the legitimate holders of power. But it is not! It is a lively, empathetic description of people trying to create their own spontaneous order in a chaotic and desperate situation. The title is odd: women played a more conspicuous role in the Paris Commune than in any previous uprising. Many of the furious press condemnations of the short-lived regime dealt with women. Zeller in fact also mentions a few women, above all the young Russian follower of Marx Elisabeth Dmitrieff, who at the age of nineteen turned up at the Marx family home and won everyone's confidence. She was additionally one of the founders of the Russian section of the International, and during the Commune she played a central role in the *Union des femmes* that organized women from various parts of Paris for the purpose of strengthening the Commune and giving women a central place in it.

Old General Zeller had one main criticism of the Commune:

it lacked leaders. There was neither a Lenin nor a Trotsky, he argued. It is easy to agree with him that the Commune was odd in the respect that it is difficult to even discern a group of leaders. So many names parade by in the records; in Bruhat's major work, the number of pictures of faces is almost stunning.

Zeller, at least, had a favourite: Louis Rossel. He was a gifted young officer who refused to accept the French capitulation. This was primarily why he joined the leading group of the Commune, known as the Communards. At the age of twenty-two, he served as their military leader for eleven days. But problems soon arose – most likely through infiltrations from the enemy's side – and chaos broke out. Rossel refused to shoot any alleged traitors, resigned his commission, and was declared to be arrested but hid in an apartment in central Paris. Ultimately, it was the enemy who captured him after the defeat of the Commune and executed him after a sham trial.

Bruhat is not as enthusiastic. Rossel was a good organizer but armed with military prejudices, he said. He wanted to introduce a system so strict that it could not fit a revolutionary situation. The rumours that he had ambitions to create a dictatorship may possibly have been true.

Bruhat follows in Marx's footsteps when he evaluates the Commune and its many actors. It is typical that his conclusions on what went wrong reproduce statements by Marx (and also Lenin).[46] Marx himself knew that his influence on developments was highly limited. A good many of the leading representatives of the Commune had joined the International, but as we know there were several shades of opinion within the International. Proudhon still had followers in the French section, and the same applied to Blanqui. The anarchists were gaining ground. Marx had a few faithful followers: Elisabeth Dmitrieff was one of them, the shoe-maker Auguste Serraillier another. But they were in no way crucial to the course of events.

It is easy for posterity to view the Commune either as the result of an underhanded plot staged by various conspiratorial elements within the International, or as a proper revolution in the same suite as its predecessors in 1789, 1830, and 1848. But it was neither of those things. If anything, it was the result of a series of coincidences.

The background was a devastating war. In that respect, the Commune had similarities with the Russian revolutions of 1905 and 1917, as well as with the Chinese Revolution of 1949. France had suffered a total defeat. Paris had been abandoned to the enemy. A provisional French government had been constituted, but it had no real authority in the capital. Dissatisfaction was fermenting in the National Guard (*La garde nationale*), which included all men old enough for military service. The provisional government had agreed to disarm the Guard, but the Guard wanted nothing to do with the agreement. The violence escalated when seventy-three-year-old Adolphe Thiers took over government power. He tried to calm the citizens of Paris in vain. Two generals, Jacques Léon Clément-Thomas and Claude Lecomte, were both shot by their own troops. These were not planned actions, as Thiers and others maintained, but unplanned outbreaks of fury. Thiers immediately gave the order to evacuate Paris, and fled the city himself. Zeller scornfully comments that Thiers always did this when the ground began burning under his feet. Cutting and running had also been his weapon in 1830 and 1848, as well as in 1851 when Louis Bonaparte seized power.[47]

All this happened on 18 March, the first day of the Commune. The people in power had left Paris; it was now a question of establishing the people's own power. The only model on hand was the one from 1792. Many of those taking the initiative regarded themselves as Jacobins; the followers of Blanqui, Proudhon, Bakunin, or Marx had no alternate model. Marx had warned against every attempt to repeat the past, but had said nothing about how to avoid it.

Suddenly, there was a power vacuum in Paris. The first person who could speak and act with any authority would thus seize the initiative. It became a collective affair: a *Comité central* – Central Committee – took on the task of guiding the free city towards the future. The first proclamations were already coming out on 18 March: 'Citizens, the people of Paris have cast off the yoke they wanted to put on us', it said.[48] But the Central Committee's position of power was not undisputed; opponents also announced themselves. In order to create legitimacy, general elections were quickly arranged after four days, on 22 March. But even this decision received criticism. Weapons were more important than opinions, the critics argued.

Through the election – in which participation was weaker than expected – each of the twenty *arrondissements* of Paris received four representatives, thus a total of eighty in all. On 28 March, the Commune was proclaimed.

So far, this was a rather undramatic history – a respite in the middle of the noise of the battle. But, outside Paris, the rumours were flying, each one worse than the last. Forgeries circulated and gained credence. Even Marx came in for his share. Newspapers that were hostile to developments in Paris published a forged letter in which Marx criticized the Parisian members of the International for devoting themselves to politics too much. Marx and Engels wrote a clarification to *The Times*.[49]

The Commune divided responsibility among its leading members; all areas were to be covered. But external threats soon became impossible to ignore, and on 10 April Marx judged the situation to be hopeless. It was the Communards' own fault, he said; they had shown entirely too much 'civility' (*honnêteté*). They did not want to appear like usurpers, but devoted their time to electing committees. Their chances lay in starting a civil war, but instead they had given free rein to 'that mischievous *avorton* Thiers'.[50]

It is not easy to know how Marx imagined a civil war when the strongest army in Europe – the German – stood outside the city. But his attitude towards the Parisian drama contains many other nuances. This is clear from a letter he wrote only six days later to Ludwig Kugelmann. 'What resilience, what historical initiative, what a capacity for sacrifice in these Parisians!', he exclaimed enthusiastically. In fact, he went further: 'History has no like example of a like greatness.' Nevertheless, compunctions meant that the crucial moment had been lost. Entirely too rashly, the Central Committee had turned over power to the Commune.

Marx noted with satisfaction that his prediction from *The Eighteenth Brumaire of Louis Bonaparte* had come true: the next attempt at a French Revolution should not amount to taking over the bureaucratic-military machinery, but smashing it.[51]

Kugelmann received a new letter from Marx on 17 April. New

ideas were crying out to be expressed. World history would be easy if it played out under purely favourable circumstances and if chance did not play a role, Marx wrote. The characters of those in the leadership of the movement also belonged to chance.[52]

In two drafts, Marx addressed precisely two such leading persons (the completed letters have been lost). One was Leo Frankel (or Fränkel), a Hungarian who joined the International and made his name in the Commune through his efforts to establish a Committee for Public Security (*Comité de salut public*), and the other was Louis-Eugène Varlin, who was also a member of the International but was chiefly a Proudhonist. Marx encouraged them to see to it that papers that compromised Thiers and other enemies of the Commune were preserved in a safe place. He also criticized the Commune for devoting entirely 'too much time over trifles and personal squabbles'.[53]

There are no letters in Marx's hand from the time of the 'bloody week'. On 12 June, when London was flooded with refugees from the massacres in May, Marx formulated a few summary assessments in the letter to Edward Spencer Beesly that has already been discussed. He noted that the nonsense *(Unsinn)* of the Paris press about his own writings and his relationship to the Commune testified to the fact that the police were sitting on greatly insufficient material. But he exclaimed in the same breath: 'If only the Commune had listened to my warnings!' He had advised them to fortify the heights to the north towards the Prussian side, otherwise they would end up in a rat trap, and he had told them to send all papers that compromised the Thiers regime to London. They had done neither.[54]

The Paris Commune made Marx notorious across all Europe – in fact, over large parts of the world. Previously he had lived somewhat in the background, watched by a police spy or two; he had become briefly known as a journalist and acquired a certain, very limited reputation as a scholar, but now his name was being spread everywhere and roused horror or rapture. He was not unaffected by the fame. He wrote to Kugelmann with a satisfied smile that 'throughout the period of the last Paris revolution' he had incessantly been called '*le grand chef de l'Internationale*' (the big boss of the International) in the hostile press.[55]

Kugelmann knew as well as Marx that it was not true. As we have seen, Marx's influence over the Paris Commune was limited, and the very birth of the Commune was neither calculated nor pushed forward by anyone. It arose out of the chaos the war had created.

But, once the Commune was a fact, Marx – true to habit – tried to keep accounts of what was happening. He composed several drafts before publishing in June 1871 – when everything was over – *The Civil War in France*, a nearly forty-page 'Address' that constituted the official position of the International on the events in Paris and in France. It is above all a history of the background of the Commune, its character, and its bloody conclusion, more than the course of events.

The interesting thing is Marx's analysis of the Commune as a political phenomenon. He starts with a small exposition on the development of the state. Its permanent attributes of a standing army, police, bureaucracy, and so on are a consequence of the absolute monarchy. But the state gradually developed to strengthen the power of the capitalists over labour; it serves, in the words of Thiers, to keep the 'vile multitude' in check. This took on an extreme form in the Second Empire, during which the rich got tremendously richer and the working class had to toil and starve.

It is in this light that the Commune should be viewed. It was, Marx said, 'the direct antithesis to the Empire'. Here, he was reaching directly back to Hegel, who argued that the revolution of 1789 constituted the antithesis to absolutism. But Marx did not then follow in Hegel's footsteps: for Hegel, the negation of absolute royal power must also meet its negation, in this case the rule of the first Napoleon. Marx, naturally, did not see the bloody repression of the Commune as such a step forward – quite the contrary.

But how did the Commune itself appear as an antithesis to what preceded it? The Commune had rid itself of the Army, replacing it with the National Guard which consisted of 'the working men'. The Commune was to be a working assembly, not a parliamentary one, and it was to be simultaneously executive and legislative. Once the Commune had got rid of the police and the standing army, it was also eager to free itself from the power of the priests.

In a vision reminiscent of Charles Fourier, Marx saw all of France covered by nothing but communes down to the smallest village. Each and every one had its sovereignty, at the same time as they were joined together in decision-making assemblies both regionally and centrally in Paris. At the higher levels, it was thus a representative system.

Marx said optimistically that, just as private businesses have a splendid ability to put the right person in the right place (here he undoubtedly got his information from Engels), so would the communes and the network of communes find their ideal executor of all the tasks a society requires to function.

After this summary plan for a new type of society, Marx returned to a more theoretical level. Much earlier, he had preferred to use a classic pair of concepts – form and content (or form and substance) – to elucidate his views on society in general. Once again, this was put to use. These were, he said, entirely new historical creations that should not be confused with certain earlier forms of social life, with which they may have a certain external similarity. They were thus not any new variant of the medieval communes, nor do they constitute a new attempt at breaking down large political entities into small states. Nor did it involve a return to the communal division of the 1790s. On the contrary, they constitute a thoroughly expansive political form, whereas all previous forms had been repressive. This form aims at turning the means of production, land and capital, into simple tools for free and associated labour. This is, Marx emphasized, pure communism.

The working class expected no miracles from the Commune, and they had no pre-set utopias. They saw before them a long series of future battles, which would change both circumstances and people. International cooperation would always be important.

The Commune showed wisdom and moderation, Marx wrote. Like the English oligarchs, the German Empire had created an important part of its wealth through robbing the Church of its riches at one point, and now they professed horror at the fact that the Commune had taken 8,000 francs from the Church.

But despite his admiration, he admitted that the past had

strongly made itself felt during the months the Commune existed. His words are a faint echo of the classic ideas in *The Eighteenth Brumaire of Louis Bonaparte*, written nearly twenty years earlier, where he talked about the past weighing like a nightmare on those that came after. Now, he was more hopeful: time would shake these regressions off. With these words, he definitively distanced himself from the Jacobins who played an important role in the first Commune.

But he also emphasized the significance of women in the Commune as 'heroic, noble, and devoted, like the women of antiquity'.

At the end of the document, he defended the decision of the Commune to take hostages – including the Archbishop of Paris – when the threat from outside became urgent. Marx pointed out that the Communards offered again and again to exchange the prelate, and even additional priests, for one man – namely Blanqui, who was being held prisoner by their opponents. Thiers refused, since 'he knew that with Blanqui he would give to the Commune a head, while the Archbishop would serve his purpose best in the shape of a corpse'.

The Commune ended with a civil war under the supervision of the foreign invaders. Thiers's troops displayed a cruelty that can only be compared with the worst Roman generals. But Marx assured his readers that the defeat of the Commune did not mean the end; the battle would be taken up again and again ever more intensively.[56]

The address is an important document. It acquired great historical significance especially because it guided Lenin to such a great degree. It is not as obvious that it completely expresses Marx's understanding. His earlier addresses in the name of the International had been products of compromise. This one has such features as well. Marx suppressed the criticism he gave free rein to in his correspondence. When he pointed out Blanqui as the possible leader of the Commune, he was scarcely expressing his own assessment of the foremost advocate of what he called the 'tactic of the Putsch'. Rather, he was placating the influential Blanquists in the International with his words.

But what can be said about his words on the Commune as a promising start to a social revolution? Here there is more that squares with his deepest convictions. He expressed the ideas on free association of people in many other places. His views on politics as a form of the real content of society – humanity's metabolism with nature – are unmistakably his own.

It is clear that the Commune affected him deeply, and in certain important aspects actually changed his convictions – at least for the time being. Above all, he now saw bloody conflicts as a part of social development that would be hard to avoid. His thought that the Commune was only the first of a series of increasingly far-reaching class struggles contrasted with his earlier warnings against establishing a commune in Paris. It is completely possible that he was influenced by Engels, who was growing even closer to him now that they both lived in London and Engels was actively involved in the innermost circles of the International. Engels, as we know, was a man with military ideas and ideals, in contrast to the eternal civilian Marx.

One question the reader gets no response to is how political development as Marx outlined it here relates to the concentration of capital. Would the future not also contain ever greater businesses – though communally owned – alongside all the communes? How would this affect the communes? It is clear that the Commune had become extraordinarily important for Marx. It is nonetheless risky to fully identify his political ideas with what he expressed in his letters and addresses about the striking and harrowing months in Paris in the spring of 1871. We will soon see why.

The Dissolution of the International

After the Commune, the centres of power – with Bismarck at their head – regarded Marx as the most dangerous man in Europe. Marx was not displeased with the role after years in the background. At the same time, political problems were piling up for him. In the International, the British delegation had set the tone; this also helped him into the central position he obtained in the

organization. But the British, without exception, thought poorly
of the Paris Commune. Systematic union work stood at the centre
for them, and, in that light, the French experiment appeared to be
senselessly rash and fundamentally hopeless.

Marx estranged himself from the British with his address on
the Commune, choosing instead to enter into competition with
Bakunin and the anarchists. The anarchists argued that the
Commune showed they were right in relation to Marx about the
path to a free and equal society. The spontaneity in the process
spoke to their advantage. At the same time, neither Marx nor
Bakunin had counted on such a social experiment having the
misery and suffering of war as its immediate basis, but the anonymous shots from the embittered soldiers who killed two generals
became the starting signal for the Commune.

In the words of Wolfgang Schieder, Marx's address – held when
the commune had already been crushed – was one of his 'politische
Meisterlösungen' (political master solutions).[57] Marx interpreted
the Commune with its own categories – the Communards thus
did not annihilate state power, which the anarchists had as a goal,
but fundamentally changed it for their own purposes. They did
not seek to repeat the communal experiment of the 1790s – what
Marx had warned against – but created something completely
new that could be developed further in the future.

But the anarchists were not convinced. On the contrary,
they gained ground. The Italian and Spanish sections sided
with Bakunin, and the Russians strengthened their position
in France. Marx – with Engels at his side – sought to seize the
initiative through a smaller conference in London in September
1871. Marx completely dominated it – according to a careful
calculation, he spoke 100 times[58] – and rode completely rough-
shod over his chief opponent, the Spaniard Anselmo Lorenzo,
who stood very close to Bakunin. Marx behaved in a more
conciliatory manner towards the Blanquist (and Communard)
Édouard Vaillant, but did not accept the thesis that insurrection
was the only way to go. No, Marx declared, parliamentarism
was an alternative to revolutionary opposition.[59]

This is a standpoint that does not emerge in the address
on the Commune. But it is nonetheless probable that it lies

closest to Marx's actual political convictions at the time. By all appearances, he was quite disillusioned in his views on the International. In a letter to Danielson, he likened the organization to a prison. Jenny Marx told Liebknecht that her husband was upset about all the accusations after the Commune. Her letter in general is marked by a great melancholy, both her own and on behalf of Karl and the International. 'Now I have grown too old to hope for much and the recent terrible events have completely shattered my peace of mind', she wrote.[60]

But one final battle still remained for the International. Marx and Engels both travelled to the Congress in The Hague in September 1872, the first and last of the International's congresses that both participated in. Marx's followers had a narrow majority over the anarchists, with Bakunin at their head. Their opponents could thus be thrown out of the International. But the victory was not worth much. Bakunin was able to quickly gather his troops into a counter-congress. Marx's last desperate attempt was to move the centre of the International to New York. He had great confidence in the future of the workers' movement in the United States, to be sure, but he undoubtedly had no illusions that the International would be able to attain its earlier position so far away from most of the associated workers' organizations.[61] In 1874, the International dissolved.

The German Social Democrats

It was only now that Marx seriously began occupying himself with the development of the workers' movement in Germany. In his eyes, Germany had always lagged behind Great Britain, and was several steps behind France. The Germans had not even had their own bourgeois revolution.

In the initial phase of the International, British trade union leaders had been his most important support. As a result of the Commune, France came into focus. But once the Commune had been crushed and its surviving activists forced into a bitter life as refugees in London, at the same time as Bakunin had attained decisive influence over the workers' movement of southern Europe, the new German Reich appeared as the remaining alternative for Marx's and Engels's political involvement.

There had been a growing German workers' movement ever since the early 1860s in this new kingdom. Its pioneer was Ferdinand Lassalle. Lassalle was seven years younger than Marx and had much in common with him. Both had Jewish backgrounds, both studied in Berlin and were decisively influenced by Hegel's thought, both stayed a few years in Paris, and both had a burning interest in Ancient Greece; Lassalle's interest materialized in a two-volume work on Heraclitus and his philosophy.

Both also had a great interest in literature. Marx had given up writing poetry early on in his youth, but Lassalle was more persistent. In 1859, he sent Marx a drama titled *Franz von Sickingen* after the German knight from the time of Luther who acquired great power and great wealth through various tricks. Lassalle was eager to get his older friend's assessment of the document, and Marx wrote a proper review in his response.

First came the praise: the construction was good, as was the plot (more than could be said about most modern German dramas, he added sourly). Reading it had quite simply livened him up. The iambs limped, to be sure, but that did not need to be a disadvantage. The tragic plot reminded him of the revolutionary party of 1848–49, which rightly came to grief. It was a worthy theme for a drama. But – and now came the objections – was the chosen subject really suitable for illustrating the current failures? The parallels stumbled. Franz von Sickingen had gone under because as a knight, he belonged to a social class on the decline. He only imagined that he was revolutionary. Marx also criticized the characteristics of the other characters in the play. Sickingen appeared entirely too abstract, and the rest of the cast devoted too much time to reflection. Lassalle's unfortunate partiality for Schiller's brooding heroes shone through. Marx ultimately toned the criticism down a bit by saying that his wife Jenny had enjoyed reading the play.[62]

Lassalle's drama gradually became the subject of a large and involved literary debate. But Marx had already done his part with the review in his letter, which itself testifies to the fact that strong intellectual and aesthetic interests brought him and Lassalle together.[63]

Marx would also become interested to some extent in a woman who played a special role in Lassalle's life: the countess Sophie von Hatzfeldt. Lassalle had made her acquaintance in Berlin. At a very young age, Sophie von Hatzfeldt had been forced into a marriage with a man from the high nobility who turned out to be a scoundrel and a tormentor. Lassalle, who like Marx knew a lot about the law, took up her case and conducted lawsuits against her husband for nearly nine years. He was successful; the countess was awarded a significant part of the family fortune, and from it she endowed Lassalle with a generous annual sum. It is unclear whether the countess and the young socialist were united by any amorous connections. In any case, the political harmony between the two was palpable. Sophie von Hatzfeldt became 'the red countess' and played an important role in the early German workers' movement.

It was Lassalle who founded the first workers' party in Germany in 1863. It was actually not called a 'party' but an 'association': *Allgemeiner Deutscher Arbeiterverein* (ADAV, The General German Workers' Association). Lassalle was only with the party during its first years. At the age of thirty-nine, he fell in a duel with a rival – a Romanian boyar named Janko von Racowitza – over the favours of a young woman.

The relationship between Marx and Lassalle was full of contradictions. Marx, who was used to playing first fiddle when meeting people with leftist opinions, found the incessantly talkative, enthusiastic, self-confident and conceited – yet extremely versatile – Lassalle difficult. Upon receiving message of the fatal outcome of the duel, Engels wrote appreciatively to Marx: 'Whatever Lassalle may have been in other respects as a person, writer, scholar – he was, as a politician, undoubtedly one of the most significant men in Germany.' Marx responded that despite everything, Lassalle was 'one of the *vieille souche* and the foe of our foes'. Marx found it difficult to imagine that the mouth that had spoken so incessantly was now forever silenced.

But he would soon become more negative once he had acquainted himself with the social theory Lassalle had allowed to serve as guidance for the political movement he started. He had taken essential elements from Marx, to be sure, but without referring to his guide; Marx was extremely irritated with those who did not acknowledge his priority. It was worse with Lassalle's political positions. Lassalle, who came from Breslau (now Wrocław) in Silesia, did not share Marx's loathing for Prussia. On the contrary, he hailed Prussia's advances with satisfaction.

He and Marx also had entirely different ideas about the best strategy for the working class. Marx stuck to his understanding from 1848 that the German still had to undergo a bourgeois revolution, and that the working class must therefore ally with the bourgeoisie (or 'middle class', to use the term he used in the Inaugural Address). Lassalle and his followers, on the other hand, indicated the capitalists as the immediate enemy and saw the landowning class as a natural ally.

He also had a completely different attitude towards state power as such, arguing that a socialist party should be able to make direct use of the state. Bismarck, the powerful and victorious chancellor of Germany, took a certain amount of interest in Lassalle and even initiated written correspondence with him. The letters remained unknown and were not published until 1928. It is easy to imagine how furious Marx would have been if he had learned about the correspondence.[64]

After Lassalle's death, other forces took over his party. A newspaper named *Der Sozial-Demokrat* appeared as a party organ. Its editor-in-chief was named Johann Baptist von Schweitzer, a young man from a good family. Schweitzer tried to get Marx and Engels as contributors. Marx actually contributed a few articles, but soon became deeply displeased with the newspaper and with Schweitzer. One of the reasons was that Schweitzer, like Lassalle earlier, turned out to be rather positive not only towards Prussia but also to Bismarck.

Schweitzer's most immediate opponents, however, were in Germany. One of the most important was Wilhelm Liebknecht, a close acquaintance of the Marx family during his years as a young refugee in London and now busy supporting himself as a journalist, with varying success. He had tried contributing to Schweitzer's newspaper at one time, but the contradictions became too great. In Leipzig, Liebknecht met August Bebel, a young carpenter who had given himself over to journalism and politics, and they both founded the Sächsische Volkspartei (People's Party of Saxony), in which socialists and liberals agreed on their anti-Prussian convictions.[65] But the ideological framework soon became too vague for both socialists, who in 1869 created Germany's second social democratic party, *Die sozialdemokratische Partei Deutschlands* (The Social Democratic Party of Germany) in the Thuringian city of Eisenach. The party was more openly revolutionary than Lassalle's and Schweitzer's, and Liebknecht was forced to spend several years in prison.

Ideologically, Liebknecht and Bebel stood closer to Marx than Lassalle or Schweitzer. But both Marx and Engels were constantly displeased, particularly with Liebknecht who they often branded as slow-witted and lacking in judgement. In his role as the chief spokesman for the International, Marx also tried to have diplomatically acceptable relations with both German parties, even if it was only Liebknecht and Bebel who were formally linked to the organization.

By the end of the 1860s, the International had become a force to reckon with in Germany. Whereas Schweitzer had once spoken with contempt about 'the antiquated Marxist clique', Marx's influence grew dramatically during the victorious years of the International. Roger P. Morgan points out that the person who above all contributed to its success was Johann Philipp Becker, who lived in Switzerland, it is true, but was untiring and successful in bringing forth new members in Germany as well.[66]

At that time, the political landscape was also changing dramatically. The tactic of Lassalle and his party – seeking cooperation with the landowning class – was rendered defunct when the liberals allied themselves with Bismarck's conservative grouping during Prussia's years of victory in the 1860s. As representatives of the working class, both social democratic parties now stood alone. After the Paris Commune, repression became palpably more severe in the now-unified German Reich. Bebel ended up in prison, as did Liebknecht.

Unifying both parties came naturally in this awkward situation, and this was achieved during a conference in 1875 in Gotha, a city in Thuringia. Marx wrote a temperamental criticism of the proposed unified party programme. His *Critique of the Gotha Programme* is one of his most important and most influential political texts. He did not send the text to Liebknecht – with whom he was extremely displeased at that point in time – but to Wilhelm Bracke, another person who was ideologically close. In the furious letter that accompanied it, he was horrified that he and Engels were generally regarded as the spiritual fathers of the German Social Democrats. If the programme became reality, he and his friend would publicly 'entirely dissociate ourselves from said programme'.

Engels had already sent critical letters on the draft programme to both Wilhelm Bracke and August Bebel. He anticipated some of Marx's critical points in it but only some of them; there is no counterpart to Marx's heavy criticism based in the social sciences. It is also worth knowing that he talked about 'our party' – that is, the party that Marx said they were both so far away from.[67]

But it was Engels who much later – in 1891 – published Marx's critique of the Gotha programme. By then, it would soon be time for a new programme for the large, extraordinarily successful German Social Democratic Party. The programme they agreed on in Erfurt in 1891 became the most palpably Marx-inspired in the party's history. But by that time, Marx was already dead. In 1875, the unpublished document that Marx sent to Bracke was not given much importance. Two parties were to be united in Gotha, and Marx's criticism did not have the effect on that work he undoubtedly expected. Nor did he put his threat of a public repudiation into effect.[68]

Critique of the Gotha Programme

The Marx who criticized the Gotha programme is very different from the Marx who wrote the most important documents of the International. In the latter, he sought to bridge antagonisms; here, he was prepared for confrontation. The International no longer existed, and now his most important goal was to clean everything reminiscent of Ferdinand Lassalle's ideas out of German social democracy. Moreover, both he and his audience were still living in the shadow of the Commune. The Commune had given him and many others new ideas of what was politically possible and desirable. After the era of repression in the 1850s and of new hopes in the 1860s came the Commune, born in a vacuum of power and crushed by merciless opponents. Where once a brighter path towards a classless society seemed to open up, only confrontation now remained.

It was in this spirit that Marx set about critiquing the Gotha programme. It was an almost furious reckoning. It began as a lecture in the world of ideas of *Capital*. 'Labour is the source of all wealth and all culture,' the authors of the programme stated. No, Marx said, *nature* is just as much a source of the use values that people live on. Labour itself is the expression of a natural force. The conception of the '*supernatural creative power*' of labour is bourgeois.

Here, Marx's criticism is independent of varying political conjunctures, touching on the often overlooked core itself of the theoretical structure of *Capital*. Humanity is a part of nature; society and its culture develop out of nature. Class society creates a gap between society and its source. Society appears as something supernatural, something standing over nature: humanity can own the nature from which it has sprung. The goal is to bridge the gap; this requires a grand development of the productive forces of labour and the workers' collective striving for a society of free associations.

In the rest of the text, Marx goes through the proposed programme line by line, noting embarrassing trivialities, questionable inferences, and fine truths. His tone increases markedly as soon as he sees Lassalle's surviving thoughts behind the text. He angrily objected to Lassalle's phrase '*unverkürzter Arbeitsertrag*' – undiminished proceeds of labour – which he found incompatible with all reasonable economic thinking. In addition, the idea that the worker should receive the full value in wages of what their labour produced is unrealistic. One part of it necessarily had to go to administrative costs, another to schools and healthcare and so on, a third to those who cannot work at all or those who can no longer work.

Marx also detects the remainder of Lassalle's and his party's ideas in the proposal that the working class should ally with the landowners. Only the capitalists were pointed out as opponents.

The question of how Marx views morals is an interesting one. There is the trace of a declaration in what he says about justice. The programme's proposal talks about 'equitable allocation'. But what is equitable allocation under the prevailing method of production? Marx asked himself. Is such allocation not a chimera when certain classes possess economic power over production? It will be otherwise only in a society where class power is broken. But then, justice would not mean that everyone gets the exact same compensation for their labour. Some people are physically or intellectually superior to others, but these natural differences should not single out the less fortunate for discrimination. Some people are married, others are not. Some have more children than others.

Marx distinguished between a lower and a higher stage under communism. Only in the higher stage are individuals no longer subordinate to the division of labour. The antithesis between physical and intellectual labour is abolished, and individuals are equal to their productive forces. 'Only then can the narrow horizon of bourgeois right be crossed in its entirety, and society inscribe on its banners: From each according to his abilities, to each according to his needs.' In short, it is only in such a society that true justice can prevail.

This is the culmination of the critique – what follows after seems like marginal notes in comparison. Marx notes a slipshod use of the term 'reactionary mass'. The bourgeoisie was and is a revolutionary class; who would dare cry out to craftsmen, minor industrialists, and farmers that they were a reactionary mass?

Another criticism deals with the tension between nation and internationalism. Marx says that the class struggle is only national in its form, whereas it is international in its content. That is: its immediate targets of attack are the class relations of its own nation, but the same struggle must take place in each individual country.

Marx has a particular eye for the 'iron law of wages' – Ricardo's concept that he still embraced in the *Manifesto*. Now, he unhesitatingly rejects it.

Even more hateful to him are the hopes that Lassalle and his followers placed in a neutral state. Marx's views of the existing state were dark. Freedom cannot be sought there, but consists in the state being transformed from a controlling body to a subordinate one.

The road to freedom passes through '*the revolutionary dictatorship of the proletariat*'. The concept of the dictatorship of the proletariat thus turns up again here. Between 1850 and the Paris Commune, it was conspicuous by its absence in everything he wrote. It did not disappear by chance, nor was it by chance that it came back in a situation reminiscent of the revolutions of 1848–49. It could still be of use in 1875.

Marx had expressed the sentiment many times that universal and equal suffrage was an important step on the path towards another society. Now he lessened its significance: it already existed in Switzerland and the United States, he said. It was a truth with a large modification. At the time Marx wrote that, Switzerland had a very particular type of democracy, and in the United States it would be a long time before all men (for example, Native Americans and African Americans) could vote in general elections. Women were given the right to vote in 1920 in the United States, and in Switzerland only in 1971.

Marx placed less confidence here in the possibility of changing society via the ballot box than he did during his years in the International. The Paris Commune and Bismarck's hardening grip over German politics had given him new ideas. But the understanding he expressed precisely in his critique of the Gotha programme was not set in stone, either.

The text on the Gotha programme ends with a sentence in Latin: *Dixi et salvavi animam meam* (I have spoken and saved my soul). This origin is found in the Bible, more specifically in Ezekiel 3:19; it is known in the wording Marx used from the Roman Catholic Bible. Marx had unburdened his political conscience.[69]

His political influence did not increase in Germany after the criticism; if anything, it decreased. When both he and Engels left the party, not even Liebknecht felt that they both could play a role any longer for its continued development.[70]

The development of the new, united Social Democratic Party underwent a strange trajectory. In 1878, Bismarck forced through his 'Anti-Socialist Law' (or, as it was officially named, *Gesetz gegen die gemeingefährlichen Bestrebungen der Sozialdemokratie*, the Law against the public danger of Social Democratic endeavours). The law, in force between 1878 and 1890, simply banned the party and with it all socialist propaganda as well. Even so, individual Social Democrats could be elected to governing bodies. Their influence grew, even during the years the law was in force. It was a matter of pride for Bismarck that the law remained on the books, but his defence had fateful consequences for himself; this law more than anything contributed to him being forced to leave his post as chancellor. It was rejected with him, and German social democracy emerged even stronger from its struggle for recognition. In 1890, the party was more organized than any other political party up to that point, and its election results were brilliant.[71] Engels realized early on that if anything, the prohibition would strengthen the cause of the workers in Germany. The Anti-Socialist Law will favour us, he declared in 1879. 'It will complete the revolutionary education of the German workers.'[72]

Marx would never live to see whether Engels had been right in his predictions. As we have seen, he devoted himself in his final years to studies in a number of different fields, and what he made public was limited to various brief corrections and forewords to new editions. He rebuked a seriously erroneous history of the International; authored a brief foreword to a new edition of his reckoning with Proudhon, *The Poverty of Philosophy*; worked up a 'Workers' Questionnaire' for a French socialist periodical; and he and Engels together wrote a series of short articles in which Engels's typical style shows through.[73] During these years, Marx's health worsened, at the same time that he was once again in full swing testing the foundations for his social theory. In politics, there was above all one area that occupied his thoughts: developments in Russia.

The Russian Road

Marx did not publish much at the end of his life. After the French version of *Capital* in 1875, it was not much more than sporadic

trifles. The rumour that he had given up or left all the responsibility to Engels began to stick. Franz Mehring, who published
the first full-scale biography of Marx in 1918, felt called upon
to emphasize that his subject did remain continuously active up
until the end. This did not prevent David Riazanov, the untiring
publisher of Marx's and Engels's writings, to assert in his double
biography of both men that from 1873 Marx was in such a bad
way that he was only capable of devoting himself to his always
incomplete *Capital* project. The idea turns up even later, at least
in the English literature. David McLellan circulated it in his biography from 1973. Even Tristram Hunt fell victim to the same idea
in his book on Engels from 2009; Gareth Stedman Jones does the
same in his biography of Marx.[74]

On the contrary, the thousands of pages of excerpts and other
notes that Marx produced at the end of his life testify to his inexhaustible energy. A careful study of these shows that he was busy
re-examining much of what he had previously concluded, and in
particular, broadening his horizons.

Several outstanding specialists have brought up the idea of
speaking about 'the late Marx' of the 1870s and early 1880s,
in contrast to 'the young Marx' before 1850 and 'the mature
Marx' of the 1850s and 1860s. Above all, Polish-British sociologist Teodor Shanin and Japanese historian Haruki Wada have
advanced this idea. Wada developed it in a monograph in Japanese, later providing a summary in the 1983 anthology *Late
Marx and the Russian Road*, which Shanin edited. Shanin himself
contributed an article on the subject; two British sociologists,
Derek Sayer and Philip Corrigan, agree with the main thesis but
also want to accurately define it.[75]

What is there to say about this? The division itself into distinct
periods seems exaggerated to me. It is reminiscent of what music
historians usually say about Beethoven and literary historians
about Strindberg. Unity can be glimpsed behind the boundaries
drawn up.

It is easy to recognize Marx in everything he wrote, from the
1840s to the 1880s; at the same time, he was an author and
thinker who constantly re-examined his theses. This is seen most
clearly as regards politics. The 'late Marx' that Wada and Shanin

speak about is in many respects Marx after the Paris Commune of 1871. But there is yet another principal moment of change: the interest in things Russian.

Ever since his youth, Marx had seen the Russia of the tsars as the great menace. Early on, it is true, he had got to know radical Russian emigrants who represented an entirely different Russia. But it was only when some of these exiles decided to translate *Capital* into their own language that his interest in Russian culture and Russian society awakened in earnest. When one of his friends, Nikolai Danielson, sent him a book in Russian by one N. Flerovsky about the working class in Russia, he became so interested that he decided to teach himself Russian. After a hectic period of learning he could spell out Flerovsky's text, and he was impressed by it.[76]

His interest in Russia would soon increase further; the most important inspiration came from the Paris Commune. By reading additional Russian literature – especially texts by Nikolai Chernyshevsky, the most outstanding author and intellectual of the time – he came in contact with the powerful Russian political current called *narodniki*, or 'Friends of the People'. (The name comes from *narod*, the Russian word for 'people'.) It was, as Teodor Shanin points out, a very broad movement, with everyone from revolutionary terrorists to peaceful philanthropists.[77]

Chernyshevsky belonged to the radical wing and was its most influential author. The tsarist regime found him entirely too dangerous and had jailed him in the 1860s. As a prisoner, he wrote his most read and admired work: *What is to be Done?*, a didactic novel that played an enormous role in his home country. But the texts by Chernyshevsky that Marx was above all influenced by were on the one hand an article on the Russian peasant commune (*obshchina*) and on the other a few fictional letters that dealt partially with the same subject.

In these texts, Chernyshevsky declared that he was a follower of neither Schelling's nor Hegel's systems, but that he had learned from the theses of these philosophers that the highest form of development resembled the first, original stage more than the intermediate ones. Chernyshevsky applied this thesis to Russian developments. Critics usually say that the peasant community, characterized by common ownership, is primitive in relation to the private ownership of land. But is there not another form that is higher than private ownership, a form that repeats important elements in the original *obshchina*?[78]

It is this idea that took hold of Marx. The immediate background to his fascination lay in his conviction that the Commune of 1871 represented a higher social form than the one that capitalism had produced. He drew additional inspiration from the literature by Lewis H. Morgan and others on primitive societies, from which he enthusiastically composed excerpts.

He had reason to attempt to formulate his understanding a few times on issues that concerned the future of Russia. Part of it was that his name had become well known in radical Russian circles through the translation of *Capital*. In 1877, the Russian periodical *Otechestvennye zapiski* (Notes from the Homeland) had commented on the book, and Marx found reason to write a clarification in which he questioned whether Russia was following the Western European pattern of development. He never completed the text; Engels found it among the piles of manuscripts he went through after Marx's death.[79]

There were also several longer drafts of a letter to the Russian revolutionary Vera Zasulich, who was in exile in Switzerland after having carried out an assassination attempt in St Petersburg. Zasulich had been deeply influenced by *Capital*, but had got into discussions with a number of other Russians about what Marx's writing could mean for the future of Russia. Her opponents, who called themselves Marxists, maintained that Russia necessarily had to go through a capitalist stage for the country to achieve a classless society. As proof, they found in Marx such things as a quote in *Capital* that England had undergone development and other countries had to follow.[80]

Marx took Zasulich's questions very seriously. He wrote three longer drafts as a response but discarded them all and only sent a fourth, significantly shorter one. One central piece of information was common for all the drafts: the quote from *Capital* that he cited in the draft to *Otechestvennye zapiski* only said that the West European countries were fated to go through the same development as Great Britain. He thus did not comment there about the future of Russia.

On the other hand, in only one of the drafts – the one he wrote first – did he take up Zasulich's reference to some Russians that saw themselves as Marxists. 'The Russian "Marxists" of whom you speak are quite unknown to me,' he said, with deprecating quotation marks around the term 'Marxist'. The Russians he knew had opinions directly opposed to theirs, he assured her. There was no inevitable dissolution of common peasant property in Russia, not even for Marx himself.

In the typical Russian village, the *obshchina*, property was held partially in common. Such ownership was threatened when capitalism began to permeate Russia. But the development was not inexorable, Marx assured her.

In all four drafts, Marx argued against a deterministic understanding of Russian developments. Only the wording was different; Marx was evidently striving to find the right formulations to express his standpoint. He emphasized that Russia did not need to go through the same technological development as western Europe. Steam power had a long history before it was able to transform industry and communications in Western Europe, but now it was available to be put to immediate use in Russia as well. It was thus with all types of technology. Russia should simply be able to hop over the development that marked Western Europe.

But Marx's reasoning, which varied from draft to draft, also contains other elements. In the 'first' draft (which probably was written as number two in order), he also cites Lewis H. Morgan's theses on 'primitive societies', quoting his words that archaic forms of society were reborn in more advanced societies. Here, an entirely different pattern is cited. Humanity's path led from homogeneous societies through splits and conflict back to a unity that is more complex and advanced than the first one. It is Hegel's dialectic that ultimately seems to be guiding his thoughts, although it is Morgan he cites.

In the next breath, Marx emphasized that knowledge about the dissolution of early societies is extremely imperfect and sketchy. Those familiar with the subject knew that it was often war that tore communities to pieces. But certain forms of common ownership turned out to be more viable than others. Marx recalled that in his own home districts outside Trier (that is, Hunsrück), archaic forms characterized by large common lands had survived up to the present time.

Clarity can only be obtained from this uneven picture if it is regarded purely theoretically and normal conditions of life are reckoned with. The requirement Marx imposed is rather obvious: all the conformities to laws that science can establish are valid under certain ideal circumstances.

The crucial factor with Russian village communities is that, unlike older societies with common ownership, they are not built on blood ties. It thus constitutes a higher form, which he designates *communes agricoles* – agricultural communities or, if you like, agricultural communes. Within this form, circumstances can cause great variations.

Marx also pointed out that Russia was suited to this form through the quality of its soil. He was quite simply optimistic about the possibility of developing it to a higher level. But, he said by way of conclusion, this required a Russian revolution.

So ends the longest draft of his response. But he obviously was not satisfied with it, and it is easy to understand why: he took up entirely too many threads, and the quote from Morgan opened up a historical and philosophical discussion whereas the reasoning about the purely theoretical standpoint faces towards scientific theory.

He thus made a third attempt, concentrating there on different variations of primitive societies. He set the Russian and the German village communities against each other. The German form did not yet exist at the time of Julius Caesar. It is not known when it arose, but Marx called it medieval and also brought out his home districts as a robust example. What was new, on the other hand, was that he emphasized that there was attention between the common and the private and agricultural communes, and that this tension could lead to their dissolution. But this was not an inevitable development. He pointed to different variations in Russia, but broke off abruptly in mid-sentence.[81]

Clearly, the reasoning had become too much for him. An investigation into the various types of simple societies with large amounts of common ownership would require an entire dissertation, and Marx was not ready to write that. He thus satisfied himself with a much shorter, fourth version in which he began by explaining that he had delayed his response (it had been twenty days) because he had been struck with an illness that he had periodically suffered from for over ten years. That was why he could not write anything intended for publication. He just established, once again, the fact that in *Capital* he only expressed an opinion on Western Europe and gave no proof either for or against the viability of the village community. On the other hand, he had gathered material from original sources that convinced him that the village community was the 'point of support for Russia's social rebirth'.[82]

It is thus the later material that he was trying to bring to the fore in the three drafts, but without having succeeded. Marx was, and remained, the master of the unfinished work.

After Marx died, Engels wanted to have the drafts published, as well as the fragment intended for *Otechestvennye zapiski*. But the Russians concerned delayed the process, and a Russian translation was published only in 1886. It roused differing feelings. Many who saw themselves as carrying Marx's line further, including Lenin, tried to minimize the significance of the letter. David Riazanov, the scholarly publisher of Marx's and Engels's writings, even maintained that texts testified to Marx's intellectual capacity having declined.

Haruki Wada asserts that the negative reactions were early examples of a powerful tendency to protect their own image of Marxism against Marx's own words.[83] It is easy to agree with him. The drafts do not testify to any reduced intellectual vitality, but surely to an exciting new orientation to a large complex of problems that was difficult to survey.

The Forms of Politics

On the whole, Marx's fundamental social theory had retained its identity since the mid-1840s. His political understanding, on the other hand, underwent several sudden changes, especially from the 1850s up until his death.

Considering the essential features of his thinking, this change-ability is hardly surprising. The distinction between the *content* of the society and its *form* is crucial. The content is the interaction between the forces and the relations of production. In Marx's time, it was thus the relationship between the productivity of labour on the one hand, and the struggle between capitalists and workers on the other. Politics, on the other hand, was one form this content took. Form is extraordinarily important; it is there that a social class can change its conditions in competition with other classes. But, at the same time, the political stage is changeable. Opportunities open and close. Sometimes periods of calm prevail; the established power is unchallenged. But new possibilities in the face of the future crop up, and then it is a matter of seizing the day.

Marx was thoroughly optimistic about the possibility of decisive changes. He was not a meek and cautious commentator; on the contrary, he was quick to point out the new and epochal. So it was under the revolutionary years of 1848–49, so it was when the British Workers' Parliament assembled in 1854, and so it was in the face of the economic crisis that gathered over Europe after the mid-1850s. He was hesitant before the International at first, but gradually became increasingly hopeful in the face of the opportunities to assemble the international workers' movement for a decisive showdown with capitalists and landowners. We saw how, during the Franco-Prussian War of 1870–71, he revealed uneasiness about creating a new Paris Commune on the model of 1792. But once the Commune existed, he saw not the past but the future in it. Contact with the Russian *narodniki* got him to develop ideas on another path towards the society of the future than the one that ran through Western European capitalism.

This time as well, his hopes for revolutionary change got support from a concrete political event. When war broke out between Russia and Turkey he was sure that the Turks – 'the gallant Turks' – would be victorious. He wrote to his friend Sorge that this victory would trigger a revolution in Russia. He said that he himself had carefully studied official and unofficial sources that his friends in St Petersburg had let him acquaint himself with, which is why he knew that the country was already 'in a state of decomposition' before the war.[84]

When it turned out that, despite his conjecture, Russia came out of the war victorious and the regime could gather its forces in order to take the wind out of the radical opposition, Marx did not give up. It was then that he composed his drafts, borne by unmistakable optimism, to Zasulich.

The lines of bright optimism are bordered by an equally long series of dark disappointments. The disappointments made him angry rather than sorrowful. There was one disappointment that probably vexed him more than any other: the development of Great Britain. British trade union members had got him to involve himself in the International, and during the movement's years of success he believed that the British working class was now ready for revolution. But nothing came of it; everything ended in compromises. At the very end of his life, just before Christmas 1882, he wrote to his daughter Laura that he was delighted by the success of his theory in Russia, which was, with England, the guarantor of the old society.[85] England and Russia were now placed on the same level, and his hope was in Russia.

Marx often spoke about revolution, but he was critical of those who had that word on their lips at all times. In the same letter to his daughter Laura, he praised what her husband Paul had recently written. Previously, he had been repulsed by 'certain ultra-revolutionary turns of phrase' that were best left to the anarchists. Marx's own view on revolutions was rather simple. Like the bourgeoisie once did, only the working class itself can break its chains. It only has to be equipped with a proper theory. But revolutionary opportunities are just that – opportunities – characterized by chance.

In discussions on the similarities and differences between Marx and Engels, it is often said that Engels was marked to a greater degree than Marx by the strong evolutionism of the nineteenth century. In his opinion, society developed fundamentally in the same way as nature did. Marx, on the other hand, emphasized more the significance of upheavals.

Marx typically imagined an uninterrupted evolution – a constant increase – of productive forces under capitalism, whereas, on the contrary, the capitalist method of production itself is conservative.

One day, this method of production would burst, but his basic theory – the theory in *Capital* – does not say when this will take place. There is a reason he was entirely too optimistic as soon as signs of a revolutionary development could be anticipated. He constantly believed that the limit had been reached.

The most fruitful Marx research of the last two decades – which concentrated on the German '*neue Marx-Lektüre*' (new Marx reading) and the American *Temporal single-system interpretation*, or TSSI (see above, p. 448) but also blossomed in France, perhaps chiefly through Étienne Balibar – asserts that the crucial point in Marx's theory is the relations of production, rather than the forces of production.[86] The gap between Marx's and Engels's ideas has thus been emphasized more than previously. Engels was undoubtedly a man of the productive forces, and this applied even more to the next generation of followers with Karl Kautsky at their head. The similarity between the theories of Darwin and Marx was emphasized again and again, at the price of both being depicted in a vulgarized and superficial manner.

The difference between Marx and Engels is especially important in the area of politics. Marx spoke about the state needing to be transformed, becoming only an administrative unit over the long term. Engels, on the other hand, made use of metaphors such as the state 'withering away' or 'dying'. People seemed to become only the instruments of society's own natural processes.

The boundary between species development and humanity's historical development is more clearly marked in Marx than in Engels.[87] At the same time, the difference should not be exaggerated. It is not even certain that Marx and Engels themselves were fully aware of it. In their mutual correspondence, Marx spoke incessantly about 'our theory'.

We should remember that there was for a long time a certain degree of confusion regarding the content of the terms *socialism* and *communism*. This confusion did not lessen during the 1860s and 1870s.

Wolfgang Schieder makes an important observation in his book about Marx as a politician. In 1842, German political scientist Lorenz von Stein published his pioneering work *Sozialismus und Kommunismus des heutigen Frankreichs*, in which he spoke about socialism as a science of society. Marx took over this usage early on, and did not change it when he had heavily critical viewpoints, for example of what he called utopian socialism. When Engels began talking about his and Marx's theory as *scientific* social-ism, he thus deviated from Marx's original conception, Schieder says. He is thinking of Engels's works *Anti-Dühring* and *Die Entwicklung des Sozialismus von der Utopie zur Wissenschaft* (*Socialism: Scientific and Utopian*, translated by Edward Aveling). But Marx actually wrote a foreword to the French translation of the latter work, in which he spoke about 'what might be termed an *introduction to scientific socialism*'.[88]

This is hardly a question of a landslide in Marx's linguistic usage. On the one hand, he is referring to a scientific discussion in which different interpretations are freely contrasted with each other, and Fourier, Saint-Simon, Proudhon, and Marx himself give their interpretations free rein. On the other hand, he has in mind what he (for the time being) sees as true, and here he agrees with his own and Engels's interpretation. There is nothing strange in this. It only becomes odd when the term 'scientific socialism' hardens into a dogma with which other interpretations – regard-less of how well founded they may be – are forcibly opposed.

Schieder notes in passing that in some early writings, the term *communism* signifies a *movement*, 'eine Bewegung', but draws no conclusions from this.[89] But is it not helpful to imagine that socialism signified the doctrine or theory itself, and communism the party that would gather the workers behind it? No, the usage was not so unambiguous. For Marx (and not only for him!) communism also became the term for a certain type of society.

Starting with the Paris Commune, it became completely so. As we have seen, Marx said that the Commune represented 'pure communism' (above, p. 559), and he took a few additional steps in the same direction in his criticism of the Gotha programme a few years later. There, he differentiated between a higher and lower stage of communism; the harmonic balance between peo-ple's abilities and their needs is reached only in the higher stage.

This is the statement that his followers made the starting point for rigidly dogmatic further elaboration. The first stage of com-munism was dubbed socialism, and only the second one simply communism. In the Soviet Union, this became a profitable basis for all kinds of schematism. But that is a later story.

The newcomer to the flora of concepts, which came into existence after the revolutions of 1848–49, is the concept of *social democracy*. Its country of origin is Germany; from there, it spread above all to the Nordic countries and Russia. The word 'democracy' retains its radical character of popular governance, in which the people – the great mass – are understood in contrast to the elite holding power. It is still assumed by most that universal and equal suffrage would mean that the capitalists as well as the landowning aristocracy would be swept from power if the majority actually had the last word.

The word 'socialism' retained its ambiguity, but normally meant that the conditions of ownership would be radically changed. In its radical interpretation, ownership of the means of production – land and capital – would be subjected to joint administration under democratic control.

But from the very beginning, social democracy took different forms. The party that Lassalle founded was thus social democratic; as will be remembered, the party newspaper was called *Der Sozial-Demokrat*. Like his early followers, Lassalle saw a possibility for social democracy in an alliance with the landowners against the capitalists. The competing party founded by August Bebel and Wilhelm Liebknecht already had the word 'social democracy' in its name; when both parties united at the conference in Gotha, this became the joint term that later marched triumphantly throughout northern Europe. Battles soon flared up within the party in Germany over whether a revolution was a necessary condition for achieving the desirable type of society; in Russia, the party split into two competing tendencies, the Mensheviks and the Bolsheviks. But this is also a later story.

As far as is known, Marx did not describe himself as a social democrat. But nonetheless, the united Social Democratic Party in Germany became 'our party' for him and Engels. With his merciless criticism, he tried to turn it in the right direction.[90]

After the interlude of the International, Marx would again more wholeheartedly express his opinion that the revolution was a necessary path towards a classless society. But he did not perceive the

revolution primarily as a bloody reckoning; rather, as the breakthrough for a new social order. Once this was established, the
former ruling powers would certainly attempt to retake the position they had lost; casualties would then be unavoidable. Engels,
the old military man, was significantly more bellicose in his way
of talking about revolutions.

14

Statues, Malicious Portraits, and the Work

A book that we read for the first time develops unpredictably, like life itself. But upon rereading, the text steers purposefully towards its conclusion. The reader already knows how it goes; the first lines herald the last ones. This is also how we regard the person who has died. In the child, we anticipate the sum total of their life. Every step in their development is preparation for what is to come.

In his autobiography *Words*, Jean-Paul Sartre wrote a few memorable lines on the matter:

> In the drawing-rooms of Arras, a cold, simpering young lawyer is carrying his head under his arm because he is the late Robespierre; blood is dripping from it but does not stain the rug; not one of the guests notice it, whereas we see nothing else; five years will go by before it rolls into the basket, yet there it is, cut off, uttering gallant remarks despite its hanging jaw.[1]

The same applies to Karl Marx. But it is perhaps not the dead Marx at his writing desk, white-bearded and consumed by illness, that obscures the view of his life and work. If anything, he disappears behind his colossal horde of interpreters and followers – and even more behind the political parties and states that quoted him and his writings. Where is the living Marx, under this crowd?

It is hoped that a part of the answer has emerged in the preceding chapters. But now we must consider the part of his history

that followed his death, when he remained a constant presence –
beloved and canonized, but also hated and defamed, and often
misunderstood – among both admirers and slanderers.

Since Marx's influence is so enormous, this presentation must
necessarily be rather a number of short paragraphs about the
innumerable branches that are called the history of Marxism.
A full-scale presentation would require several volumes. Such
volumes already exist, although all of them came to be during
the period when the Soviet Union still existed. The most extensive
of these is the three-volume work by Polish-British philosopher
Leszek Kołakowski, published in English translation in 1978 as
Main Currents of Marxism. It is a very knowledgeable work,
marked by the author's bitter experiences of Polish communism.
As in his other great works, Kołakowski uses an organic metaphor
to understand the development of an ideological phenomenon:
first budding, then flowering, and finally withering away. Contemporary Marxism, he argues, is dying.[2]

Predrag Vranicki develops another view in his 1972–74 work,
Geschichte des Marxismus. Vranicki lived in Yugoslavia (specifically, what is today Croatia) and was part of the regime-critical
Praxis group, which sought to renovate Marxist theory in their
home country. His history breathes not only dissatisfaction with
the condition of things, but also a certain degree of optimism
about the future of Marxism.[3]

More limited thematically and in number of pages, but important in its effort, is Perry Anderson's 1976 book *Considerations
on Western Marxism*. Anderson, a British *Trotskyist* thinker, sees
the various Marx-inspired theories that developed above all in
Western Europe as fundamentally idealistic: ideas, not political
realities, are bandied about.[4]

In the brief version of the history of Marxism that follows here,
the view is directed at how later interpreters and followers relate
to Marx and his work. This summary presentation will serve to
provide a basis for the final question of how Marx today, more
than a quarter-century after the fall of the Berlin Wall, appears in
light of all that has been done and written with either actual or
alleged inspiration from him.

The Road from Highgate to the Winter Palace

It was Engels who gave the speech on the day in March 1883 when Marx was buried in Highgate Cemetery in North London. The group at his graveside was not a large one. Eleanor Marx was there, of course, but not her sister Laura. On the other hand, Laura's husband Paul Lafargue was there, as well as Charles Longuet, the husband of the recently deceased Jennychen. Lenchen Demuth was there, but not her son Freddy. Friedrich Lessner, who had followed Marx the whole way from *Neue Rheinische Zeitung* to London and remained one of his closest confidants, was among the group of mourners, as was another veteran of the 1840s, Georg Lochner. Wilhelm Liebknecht represented the German Social Democrats. Two outstanding natural scientists, both equally convinced of the greatness of Marx's social theory, paid him the final honours: the chemist Carl Schorlemmer and the biologist Ray Lankester. Gottlieb Lemke, one of the many London Germans, laid a wreath with a red band from the party newspaper *Der Sozialdemokrat* and from the German education association for whom Marx had meant so much.

There were not many who heard Engels speak. We do not know exactly what he said. On the one hand, he left behind a draft: on the other hand, he wrote himself in *Der Sozialdemokrat* that he gave a speech 'something like' the one that was being printed. Both texts deviate from each other greatly. Engels probably spoke rather freely, but with one eye on his draft.

In any case, he used no small words about his friend. Marx was placed alongside Darwin, he had revolutionized science both through his views on the decisive motive forces of history and with his theory on the laws of development of capitalism, and he had also made independent contributions in other areas of knowledge as well. But his scientific work was not simply something for itself; in his eyes, science was a force that could change society and he had himself contributed to this social change through both his political work and his journalistic activities.

That was why he had also become the most hated man of his time. Except when it was absolutely necessary to defend himself, he treated all these expressions of loathing like spiderwebs he could easily brush aside. And now that he was dead, he was mourned by millions of colleagues from Siberia to California. He also had many opponents, but no personal enemies.

Greetings from Russian social democrats and French and Spanish socialists were read at the graveside, and finally Liebknecht gave a speech in which he singled out Marx not only as a great social scientist but also as the creator of both German social democracy and the International Workingmen's Association.[5]

The latter were statements that Marx himself would have repudiated. But now he no longer had any say, and a monument could be raised over him – then only in words, but later also in stone. With few exceptions, the statues in stone or metal belong to the Soviet era, usually depicting Mark as a powerful, self-confident fighter gazing resolutely into the future. Sometimes he is alone, sometimes he is with Engels, but the style – as with statues of Lenin and other revolutionaries – is heroic.

Once Marx was dead, the battle over the correct interpretation of what he said and wrote began in earnest. In the beginning, there were two people who were close to him that had the greatest authority. One was of course Engels; the other Marx's youngest daughter, Eleanor. They were both close to each other; Engels had watched Eleanor grow up and had remained the family's closest friend and support. But they had somewhat different ideas of how Karl Marx's intellectual legacy should be handled. There is at least one picture of this divergence that Eleanor Marx's latest biographer, Rachel Holmes, depicts.

The Second International was formed on 14 July 1889, the hundredth anniversary of the French Revolution. Engels was the great leading figure in the new movement, and was greeted with ovations at the congresses he was able to take part in before he died in 1895. Eleanor Marx had a strong position that only initially had to do with her kinship with the great Karl. She herself possessed a formidable intellectual capacity and was additionally equipped with a great capacity for work. It was also to her advantage that she spoke perfect German and English from childhood, and taught herself equally perfect French in her youth.

At the Zürich conference of the Second International in 1893,

Margarete Greulich had painted a giant portrait of Karl Marx; under it, Engels gave a brief, eloquent, and highly acclaimed speech about his friend. Eleanor was not completely happy about the idolization of her father. The aging Engels, on the other hand, seems to have had nothing against it.[6]

As we have seen, Marx had defended himself against the designation 'Marxist'. He did not recognize himself in the roughly knocked together theory ascribed to him in both France and Russia. Even his youngest daughter sometimes had to fight against the same vulgarization. During one of her many lecture tours, she encountered a man who explained to her after her speech what her father had actually meant by social democracy. When the man had finally got to his point, Eleanor exclaimed: 'Heaven save Karl Marx from his friends!'[7]

As far as is known, Eleanor never used the term 'Marxism'. But Engels accepted it when it began to be more widely adopted around 1890, as German social democracy was enjoying great electoral success and it became legal to propagandize for the party and its ideas. For a short time, Marxism additionally became a fad among younger people, especially young students and artists. One group, chiefly concentrated in Berlin but spread across Germany, was called *Die Jungen* (The Young).

Die Jungen were active in various ways – politically, scientifically, and artistically. They found unity in Karl Marx. Students played him off against their academic teachers. One of the most prominent, Paul Ernst, wrote much later in his memoirs: 'Going from Schmoller to Marx was like going to heaven.' Gustav von Schmoller was a political economist of the 'historical school', a professor in Berlin and the architect behind Bismarck's welfare programme that was to alleviate the workers' dissatisfaction. It need hardly be said that he stood far from Marx.

Die Jungen played a role in the rapidly growing left press, and took on a leading role in newspapers such as *Volks-Tribüne* (People's Tribune) in Berlin and *Volksstimme* (The People's Voice) in Magdeburg.[8]

But the young enthusiasts who called themselves Marxists had a problem with Marx's view of history. What role did the superstructure, where they themselves intended to work, actually have?

In Engels, they saw an oracle, or least someone better able than anyone else to enter questions on the subject. He thus received a number of letters from young men. The most well-known response he wrote was to Joseph Bloch, a student in Berlin who also made a name for himself as editor of a few socialist publications. It was in the letter to Bloch where Engels pointed out that 'production and reproduction of actual life' was only '*in the final analysis*' the determining moment in the development of society.[9] The determination 'in the final analysis' has caused headaches among his interpreters. Greater clarity can be obtained if it is noted that the same expression occurs in *Anti-Dühring*. There, it was part of a polemic against Eugen Dühring, who had claimed to lay out 'conclusive truth in the final analysis' (*endgültige Wahrheit letzter Instanz*) in the fields of moral philosophy and economy. Dühring's ambition was to turn both moral philosophy and political economy into a type of more complex mechanism. Ethical truths would be as unchangeable as the laws of mechanics.

It may seem strange that Engels took over Dühring's expression 'in the final analysis' in the middle of a polemic with the latter. But he loaded the expression with new content. History (and, for example, ethics with it) is constantly changing, a process we also therefore have insufficient knowledge of. What we can say in general about history is limited to 'platitudes and commonplaces of the sorriest kind – for example, that, generally speaking, men cannot live except by labour; that up to the present they for the most part have been divided into rulers and ruled; that Napoleon died on 5 May 1821, and so on'.[10]

These were words spoken in the heat of battle. Class society is hardly a platitude, in Engels's opinion. But the meaning is clear: his words echo with what both he and Marx said many times previously – at the earliest in *The German Ideology* – namely that the general principles of history that can be established are not a timetable according to which history can be arranged. The real development only emerges in the study of concrete historical material.

This was what he meant in his letter to Bloch. But here, it is not so explanatory. He said that it is often the *form* (he italicized the word) that determines the course of events in historical conflicts;

as we know, the form is the political, legal, and ideological conditions – in fact, even personal circumstances – that can determine
the actual outcome. He referred to Marx's *Eighteenth Brumaire
of Louis Bonaparte*, to *Capital*, and to his own *Anti-Dühring*.

Engels also patiently wrote a number of other responses to
young enthusiasts who wanted clarity on the issue. But his attitude towards the movement was fundamentally negative. The
fact that *Capital* had got a number of new, conscientious readers
played no role. Engels was upset over what he saw as the young
men's conceit.

Otto von Boenigk, a young baron who complained in his
letter about the masses' lack of education, received particularly
harsh treatment. Engels was furious. He could not understand
how Boenigk could say such a thing when German workers had
just displayed their outstanding political maturity in the struggle
against the Anti-Socialist Laws. Arrogance among the 'educated'
was a greater danger. 'We' – that is, the workers' movement – lack
occupational categories such as engineers, agronomists, and architects, to be sure. But the capitalists have been able to buy such
skills, and 'we' can do that as well. Engels continued: 'But apart
from specialists like these, we shall manage very well without the
rest of the "educated" men; e. g. the present heavy influx of lite-
rati and students into the party will be attended with all sorts of
mischief unless those gentry are kept within bounds.'[11]

These were harsh words. His wrath is explained not only by
von Boenigk's pride in his education. There were also more tacti-
cal reasons. *Die Jungen* criticized the Social Democrats for taking
entirely too cautious an attitude in politics. The revolutionary
flame had died down, and the party leadership had adapted itself
to existing German society.

But Engels, like Bebel and Liebknecht, knew that it was now a
question of navigating carefully and not verbally challenging those
governing the country. Bismarck had disappeared, but a more
aggressive nationalism was developing under Kaiser Wilhelm II. A
social democratic movement that directly threatened an uprising
could be the subject of even more brutal repression than the newly
abolished Anti-Socialist Laws. The party programme itself could
indeed be radicalized – which happened at the 1891 congress in

Erfurt, where Marx's *Critique of the Gotha Programme* served as guidance. But fate should not be tempted in practical politics as long as they were at a disadvantage as regards numbers and power.

Incidentally, Engels began his letter to von Boenigk with a confession of gradual development. Socialist society is not created all at once, he explained. It is a continuous process of change. It can be implemented gradually (*graduell*) without difficulty. The communities of production and distribution – that is, cooperatives – that the workers have been able to create and make competitive prove this.

This assurance is far from the revolutionary slogans that *Die Jungen* gave vent to. But if looked at carefully, revolution – and even the dictatorship of the proletariat – can be found in the party programme that Engels would soon successfully propagandize for. On the other hand, he was afraid that Marx's *Critique of the Gotha Programme* would be leaked far too early and become a weapon in the hands of the young enthusiasts. This is how a letter he wrote to Karl Kautsky in December 1890 has to be interpreted. He enclosed the manuscript of Marx's *Critique*, but warned Kautsky to lay low with it for the time being – otherwise it could end up in the wrong hands. He promised to write a few introductory lines to the text himself, but could not say when – his hands were full with letters he had to write first. He was talking about exactly that type of correspondence we just became acquainted with.

It was typical of him to write this to Kautsky. Born in 1854, Karl Kautsky was a few years older than the members of *Die Jungen* but was still a relatively young man. He had precisely the academic background that Engels dismissed in his letter to von Boenigk, but he was an even-tempered person and had won both Marx's and Engels's confidence during a visit to London in 1881. Two years later, he had founded the periodical *Die Neue Zeit* (The New Times), which gradually found a position as the main theoretical organ of German social democracy – in fact, of all of Marxism. It was there that Engels published Marx's *Critique of the Gotha Programme* with an introductory clarification, and it was there that various feuds about the correct direction of Marxism played out.[12]

Kautsky also wrote a series of books that became important for the consolidation of Marxism. The first of them was called *Karl Marx' ökonomische Lehren* (The Economic Doctrines of Karl Marx); it was published in 1887 and became a great success. The thirteenth edition, from 1910, is now on the Internet. In the introduction, Kautsky establishes his thesis that Marx's 'individual doctrines are parts of a firmly constructed system and can only be understood in their context'. We who have followed Marx's lifelong work as researcher and author know that this is as far from the truth as can be imagined. The Marx who is continually on the road towards new horizons becomes here instead a system-builder who carefully joins together bits of his knowledge so that everything fits together, as in a puzzle. The only competent interpreter is the person who takes stock of the puzzle.

Marxism was on the way to becoming an orthodoxy. Orthodoxy both tames young hotheads and revives those who work in thoughtless routine. It is entirely natural that Kautsky took up the task of providing the correct interpretation of the new, radical party programme from Erfurt and responding to the tricky question of how ethics relates to the materialist conception of history.[13]

It is also Kautsky who must step in when his old friend and brother in the party Eduard Bernstein emerges with the demand that Marxism must be revised. According to Bernstein, experience showed that the social revolutions Marx said so much about were not necessary. The working class was already doing better; before it and its own party lay a possible path of constant improvements. Democracy was gaining ground, and through it the working class would come to power as soon as it had gained sufficient 'intellectual maturity' and was equal to economic development. Marxist theory thereby also had to be revised. Bernstein maintained that with his letters (which had been disseminated in party circles), Engels had already changed the theory and that it was a question of going further along the same road. What theory lost in uniformity, it gained as a science.

Bernstein was of the same generation as Kautsky, but had no academic background. After high school, he had made a living as a bank clerk before he gave himself over to social democracy. He had also got to know Marx and Engels personally, and he was and remained a close friend of Kautsky. It was in Kautsky's periodical *Die Neue Zeit* that he published a series of articles on the problems of socialism, which Kautsky encouraged him to develop into a book. The result was the 1899 work *Die Voraussetzungen des Sozialismus* (Evolutionary Socialism).

This 'revisionism battle' continued up until the First World War, with Kautsky and Bernstein as the main combatants. August Bebel, the leader of the party, sided with Kautsky's interpretation; it thus became the official Social Democratic line up until Bebel's death in 1913.[14]

But despite the orthodoxy, the German Social Democratic Party had fundamentally changed. When a militant nationalism gripped people's minds during the new century, the German Social Democratic Party was unresisting, despite all its commitments in the Second International. Only two members of parliament, Rosa Luxemburg and Karl Liebknecht (the son of Wilhelm), voted against the war credits the Kaiser demanded to throw the country into war. The party had revised its line in a more fateful way than Bernstein had intended.

One of the early contributors to Kautsky's *Die Neue Zeit* was the Russian Georgi Plekhanov. He wrote an article on Hegel that Engels found 'ausgezeichnet' (excellent), but which is memorable above all because it was there that the term 'dialectical materialism' was coined. Henceforth it became the name of the philosophy that Engels had drawn up the outlines for.[15]

In dialectical materialism, as it was now being outlined, Marx came ever closer to Darwin. Marx himself said that Darwin's theory was the foundation of his own and Engels's theory, but it also underlined the difference: humanity changed their environment, and thereby themselves, through production. This crucial difference was toned down step by step in the development of what was now being called Marxism. Everything was subject to evolution, species as well as societies. Determinism also took hold all the more firmly. Everything that Marx had said about the play of chance ended up in the background. The future was like a ball of yarn being unravelled, turn after turn. The difference between predictions and appeals was forgotten.

Marxism became dogmatic. This was not only a development in Germany, but in France and the Nordic countries as well, even if the desire to build systems was not as conspicuous there. The first Italian to emerge as a Marxist of some importance was the professor of philosophy Antonio Labriola. He already had a long intellectual development behind him when he became a convinced follower of Marx and Engels. (Incidentally, he exchanged some interesting letters with Engels; only Labriola's letters are preserved, however, and not Engels's.) Labriola avoided dogmatic excesses, could comment critically on far-reaching determinism, and emphasized that Marxism was a philosophy of action, of *praxis*. He thereby heralded the most innovative Italian Marxist, Antonio Gramsci.[16]

But the most decisive development was Russian. Plekhanov long remained the guiding name. Through his proximity to Engels and his contributions to *Die Neue Zeit*, he gained particular authority. It was only much later that one of his followers – Vladimir Ilyich Ulyanov, known as Lenin – would overshadow him.

Lenin's life is so well known that it can be depicted quite summarily: his background was solidly bourgeois; an older brother, Alexander, was active as a revolutionary *narodnik* and was executed when Vladimir was seventeen years old. Vladimir decided to complete his work. He earned a degree in law and became a Marxist, got involved in the Russian Social Democratic Party, was exiled to Siberia and escaped to Western Europe, where – with the brief exception of the first Russian Revolution in 1905 – he remained until 1917 when the Tsar was overthrown.

There were many other Russian social democratic refugees in Western Europe, and it was there that the party's politics were pursued; in Russia their activities had to be strictly underground. There were no former followers of Lassalle or Proudhon among the Russians, nor were there any revisionists. The great majority had a background as *narodniki*, but had now become Marxists. But this harmony was only illusory. Marx's work could be interpreted in various ways, and stress could be laid differently. Above all, it was difficult to talk about a uniform and natural political line in Marx.

The immigrants themselves constituted a variegated collection of people with different images of what a good society should be and what the road there should look like. There were heated clashes of opinion that culminated at the 1903 congress, held in Brussels and London. Lenin led the group that had the majority and were therefore called *Bolsheviks*, whereas their opponents – led by Julius Martov – correspondingly became *Mensheviks*, the representatives of the minority. The most important subject of contention was how the party should be governed. The year previously, in 1902, Lenin had made his position clear with the book *What Is to Be Done?* He argued that a group of intellectuals schooled as professional revolutionaries had to lead party work with a firm hand.[17] This was far from Marx's ideal of the revolution as the act of the working class itself, but better corresponded to the actual Russian situation with the party's leading figures isolated in Western Europe while the people remained under the rule of the Tsar. Even among the *narodniki*, there had been believers that politically devoted intellectuals should lead the masses to their own liberation.

The danger of a party led by a few people holding power was not as obvious in the isolation of exile, even if it was criticized by the Mensheviks as well as by social democrats from other countries. But Lenin argued that it was he and his group who were bringing the inheritance from Marx and Engels into the new century. As we have seen, Marx had no prepared political theory, but could seek openings towards the future in shifting political forms. The same went for Engels. Lenin's theory of the party, however, was firmly constructed.[18]

Marxism was for him a teleological process; step by step, Marx and Engels had revealed reality as it was and he himself could now tear away yet another corner of the veil that hid both nature and society from humanity's gaze. In 1913, he explained in an article titled 'The Three Sources and Three Component Parts of Marxism': 'The Marxist doctrine is omnipotent because it is true.' In addition, it is 'comprehensible and harmonious, and provides men with an integral world outlook'. The Russian original also speaks of 'Marx's teachings', and there Marx thus had to bear the weight of his doctrine alone. But in this brief text, written in an effective lapidary style, Lenin also gives Engels a part of the honour through *Anti-Dühring* and the book on Feuerbach. The end pieces deal with politics, and there Lenin certainly knows that he himself has taken numerous steps beyond both Marx and Engels.[19]

But before Lenin could be content with the completed system, he had been forced to demand a course correction among his closest followers – the Bolsheviks – as well. In 1909, his most important philosophical work, *Materialism and Empirio-Criticism*, was published. The background is an interesting one. Around the turn of the twentieth century, the Austrian physicist and philosopher Ernst Mach (whose surname is now the unit for the speed of sound) had become a thinker who appealed to the young generation of radicals and revolutionaries. It is above all his main philosophical work from 1886, *Beiträge zur Analyse der Empfindungen* (Contributions to the Analysis of Sensations), that made an impression. Mach advocated an extreme form of empiricism that anticipated the logical positivism that distinguished the Vienna Circle, asserting that the only thing that existed was sensory perceptions. From them, we construct both the external world, and the idea of our own ego and what it contains.

With his theory, Mach got into a polemic with Albert Einstein, who embraced a realist theory of knowledge: atoms had a real, independent existence.[20] For Lenin, it was more important that Mach's theses conflicted with the doctrine that Engels had worked out, which contained both a realist theory of knowledge (we can achieve real knowledge of an external world that is independent of us) and an ontological materialism (there are no idealistic magnitudes that are not grounded in some type of substance).

Many young revolutionaries, on the other hand, saw Mach's empiricism as better suited to their cause. In the period around the turn of the twentieth century, reality itself could seem precarious. Europe was teetering on the brink of a great war, commerce was being reshaped with electricity playing a role that was hard to grasp, the economy was concentrating large capital in the banks as never before, art was seeking new forms of expression, and physics and chemistry were undergoing their great fundamental crises that would result in the theory of relativity and quantum physics. Nietzsche was capturing minds on both the left and the

right. Everything seemed undefined, bordering between threatening and hopeful. Realism and materialism did not fit in such a
disorganized reality.

But Lenin wanted to preserve Marxism as Engels had left
it. It particularly aggrieved him that his opponents among the
Mensheviks were more inclined to stick to Engels, while several
of the leading young Bolsheviks followed in Mach's footsteps.
So it was, for example, with Alexander Bogdanov, a polymath
who competed with Lenin for power among the Bolsheviks, and
Anatoly Lunacharsky, who after the revolution would be the
People's Commissar for Education in the Soviet Union. They, and
a number of other Bolsheviks, assembled at a conference that
resulted in a document in which they attempted to unite Marx
and Mach.

It can be seen from Lenin's correspondence how he tried to
gather his forces for a counterattack. The great deathblow would
be *Materialism and Empirio-Criticism*, in which above all Engels
was set against Mach and where his opponents were castigated
in more than 300 pages. The image of a uniform Marxist outlook
is constructed here, and dialectical materialism constitutes the
very foundation for Lenin's theories on society, on capitalism,
and on socialism. Modify the foundation, and the whole construction falls.[21]

There are two reasons for Lenin's ardour. On the one hand, he
had to compete with the Marxist system that Karl Kautsky had
already constructed. Lenin was not at all as much of an evolu-
tionist and Darwinist as Kautsky; revolutionary leaps were more
important to him. But the most important difference was his
political theory. He put the responsibility on a revolutionary elite;
Kautsky, the chief ideologist for a large, successful party machinery, looked to the future with calm confidence. Development
would bring forth the socialist society just as certainly as the bud
would burst forth in bloom.

The other reason for Lenin's fervour was that a closed system
could be a powerful force. If the party – or rather, its Bolshevik
section – could unite around a closed ideology, that would be a
strength. But if Mach is given a place in the centre of Marx's and
Engels's theories, who would come next?

If the theory is unconditional, then one day it could become omnipotent. Lenin won the decisive battle over Bogdanov and the other followers of Mach at a meeting in Paris; Bogdanov was expelled from the party and left politics for several years.

The outbreak of war in 1914 drove Lenin to Switzerland, and there it soon turned out that he himself had not finished with the fundamentals of Marxism. He tried to deal with his disappointment over the betrayal of the European workers' movement by grappling with one of the most demanding works of the history of philosophy, Hegel's *Wissenschaft der Logik* (Science of Logic). The background is, of course, that he knew that the work played a large role for Marx, and he himself declared that *Capital* could not be understood without knowing something about Hegel's *Logic*. In his notes, he emerges as an ambitious student who, with pen in hand, underlined important parts and added notes such as 'NB', 'subtle and profound', and even 'ha ha!' Often he got into longer commentary, agreements, or repudiations. He wrote 'cf. Machism' in the margins when he referred to Hegel's reckoning with Kant; his reckoning with Bogdanov was still fresh in his memory. He also sought support in Hegel for his striving for a uniform and closed philosophy: 'The general laws of *movement of the world and of thought*.'[22]

But Lenin's philosophical studies, in which Hegel's *Logic* constituted the natural centre, also led him out onto partially new terrain. The relationship between evolution and revolution found itself at the centre of his interest. The tendency from Engels, and more so from Kautsky, had been the emphasis on a process of continual advance. But what place do dialectical leaps have in such a world of ideas? Is there a place for any revolution in general? Lenin summarized his thoughts in an unfinished text titled 'On the Question of Dialectics'. Every change is a struggle between opposing forces, and the struggle occasionally results in radical changes. In the fragment, he talks above all about human knowledge, but he found the same rhythm in the shufflings of reality.[23]

It would be a few years before he himself was part of creating such a radical change. Russia suffered appalling losses during the war, and the sacrifices led to the Tsar being overthrown. After the February Revolution in 1917, Lenin hastily made his way to Russia; once there, he surprised his comrades with the declaration that it was now time for the Bolsheviks to seize power. They actually succeeded, in what is called the October Revolution of 1917. It is often pointed out that it was more of a coup than a revolution. On the other hand, revolutions are rarely military events in a grand style (the Chinese Revolution of 1949 is an exception); more often they are a clever exploitation of a vacuum in power. The measure of a revolution perhaps has more to do with the extent to which a society is changed through it. In that sense, Lenin's revolution had colossal dimensions. The storming of the Winter Palace, the centre of power, was at least a symbol that could then be used on every anniversary of the revolution up to the fall of the Soviet Union in 1991.

The Soviet Union, Orthodoxy, and Deviationists

When Lenin challenged Kautsky's orthodoxy with his own at the beginning of the century, it seemed to be a hopeless competition with a large, successful party apparatus. Lenin only had a part of Russian social democracy, whose leading figures were in exile, behind him. But the world war changed everything. German social democrats had lost their prestige, whereas Lenin succeeded in seizing and keeping power despite opposition that long seemed to be insurmountable. Russian developments after 1917 are well known and depicted in an enormous amount of literature. These will not be described here.[24]

The future that the Bolsheviks were throwing themselves (and their country) into was still an unwritten page. Socialism would now be built, Lenin announced the morning after the seizure of power. There were two different power bases for the task. One was the party, governed according to Lenin's principles, with an elite holding power at the top. The system of Soviets was the antithesis. Ordinary people would decide in these councils of workers, peasants, and soldiers. They themselves elected their leading representatives, and their mandates would vary. In the long run, it was the party that gathered more and more power into its hands.

The dream of direct democracy through the Soviets remained, but increasingly in the shadow of the party apparatus.

The party, which in 1918 began calling itself Communist, encountered a hostile world: fourteen different nations sent troops to crush the new regime, but all were unsuccessful. The Communists also met domestic opposition, especially from other left-wing groups. The conflicts culminated in the Kronstadt uprising of 1922. The sailors in the Kronstadt fortress fought for Soviet power, but were mowed down by the army.

Leon Trotsky played the decisive role in this course of events. He was Lenin's most important collaborator during the revolution and for a few years afterwards; he was extraordinarily gifted, versatile, and a brilliant speaker and writer – but also merciless towards those who offered him resistance.

When Lenin, stricken with illness, became increasingly unable to lead the party, Trotsky seemed to be the obvious candidate as his successor. But he soon met a superior opponent in Iosif Dzhugashvili, a Georgian known under his revolutionary pseudonym Stalin. Stalin did not have Trotsky's intellectual capacity, but he was an unrivalled player at the game of power who went further in unscrupulousness than Machiavelli had ever imagined.[25]

Before Stalin gradually strangled all political, philosophical, and cultural debate, however, magnificent intellectual energy was developing. Experiments in form flowed freely for a few feverish years; everything would be created anew, and a new type of person would emerge from the process of re-smelting. The direction was not a given, even in the field of the economy. Lenin was still in power when the New Economic Policy, with elements of the free market, was proclaimed; Stalin put a definitive stop to it only when he pushed through his Five-Year Plan.

Intense debates were conducted in the field of fundamental Marxist theory as well. How would a society actually develop after a proletarian revolution? Did culture, philosophy, and politics not also have to be transformed? Or was that something that more or less occurred by itself?

Quite simply, the debate concerned the issue of determinism. A battle was brewing; not with weapons, but with words. The main combatants were Abram Deborin on one side, and on the

other a group of 'mechanists' who asserted that after the revolution, the alteration of the whole of society would run more or less
automatically. Nikolai Bukharin was relatively close to the latter
group.

Deborin – who was Plekhanov's confidant before the revolution – emphasized the leap in development, the unpredictable.
Bukharin, who had a central position in the party – he was its
darling, as Lenin phrased it – emphasized that the course of
events conformed to laws, and pointed out the danger of a dialectic run wild that gave too much space to ideas, and perhaps
passing fancies. Deborin tried to bring Lenin – who had a weakness for Hegel's *Logic* – to his side, but Lenin was already out of
the running.

The central point of the debate was over the question of
whether there had to be a unique cultural revolution after the
October Revolution. Deborin said yes; his opponents said no.
But the showdown also revealed that Lenin's assertion about
Marxism constituting a closed system did not add up. On the
contrary, there could be disagreement about central issues such as
determinism and the dialectic.

It was that type of uncertainty that Stalin saw as a direct threat
to the power he was on the verge of establishing. In field after
field, he therefore staked out a general line that no one could
deviate from. In philosophy, this took place in late 1930 to early
1931. A resolution from the main philosophical organs came out
in December; on New Year's Day 1931 Mark Borisovich Mitin –
one of Stalin's closest men in the field – gave a lecture in which
he critiqued Deborin and also Bukharin. On the other hand, he
called attention to *The Foundations of Leninism*, the document in
which Stalin codified the term 'Leninism'. Engels's *The Dialectics
of Nature* had been published in the 1920s and was now, in all its
incompleteness, a part of the orthodox arsenal. The laws of the
dialectic were exactly three, not two or four as Engels had also
ventured.

Neither dialecticians nor mechanists were awarded the victory
in Mitin's lecture. If anything, the general line entailed a middle
way: the dialectic was given a place, but on the foundation of strict
materialism. Development has its leaps – but in moderation. More

important was that Mitin (and through him Stalin) demanded that the general line should permeate all scientific research. As we have seen, this had fateful consequences in genetics in particular.

The distance between Marx's incessant reappraisals and new orientations and this closed system – open only to the arbitrariness of those in power – is tremendous.[26]

The Range of Deviationists

The Soviet Union survived its first period of upheaval. Most observers believed that the revolutionary outbreak would be put down as quickly as it had been in Hungary, Bavaria, and other places where uprisings had broken out in the shadow of the world war. But the Soviet Union endured, and after a few tumultuous years it emerged as a stable country. It was particularly so when the capitalist world entered deep crisis around 1930. Unemployment was epidemic, and many people were radicalized. The Soviet Union appeared for many as a safe path towards a better, more just future. Eric Hobsbawm – whose same admiration led him to became a communist – wrote in his masterly 1994 book about the twentieth century, *Age of Extremes*, about how the world appeared to young radicals in crisis-stricken Europe. Hobsbawm's reaction was not unusual. An intellectual elite was also attracted. In Great Britain – the country that Marx finally gave up hope on – as well as in the United States, France, Germany, and Italy, brilliant young minds gathered around the dry catechism of Marxism–Leninism. They saw misery, poverty, and hopelessness in their own suffering countries, and imagined the realization of their ideal in Stalin's Soviet Union. Long afterwards, it is easy to forget the enthusiasm that the country to the east could arouse in the strongholds of capitalism. Marxism–Leninism was not seen as a distortion of Marx's work, but its completion.[27]

Lenin had created a Third – Communist – International, and it was steered with a tight rein from Moscow. Exiled by Stalin, Trotsky created a Fourth International, offering through it an ideological home for those who had turned away in horror from Stalin's collectivization, show trials, and mass purges.

But the Soviet Union remained a powerful centre for Marxist–
Leninist propaganda up until its dissolution in 1991. The
production of books, articles, and films was immense. Those who
considered themselves followers of Marx but critical of the Soviet
system – wherever they lived in the world – became deviationists
from the norm that political power had created.

As soon as an orthodoxy is established, revisionists and heretics
turn up. A Kautsky requires a Bernstein. Bernstein revised Marx,
it is said; but Marx's theories did not suddenly become a monolith on the day he died. Lenin's system, which Stalin codified as
Marxism–Leninism, invariably made revisionists out of everyone
who tried to think further on their own.

Rosa Luxemburg herself had attacked Bernstein's revisionism.
With her studies of the development of finance capital, she passed
on the inheritance from Marx in an independent fashion. Early on,
she had criticized the Bolsheviks' ideas of a ruling party elite, and
when after the October Revolution Lenin drove out all competing
tendencies from the power apparatus, Luxemburg was merciless
in her criticism. But she was soon silenced by a right-wing militia
that murdered her and Karl Liebknecht on 15 January 1919.[28]

With the establishment of Soviet power and its orthodoxy,
revisionism remained a constant shadow. The watch around the
ideological line decreed was sometimes stricter, sometimes more
generous. But it was always there, and was a concern for the
innermost circles of power.

Helga Grebing wrote a book on the history of revisionism from
Bernstein up to the Prague Spring. It was published back in 1977,
when the Soviet Union still appeared to be the most stable of
powers, unthreatened by anything except the Third World War.
The Austro-Marxists who tried to unite Marx with Kant were
given their own section; their role within Austrian social democracy was important during the interwar period.

The first big individual name in Grebing's book is the Hungarian
philosopher and literary historian Georg Lukács. His 1923 book
History and Class Consciousness attracted sharp criticism in the
Soviet Union. Lukács questioned the orthodoxy that had taken
form on many points. Marxism did not entail a belief in one

or another of the theses in Marx; it is thoroughly a method of studying reality, he asserted, and he repudiated the copy theory of knowledge that Lenin had established with inspiration from Engels. In addition, he criticized Engels's method of extending the dialectic to nature as well. Lukács would himself repudiate his theses, and thereafter remained somewhat loyal to Soviet orthodoxy up until 1956, when he sided with the uprising in his home country and once again fell into disfavour.[29]

One unique and fascinating Marxist was Ernst Bloch, who developed a number of themes in his own headstrong way: materialism that opened broad horizons towards the diversity of life and culture; atheism that did not exclude the emotional intensity of religion; utopias that drove people constantly forward on the way to the 'home everyone longs for, but where no one has yet been' – the final words in his colossal 1959 work *Das Prinzip Hoffnung* (The Principle of Hope). When Bloch returned to Germany after exile in the United States, he chose the GDR and was allowed to start a new philosophical journal – *Deutsche Zeitschrift für Philosophie* (German Journal for Philosophy) – but soon turned out to be entirely too obstinate for the regime and sought refuge in West Germany, where he lived out his final years, a celebrated teacher of radical students.[30]

Both Lukács and Bloch were part of the group of intellectuals who, according to French philosopher Michael Löwy, gave expression to the hope for a happy ending to history that is typical of Jewish messianism. Löwy argues that such utopian thinking was common in the decades around the turn of the twentieth century. One question that then presents itself is whether Marx's ideas can be seen as a forerunner of this tradition. This seems doubtful; Marx was rather unaffected by the Judaism of his ancestors, and his statements on the subject do not even indicate any closer familiarity.[31]

From the 1920s onwards, the publication of Marx's unfinished works, which had been interrupted after Kautsky, was taken up again. The driving force in this project was David Riazanov, who was active in the Soviet Union under increasingly difficult conditions. He was eventually murdered in the great wave of terror in 1938. The corresponding work in Germany could be carried out under freer conditions before Hitler's seizure of power. In the years around 1930, the publication of a large critical edition of Marx and Engels's work was underway; even though it had to be discontinued in 1933, it had far-reaching consequences. A new Marx could be glimpsed in part, above all in and through the previously unknown *Economic and Philosophic Manuscripts*.[32]

One of the leading interpreters of this text was Herbert Marcuse. At that time, Marcuse was also a contributor at the Institut für Sozialforschung (Institute for Social Research) that had been established in Frankfurt am Main, where researchers such as Theodor Adorno and Max Horkheimer were working. Characteristic of this 'Frankfurt School' was that Marx was treated as a classical scholar and inspiration alongside several others, above all Hegel, Freud, and gradually Max Weber as well. This tradition has been maintained in new forms. Jürgen Habermas has attempted to reconstruct historical materialism; even a number of somewhat younger talents, with Axel Honneth at their head, have developed interesting ideas on Marx's topicality.[33]

The thinkers usually counted among the Frankfurt School were without exception sharp critics of the Soviet Union and its Marxism–Leninism. French Marxists had a more ambiguous relationship to the rule of Stalin and his successors. After the Second World War, the French Communist Party grew stronger, attracting many young intellectuals. Michel Foucault was one of them; he said that at the time he disliked Jean-Paul Sartre, who polemicized against the communists. Gradually, their roles changed. Sartre took up a conciliatory attitude towards most of what the Soviet Union was doing. But in his great work from 1960, *Critique de la raison dialectique* (Critique of Dialectical Reason), he was at least a biting critic of the 'lazy Marxism' that in his opinion characterized official Soviet ideology.[34]

Sartre's own Marxism bore the stamp of humanism: the Marx of the *Manuscripts*, who spoke about humanity's essence and its alienation, became normative. A few years into the 1960s, this interpretation was subjected to merciless criticism by French philosopher Louis Althusser, who as we have already seen maintained that the early Marx, the author of the *Economic and Philosophic Manuscripts*, differed crucially from the mature Marx.

Italy also had a strong Communist Party, but it developed in another, freer direction. One of its founders was Antonio Gramsci. Together with Rosa Luxemburg, Gramsci was the most innovative Marxist of the first half of the twentieth century. But the conditions for his work were extremely unique: it was in Mussolini's prisons between 1926 and 1937 that he composed his famous *Quaderni di carcere* (Prison Notebooks). That is why posterity has above all taken notice of his theories on cultural hegemony. He took one of his starting points from the third of Marx's Theses on Feuerbach: that the educator himself also has an educator. A person's convictions are not determined only by the social position they have. In capitalist society, the bourgeoisie also has the role of pedagogue, thereby possessing power over thinking. It would remain so even if the working class conquered political power, Gramsci argued. The workers therefore had to create their own convictions, values, and norms, getting help from those intellectuals who stood on their side.

During his time as an active politician, Gramsci was a more mainstream communist. In prison – where he could follow the ravages of fascism, the victory of Nazism in Germany, and the degeneration of the Soviet Union – he arrived at his new convictions. It was the late 1950s before his ideas gained real influence; over the following decades, he was among the most important providers of impulse for the left then taking form in Europe and other parts of the world.[35]

Gramsci became one of the fathers of Eurocommunism, a short-lived movement that was important in its time. Its chief proponent was Enrico Berlinguer, the leader of the Italian Communist Party who struck a 'historic compromise' with the ruling Christian Democrats in Italy. Nothing came of it, however, and Eurocommunism quickly lost its power of attraction over the course of the 1980s.[36]

The leading ideologues in the Soviet Union of course condemned Eurocommunism as yet another form of revisionism. In the same way, they had managed to dismiss and persecute numerous deviationists on the home front. Tellingly enough, these persecuted heretics often sought their inspiration in Marx's own writings.

A showdown that attracted a great deal of attention in its time played out in Poland between the young philosopher Leszek Kołakowski and the then 'chief ideologist' of the Communist Party, Adam Schaff. We have already become acquainted with their debate (see above, p. 134). Tellingly enough, Schaff soon lost his central position and was ultimately driven to leave Poland in connection with the wave of government-supported anti-Semitism that gushed forth in 1968. Kołakowski had been forced to emigrate earlier.

In almost all Soviet-dominated countries, similar oppositional interpretations of Marx and Marxism developed. The Praxis group in Yugoslavia has already been mentioned. In Hungary, students of Lukács – with Agnes Heller as the most famous representative – formed their own pocket of resistance. But she and her fellow thinkers were gradually forced into exile. Among other things, Heller wrote a book that attracted a great deal of attention, titled *The Theory of Need in Marx* in its English translation. She made frequent use of Marx's writings from his youth, as well as the *Grundrisse* and *Capital* – briefly put, all of his writings far outside the narrow and doctored selection of orthodoxy.[37]

Free thought also played a role in the Prague Spring of 1968 when a new regime in Czechoslovakia sought to create 'socialism with a human face'. The attempt was brutally put down, and those who wanted to go their own way were forced into silence. Their chief representative was Karel Kosík, author of the remarkable and magnificent work *Dialectics of the Concrete*. Kosík sought to escape the soulless orthodoxy of Marxism–Leninism through drawing inspiration from Marx himself – both the young Marx and the author of *Capital* – and also from Hegel and even Heidegger. A central concept in Kosík was *praxis*, which he distinguished from labour with its character of a load or a burden. There is freedom and innovation in praxis, something that every person is capable of. But existing society, which Kosík by way of precaution only called capitalist, smothers freedom with its abstractions.[38]

The left-wing wave that rolled over Western Europe and the United States from the late 1960s through the following decades had much to learn from the intellectual opposition in the Soviet Union. But this only happened by way of exception. Everything associated with the Soviet Union, even its opposition, appeared tainted with melancholy.

People sought inspiration further afield. China, with Mao Zedong, aroused enthusiasm among many. Like the Russian Revolution and the Paris Commune, the Chinese Revolution of 1949 came after a devastating war. The difference was that Mao appeared as the victor of the war. In the beginning, he followed the Soviet Union's path, and China was flooded by Soviet experts. After Khrushchev's speech at the Twentieth Party Congress in 1956, the friendship turned into hostility; the Chinese Communist Party was not ready to rid itself of its inheritance from Stalin. But the cause of the schism also lay on another, deeper level. Mao and his party may have embraced Marxist orthodoxy, but they also carried another intellectual inheritance rooted in China's long history. The old imperial dynasties had had the 'Mandate of Heaven'. Mao may not have spoken about heaven, but his regime was the one that would carry China further through the new centuries.

Their long-term perspective was united with a short-term one. Chinese politics after the revolution was characterized by extreme irregularity. The 'Great Leap Forward', which would industrialize the country in a single stroke, ended in catastrophe with famine and mass death. The Cultural Revolution would put an end to class society and the rule of the political elite, and create an equal China. The results were years of unhappiness for millions of people, while enthusiasm for the great goal also gradually died down among the young people that had supported the revolution.

But it was precisely the Cultural Revolution that captivated many who wanted to get away from capitalism, consumerism, and vacillating social democracy in Europe and the United States. The hardness of heart of the Western world and the Soviet Bloc contrasted with Mao's vital innovative thinking and the fighting spirit of the Red Guards. Many became Maoists, and schooled themselves in what was called Marxist–Leninist–Maoist thought.[39]

Others were swayed by the Cuban Revolution of 1959. It meant liberation from a regime of oppression supported by the United States. The country only gradually became communist when the Soviet Union offered the only bulwark against the powerful enemy to the north, which considered itself as having the right to choose regimes in Latin America to its liking. Cuba gradually became more and more like other Soviet-supported regimes, with food shortages and political dissidents in prison.

It was not primarily Fidel Castro, revolutionary leader and later on president, who inspired enthusiasm among radicals in Latin America, the United States, and Western Europe; it was his closest comrade, the Argentinian Ernesto Guevara, known as Che. Che Guevara saw his task as liberating all of Latin America from poverty, right-wing dictatorships, and dominance by the United States; he imagined the next opportunity for revolution was in Bolivia. He thought he would encounter a dilapidated Bolivian army, but on the contrary found himself face to face with an enemy trained and equipped by the CIA. He was executed in 1967, and immediately became an icon who still holds a certain charm many decades later.

At the beginning, it was Guevara's theory of revolution – the 'foco' theory – that aroused interest and, at least in Latin America, a following. This meant that the uprising against the regime of oppression would be concentrated on a single crucial point, like sunbeams in a magnifying glass. That was how Guevara interpreted what had happened in Cuba – a limited group of men had overthrown the old regime by concentrating their attack on their opponent's weakest point. It was an idea that inspired many across the entire continent. Latin America was regarded as a unity – in fact, a single country from Mexico to Patagonia. Now this enormous territory was to be liberated from oppression.[40]

But the United States started large-scale training for combating guerrillas in Panama, and attempts at uprising failed everywhere. Even a democratically elected socialist president, Salvador Allende, was overthrown in 1973 in a military coup for which US Secretary of State and Nobel Peace Prize winner Henry Kissinger was primarily responsible. Chile instead became one of a number of brutal right-wing dictatorships that left their mark on the continent at the time.

Only around the turn of the twenty-first century could a number of more or less socialist-minded regimes come to power in Latin America. But by then the Soviet Union had fallen, and the grip of the United States on the continent had weakened. The *foco* theory no longer had any drawing power.

It would not be possible to obtain a correct image of the singular history of Marxism without also saying something about its equally lively counter-history. Statues of Marx have been raised, but the malicious portraits, abuse, and more or less conscious distortions are equally numerous. The Soviet propaganda apparatus was met with an American one. The free world was never so free as it was during the time of Joseph McCarthy in the early 1950s, when the mildest liberal could be accused of being a communist. It remained free despite bloody regimes in Spain, Portugal, and Latin America, and the Apartheid system in South Africa could only fall once the Soviet Union was gone.

The oddest propaganda efforts could also find a place among seemingly serious researchers. The 1947 biography of Marx by the German sociologist Leopold Schwarzschild, translated into English in 1986 as *The Red Prussian*, was a work of hatred that suited the atmosphere of the Cold War. (Even the title of the work is strange; as we know, Marx was not from Prussia, but from the Palatinate.) But in its time, the book met with great approval in circles where perhaps not Marx, but the Soviet Union was seen as a major threat.[41]

The list of writing in the same tradition is a long one, and it has not stopped yet. It is more common now that Marx is dismissed with some brief, conventional summary of the idea behind his work. A few terms such as base and superstructure, and socialism and communism, are brought together, and if necessary, the dish is spiced with a few well-known quotes taken from writings and letters that came out at various stages of his life. Above all, according to these caricatures, there is a straight line from Marx through Lenin to Stalin and Mao. Everything that had been realized in the Soviet Union and China is found in Marx.

The actual history of Marxism began with Marx's death, gaining its fixed form when Kautsky and Lenin each created their own closed system. Everyone who did not feel at home within these narrow frameworks but nonetheless sought inspiration and Marx's writings thus became deviationists and were dismissed as revisionists or renegades. Within the Soviet sphere of power, many who went their own way paid with their lives or were exiled to the 'gulag archipelago' of work camps. At best, they were pushed out into obscurity like Deborin. Only in periods of ideological thaw could those who thought independently make themselves heard without repression. Even those who lived outside direct Soviet influence were forced to constantly declare whether they accepted or deviated from accepted Marxism.

When the Soviet Union fell in 1991, the Communist Parties – recently so powerful – became mere fragments of what they had been, with no possibility of maintaining more than a trickle of the enormous torrent of propaganda material. Trotsky's Fourth International still remains, but with no power other than words can provide.

The changes in China were equally radical. They had begun much earlier, as a result of Deng Xiaoping's return to the centre of power in the late 1970s after more than a decade out in the cold. Deng and his closest collaborators pushed through a radical change of China's economic policy, with increasingly larger features of a capitalistic market economy. In 1989, when large parts of Eastern and central Europe were already melting down, a growing movement of primarily young Chinese demanding freedom of expression, the press, and assembly reached its culmination. The movement was crushed on 3 June in Beijing, in a bloody massacre in Tiananmen Square. Deng wanted a free market, with politics entirely dominated by the Chinese Communist Party. The party would decide what could be said and written in the country.

More than a quarter-century later, long after Deng's death, raw capitalism and raw communism are still united in a China that has now become an economic world power. The party pays lip service to Marxism–Leninism; literature in the names of Marx, Lenin and Mao Zedong is still being produced; and there are still mildly oppositional politicians demanding more ideology, more Marxism, and above all more Mao Zedong in politics. Their criticism is now benevolently taken up by those in authority, who in their own way unite Marx with what can be termed a neoliberal economic policy. The Chinese regime is stable so long as it is economically successful. The day it is *not*, it will be threatened by collapse.[42]

When the state Marxist traditions collapsed or disappeared into impotence, it became much easier to concentrate on Marx's texts without the risk of various official interpreters interrupting. But the dark tradition that signed a contract for Marx over a large part of the twentieth century inevitably raises the question of what there is in his works that could inspire such a catastrophic development. That question will soon also be asked here. But, like the question of what is still useful and capable of development in his works, this will require a careful study of the texts.

The Sum Total of Marx

Marx built no system. He was, on the other hand, constantly working on his grand theory of society. This theory occupied him for almost forty years, and he still was reshaping it at the end of his life. In the foreword to *A Contribution to the Critique of Political Economy* from 1859, he formulated what he called his 'thread' through the research. Many of his followers made this thread a guiding principle. This entailed a great change. Threads are followed to find a way out of the labyrinth of society. But many of Marx's followers seemed instead to find a map that they could then supplement and change (or 'develop') more or less arbitrarily.

Marx warned against temptation of finding a formal schema in his work. Only careful study of the full diversity of reality provides real knowledge. He himself became a major specialist of the capitalist epoch as far as he managed to follow its development.

Capital stands at the centre of this work. It is not, as many believe, simply a work about economics, but deals with society in its various ramifications; it is just as much sociology and modern history, and to a certain extent also political science and cultural history. Through the term 'character mask', it contains an important bit of social psychology; in Marx's opinion, it does not matter if the capitalists are greedy, but the system drives them to act as if they were.

The concept of class was at the centre of Marx's interest early on. The rhetorical flourish in the *Communist Manifesto* that all hitherto existing society is the history of class struggle was not simply a slogan, but a powerful exhortation to realize the crucial significance of social classes and class antagonism in history. The class relations that Marx studied in detail are those specific to capitalism, or more precisely the relationship between the three classes that dominate the means of production: landowners, capitalists, and workers. The power of the landowners dates back to earlier historical stages, but changes character in this new society. Owing to their power over the land, they reap a portion of the profits, of which the capitalists run off with the lion's share. The workers create profits through their labour, and receive wages that make it possible for them to survive and reproduce themselves. By associating in trade unions, they can secure a somewhat larger share. This pushes the development of the forces of production, as does legislation forbidding inhuman working conditions. The workers can thus produce more in a shorter time. For this reason, technology must be developed and scientific research must be engaged.

Rapidly increasing productivity is the chief achievement of capitalism. The dark side is the lack of freedom and the destitution it brings the working class. Even the capitalists are victims of the compulsion to constantly guard their positions and to continuously rationalize production. All other occupational categories in society are affected as well: 'All that is solid melts into air.'

Capitalism creates its own world of illusions. Marx calls this commodity fetishism; this means that passive objects – commodities – appear as living, while people (that is, those who produce these commodities) on the contrary seem inactive. Commodity fetishism is capitalism's own religion. Like all religions, it is humanity's spontaneous way of both making sense of and finding comfort in a world that otherwise seems as mysterious as it is threatening. What was once called Fate or God is called the Market in capitalism.

Humanity's relationship with nature is changed as a result of the capitalist mode of production. It is itself a part of nature, living off what nature produces, at the same time as it exceeds nature, extracting more and more through its creative power. But capitalism creates a widening gap between humanity and nature; nature is treated so that its products become maximally profitable without regard to the conditions for its continued existence.

According to Marx, there is also a self-destructive dynamic in the capitalist system. Capital appropriates the surplus value that labour creates, but surplus value is at the same time a growing burden that allows dead labour (labour that has already created value) to encroach upon living labour. The past weighs ever heavier on the productive present. The system must finally be crushed under its own weight.

Marx is speaking of a tendency here, but makes no predictions. He can, if anything, be compared with a geologist who declares that a major earthquake must occur sooner or later somewhere along the San Andreas Fault in California. In practice, Marx prepared himself for the fall of capitalism as soon as the clouds of crisis piled up over larger or smaller parts of the world. So it was in 1848–49, and again in 1856–57. His life in the 1860s was devoted to research and the International, but the Paris Commune in 1871 readied him once again for the great metamorphosis.

Marx was no politician. He saw politics as a changeable form for the actual content of society; his ideas about its possibilities were also quickly changeable. Only those who made him a system builder have padlocked him into certain statements he made in definite situations and transformed them into dogmas. He used the term 'dictatorship of the proletariat' both around 1850 and in connection with the Paris Commune. The idea was that the working class that had seized power in a revolution would safe-guard it against all possible competitors during a brief transition period in order to prepare the way for a new classless society. During the more than twenty years between the revolutions of 1848–49 and the Paris Commune, the concept faded away. Marx was then more interested in the opportunities that universal suffrage could open for the rapidly growing working class.

Marx never saw himself as the leader of a revolution. Liberation was the act of the working class itself. He would contribute clear, unbiased insight into how society worked, and what opportunities were opening up for the oppressed. The idea that a small elite of intellectuals, schooled in the craft of revolution, would lead a firmly constructed party to a socialist society was foreign to him. During his lifetime, incidentally, only the beginning of the modern party system could be seen.

One controversial question in all Marx research is the question of alienation. In the opinion of many, the concept only belongs to a few early writings, above all the *Manuscripts*. As soon as Marx abandoned the idea that humanity had an essence that could be realized in the future, later talk of alienation (*Entfremdung*, *Entäussering*) became only meaningless reminiscences. This is a mistake. Marx did not say that humanity did not have an essence; he said that its essence is formed by the society they live in. Furthermore, one of his important ideas is that capitalism creates immeasurable wealth but still forces the worker into destitution. In a classless society, workers would be able to enjoy the prosperity that now only the bourgeoisie and the upper classes do. Even the people of India, he says – blessed by the British with the driving forces of modern development but at the same time deeply oppressed – have a decent existence within reach. For Marx, alienation is the distance between possibility and current reality.

Another concept his interpreters have difficulty agreeing on is the dialectic. Here as well, many stop before a large either/or: either the dialectic must govern everything from the class struggle to water that freezes into ice at a certain temperature, or it only has a decorative function in Marx's writings. It is not so simple. Marx said neither yes nor no to Engels's innovation of a natural dialectic; the essential thing is that it plays no role whatsoever in his own writings despite his commenting quite a lot on both nature and the natural sciences. On the other hand, the dialectic is extremely important for the entire structure of *Capital*. As Hegel did in both the *Phenomenology* and *Logic*, he followed the path from the simple to the increasingly complex. For the sake of historical concreteness, he also wove in sections on, for example, the working day and the development of machinery under capitalism. The totality must take on the form of a work of art, he himself said.

Other dialectical core concepts also figure often in Marx's texts. Form and content are central: he uses them more often than the conventional and misleading base and superstructure. Material production and the class relations connected with it constitute society. Politics – like the legal apparatus, religion, art, and the predominant way of thinking – are the forms of this content. The forms are in no way passive; it is in and through them that the conscious life of humanity is played out. But they are always dependent upon the content.

Surface and depth are other dialectical concepts that have an important place in Marx. Use value is the sensuous surface, while (exchange) value is not visible on the outside. In the second edition of the first volume of *Capital*, Marx clarifies that value in turn also has depth and surface. The surface is the exchange value that the constantly changing price constitutes; under that is the value that, according to Marx, is determined by the amount of labour put into its production.

The relationship between the forces and the relations of production can also be grasped dialectically. The capitalist mode of production pushes the forces of production towards constantly greater heights, compelled by its own hunger for surplus value. But the growth of the forces of production also exposes capitalism to increasingly harsher strains.

The key concept in Hegel's dialectic – *Aufhebung*, with its triple meaning of abolition, preservation, and lifting up to a higher level – is also important for Marx. Like Hegel, he sees every major social change as an *Aufhebung* of what previously existed. From first to last, a revolution worth the name is an *Aufhebung*. Even capitalism will someday be abolished.[43]

Lastly, we can say that Marx underestimated the ability of capitalism to integrate new technologies. He himself lived to see the start of the second Industrial Revolution, fully realizing the potential of both electricity and the chemical industry. But he did not imagine that they both would give capitalism a new life. Even less did he imagine the third revolution – of electronics and biotechnology – that began in the second half of the twentieth century. This revitalized capitalism as well. It was during this same period that the Marx-quoting 'really existing socialism' foundered.

The study of *Capital* over the last two decades has increasingly emphasized the significance of the relations of production at the expense of the forces of production. This is a major reversal from Kautsky's belief, grounded in biology, of technological development that would soon burst capitalism from within. *Die neue Marx-Lektüre* – the new reading of Marx – shifts the emphasis to capitalism with its inherent ability for renewal. Attention has thus been directed towards features of his theory whose consequences Marx himself did not completely draw out. He was entirely too keen on imagining a revolution behind the next corner of development.

Marx said he was not writing recipes for the kitchen of the future.[44] On the other hand, he said that the society he was living in had to give way to an entirely different sort of society. Capitalism was not an eternal condition. It had arisen once centuries ago, and it would go under in the same way.

His explanations of this new society are few and sporadic. The labour of the future must be universal and free, at the same time characterized by the seriousness that distinguishes freedom, he said in the *Grundrisse*. The realm of freedom should spread alongside that of necessity, it says in *Capital*. 'From each according to their ability, to each according to their need,' as it is written in *Critique of the Gotha Programme*.

But what kind of statements are these? Are they of the same type as calculations of future solar eclipses? Absolutely not; they said nothing about a point in time. Nor are they appeals to action of the 'Let us come together to create a better society' type. If anything, one can think of the magnificent phrase in *The Eighteenth Brumaire of Louis Bonaparte* that people create their own history – not freely, but based on immediately given circumstances. The circumstances are given, but what we do with them is not.

How, for example, do we make use of the insight that society produces riches never before seen at the same time as the

mercilessness of class society means that so many live impoverished, hard, often unendurable lives? For Marx, this insight is
enough for people to join together and, *under the given circumstances*, create a new and better society.

Above all, Marx was a critic of the capitalist social system. The
word 'critic' bears Kant's stamp. Marx wanted to lay bare the
conditions for all of society, the foundations of its strength and its
vulnerability. The project as such was almost too large, and given
Marx's ambitions he could not completely bring it to a close.[45]

Marx completed much else. He was a brilliant journalist and
author of shorter works. There, his stylistic mastery reached outstanding heights. One need only think of the first section of the
Communist Manifesto, his words about religion as the opium of
the people, or the chain of aphoristically incisive phrases in the
introduction to *The Eighteenth Brumaire*.

One important foundation for his linguistic brilliance was the
wide reading he conducted early on, which reached from Ancient
Greece up to the time he lived in, from Aeschylus to Balzac. He
constantly scattered literary quotes in his text, preferring to do so
in the original.

His wide reading in different types of nonfiction became even
more impressive with time. He was a tireless devourer of books
who fearlessly dove into one technical field after another as soon
as it appeared important to him for the project he was working
on. This was more than diligence; it was a kind of obsession.
When some time in the late 1860s he was asked his favourite
pastime, he wrote 'in Büchern wühlen' (Bookworming).[46] He submitted this information in what were called 'Confessions', which
young women gladly harassed their families and their friends with
at that time. Here, it was his daughter Jennychen who demanded
his responses; her sister Laura wanted the same, and he varied his
answers somewhat but not by much.

We already know his favourite poets: Dante, Aeschylus,
Shakespeare, and Goethe. Among the prose authors, he mentions
not only Balzac but also Diderot, Lessing, and Hegel. The two
real-life heroes he indicates are an ill-matched pair: Spartacus,
the leader of the great slave uprising of antiquity, and Kepler, the

scientific genius. He takes his heroine from Goethe: Gretchen, the
victim of Faust's perfidious lust. His responses to the questions
about his favourite masculine and feminine qualities run in the
same style: strength and weakness. This is a response befitting a
Victorian family man, but hardly Karl Marx.

The maxim he saw as his own is classic for a humanist: *Nihil
humani a me alienum puto* (Nothing human is alien to me). His
motto could be a helpful memento for those who see a dogmatist
in him: *De omnibus dubitandum* (Question everything).

These 'confessions', of course, say nothing more than that Marx
wanted to appear this way to his family. But even a self-portrait
of this kind has informational value. Marx never wrote anything
closer to an autobiography than these 'confessions'.

Marx and Posterity

How does the historical Marx relate to the image – idol or bogey-
man – that posterity has created of him? This question cannot have
any definite answer. The person answering it themselves has only
an image of Marx – however nuanced it may be – and that image
is marked by the time and the environment that person is living
in. But there is nevertheless much we can say with certainty. Once
he was dead, he could no longer sum up his work himself; others
had to take on the task. He can be glimpsed behind Marxism – or
rather, the different kinds of Marxism.

Long afterwards, and with access to nearly all of his work, we
can compare what he and his followers asserted. We can see that
he emphasized the difference between his and Darwin's theories
more powerfully than Kautsky. We can see that his views on party
and party leadership differed markedly from Lenin's. But can we
then say that Marx had no presence in what either Kautsky or
Lenin did?

He did, of course. There are important elements in Marx's
works that reverberate in both Kautsky and Lenin. Despite the
abundant intellectual wealth in *Capital*, there is a tendency in it
towards ignoring the concrete problems of society that becomes
even clearer in Marx's political and journalistic work. Nationalism

is a central example. It began its modern career sometime after the French Revolution; German culture was an important breeding ground. Marx condemned all this as reactionary drivel. Similarly, he was blind to the nationalist overtones in the Second French Empire. It was above all the rural masses in the countryside, otherwise untouched by the Enlightenment, who supported Napoleon III in the frequent referendums. If the occasional worker also supported the emperor, this was due to his false rhetoric that hinted at a social conscience. Towards the end of the nineteenth century, the nationalist mass movements that would leave a mark on the twentieth began to take form. They competed, often successfully, with the workers' movement on its own territory. What is more, the demand for socialism could be united with national enthusiasm.

Marx was not solely responsible for the clumsiness – defencelessness, in fact – in the face of this nationalism. But he was one of those responsible. He and his fellow thinkers did not see that nationalism was just as natural an element in modern society as its opposite, internationalism. In 1914, nationalism commanded almost the entire political field. Even most social democrats and socialists were seized by a bloody fervour for their own countries.[47]

In general, Marx had not paid sufficient attention to the irrational sides of human life. He himself was a passionate man, and through literature he had obtained great knowledge about the furthest depths of the soul. But when he spoke about the future, in which the workers' movement would march victoriously forward, it was as if he ignored these insights. People would then act entirely based on their social position. Workers would act as workers, and not also as German or French, Catholics, Protestants, or atheists.

Sexuality, and erotic passion in general, was another field where Marx did not have much to say. People would surely devote themselves to the pleasures and torments of love in another kind of society as well, but Marx did not utter a word about this. Sigmund Freud took up the question of communism in love in his book on the unpleasantness of culture. Even in a country such as the Soviet Union, sexual relations had to remain 'the source of the strongest dislike in the most violent hostility among men who in other respects are on an equal footing', he wrote.[48] This would hold true even if the Soviet Union had developed into the ideal society it never achieved.

As regards the position of woman, Marx was conspicuously silent. He certainly imagined that woman would be liberated as women in a future classless society. But when it came to concrete analyses, he most often forgot the oppression they lived under. Even where concrete things such as women's place in industry were concerned, he displayed a noteworthy thoughtlessness. Only here and there – such as in the case of the Paris Commune of 1871 – could he call attention to women's efforts.

Here, his friend Engels was more observant. It was he who wrote *The Origin of the Family, Private Property, and the State*, a classic in the genre, in 1884. Even earlier August Bebel, the leading name of German Social Democrats, had written a book in which women were entirely in focus: *Woman Under Socialism* (1879).[49]

Soon enough, women would play a prominent role in the movement that in many respects originated with Karl Marx. His daughter Eleanor is one example among many; Clara Zetkin is another. Among other things, Zetkin wrote a book about the situation of women factory workers that attracted a great deal of attention, and she was the one who took the initiative for International Women's Day in 1910. It was thus from the beginning a completely socialist initiative, but 8 March would gradually come to be celebrated by others as well.[50]

Neither Lenin nor others were unfamiliar with the fact that the idea of a ruling party elite was foreign to Marx. But does that mean that Lenin's great project had nothing to do with Marx?

That would be a hasty conclusion. Marx was never in doubt about the dominant role of the workers in every workers' movement. But where did he find himself? He was the one who developed the theory of capitalist society and its internal contradictions. It was thus also he who could determine what was possible to do, and what was futile or dangerous.

During certain periods, he was a man of compromise who only cautiously attempted to win a hearing for his own interpretation.

But as soon as the contradictions sharpened, he did not hesitate to polemicize, harshly and mercilessly, with those who thought otherwise. He could be ruthless in his polemics against those with opposing opinions, regardless of their background. He was equally as sharp with the journeyman tailor Weitling as he was with the nobleman Bakunin. Proudhon the typographer was spared no more than Vogt the professor. Marx was certain that he was the one who possessed the best theory of society. This resoluteness, which not infrequently intensified into irreconcilability, can seem reminiscent of Lenin's manner of acting. Theory pointed out one single path, and it was to be followed.

This unwillingness to compromise of course had another side: the magnificence of the project. The essential thing for Marx was the social revolution – that is, the transformation of the funda-mental conditions of society. The political seizure of power was only a means, which he could imagine in various ways. In con-trast to Marx, Lenin was a pure politician; he was also someone who actually gained power, something Marx completely lacked. But Lenin soon found that this power was limited as well. The Russian bureaucracy lived on, and he found no way of abolishing the dictatorship of the proletariat. In his Testament, he warned his closest collaborators about Stalin, but even on this point his words had no influence. Stalin became his successor, burying him in a mausoleum and – even more effectively – within a doctrine called Leninism over which Stalin alone reigned. What then took place had no connection with Karl Marx, who in fact became an increasingly censored author in the country that claimed it was carrying his work forward.

Marx's influence remained quite great in the social democratic parties that remained in the Second International. But even there, it concerned a closed Marxism, even if it was of a Kautskyan vintage. The question of what this Marxism meant for practical politics is a subject of discussion we will not go into here. It is telling that this strain thinned out in party programme after party programme. This was so even in Germany; the last remnants disappeared in the programme the German Social Democrats adopted at Bad Godesberg in 1959.

After the First World War, it was Lenin and his Communist International that set the norm for Marxism. Rosa Luxemburg became the first deviationist, but quickly disappeared from the scene. Her words have long been forgotten: 'Far from being a sum of ready-made prescriptions which have only to be applied, the practical realization of socialism as an economic, social and juridical system is something which lies completely hidden in the mists of the future.'[51]

Antonio Gramsci was essentially also a deviationist, but his notes from prison reached the world posthumously. It was only then that they could inspire freethinkers in opposition to Soviet dogmatism.

An important part of the anti-Soviet tradition of thought reaches back to Marx's own writings, both *Capital* or such things as were yet unpublished. This is how the young Marx, the author of the *Manuscripts*, was discovered, and also how the *Grundrisse* came into focus for interpreters of Marx.

It has been a long time since the Soviet Union and its satellites collapsed. At that time, there were many who were glad that Marx too would now definitively be sent off to the past, to be remembered only by historians of the nineteenth century and additionally the occasional nostalgist.

But that is not how it turned out. Marx has maintained his topicality. More than that – in many respects, he has been liberated from the history of Marxism that concealed him behind various dogmatic disguises. Naturally, he will never be completely free of this history – as we have seen, there are things in his own works that anticipated both Kautsky and Lenin. But it is only now, with the perspective of distance, that we can clearly see the relationship between his works and the traditions that invoked him.

The biggest difference lies in the fact that Marx never arrived at any summation of his work, much less any system. He followed a thread, which guided his path through the labyrinth of society. But the map his followers began sketching out as soon as he had died was not his work. He certainly would have liked to have drawn such a map himself. But new questions, new material, and new books continually turned up in his path.

On the other hand, he developed an entire toolbox of critical instruments. The central element in his work, as we have seen, is criticism of political economy and of the ideas and theories, the institutions and cults and myths, that develop out of the system. In fact, this criticism applies to the whole of the capitalist society that Marx lived in and that we still live in – even if on another level.

It is true that he always saw this reality on its way towards dissolution. There was a limit to its conditions of possibility, and on the other side of this limit a new kind of society would be created – a classless society where everyone could freely act as individuals in community with others. The conception of this society – socialist, communist; the terms were fluid – was already lively and strong when Marx became acquainted with the new radicalism of the 1840s, and it continued to be fluid over a large part of the twentieth century. In the Soviet Union, it was often said that this good society could only be achieved after enormous hardships: the misery was a precondition for a happy future. This was not Marx's thinking. He did not ignore the risk of bloody conflicts, but he had no conception of any grind that people had to go through in order to attain a better society. Nor was the ambition to 'create a new human' his. He dreamed of polytechnical education in the future, through which the gulf between manual and intellectual occupations would be bridged. He probably imagined a school system that would also include the kind of education he himself possessed in such ample measure.

On the other side of the fall of the Soviet Union and China's development into the most expansive capitalist economy of the twenty-first century, the term 'Marxism' itself has lost its topicality. There is no longer a norm to follow or oppose for those who want a way out of the world that has taken shape over the last two decades. So far, the opponents of this new capitalism have assembled under the slogan 'Another world is possible'. Many different tendencies can gather under this banner: Marxist–Leninists and anarchists, Maoists and feminists, radical Christians and Muslims, environmental activists and anti-militarists.

A WORLD TO WIN

But one name continually turns up in this new age: Karl Marx. It is no longer Marx the supposed system-builder who attracts people. It is instead the Marx who constantly sought to push deeper into the labyrinths of the age he lived in, the Marx who was never content with the magnificent discoveries he made but who saw new horizons opening over the top of every hill and therefore had to continue on his way.

This Marx is subtle enough to form the basis for precise, philosophically demanding analyses such as the 2004 work by American philosopher Anne Fairchild Pomeroy, *Marx and Whitehead*. Through a parallel reading of Marx and British philosopher and mathematician Alfred North Whitehead, Pomeroy seeks to show that both, in their own way, sought to overcome the gulf between subjectivism and objectivism – one with the concept of *process*, the other with the dialectic.[52] But Marx is also resolute and direct enough to still inspire topical criticism of capitalism's latest achievements, the failings of politics, and the genuflection of the contemporary world of ideas before a fetish like the market.

In both cases, it is the Marx of the nineteenth century, not the twentieth, who can attract the people of the twenty-first. Today, the world is globalized in much the same way as it was before 1914. Communications move much more quickly, but this is a degree of difference and not of type. People, messages, and ideas are flung around the globe. Money circulates between continents in a never-ceasing stream, poverty lives side-by-side with wealth, and capital exercises its impersonal power over all and sundry. In this world, Karl Marx lives on.

His path in our present era and our future is not a subject for this book. Here it is the Marx of the nineteenth century that has been in focus. We have followed the winding path through his life and his writings. What is the image of him that ultimately emerges?

For me, it is without a doubt Faust, the restless doctor in his dark study who is constantly seeking to increase his knowledge of the world. Marx certainly struck no deal with the Devil; in his eyes, this potentate is as much an ingredient as God is in the opium of the people called religion. No; Marx allied himself with the working class. He wanted to work for the liberation of the workers; in their liberation, he saw the liberation of all humanity.

He has no unequivocal answer to the question of the path to such liberation: the ballot box, bloody uprisings, or a combination of both. But it is not with his answers that he maintains his contemporaneity. He lives on as the great critic of capitalism. As a critic, he sometimes lets us imagine a positive contrasting picture of human activity, in which solidarity can coexist with freedom, and pleasure with seriousness. It is a possible utopia for our time as well.

Postscript

I have had a number of helpful readers who provided valuable points of view on what I have written. As always, my dear Eva-Maria has been my first reader. Some have closely scrutinized chapter after chapter as I wrote them: Maria Johansen, Per Magnus Johansson, Thomas Karlsohn, David Karlsson, and Per Arne Tjäder. Others took a position on the entire book: Michael Azar, Sten Dahlstedt, Claes Ekenstam, Victoria Fareld, and Edda Manga. Johan Lönnroth read the chapter on *Capital* ('The Unknown Masterpiece'). Elena Namli provided valuable information, as has Per Magnus Johansson.

Marx Chronology

1818   **Karl Marx is born (May 5).**
1825   The first passenger railroad opens.
1830   The July Revolution in France.
1830s   Balzac is a success with his novels in a realistic style.
1840   The term 'anarchism' is coined. Its competitors – liberalism, conservatism, socialism, and communism – are not that much older.
1841   Marx finishes his doctoral thesis.
1843   Karl Marx and Jenny von Westphalen are married.
1843   Marx begins a major work on Hegel, the introduction to which is published after Marx's death.
1843   Karl and Jenny move to Paris.
1844   Daughter Jenny (Jennychen) is born.
1844   The weavers' uprising in Silesia.
1844   The cooperative movement begins in Rochdale.
1845   Marx is deported from Paris.
1845   Daughter Laura is born.
1845   Marx and Engels write *The German Ideology*, which remained in manuscript form until 1932.
1847   The Bund der Kommunisten (Communist League) forms and adopts the slogan 'Workers of all countries, unite!' Marx and Engels are tasked with drawing up a programme. Marx designs the final version, which is called a manifesto.
1847   The ten-hour workday is introduced in Great Britain.
1848   The *Communist Manifesto* is published.
1848   The February Revolution in Paris.

1848   The March Revolution in Berlin.

1848   The National Assembly begins to meet in Frankfurt am Main.

1848   Marx and Engels publish the *Neue Rheinische Zeitung*, 'an organ for democracy'.

1849–55 Four of Karl and Jenny's children die.

1851   The Great Exhibition in London's Crystal Palace.

1852–61 Marx writes a long series of articles in the *New York Daily Tribune*.

1853–56 The Crimean War.

1855   Daughter Eleanor is born.

1856–57 Economic crisis in Europe and the United States.

1857–58 Marx writes the *Grundrisse* (Foundations of the Critique of Political Economy), published posthumously.

1859   War between France and Austria.

1859   Darwin's *On the Origin of Species* is published.

1861–1865 The American Civil War.

1861   Serfdom is abolished in Russia.

1864   The Marx family moves to their own house in London.

1864   The International forms. Marx has great significance for the organization.

1864–65 Marx draws up the version of the third volume of *Capital* that Engels revised and published in 1894. During the 1860s and 1870s, Marx writes six different versions of the second volume of *Capital*, which formed the basis for Engels's edition in 1885.

1867   The first volume of *Capital* is complete.

1870   Engels moves to London.

1870–71 The Franco-Prussian War. Germany conquers Alsace and Lorraine. Bismarck's power increases.

1871   The Paris Commune is proclaimed, but is brutally crushed after less than two months.

1874   The International dissolves.

1875   Germany's two social democratic parties unite in Gotha.

1875   Marx writes *Critique of the Gotha Programme*.

1876   Engels begins writing *Anti-Dühring*.

1878   The Social Democratic Party is banned in Germany.

1880s Electric light bulbs become commonplace.

1881   The International Exposition of Electricity in Paris, and in
       Berlin the following year.

1881   Jenny Marx dies (December 2).

1883   Jennychen dies (January 11).

1883   **Karl Marx dies (March 14).**

1889   The Second International is founded.

1890s The term 'Marxism' spreads.

1895   Engels dies.

Notes

1 The Great Project

1. Lankester turns up in *Europa*, a 1935 novel by the social anthropologist Robert Briffault (p. 234). As a novelist, Briffault was distinguished by having a number of real people speaking almost authentic lines. He knew Lankester personally, and he himself shared the man's deep fascination with Marx. The quote naturally has no value as source criticism, but says something typical about the view of Marx among a number of the outstanding intellectuals of the time, especially in Great Britain. Lewis S. Feuer, 'The Friendship of Edwin Ray Lankester and Karl Marx: The Last Episode in Marx's Intellectual Evolution', *Journal of the History of Ideas* 40, no. 4 (1979), deals with the relationship between Lankester and Marx.
2. Jacques Derrida, *Spectres de Marx: L'État de la dette, le travail du deuil et la nouvelle Internatio- nale* (Paris: Galilée, 1993).
3. Étienne Balibar, *La philosophie de Marx* (Paris: Éditions La Découverte, 1993). Balibar's position is interesting; in his youth, he was very close to Louis Althusser. But at the time he published his book on Marx's philosophy, he had gone in-depth into a field to which Marx himself had not devoted any deeper study, namely nationalism and racism. Together with American sociologist Immanuel Wallerstein, he wrote the epoch-making Étienne Balibar and Immanuel Wallerstein, *Race, Nation, Class: Ambiguous Identities* (London: Verso,1991).
4. John Cassidy 1993 in the *New Yorker*. Similar strains were heard at the same time from American Marxist Marshall Berman: Marshall Berman, *Allt som är fast förflyktigas: modernism och modernitet*, Swedish translation by Gunnar Sandin (Lund: Arkiv förlag, 1987), p. 266, whose final page reads: 'All of a sudden, the iconic looks more convincing than the ironic, that classic bearded presence, the atheist

as biblical prophet, is back just in time for the millennium.' On the phenomenon itself, see Randy Martin, *On Your Marx: Rethinking Socialism and the Left* (Minneapolis: University of Minnesota Press, 2001), in particular p. 229. Even Indo-British economist and politician Meghnad Desai was ready to talk about Marx's return at that time; see Meghnad Desai, *Marx's Revenge: The Resurgence of Capitalism and the Death of Statist Socialism* (London: Verso, 2002).

5. 'Marx the Millennium's "Greatest Thinker"', BBC News Online, 1 October 1999, bbc.co.uk.

6. On Soros, Eric Hobsbawm, *How to Change the World: Marx and Marxism, 1840–2011* (London: Little, Brown, 2011), p. 6. One politician who has attracted a great deal of attention over the past few years, former Greek finance minister Yanis Varoufakis, has also expressed ideas about Marx's topicality. The present era needs Marx for his insight that capitalism is not chiefly unjust but irrational, he says. Capitalism dooms entire generations to unemployment and turns the capitalists into anxiety-ridden automatons. It creates the 'democratic deficit' that he wants to explain, with Marx's help, of liberalism's ambition to distinguish politics from economics. But Varoufakis is no uncritical admirer of Marx. He says that the current era can learn from Marx's mistakes – both his failure to warn his followers not to amass their own unjust power and his ambition to create a mathematically exact theory from something that in his own opinion was impossible to quantify: concrete labour. See Yanis Varoufakis, 'How I Became an Erratic Marxist', *Guardian*, 18 February 2015. Rahel Jaeggi, 'Was (wenn überhaupt etwas) ist falsch Im Kapitalismus? Drei Wege der Kapitalismuskritik', *Nach Marx: Philosophie, Kritik, Praxis* (Frankfurt am Main: Suhrkamp, 2013) is an excellent article on how today's critique of capitalism, often weighed down with clichés, could be sharpened from Marxian starting points.

7. Thomas Piketty, *Le Capital au XXIe siècle* (Paris: Seuil, 2013), p. 29 and *passim*.

8. Göran Therborn, *The Killing Fields of Inequality* (Cambridge: Polity Press, 2013).

9. Göran Therborn, *From Marxism to Post-Marxism?* (London: Verso, 2008).

10. John Bellamy Foster, *Marx's Ecology: Materialism and Nature* (New York: Monthly Review Books, 2000). More on Foster below (pp. 71, 490).

11. Naomi Klein, *This Changes Everything: Capitalism vs. the Climate* (New York: Simon & Schuster, 2014), p. 177.

12. Guy Standing, *Prekariatet: den nya farliga klassen* (2011, översättning Joel Nordquist, Göteborg: Daidalos, 2013). See also Guy

Standing, *A Precariat Charter: From Denizens to Citizens* (London and New York: Bloomsbury Academic, 2014) on possible solutions.

13. On the opium metaphor, see p. 99.

14. On Eleanor Marx's plans for a biography, see Rachel Holmes, *Eleanor Marx: A Life* (London, New Dehli, New York and Sydney: Bloomsbury, 2014), pp. xvf and 195ff. Her notes have been published in the original in several editions, for example in Hans Magnus Enzensberger (ed.), *Gespräche mit Marx und Engels* (Frankfurt am Main: Insel Verlag, 1973).

15. Franz Mehring's *Karl Marx: hans livs historia* (Stockholm: Gidlunds, 1983) is also found in English translation.

16. Gemkow's biography has been published in four editions, the latest of which is from 1975; see Heinrich Gemkow, *Karl Marx: eine Biographie* (Berlin: Dietz, 1975).

17. Elster has also written a more comprehensive study of Marx, with the expressive title *Making Sense of Marx* (Cambridge: Cambridge University Press, 1985). Another representative of analytical Marxism is Melvin Rader, *Marx's Interpretation of History* (New York: Oxford University Press, 1979). British philosopher Gerald Cohen's *Karl Marx's Theory of History*, however, is probably the book from the analytical Marxist tradition that has garnered the most attention; see p. 375. American sociologist Erik Olin Wright is also sometimes counted among them. He has chiefly written interesting things about the concept of class; see Erik Olin Wright, *Class Counts: Comparative Studies in Class Analysis* (Cambridge: Cambridge University Press, 1997).

18. For Marx's literary appetite, see Jonathan Sperber, *Karl Marx: A Nineteenth-Century Life* (New York and London: Liveright, 2013), p. 489; on his piles of manuscripts, see pp. 487f.

19. Stefano Petrucciani, *Marx* (Rome: Carocci editore, 2009).

20. Stefano Petrucciani, *A lezione da Marx: nuove interpretazioni* (Rome: manifestolibri, 2012).

21. Nello Ajello, *Il lungo addio: intellettuali e PCI dal 1958 al 1991* (Rome-Bali: Editori Laterza, 1997) is a rewarding account of the development and dissolution of the Italian Communist Party.

22. Rolf Peter Sieferle's *Karl Marx zur Einführung* (Hamburg: Junius, 2007) is another introduction in German; it is a solid, knowledgeable, but unnecessarily detailed – and somewhat boring – book.

23. For further debate, see Ingo Elbe, 'Die Beharrlichkeit des "Engelsismus": Bemerkung-en zum Marx-Engels-Problem', *Marx-Engels-Jahrbuch*, 2007.

24. One article about the often ideologically conditioned shortcomings in the early volumes of MEGA is Rolf Dlubek's 'Die Entstehung der zweiten Marx-Engels-Gesamtausgabe im Spannungsfeld von

legitimatorischem Auftrag und editorischer Sorgfalt', *MEGA-Studien Journal 1994/1* (Amsterdam: International Institute of Social History, 1994), pp. 60–106.

25. On Engels's editing of Volumes II and III of *Capital*, see Regina Roth, 'Die Herausgabe von Band 2 und 3 des *Kapital* durch Engels', *Marx-Engels Jahrbuch 2012–13* (Berlin: Akademie-Verlag, 2013), pp. 168–82.

26. On Jenny Marx's possible contributions to the *Manifesto*, see p. 232.

2 The Time of Revolutions

1. On the term 'industrial revolution', see D. C. Coleman, *Myth, History and the Industrial Revolution* (London: The Hambledon Press, 1997), pp. 3–27, and Hans-Werner Hahn, *Die industrielle Revolution in Deutschland* (Munich: Wissenschaftsverlag, 2005), p. 51.

2. On the expansion of the railroads according to Eric Hobsbawm, see his *How to Change the World: Marx and Marxism, 1850–2011* (London: Little, Brown, 2011), p. 63.

3. The literature on the genesis and early organizations of struggle of the working class is enormous. The classic work regarding England is E. P. Thompson, *The Making of the English Working Class* (Harmondsworth, Middlesex: Pelican Books, 1968). Chartism and the formation of class consciousness come late in the account, after nearly 800 and 950 pages respectively. Some relatively fresh literature on Chartism is John K. Walton, *Chartism* (London: Routledge, 1999) and Miles Taylor, *Ernest Jones, Chartism, and the Romance of Politics 1818–1869* (Oxford: Oxford University Press, 2003).

4. Thomas Carlyle, *Selected Writings* (Harmonsdsworth: Penguin Books, 1984), pp. 75, 152–68, 211.

5. James Phillips Kay, *The Moral and Physical Condition of the Working Classes Employed in the Cotton Manufacture in Manchester* (London: James Ridgway, 1832). On the Manchester environment as a source of social anxiety and dark future scenarios, see Stephen Marcus, *Engels, Manchester, and the Working Class* (New York: Random House, 1974).

6. On the new content of the word 'revolution' as a thoroughgoing renewal, see Bernhard I. Cohen, *Revolution in Science* (Cambridge: Harvard University Press, 1985), pp. 51–90.

7. The term 'the second Industrial Revolution' was coined by Scottish polymath Patrick Geddes, who is best known as the father of the garden city; see Patrick Geddes, *Cities in Evolution: An Introduction to the Town Planning Movement and the Study of Civics* (London:

Williams & Norgate, 1915), Chapter 3. The American technology historian David Landes clarified the term; see David Landes, *The Unbound Prometheus: Technological Change and Industrial Development in Western Europe from 1750 to the Present* (Cambridge: Cambridge University Press, 2003).

8. Another biologist, Alfred Russel Wallace, developed a theory that was rather like Darwin's, thus rushing Darwin to fully work out his own discovered in *The Origin of Species*. Amabel Williams-Ellis's *Darwin's Moon: A Biography of Alfred Russel Wallace* (London: Blackie, 1966) is a biography of the remarkable and contradictory Wallace. The literature on Darwin is incalculably great; one splendid account of Darwin's place in his time is Adrian Desmond and James Moore, *Darwin* (London: Penguin Books, 1992).

9. The standard work on social Darwinism, in particular in the United States, is Eric Hofstadter, *Nations and Nationalism since 1790: Programme, Myth, Reality* (Cambridge: Cambridge University Press, 1992).

10. The great comprehensive biography of Virchow and his work is Constantin Goschler, *Rudolf Virchow: Mediziner, Anthropologe, Politiker* (Köln: Böhlau, 2009).

11. The nineteenth-century history of psychology and sociology is the subject of a large and growing amount of literature. Robert Smith's *The Fontana History of the Human Sciences* (London: Fontana, 1997) is a useful summary.

12. Peter Gay's *Freud* (Stockholm: Bonniers, 1990) is a good, reliable biography of Freud.

13. On the development of statistics, see Stephen M. Stigler, *The History of Statistics: The Measurement of Uncertainty Before 1900* (Cambridge: Harvard University Press, 1986).

14. Joseph Schumpeter's *History of Economic Analysis* (New York: Oxford University Press, 1954) is still the standard work on the history of economic thinking.

3 The Darling of Fortune

1. Basic information on Marx's background and the environment he grew up in can be found in Heinz Monz, *Karl Marx: Grundlagen der Entwicklung zu Leben und Werk* (Trier: NCO-Verlag, 1973), which is otherwise a greatly expanded second edition of his *Karl Marx and Trier*.

2. On Wyttenbach, see above all Tina Klupsch, *Johann Hugo Wyttenbach: Eine historische Biographie* (Trier: Kliomedia, 2012). On Wyttenbach's attitude towards the French Revolution and his

criticism of Napoleon, ibid., pp. 167–71; his rising Prussian nationalism, p. 180; his political resignation, p. 201.

3. On Ludwig Gall, see Heinz Monz, *Karl Marx: Grundlagen der Entwicklun zu Leben und Werk* (Trier: NCO-Verlag, 1973), p. 105; on *Triersche Zeitung*, ibid., p. 107.

4. On Heinrich Marx's cautious attitude at the Casino party, see ibid., p. 261.

5. On Karl's family and his siblings, see Monz, *Karl Marx*, pp. 228–38.

6. Heinrich Marx's letter about Hermann, MEGA III/1, p. 301; on Eduard, ibid., p. 319.

7. The letter in which Emilie claims she is similar to her brother was addressed to Karl and Jenny Marx's youngest daughter Eleanor, 17 March 1883; see ibid., p. 237.

8. On Marx's exemption from military service, see the letter from Karl Friedrich Köppen, 3 June 1841, MEGA III/1, pp. 360–3. Köppen, a friend from Berlin and himself rejected from military service, wondered somewhat ironically 'what that pretty little lady', the future Jenny Marx, thought about this 'incapacity'. His father's concern for Karl's lungs are detailed in a letter of May–June 1836, MEGA III/1, p. 297. For his mother's term for Karl as 'ein Glückskind', see the letter from Heinrich Marx to Karl, 9 September 1836, MEGA III/1, p. 300.

9. Edgar von Westphalen, Karl's schoolmate and future brother-in-law, described him as a 'Protestant à la Lessing' – a tolerant man with an ecumenical bent who believed in reason. Heinz Monz, *Karl Marx: Grundlagen der Entwicklung zu Leben und Werk* (Trier: NCO-Verlag, 1973), p. 250.

10. On Heinrich Marx's education and career, and his and his family's conversion to Protestantism, see Monz, *Karl Marx*, pp. 239–96. Jonathan Sperber, *Karl Marx: A Nineteenth-Century Life* (New York: Liveright, 2013), p. 13, puts great effort into tracing Heinrich's legal education, and comes to the conclusion that it was rather shaky. If that is the case, it should be added that this did not prevent him from becoming a successful lawyer.

11. The exhaustive account of the relationship between Heinrich and Karl Marx, including Eleanor Marx's testimony, is Manfred Schönke, *Karl Marx und Heinrich Marx und ihre Geschwister: Lebenserzeugniss – Briefe – Dokumente* (Bonn: Pahl-Rugstein Nachfolger, 1993).

12. Marx to Lassalle, 8 May 1861, MEGA III/1, p. 143, MEW 30, p. 602, CW 41, p. 283. The old woman intrigues him: 'wegen ihres sehr feines esprit und der unerschütterlichen Charactergleichheit', MEW 30, p. 602.

13. On little Karl's tyranny towards his sisters, for example, see Sperber, *Karl Marx*, p. 25. The basis of this tradition is, again, Eleanor Marx's

notes; her aunts are said to have told her about this; see Hans
Magnus Enzenberger, *Gespräche mit Marx und Engels* (Frankfurt
am Main: Insel Verlag, 1973).

14. Marx's student writings are reproduced in MEGA I/1, pp. 449–70.
The German essay is translated in CW 1, pp. 3–9, the essay on
Christianity and Latin, ibid. pp. 636–42.

15. Heinrich Marx to Karl regarding Vitus Loers in a letter of 18–29
November 1835, MEGA III/1, pp. 291f., CW 1, p. 647.

16. Marx's poetry is collected in MEGA I/1. *Buch der Lieder* can be
found there on pp. 557–612. There are English translations in
CW 1, pp. 517–632. It is not unreasonable to assert that a streak
of Romanticism remains in Marx's thinking even after he settled
accounts with the enthusiasm of his youth. In at least one description, he remains a Romantic throughout his life: Ernst Eduard Kux,
Karl Marx – die revolutionäre Konfession (Zürich: Buchdruckerei
Neue Zürcher Zeitung, 1966), but this is a great exaggeration.

17. Heinrich Marx's first reaction to Karl's poetry, letter of 18–29
November 1835, MEGA III/1, pp. 291f. The poem 'Wunsch' can be
found in MEGA I/1, pp. 718ff; presumably, this is the poem Heinrich Marx also comments on in MEGA III/1, p. 724.

18. The letter in which Heinrich Marx regrets not being of a poetic
nature himself was written between February and the beginning of
March 1836, ibid., p. 294, CW 1, pp. 649ff.

19. 'als schwacher Zeichen ewiger Liebe', MEGA I/1, p. 617. The letter
is not reproduced in CW.

20. 'The Stupid Germans', MEGA I/1, p. 643, CW 1, p. 575.

21. The Hegel poem, MEGA, p. 644, CW 1, p. 477; *Scorpion and Felix*,
MEGA, pp. 688–703, CW 1, p. 616.

22. On Ludwig von Westphalen, his family background, his careers, and
their differing views on Jenny's relations with Karl Marx, as well as
on his elder son Ferdinand and his unfavourable attitude towards
the relations between Jenny and Karl, see Monz, *Karl Marx*, pp.
319–42.

23. The letter in which Heinrich Marx reminds his son of his advantages
was written on 17 November 1837 and can be found in MEGA
III/1, p. 321 and CW 1, p. 684.

24. Letter from Sophie, 28 December 1836, MEGA III/1, p. 304, CW
1, pp. 666f.

25. The poem that is reminiscent of Friedrich's painting is called 'Sehn-
sucht' (Yearning), MEGA I/1, pp. 574ff. 'To Jenny' is reproduced
there, pp. 581f, and in CW 1, p. 521f. Goethe's *Egmont: ein Trauerspiel in fünf Aufzügen* in Johann Wolfgang von Goethe, *Egmont:
ein Trauerspiel in fünf Aufzügen, Goethes sämtliche Werke nach
Epochen seines Schaffens* (München: Carl Hanser, 1990), p. 286.

26. First letter from Heinrich to Karl Marx, 8 November 1835, MEGA III/1, CW 1, p. 661.

27. The letter in which his father reminds Karl that he is not the only child is from 19 March 1836, and is reproduced in MEGA III/1, p. 296, CW 1, pp. 652f.

28. The complaint about the lack of order is made in a letter written sometime in February or the beginning of March 1836, MEGA III/1, p. 293, CW 1, p. 650.

29. Heinrich Marx's letter of attorney on a change of place of study, 1 July 1836, MEGA III/1, p. 299, CW 1, p. 655.

30. The admonitions about moderation and orderliness are found in the previously cited letters from the fall of 1835 and the spring of 1836. For the father's description of the son in a letter of 12 August 1837, see MEGA III/1, p. 311f, CW 1, pp. 674f. The last, resigned letter was written 10 February 1838, MEGA III/1, p. 328f, CW 1, pp. 691ff.

31. Letter to his father, 10–11 November 1837, MEGA I/1, pp. 9–18, CW 1, pp. 10–21.

32. That Marx was likely the only one who spoke of a 'Doctor's Club' is evident from Wolfgang Essbach, *Die Junghegelianer: Soziologie einer Intellektuellengruppe* (München: Wilhelm Fink Verlag, 1988), p. 69. Essbach's investigation of the Young Hegelians is the most detailed. The literature on the subject is great. Karl Löwith *Die hegelsche Linke* (Stuttgart: Friedrich Frommann Verlag, 1962), an anthology of texts with a long introduction by Löwith – has almost classic status. One counterpart from the era of the GDR is Manfred Buhr, *Die Hegelsche Linke: Dokumente zu Philosophie und Politik im deutschen Vormärz* (Leipzig: Philipp Reclam Verlag, 1985), likewise with a comprehensive introduction and a very large selection of texts containing numerous letters. One American counterpart is Lawrence S. Stepelevich, *The Young Hegelians: An anthology* (New York: Cambridge University Press, 1983). Monographs besides Essbach's are William J. Brazill, *The Young Hegelians* (New Haven and London: Yale University Press, 1970) and Warren Breckman, *Marx, the Young Hegelians, and the Origin of Radical Social Theory: Dethroning the Self* (Cambridge: Cambridge University Press, 1999). It is customary to point out Hegel's disciple, professor of law Eduard Gans, as an important inspiration for the Young Hegelians and Marx as well, who attended Gans's lectures during his studies. It is difficult, however, to support the assertion that Marx would have been more deeply influenced by him. On Marx as a pupil of Gans, see Auguste Cornu, *Karl Marx et Friedrich Engels: leur vie et leur œuvre*, bd 1, *Les années d'enfance et de jeunesse, La gauche hégélien- ne: 1818/1820–1844* (Paris: P.U.F., 1955), pp. 85–9.

33. David Friedrich Strauss, *Das Leben Jesu kritisch bearbeitet* (Tübingen: C.F. Osiander, 1835–6).

34. See Brazill, *The Young Hegelians*. The assertion that Marx was not a Young Hegelian goes back to Cornu, *Karl Marx et Friedrich Engels*, and played a role in the same assertion turning up in Althusser.

35. Johann Albrecht Friedrich von Eichhorn lived between 1779 and 1856. Engels's letter to Ruge, 26 July 1842, MEGA III/1, p. 235.

36. Schelling's lecture series in Berlin has been depicted countless times. A living picture can be gleaned from Arsenij Gulyga, *Schelling: Leben und Werk* (Stuttgart: Deutsche Verlags-Anstalt, 1989), pp. 356–62. Schelling's lectures are reproduced in F. W. J. Schelling, *Sämtliche Werke* (Stuttgart-Augsburg: J. G. Cotta'scher, 1861). Kierkegaard's reactions are summarized by Joakim Garff, *Søren Aabye Kierkegaard: en biografi* (Nora: Nya Doxa, 2002), p. 182. Engels's writings on Schelling and his lectures can be found in MEGA I/3, pp. 256–338, MEW: Engänzungsband, Zweiter Teil, pp. 163–245, and in CW 2, pp. 181–264. 'Hegeling', MEGA, p. 272, MEW, p. 176, and CW, pp. 196f.

37. On the persecution of Hegel's students and his engagement for them, see for example Jacques d'Hondt, *Hegel secret: recherches sur les sources cachées de la pensée de Hegel* (Paris: Épiméthée, 1968).

38. G. W. F. Hegel, *Grundlinien der Philosophie des Rechts* (Frankfurt am Main: Suhrkamp, 1821) § 297, p. 464.

39. 'What is rational …', G. W. F. Hegel, *Elements of the Philosophy of Right* (Cambridge: Cambridge University Press, 1991), p. 20.

40. On Hegel's lectures in legal philosophy, see for example Hegel, *Philosophie des Rechts: Die Vorlesungen von 1819/20 in einer Nachschrift* (Frankfurt am Main: Suhrkamp, 1983), and there above all Dieter Henrich's 'Einleitung', p. 15.

41. On the ideas of a 'beamtete Intellgenz' that could reform society in the desired direction, see Wolfgang Essbach, *Die Junghegelianer: Soziologie einer Intellektuellengruppe* (München: Wilhelm Fink Verlag), pp. 103–7; quote from Ruge, p. 106; on Bauer and his dashed hopes, pp. 117–31.

42. Twelve letters to Marx in Bruno Bauer's hand are preserved: the first from 11 December 1839 and the last from 13 December 1842. They are reproduced, along with other letters to Marx, in MEGA III/1, pp. 335–86.

43. The letter from Marx to Bachmann is reproduced in MEGA III/1, p. 19 and CW 1, p. 379.

44. Bachmann's insert into the minutes of the faculty of 13 April 1841 is reproduced in MEGA III/1, Apparatus, p. 565.

45. On Leibniz, see MEGA I/1, p. 24, CW 1, pp. 37f; on Hegel, ibid.,

pp. 13 and 29. Hegel's pronouncement on the subject, see G. W. F. Hegel, *Vorlesungen über die Geschichte der Philosophie*, vol. II, G. W. F. Hegels Werke, bd 19 (Frankfurt am Main: Suhrkamp, 1986), in particular p. 312.

46. MEGA I/1, p. 13, CW 1, p. 29.

47. On the difference between the conceptions of Epicurus and Democritus, MEGA I/1, pp. 27–40, CW 1, pp. 39–53; on Epicurus, the deviation from the correct line and later criticisms of this, pp. 36 and 49 respectively; the defence of Epicurus and the polemic against Democritus in the Hegelian spirit, pp. 39 and 52 respectively, and *passim*. The thesis that Marx was the first to clearly expound the difference between the conceptions of Democritus and Epicurus on necessity and chance goes back to Cyril Bailey, *The Greek Atomists and Epicurus* (Oxford: Clarendon Press, 1928). See also Benjamin Farrington, *The Faith of Epicurus* (London: Weidenfeld and Nicolson, 1967), pp. 7–9, 113–19.

48. John Bellamy Foster, *Marx's Ecology: Materialism and Nature* (New York: Monthly Review Books, 2000), pp. 60 and 32. On Darwin's and Marx's materialism, pp. 178 and 196. On Epicurus's philosophy and its early effects, see James Warren (ed.), *The Cambridge Companion to Epicureanism* (Cambridge: Cambridge University Press, 2009). It is not only Foster who emphasizes how important the philosophy of Epicurus remained for Marx. Italian philosopher Costanzo Preve talks about 'four masters' for Marx: Epicurus, Rousseau (equal democracy), Adam Smith, and Hegel; Constanzo Preve, *l lo di Arianna: quindici lezioni di loso a marxista* (Milano: Vangelista, 1990).

49. Marx quotes Aeschylus, MEGA I/1, pp. 14f, CW 1, pp. 30f. The quote is from Aeschylus's *Prometheus Bound*, lines 966–9.

50. Polemic regarding interpretations of Hegel, ibid., pp. 66–70 and 84–8 respectively.

51. Letter from Bauer to Marx, 12 April 1841, MEGA III/1, p. 357. On morals (*die Moralität*) in contrast to ethics, see for example G. W. F. Hegel, *Wissenschaft der Logik* (Frankfurt am Main: Suhrkamp, 1969), §141, pp. 286–91. On Hegel's followers, MEGA I/1, pp. 66–70. Marx develops this criticism in more detail in *Zur Kritik der Hegelschen Rechtsphilosophie*; see p. 94.

52. Dedication to Ludwig von Westphalen, MEGA I/1, p. 12, CW 1, pp. 27f.

53. Letters to Ruge, 9 July 1842, MEGA III/1, p. 28, CW 1, p. 389; 25 January 1843, ibid., pp. 43 and 397; and 13 March 1843, ibid., pp. 44 and 399.

54. On Caroline von Westphalen, see Rachel Holmes, *Eleanor Marx: A Life* (London: Bloomsbury, 2014), pp. 23, 29, 33, and 36. According

to David McLellan, the reason Caroline set out for Bad Kreuznach with her daughter and future son-in-law was that her stepson Ferdinand von Westphalen, a vehement opponent of his half-sister's marriage, had obtained a prominent position in Trier.

55. The painting of Jenny von Westphalen I have in mind is by an unknown artist. It is reproduced in Monz, *Karl Marx*, fig 18. There is, however, a more beautiful medallion, reproduced in Heinrich Gemkow, *Karl Marx: eine Biographie* (Berlin: Dietz, 1967).

56. Quote about Marx after David McLellan, *Karl Marx: His Life and Thought* (St Albans: Paladin, 1973), p. 53.

57. The letter in French from Jenny to Karl, 10 February 1845, MEGA III/1, pp. 453f.

58. Letter from Bauer, 31 March 1841, MEGA III/1, p. 354.

59. Early letters from Jenny von Westphalen to Karl Marx quoted and cited here are from 10 May 1838 (MEGA III/1, p. 331), 24 June 1838 (pp. 332f) and 1839–40 (pp. 337ff).

60. The letter on the lot of women from early March 1843, MEGA III/1, p. 396.

61. According to Albert Rosenkranz, priest in Bad Kreuznach, the Pauluskirche was temporarily closed for repairs and the Wilhelmskirche replaced it. 'Pauluskirche (Bad Kreuznach)', Wikipedia.org.

62. *L'opinion publique* is an important concept in Rousseau. It has, however, many grounds in the French philosopher; for a thorough study, see Colette Ganochaud, *L'Opinion publique chez Jean-Jacques Rousseau* (Lille: Université de Lille III, 1978).

63. Carl Adolph Agardh, 'Opinions magt (I anledning af Europas ställning år 1830)', *Skånska Correspondenten* 1832, after Liedman *Att förändra världen – men med måtta: det svenska 1800-talet speglat i C A Agardhs och C J Boströms liv och verk* (Stockholm: Förlaget Arbetarkultur, 1991), p. 209.

64. The complete title of Ruge's periodical is *Anekdota zur neuesten deutschen Philosophie und Publicistik*, and it was published in two volumes in 1843 (Zürich/Winterthur: Literarisches Comptoir, I–II, 1843). An account of Marx's early journalistic work is given in MEGA I/1, Apparatus, pp. 963–83. Letter to Ruge 20 March 1842, MEGA III/1, CW 1, p. 385.

65. 'Comments on the latest Prussian Censorship Instruction', MEGA I/1, pp. 97–118, CW 1, pp. 109–31.

66. Ruge's opinion of Marx quoted according to MEGA I/1, Apparatus, p. 966. Hess made his judgement of Marx in a letter to Berthold Auerbach of 2 September 1842, which is reproduced in Moses Hess, *Briefwechsel*, published by Edmund Silberner with the assistance of Werner Blumenberg, bd II ('s-Gravenhage: Mouton & Co., 1959). The quote is reproduced in the great standard biography of Hess by

Edmund Silberner, *Moses Hess: Geschichte seines Lebens* (Leiden: E. J. Brill, 1966), p. 95, as well as in various Marx biographies, for example Siegel 1978, p. 78.

67. 'Proceedings of the Sixth Rhine Province Assembly', MEGA I/1, pp. 121–69, CW 1, pp. 132–81.

68. 'Comments on the latest Prussian Censorship Instruction', MEGA I/1, pp. 97–118, CW 1, pp. 101–31.

69. MEGA I/1, p. 100, CW 1, pp. 111f.

70. Ibid., pp. 104 and 116.

71. MEGA I/1, pp. 127 and 133, CW 1, pp. 139 and 144.

72. Ibid., pp. 146 and 158.

73. Ibid., pp. 161–5 and 177.

74. Ibid., pp. 143 and 155.

75. This statement was not published until 1922, three years after Luxemburg's death, Rosa Luxemburg, *Världskriget och de europeiska revolutionerna: Politiska skrifter i urval 1914–1919* (Lund: Arkiv, 1985), p. 83.

76. MEGA I/1, pp. 172–90, CW 1, pp. 184–202.

77. 'Proceedings of the Sixth Rhine Province Assembly. Third Article Debates on the Law on Thefts of Wood', MEGA I/1, pp. 199–236, CW 1, pp. 224–63. The quotes from pp. 210 and 235 respectively. Marx uses the word 'class' several times, including on pp. 209 and 234.

78. The censors' reactions are reproduced in detail in MEGA I/1, Apparatus, p. 1022.

79. 'Communism and the Augsburg *Allgemeine Zeitung*', MEGA I/1, pp. 237–42, CW 1, pp. 215–23.

80. 'The Divorce Bill: Criticism of a Criticism', MEGA I/1, pp. 260–3 and 287–90, CW 1, pp. 274–6 and 307–10.

81. 'Justification of the Correspondent from the Mosel', MEGA I/1, pp. 296–327, CW 1, pp. 332–58, 313. On head and heart, pp. 313 and 349 respectively; on anonymity, ibid., pp. 297 and 333; on distress and necessity, pp. 301 and 337 respectively.

82. The decision to shut down the paper is reproduced in MEGA I/1, Apparatus, pp. 1108. 'Announcement' that the editorial board is finished, MEGA I/1, p. 366, CW 1, p. 376.

83. Marx W. Wartofsky, *Feuerbach* (Cambridge: Cambridge University Press, 1977), pp. 141, 190, and 210.

84. The Engels quote in MEGA I/3, p. 225, CW 2, p. 197 and I/30, p. 263, CW 26, p. 364.

85. On Feuerbach and Marx, see for example Werner Schuffenhauer, *Feuerbach und der junge Marx: zur Entstehungsgeschichte der marxistischen Weltanschauung* (Berlin: VEB Deutscher Verlag der Wissenschaften, 1965) and Ferdinand Maier, *Wirkungsgeschichte*

als Dialektik von Assimilation und Verdrängung: Ludwig Feuerbachs kritischer Humanismus und die marxsche Metakritik (Cuxhaven and Dartford: Traude Junghaus, 2000). Feuerbach is placed in another context in an interesting way in Peter C. Caldwell, *Love, Death, and Revolution in Central Europe: Ludwig Feuerbach, Moses Hess, Louise Dittmar, Richard Wagner* (New York: Palgrave Macmillan, 2009).

86. Feuerbach's 'Principles of the Philosophy of the Future' is reproduced in Ludwig Feuerbach, *Philosophische Kritiken und Grundsätze i Sämtliche Werke* (Stuttgart-Bad Cannstatt: Fromman Verlag, 1959), pp. 245–320, and in an English translation in Feuerbach 1986. The article was originally published in Arnold Ruge's journal *Anekdota* in 1843.

87. Marx's letter to Feuerbach of 3 October 1843, MEGA III/1, pp. 58ff, CW 3, pp. 349ff.

88. Feuerbach's drafts and letter, MEGA III/1, pp. 413–7 and 419f.

89. Marx's letter to Feuerbach, 18 October 1844, MEGA III/1, CW 3, pp. 354–7. On this letter, see Schuffenhauer, in the files, pp. 87–135.

90. On Feuerbach's draft, see MEGA III/1, Apparatus, pp. 797–800. See further Werner Schuffenhauer, *Feuerbach und der junge Marx: zur Entstehungsgeschichte der marxistischen Weltanschauung* (Berlin: VEB Deutscher Verlad der Wissenschaften, 1965), pp. 66–86.

91. On Feuerbach and *Capital* see Marx W. Wartofsky, *Feuerbach* (Cambridge: Cambridge University Press, 1977), p. 451.

92. Hildegard von Bingen (1098–1179) was a famous abbess, mystic, and author. A good picture of her and her work can be found in Christine Büchner, *Hildegard von Bingen: eine Lebensgeschichte* (Frankfurt am Main: Insel-Verlag, 2009).

93. MEGA I/2, pp. 11 and 24f, MEW 1, pp. 209 and 224, CW 3, pp. 10f and 24f.

94. Marx's translation into everyday language, MEGA I/2, pp. 26, MEW 1, pp. 226, and CW 3, p. 25.

95. MEGA I/2, p. 88, MEW 1, p. 296, and CW 3, p. 91.

96. On mysticism MEGA I/2, pp. 8, 10, and 92, MEW 1, pp. 206, 208, and 287, and CW 3, pp. 7f, 9, and 83.

97. On the nobility, MEGA I/2, pp. 114ff, MEW 1, pp. 310ff, and CW 3, pp. 105ff. Blumenbach developed his racial doctrine for the first time in Johann Friedrich Blumenbach, *De generis humani varietate nativa liber* (Goettingae, 1776); the Latin title means 'Book on the Natural Variations of the Human Species' in English.

98. For Hegel's modernity, his adaptability and his defence of private ownership, see MEGA I/2, pp. 104–10, MEW 1, p. 299–305, and CW 3, pp. 95–101.

99. On democracy, MEGA I/2, pp. 30f, MEW 1, pp. 231ff, and CW 3, pp. 29–32. On atomized society, pp. 88, 283, and 79; the quote on individualism, pp. 90f, 285, and 81. On communist essence, pp. 88, 283, and 81. (In CW the translation actually reads 'communal being', but the charge in Marx's text is thus thwarted.)

100. The most exhaustive account on religion as opium of the people in German philosophy is found in Michael Löwy, 'Über Religion und Kritik', *Friedrich Engels – ein Klassiker nach 100 Jahren* (Hamburg: VSA-Verlag, 1996), p. 95.

101. 'Contribution to the Critique of Hegel's Philosophy of Law, Introduction' is found in MEGA I/2, pp. 170–83, MEW 1, pp. 378–91, and CW 3, pp. 175–87. The quotes are on pp. 170, 378, and 175f.

102. 'On the Jewish Question' is reproduced in MEGA I/2, pp. 141–69, MEW 1, pp. 347–77, and CW 3, pp. 146–74. The quotes are in MEGA I/2, pp. 146 and 165, MEW 1, pp. 352 and 373, CW 3, pp. 151 and 170f. Thomas Hamilton, *Men and Manners in America* (Cambridge: Cambridge University press, 2009 [1833]).

103. Michael Löwy, *Förlossning och utopi* (Göteborg: Daidalos, 1992 [1988]), p. 7, on the flowering of Jewish culture in Central Europe; on the idea that Marx could be a messianist in disguise, p. 23.

104. Arnold Künzli, *Karl Marx: eine Psychographie* (Wien: Europa Verlag, 1966).

105. On the 'Jewish joke', see for example Adam Sutcliffe, 'Ludwig Börne Jewish messianism, and the politics of money' (*Leo Baeck Institute*, 2012), pp. 213–37.

4 In Paris

1. One important gateway to knowledge of French socialism and communism, for Marx as for so many other young Germans, was Lorenz Stein's *Der Sozialismus und Kommunismus des heutigen Frankreichs* (Socialism and Communism in Present-Day France, 1842). Stein was no sympathizer; on the other hand, he wrote a good, conscientious introduction. Lorenz von Stein, *Der Sozialismus und Kommunismus des heutigen Frankreichs: ein Beitrag zur Zeitgeschichte* (Leipzig: O. Wigand, 1848 [1842]). Once in Paris, Marx could personally acquaint himself with the new movements.

2. The literature on Marie d'Agoult is extensive. The most detailed is Jacques Albert Vier, *La comtesse d'Agoult et son temps*, vol. 1–6 (Paris: A. Colin, 1955–1963). Among the newer biographies, Phyllis Stock-Morton, *The Life of Marie d'Agoult, Alias Daniel Stern* (Baltimore: Johns Hopkins, 2000) and Charles Dupêchez, *Marie d'Agoult, 1805–1876* (Paris: Perrin, 2001). On the chiefly German

exiles in Paris, see for example Lloyd S. Kramer, *Threshold of a New World: Intellectuals and the Exile Experience in Paris, 1830–1848* (Ithaca, N.Y.: Cornell University Press, 1988).

3. Jacques Attali, *Karl Marx ou l'esprit du monde* (Paris: Fayard, 2005), p. 88. Cornu devotes no attention whatsoever to life in the salons, nor does he say anything about the socialist ideas with either Marie d'Agoult or George Sand.

4. Letter from Hermann Ewerbeck to Karl Marx, 31 October 1845, MEGA III/1, p. 489.

5. Heine's importance to Marx is toned down, for example, in Jerrold Seigel, *Marx's Fate: The Shape of a Life* (Princeton: Princeton University Press, 1978), pp. 95f.; Francis Wheen, *Karl Marx: en biografi* (Stockholm: Norstedts, 2000), p. 67; and Attali, *Karl Marx ou l'esprit du monde*, pp. 86–92. The only person who emphasizes Heine's particular significance is Auguste Cornu, *Karl Marx et Friedrich Engels: leur vie et leur œuvre*, vol. 3, *Marx à Paris* (Paris: P.U.F., 1962), pp. 27–35. But true to habit, Cornu only has eyes for the political dimension and not the cultural one. A remarkable account of Heine's development during his Paris years after 1831 and up to the February Revolution of 1848 can be found in Peter Uwe Hohendahl, *Heinrich Heine: europäischer Schriftsteller und Intellektueller* (Berlin: Erik Schmidt Verlag, 2008), pp. 65–80.

6. The creator of Saint-Simonism was Claude Henri de Rouvroy, Count of Saint-Simon (1760–1825), whose influence was to a great degree posthumous. He developed an extraordinarily complex doctrine concerning a socialist society of the future. On the one hand, society would be led by the real future elites – practitioners of science and industrialists – and on the other it would be permeated by arts and music, and even a kind of earthly religiosity. It is no wonder that the Saint-Simonist movement was characterized by internal splits. But its influence in France became enormous, reaching long into the future – perhaps even up to Charles de Gaulle (1890–1970). See for example Rolf Peter Fehlbaum, *Saint-Simon und die Saint-Simonisten: Vom laissez-faire zur Wirtschaftsplanung* (Basel: Veröffentlichen der List Gesellschaft, 1970), pp. 590–640.

7. On the letter to Marx and its publication, see Claude Malécot et al., *Le monde de George Sand* (Paris: Éditions, du Patrimoine, 2003), p. 164.

8. The depiction of Parisian cultural life in Marx's time in Paris is found in George Sand, *Œuvres autobiographiques*, vol. II (Paris: Bibliotèque de la Pléiade, Gallimard, 1971), in particular p. 390. Like many others, Heine was in love with George Sand and wrote enthusiastically about her in his book on Paris and France: 'the greatest author France had produced after the July Revolution [of

1830], that daring and solitary genius'; Heinrich Heine, *Lutetia: Correspondences sur la politique, l'art et la vie* (Paris: Michel Lévy, 1863), p. 39. Furthermore, Sand was said to have an 'admirable beauty' – in fact, Heine compares her with the Venus de Milo, p. 48. George Sand's attempt to create French proletarian literature found expression, for example, in her encouraging the Toulon blacksmith Charles Poncy to write. See Claude Malécot et al., *Le monde de George Sand* (Paris: Éditions du Patrimoine, 2003), p. 48.

9. Letter to Feuerbach, CS 3, pp. 355f. Édouard de Pompery, *Exposition de la science sociale, constituée par C. Fourier* (Paris: Librarie sociale, 1840), pp. 13 and 29.

10. There is a gigantic body of work on Saint-Simon, Fourier, and Owen. A standard work that is far from unobjectionable is Frank E. Manuel and Fritzie P. Manuel, *Utopian Thought in the Western World* (Cambridge, Mass.: Belknap Press of Harvard University Press, 1979).

11. Marx, 'On Proudhon', MEW 16, pp. 25–32, CW 20, pp. 26–33.

12. Letter from Proudhon to Marx, 17 May 1846, MEGA I III/2, p. 206. It was Jacques Pierre Brissot who first spoke of property as theft, in Jacques Pierre Brissot de Warville, *Recherches philosophiques sur le droit de propriété et sur le sol considérés dans la nature et dans la société, par un jeune philosophe* (Paris: publisher unknown, 1780). The literature on Pierre-Joseph Proudhon is quite large. One interesting work is Gilda Manganaro Favaretto, *Possibilitá e limiti nel 'socialism scientifico' di P. J. Proudhon* (Rom: Edizioni dell'Ateneo, 1983).

13. On Bakunin's later assessment of Marx, see Auguste Cornu, *Karl Marx et Friedrich Engels: leur vie et leur œuvre*, vol. 3, *Marx à Paris* (Paris: P.U.F., 1962), pp. 46.

14. On the various revolutionary associations, see Otto Büsch, *Die frühsozialistischen Bünde in der Geschichte der deutschen Arbeiterbewegung* (Berlin: Colloquium Verlag, 1975).

15. On the police spies' reports, see Cornu, *Karl Marx et Friedrich Engels*, p. 7.

16. Letter from Marx to Ruge, September 1843, MEGA III/1, p. 56. The letter is not reproduced in *Collected Works*; it is, on the other hand, in the Marxist Internet Archive: 'Letter from Marx to Arnold Ruge in Dresden', Marxists.org.

17. Peter C. Caldwell, *Love, Death, and Revolution in Central Europe: Ludwig Feuerbach, Moses Hess, Louise Dittmar, Richard Wagner* (New York: Palgrave Macmillan, 2009) describes how Marx was preferred as editor over Hess, p. 47. The great Hess biography is Edmund Silberner, *Moses Hess: Geschichte seines Lebens* (Leiden: E. J. Brill, 1966).

18. Letter from Hess to Marx, 3 July 1844, MEGA III/1, pp. 434f.

19. Weitling, *Garantien der Harmonie und Freiheit*. 1842, accessible at archive.org. On progress as natural law XI; on property as the origin of all evil, p. 18; on the second Messiah, p. 243; on the children who would be part of a school army, p. 188. Regarding the latter, compare with Charles Fourier, *Slaget om de små pastejerna: skrifter i urval* (Stockholm: Federativs klassiker 9, 1983), the chapter 'Industrial Armies', pp. 116–19. On women, pp. 184–7; on freedom of the press, pp. 214–8; on freedom of choice, p. 225; on the people's monarchy p. 251.

20. Kurt Aspelin, *Det europeiska missnöjet: samhällsanalys och histo-riespekulation: studier i C.J.L. Almqvists författarskap åren kring 1840* (Stockholm: Norstedts, 1979), writes about utopian mysticism, pp. 19–26. The same tradition is described in a more general manner in Manuel and Manuel, *Utopian Thought in the Western World*. See, for example, the section on Enfantin, pp. 615–40.

21. Heine's letter to Marx, 21 September 1844, MEGA III/1, pp. 443f. On the world turned upside down, see for example Christopher Hill, *The World Turned Upside Down: Radical Ideas During The English Revolution* (Harmondsworth: Penguin Books, 1984) and Le Roy Ladurie, *Karnevalen i Romans: från kyndelsmäss till askonsdag 1579–1580* (Stockholm: Atlantis, 1982 [1979]).

22. On the economic background to early German industrialization, see Hans-Ulrich Wehler, *Deutsche Gesellschaftsgeschichte*, vol. 2, *Von dem Reformära bis zur industriellen und politischen 'Deutschen Doppelrevolution' 1815–1845/49* (München: C. H. Beck, 1987), pp. 585–684. On Gerhart Hauptmann's drama, see Hans Schwab-Felisch, *Gerhart Hauptmann: Die Weber: Dichtung und Wirklichkeit* (München: Ullstein, 2000). Käthe Kollwitz's images from the weavers' uprising are richly represented in the Käthe Kollwitz museums in Berlin and Cologne.

23. There is a great deal of literature on pauperism. See, for example, Karl Williams 1981 and Gertrude Himmelfarb, *The Idea of Poverty: England in the Early Industrial Age* (London: Faber, 1984).

24. Marx, 'Critical Marginal Notes on the Article "The King of Prussia and Social Reform. By a Prussian" ', MEW 1, pp. 392–409, CW 3, pp. 189–206.

25. Sigmund Freud, *Das Unbehagen der Kultur*, vol. 14 Gesammelte Werke (London: Imago, 1948 [1930]).

26. On the consciousness of the weavers and Weitling's efforts, see 'Kritische Randglossen', MEGA I/2, pp. 458f, MEW 1, pp. 404f, and CW 3, pp. 201f.

27. Letter from Weitling to Marx, 18 October 1844, MEGA III/1, p. 445.

28. 'Vorwort zur Gesamtausgabe', MEGA I/1, pp. 18ff. The person who

went furthest in emphasizing the distance between Marx and Engels is Norman Levine, *The Tragic Deception: Marx contra Engels* (Oxford and Santa Barbara: Clio Books, 1975). Even more broadly arranged is Norman Levine, *Dialogue within the Dialectic* (London: George Allen & Unwin, 1982), in which the author goes up through Lenin, Stalin, and Mao, and their way of (poorly) managing the inheritance from Marx. Above all, Tristram Hunt exaggerates the importance of Engels for *Capital*, for example in *Marx's General: The Revolutionary Life of Friedrich Engels* (New York: Metropolitan, 2009), pp. 234f.

29. Late in life, Engels remembered in a letter to Franz Mehring that initial 'distinctly chilly meeting' with Marx; letter from Engels to Mehring, end of April 1895, MEW 39, p. 473, CW 50, p. 503.

30. On the environment in Manchester, see Marcus, *Engels, Manchester and the Working Class*.

31. 'Outlines of a Critique of Political Economy', MEGA I/3, pp. 467–94, MEW 1, pp. 499–524, CW 3, pp. 418–43, and on liberal theory, pp. 472, 502, and 421.

32. Engels on Smith as Luther, MEGA I/3, p. 476, MEW 1, p. 503, and CW 3, p. 422.

33. On the theory of value and the importance of inventions for the forces of production, ibid., pp. 477ff, 507ff, and 426ff. Smith opens the text of *Wealth of Nations* itself (Book I, Chapter 1) with the assertion that the greatest improvement of the 'productive powers' of work is the increased division of labour, Adam Smith, *Inquiry into the Nature and Causes of the Wealth of Nations*, Glasgow edition of the works and correspondence of Adam Smith (Oxford: Clarendon Press, 1976), p. 4.

34. 'Entzweiung' (dichotomy), Engels, MEGA I/3, p. 481, MEW 1, p. 511, and CW 3, p. 430.

35. Atoms, the human species being, and stock exchange speculation, ibid., pp. 484f, 515f, and 434f. On John Dalton, see Arnold Thackeray, *John Dalton: Critical Assessments of His Life and Science* (Cambridge, Mass.: Harvard University Press, 1972).

36. On the society of the future, MEGA I/3, p. 476, MEW 1, p. 505, or CW 3, p. 424. On Fourier and peaceful rivalry, ibid., pp. 485, 516, and 435.

37. The final words in the article, ibid., pp. 494, 524, and 443.

5 The Manuscripts

1. Marcuse's early article in Herbert Marcuse, 'Neue Quellen zur Grundlegung des historischen Materialismus', *Die Gesellschaft* 9

(Berlin 1932), pp. 136–74.

2. Roger Garaudy, *Humanisme marxiste* (Paris: Éditions sociales, 1957). Jean-Yves Calvez, *La pensée de Karl Marx* (Paris: Points, 1956). Jean-Paul Sartre, *Critique de la raison dialectique*, vol. 1 (Paris: Gallimard, 1960).

3. T. I. Oizerman, 'Das Problem der Entfremdung in Zerrspiegel der bürgerlichen und revisionistischen "Kritik" des Marxismus', *Deutsche Zeitschrift für Philosophie*, 1962, p. 9. On the French scene, see for example Mark Poster, *Existential Marxism in Postwar France: From Sartre to Althusser* (Princeton: Princeton University Press, 1975).

4. In the MEGA critical edition, it was decided to reproduce Marx's manuscript in two versions – first in the order Marx probably wrote down his notes (MEGA I/2, pp. 187–322) and then in a more logical structure (MEGA I/2, pp. 323–438). Both versions will be of use here. The MEW version is found in Ergänzungsband 1, pp. 467–588. The English version is found in CW 3, pp. 229–346.

5. 'Vorrede', MEGA I/2, pp. 325f, MEW Ergänzungsband 1, pp. 467–70, CW 3, pp. 231–4.

6. On Hegel's reservations regarding forewords and other unsystematic descriptions, see Hegel 1977, 1ff and G. W. F. Hegel *Wissenschaft der Logik*, vol. 1, *Hegels Werke* (Frankfurt am Main: Suhrkamp, 1969 [1831]), 'Vorrede zur zweiten Auflage', pp. 19–34.

7. Letter from Engels to Marx, 20 January 1845, MEGA III/1, pp. 260f, CW 38, p. 17.

8. Letter from Jung to Marx, 18 March 1845, MEGA III/1, pp. 458f.

9. Moses Silberner, *Moses Hess: Geschichte seines Lebens* (Leiden: E. J. Brill, 1966), p. 191.

10. Quote MEGA III/1, p. 335, MEW Ergänzungsband 1, p. 479, CW 3, p. 343. Wilhem Schultz, *Die Bewegung der Production: eine geschichtlich-statistische Abhandlung zur Grundlegung einer neuen Wissenschaft* (Zürich och Winterthur: Verlag des literarischen Comptoirs, 1843), p. 72. Schultz, *Die Bewegung der Production*.

11. On working wages, MEGA I/2, pp. 327–38, MEW Ergänzungsband 1, pp. 471–83, CW 3, pp. 234–46. Cf. the chapter 'On the Wages of Labour', Adam Smith, *Inquiry into the Nature and Causes of the Wealth of Nations*, Glasgow edition of the works and correspondence of Adam Smith (Oxford: Clarendon Press, 1976), pp. 82–104.

12. Section 'Gewinn des Kapitals', MEGA I/2, pp. 338–51, MEW Ergänzungsband 1, pp. 483–97, CW 3, pp. 246–58. Pecqueur's most important writings are now available as an electronic resource. Marx cites Constantin Pecqueur, *Théorie nouvelle d'économie sociale et politique, ou Etude sur l'organisation des sociétés* (Paris: Chapelle, 1842). On Pecqueur in *Capital*, see *Das Kapital*, MEGA II/6, p. 562,

CW 35, pp. 609, 749.

13. Section 'Grundrente', MEGA I/2, pp. 351–63, MEW Ergänzungs-band 1, pp. 497–510, CW 3, pp. 259–70.

14. The text 'Estranged labour' is reproduced in MEGA I/2, pp. 363–75, MEW Ergänzungsband 1, pp. 510–22, and in English in CW 3, pp. 270–82.

15. The 'concept' is the subject of systematic treatment in G. W. F. Hegel, *Wissenschaft der Logik*, vol. 1, *G.W.F. Hegels Werke* bd 5 (Frankfurt am Main: Suhrkamp, 1969 [1831]).

16. On Marx at Steffens's lectures in Berlin, see Auguste Cornu, *Karl Marx et Friedrich Engels: leur vie et leur œuvre, bd 1, Les années d'enfance et de jeunesse, La gauche hégélienne: 1818/1820–1844* (Paris: P.U.F., 1955), pp. 81 and 89. Heinrich Steffens, *Anthropologie* (Breslau: Josef Mar, 1822), p. 8. Steffens, Heinrich. *Anthropologie*, vol. 2.

17. The sections 'Private property' and 'Private Property and Communism' can be found in MEGA I/2, pp. 376–99 and MEW Ergänzungsband 1, pp. 523–46, and in English translation in CW 3, pp. 283–306.

18. The section on the different kinds of communism in MEGA I/2, pp. 386–9, MEW Ergänzungsband 1, pp. 534–7, and CW 3, pp. 294–8.

19. Moses Hess had formulated the criticism of raw communism in, for example, an article in *Kölnische Zeitung* on 27 September 1843, and in other quarters as well. Edmund Silberner, *Moses Hess: Geschichte seines Lebens* (Leiden: E. J. Brill, 1966), pp. 173 and 198.

20. On *sursumer*, see Gwendoline Jarczyk and Pierre-Jean Labarrière, *Hegeliana* (Paris: P.U.F., 1986), pp. 102–20.

21. On Spinoza and Marx, see Yovel 1989, 78–103. For a criticism of Yovel's interpretation of Marx, see Allison 1992.

22. John Locke, *Two Treatises of Government* (Cambridge: Cambridge University Press, 1967), primarily § 25–51, pp. 303–20.

23. Quote from MEGA I/2, pp. 392f; MEW Ergänzungsband 1, pp. 539f; CW 3, pp. 299f.

24. 'The *forming* of the five senses' and music 'awakens in man the sense of music', MEGA I/2, pp. 294f, MEW Ergänzungsband 1, pp. 541f, CW 3, p. 302. There is rather extensive research into Marx's relationship with the arts, especially literature. The great pioneering work is Mikhail Lifshitz's book on Marx's aesthetic thinking. Lifshitz, who was close to Lukács, developed a fairly conservative conception of the arts; it is hardly likely that Marx would have shared it, had he been a contemporary of Lifshitz. But the book is exhaustive and scholarly. See Mikhail Lifshitz, *The Philosophy of Art of Karl Marx* (London: Longwood Publishing Group, 1980). On Lifshitz's aesthetic conservatism, see Stanley Mitchell,

'Mikhail Lifshits: A Marxist Conservative', in Andrew Hemingway (ed.), *Marxism and the History of Art: From William Morris to the New Left* (London: Pluto Press, 2006), pp. 28–44. There is an odd synthesis of Marx's philosophy of art – or, more correctly, that of the dominant Marxist tradition – with Proudhon's and Picasso's by the German art historian Max Raphael. Max Raphael, *Proudhon-Marx-Picasso: Three Studies in the Sociology of Art* (London: Lawrence & Wishart, 1980); on Marxism, pp. 75–112. A comprehensive review of Marx's relationship, primarily to literature, is S. S. Prawer, *Karl Marx and World Literature* (Oxford: Clarendon Press, 1976). An important section deals with the manuscripts, pp. 71–85. An intelligent, independent account of how Marx, and the traditions after him, related to culture in general and literature in particular is Raymond Williams, *Marx och kulturen: En discussion kring marxistisk kultur- och litteraturteori* (Stockholm: Bonniers, 1977). Marx talks numerous times about Mozart, above all in his newspaper articles. For example, see Prawer, *Karl Marx and World Literature*, pp. 255f. Marx could also refer to Beethoven's *Ninth Symphony*, in which Schiller's 'Ode to Joy' fit the revolutionary hopes of 1848; so it was in his article 'Die revolutionäre Bewegung' (The Revolutionary Development), published on New Year's Day 1849, MEW 6, p. 148, CW 8, p. 213. Marx's views on Wagner were more critical and ironic. When, in 1876, Marx and his youngest daughter, Eleanor, were on the way to Karlsbad to take the cure and considered spending the night in Nuremberg, they found that there was not a single hotel room available. The city was filled with people 'from all corners of the globe, who were setting off from there for the fools' festival with the town musician Wagner in Bayreuth', he wrote in a letter to Engels. In a postscript, he added drily, 'Just now everything's future here after the drums of the music of the future at Bayreuth.' His words give no hint of any appreciation of Wagner's music. Letter of 19 August 1876, MEW 34, p. 23, CW 45, p. 137. Wagner turns up again in a later letter to his daughter Jenny Longuet in which Marx talks about Liszt's daughter Cosima, who abandoned her husband, the conductor von Bülow, and became Wagner's wife instead. You could not imagine a better libretto for an Offenbach opera, Marx exclaimed. Letter of August–September 1876, MEW 34, p. 193, CW 45, p. 143.

25. 'The *open* book', MEGA I/2, p. 396, MEW Ergänzungsband 1, p. 542, and CW 3, p. 302.

26. Regarding '*sensuous, alien*', ibid., p. 397, p. 543, and p. 303, respectively.

27. Regarding 'a *chimerical illusion*', see ibid., pp. 397, 543, and 303, respectively.

28. Regarding 'for the socialist man', MEGA I/2, p. 398, MEW Ergän-zungsband 1, p. 546. Alfred Schmidt, *Der Begriff der Natur in der Lehre von Marx* (Frankfurt am Main: Europäische Verlagsanstalt, 1971).

29. Regarding 'A dwelling ...', see MEGA I/2, p. 420, MEW Ergän-zungsband 1, p. 548, CW 3, pp. 307f.

30. The sections 'Human Requirements and Division of Labour Under the Rule of Private Property' and 'The Power of Money' respectively are found in MEW Ergänzungsband 1, pp. 546–67, and in CW 3, pp. 306–26. In MEGA I/2 with its different grouping, we find them on pp. 429–38.

31. Regarding 'a mere thing', MEGA I/2, p. 437, MEW Ergänzungsband 1, p. 565, and CW 3, p. 325.

32. The section on Hegel's dialectic is found in MEGA I/2, 399–418, MEW Ergänzungsband 1, p. 568–88, and CW 3, p. 326–46.

33. Hannah Arendt, *The Human Condition* (Chicago: Chicago University Press, 1958).

6 The Years of Ruptures

1. 'Critical criticism' was in fact a concept that had been coined before Marx. See Bernd Kast, 'Nachwort des Herausgebers', in Max Stirner, *Der einzige und sein Eigentum* (Freiburg/München: Verlag Karl Alber, andra upplagan, 2013), p. 371.

2. Letter from Löwenthal to Marx, 27 December 1844, MEGA III/1, p. 447.

3. Engels's reaction to the title in a letter to Marx, 22 February–7 March 1845, ibid., p. 269, CW 38, p. 25.

4. On Edgar Bauer and the workers, MEW 2, pp. 55f, CW 4, p. 53.

5. Regarding 'the studiousness, the craving for knowledge ...', MEW 2, pp. 88f, CW 4, p. 84.

6. On the chasm between Bauer and the multitude, ibid., pp. 105ff and pp. 99ff respectively.

7. On the Jewish question, ibid., pp. 112ff and 106ff respectively.

8. On ideas and revolutions, ibid., pp. 126 and 119 respectively. A systematic and critical study of Marx and the French Revolution is François Furet, *Marx et la révolution française; suivi de textes de Karl Marx réunis, présentés, traduits par Lucien Calvié* (Paris: Flammarion, 1985), which also contains Marx's texts on the subject translated into French. Furet starts from Marx's sharp distinction between the social and the political (pp. 17, 24). If social conditions are decisive, how is it then that politics can take so many forms – that for a time Napoleon could be the man of the bourgeoisie,

or that democracy could adopt such varied manifestations? Marx never gave such questions any systematic treatment, according to Furet (pp. 35, 41). It can be argued that Marx developed an understanding of the question, an understanding that, if anything, meant that it was not possible to reach a systematic treatment; see p. 94ff.

9. On the individual and society, MEW 2, p. 127, CW 4, p. 120.

10. On the history of materialism, Spinoza, and Hegel, ibid., pp. 131–41 and pp. 124–34 respectively.

11. On Herr Szeliga, ibid., pp. 57–81 and pp. 55–77 respectively; the quote, p. 58 and p. 56 respectively.

12. The chapter on Sue's novel *Mystères de Paris* can be found in MEW 2, pp. 172–221 and CW 4, pp. 162–209.

13. The final scene, ibid., pp. 222f and 210f respectively.

14. Letter from Jung to Marx, 18 March 1845, MEGA III/1, p. 458.

15. Letter from Jenny to Karl, 2 October 1845, MEGA III/1, pp. 453f, CW 38, pp. 525f.

16. On Helene Demuth, see Heinrich Gemkow, *Karl Marx: eine Biographie* (Berlin: Dietz, 1967); Tristram Hunt, *Marx's General: The Revolutionary Life of Friedrich Engels* (New York: Metropolitan, 2009); and Jonathan Sperber, *Karl Marx: A Nineteenth-Century Life* (New York: Liveright, 2013).

17. Letter from Engels to Marx, 22 February–7 March 1845, MEGA III/1, pp. 266–9, CW 38, pp. 21–6, and 17 March 1845, ibid., pp. 270–3 and pp. 26–30 respectively.

18. Letter from Bürgers to Marx from the end of February 1846, MEGA III/1, pp. 506ff.

19. Roland Daniels to Marx, 7 March 1846, ibid., pp. 513ff.

20. Letters from Engels to Marx, 19 November 1844 and 20 January 1845, MEGA III/1, pp. 250–6 and 259–63 respectively, CW 38, pp. 9–14 and 15–20 respectively.

21. On Hess in *The German Ideology*, see above all MEW 3, pp. 478f, CW 5, pp. 491f.

22. On the goal of Marx's and Engels's trip to England, Rumyantsev, 'Über die Studien von Marx und Engels während ihres Augenhaltes in Manchester im Juli/August,' *Beiträge zur Marx-Engels-Forschung* 22, 1987, pp. 49–58, and Ljudmilla Wassina, 'Die Manchester-Exzerpthefte von Marx im Sommer 1845', *Marxistische Studien. Jahrbuch des IMSF* 12, 1987, pp. 141–51.

23. Like much else that Marx (and in this case Engels as well) wrote, *The German Ideology* has the character of a project rather than a completed work. Terrell Carver has recently questioned whether in general we can speak of a unity, considering how the manuscript looks. Terrell Carver, 'The German Ideology Never Took Place', 2010, *The Postmodern Marx* (Manchester: Manchester University

Press, 1998). In addition, it could be said that Marx and Engels were undoubtedly striving to publish a book together, and that they also searched in vain for a publisher. The work they later left to the gnawing criticism of the mice (Marx's words) is scarcely a rounded totality.

24. Michael Heinrich, *Die Wissenschaft vom Wert: Die Marxsche Kritik der politischen Ökonomie zwischen wissenschaftlicher Revolution und klassischer Tradition* (Verlag Westphälisches Dampfboot, 2011), p. 130.

25. Althusser summarizes his standpoint in above all Althusser 2010. He already lays it out in the introduction, pp. xix–xxxviii.

26. Israel 1979. István Mészáros, *Marx's Theory of Alienation* (London: Merlin Press, 1976); Bertel Ollman, *Alienation: Marx's Conception of Man in Capitalist Society* (Cambridge: Cambridge University Press, 1976); Takahisa Oishi, *The Unknown Marx: Reconstructing a Unified Perspective* (London: Pluto Press, 2001).

27. Heinrich, *Die Wisenschaft vom Wert*, pp. 141ff. Heinrich also takes other important breaks into account. For example, the concept of theory is undeveloped in *The German Ideology*; Marx and Engels appear there as pure empiricists, ibid., p. 139.

28. *Ludwig Feuerbach and the End of Classical German Philosophy* is part of MEGA IV/3 and is translated into English in volume 26 of the *Collected Works*. The quote is from CW 26, p. 520. Engels uses the adjective 'genius', in German a stronger word than 'brilliant'. The *Theses on Feuerbach* are found in CW 5, pp. 5–8, first in Marx's original and then as edited by Engels. The theses were formulated in a notebook that otherwise contained various lists of books. Marx used the notebook between 1844 and 1847. The *Theses*, which Marx himself only titled '1) ad Feuerbach' can be found there, pp. 19ff.

29. On the distinction between praxis, technique, and theory, see the major article R. Bien, 'Praxis, praktisch', *Historisches Wörterbuch der Philosophie* (Darmstadt: Schwabe, 1989), pp. 1227–307 and the literature cited there. Kant on the practical (or moral–practical) and the technical–practical in Immanuel Kant, *Kritik der Urteilskraft*, XI–XVI (Frankfurt am Main: Suhrkamp, 1974), pp. 78f. 'Spirit of practicality', G. W. F. Hegel, *Wissenschaft der Logik* (Frankfurt am Main: Suhrkamp, 1969), p. 14; English translation G. W. F. Hegel, *Science of Logic*, transl. by A. V. Miller (London: Allen & Unwin, 1969), p. 26.

30. On the changed content of the concept of work, see Herbert Applebaum, *The Concept of Work: Ancient, Medieval, and Modern* (Albany: State University of New York Press, 1992).

31. The chapter on Bruno Bauer in MEW 3, pp. 81–100, CW 5, pp. 97–116.

32. The best edition of *Der Einzige und sein Eigentum* is Max Stirner, *Der einzige und sein Eigentum* (Freiburg/München: Verlag Karl Alber, 2013). The latest English used is *The Ego and Its Own* (Cambridge: Cambridge University Press, 1995).

33. One example of Stirner's anti-Semitic outbursts can be found in the aforementioned editions, ibid., pp. 30 and 39 respectively.

34. Stirner on God and love, ibid., pp. 57f and 47 respectively.

35. On Blumenbach and the racial doctrine, see p. 97. Stirner on the races and intellectual development in Stirner, *Der einzige und sein Eigentum*, pp. 76ff and 62ff respectively. The Goethe quote from the 1806 poem 'Vanitas! vanitatum, vanitas!' is reproduced in Goethe 1986, p. 93.

36. Marx and Engels on the trisection in Stirner, MEW 3, pp. 114ff, CW 5, pp. 130ff.

37. Stirner the schoolteacher, MEW 3, p. 246, CW 5, p. 263.

38. Franz Mehring, *Karl Marx: hans livs historia* (Stockholm: Gidlunds, 1983), p. 192. Francis Wheen, *Karl Marx: en biografi* (Stockholm: Norstedts, 2000), p. 94. Sperber, *Karl Marx*, p. 166. Tristram Hunt, *Friedrich Engels: Kommunist i frack* (Stockholm: Leopard förlag, 2013), pp. 127f. Paul Thomas, 'Karl Marx and Max Stirner', *Political Theory* 3: 2, May 1975, pp. 159–79. Thomas, and a number of other contributors as well, also handle the question in Saul Newton, *Max Stirner* (New York: 2011). Daniel Brudney, who wrote what is probably the most comprehensive study of Marx's philosophical manuscripts between 1844 and 1846, certainly takes up the long chapter on Stirner but without any great analytic clarity. The point itself, as I demonstrate here in Marx's and Engels's account, does not come through. Daniel Brudney, *Marx's Attempt to Leave Philosophy* (Cambridge, Mass.: Harvard University Press, 1998), pp. 265–78.

39. Stirner ignores all historic concreteness, MEW 3, p. 112, CW 5, p. 129. History as simply the philosophy of history, ibid., pp. 114 and 130f respectively. Humans and nature, ibid., pp. 169 and 186 respectively.

40. Political liberalism, economics, and the sublation of labour, ibid., pp. 176–86 and 193–205 respectively.

41. 'Is not a matter...', ibid., pp. 186 and 205 respectively.

42. Masturbation and sex, ibid., pp. 218 and 236 respectively.

43. The criticism of Feuerbach and Stirner, and the emphasis on his own earlier articles, ibid., pp. 216f and 236 respectively.

44. Philosophers live in an upside-down world, ibid., pp. 432f and 446f respectively. The foreword, ibid., pp. 13f and 23f respectively.

45. French and British movements *contra* German ideas, ibid., pp. 441 and 455 respectively.

46. On the early French development of the concept of ideology, see Emmet Kennedy, *Destutt de Tracy and the Origins of 'Ideology'* (Philadelphia: Memoirs of the American Philosophical Society, 1978), in particular pp. 44ff.
47. Friedrich Rohmer is mentioned in MEW 3, p. 526, CW 5, p. 536.
48. Engels's article is a regular review and is called simply 'Alexander Jung, "Lectures on Modern German Literature"', MEGA I/3, pp. 361–75, CW 2, pp. 284–97. For Jung's response, see Alexander Jung, 'Ein Bonbon für den kleinen Oswald, meinen Gegner in den deutschen Jahrbüchern, *Königsberger Literatureblatt* 42, 1842. Engels commented positively about this response in a letter to Arnold Ruge on 26 July 1842, MEGA III/1, p. 235, CW 2, p. 456. Heine spoke on the 'airy kingdom of dreams' (*Luftreich des Traums*) in one of his poems ('Caput VII'), Heinrich Heine, *Atta Troll: ein Sommernachtstraum; Deutschland; ein Wintermärchen, Historisch-kritische Gesamtausgabe der Werke* (Hamburg: Hoffmann und Campe, 1985), and the quote is reproduced in MEW 3, p. 457. On the German-language development with Rohmer and Jung, see Sven-Eric Liedman, *Motsatsernas spel: Friedrich Engels' filosofie och 1800-talets vetenskaper* (Lund: Cavefors, 1977), pp. 169ff.
49. Stirner and the division of labour, MEW 3, p. 273, CW 5, pp. 291f.
50. Hunter, fisherman, etc., in one single person, MEW 3, p. 33, CW 5, p. 47.
51. On genius and the division of labour, MEW 3, pp. 377f, CW 5, pp. 393f.
52. Stirner on association, state, and society, Max Stirner, *Der einzige und sein Eigentum* (Freiburg/München: Verlag Karl Alber, 2013), p. 359.
53. The criticism of this in MEW 3, pp. 312f, CW 5, pp. 330f.
54. Communism: Stirner, *Der einzige und sein Eigentum*, p. 231. The criticism in *The German Ideology*, MEW 3, p. 229, CW 5, p. 247
55. 'True socialism' as a typical expression for Germany, MEW 3, p. 443, CW 5, p. 457.
56. MEW 3, p. 447, CW 5, p. 460.
57. On Karl Grün, ibid., pp. 473–520 and pp. 484–530 respectively. Sperber on Marx and Grün in Jonathan Sperber, *Karl Marx: A Nineteenth-Century Life* (New York and London: Liveright, 2013), pp. 181–5.
58. 'The ideas...', MEW 3, p. 48, CW 5, p. 59. 'In direct contrast...', ibid., pp. 26 and 36 respectively.
59. 'These abstractions...', ibid., pp. 27 and 37 respectively.
60. The four conditions, ibid., pp. 28ff and pp. 41–4 respectively.
61. Alienation, ibid., pp. 34 and 48 respectively.

62. Letter from Marx to C. W. J. Leske, 1 August 1846, MEGA III/2, pp. 22f. Response from Leske 15 September 1846, MEGA III/2, pp. 309f.

63. On the gnawing criticism of the mice in *Preface to a Contribution to the Critique of Political Economy*, MEW 13, p. 10, CW 29, p. 264.

64. On the Correspondence Committee, see Herwig Förder, *Der Bund der Kommunisten. Dokumente und Materialen*, vol. 1 (Berlin: Dietz Verlag, 1970–84).

65. Philippe-Charles Gigot (1819–1860) was active in the communist movement in the 1840s, at the same time as he was working as an archivist. Marx's letter to Proudhon, 5 May 1846, MEGA III/2, pp. 7f, CW 38, pp. 38ff.

66. Proudhon's response, 17 May 1846, MEGA III/2, pp. 203f.

67. Engels's letters from Paris to the Correspondence Committee, for example 19 August, 16 September, and 23 October 1846 in MEGA III/2, pp. 30ff., 34–9, and 53–9, CW 38, pp. 56–60, 60–7, and 81–6. Letters from Engels to Marx, for example 18 September, 18 October and 23 October 1846, in MEGA III/2, pp. 40–5, 48–52, and 60f, and CW 38, pp. 67–73, 75–81, and 86ff.

68. August Hermann Ewerbeck to Marx, 14 Aug 1846, MEGA III/2, p. 284. The letter is a response to something Marx wrote that has since been lost.

69. Annenkov's story from 1880 reproduced in Hans Magnus Enzensberger, *Gespräche mit Marx und Engels*, vol. 1 (Frankfurt am Main: Insel Verlag, 1973), pp. 60ff.

70. A meticulous, somewhat wordy biography of Weitling is Waltraud Seidel-Hopper, *Wilhelm Weitling (1808–1871): Eine politische Biographie* (Frankfurt am Main: Peter Lang, 2014). Another biography is Selcuk Cara, *Wilhelm Weitling – Gefangen zwischen Gott und Kommunismus: Tragikomödie in vier Akten* (München: Drei Masken Verlag, 2008).

71. The articles against Kriege have been given the title 'Circular Against Kriege' in CW, MEW 4, pp. 3–17 and CW 6, pp. 35–51.

72. Wilhelm Wolff, *Gesammelte Schriften. Nebts einer Biographie Wolffs von Friedrich Engels. Mit Einleitung und Anmerkungen* (Berlin: Jubiläums-Ausgabe, Buchhandlung Vorwärts, 1909).

73. A selection of Weerth's writings can be found in Georg Weerth, *Nur unsereiner wander mager durch sein Jahrhundert: Ein George-Weerth-Lesebuch* (Bielefeld: Aisthesis, 2008). Floran Vassen, *Georg Weerth: ein politischer Dichter des Vormärz und der Revolution von 1848/49* (Stuttgart: Metzlersche Verlagsbuchhandlung, 1971) is a biography of Weerth with an emphasis on his political poetry.

74. Letter from Annenkov to Marx, 1 November 1846, MEGA III/2, p. 316.

75. Marx's response, 28 December 1846, MEGA II/2, pp. 70–80.

76. Proudhon's book is actually called *Système des contradictions économiques, ou Philosophie de la misère* (Proudhon 1846). Another edition came out in 1850.

77. The full title of Marx's book is *Misère de la philosophie: réponse à La philosophie de la misère de M. Proudhon* (Marx 1847). Engels's foreword to the 1885 German edition was also appended. The German translation can be found in MEW 4, pp. 63–182. The critical edition in the *Marx-Engels-Gesamtausgabe* is still forthcoming and has been for some time. Marx's text can be found in English translation in CW 6, pp. 105–212.

78. On Bray etc., MEW 4, pp. 98–105, CW 6, pp. 138–44. Bray was an English and American socialist, and primarily an adherent of Owen's economic theories.

79. Robinson Crusoe is dealt with early on, in Section I:1 of the text. In the German edition this corresponds to MEW 4, p. 68; in the English to CW 6, p. 112.

80. Division of labour in factories and in society at large is dealt with in Section II:2, or MEW 4, pp. 150f and CW 6, pp. 184f.

81. The thesis that no product is useful in and of itself and that neither producers nor consumers are free is found at the end of Section I:1, or in MEW 4, p. 75 and CW 6, p. 118f.

82. On Ricardo and cynicism, ibid., pp. 78–84 and 120–5 respectively.

83. On Proudhon's mistake, Ricardo, and Smith, ibid., pp. 86–9 and 127–31 respectively.

84. Hard alcohol, ibid., pp. 92 and 133 respectively.

85. On the division of labour and machines, Section II:2, pp. 147–57 and 181–90 respectively. On oxen and machines that are not economic categories, in contrast to the factory, which is 'un rapport social de production, une catégorie économique', as it reads in the original.

86. *Verhältnis* is a central concept in Hegel. See, for example, the section 'Das quantitative Verhältnis' in his *Wissenschaft der Logik* (Frankfurt am Main: Suhrkamp, 1969), pp. 372–86; or 'Das wesentliche Verhältnis' in the same work, pp. 164–85. The English translation speaks of 'relation', which is not completely accurate.

87. Charles Babbage, *On the Economy of Machinery and Manufactures* (London: Charles Knight, 1835). Babbage played an important role in the prehistory of the computer; see Michael Lindgren, *Glory and Failure: The Difference Engines of Johann Müller, Charles Babbage and Georg and Edvard Scheutz* (Cambridge, Mass.: MIT Press, 1990).

88. Marx quotes Babbage, MEW 4, p. 153, CW 6, pp. 186f. He also had detailed excerpts of Babbage's works, MEGA IV/3, pp. 325–41.

89. Marx quotes Ure in MEW 3, pp. 155f, CW 6, pp. 188ff. Excerpts

from Ure's work are reproduced in MEGA IV/3, pp. 342–51.

90. Agricultural chemistry, MEW 4, p. 172, CW 6, p. 204.

91. The origin of manufacture, ibid., pp. 152 and 185f respectively.

92. On money created by the sovereign, ibid., pp. 109 and 147 respectively.

93. MEW 4, p. 162, CW 6, p. 194.

94. MEW 4, pp. 175–82, CW 6, pp. 206–12. *Jean Ziska* is available on the Internet in several versions, including through Project Gutenberg. Quote from the introductory 'Notice'.

95. The future society, MEW 4, p. 93, CW 6, p. 134.

96. Engels notified Marx of the sales figures in a letter dated 23–24 November 1847 (MEGA III/2, p. 121, CW 38, p. 146), and Marx wrote to his Russian friend Annenkov on 9 December 1847 that it had sold 'very well' (ibid., pp. 125 and 151 respectively). According to a letter to Marx on 21 September 1847 from publisher Carl Georg Vogler, between 500 and 600 copies appear to have been sold (MEGA III/2, p. 361). Engels on the visit to Louis Blanc in a letter to Marx, 25–26 October 1847 (ibid., pp. 111f and 133f respectively), and 21 January 1848 (ibid., pp. 130 and 155f respectively).

97. The letter to Annenkov in which Marx begged for money is the one just mentioned (MEGA III/2, CW 38, pp. 150f).

7 The *Manifesto* and the Revolutions

1. Heinrich Otto Lüning to Marx, 16 July 1847, MEW III/2, pp. 346f.

2. Heinrich Bürgers to Marx 30 August 1847, ibid., pp. 351–7, in particular pp. 353f.

3. Schapper's letter to Marx, 6 June 1846, ibid., pp. 219–23.

4. Friedrich Feuerbach was the younger brother of the more famous Ludwig, and distinguished himself first as a philologist with translations from Sanskrit and other languages. Ludwig's books, particularly *The Essence of Christianity* (Ludwig Feuerbach, *Das Wesen des Christentums,* Stuttgart: Reclam, 1994), inspired Friedrich to write philosophical works in the same style, above all Friedrich Feuerbach, *Die Zukunft der Religion* (Zürich and Winterthur: Verlag des literarischen Comptoirs, 1843). The later instalment came out in 1847.

5. The new letter from Carl Schapper et al. is dated 17 July 1846, MEW III/2, pp. 250–5. The professor, who was named Eduard Wilhelm Sievers, did not live in Paris; he had only taken a trip to France and England to study the educational systems there. Otherwise, he was a teacher in Gotha, in the German province of Thuringia; he was a philologist and philosopher and is renowned as an expert

on Shakespeare. In the revolutionary year of 1848, he published a revolutionary paper. The student remained nameless, and nothing in more detail is known about Adolf von Ribbentrop.

6. Letter from Harney to Marx, 20 July 1846, ibid., pp. 263f. On Harney, see R. Schoyen, *The Chartist Challenge: A Portrait of George Julian Harney* (London: Heinemann, 1958).

7. Moll's authorization is signed and dated 20 January 1847, MEGA III/1, p. 327.

8. There is a great amount of documentation on the activities of the League of the Just/the Communist League, the congresses in London, and more; for example Herwig Förder, *Der Bund der Kommunisten. Dokumente und Materialen* (Berlin: Dietz Verlag, 1970–84), Bert Andréas, *Gründungsdokumente des Bundes der Kommunisten* (Hamburg: Hamburg State and University Library, 1969), Jacques Grandjonc, *Statuten des "Communistischen Arbeiter-Bildungs-Vereins" London 1840–1914* (Trier: Karl-Marx-Haus, 1979), and Martin Hundt, *Bund der Kommunisten 1836–1852* (Berlin: Akademie-Verlag, 1988). See also Karl Obermann, *Zur Geschichte des Bundes der Kommunisten 1849 bis 1852* (Berlin: Dietz Verlag, 1955).

9. Letter from *Zentralbehörde des Bundes der Kommunisten* to the correspondence committee in Brussels, 18 October 1847, MEGA III/2, pp. 368ff.

10. On Engels's arrogance and vanity, in letters from Heinrich Bürgers and Roland Daniels, 11 August 1846, ibid., pp. 281ff.

11. This Gustave Oebom was actually named Napoleon Berger; in 1838, under the pseudonym Per Fas, he had published a pamphlet in Stockholm: *Den röda boken, eller några af dagens frågor* [The Red Book, or some of the issues of the day]. The book was considered criminal; Berger was put on trial and sentenced to hard labour but fled Sweden. After wandering through Europe – during which he both lost an eye and escaped from a Russian prison – he ended up in Switzerland. He resided there for ten years before setting off across the Atlantic. In the United States, he had greater success as a journalist. The question has even been asked whether he was not the first Swedish journalist in the new country. On Oebom, in the letter to the Brussels circle, MEGA III/2, p. 369. On the trial of Napoleon Berger, see Bo G. Nilsson 1980, pp. 2–18. This hater of learning, Berger/Oebom, probably chose the pseudonym Per Fas from the Latin motto *per fas et nefas* – 'through legal and illegal means'. On his journalism in the United States, see Nils William Olsson, 'Was Napoleon Berger the First Swedish Journalist in America?', *Swedish-American Historical Quarterly* 3:1, 1952, pp. 19–29. Berger was born in 1812 and died in 1870.

12. E. P. Thompson, *The Making of the English Working Class*

(Middlesex: Pelican Books, 1968) is and remains the great study of the development of the working class in Great Britain. On the desire to return to the land, for example pp. 253ff; on the Luddites and the nostalgia their actions expressed, pp. 537–45, pp. 598–649; on the craftsmen pp. 259–96. Gareth Stedman Jones has devoted great interest to the British workers' movement; see above all the essays in connection with E. P. Thompson's works, on Chartism, and on early workers' culture in Gareth Stedman Jones, *Language of Class: Studies in English Working Class History, 1832–1982* (Cambridge: Cambridge University Press, 1983). In Stedman Jones's recent Marx biography, *Karl Marx: Greatness and Illusion* (Allen Lane: London, 2016), there is a comprehensive, although not complete, account of their activities. On the programme of the Chartists to give industrial workers the opportunity for a more secure existence as small farmers, see John K. Walton, *Chartism* (London: Routledge, 1999), pp. 30f. James Philips Kay, *The Moral and Physical Condition of the Working Classes Employed in the Cotton Manufacture in Manchester* (London: James Ridgway, 1832).

13. Marx, 'Moralising Criticism and Critical Morality. A Contribution to German Cultural History. Contra Karl Heinzen', *Deutsche-Brüsseler-Zeitung* 28 October–25 November 1847 (5 parts), MEW 4, pp. 331–59, CW 6, pp. 312–40.

14. Marx's lecture is given in German translation in MEW 4, pp. 444–58, and in English in CW 6, pp. 450–65. It is also easily accessible on the Internet: Marx, 'Discours sur la question du libre-échange', Marxists. org. On the lecture and its enthusiastic reception, see Bert Andréas, *Association Démocratique ayant pour but l'union de la fraternité de tous les peuples: Eine frühe international demokratische vereinigung in Brüssel 1847–48* (Karl-Marx-Haus, 2004).

15. Adrian Velicu, *Civic Catechisms and Reason in the French Revolution* (Farnham: Ashgate, 2010).

16. Engels in a letter to Marx, 23–24 November 1847, MEGA III/2, pp. 121f, CW 38, p. 149.

17. Engels's 'Principles of Communism' can be found in MEW 4, pp. 361–80, CW 6, pp. 341–57. On the need to 'manifest' according to the 'Preface to the 1872 German Edition', p. 57, which corresponds to MEW 4, p. 573, CW 23, p. 174.

18. Engels's preface to the 1883 German edition in MEW 21, p. 3, CW 26, p. 118.

19. On Jenny Marx's possible contribution to the wording of the Manifesto, see Ulrich Teusch, *Jenny Marx: die rote Baronesse* (Zürich: Rotpunktverlag, 2011), p. 74 and the facsimile in the picture section (between pp. 110 and 111).

20. The quotes are taken from CW 6, pp. 483, 486f, and 487. In MEW

4 the corresponding pages are pp. 461, 464f, and 465.

21. 'The lower middle class ...', MEW 4, p. 472, CW 6, p. 494.

22. 'converted the physician ...', ibid., pp. 465 and 487 respectively.

23. 'Now and then ...', ibid., pp. 471 and 493 respectively. Marx later distances himself from the iron law of wages; pp. 159 and 570.

24. 'All are ...', ibid., pp. 469 and 491 respectively.

25. 'bourgeois property', ibid., pp. 475 and 498 respectively; 'a social power', ibid., pp. 475 and 499 respectively.

26. The *Manifesto* on the family, ibid., pp. 478f and 502 respectively.

27. Engels, 'Principles', MEW 4, p. 377, CW 6, p. 354.

28. 'Certain common forms', ibid., pp. 480f and 504 respectively.

29. The enumeration of measures after the revolution in 'Principles', MEW 4, pp. 373f and CW 6, pp. 350f; in MEW 4, pp. 481f and CW 6, pp. 505 respectively.

30. Engels on the various socialist movements in MEW 4, pp. 377f and CW 6, pp. 355f.

31. On 'Feudal Socialism', ibid., pp. 482ff and 507f respectively.

32. 'Petty-Bourgeois Socialism', ibid., pp. 484f and 509f respectively.

33. 'German, or "True", Socialism', ibid., pp. 485–8 and 510–13 respectively.

34. 'Conservative, or Bourgeois Socialism', ibid., pp. 488f and 513f respectively.

35. 'Critical-Utopian Socialism and Communism', ibid, pp. 489–92 and 514–7 respectively. The numerous attempts at small utopian societies are dealt with in Frank E. Manuel and Fritzie Manuel, *Utopian Thought in the Western World* (Cambridge, Mass. Belknap Press of Harvard University Press, 1979). One account of the specifically American experiments is Brian J. L. Berry, *America's Utopian Experiments: Communal Havens from Long-Wave Crises* (Hanover and London: Dartmouth College, 1992). Especially interesting are the experiments in the spirit of Fourier (pp. 83–92) and the attempt to realize Cabet's Icaria, for which Cabet himself – having left Europe, where it was difficult to work – was (as time went on) the increasingly dictatorial leader (pp. 107–15). The especially American variant that arose under the name of 'perfectionism', created by John Humphrey Noyes, is also of particular interest. Its ideology was called 'Bible communism', and the experimental society practised common property and general promiscuity under the name of 'mixed marriage'. Each member had to submit to the criticism of the others in a way that is reminiscent of the Cultural Revolution in China. But the leader himself was exempt from that kind of ordeal (pp. 92–8).

36. The last pages of the *Manifesto*, 'Position of the Communists in Relation to the Various Existing Opposition Parties', MEW 4, pp.

92f, CW 6, pp. 518f.

37. On translations according to Marx and Engels, see MEW 30, p. 573, CW 23, p. 174.

38. As far as I know, the only literature on Götrek is in Swedish, above all Erik Gamby, *Pär Götrek och 1800-talets svenska arbetarrörelse* (Stockholm: Tidens förlag, 1978); regarding the translation of the *Manifesto*, see pp. 200–11. Hesiod, *Works and Days*, verse 763.

39. Marx's letter to Engels, 23 February 1851, CW 38, pp. 295f. On Helen Macfarlane's life and work, see David Black, *Helen Macfarlane: A Feminist, Revolutionary, and Philosopher in Mid-Nineteenth-Century England* (New York: Lexington Books, 2004).

40. The literature on the revolutions of 1848–9 is enormous. Currently, the best account of the French revolution is probably Arnaud Coutant, *1848, quand la République combattait la Démocratie* (Paris: Éditions Mare et Martin, 2009). Classic depictions are Marie d'Agoult's, previously mentioned (Marie d' Agoult, *Histoire de la Révolution de 1848*, Paris: G. Sandré, 1850–53), published under the pseudonym Daniel Stern, and Alexis de Tocqueville, *Souvenirs* (Paris: Gallimard, 1964); Marx naturally wrote on the subject. The subsequent March revolution in a number of German states has been treated in works such as Wolfgang J. Mommsen, *1848 – Die ungewollte Revolution* (Frankfurt am Main: Fischer Taschenbuch, 2000), Helmut Bleiber, Rolf Dlubek, Rolf Schmidt, *Demokratie und Arbeiterbewegung in der deutschen Revolution von 1848/49: Beiträge eines Kolloquiums zum 150. Jahrestag der Revolution von 1848/49 am 6./7. Juni 1998 in Berlin* (Berlin: Gesellschaft – Geschichte – Gegenwart Band 22, trafo verlag, 2000), and Jonathan Sperber, *The European Revolutions: 1848–1851* (Cambridge: Cambridge University Press, 2005).

41. The congratulations to Paris in 'An die Bürger Mitglieder der Provisorischen Regierung der Französischen Republik', MEW 4, pp. 605f. Not found in CW.

42. Jenny Marx, 'Kurze Umrisse eines bewegten Lebens' is found together with other documents and letters in Jenny Marx, *Jenny Marx: Kurze Umrisse eines bewegten Lebens* (Berlin: Dietz Verlag, 1989). The original has been partially preserved and was donated in 1950 to the Institute for Marxism–Leninism in Moscow. An English translation with the title 'Short Sketch of an Eventful Life' is included in the collection volume Marx–Engels 1959.

43. Marx's notes in MEW 4, p. 611, CW 6, pp. 581f, and his article in *La Réforme*, MEW 4, pp. 536ff, CW 6, pp. 564ff.

44. On Herwegh, see Michael Krausnick, *Die eiserne Lerche: Georg Herwegh, Dichter und Rebell* (Baden-Baden: Signal-Verlag, 1993).

45. Marx and Engels, 'Demands of the Communist Party in Germany',

MEW 5, pp. 3ff, CW 7, pp. 3–7.

46. Letter from Weerth to Marx, 12–26 or 27 March 1848, MEGA III/2, p. 414.

47. The latest biography of Gottschalk is Klaus Schmidt, *Andreas Gottschalk. Armenarzt und Pionier der Arbeiterbewegung. Jude und Protestant* (Köln: Greven, 2002). On Gottschalk's feuds with Marx, see pp. 118–29.

48. On the German National Assembly, see Wilhelm Ribhegge, *Das Parlament als Nation, die Frankfurter Nationalversammlung 1848/49* (Düsseldorf: Droste, 1998). The satirical poem reads in the original: 'Dreimal 100 Advokaten – Vaterland, du bist verraten; dreimal 100 Professoren – Vaterland, du bist verloren!'

49. 'The Democratic Party', MEW 5, pp. 22ff.

50. Marx on Camphausen, 3 June 1848, MEW 5, pp. 25–8 and 32f, 30–33 and 39f respectively. 'The Downfall of the Camphausen Government', pp. 96f and 107f respectively. The author of the article is not known with certainty, but everything speaks to Marx having written it – there are both quotations from poems and an aphoristically incisive sentence: 'Herr Camphausen has sown reaction as envisaged by the big bourgeoisie, and he has reaped reaction as envisaged by the feudal party'.

51. The first article on Hansemann is also unattributed, but the Heine quotation indicates Marx: 'The Hansemann Government', *Neue Rheinische Zeitung*, 24 June 1848, MEW 5, pp. 101f, CW, pp. 111f. On the press laws, 20 July 1848, pp. 240ff and 250ff respectively.

52. The quote from *The Marriage of Figaro* from the article about the threat to deport Schapper in 'The German Citizenship and the Prussian Police', ibid., pp. 364f and 383f respectively.

53. 'The Pfuel Government', 14 October 1848, ibid., pp. 422 and 466 respectively.

54. A morganatic marriage (from the medieval Latin *matrimonium morganaticum*, a new formation from the medieval German *morgenga*, 'morning gift') was a way for kings to assume the right of regularizing their relationships to mistresses or to remarry with an untitled woman when his spouse from his first marriage had died. Marx, 'Counter-Revolution in Berlin', *Neue Rheinische Zeitung*, 12 Nov 1848, MEW 6, pp. 7–12, CW 8, pp. 14–19.

55. The article is called 'Impeachment of the Government' and is found in MEW 6, pp. 21f and CW 8, pp. 25f.

56. The article in *Preussischer Staats-Anzeiger* was published on 25–26 Nov 1848. The response in *Neue Rheinische Zeitung* came out on 30 Nov, MEW 6, pp. 81f, CW 8, pp. 106f, under the title 'German Professional Baseness'. 'A Decree of Eichmann's', 19 Nov, ibid., pp. 31f and 37f respectively.

57. The March Revolution as a parody of the French in Marx's article 'The Bill Proposing the Abolition of Feudal Obligations', *Neue Rheinische Zeitung*, 30 July 1848, MEW 5, p. 282, CW 7, p. 294.

58. Marx, 'The Crisis and the Counter-Revolution', 12–15 Sept 1848, MEW 5, pp. 398–404, CW 7, pp. 427–33; the quote, ibid., pp. 402 and 431 respectively.

59. On Germany's ever deeper degradation in 'Report of the Frankfurt Committee on Austrian Affairs', 28 Nov 1848, MEW 6, pp. 69–74, CW 8, pp. 88–93.

60. Marx, 'The June Revolution', 29 Jun 1848, MEW 5, pp. 133–7, CW 7, pp. 144–9. Engels's articles on the workers' uprising in Paris in MEW 5, pp. 123–32, CW 7, pp. 130–43.

61. On the meeting and friendship between Bakunin and Wagner, see Richard Wagner, *Mein Leben* (München: Bruckmann, 1911); quoted according to Anthony Masters, *Mathematische Manuskripte* (Kronberg Ts.: Scriptor, 1974), pp. 106f.

62. On the arrest, see the articles in *Neue Rheinische Zeitung*, 4–5 July 1848, MEW 5, pp. 165–8, CW 7, pp. 176–9 (author uncertain).

63. Marx's defence for the charges in 'Legal Proceedings against the *Neue Rheinische Zeitung*', 7 July 1848, MEW 5, pp. 175ff, CW pp. 186–8 and 11 Jul 1848, ibid., pp. 198–201 and pp. 208–11 respectively. Marx, 'Public Prosecutor "Hecker" and the *Neue Rheinische Zeitung*', 29 Oct 1848, MEW 5, pp. 440–4, CW 7, pp. 485–9. The joint title for Marx's and Engels's pleas is 'The First Trial of the *Neue Rheinische Zeitung*' and was published in the newspaper. Marx's defence speech is reproduced in MEW 6, pp. 223–34, CW 8, pp. 304–17; Engels's in ibid., pp. 234–9 and 317–22 respectively. Marx, 'The Trial of the Rhenish Committee of Democrats', 23 February, ibid., 240–57 and 323–39 respectively. Marx on the charges against the newspaper in an untitled article, 19 May 1849, ibid., pp. 503–6. In CW 9, p. 473, only the declaration itself that the newspaper will cease to appear is reproduced.

64. On the celebration of anniversaries in an article also untitled, 18 March 1849, ibid., pp. 362 and 108 respectively.

65. 'To the Workers of Cologne', 19 May 1849, ibid., pp. 519 and 467 respectively.

66. Engels on the events in Elberfeld in an untitled article, 17 May 1849, MEW 6, pp. 500ff, CW 9, pp. 447ff.

67. Engels's mother's letter, 20 October 1848, MEGA III/2, p. 513; and 5–6 December 1848, ibid., pp. 527ff. On anecdotes and other items concerning Engels's days in Elberfeld, see Tristram Hunt, *Friedrich Engels: Kommunist i frack* (Stockholm: Leopard förlag, 2009), pp. 171f.

68. Marx, 'Wage-Labour and Capital', *Neue Rheinische Zeitung*, 5–11

April 1849, MEW 6, pp. 397–423, CW 9, pp. 197–228.

69. Engels's preface to the 1891 edition is reproduced in MEW 22, pp. 202–9, CW 27, pp. 194–201.

70. Jenny Marx to Lina Schöler, 29 June 1849, MEGA III/3; she and Karl to the same addressee, 14 July 1849, ibid., pp. 28f. Karl's contribution to the letter is a few short closing lines.

71. Marx, 'The 13th of June', *Der Volksfreund*, 29 June 1849, MEW 6, pp. 527f, CW 9, pp. 477ff. Marx in an open letter to the editor of *La Presse* in French, *La Presse*, ibid., pp. 529 and 480f respectively. Marx to Engels, 17 August 1849, MEGA III/3, pp. 40–3, CW 38, pp. 212f. On Gottschalk's death in the cholera epidemic, see Klaus Schmidt, *Andreas Gottschalk. Armenarzt und Pionier der Arbeiterbewegung. Judge und Protestant* (Köln: Greven, 2002), pp. 143–8.

72. Marx to Engels, 23 August 1849, MEGA III/3, p. 44, CW 38, pp. 212f. Engels to George Julian Harney, 5 October 1849, ibid., pp. 49 and 217 respectively.

8 Difficult Times, Difficult Losses

1. Edmund Burke, *Reflektioner om franska revolutionen* (Stockholm: Contra, 1790).

2. Marx/Engels, 'The Prussian Refugees', *Sun*, 15 June 1850; 'Prussian Spies in London', *Spectator*, same day; and 'To the Editor of *The Globe*', mid-June 1850, MEGA I/10, pp. 343–9, CW 10, pp. 378–86.

3. Marx, *Enthüllungen über den Kommunisten-Prozess zu Köln*, MEGA I/11, pp. 363–422, MEW 8, pp. 405–70, CW 11, pp. 395–457. The quote, ibid., pp. 412, 456, and 445 respectively.

4. On Chartism during 1848, see John Saville, *1848: The British State and the Chartist Movement* (Cambridge: Cambridge University Press, 1987), pp. 80–101, and John K. Walton, *Chartism* (London: Routledge, 1999), pp. 32ff.

5. On the ideological change around 1850, see Frederick Gregory, *Scientific Materialism in Nineteenth Century Germany* (Dordrecht and Boston: D. Reidel Publishing Company, 1977).

6. On Virchow, see Constantin Goschler, *Rudolf Virchow: Mediziner, Anthropologe, Politiker* (Köln: Böhlau, 2009). On his reaction to the typhus epidemic, pp. 59–64; on his views on communism and socialism, p. 72; on his closeness to Marx, p. 78. A good summary of Virchow's changed views on progress, revolutions, and more gradual development, pp. 301ff, 305ff, and *passim*.

7. Georges Cuvier, *Discours sur les revolutions de la surface du globe et sur les changements que'elles ont produits dans le règne animal* (Paris: Dufours, 1825). On Cuvier and catastrophe theory, see for

example Dorinda Outsam, *Georges Cuvier: Vocation, Science and Authority in Post-Revolutionary France* (Manchester: Manchester University Press, 1984) and Laurent Goulven, *Paléontologie et évolution en France de 1800 à 1860: Une histoire des idées de Cuvier et Lamarck à Darwin* (Paris: C.T.H.S., 1987). Copernicus's great work from 1543 is called *De revolutionibus orbium cœlestium* (On the Revolutions of Heavenly Spheres). On the changes to the concept of revolution and studies concerning this, see p. 26.

8. The literature on Lyell, Malthus, and in particular Darwin is vast. One Darwin biography that sums up the whole problem area in question quite well is Adrian Desmond and James Moore, *Darwin* (London: Penguin Books, 1992). On Malthus's criticism of Condorcet and Godwin, see A. M. C. Waterman, *Revolution, Economics and Religion: Christian Political Economy, 1798–1833* (Cambridge: Cambridge University Press, 1991).

9. Liebknecht's *Biographical Memoirs of Karl Marx* came out in the original in 1896. See Wilhelm Liebknecht, *Karl Marx zum Gedächtnis: ein Lebensabriss und Erinnerungen* (Nürnberg: Wörlein and Comp., 1896). The complete and critically guaranteed version is the English translation in William A. Pelz's edition of central Liebknecht documents: *Wilhelm Liebknecht and German Social Democracy: A Documentary History* (Westport: Greenwood, 1994). On Jenny Marx there, pp. 86f.

10. Ulrich Teusch, *Jenny Marx: die rote Baronese* (Zürich: Rotpunktverlag, 2011), pp. 81ff.

11. Jenny's memoirs 'Short Sketch of an Eventful Life' in Jenny Marx, *Jenny Marx: Kurze Umrisse eines bewegten Lebens* (Berlin: Dietz Verlag, 1989); also in Hans Magnus Enzensberger, *Gespräche mit Marx und Engels* (Frankfurt am Main: Insel Verlag, 1973), I, pp. 241f.

12. On Engels's entry into Ermen & Engels and the doings that got his father to believe in him, Tristram Hunt, *Friedrich Engels: Kommunist i frack* (Stockholm: Leopard fölag, 2009), pp. 187f.

13. Jenny Marx to Engels, 27 Apr 1853, MEGA III/6, p. 452, CW 39, pp. 581.

14. Marx to Engels, 8 Sep 1852, MEGA III/6, p. 11, CW 39, p. 181.

15. Selected portions of the spy's report are reproduced in many biographies, for example Isaiah Berlin, *Karl Marx: His Life and Environment* (Oxford London New York: Oxford University Press, 1978), pp. 142f; David McLellan, *Karl Marx: His Life and Thought* (St Albans: Paladin, 1976), pp. 268f. The entire document can be read in Carl Grünberg, *Archiv für die Geschichte des Sozialismus und der Arbeiterbewegung* (Leipzig: Verlag von C.L. Hirschfeld, 1922), pp. 56ff as well as in Enzensberger 1973, I, pp. 251ff.

16. Jenny to Karl in August 1851, MEGA III/3, pp. 612ff, not in CW.

17. Marx's letter to Engels about his son's death, 19 Nov 1850, MEGA III/3, p. 91, MEW 27, p. 143, CW 38, p. 241. Engels's comforting letter to Jenny Marx has not been preserved; on the other hand, Marx's letter has, in which he says that Engels's thoughtfulness had been a help, 23 Nov 1850, MEGA III/3, p. 92, CW 38, p. 242.

18. Jenny's letter, quoted according to Teusch, *Jenny Marx*, p. 105. Jenny's memoirs about Franziska's death in Jenny Marx, *Jenny Marx*.

19. Marx wrote a series of letters to Engels about Edgar's illness, vacillating between hope and despair: 3, 8, 16, and 30 March 1855, MEGA III/7, pp. 182, 183, 185, 186, and 187, CW 39, pp. 524f, 526, 528, 529f, and 530. The letter concerning his son's death follows on 6 April 1855, ibid., p. 188. In the last of these letters, he wrote: 'I shall never forget how much your friendship has made to make this ghastly time easier for us.' A few days later, on 12 April, he wrote: 'I cannot tell you how we miss the child at every turn', MEGA III/7, p. 189, CW 39, p. 533. Jenny's memoirs in Jenny Marx, *Jenny Marx*, p. 40. Liebknecht on Marx's sorrow, Pelz, *William Liebknecht*, pp. 117f.

20. Jacques Attali, *Karl Marx ou l'esprit du monde* (Paris: Fayard, 2005), p. 256. Rachel Holmes, *Eleanor Marx: A Life* (London: Bloomsbury, 2014), p. 226 after Aaron Rosebury, 'Eleanor, Daughter of Karl Marx: Personal Reminiscences', *Monthly Review* 24, no. 8 (Jan 1973), pp. 45f. 'Tussy *is* me,' Holmes, *Eleanor Marx*, p. 357.

21. The letter to Engels about the birth of their last child, 8 Jul 1857, MEW 29, p 150, CW 40, p. 143.

22. Letter from Jenny to Karl, 19 Jun 1852, MEGA III/5, pp. 411f, not in CW.

23. Pelz, *William Liebknecht*, p. xxx.

24. Marx to Engels on his and Jenny's horrible daily life, for example, see a letter to Engels, 15 July 1858, MEW 29, p. 340, CW 40, p. 328.

25. Marx to Paul Lafargue, 13 August 1866, MEW 31, p. 519, CW 42, p. 308.

26. Karl to Jenny 21 June 1856, MEGA III/8, pp. 262f, MEW 29, pp. 532–6, CW 40, pp. 54–7.

27. Karl to Jenny, 15 December 1863, MEGA III/12, pp. 453f, MEW 30, pp. 463, CW 41, p. 499.

28. Eleanor on her parent's mutual desire to laugh, see Teusch, *Jenny Marx*, p. 142f.

29. On the photo of Marx with his new elegant topcoat, see the letter from Jennychen to Karl in early May 1867, and from Laura to the same, 8 May 1867, in Olga Meier, *Die Töchter von Karl Marx: unveröffentliche Briefe* (Hamburg: Fischer Taschenbuch, 1983), pp. 46 and 51 respectively.

30. Terrell Carver is among those experts who frankly deny that the copy of Freyberger's letter has any weight as evidence; see his 'Marx's "illegitimate son" … or Gresham's Law in the world of scholarship' on the website *Marx Myths and Legends*, Marxmyths.org. Carver also points out the letter from Marx to Engels of 25 Aug 1851 that I mention in the text (MEGA III/4, pp. 187–93, CW 38, pp. 436–43). Among the slanderers given prominence is Arnold Ruge. The other, stronger evidence is from the letter of 31 August 1851 (ibid., pp. 195–8 and 445–9 respectively). 'Skizzen über die deutsche kleinbürgerliche Emigration in London im Sommer 1851' is reproduced in MEGA I/11, pp. 86–92, but not in CW.

31. Jonathan Sperber, *Karl Marx: A Nineteenth-Century Life* (New York: Liveright, 2013), p. 263. Jacques Attali maintains that Jenny was travelling at the point in time in question; Attali, *Karl Marx*, p. 191. Holmes, *Eleanor Marx*, p. 161 does the same.

32. On the interruption to Jenny's long series of pregnancies, Teusch, *Jenny Marx*, p. 166.

33. On the rumours among leading social democrats at the turn of the twentieth century, see Rolf Hecker, 'Unbekannte Dokumente über Marx' Sohn Frederick Demuth', *Beiträge zur Geschichte der Arbeiterbewegung* 43 (1994), pp. 43–59.

34. Eleanor's letter to Laura according to Holmes, *Eleanor Marx*, pp. xvi and 195ff.

35. Holmes, *Eleanor Marx*, in particular pp. 381–402, but also a general picture of Lenchen's role in the Marx family. In her introduction to a volume of letters from the Marx daughters, Margarete Mitscherlich-Nielsen places Karl Marx on an equal footing with Eleanor Marx's notoriously unfaithful and villainous lover Edward Aveling. This is not a reasonable comparison. We have no end of testimony regarding Aveling's way of treating both his wife and Eleanor; regarding Karl's mistakes, on the other hand, we have only this. From this silence, we can of course not draw any certain conclusions, but only probable ones. But this is what we have to go on here. Margarete Mitscherlich-Nielsen, *Die Töchter von Karl Marx. Unveröffentliche Briefe* (Köln: Kiepenheuer and Witsch, 1981). In Japan, where interest in the matter has long been great, particular documentation has been gathered indicating that Karl Marx was the father of Frederick Demuth: Izumi Omura, *Karl Marx Is My Father: The Documentation of Frederick Demuth's Parentage* (Far Eastern Booksellers, 2011). The first great monograph in which Marx's paternity was asserted was by a Japanese author, Chushichi Tsuzuki, *The Life of Eleanor Marx: A Socialist Tragedy* (Oxford: Clarendon Press, 1967), pp. 243f and *passim*. In the Soviet Union and the GDR, where a prudish view of marriage and adultery prevailed, the

issue of Freddy's ancestry was a hot potato. See Carl-Erich Vollgraf, 'Nochmals zur Kommentierung in der zeiten MEGA: Fallstudien', *Beiträge zur Marx-Engels-Forschung: Neue Folge* (Hamburg: Argument, 1993), p. 73. By all appearances, Marx was unaffected by the feminist tradition that started with Mary Wollstonecraft and her epoch-making 1792 work *A Vindication of the Rights of Woman*. The tradition was not unknown to the Chartists, whom Marx stood close to in other respects and who counted many women in their number. On this, see Jutta Schwarzkopf, *Women in the Chartist Movement* (Basingstoke: Macmillan, 1991).

9 Journalist on Two Continents

1. Marx's letter to Weydemeyer, 4 Feb 1850, MEGA III/3, p. 61, CW 38, p. 226.
2. Heinrich Bürgers wrote to Marx on 27 Mar 1850 that the newspaper *Westdeutsche* was the only one representing the Social Democratic Party in Germany, though in a modest fashion, MEGA III/3, p. 502.
3. Letter from Marx to Louis Bauer, 30 November 1849, MEGA III/3, p. 50, CW 38, p. 218.
4. Eduard von Müller-Tellering's letter to Marx, 27 September 1849, MEGA III/3, pp. 394f, and Marx's letter to von Müller-Tellering 12 March 1850, ibid., pp. 68–71. A facsimile of the letter is reproduced in ibid., p. 69. The letter is also in CW 38, pp. 229f.
5. On Willich and his philosophy, see Loyd David Easton, *Hegel's First American Followers: The Ohio Hegelians: John B. Stallo, Peter Kaufmann, Moncure Conway, and August Willich, with Key Writings* (Athens: Ohio University Press, 1966).
6. The duel between Willich and Schramm can be glimpsed in Marx and Engels's correspondence; see for example George Julian Harney's letter to Engels of 11 September 1850, Mega III/3, p. 643. Percy Hotspur (actually named Henry Percy) is an important character in *Henry IV*. This play is also where the word *hotspur* comes from. Marx, *Herr Vogt*, MEGA I/18, p. 113, MEW 14, p. 445, CW 17, p. 86.
7. Letter from Marx to Joseph Weydemeyer, 19 December 1849, MEGA III/3, pp. 51f, CW 38, p. 219.
8. Marx wrote the introductory text to the journal. It is true that it was signed by Carl Schramm, the journal's 'Gerant' (the person legally responsible for it), but the style is unmistakably Marx's. MEGA I/10, pp. 17f, CW 10, pp. 5f.
9. It was to Weydemeyer that Jenny Marx turned in her despairing

letter of 20 May 1850 with the request for money, expressing her disappointment that their friends in Cologne had proven unwilling to work for the journal despite Karl investing so much money in it during his period as editor-in-chief; pp. 733f, CW 38, pp. 555f. Weydemeyer responded to Karl on 24 May 1850, pointing out how difficult it was to get any buyers, MEGA III/3, pp. 549f. Weydemeyer to Karl Marx on workers who had become petty bourgeois, 15 June 1850, MEGA III/3, pp. 563f. On distribution that was not working, see for example Hermann Wilhelm Haupt in Hamburg to Marx, 3 December 1850, ibid., pp. 686–9. On late submission of manuscripts, see letter from Theodor Hagen, musicologist in Hamburg, 28 June 1850, ibid., p. 572.

10. Marx, 'The Class Struggles in France, 1848 to 1850', *Neue Rheinische Zeitung*, January 1850, MEGA I/10, pp. 119–96, CW 10, pp. 45–145. The quotes therefrom, pp. 121, 128, 147 and 49, 58, 78 respectively.

11. Ibid., pp. 187 and 122 respectively.

12. The review of Guizot's books were published in the second issue of *Neue Rheinische Zeitung: Revue* and are reproduced in MEGA I/10, pp. 205–10, CW 10, pp. 251–6. The publisher of MEGA assumes that it was Marx who wrote about Guizot (MEGA I/10, Apparatus, p. 820), which is also likely but not completely certain. The most distinctive elements in his way of writing are missing.

13. The classic English translation of this Greek epic was by George Chapman around 1600, and was last published in 2001: *Homer's Batrachomyomachia, Hymns and Epigrams*. As has been seen, authorship has been ascribed to Homer – a greatly controversial attribution.

14. 'Review, January–February 1850', MEGA I/10, pp. 211–23, CW 10, pp. 257–70. According to MEGA I/10, Apparatus, p. 825, Engels spoke in a few letters – among them one to Marx – about a joint work, whereas in *Herr Vogt* Marx claimed all the honour.

15. The review of Carlyle 1850 was published in the April issue of *Neue Rheinische Zeitung*, MEGA I/10, pp. 265–75, CW 10, pp. 301–10.

16. Engels, 'The Peasant War in Germany', published in the May–October number of *Neue Rheinische Zeitung* (Nos. 5–6), MEGA I/10, pp. 367–443, CW 10, pp. 397–482.

17. Marx and Engels. 'Review. May–October', signed 1 November 1850, MEGA I/10, pp. 448–88.

18. Letter from Haupt to Marx, 1 October 1850, MEGA III/3, pp. 650f.

19. Marx, 'Skizzen über die deutsche kleinbürgerliche Emigranten …', MEGA I/11, pp. 86–92. Marx and Engels 'under Mitwirkung von Ernst Dronke', *The Great Men of the Exile*, MEGA I/11, pp. 221–311, CW pp. 227–326. 'Character mask', pp. 260 and

268f respectively. The Heine quote from the poem cycle *Atta Troll.
A Midsummer Night's Dream*, Canto 24, in Heinrich Heine, *Atta
Troll: ein Sommernachtstaum; Deutschland; ein Wintermärchen,
Historisch-kritische Gesamtausgabe der Werke* (Hamburg: Hoff-
mann und Campe, 1985), p. 79, line 48.

20. Marx and Engels, 'Address of the Central Authority of the League,
March 1850', MEGA I/10, pp. 254–63, CW 10, pp. 257–87. 'The
revolutionary Babylon', pp. 256 and 279 respectively.

21. 'Less than nothing', according to Teusch, *Eleanor Marx*, p. 99. Laura
Lafargue to Jenny Longuet, 28 February 1869, in Mitscherlich-
Nielsen, *Die Töchter von Karl Marx*, p. 63.

22. The critical edition of *The Eighteenth Brumaire of Louis Bonaparte*
is found in MEGA I/11, pp. 96–189. Also useful is MEW, 8, pp.
115–207. In English in CW 11, pp. 99–197.

23. 'Utopian nonsense' and 'the most colossal event ...', MEGA I/11,
pp. 104f, CW 11, p. 110.

24. The farmers constitute a 'vast mass', ibid., pp. 180 and 187
respectively.

25. Louis Althusser, *Filosofi från en revolutionär klasståndpunkt* (Lund:
Cavefors, 1976), pp. 35–77.

26. 'And as in private life ...', MEGA I/11, p. 122, CW 11, p. 128.

27. On interest as a political and economic term, see the detailed article
by Hans Wolfgang Orth, Jörg Fisch, and Reinhart Kosseleck, 'Inter-
esse', *Geschichtliche* Grundbegriffe (1982). On Marx's early use
of the term, pp. 341ff. The example concludes, however, with the
Communist Manifesto and thus does not concern the most typical
writings from the early 1850s. Marx in general is not mentioned in
Johan Heilbron's brief article in the *International Encyclopedia of
the Social and Behavioral Sciences*; see Johan Heilbron, 'Interest:
History of the Concept', *International Encyclopedia of the Social
and Behavioral Sciences* 11 (2001). The economic significance
often has the monopoly in the major Marxist glossaries, such as
in Georges Labica, *Dictionaire critique du marxisme* (Paris: P.U.F.,
1982), pp. 469–73. It is not even included in Tom Bottomore, *A Dictionary of Marxist Thought* (Oxford: Blackwell Reference, 1983).
On the other hand, there is an interesting article in Lotter, Meiner,
and Treptow's *Das Marx-Engels-Lexikon* with important quotes:
Karl Lotter, Reinhard Meiners, Elmar Treptow, *Das Marx-Engels
Lexikon: von Abstraktions bis Zirkulation* (Köln: PapyRossa Verlag,
2013), pp. 167–70.

28. On the repetitions of history, see G. W. F. Hegel, *Enzyklopädie der
philosophischen Wissenschaften* (Frankfurt am Main: Suhrkamp,
1986), p. 506 and Hegel, *Wissenschaft der Logik, Band II*, vol. 6
(Frankfurt am Main: Suhrkamp, 1986), p. 339. Engels talks about

Hegel's thinking in a letter to Marx of 3 December 1851. In fact, Marx took his example in part from this letter, MEGA III/4, pp. 260–3, CW 38, p. 505. Marx only formulated the parallel better.

29. On freedom and tradition, MEGA I/11, pp. 96f, CW 11, p. 103. The poetry of the future, ibid., pp. 101 and 106 respectively.

30. Marx's comparison between his own work, Hugo's, and Proudhon's in the 1869 afterword, MEW 16, pp. 398ff, CW 21, pp. 56ff.

31. On the *New York Daily Tribune,* Horace Greeley, and Charles Anderson Dana, see Richard Kluger, *The Paper: The Life and Death of the New York Herald Tribune* (New York: Knopf, 1986). On Greeley's socialist ideas and Dana's and Ripley's lives at Brook Farm, pp. 51f, 53f, and 70 respectively. On Charles A. Dana and Napoleon III, p. 72. His firing and his new career, pp. 106f, 141.

32. On Marx not writing the articles on Revolution and Counterrevolution, MEGA I/11, pp. 3 and 637. Rachel Holmes put Marx's inability to write the first articles in the context of his troubles at home after Lenchen Demuth gave birth to Freddy. Holmes, *Eleanor Marx,* p. 394. Sperber on Marx's English in Sperber, *Karl Marx,* p. 314.

33. The current standard work on the Atlantic cable and Cyrus W. Field's efforts is John Steele Gordon, *A Thread Across the Ocean: The Heroic Story of the Transatlantic Cable* (London: Simon & Schuster, 2002).

34. Karl Marx, *Marx on China, 1853–1860: Articles from the New York Daily Tribune* (London: Lawrence and Wishart, 1951) is also available on the Internet at Marxists.org. The articles on India are found in Karl Marx, *Karl Marx on India: From the New York Daily Tribune* (New Delhi: Tulika Books, 2005).

35. The example headlines are from articles in the *New York Daily Tribune,* 22 June 1853, MEGA I/12, pp. 157ff, CW 12, pp. 115ff, 19 September 1853, ibid. pp. 269ff, and 28 November 1853, pp. 488ff and 239ff respectively.

36. On the number of horsepower and other statistics, see 'Political Prospects – Commercial Prosperity – Case of Starvation', *New York Daily Tribune,* 2 February 1853, MEGA I/12, pp. 8ff, CW 11, pp. 477ff.

37. *The Times* and 'that mendacious wire', *New York Daily Tribune,* 14 February 1853, MEGA I/12, p. 155, CW 12, p. 113.

38. On von Westphalen's ultra-Prussian attitude, 18 April 1853, ibid. pp. 89ff and 28ff respectively.

39. On Grundtvig's' criticism, *New York Daily Times,* 9 September 1853, ibid., pp. 137 and 101 respectively.

40. On Great Britain as an enchanting land that was difficult to live in, *New York Daily Tribune,* 4 April 1853, MEGA I/12, pp. 66, 539, CW 11, p. 539.

41. 'On Chartism', *New York Daily Tribune,* 25 Aug 1852, MEGA I/11,

pp. 324–7, CW 11, pp. 333–41.

42. The first article on the workers' parliament was published 24 March 1854 and had to share space with the British war budget: 'Opening of the Labour Parliament – English War Budget', MEGA I/13, p. 100, CW 13, pp. 50–6. The letter to the parliament was published in *The People's Paper*, 18 March 1854, under the title 'Letter to the Labour Parliament', ibid., pp. 115f and 57f respectively, and the article 'The Labour Parliament' in the *New York Daily Tribune*, 29 March 1854, ibid., pp. 111–15 and 61–4 respectively. On Ernest Jones, see Miles Taylor, *Ernest Jones, Chartism, and the Romance of Politics 1818–1869* (Oxford: Oxford University Press, 2003).

43. Marx, 'Speech on the Anniversary of *The People's Paper,*' 14 April 1856, MEW 12, pp. 3f, CW 14, pp. 655f.

44. Marx, 'Condition of Factory labourers', *New York Daily Tribune*, 22 April 1857 and 'The English Factory System', ibid., 28 April 1857, MEW 12, pp. 183–93, CW 15, pp. 251–61. The quote, 185 and 253 respectively. Marx, 'The State of British Manufactures', *New York Daily Tribune*, 15 March 1859, MEW 13, pp. 202ff, CW 16, pp. 190–6. Compare also the continuation under the same title in *New York Daily Tribune*, 24 March 1859, MEW 13, pp. 220ff, CW 16, pp. 206–10.

45. Marx's articles under the title 'The State of British Manufacturing Industry', 6 August 1860, MEW 15, pp. 78–88, CW 17, pp. 410–20. On cooperation, see Johnston Birchall, *Co-op: The People's Business* (Manchester and New York: Manchester University Press, 1994).

46. See articles in the *New York Daily Tribune*, 16 and 23 September 1859, MEW 13, pp. 490–9, CW 16, pp. 487–96. A. H. Hassall, *Adulteration Detected, Or, Plain Instruction for the Detection of Frauds in Food and Medicine* (London: Longman, Brown, 1861). Marx refers to Hassall's book in *Capital*, vol. 1, MEGA II/5, pp. 190 and 253, MEW 23, pp. 189 and 263, and CW 35, pp. 184 and 256. On bakeries of the time and the imagined future, 'Bread Manufacture', *Die Presse*, 20 October 1862, MEW 15, pp. 554–7, CW 19, pp. 252–5.

47. Marx, 'A Meeting', *Neue Oder-Zeitung*, 24 March 1855; MEW 11, pp. 135ff, CW 14, pp. 98–101. Untitled, *Neue Oder-Zeitung*, 11 November 1855, MEW 10, pp. 602ff, CW 13, pp. 571–8.

48. The latest major biography of Palmerston, chiefly engaged with his liberal world of ideas, is David Brown, *Palmerston: A Biography* (New Haven and London: Yale University Press, 2010). Marx's series of articles on Palmerston were published in their entirety in *The People's Paper*, 22 October–24 December 1853, MEGA I/12, pp. 393–442, MEW 9, pp. 353–418, CW 12, pp. 341–406.

49. On Palmerston in *Neue Oder-Zeitung*, 16 and 19 February, 24

March, and 26 July 1855, MEGA I/14, pp 123ff, 125ff, 163ff, and 571–4, MEW 11, pp. 60–8, 100–3, and 376–9, CW 14, pp. 14–20, 49–52, 367–70.

50. Lord Aberdeen as jester in the *New York Daily Tribune*, 17 April 1854, MEGA I/13, p. 181, MEW 10, p. 177, CW 13, p. 132.

51. Marx on Disraeli's budget in the *New York Daily Tribune*, 7 May 1858, MEW 12, pp. 445–9, CW 15, pp. 510–14.

52. On the approaching crisis, in the *New York Daily Tribune*, 24 March 1855, MEGA I/14, pp. 166–9, MEW 11, pp. 100ff, CW 15, pp. 59–62.

53. On the Hamburg stock exchange in the *New York Daily Tribune*, 22 December 1857 and 5 January 1858, MEW 12, pp. 339ff and 344ff, CW 15, pp. 410ff and 413–8.

54. On the French crisis in an article on the position of Napoleon III, *New York Daily Tribune*, 1 April 1858, MEW 12, pp. 412ff, CW 15, pp. 477–81. The article began with a quote from the Italian poet Torquato Tasso.

55. On the coming revolution in Great Britain in the *New York Daily Tribune*, 21 June 1858, MEW 12, pp. 497ff, CW, pp. 560–5.

56. More essential descriptions of the economic crisis itself in the *New York Daily Tribune*, 4 October 1858, MEW 12, pp. 570ff, CW 16, pp. 33–6. 'The Crisis in England', *Die Presse*, 6 November 1861, MEW 15, pp. 348ff, CW 19, pp. 53–6.

57. Jonathan Sperber accounts in detail, and with reasonable consideration, the relationship between Marx and Urquhart in Sperber, *Karl Marx*, pp. 306ff.

58. On Cobden and the Muslims, 'Debates in Parliament', *New York Daily Tribune*, 9 March 1854, MEGA I/13, pp. 71f, MEW 10, p. 83, CW 13, p. 14.

59. On the Grand Mufti and Christian societies, 'Declaration of War – On the History of the Eastern Question', *New York Daily Tribune*, 15 April 1854, MEGA I/13, pp. 150f, MEW 10, pp. 169ff, CW 13, pp. 11–25.

60. The nine articles on Spain with the common headline 'Revolutionary Spain' were published in the *New York Daily Tribune* between 9 September and 2 December 1854, MEGA I/13, pp. 416–66, MEW 10, pp. 433–85, CW 13, pp. 389–446. The fragments of the article 'Spain – Intervention' are reproduced in MEGA I/13, pp. 473ff, MEW 10, pp. 631–4, CW 13, pp. 654–9. Marx wrote about the designation 'liberal' 1 December 1854, MEGA I/13, p. 448, MEW 10, p. 474, CW 13, p. 435. The priority of the Spanish liberals for example in Rudolf Vierhaus, *'Liberalismus', Geschichtliche Grundbegriffe* (Stuttgart: Klett-Cotta, 1982), p. 751 and E. K. Bramsted and K. J. Melhuish (eds), *Western Liberalism: A History in Documents*

from Locke to Croce (London and New York: Longman, 1978), p. 3. On economic liberalism, see Rudolf Vierhaus, *'Wirtschaftlicher Liberalismus'*, *Geschichtliche Grundbegriffe* (Stuttgart: Klett-Cotta, 1982).

61. Developments in India came under discussion in various early articles by Marx: 'The Russian Humbug – Gladstone's Failure – Sir Charles Wood's East Indian Reform', *New York Daily Tribune*, 25 June 1853, MEGA I/12, pp. 162–5, MEW 9, pp. 127ff, CW 12, pp. 120–4; 'The Turkish War Question – The *New York Tribune* in the House of Commons – The Government of India', *New York Daily Tribune*, 20 July 1853, MEGA I/12, pp. 204–14, MEW 9, pp. 176–87, CW 12, pp. 174–84; 'Layard's Motion – Struggle over the Ten Hours' Bill', ibid., 22 July 1853, MEGA I/12, pp. 220–5, MEW 9, pp. 188ff, CW 12, pp. 185–91; 'The War Question – Doings of Parliament – India', 5 August 1853, MEGA I/12, pp. 244–7, MEW 9, pp. 212ff, CW 12, pp. 209–15; and 'The Future Results of the British Rule in India', 8 August 1853, MEGA I/12, pp. 248–53, MEW 9, pp. 220ff, CW 12, pp. 217–22. The last of these is where the controversial statements quoted can be found. Marx never really felt at home discussing the problems of India. He could not write an overview of India, he explained in a letter to Engels on 13 August 1858, MEGA III/9, p. 201, CW 40, p. 339.

62. Edward Said, *Orientalism* (Stockholm: Ordfront, 1978), pp. 154–7.

63. Aijaz Ahmad, *In Theory: Classes, Nations and Literatures* (London: Verso, 2008), in particular pp. 227ff.

64. 'The Revolt in India', *New York Daily Tribune*, 4 April 1858, MEW 12, pp. 238ff, CW 15, pp. 305–8, and 'The Indian Insurrection', *New York Daily Tribune*, 16 September 1857, MEW pp. 285ff, CW 15, pp. 327–30. Marx wrote an additional series of articles on the Indian rebellion, but they do not have the same fundamental interest at all. Engels analysed the military operations in other articles.

65. Marx, 'Revolution in China and Europe', *New York Daily Tribune*, 14 June 1853, MEGA I/12, pp. 147–53, MEW, pp. 95–102, CW 12, pp. 93–100. Stephen R. Platt, *Autumn in the Heavenly Kingdom: China, the West, and the Epic Story of the Taiping Civil War* (New York: Knopf, 2012).

66. 'History of the Opium Trade', *New York Daily Tribune*, 20 and 25 September 1858, MEW 12, pp. 549–56, CW 16, pp. 13–20. Marx, 'Chinese Affairs', *Die Presse*, 7 July 1862, MEW 15, pp. 514ff, CW 19, pp. 216ff. The quote, pp. 515 and 217 respectively.

67. On the linking together of China and Great Britain, see the aforementioned article 'Revolution in China and Europe', *New York Daily Tribune*, 14 June 1853, MEGA I/12, pp. 147–53, MEW 9, pp. 95ff, CW 12, pp. 93–100. The article that led to the conflict with

Dana is called 'The British and Chinese Treaty', *New York Daily Tribune*, 15 October 1858, MEW 12, pp. 584–9, CW 16, pp. 46–50. His letter on the matter to Engels, 17 December 1858, MEGA III/9, pp. 259f, MEW 29, pp. 376f, CW 40, pp. 362f. 'The War Against Persia', *New York Daily Tribune*, 14 February 1857, MEW 12, pp. 117ff, CW 15, pp. 177–80.

68. On the rebellion in Haiti, see for example Philippe R. Girard, *Ces esclaves qui ont vaincu Napoléon: Toussaint Louverture et la guerre dindépendance haïtienne (1801–1804)* (Rennes: Les Perséides, 2013) and Carolyn Fick, *Haïti, naissance d'une nation: La Révolution haïtienne vue d'en bas* (Rennes: Les Perséides, 2013).

69. Marx, 'The British Government and the Slave-Trade', *New York Daily Tribune*, 2 July 1858, not yet in MEGA, MEW 12, pp. 507ff, CW 15, pp. 570–74.

70. Marx, 'The American Question in England' and 'The Londoner *Times* and Lord Palmerston', *New York Daily Tribune*, 11 and 21 October 1861 respectively, MEW 15, pp. 304ff and 318ff, CW 19, pp. 7–16 and 21–6.

71. For a brief and pithy account of Great Britain during the Civil War and in particular in connection with the *Trent* affair, see Llewellyn Woodward, *The Age of Reform 1815–1870* (London: Clarendon Press, 1962), above all pp. 308–12. (The book is included in *The Oxford History of England.*)

72. Marx's last articles in the *New York Daily Tribune* were published 25 December 1861 and 10 March 1862 respectively, MEW 15, pp. 395ff and 439ff, CW 19, pp. 110–14 and 172–7. He had by then written several reports on the Civil War and the official hesitation of Great Britain in *Die Presse*, for example 20 October and 7 November 1861, MEW 15, pp. 329ff and 339ff respectively, CW 19, pp. 32–42 and 43–52. On the *Trent* affair in *Die Presse*, 18 January and 2 February 1862, MEW 15, pp. 445f and 454ff, CW 19, pp. 145–8 and 153–6.

73. On Napoleon III and the war against Austria, *New York Daily Tribune*, 24 January and 1 February 1859, MEW 13, pp. 161ff and 177ff, CW 16, pp. 148–53 and 167–70. On the prospects of war in the *New York Daily Tribune*, 31 March 1859, MEW 13, pp. 280ff, CW 16, pp. 261–6.

74. 'Anti-Semitism in Vienna', in the *New York Daily Tribune*, 6 June 1859, MEW 13, pp. 333ff, CW 16, pp. 320–7. 'The Peace', *New York Daily Tribune*, 28 July 1859, MEW 13, pp. 420ff, CW 16, pp. 412–15.

75. On the rumours of an impending Franco-British war, see 'The Invasion Panic in England', *New York Daily Tribune*, 9 December 1859, MEGA I/18, pp. 22ff, MEW 13, pp. 545ff, CW 16, pp. 545ff.

'Mazzini and Napoleon', *New York Daily Tribune*, 11 May 1858, MEW 12, pp. 420ff, CW 15, pp. 485–9. Napoléon-Louis Bonaparte, *Extinction du pauperisme* (Paris: Pagnerre, 1844). Friedrich Wilhelm IV and his mental health in the *New York Daily Tribune*, 23 October 1858, MEW 12, pp. 594ff, CW, pp. 54–8.

76. The King's abdication and his successor, *New York Daily Tribune*, 23 October and 3 November 1858, MEW 12, pp. 604ff and 613ff, CW 15, pp. 65–9 and 74–7. The matter was later commented on in several articles that followed rapidly. 'Public Feeling in Berlin', *New York Daily Tribune*, 28 April 1860, MEGA I/18, pp. 412ff, MEW 15, pp. 39ff, CW 17, pp. 367ff.

77. On the Swedish Crown Prince in the *New York Daily Tribune*, 5 September 1857, MEW 12, pp. 266f, CW 15, pp. 33–335. The best biography of Carl XV is in Swedish, Sven Eriksson, *Carl XV* (Stockholm: Wahlström and Widstrand, 1954). In English there is nearly nothing, apart from articles in the *Encyclopaedia Britannica*.

78. George Ripley and Charles Dana, *The New American Cyclopaedia: A Popular Dictionary*, vol. 1 (New York: A. Appleton and Company, 1858). Engels's letter to Marx about Bernadotte, 21 and 22 March 1857, MEW 29, pp. 180–7, CW 40, pp. 174–80. The article on Bernadotte is reproduced in German translation in MEW 14, pp. 154–63, and in the English original in CW 18, pp. 149–58.

79. 'Ireland's Revenge', *Neue Oder-Zeitung*, 16 March 1855, MEW 11, pp. 117ff, CW 14, pp. 78ff, and 'O'Connor's Funeral', 15 September 1855, MEW 11, p. 529, CW 14, p. 524. Stedman Jones goes through the attitude of the entire Marx family towards the Irish question and Fenianism, pp. 478–85.

80. Sperber points out that the journalism of the '50s and '60s is usually overlooked, but himself does not make any in-depth study of them; Sperber, *Karl Marx*, pp. 291ff. Significantly more detailed is Jones, *Karl Marx*, in particular pp. 353–63. He does not, however, devote himself to any comprehensive review of this journalism.

10 The Most Intensive Effort

1. Jenny Marx's letter to Conrad Schramm, 8 December 1857, MEGA III/8, pp. 211f, MEW 29, p. 645, CW 40, p. 566.

2. Karl Marx to Engels the same day, MEGA III/8, p. 208, MEW 29, p. 232, CW 40, p. 217. To Lassalle, 21 December 1857, MEGA III/8, pp. 223f, MEW 29, p. 548, CW 40, p. 226. To Engels, 11 January 1858, MEGA III/9, p. 18, MEW 29, p. 256, CW 40, p. 244. Second letter to Lassalle, 22 February 1858, MEGA III/9, pp. 71ff, MEW 29, pp. 50f, CW 40, p. 270. On the disarray in the manuscript, to

Engels, 31 May 1858, MEGA III/9, p. 157, MEW 29, p. 330, CW 40, p. 318. Letter to Lassalle, 12 November 1858, MEGA III/9, pp. 238f, MEW 29, p. 566, CW 40, p. 354.

3. Karl Marx, 'Einleitung zur Kritik der politische Oekonomie', *Die Neue Zeit* 31 (1903). Max Adler, *Marx als Denker: zum 25. Todestag von Karl Marx* (Berlin: Volksbuchhandlung, 1908). Georg Lukács, *Historia och klassmedvetande* (Lund: Cavefors, 1968), pp. 43ff.

4. Karl Marx, *Grundrisse der Kritik der politischen Ökonomie* (Frankfurt am Main: Europäische Verlagsanstalt, 1953).

5. Antonio Negri, *Marx oltre Marx* (London: Pluto, 2003).

6. Michael Hardt and Antonio Negri, *Imperiet* (Göteborg: Glänta produktion, 2003), *Multituden: krig oder demokrati i imperiets tidsàlder* (Hägersten: Tankekraft, 2007), *Commonwealth* (Cambridge, Mass: Harvard University Press, 2009) and *Förklaring* (Hägersten: Tankekraft, 2013). Among Slavoj Žižek's many works, *The Sublime Object of Ideology* (London: Verso, 1989) and *Less Than Nothing: Hegel and the Shadow of Dialectical Materialism* (London: Verso, 2012) can be mentioned. Žižek also belongs to those followers of Marx who, during the early 2000s, showed great interest in religion, and Christianity in particular. He declares himself an atheist and a materialist, it is true, but at the same time he asserts that in Christianity is found the same type of liberation thinking as in Marxism. In an interesting study, Swedish theologian Ola Sigurdson compared Žižek's interest in religion with Terry Eagleton's. Eagleton is a self-professed Catholic, and in that respect stands far from Žižek. But Sigurdson showed that both are united in their idea that both Christianity and Marxism raise the question of hope, or the hope in a future liberation. Ola Sigurdson, *Theology and Marxism and Eagleton and Žižek: A Conspiracy of Hope* (New York: Palgrave Macmillan, 2012), particularly the concluding chapter 'An Anatomy of Hope', pp. 163–203. Jürgen Habermas, one of the leading representatives of critical theory, or the Frankfurt School, has also become interested in religion, although from another starting point. He notes that two tendencies have become dominant in the present: on the one hand, a naturalism that intends to reduce everything human to nature, and on the other a number of religious orthodoxies that have won increasing political influence. In this situation, Habermas seeks a way beyond these extremes – a way that admits both the conquests of the natural sciences and the sincerity of religious feeling but provides independent space for secular human culture as its own independent field. Jürgen Habermas, *Zwischen Naturalismus und Religion: Philosophische Aufsätze* (Frankfurt am Main: Suhrkamp, 2005). It is worth noting that in these discussions of religion, Marx's theory of the genuine expression of religion in

capitalism – commodity fetishism – plays a negligible role. Thomas M. Kemple, *Reading Marx Writing: Melodrama, the Market, and the 'Grundrisse'* (Stanford, CA: Stanford University Press, 1995).

7. Roman Rosdolsky, *Zur Entstehungsgeschichte des Marxschen Kapital: Der Rohentwurf des Kapital* (Wien: Europa Verlag, 1968) and Roman Rosdolsky, *'Kapitalets' tillkomsthistoria* (Göteborg: Röda Bokförlaget, 1977–79). Many have continued on Rosdolsky's path. Fred Schrader, *Restauration und Revolution: die Vorarbeiten zum 'Kapital' von Karl Marx in seinen Studienheften 1850–58* (Hildesheim: Gerstenberg, 1980) in particular deserves to be pointed out.

8. 'Einleitung', MEGA II/1.1, pp. 7*–23*. In the *Marx Engels Werke* (MEW), the *Grundrisse* was only published much later, in 1983 – long after the other volumes. In the preface to the nearby *Zur Kritik der politischen Ökonomie*, Lenin can confirm the significance of what Marx had said: MEW 13, pp. v–xxvi, in particular p. vii. Marx's new, intensive occupation with Hegel's philosophy in connection with the *Grundrisse* was hard to swallow in the Soviet tradition, where it was claimed that by the mid-1840s Marx had laid the foundations of his materialism in opposition to Hegel once and for all. See further Dieter Riedel, *'Wie Hegel das richtig gesagt hat,' Beiträge zur Marx-Engels-Forschung: Neue Folge* (Hamburg: Argument, 1993), pp. 122ff.

9. Michael Heinrich, *'Entstehungs- und Auflösungsgeschichte des Marxschen 'Kapital,' Kapital und Kritik* (Hamburg: VSA Verlag, 2011), pp. 163 and 345–51.

10. 'Gattungswesen', MEGA II/11, p. 167, 'Species-being', CW 28, p. 176.

11. 'Bastiat und Carey', MEGA II/1, pp. 1, 3–15, CW 28, pp. 5–16. 'Einleitung', ibid., pp. 21–45 and 17–48 respectively.

12. Letter from Marx to Engels, 16 January 1858, MEGA III/9, p. 25, MEW 29, p. 260, CW 40, p. 249. Letter from Marx to Joseph Dietzgen, 9 May 1868, MEW 32, p. 547, CW 43, p. 31. Hegel literature in Marx's and Engels's libraries according to MEGA IV, pp. 315–22. *The Science of Logic* is registered there as pp. 321f, number 553 in the current catalogue. Freiligrath, like Marx, was living in London at the time. On Marx's studies of Hegel's *Logic*, see MEGA IV/32, pp. 321f.

13. Marx's words on the manuscript to *The German Ideology* can be found in MEGA II/2, p. 102, MEW 13, p. 10 and CW 29, p. 264.

14. 'definite individuals ...', MEW 3, p. 25, CW 5, p. 35. 'Individuals producing ...', MEGA II/1.1, p. 21, CW 28, p. 17.

15. The introductory arguments on individualism, production, and distribution in MEGA II/1.1, pp. 21–4, CW 28, pp. 17–26. John Stuart

Mill on production and distribution in *A System of Logic, Ratiocinative and Inductive; Being a Connected View of the Principles of Evidence, and the Methods of Scientific Investigation*, Collected Works of John Stuart Mill 7–8 (Toronto: University of Toronto Press, 1973–74), pp. 199ff. His *System of Logic* can be found in the same source. Graeme Duncan, *Marx and Mill: Two Views of Social Conflict and Social Harmony* (Cambridge: Cambridge University Press, 1973) concludes in a comparison between Marx and Mill. Unfortunately, the author does not go into their different views on the relationship between distribution and production. An independent and worthwhile commentary on Marx's introduction is Stuart Hall, *A 'Reading' of Marx's 1857 Introduction to the Grundrisse* (Birmingham: Centre of Contemporary Cultural Studies, 1973).

16. Jindřich Zelený, *The Logic of Marx*, trans. by Terrell Carver (Oxford: Blackwell, 1980), pp. 15–22 and *passim*.

17. The anatomy of humans and of apes in MEGA II/1.1, p. 40, CW 28, p. 42. For serious commentaries, see for example Heinrich, above all p. 178.

18. 'nothing is simpler ...', MEGA II/1.1, p. 30, CW 28, p. 31. 'Totality', ibid., pp. 34 and 36 respectively.

19. 'identical, but that ...', MEGA II/1.1, p. 35, CW 38, p. 36.

20. MEGA II/1.1, p. 36, CW 28, p. 38.

21. Hegel's most exhaustive presentation on the concept of reflection can be found in *The Science of Logic*, Part II, Hegel 1969, pp. 393–478. A good elucidation of Hegel's concept of reflection can be found in W. van Dooren, *Het Totalitetsbegrip bij Hegel en zijn Voorgangers* (Diss., Assen, 1965).

22. 'greift über ...', MEGA II/1.1, p. 35, English translation 'dominant moment', p. 36.

23. Hegel's example of the character and customs of a people and their legislation can be found in G. W. F. Hegel, *Enzyklopädie der philosophischen Wissenschaften* (Frankfurt am Main: Suhrkamp, 1986), pp. 346f. On *Verhältnis* and *Beziehung* in Hegel, see above, p. 210.

24. Louis Althusser, *For Marx* (London: Verso, 2005), p. 56.

25. 'Conceptual totality', MEGA II/1.1, p. 27, CW 28, p. 38. Marx also spoke of a *Gedankenkonkretum*, which in the *Collected Works* is very freely translated as 'a product of the thinking mind'.

26. On *'the unequal development'*, see ibid., pp. 44f and 46 respectively.

27. The reckoning with Karl Vogt, see, p. 530. Vogt was counted among the same grouping of materialists as Ludwig Büchner and Jacob Moleschott in this biological and philosophical debate. See Carl Vogt, *Köhlerglaube und Wissenschaft* (Giessen: J. Ricker'sche Buchhandlung, 1855), in which he certainly does not allow any freedom from the fundamental laws of matter, whether for humanity, art,

or anything else. Vogt and the others appear in the context of their times in the omnibus volume Kurt Bayertz, Walter Jaeschke, Myriam Gerhard, *Weltanschauung, Philosophie und Naturwissenschaft im 19. Jahrhundert: Der Materialismusstreit* (Hamburg: Meiner, 2007).

28. On the history of Aristotelian logic, see Heinrich Scholz, *Abriss der Geschichte der Logik* (Freiburg im Breisgau: Alber, 1959) and Wilhelm Risse, *Die Logik der Neuzeit* (Stuttgart-Bad-Cannstadt: Frommann, 1964–70).

29. On Hegel's *Science of Logic* and Marx's *Capital*, see Abbas Alidoust Azerbaijani, *Aufhebung Hegels Wissenschaft der Logik in Marx' Das Kapital* (Bern: Peter Lang, 2010).

30. MEGA II/1.1, pp. 26f, CW 28, p. 27.

31. MEGA II/1.1, pp. 26f, CW 28, p. 27. The living work that brings the dead to life through consuming it, pp. 272 and 285f respectively.

32. On the extremes, on the spiral or the increasing curve, MEGA II/1.1, p. 189, CW 28, p. 197.

33. MEGA II/1.1, p. 132, CW 28, p. 138.

34. Calculations of surplus value, MEGA II/1.1, pp. 277–309, CW 28, pp. 291–328. To Engels about arithmetical errors, 11 November 1858, MEW 29, p. 256, CW 40, p. 244. On the circulation of capital, MEGA I/1.2, pp. 563ff, CW 29, pp. 72ff.

35. Letter to Engels 2 Apr 1858, MEGA III/9, pp. 121–5, MEW 29, pp. 311–18, CW 40, pp. 297–304. The summary in the *Grundrisse*, MEGA I/1.1, p. 43, CW 28, p. 45.

36. Engels's response, April 1858, MEGA III/9, pp. 126ff, MEW 29, pp. 319ff, CW 40, pp. 304ff.

37. Marx's letter 29 April 1858, ibid., pp. 134f, 323f, and 309f respectively. Marx himself was well aware of how elusive this portion of his presentation was, even in the finished work. To his old friend Joseph Weydemeyer – then residing in the United States – he wrote on 1 February 1859 that 'the analysis of simple money forms is, you know, the most difficult because the most abstract part of political economy', MEGA III/9, p. 295, MEW 29, p. 573, CW 40, p. 377.

38. Marx's letter of thanks, 31 May 1858, ibid., pp.156f, 329f, and 317f respectively. The details in the agreement with Duncker are evident from many letters from this time, for example to Engels, 29 March 1858, ibid., pp. 115f, 309f, and 295 respectively. Against a certain amount of compensation, Duncker pledged to publish three instalments that Marx would deliver on a continuing basis. After three instalments, Duncker would evaluate the results and, if it proved successful, would draw up a formal contract. Marx would only finish one instalment and delivered it later than promised.

39. Marx's index of the *Grundrisse* in MEGA III/2, pp. 3–14 and CW

29, pp. 421–9. He then wrote an initial version of the instalment at a rapid pace, ibid., pp. 19–94 and pp. 430–507 respectively.

40. The preface, MEGA II/2: pp. 99–103, CW 29, pp. 261–265. In the German original, it says 'erst zu bewiesende Resultate', that is, stronger than the 'substantiated' of the English translation ('results that still have to be substantiated').

41. Gerald Allen Cohen, *Karl Marx' Historieteori: Ett försvar* (Lund: Arkiv, 1978), pp. 278–296. MEGA II/6, p. 278, CW 35, p. 281.

42. *Leitfaden* corresponds to the less expressive 'guiding principle' in the English translation.

43. 'Base' in the *Grundrisse*, MEGA II/1.2, pp. 380f, CW 28, pp. 400f. In the *Collected Works*, 'Basis' is translated as 'foundation' (CW 29, pp. 265), while Cohen starts out from the translation 'basis'. The meaning is the same.

44. The analysis of the commodity, and use and exchange value, in MEGA II/2, pp. 107–30, CW 29, pp. 269–92. The accumulation of commodities, MEGA II/2, p. 107 and MEGA II/5, p. 17, CW 29, p. 269.

45. The historical overview, MEGA II/2, pp. 130–9, CW 29, pp. 292–302. *Theorien über den Mehrwert* was published by Karl Kautsky in a three-volume edition between 1905 and 1910. The text can be found in MEW 26, vols 1–3; it is found in a scientifically more satisfying edition in MEGA II, p. 3. The English translation in CW vols 31 and 32. Steuart's influence on Hegel is brought out in a large amount of literature on Hegel. One fundamental work is Paul Chamley, *Économie poli- tique et philosophie chez Steuart et Hegel* (Strasbourg: Muh-Le Roux, 1963).

46. Methods of research and presentation in the postscript to the second edition of *Capital* (1872), MEGA II/6, p. 709, CW 35, p. 19.

47. All Marx's digressions in parentheses, MEGA II/1.1, pp. 94ff, CW 28, pp. 98ff.

48. The globalized world of the department store, MEGA II/2, p. 158, CW 29, p. 324.

49. The pillar saints, MEGA II/2, p. 201, CW 29, p. 367.

50. Going from value to price, MEGA II/2, pp. 162f, CW 29, pp. 338ff.

51. Postage from Engels: Letter from Marx to Engels, 21 and 22 January 1859, MEGA III/9, pp. 519ff, MEW, pp. 385ff, CW 40, p. 369. Marx on getting to work on the second part in a letter to Engels, 21 February 1859, MEGA III/9, p. 318, MEW 29, p. 399, CW 40, p. 389. (The publishers of *Marx Engels Werke* have clearly misunderstood what he was saying, and believe that he was referring to the first instalment; compare note 332, MEW 29, p. 701. But that instalment had already been completed and printed!)

52. Engels's reviews in *Das Volk*, 6–20 August 1859, MEGA II/2, pp. 246–55, CW 16, pp. 465–77.

53. Marx himself reproduced the remark in a letter to Engels, 22 July 1859, MEW 29, p. 463, CW 40, p. 473.

54. 'the real ...', MEGA II/1.1, pp. 168f, CW 28, p. 176.

55. The socialists' mistake, ibid., pp. 171f and 180 respectively.

56. Marx on power, ibid., pp. 266 and 278 respectively.

57. 'Society does not ...', pp. 188 and 195 respectively.

58. The text on various pre-capitalist modes of production can be found in MEGA II/1.2, pp. 378–415, CW 28, pp. 399–439.

59. Eric Hobsbawm, *How to Change the World: Marx and Marxism, 1840–2011* (London: Little, Brown, 2011), pp. 127–75. Gianni Sofri, *Det asiatiska produktionssättet* (Stockholm: Prisma, 1969).

60. On Spivak's preference for the *Grundrisse*, see Kemple, *Reading Marx Writing*, p. vii. Gayatri Chakravorty Spivak, *Selected Subaltern Studies* (Oxford: Oxford University Press, 1988) provides a useful compilation of subaltern studies. The quote from the preface to *A Contribution*, MEGA II/2, p. 101.

61. Marx's starting point, MEGA II/1.2, p. 399, CW 28, p. 419. The tautology, ibid., pp. 393 and 413 respectively.

62. Marx's statements on the Asiatic production are quite scanty; see above all ibid., pp. 380f and 400ff respectively.

63. On property, the most concentrated (and difficult to read!), ibid., pp. 398ff and 416f respectively, and *passim*.

64. Hobsbawm, *How to Change the World*, pp. 154ff.

65. *Grundrisse*, MEGA II/1.2, pp. 368f, CW 28, pp. 387f.

66. 'eternal right', pp. 407 and 428 respectively.

67. Marx promises more on landed property, ibid., pp. 400 and 421 respectively.

68. On work before, during, and after capitalism, ibid., pp. 498–502 and 529–33 respectively. 'Really free work ...' and 'Work involved ...', ibid., pp. 499 and 530.

69. David McLellan, 'Introduction', *Karl Marx's Grundrisse* (London: Macmillan, 1971), p. 15. Martin Nicolaus, 'The Unknown Marx', *Ideology in Social Science: Readings in Critical Social Theory* (Suffolk: Fontana/Collins, 1972), p. 333.

70. Kemple, *Reading Marx Writing*.

11 The Unfinished Masterpiece

1. Marx writes about his attempt to become a railroad employee in a letter to Ludwig Kugelmann, 28 December 1862, MEGA III/12, p. 297, MEW 30, p. 640, CW 41, p. 436.

2. The letter about Mary Burns's death and Engels's reactions, 7, 8,

13, 24, and 26 January 1863, MEGA III/12, pp. 307–16, MEW 30, pp. 309–18, CW 41, pp. 441–8.

3. Wolff's will is commented on in a number of letters in Marx and Engels's correspondence, for example from Engels to Marx, 3 June 1864, and from Marx to Engels, 7 June 1864, MEGA III/12, pp. 377f and 381, MEW 30, pp. 405–9, CW 41, pp. 535–8. Marx genuinely mourned his friend. He wrote about the funeral in a letter to Jenny on 13 May 1864 (MEGA III/12, pp. 528f, MEW 30, pp. 659f, CW 41, pp. 525f), which indicates among other things that Marx himself spoke at the graveside and was so touched that his voice failed him several times. Wolff, during his years in England, had worked as a respected private teacher in Manchester.

4. Marx's carbuncles had been a recurrent theme in his correspondence since the autumn of 1863. Sperber, *Karl Marx*, pp. 350f.

5. For the development of Marx's economic criticism after 1850, see Marcello Musto, 'Marx und die Kritik der politischen konomie: von den frühen Studien bis zu den "Grundrissen", *Kapital und Kritik* (Hamburg: VSA Verlag, 2011), pp. 130–54, and Michael Heinrich, 'Entstehungs– und Auflösungsgeschichte des Marxschen "Kapital"', *Kapital und Kritik* (Hamburg: VSA Verlag, 2011), ibid., in particular pp. 159f.

6. On 'the economic stuff' and 'the vile business', respectively (in both cases, Marx uses a much coarser German word, *Scheiss*, 'shit'), Marx to Engels, 2 April 1851, MEGA III/4, p. 85, MEW 27, p. 228, CW 38, p. 325, and 14 August 1867, not yet in MEGA, MEW 31, p. 321 and CW 42, p. 400.

7. Marx to Kugelmann 28 December 1862, MEGA III/12, pp. 296ff, MEW 30, pp. 639ff, CW 41, pp. 435ff.

8. The manuscripts between 1861 and 1863 comprise six parts of the MEGA – more precisely, MEGA II/3–6. These correspond to Volumes 30–34 of the CW. 'Value, price and profit' is reproduced in MEGA II/4.1, pp. 385–432, but in CW 20, pp. 101–49. The lecture was held on two occasions, 20 and 27 Jun 1865.

9. The work is 'an artistic whole', letter to Engels, 31 July 1865, MEGA III/13, p. 510, MEW 31, p. 132, CW 42, p. 173.

10. The letter about creative intoxication and the outbreak of a new illness, to Engels, 10 Feb 1866, MEW 31, pp. 174f, CW 42, p. 223f.

11. Marx communicates his hopes of being finished in August to Engels, 7 July 1866, MEW 31, p. 232, CW 42, p. 289. The hopes of being finished in a week, 10 Nov. 1866, MEW 31, p. 263, CW 42, p. 332.

12. On his stay with the Kugelmanns, see the letters to Engels, 24 Apr. and 7 May 1867, MEW 31, pp. 299ff and 296–9 respectively, CW 42, pp. 259–62 and 370–4 respectively.

13. Marx's question to Engels in a letter dated 24 Aug. 1867, MEW 31, p. 327, CW 42, pp. 407f.

14. Engels's letter to Marx, 27 Apr. 1867, MEW 31, p. 292, CW 42, p. 362.

15. Engels's review for *Elberfelder Zeitung* is reproduced in MEW 16, pp. 214f, CW 40, pp. 214f. Engels's review in *Rheinische Zeitung*, MEW 16, pp. 210–13, CW 20, pp. 210–13. The quote, p. 213 in both.

16. The review intended for *Fortnightly Review*, ibid., pp. 288–309 and 238–59 respectively.

17. Dühring's review of *Capital* was originally published in Eugen Dühring, *Cursus der Philosophie als streng wissenschaftlicher Weltanschauung und Lebensgestaltung* (Leipzig: Erich Koschny, 1867), pp. 182–6.

18. Marx's letter to Engels, 8 Jan 1868, and to Kugelmann 11 Jan and 6 Mar 1868, MEW 32, pp. 9, 533, and 538 respectively, CW 42, 514, 522, and 543f respectively.

19. On Marx's relationship to Russian populism, see Maximilien Rubel, 'Karl Marx et le socialisme populiste russe,' *La revue socialiste* (1947) and Henry Eaton, 'Marx and the Russians,' *Journal of the History of Ideas* (41/1, 1980). 1980 and above all Teodor Shanin, *Late Marx and the Russian road: Marx and 'The Peripheries of Capitalism'* (London, Melbourne, Henley: Routledge and Kegan Paul, 1983). See further below, p. 572.

20. The statement of the Russian censors after Jacques Attali, *Karl Marx ou l'esprit du monde* (Paris: Fayard, 2005), p. 362f.

21. Marx's letter to Danielson, 7 Oct 1868, MEW 32, p. 563, CW 43, p. 123ff.

22. The section 'Ergänzungen und Veränderungen zum ersten Band des Kapitals', which was prepared between December 1871 and January 1872, can be found in MEGA II/6, 1–54. The apparatus volume related to it provides additional detailed information. 'Afterword to the Second German Edition' on its greater scientific 'strictness', ibid., 700, CW 35, p. 12.

23. Marx on Roy's translation efforts in a letter to his son-in-law Paul Lafargue, 21 Mar 1872; to the Russian translator Nikolai Frantsevich Danielson, 28 May 1872; to Friedrich Adolph Sorge, 21 Dec 1872; to Maurice Lechâtre, 12 May 1873; MEW 33, pp. 437, 477, 552 and 626 respectively, CW 44,347, 385, 460, and 495 respectively. Marx 1875, new critical edition in MEGA II/7. Engels did not include all Marx's corrections, ibid., 12*. On the unique position of the French version, see Heinrich 2011, p. 160f.

24. On the new reading of Marx, see Werner Bonefeld and Michael Heinrich, *Kapital und Kritik: nach der 'neuen' Marx-Lektüre* (Hamburg: VSA:Verlag, 2011).

25. On use value, exchange value, and value, see the second edition of *Capital*, MEGA II/6, 69–113, CW 35, pp. 45–80. On sharpening the distinction between value and exchange value, see the editorial investigation, 27*, and Marx's own 'Ergänzungen und Veränderungen ...', 7 and *passim*. The otherwise very readable Johan Fornäs, *Capitalism: A Companion to Marx's Economic Critique* (London and New York: Routledge, 2013) asserts that the distinction between exchange value and value is 'slightly confusing', which probably refers to the text of the first edition. Every misunderstanding is cleared away after Marx's explanation in the second edition.

26. Adam Smith uses the term 'productive force' at the very beginning of *The Wealth of Nations*; Adam Smith, *Inquiry Into the Nature and Causes of the Wealth of Nations* (Oxford: Clarendon Press, 1976), 13. The quote from *Capital* is from the English translation, CW 35, p. 50; the original is in MEW II/6, p. 74. It can be questioned whether the English translation of *Produktivkraft* with 'productiveness' is reasonable; *Produktivkraft* is, however, a specific, technical term in Marx as it was previously in Smith.

27. On commodity fetishism, MEGA II/6, pp. 102–113, CW 35, pp. 81–94; the quote 102 and 81f respectively. The account of commodity fetishism breaks stylistically from the section preceding it. No one has described this better than David Harvey. Marx was now writing in a literary style; his language is 'metaphoric, imaginative, playful and emotive, full of allusions and references to magic, mysteries, and necromancies'. David Harvey, *A Companion to Marx's Capital* (London and New York: Verso, 2010), p. 38.

28. The formula C–M–C, pp. 131 and 115 respectively, The linen, the Bible, and the whisky, pp. 135 and 120 respectively.

29. Marx's definition of the machine, pp. 364f and 376f respectively.

30. The inevitable end of capitalism, pp. 683 and 751 respectively.

31. A detailed and competent account for the creation of Volume II is given in the MEGA edition, II/13, pp. 497–548 (apparatus volume). On the statement from 1864, p. 502.

32. Engels on Marx's condition in the foreword, MEGA II/13, pp. 5ff, CW 36, pp. 7ff. The literature on Engels's editing of Marx's manuscripts included Carl-Erich Vollgraf and Jürgen Jungnickel, '*Marx in Marx' Worten? Zu Engels Edition des Hauptmanuskripts zum dritten Buch des 'Kapitals,'* MEGA-Studien 1994/2, pp. 3–55; Michael Heinrich, *Engels' Edition of the Third Volume of 'Capital and Marx' Original Manuscript, Science and Society* 60:4 (1996–97), pp. 452–66; Michael Krätke, 'Das Marx-Engels-Problem: warum Engels das Marxsche Kapital nicht verfälscht hat', *Marx–Engels Jahrbuch* (2006), pp. 142–70; and Ingo Elbe, 'Die Beharrlichkeit des

"Engelsismus": Bemerkung- en zum Marx-Engels-Problem', *Marx-Engels-Jahrbuch* (2007), pp. 92–105.

33. 'locate and describe' in Marx's manuscript, MEGA II/4.2, p. 7, MEW 25, p. 33, CW 37, p. 27.

34. 'Our present analysis ...', MEGA II/4.2, p. 251, MEW 25, p. 174, CW 37, p. 164.

35. 'the nature ...', ibid., 287, 223, and 211 respectively. The German original has *Wesen*, essence, and not *Natur*.

36. 'most external ...', ibid., pp. 461, 404, and 355 respectively.

37. The Trinity Formula, ibid., pp. 834ff, 822ff, and 801f respectively. Engels here wrote about Marx's original text; to a great extent he abbreviated and simplified it, bringing it into closer harmony with Volume I.

38. Eric Hobsbawm, *How to Change the World: Marx and Marxism, 1840–2011* (London: Little, Brown, 2011), pp. 179ff.

39. Eugen Böhm-Bawerk, 'Zum Abschluss des Marxschen Systems' (1896), in Eugen Böhm Bawerk, *Gesammelte Schriften* (Wien: Holder-Pichler-Tempsky, 1924).

40. On Hilferding's life and work, see William Smaldone, *Rudolf Hilferding: The Tragedy of a German Social Democrat* (DeKalb: Northern Illinois University Press, 1998). On the similarities between the concentration of wealth before 1914 and in the 2010s, see Thomas Piketty, *Le Capital au XXIe siècle* (Paris: Seuil, 2013), pp. 75ff and *passim*.

41. Rosa Luxemburg, *The Accumulation of Capital*, trans. by Agnes Schwarzschild (London: Macmillan & Kegan Paul, 1951).

42. V. I. Lenin, *Imperialismen som kapitalismens högsta stadium* (Göteborg: Proletärkultur, 1983). Rosa Luxemburg, *Världskriget och de europeiska revolutionerna: Politiska skrifter i urval 1914–1919* (Lund: Arkiv, 1985), p. 83.

43. Georg Lukács, *History and Class Consciousnes: Studies in Marxist Dialectics*, trans. by Rodney Livingstone (Cambridge, Mass.: MIT Press, 1967).

44. There is substantial literature on the Frankfurt School; Rolf Wiggershaus, *Die Frankfurter Schule: Geschichte, Theoretische Entwicklung, Politische Bedeutung* (München: Dt. Taschenbuch Verlag, 1997) and Martin Jay, *The Dialectical Imagination: A History of the Frankfurt School and the Institute of Social Research* (Berkeley: University of California Press, 1996) provide good introductions.

45. Paul Baran and Paul Sweezy, *Monopolkapitalet* (Stockholm: Rabén & Sjögren, 1966).

46. Louis Althusser, *Lire Le capital* (Paris: Maspéro, 1966), second edition Louis Althusser and Étienne Balibar, *Att läsa Kapitalet* (Staanstorp: Cavefors, 1970).

47. 'continent of history', Louis Althusser, *Filosofi från en revolutionär klasståndpunkt*, Göran Therborn (ed.) (Lund: Caverfors, 1976), p. 56.

48. Examples of early capital-logic works are Helmut Reichelt, *Zur logischen Struktur des Kapitalbegriffs bei Karl Marx* (Frankfurt am Main: Europäische Verlagsanstalt, 1970) and Hans-Jørgen Schanz, *Til rekonstruktionen af kritikken af den politiskeøkonomis omfangslogiske status* (Aarhus: Modtryk, 1973).

49. On the movement in general, Ingo Elbe, *Marx im Westen: die neue Marx-Lektüre in der Bundesrepublik seit 1965* (Berlin: Politische Ideen, 2010) and Werner Bonefeld and Michael Heinrich, *Kapital und Krikik: nach der 'neuen' Marx-Lektüre* (Hamburg: VSA: Verlag, 2011).

50. Hans-Georg Backhaus, *Dialektik der Wertform. Untersuchungen zur Marxschen Ökonomierkritik* (Freiburg im Breisgau: ça ira-Verlag, 1997). His own version of how *die neue Marx-Lektüre* arose and what characterizes it is presented in a longer introductory text, pp. 9–40. Reichelt summarizes his efforts even later in Helmut Reichelt, *Neue Marx-Lektüre: zur Kritik sozialwissenschaftlicher Logik* (Freiburg im Breisgau: ça ira, 2013).

51. Prokla was founded in 1970. Altvater has now left the Greens and gone over to Die Linke (The Left).

52. Michael Heinrich's most important work is *Die Wissenschaft vom Wert: Die Marxsche Kritik der politischen Ökonomie zwischen wissenschaftlicher Revolution und klassischer Tradition* (Verlag Westphälisches Dampfboot, 2011). On the polemic with Backhaus/Reichelt, pp. 171f. On the particular level of theory in Marx, pp. 17f and *passim*. Heinrich's most accessible exposition of the monetary theory is found in Michael Heinrich, *An Introduction to the Three Volumes of Karl Marx's Capital*, trans. by Alexander Locascio (New York: Monthly Review Press, 2004), pp. 180ff.

53. Hans-Georg Backhaus, 'Materialen zur Rekonstruktion der Marx-schen Werttheorie', *Gesellschaft: Beiträge zur Marxschen Theorie 3* (Frankfurt am Main: Suhrkamp, 1975), p. 123.

54. Peter Ruben, 'Über Methodologie und Weltanschauung der Kapitallogik', *Sopo* 42 (1977), pp. 40–64.

55. Heinrich, op. cit, pp. 220–33 and in particular in the summarizing paragraphs, p. 250f.

56. Robert Kurz, *Geld ohne Wert: Grundrisse zu einer Transformation der Kritik der politischen Ökonomie* (Berlin: Horlemann Verlag, 2012). Roswitha Scholz, *Differenzen der Krise – Krise der Differenzen: die neue Gesellschaftskritik im globalen Zeitalter und der Zusammenhang von 'Rasse', Klasse, Geschlecht und postmoderner Individualisierung* (Berlin: Horlemann Verlag, 2005). Scholz and Kurz were married to each other.

57. *Historisch-kritisches Wörterbuch des Marxismus* (see Wolfgang Fritz Haug, *Historisch-kritisches Wörterbuch des Marxismus* (Hamburg: Argument, 1994). The work has reached Volume 8:1, but much remains. Wolfgang Fritz Haug, *Hightech-Kapitalismus in der grossen Krisen* (Hamburg: Argument, 2012).

58. Haug's latest introduction to *Capital* is Wolfgang Fritz Haug, *Neue Vorlesungen zur Einführung ins Kapital* (Hamburg: Argument, 2005). Heinrich's shorter introduction to *Capital* is Heinrich 2012. So far, two volumes of the more comprehensive reading guides have been published: Michael Heinrich, *Wie das Marxsche Kapital lessen?*, vol. I, (Stuttgart: Schmetterling Verlag, 2008) and Michael Heinrich, *Wie das Marxsche Kapital lessen?*, vol. II (Stuttgart: Schmetterling Verlag, 2013). Johan Fornäs, *Capitalism: A Companion to Marx's Economic Critique* (London and New York: Routledge, 2013). Fredric Jameson, *Representing 'Capital': A Reading of Volume One* (London: Verso, 2011). David Harvey, *A Companion to Marx's Capital* (London: Verso, 2010) and David Harvey, *A Companion to Marx's Capital: Volume 2* (London: Verso, 2013). Harvey's lectures can be found on the Internet. Andrew Kliman, *Reclaiming Marx's 'Capital': A Refutation of the Myth of Inconsistency* (Lanham, MD: Rowman and Littlefield, 2007).

59. Mark Moiseevitch Rozental, *Die dialektische Methode der politischen Ökonomie von Karl Marx* (Berlin: Dietz Verlag, 1973). See above all pp. 311–20.

60. Heinrich, *Die Wissenschaft vom Wert*, pp. 144–8.

61. The sixth thesis on Feuerbach, CW 5, p. 7.

62. 'Every beginning …', MEGA II/6, p. 65, CW 35, p. 7.

63. 'Ergänzungen zum ersten Band des "Kapitals"', MEGA II/6, pp. 22f. Cf. also the publisher's 'Einleitung (Introduction)', ibid., p. 27*.

64. 'mode of existence of value', ibid., pp. 83 and 60 respectively. In the first edition it reads: 'Wenn wir künftig das Wort '*Werth*' ohne weitere Bestimmung brauchen, so handelt es sich immer vom *Tauschwert*' (When we use the word 'value' below without a more precise determination, it always concerns *exchange value*). MEGA II/5, p. 19. It is likely this sentence that made Fornäs remark that the distinction is perhaps slightly confusing; Fornäs 2013, 32). The bandying about of the terms 'use value', 'exchange value' (or 'value form') and 'value' continue throughout the entire first chapter of *Capital*. See in particular MEGA II/6, pp. 80–98, CW 35, pp. 58–78.

65. The Aristotle quote, ibid., pp. 91 and 69 respectively.

66. On the history and continued topicality of the concepts of form, substance, and content, see Sven-Eric Liedman, *Stenarna i själen: form och materia från antiken till våra dagar* (Stockholm: Bonniers, 2006). On Aristotle there, pp. 67–94. Among later interpreters,

Gareth Stedman Jones has called attention, though briefly, to the significance of the concepts of form, substance, and content in *Capital*.
Jones, *Karl Marx*, p. 390

67. The twofold nature of labour, MEGA II/6, pp. 75, CW, pp. 35, 51.
The quote reproduced is from Revelation (King James Version).
Capital, MEGA II/6, pp. 115f, CW 35, p. 97.

68. The commodity 'an object outside us', pp. 69 and 45 respectively.

69. 'übernatürlich' in the original, p. 89. 'Non-natural' in CW 35, p. 67.

70. 'Transubstantiation', pp. 133 and 117 respectively.

71. Capital 'is not a thing …', MEW 25, p. 822, CW 37, p. 801. Marx's
own corresponding text can be found in MEGA II/4.2, p. 843. Even
if it is less well organized than Engels's editing, it is for the matter
itself more illustrative and the nature/society opposition is more
sharply marked.

72. 'Realm of freedom', ibid., pp. 828 and 807 respectively. In his
editing, Engels followed Marx's manuscript word for word regarding the realms of freedom and necessity, MEGA II/4.2, p. 838.

73. Marx on freedom, equality, and so on, MEGA II/6, p. 191, CW 35,
p. 186.

74. 'a dead dog', MEGA II/6, p. 709, CW 35, p. 19. The relationship
between Marx and Hegel has constantly been controversial. Robert
Fine, who speaks of Hegel as 'Marx's *doppelgänger*', makes an
attempt at moving Marx much closer to Hegel; Robert Fine, *Political Investigations: Hegel, Marx, Arendt* (London: Routledge, 2001),
pp. 79–96. When Marx said that Hegel's dialectic was the antithesis
of his own, he was simply not speaking the truth, Fine maintains;
Hegel did not build the kind of idealistic constructions Marx alleged
he did at all. Fine obviously does not take the essential differences
between Marx and Hegel into sufficient consideration, for example
that Hegel's schematizations are missing in Marx and that there is a
structural difference between Hegel's idealism and Marx's materialism. Nor is there any equivalent to Marx's striving after exactitude
in Hegel.

75. 'with the precision of natural science', MEGA II/2, p. 101, CW 29,
p. 263.

76. 'Senior's "Last Hour"', MEW II/6, pp. 232–6, CW 35, pp. 233–8.
On the portion of necessary work time in the whole, MEGA II/6,
pp. 219, CW 35, pp. 218f.

77. The examples are later developed in the chapters on the rate of
surplus value and on the working day, ibid., pp. 221–303 and
221–307 respectively.

78. The law on the mass of surplus value, ibid., pp. 304 and 308
respectively.

79. On the transition from value to price, MEW 25, pp. 164–75, CW

37, pp. 153–65. 'The cost price' and 'Our present analysis …', MEW 25, pp. 175f, CW 37, p. 164.

80. Marx's original version in MEGA II/4.2, pp. 230–42. 'In der Wirklichkeit …', ibid., p. 234.

81. Ladislaus von Bortkiewicz's 1907 article is included in Ladislaus von Bortkiewicz, *Wertrechnung und Preisrechnung im Marxschen System* (1907, Lol- lar/Giessen: Achenbach, 1976).

82. Paul M. Sweezy, *The Theory of Capitalist Development: Principles of Marxian Political Economy* (New York: Modern Reader Paperbacks, 1970), p. 123.

83. Michael Heinrich, *Die Wissenschaft vom Wert: Die Marxsche Kritik der politischen Ökonomie zwischen wissenschaftlicher Revolution und klassischer Tradition* (Verlag Westphälisches Dampfboot, 2011), pp. 270f.

84. Andrew Kliman, *Reclaiming Marx's Capital: A Refutation of the Myth of Inconsistency* (Lanham, MD: Rowman & Littlefield, 2007) provides a history of the controversies around the transformation problem (pp. 41ff), presents his method of interpretation (pp. 55ff), and attacks competing interpretations (pp. 75ff). One of Kliman's most important targets of attack is what he calls 'physicalism' (not to be confused with the physicalism developed by certain representatives of neopositivism). By physicalism, he means that value is determined both by the technology (the machines) that are put to use in production, and by workers' wages. It is easy to agree with Kliman here. The strict boundary Marx drew between nature (including machinery) and the societal level ('supernatural') squares with an interpretation of this kind.

85. Heinrich develops his interpretation of *Capital* as a project that had been in progress for many years most consistently in 'Entstehungs- und Aufl.sungsgeschichte des Marxschen "Kapital"', pp. 155–93. Marx in a letter to Danielson, 13 December 1881, MEW 35, p. 246, CW 46, p. 161. One economist who often appears in the context is Piero Sraffa, an Italian largely active at Cambridge. His central work is Piero Sraffa, *Production of Commodities by Means of Commodities: Prelude to a Critique of Economic Theory* (Cambridge: Cambridge University Press, 1960). Sraffa certainly took up the transformation problem, but his main business was a reckoning with marginalism. He is usually characterized as a neo-Ricardian, and thus not a Marxist. A number of researchers using matrix algebra have shown that it is not possible to demonstrate a connection between value and prices; see Ian Steedman, *Marx After Sraffa* (London: NLB, 1977) and Michio Morishima, *Marx's Economics: A Dual Theory of Value and Growth* (Cambridge: Cambridge University Press, 1973).

86. '[O]nly in the shape of money', MEGA II/6, pp. 172, CW 35, p. 165.
87. Helmut Reichelt, *Zur logischen Struktur des Kapitalbegriffs bei Karl Marx* (Frankfurt am Main: Europäische Verlagsanstalt, 1970) still deals in detail with the question of the relationship between historical materialism and a critique of capital, calling attention above all to the difference between concretion and precision (pp. 19–72) and also pointing out what is misleading in imagining that Marx, in his particular theory, applied a dialectical method (p. 81). Schanz *Til rekonstruktione*, p. 693 is significantly more resolute in his rejection of historical materialism (pp. 19ff and *passim*). Heinrich, in 'Entstehungs- und Aufl.sungsgeschichte des Marxschen "Kapital"', is entirely unhesitating in his dismissal.
88. Marx on trade and usury capital, MEGA II/6, pp. 180ff, CW 35, pp. 174–7.
89. Gödel's First Incompleteness Theorem: 'Any consistent formal system F within which a certain amount of elementary arithmetic can be carried out is incomplete; i.e., there are statements of the language of F which can neither be proved nor disproved in F.' See Peter Smith, *An Introduction to Gödel's Theorems* (Cambridge: Cambridge University Press, 2007).
90. Note 89, MEGA II/6, p. 364, CW 35, pp. 375f.
91. On Marx's changed view of the relationship between value and money, see Heinrich 'Entstehungs- und Aufl.sungsgeschichte des Marxschen "Kapital"', p. 176.
92. On 'high-tech capitalism', Wolfgang Fritz Haug, *High-tech-Kapitalismus in der grossen Krise* (Hamburg: Argument, 2012). Werner Sombart discerned a late capitalist stage back in 1902. A later edition is Werner Sombart, *Der moderne Kapitalismus* (München and Leipzig: Duncker and Humblot, 1916–28). Sombart gradually distanced himself more and more from Marx. Ernest Mandel, *Senkapitalismen* (Stockholm: René Coeckelberghs, 1974–5) and Jürgen Habermas, *Legitimationsprobleme im Spätkapitalismus* (Frankfurt am Main: Suhrkamp, 1973). A good account of postmodernism is Krishan Kumar, *From Post-Industrial to Post-Modern Society: New Theories of the Contemporary World* (Hoboken, NJ: John Wiley and Sons, 2009). Kumar takes up Marx's and Marxism's position in the postmodern debate in particular, for example pp. 114ff and 194ff. Jameson, *Postmodernism, Or, the Cultural Logic of Late Capitalism*, pp. xxi and 260–78. Terrell Carver, the assiduous British expert on Marx, even created a postmodern Marx: a Marx who would not (like the modern Marx) be regarded as a thinker with a uniform outlook or theory, and who therefore could have new interpretations evolved depending on what was being focused on in his work. It can be said that Carver succeeds

in surveying important changes in Marx's development, just as he can also show that older text editions create seemingly uniform works. But the question is what use there is of the term 'post-modern'. Talking about a post-Soviet Marx would probably be more apposite. Terrell Carver, *The Postmodern Marx* (Manchester: Manchester University Press, 1998). The principles in *The German Ideology*, p. 172.

93. Humanity's labour in relation to nature and in contrast to the activities of animals; MEGA II/6, pp. 192f, CW 35, p. 187. In the English translation, the important German word *Stoffwechsel* has often been replaced by the meaningless 'material actions'. One of the pioneers in the area was the great chemist Justus von Liebig, of whose work Marx was a zealous reader. Justus Liebig, *Die Thierchemie, oder die organische Chemie in ihrer Anwendung auf Physiologie und Pathologie* (Braunschweig: Verlag Vieweg, 1842), which was also published in many later editions, was of particular significance for the doctrine of metabolism.

94. On Marx's naturalism, see Johan Fornäs, *Capitalism: A Companion to Marx's Economic Critique* (London: Routledge, 2013), pp. 297f.

95. The French translation, MEGA II/7, pp. 145f.

96. François Mitterrand, *L'abeille et l'architecte: chronique* (Paris: Flammarion, 1978).

97. 'Ich arbeite wie toll die Nächte durch', Marx to Engels, 8 December 1857, MEGA III/8, pp. 210, MEW 29, p. 225, CW 40, p. 217.

98. 'Mir war das Ekelhafteste die Unterbrechung meiner Arbeit', Marx to Engels 10 February 1866, MEW 31, p. 174, CW 42, p. 223. On the expanded concept of labour, see for example Pierre Jaccard, Histoire du travail de l'antiquité à nos jours (Paris: Payot, 1960).

99. 'Nach Hobbes ist die *Wissenschaft*, nicht die *ausführende Arbeit*, die Mutter der Künste', MEGA II/3.4: Beilagen, MEW 26, pp. 1, 329.

100. On technicians in Germanophone Europe as against Great Britain, see Mikael Hård, *Machines Are Frozen Spirit: The Scientification of Refrigeration and Brewing in the Nineteenth Century: A Weberian Interpretation* (Frankfurt am Main: Campus, 1994), pp. 97ff and *passim*.

101. 'the soul of capital', MEGA II/6, pp. 239, CW 35, p. 241. 'You may be a model citizen ...', ibid., pp. 241 and 242 respectively.

102. The reserve army, ibid., pp. 573–83 and 623–34 respectively.

103. On the British census, ibid., pp. 427f and 449f respectively.

104. The interrupted chapter on classes is now found in a critical edition after Marx's manuscript in MEGA II/4.2, pp. 901f. It turns out that Engels did not make any changes, MEW 25, pp. 892f, CW

37, pp. 870f. In Marxian traditions, on the other hand, the interest in his concept of class has often been great. It is still so in the post-Soviet epoch. Erik Olin Wright's *Class Counts* is an ambitious work, in which the author strives to capture the class structure of present-day capitalist society, with its great, diffuse middle class, on the basis of certain fundamental ideas in Marx. Erik Olin Wright, *Class Counts: Comparative Studies in Class Analysis* (Cambridge: Cambridge University Press, 1997).

105. On factory legislation and the demands in it, MEGA II/6, pp. 460–75, CW 35, pp. 483–505; the quote, pp. 463 and 486 respectively.

106. Robin Small, *Karl Marx: The Revolutionary as Educator* (Dordrecht: Springer Netherlands, 2014) is an account of Marx's ideas on education and his polytechnic ideal. The book unfortunately has a somewhat devout tone and never goes into detailed analysis.

107. Marx to Engels, 25 February 1867, MEW 31, p. 278, CW 42, pp. 347f.

108. Balzac's 1840 comedy was christened by its author as *Le faiseur* but was performed on stage after his death under the name *Mercadet*. See Étienne Balibar, *La philosophie de Marx* (Paris: Éditions La Découverte, 1993). 'Le Chef-d'œuvre inconnu' was originally included in the second edition of Balzac's 1831 debut, *Romans et contes philosophiques*. 'Melmoth réconcilé' was first published in 1835 in the collection *Le livre des conteurs*. Honoré Balzac, *Le livre des* conteurs, vol. 6 (Paris: Lequien ls, 1835). On the story as a parody of the fantastic novels of the Romantic period, see Ruth Amossy, 'Melmoth réconcilié ou la parodie du conte fantastique', *L'année balzacienne* (Paris: P.U.F., 1978), pp. 149–67. Marshall Berman, *Allt som är fast för yktigas: modernism och modernitet* (Lund: Arkiv förlag, 1987) provides a convincing account of Faust's period of capitalistic entrepreneurial spirit.

109. On the significance of the story for Marx, see Isaiah Berlin, *Karl Marx: His Life and Environment* (Oxford: Oxford University Press, 1978), p. 2; Jerrold Seigel, *Marx's Fate: The Shape of a Life* (Princeton: Princeton University Press, 1978), p. 388; Jacques Attali, *Karl Marx ou l'esprit du monde* (Paris: Fayard, 2005), p. 250; Francis Wheen, *Karl Marx: en biografi* (Stockholm: Norstedts, 2006), pp. 1–6 and 111.

12 Twin Souls or a Tragic Mistake?

1. The phrase is alluded to in the title of Norman Levine's *The Tragic Deception: Marx Contra Engels* (Oxford: Clio Books 1975).

2. After Marx died, Engels became uneasy about suddenly being forced to play a leading role. 'I have spent a lifetime doing what I was fitted for, namely playing the second fiddle,' he wrote to one of Marx's most zealous followers, the Swiss revolutionary Johann Philipp Becker (15 October 1884, MEW 36, p. 218). 'And I was happy to have so splendid a first fiddle as Marx.' But now the matter had become more difficult: now, he suddenly had to take over Marx's role, and he trembled at the thought.

3. Letter from Engels to Marx, 3 August 1859, MEGA III/9, p. 534, MEW 29, p. 468.

4. The first edition of Engels's notes was called *Natur und Dialektik*. Only later was it changed to the title we know today. Critical edition MEGA I/26, in English CW 25, pp. 313–588.

5. Letter from Marx to Engels, 31 May 1873, MEW 33, p. 82, CW 44, p. 504.

6. Marx's mathematical manuscripts, see Karl Marx, *Matematičeskie rukopisi* (Moscow: Izdatel'stwo 'Nauka', 1968). The German edition, Marx, *Mathematische Manuskripte* (Scriptor, 1974). Endemann's foreword and introduction, pp. 7–49. The polemic with Yanovskaya, p. 7; inner connections, p. 11.

7. The negation of the negation, ibid., p. 51.

8. 'only a symbolic indication', ibid., pp. 85f.

9. He devoted twenty-seven pages, ibid., pp. 102–29, to a historical review.

10. Engels's vain search for a manuscript by Marx on the dialectic, letter to p. L. Lavrov, 2 April 1883, MEW 36, p. 3, CW 47, p. 3.

11. Engels to Marx, 18 August 1881, MEW 35, pp. 23ff, CW 46, pp. 130ff. According to Engels, Marx's innovation was that dy/dy could be replaced with o/o.

12. The origins of mathematics, MEW 20, p. 35, CW 25, p. 36. Zero is not devoid of content but the centre of the number series, MEW 20, p. 524, CW 25, pp. 539f.

13. On Mao and the transformation of Beijing, Johan Lagerkvist, *Tiananmen redux: den bortglömda massakern som förändrade världen* (Stockholm: Bonniers, 2014), p. 104.

14. On Marx's early contact with the natural sciences, see John Bellamy Foster, *Marx's Ecology: Materialism and Nature* (New York: Monthly Review Books, 2000), pp. 117f.

15. MEGA I/1, p. 16, CW 1, p. 18.

16. 'liebes Männchen von der Eisenbahn', letter from Jenny von Westphalen to Karl Marx, 10 August 1841; MEGA III/1, p. 365, CW 1, p. 709.

17. William Thomson and Peter Guthrie Tait, *Treatise on Natural Philosophy*, vol. I (Oxford: Clarendon Press, 1867). Thomson later

became Lord Kelvin, the name by which he is still remembered. Gustav Wiedemann, *Die Lehre vom Galvanismus und Elektromagnetismus*, vol. I–II (Braunschweig: Vieweg, 1872). Engels's excerpts of these works are in MEGA IV/31, pp. 478–511 and 527–602 respectively.

18. On Marx and Kirchhoff, see Jacques Attali, *Karl Marx ou l'esprit du monde* (Paris: Fayard, 2005), p. 159.

19. On the 1851 London exhibition, see Jeffrey A. Auerbach, *The Great Exhibition of 1851: A Nation on Display* (New Haven: Yale University Press, 1999). The exhibition turns up in passing in Marx and Engels's correspondence; see for example the letter from Marx to Engels, 21 May 1851, and from Engels to Marx, 6 July 1851, MEGA III/4, pp. 122 and 142 respectively, MEW 17, pp. 264 and 277 respectively, CW 38, pp. 361 and 379 respectively. Marx's reactions to the London exhibition, Attali, *Karl Marx*, pp. 188f.

20. Marx, regarding the electricity exhibition in Munich in a letter to Engels, 8 November 1882, Engels's response to him, 11 November 1882, MEW 25, pp. 104 and 108 respectively, CW 46, pp. 364 and 373 respectively.

21. Hospitalier 1882. Marx's excerpts, MEGA IV/31, pp. 467–73. On the underlining, see ibid. 875f. On the copy in his library, see MEGA IV/32, p. 330.

22. Letter from Engels to Bernstein, 27 Feb–1 March 1883, MEW 35, pp. 444f, CW 46, p. 149. On the second Industrial Revolution, see above, p. 24.

23. On the significance of Liebig for Marx, see Foster, *Marx's Ecology*, pp. 20 and 147–77. On Liebig and Schönbein as more important than all political economists, Marx in letters to Engels, 13 and 20 February 1866, MEW 31, pp. 178 and 183, CW 42, pp. 227 and 232.

24. Fraas 1842. Marx in a letter to Engels, 25 March 1868, MEW 32, pp. 52f, CW 42, pp. 558f. Engels composed a few brief excerpts of Fraas's book in the early 1880s, largely drawing the same conclusions as Marx, MEGA IV/31, pp. 512–15. In *The Dialectics of Nature* he repeated the same ideas, though without mentioning Fraas's name, MEW 20, p. 453, CW 25, p. 461.

25. Justus von Liebig, *Die organische Chemie in ihrer Anwendung auf Agricultur und Physiologie* (Braunschweig: Vieweg, 1840), and many later editions and translations. The classic monograph on Liebig and his efforts is Richard Blunck, *Justus von Liebig: die Lebensgeschichte eines Chemikers* (Berlin: Hammerich und Leser, 1946). Significantly newer is William H. Brock, *Justus von Liebig: The Chemical Gatekeeper* (Cambridge: Cambridge University Press, 1997). Brock concentrates one-sidedly on Liebig's British contacts,

but objectively the account of agrarian chemistry is valuable, see pp. 145–82. In contrast to Engels, Marx, as was his custom, composed many detailed excerpts above all of von Liebig, *Die organische Chemie* (or, more correctly, of the fourth edition from 1842). The excerpts are included in what are known as the 'London Notebooks', which date from 1850 to 1853. The Liebig excerpts are printed in MEGA IV/9, pp. 172–213.

26. Marx, MEGA II/6, p. 477, CW 35, pp. 507f.

27. Marx's own manuscript from 1864, MEGA II/4.2, p. 753. Engels moves the expression *unheilbarer Riss* forward an entire chapter; see MEW 25, p. 821 and CW 37, p. 799, which most closely corresponds to MEGA II/4.2, p. 833.

28. Foster, *Marx's Ecology*, pp. 147–74 and *passim*.

29. On the history of the concept of metabolism, see Franklin C. Bing, 'The History of the Word "Metabolism"', *Journal of the History of Medicine* 26:2, pp. 158–80.

30. On Marx's use of the concept of nature, see Foster, *Marx's Ecology*, pp. 155ff.

31. Marx in a letter to Engels, 28 January 1863, MEW 30, pp. 320ff, CW 41, p. 449. Lukács wrote about Marx's notebooks in an article originally published in 1925, and printed in English in Georg Lukács, 'Technology and Human Relations', *New Left Review* 39, 1966 (1925). One monograph on the subject is Amy E. Wendling, *Karl Marx on Technology and Alienation* (Houndmills: Palgrave Macmillan, 2009). Unfortunately, it does not go into the particulars but discusses issues on a more general level.

32. Tristram Hunt at least mentions the name of Schorlemmer and indicates his significance for Engels, Hunt, *Friedrich Engels*, pp. 230 and 314.

33. Engels, 'Carl Schorlemmer', MEW 22, p. 314, CW 27, p. 305.

34. The letter from Engels to Schorlemmer is kept in Manchester University Library, Special Collections, and provides information on a few Greek words of interest to the history of chemistry. The letter, written on 27 January 1891, is reproduced in MEW 38, p. 14, CW 49, p. 111. Four letters from Schorlemmer to Engels are preserved in *IISG Marx-Engels Nachlass, IML ZPA*, 1:5, p. 2318. The letters from Schorlemmer to Marx, ibid., pp. 3986–92, 1:5, p. 3311.

35. Letter from Engels to Marx, 6 March 1865, MEW 31, p. 92, CW 42, p. 117.

36. Henry Ensfield Roscoe, '*Carl Schorlemmer*', *Proceedings of the Royal Society of London*, vol. 8, and 'Carl Schorlemmer, L.L.D., R.R.S.', *Nature*, vol. 46, p. 365.

37. The nickname Jollymayer turns up in numerous letters, for example from Marx to Engels, 24 October 1868, MEW 32, p. 191, CW 43,

p. 143; Engels to Laura Lafargue, 2 June 1883, MEW 36, p. 33, CW 37, p. 31; and Engels to Schorlemmer, 27 January 1891, MEW 38, p. 14, CW 49, p. 111. On the ill and melancholy Schorlemmer, for example, see a letter from Engels to Laura Lafargue, 20 July 1891, MEW 38, p. 138, CW 49, p. 220: 'but he is getting more and more Tristymeier, you have to work very hard to get a smile out of him now'.

38. On Schorlemmer's travelling life, see for example Engels to Pauli 25 April 1876, MEW 34, p. 181, CW 45, p. 116; Engels to Marx 7 July 1881, MEW 35, pp. 5f, CW 46, p. 104; Engels to Jenny Longuet, 7 December 1881, MEW 25, p. 240, CW 46, p. 156. On the trip to America, see Engels to Laura Lafargue, 6 August 1888, MEW 37, pp. 82f, CW 48, pp. 202ff; and Engels to F. A. Sorge, 28 August 1888, MEW 37, pp. 86f, CW 48, p. 206 and 31 August 1888, ibid., 87f and 207f respectively. On the trip, see Tsuzuki 1967, 175f and Holmes 2014, 306ff. On Schorlemmer's trip to Paris, see Engels to Laura Lafargue, 3 October 1883, MEW 36, p. 66, CW 47, pp. 60f and Schorlemmer to Laura Lafargue, *IISG Amsterdam Marx-Engels Nachlass*, p. 348.

39. Roscoe, *'Carl Schorlemmer'*, VIII, and 'Carl Schorlemmer, L.L.D., R.R.S.', *Nature*, p. 365.

40. Carl Schorlemmer, 'On the Actions of Chlorine Upon Methyl', *Proceedings of the Royal Society of London*, vol. 12, 1864.

41. The standard work on the early history of oil is R. J. Forbes, *Studies in Early Petroleum History*, vols 1–2 (Leiden: Brill, 1958–59). On the efforts of Schorlemmer, see Part II, pp. 64ff. On Schorlemmer's early analyses, see the letter from Schorlemmer to E. Erlenmeyer, 6 November 1882, *Bibliothek des deutschen Museums*. Carl Schorlemmer, 'On the Normal paraffin', *Philosophical Transactions of the Royal Society of London*, vol. 162, 1872, pp. 111ff.

42. On chemistry, see the letter from Marx to Engels, 22 June 1867 and Engels's response, 24 June 1867, MEW 31, pp. 306 and 309 respectively, CW 42, pp. 385 and 387f respectively.

43. The note is found in the first edition of *Das Kapital* in MEGA II/5, p. 246, in the second edition MEGA II/6, p. 308, and in the French translation MEGA II/7, 262. In the third German edition, Engels made in addition to Marx's brief note, although without changing the content in any way. This addition is found in the English translation, CW 35, p. 313. G. W. F. Hegel, *Wissenschaft der Logik* (Frankfurt am Main: Suhrkamp, 1969), pp. 82–115 (Qualität), 209–445 (Quantität), and 445–55 (the relationship between both); English translation G. W. F. Hegel, *Science of Logic*, transl. by A. V. Miller (London: Allen & Unwin, 1969), pp. 81–103, 185–325, and 332–347 respectively. On law, Hegel, *Wissenschaft der Logik*,

pp. 150–6.

44. William Robert Grove, *Correlation of Physical Forces* (London, Longman, 1846). Engels on the forms of movement, MEGA I/26, p. 409, CW 25, p. 370. Marx on Grove's book in a letter to Engels, 31 August 1864, and to Philips, 17 August 1864, MEW 25, pp. 424 and 670 respectively, CW 41, pp. 553 and 551 respectively.

45. Engels on 'heat death' to Marx, 21 March 1869, MEW 32, pp. 286f, CW 43, p. 246. Rudolf Clausius, *Die mechanische Wärmetheorie* (Braunschweig: F. Vieweg & Sohn, 1867).

46. The polemic in *The Dialectics of Nature*, MEGA I/26, pp. 458 and 517 respectively, MEW 20, pp. 535 and 545 respectively, and CW 25, pp. 535 and 562 respectively. The notes were authored in 1873 and 1875 respectively. Clausius, *Die mechanische Wärmetheorie*. Engels refers to Clausius's book in notes from 1880 in 1881, MEGA I/26, pp. 435, 469, and 517f, MEW 20, pp. 382, 391, and 545, CW 25, pp. 390, 398, and 563.

47. Kant deals with works of art and organisms respectively in different parts – the latter is dealt with in Immanuel Kant, *Kritik der Urteilslzraft*, XI–VI (Werkausgabe: Frankfurt am Main, 1974), pp. 334–456. The differences between both areas is dealt with in the introduction, pp. 78–109. Foster, *Marx's Ecology*, p. 232f.

48. The postscript to the second edition of *Capital*; MEGA II/6, p. 709, CW 25, p. 19. There is a large amount of literature on emergent phenomena of different types. See for example Victoria N. Alexander, *The Biologist's Mistress: Rethinking Self-Organization in Art, Literature and Nature* (Litchfield Park, AZ: Emergent Publications, 2011).

49. Letter from Engels to Marx, 30 May 1873 (with Schorlemmer's comments) and from Marx to Engels, 31 May 1873, MEW 33, pp. 80f and 82ff respectively, CW, pp. 500–4 and 504ff respectively.

50. On the appeals to Marx and his refusal, see William Liebknecht, *Briefwechsel mit Karl Marx und Friedrich Engels* (Mouton & Co., 1963), pp. 190 and 195ff.

51. Engels, 'Old Preface', MEGA I/26, p. 328, MEW 20, p. 328, CW 25, p. 336.

52. Letter from Engels to Marx, 24 May, Marx to Engels 25 May, Engels to Marx 28 May and 25 July 1876, MEW 34, pp. 12f, 14, 17ff, and 20 respectively, CW 45, pp. 117ff, 119ff, 122ff, and 130f respectively. Letter from Marx to Liebknecht, 7 October 1876, MEW 34, p. 209, CW 45, p. 154.

53. The section on Büchner is in MEW 20, pp. 472–6, CW 25, pp. 482–7.

54. 'Hard and fast lines', ibid., pp. 482 and 493 respectively.

55. On thought and reality in particular see the section titled 'Abstract Identity' (written in 1874), MEW 20, pp. 483f, CW 25, p. 495.

56. Upon publication in the 1920s, the note on the dialectics was given the title *(a) Allgemeine Fragen der Dialektik. Grundgesetze der Dialektik*, translated into English as (a) General Questions of Dialectics. The Fundamental Loss of Dialectics, MEW 20, pp. 418f, CW 25, p. 492.

57. 'Der dumme Wilhelm', Engels to Marx 24 May 1876, MEW 34, p. 13, CW 45, p. 18. '[T]he tedious Dühring', 28 May 1876, MEW 34, p. 17, CW 45, p. 122.

58. Engels thanks Marx for the text in a letter on 6 March 1877, MEW 34, p. 37, CW 45, p. 206. Marxist section is called 'From the *Critical History*' in the book version, MEGA I/27, p. 494, MEW 20, pp. 210–38, CW 25, pp. 211–43.

59. '[J]ournalistic activities', letter from Engels to Eduard Bernstein, 26 June 1879, MEW 34, p. 379, CW 45, p. 361.

60. More appreciatively, for example in a letter to the same Bernstein, 11 April 1884, MEW 36, p. 136, CW 47, p. 126; or to August Bebel, 3 December 1892, MEW 38, p. 356, CW 50, pp. 50f. Engelsism, compare with my article 'Engelsismus' in *Kritisches Wörterbuch des Marxismus*, 1997.

61. Quantity and quality, MEGA I/27, pp. 317–25, MEW 20, pp. 111–20, CW 25, pp. 110–19; negation of the negation, MEGA I/27, pp. 326–38, MEW 20, pp. 120–33, CW 25, pp. 120–32.

62. Ibid., pp. 336, 131, and 131 respectively.

63. The four different dialectical laws, MEGA I/26, p. 293, MEW 20, p. 307, CW 25, p. 313.

64. The normative presentation with three laws, ibid., I/26, pp. 307ff, 348ff, and 356ff respectively.

65. MEW 20, p. 9, CW 25, p. 9.

66. *Ludwig Feuerbach*, MEGA I/30, pp. 122–62, MEW 21, pp. 261–307, CW 25, pp. 353–98.

67. Engels to Marx, 11 or 12 December 1859, MEGA III/10, p. 127, MEW 29, p. 524, CW 40, p. 551.

68. MEW 13, p. 470, CW 16, p. 469.

69. Marx on *The Origin of Species* to Engels, 19 December 1860, MEGA III/11, p. 271, MEW 30, p. 131, CW 41, p. 232.

70. Marx's letter to Lassalle 16 January 1861, MEW 30, p. 578, CW 41, pp. 246f.

71. A lively description of how Darwin absorbed Malthus's ideas on overpopulation and then applied them to the principles of natural selection is given in Adrian Desmond and James Moore, *Darwin* (London: Penguin Books, 1991), pp. 264ff and *passim*. It is in the third chapter of *The Origin of Species*, 'Struggle for Existence', that the influences from Malthus appear most clearly.

72. On Darwin and Malthus, see the letter from Marx to Engels, 18

June 1862, MEW 30, p. 249, CW 41, p. 381.

73. Friedrich Albert Lange, *Die Arbeiterfrage in ihrer Bedeutung für Gegenwart und Zukunft* (Duisburg: Bleuler-Hausheer, 1875), pp. 75, 29ff. On the struggle for the best conditions of life, ibid., pp. 5f. On the struggle for wages, p. 13. On the dissemination of talents, pp. 46ff. Moral advances, p. 15.

74. Marx on Lange in a letter to Kugelmann, 27 June 1870, MEW 32, pp. 658f, CW 42, pp. 527f.

75. MEW 3, p. 31, CW 5, p. 31.

76. Pierre Trémaux, *Origine et transformations de l'homme et des autres êtres* (Paris: Librairie de L. Hachette, 1865), pp. 13, 129, 160ff. Trémaux was said to have put forward a great law of nature: *la loi de coïncidence du sol et des types*, a law on the concordance between the soil and the races/species. The law was formulated as follows: 'La perfection des êtres est ou devient proportionnelle au degré d'élaboration du sol sur lequel ils vivent' – the perfection of beings is or becomes proportional to the extent that the soil on which they live has been worked. Trémaux, Origine, pp. 11 and 17. Pierre Trémaux had arrived at his results during various anthropological field studies in locations such as Sudan. His book is based on limited biological material. The discussion about Darwin and other early evolutionary biologists is meagre.

77. Marx on Trémaux to Engels, 7 August 1866, MEW 31, pp. 248f, CW 42, pp. 304f. Engels's response, 2 October 1866, ibid., 256 and 320 respectively; Marx's reply, 3 October, and Engels's final judgment, 5 October 1866, ibid., 257ff and 322ff respectively.

78. *Das Kapital*, MEGA II/6, pp. 337 and 364, CW 35, pp. 346 and 375.

79. Desmond and Moore, *Darwin*, pp. 601f.

80. On the friendship between Marx and Lankester, see Lewis S. Feuer, 'The Friendship of Edwin Ray Lankester and Karl Marx: The Last Episode in Marx's Intellectual Evolution', *Journal of the History of Ideas*, vol. 40, no. 4, 1979, pp. 633–48. Lankester's fight against fraudulent media, see ibid., pp. 624f. On Lankester and Marx, see Foster, *Marx's Ecology*, pp. 221–4. On Darwin and Marx as the great materialists of the nineteenth century, ibid., pp. 1 and *passim*. In his great Marx biography, Gareth Stedman Jones misunderstands the basis for Marx's initial hesitancy towards Darwin. He does not see that the reason is the influences of Malthus, but believes that it concerns the thesis that biological development is random. To this, it can be said that this consequence of Darwin's theory did not represent the time in which he lived, and probably not even for Darwin himself; in *The Origin of Species*, he could talk about the development of species as development towards greater physiological

differentiation. What was clear to Darwin, and what Marx immediately emphasized, was that all teleological argumentation could
be dismissed from the field of the development of species. Stedman
Jones, *Karl Marx,* pp. 567f.

81. On the significance of the discovery of Neanderthals for their views on
the earliest history of humanity, see Foster, *Marx's Ecology,* pp. 212f.

82. Herbert Spencer, *Utvecklingsläran* (Uppsala: U. Almqvist & J.
Wiksell, 1883), § 121, 307.

83. Lewis H. Morgan, *Ancient Society or Researches in the Lines of
Human Progress from Savagery through Barbarism to Civilization*
(London: MacMillan and Company, 1877). On the Scottish Enlight-
enment thinkers' ideas about progress, see David Spadafora, *The
Idea of Progress in Eighteenth Century Britain* (New Haven: Yale
University Press, 1990).

84. James George Frazer, *The Golden Bough: Studies in Magic and Religion* (Stockholm: Natur & Kultur, 1992). Frazer gradually expanded
his work so that it ultimately extended over twelve volumes.

85. Marx called Kovalevsky 'the fat boy' in documents such as a letter
to Engels on 17 September 1878, MEW 34, p. 78, CW 53, p. 22.

86. Engels in MEGA I/29, pp. 7–271, MEW 21, pp. 25–173, CW 26,
pp. 129–276.

87. Lewis H. Morgan, *Ancient Society or Researches in the Lines of
Human Progress from Savagery Through Barbarism to Civilization*
(London: MacMillan and Company, 1877), p. 34.

88. Foster, *Marx's Ecology,* p. 220.

89. Karl Marx, *The Ethnological Notebooks of Karl Marx: Studies of
Morgan, Phear, Maine, Lubbock* (Assen: Van Gorcum, 1972). Lawrence Krader reproduces all of Marx's commentary in the excerpts
of Morgan in *Ethonologie und Anthropologie bei Marx* (Frankfurt
am Main: Ullstein, 1976), pp. 26–9. On societal conditions, Morgan,
Ancient Society, p. 18. The exclamation point, Marx, *The Ethnological Notebooks,* p. 127. Engels, see MEGA I/29, p. 13, MEW
21, p. 30. The perception that Engels uses the expression 'materialist conception of history' here for the first time is corroborated in
many quarters, including Krader, *Ethonologie und Anthropologie,*
pp. 124ff. Timo Freudenberger, *Die Anthropologie in der politischen
Theorie von Karl Marx und Friedrich Engels* (München: GRIN
Verlag, 2007) also deals with Marx, Engels, and anthropology, but
adds nothing substantially new, however.

90. Production of new people, MEGA I/29, pp. 11f. MEW 21, pp. 27f.

91. Marx, *The Ethnological Notebooks,* p. 112; cited by Engels in
MEGA I/29, pp. 21f, MEW 21, p. 38, CW 26, p. 141.

92. Edward Aveling, *The Darwinian Theory: Its Meaning, Difficulties,
Evidence, History* (London: Progressiv Pub., 1884). Karl Kautsky,

Erinnerungen und Erörterungen (Haag: Mouton, 1960), pp. 214ff.

93. On Engels's *Habgier* ('greed'), see Lawrence Krader, *Ethonologie und Anthropologie bei Marx* (Frankfurt am Main: Ullstein, 1976), p. 147. Engels, see MEGA I/29, p. 269, MEW 21, p. 171, CW 26, p. 275.

94. Marx, *The Ethnological Notebooks*, p. 27. Compare Krader, *Ethonologie*, p. 31.

95. Johann Jakob Bachofen, *Das Mutterrecht: eine Untersuchung über die Gynaikratie der alten Welt nach ihrer religiösen und rechtlichen Natur* (Basel: Schwabe, 1948). Engels on Bachofen, see MEGA I/29, pp. 33ff, MEW 21, pp. 53ff, CW 26, pp. 158–61.

96. Simone de Beauvoir, *Det andra könet* (Stockholm: Norstedts, 2002); Eva Lundgren-Gothlin, kön och existens: studier i Simone de Beauvoir Le deuxième sexe (Göteburg: Daidolos, 1991).

97. Engels's note to the *Manifesto*, see MEW 4, p. 62, CW 6, p. 483. Krader, *Ethonologie*, on learned debate, p. 120.

98. Stalin's understanding is indicated, for example, by Stalin, *Problems of Leninism: Lectures Delivered at Sverdlov University* (Peking: Foreign University Press, 1976). There is a great deal of literature on Lysenko. For somewhat different critical perspectives, see David Joravski, *The Lysenko Affair* (Cambridge, Mass.: Harvard University Press, 2010). On the branding of Einstein's theory of relativity, which lasted from 1951 to 1955, see Siegried Müller-Markus, *Einstein und die Sowjet Philosophie: Krisis einer Lehre*, vols 1–2 (Alphen an den Rijn: Kluwer, 1966).

99. Andrew Delano Abbott, *The System of Professions: An Essay on the Division of Expert Labor* (Chicago: University of Chicago Press, 1988), provides a splendid modern outline of professionalization.

100. Charles Darwin, *The Descent of Man, and Selection in Relation to Sex* (London: John Murray, 1871), p. 67. Spencer, *Utvecklingsläran*, pp. 140f. Haeckel's ambitions culminated in his book *Die Welträtsel* (The Riddles of the Universe), published in 1899.

101. For a more careful investigation of the specialization of science and its effects on Marx's position, see Sven-Eric Liedman, *Motsatsernas spel: Friedrich Engels' filosofie och 1800–talets vetenskaper* (Lund: Cavefors, 1977), vol. 1, pp. 129ff, 155ff, and *passim*.

102. MEGA 20, p. 6, CW 25, p. 6.

103. MEGA II/6, p. 68, CW 35, p. 11. Dante in fact wrote *Vien dietro a me, e lascia dir le genti*, which literally translated is, 'Follow me and just let people talk.'

104. Wilhelm Roscher, *Die Grundlagen der National Ökonomie: ein Hand- und Lesebuch für Geschäftsmänner und Studierende* (Stuttgart: Cotta'sche Buchhandlung, 1854).

105. Alfred Marshall, *Principles of Economics* (London: Macmillan,

1890). On the development of the subject of economics, see the standard work, Joseph Schumpeter, *History of Economic Analysis* (New York: Oxford University Press, 1954).

106. Henry Hyndman, *England for All* (London: Gilbert & Rivington, 1881). On Hyndman and Eleanor Marx, see Rachel Holmes, *Eleanor Marx: A Life* (London: Bloomsbury, 2014), pp. 141f, 200f and 297f.

107. The literature on William Morris is abundantly rich. One good biography is Fiona MacCarthy, *William Morris: A Life for Our Time* (London: Faber & Faber, 1994). See also E. P. Thompson, *William Morris: Romantic and Revolutionary* (London: Pantheon, 1976). Marx's influence on Morris is emphasized especially strongly – possibly too strongly – by Paul Meier in his extremely comprehensive dissertation, Paul Meier, *William Morris: The Marxist Dreamer* (London: Humanities Press, 1971).

108. It was Engels who reported the utterance that Marx made to Lafargue regarding Marxism, letter from Engels to Eduard Bernstein, 2/3 November 1882, MEW 35, p. 388, CW 46, p. 356.

109. Paul Lafargue is the subject of a large and growing amount of literature. In English, there is the large two-volume monograph by Leslie Derfler, in which the origins of French Marxism are important; see Leslie Derfler, *Paul Lafargue and the Founding of French Socialism, 1842–1882* (Cambridge, Mass.: Harvard University Press, 1991) and *Paul Lafargue and the Flowering of French Socialism, 1842–1882* (Cambridge, Mass.: Harvard University Press, 1998). Françoys Larue-Langlois, *Paul Lafargue* (Paris: Punctum, 2007) is a newer, more concentrated biography. There is a monograph by Andrée Collot on Jules Guesde and his role in *Parti Ouvrier*: see André Collot, *Jules Guesde: Éducateur et organisateur du proletariat* (Paris: éd. inclinaisons, 2010).

110. On Walras as the greatest of economists, see Schumpeter, *History of Economic Analysis*, p. 827.

111. Allen W. Wood, *Karl Marx* (London: Routledge, 2004), pp. 127–32.

13 Marx the Politician

1. Letter from Marx to Edward Spencer Beesly, 12 June 1871, MEW 33, p. 228, CW 44, p. 150.

2. Teodor Shanin, *Late Marx and the Russian Road: Marx and 'The Peripheries of Capitalism'* (London: Routledge & Kegan Paul, 1983).

3. Marx to Engels, 3 February 1860, MEW 30, pp. 22f, CW 41, pp. 21f.

4. Marx reproduces the suggestion from Sasonov in *Herr Vogt*, MEGA

I/18, pp. 71f, MEW 14, pp. 401f, CW 17, pp. 41f.

5. Letter from Becker, MEGA I/18, pp. 88–93, MEW 14, pp. 420–4, CW 17, pp. 60–4. A large – predominant, in fact – part of *Herr Vogt* consists of reproduced letters, which overshadows the history of the *Bund der Kommunisten*.

6. On the German Workers' Association and the unanimous condemnation of Vogt, MEGA I/18, pp. 325f, MEW 14, p. 619, CW 17, pp. 264f. On the condemnation, also in a letter to Engels, 9 February 1860, MEGA III/10, pp. 231ff, MEW 30, p. 31, CW 41, p. 34.

7. Engels against hiring an exile publisher in a letter of 15 September 1860, MEW 30, p. 92, CW 41, p. 191. Marx holds his ground in his response on 25 September 1860, ibid., 95ff and 197 respectively. The letter indicates that he had to pay for the costs himself, 25 pounds. Others, including Ferdinand Lassalle, promised to contribute 20, but he requested the remaining five from Engels.

8. On Vogt and Napoleon III, see for example the letter from Marx to Ludwig Kugelmann, 12 April 1871, MEW 33, p. 206, CW 44, p. 132. The information dates back to *Papiers et correspondance 1870–71*.

9. Shlomo Avineri, The Social and Political Thought of Karl Marx (Cambridge: Cambridge University Press, 1968). See in particular 'Epilogue', pp. 250–8.

10. Wolfgang Schieder, *Karl Marx als Politiker* (München & Zürich: Piper, 1991), p. 10f.

11. Marx to Engels, 4 November 1864, MEGA III/13, pp. 37–44, MEW 31, pp. 10–16, CW 42, pp. 15–18.

12. Marx to Ferdinand Freiligrath, 29 February 1860, MEW 38, pp. 488–95, CW 41, pp. 80–7.

13. On Marx, the parties, and 'the Marx party', see Schieder, *Karl Marx als Politiker*, pp. 130–50.

14. Documentation of the International, like the literature concerning it, is plentiful. The first major history is David Riazanov 'Zur Geschichte der Internationale: Die Enstehung der Internationalen Arbeit er assoziation', *Marx-Engels-Archiv I*. Another is Henry Collins, 'The International and the British Labour Movement: Origins of the International in England', *La première Internationale: l'institution, l'implantation, le rayonnement* (Paris: Editions du Centre Nationale de la Recherche Scientifique, 1968). The material can be found in MEGA I/20, pp. 253–591, as well as all of MEGA I/21. The minutes are easily available online, as is all of Marx and Engels's contributions during the meetings; see International Workingmen's Association at Marxists.org. On the exact number of members in the original Central Committee, see Holmes, *Eleanor Marx*, p. 70.

15. Marx on Tolain in a letter to Engels already mentioned, 4 November

1864, MEGA III/13, p. 38, MEW 31, p. 10, CW 42, p. 17.

16. 'Address of the International Working Men's Association' is reproduced in MEGA I/20, pp. 3–12. After that comes the German version, which was given the more urgent title 'Manifest an die arbeitende Klasse Europas' and was printed in the then-new German newspaper *Der Sozial-Demokrat*, 21 December 1864, ibid. 16–25. The original English text in CW 20, pp. 5–14.

17. On the cooperative movements at that time in Marx's thinking, see Ingolf Neunübel, 'Zur Bedeutung von Marx' Studien über die Kooperativbewegung Anfang der fünfziger Jahre für die Ausarbeitung der marxistischen Genossenschaftskonzeption', *Marx-Engels Jahrbuch* (Berlin: Dietz, 1991). Neunübel's article is also historically interesting in itself: it was written when perestroika – that is, the (entirely planned) transformation of the Soviet economy advocated by Mikhail Gorbachev – was up for discussion and workers' cooperatives were seen as one of the paths to the future.

18. Oddly enough, there is no article on the concept of association in the *Historische Grundbegriffe*.

19. On the concept of brotherhood, which Marx previously criticized (see p. 297), and its long meandering history, see Wolfgang Schieder, 'Brüderlichkeit, Bruderschaft, Brüderschaft, Verbrüderung, Bruderliebe, Bruderschaft', in *Geschichtliche Grundbegriffe* (Stuttgart: Klell-Cotta, 1972) pp. 552–81. Schieder takes up Marx's and Engels's early doubts (pp. 577ff), but on the other hand he does not take up his use of the word in his address to the International. Johann Philipp Becker develops his view of brotherhood and solidarity in his own periodical *Vorbote*, no. 8, 1866. On Marx and the concept of solidarity, see Rainer Zoll, *Was ist Solidarität heute?* (Frankfurt am Main: Suhrkamp, 2000).

20. 'Provisional Rules of the Association', MEGA I/20, pp. 13ff, CW 20, pp. 14ff.

21. Marx to Engels, 4 November 1864, MEGA III/13, pp. 38–43, MEW 31, pp. 9–16, CW 42 11–19.

22. Engels's letter to Marx, 7 November 1864, MEGA III/13, pp. 38–43, 45, MEW 31, p. 17, CW 42, pp. 19f.

23. Marx to Engels, 14 November 1864, MEGA III/13, p. 54, MEW 31, p. 21, CW 42, pp. 22f. The note from Peter Fox that Marx talked about has not been preserved.

24. Marx's letters to Lincoln, reproduced in MEGA I/10, pp. 26–30 and CW 20, p. 21. The letter was also published in German in *Der Sozialdemokrat*, 30 December 1864, ibid., pp. 36f and is reproduced in MEW 16, pp. 18ff. The letter to Johnson was published in English in the *Bee-Hive Newspaper*, 20 May 1865 and is reproduced in MEGA I/20, pp. 134–7 and CW 20, p. 994, and in German in MEW

16, pp. 98f.

25. The lecture was held at the meetings of the Central Committee on 20 and 27 June 1865. The critical edition of the English original of *Value, Price and Profit* is found in MEGA I/20, pp. 141–86 as well as CW 20, pp. 101–49. There is a German translation in MEW 16, pp. 103–52. The citation from Hobbes is reproduced in MEGA I/20, pp. 167f and in CW 20, p. 128. The same citation is found in *Capital*, MEGA II/6, p. 186, CW 35, p. 180.

26. Marx in letters to Engels, 20 May and 24 June 1865, MEGA II/13, pp. 466f and 481f respectively, MEW 31, pp. 122f and 124f, CW 42, pp. 159f and 162f.

27. Engels's response, 15 July 1865, MEGA III/13, pp. 497f, MEW 31, pp. 128f, CW 42, p. 168.

28. The most comprehensive study of the relationship between Mill and Marx is Graeme Duncan, *Marx and Mill: Two Views of Social Conflict and Social Harmony* (Cambridge: Cambridge University Press, 1973). Duncan, however, does not go into any questions on Marx's and Mill's (nonexistent) personal relations. He makes a sweeping comparison between both men's theories, coming to the peculiar conclusion that the capitalist society he himself lives in has the homogeneity that both Marx and Mill saw as an ideal, p. 315.

29. Marx on Bakunin to Engels, 4 November 1864, MEGA III/13, p. 43, MEW 31, p. 16, CW 42, p. 18. Schieder *Karl Marx*, p. 77.

30. There are a number of Bakunin biographies, among which Anthony Masters, *Bakunin: The Father of Anarchism* (London: Sidgwick & Jackson, 1974), Paul McLaughlin, *Mikhail Bakunin: The Philosophical Basis of His Anarchism* (New York: Algora, 2002), and Mark Leier, *Bakunin: The Creative Passion* (London: St Martin's Press, 2006) deserve mention.

31. Marx to Engels on Bakunin's claim to power, 15 December 1868, MEW 32, p. 234, CW 43, p. 190. Letter from Bakunin to Marx, 22 December 1868, MEW 32, p. 757.

32. On Becker and Bakunin, see for example Marx's letter to Engels, 28 January 1869, MEW 32, p. 250, CW 43, p. 208; and to Paul and Laura Lafargue, 15 February 1869, MEW 32, p. 593, CW 43, p. 218. Schieder, *Karl Marx als Politiker*, p. 77.

33. The decision on Bakunin's Alliance of 22 December 1868, authored by Marx, has the title 'Association Internationale des Travailleurs', 'L'Alliance Internationale de la Démocratie Socialiste'. Circulation du Conseil Générale, 22 décembre 1868', MEGA I/21, pp. 105–9, and is reproduced in English translation in CW 21, pp. 34ff.

34. On the *Manifesto*, Marx, Engels, and the right of inheritance, see above, p. 243. 'Bericht des Generalrats über das Erbrecht', *Der*

Vorbote, October 1869, MEW 16, pp. 367ff.

35. Bakunin published a series of articles in the newspaper *L'Égalité* in 1869, including a series dealing precisely with the International and its politics: Mikhail Bakunin, 'Politique de l'Internationale', *L'Égalité*, nos 39–42, av Michel Bakounine, 1869). Marx's letter regarding Bakunin's criticism is titled 'Le Conseil général au conseil fédéral de la Suisse romande', and is reproduced in MEGA I/21, pp. 159–65; it can be found in English in CW 21, pp. 84–91. Marx also lay behind a 'Confidentielle Mitteilung' to the German Social Democrats, MEGA I/21, pp. 220–7, CW 21, pp. 112–24; the content is much the same, the tone sharper (he did not need to fear that the text would come to Bakunin's attention).

36. On the referendum of 8 May 1870, see for example André Zeller, *Les homes de la Commune* (Paris: Librairie Académique Perrin, 1969), p. 73.

37. 'The General Council of the International Workingmen's Association on the Franco-Prussian War', MEGA I/21, pp. 245–9, CW 22, pp. 3–8; the text was also published in German in Becker's newspaper *Die Vorbote*. The German version is found in both MEGA I/21 and MEW 17, pp. 3–8.

38. Marx in a letter to Engels, 20 July 1870, MEW 33, p. 5, CW 44, pp. 3f.

39. Engels wrote an impressive series of articles in the *Pall Mall Gazette* on the Franco-Prussian War, MEGA I/21, pp. 253–496, CW 22, pp. 9–258, and in German translation in MEW 17, pp. 11–264. There were a total of forty-two articles between 29 July 1870 and 18 February 1871.

40. Marx on Serraillier's journey and the risk for a new Paris Commune in a letter to Engels, 6 September 1870, MEW 33, p. 54 and CW 44, pp. 64f.

41. Marx, 'Second Address on the Franco-Prussian War', MEGA I/21, pp. 485–91, CW 22, pp. 263–70, in German translation in MEW, pp. 271–9, 490, 269, and 277.

42. Marx in a letter to Beesly 19 October 1870, MEW 33, p. 158, CW 44, pp. 88f. On the Lyon Commune, there is a thorough examination by Maurice Moissonnier, *La Première Internationale et la Commune à Lyon : 1865–1871, spontanéisme, complots et luttes réelles* (Paris: Editions sociales, 1972).

43. The text had been written back in 1866 by Jean-Baptiste Clément, who himself became an active Communard. The music was written by Antoine Renard, an ironworker who also performed as an opera tenor but did not otherwise make a name for himself as a composer. Even *La semaine sanglante* got its own song. Clément also wrote the words to that, while the music was taken from an older

song.

44. Prosper Olivier Lissagaray, *Histoire de la Commune de 1871* (Paris: M. Rivière, 1947). On the love story between Eleanor Marx and Lissagaray, see Holmes, *Eleanor Marx*, pp. 110–50.

45. Jean Bruhat, Jean Dautry, and Emile Tersen, *La Commune de 1871* (Paris: Editions sociales, 1970). The quote from Lenin, p. 380.

46. Zeller, *Les homes de la Commune*. On Elisabeth Dmitrieff, p. 299. Neither Lenin nor Trotsky, p. 251. On women in the Commune, see Holmes, *Eleanor Marx*, p. 102. The quote from *The Times*, ibid., p. 106. On her relationship with Karl Marx and her friendship with Eleanor Marx, see Bruhat et al., *La Commune de 1871*, pp. 184–7, 190f, and 372, and Holmes, *Eleanor Marx*, p. 105. On Rossel in Zeller, *Les homes de la Commune*, pp. 521–9; in Bruhat et al., *La Commune de Paris*, pp. 248–52. Bruhat et al., *La Commune de 1871*, sums up the Commune, pp. 373ff. Enumerating the Communards who were a part of the International, p. 155.

47. Zeller, *Les Hommes de la Commune*, pp. 193f on the propensity of Thiers to flee.

48. The quote from the first proclamation according to Bruhat et al., *La Commune de 1871*, p. 117.

49. On the forged letter, see the letter from Marx to Paul Lafargue, 23 March 1871, MEW 3, pp. 193f, CW 44, pp. 121ff. Marx's and Engels's clarification for *The Times* is reproduced in MEGA I/22, p. 3, CW 22, p. 285. Marx at that time was generally fully occupied with denying certain more or less malicious rumours circulating in the press. See MEGA I/22, pp. 4–10. CW 22, pp. 286–93.

50. On the entirely excessive civility of the Commune, Marx to Wilhelm Liebknecht, 6 April 1871, MEW 33, pp. 200ff, CW 22, pp. 127ff.

51. On the significance of the Commune, in a letter to Kugelmann, 12 April 1871, MEW 33, pp. 205f.

52. On chance to Kugelmann, 17 April 1871, MEW 33, p. 209, CW 44, pp. 136f.

53. On Fränkel, see Zeller, *Les hommes de la Commune*; on Varlin, Bruhat et al., *La Commune de 1871*, pp. 44 and *passim*. The draft of a letter to Fränkel alone is dated 26 April 1871, MEW 33, pp. 261f, CW 44, pp. 141f; to both Fränkel and Varlin 13 May 1871, MEW 33, pp. 226f, CW 44, pp. 148f. The second letter is the one being referred to here.

54. The letter to Beesly, 12 December 1871, MEW 33, pp. 228ff, CW 44, pp. 150ff.

55. 'le grand chef', Marx in a letter to Kugelmann, 18 June 1871, MEW 33, p. 238.

56. Marx, 'The Civil War in France: Address of the General Council of the International Working Men's Association', MEGA I/22,

pp. 123–62, CW 22, pp. 307–59. The quotes, pp. 138f and 329f respectively and (on women) pp. 148 and 341 respectively. On Blanqui, pp. 156 and 352 respectively.

57. Schieder, *Karl Marx als Politiker*, p. 88.

58. Marx's 100 contributions in Miklos Molnár, 'Die Londoner Konferenz der Internationale', *Archiv für Sozialgeschichte* 4 (1964).

59. On the London conference, see Hans-Dieter Krause, 'Der Londoner Delegiertenkonferenz von 1871', *Marx-Engels Jahrbuch* 3 (1980), pp. 196–220. Marx and Engels's contributions to the conference can be found in MEGA I/22, pp. 285–358.

60. Marx to Danielson 28 May 1872, MEW 33, p. 477, CW 44, pp. 385f. Jenny Marx's letter to Wilhelm Liebknecht, 26 May 1872, MEW 33, pp. 702f, CW 44, pp. 579ff; the quote, pp. 702 and 580 respectively.

61. The conference in The Hague, 2–7 September 1872, will be covered by MEGA I/23, which has not yet been published. On the conference in The Hague, see Schieder, *Karl Marx als Politiker*, pp. 108–14. Bakunin's various articles, letters, and incomplete manuscripts are collected in Mikhail Bakunin, *Michel Bakounine et les conflits dans l'Internationale 1872* (Leiden: Brill, 1965), including the interesting unfinished text 'Écrits contre Marx', pp. 169–219.

62. Ferdinand Lassalle, *Die Philosophie Herakleitos den Dunklen von Ephesos* (Berlin: Franz Duncker, 1857). Letter, Marx to Lassalle, 19 April 1859, MEGA III/9, pp. 389–92, MEW 29, pp. 590–3, CW 40, pp. 418–21.

63. The 'Sickingen debate' was the subject of an entire book, published by Walter Hinderer; see Walter Hinderer, *Sickingen-Debatte: ein Beitrag zur materialistischen Literaturtheorie* (Darmstadt: Sammlung Luchterhand, 1974).

64. Shlomo Na'aman, *Ferdinand Lassalle: Deutscher und Jude: Eine sozialgeschichtliche Studie* (Hannover: Schriftenreihe der Niedersächsischen Landeszentrale für politischen Bildung, 1968), takes up Lassalle's fate as a Jew and a socialist agitator in nineteenth-century Germany. The latest major work on Lassalle is Thilo Ramm, *Ferdinand Lassalle: der Revolutionär und das Recht* (Berlin: Berliner Wissenschaftsverlag, 2004). On Lassalle's death, see the letter from Engels to Marx, 4 September 1864, MEGA III/12, p. 634f, MEW 30, p. 429, CW 41, pp. 55ff; and Marx's response, 7 September 1864, MEGA III/12, p. 637, MEW 30, p. 432, CW 41, pp. 560ff. A good overview of Marx's and Lassalle's different views on working-class strategy is Roger Morgan, *The German Social Democrats and the First International, 1864–1872* (Cambridge: Cambridge University Press, 1965), pp. 2f, 20ff. The correspondence between Bismarck and Lassalle, which became known and published only in 1928, is

easily accessible on Marxists.org.

65. The latest biography of Wilhelm Liebknecht is Wolfgang Schröder, *Wilhelm Liebknecht: Soldat der Revolution, Parteiführer, Parlamentarier* (Berlin: Karl Dietz Verlag, 2013); the latest on Bebel is Jürgen Schmidt, *August Bebel: Kaiser der Arbeiter* (Zürich: Rotpunktverlag, 2013).

66. On the Marx clique, see Roger Morgan, *The German Social Democrats and the First International, 1864–1872* (Cambridge: Cambridge University Press, 1965), pp. 59; on Marx, the International and the social democratic parties in Germany, ibid., pp. 168ff and *passim*.

67. Cover letter to Wilhelm Bracke, 5 May 1875, MEW 19, pp. 13f, CW 45, pp. 69–73. Engels to Bebel 18/28 March 1875, ibid., pp. 3–9 and 60–6 respectively. Engels's letter to Bracke, 11 October 1875, MEW 34, pp. 155–63 and CW 94–103. Engels's criticism, however, lacks the sharpness of Marx's more heavy-handed reckoning.

68. Engels's foreword to Marx's criticism, ibid., pp. 521f and CW 27, pp. 92f.

69. Marx, 'Kritik der Gothaer Programms', MEGA I/25, pp. 9–25, MEW 19, pp. 15–32, CW 75–99. The quotes, ibid., MEGA I/15, pp. 10, 11f, and 15, MEW 19, pp. 16, 17f, and 21; CW 24, pp. 81, 83, 87. On the 'revolutionary dictatorship of the proletariat', MEGA I/25, p. 22, MEW 19, p. 28, CW 24, p. 95. On the dictatorship of the proletariat, Schieder, *Karl Marx*, 1991, 34.

70. Liebknecht's statement according to Schieder, *Karl Marx als Politiker*, p. 117.

71. Heidi Beutin, Wolfgang Beutin, and Holger Malterer, *125 Jahre Sozialistengesetz: Beiträge der öffentlichen Konferenz von 18.–30. November 2003* (Frankfurt am Main: Peter Lang, 2003) provides a splendid picture of the Anti-Socialist Laws and their consequences.

72. Engels, 'Sulle attuali condizioni della Germania e della Russia', MEGA I/25, pp. 169f, German translation MEW 19, pp. 148f, English translation, CW 24, pp. 251f.

73. Marx's reckoning with George Howell, once a member of the International, was published in *The Secular Chronicle*, 4 August 1878, MEGA I/25, pp. 151–7, MEW 19, pp. 142–7, CW 24, pp. 234–9; his foreword to the 1880 edition of *The Poverty of Philosophy* in MEGA I/25, p. 198, MEW 19, p. 229, CW 24, pp. 236f; his 'Questionnaire for Workers' with numerous questions about labour, health, and so on, ibid., pp. 199–207, 230–7, and 328–34 respectively.

74. Franz Mehring, *Karl Marx: hans livs historia* (Stockholm: Gidlunds, 1983), pp. 710ff. David Riazanov, *Karl Marx and Friedrich Engels: An Introduction to Their Lives and Their Work*, trans. by Joshua Kunitz (New York: Monthly Review Press, 1973), 205ff. David McLellan, *Karl Marx: His Life and Thought* (St Albans: Paladin,

1973), pp. 425–30. Tristram Hunt, *Friedrich Engels: Kommunist i frack* (Stockholm: Leopard förlag, 2009), pp. 305f. Stedman Jones, *Karl Marx*, pp. 535ff.

75. Haruki Wada, 'Marx and Revolutionary Russia', in Teodor Shanin, *Late Marx and the Russian Road: Marx and 'The Peripheries of Capitalism'* (London: Routledge & Kegan Paul, 1983), pp. 40–75, and Derek Sayer and Philip Corrigan, 'Late Marx: Continuity, Contradiction and Learning', in ibid.

76. N. Flerovsky was a pseudonym for Vasilii Bervi. His book dealt with the condition of the Russian working class and was thus a parallel investigation to Engels's writings about English conditions from 1845. Marx wrote to Engels that this was the most important book about the condition of the workers since Engels's own. Letter of 10 February 1870, MEW 32, p. 437, CW 43, pp. 423f. Marx read Bervi's work carefully, as indicated by his own copy with many margin notes, see MEGA IV/32, p. 147.

77. Shanin, *Late Marx and the Russian Road*, p. 8.

78. Chernyshevsky's *What Is to Be Done?* is available in English translations, the earliest from 1886. Excerpts from the texts by Chernyshevsky that influenced Marx can be found in a new English translation, Nikolai Chernyshevsky, 'Selected Writings', in Shanin, *Late Marx and the Russian Road*, pp. 181–203.

79. Marx's draft of a reply to *Otechestvennye zapiski*, 'L'article 'Karl Marx devant le tribunal de M. Joukowski', MEGA I/25, pp. 112–17.

80. Letter from Zasulich to Marx, 16 February 1881, is reproduced in works such as Shanin, *Late Marx and the Russian Road*, pp. 98f.

81. Marx's drafts to Zasulich in the original French, MEGA I/25, pp. 219–40, in German in MEW 19, pp. 384–406, and in English in Shanin, *Late Marx and the Russian Road*, pp. 99–123 as well as in CW 24, pp. 346–69. The second draft first, Wada, 'Marx and Revolutionary Russia', pp. 64f.

82. Letter from Marx to Vera Zasulich, 8 March 1881, MEGA I/25, pp. 241f, MEW 35, pp. 166f, CW 46, pp. 71f and Shanin, *Late Marx and the Russian Road*, pp. 123f.

83. Wada, 'Marx and Revolutionary Russia', pp. 41f.

84. Letter from Marx to Friedrich Adolph Sorge, 27 September 1877, MEW 34, p. 296, CW 45, p. 278.

85. Letter from Marx to Laura Lafargue, 14 December 1882, MEW 35, pp. 407f, CW 46, pp. 398f. On Marx's disappointment over England, see also Schieder, *Karl Marx als Politiker*, p. 98.

86. On the priority of the relations of production, see Etienne Balibar, *Cinq etudes du matérialisme historique* (Paris: Maspero, 1974), p. 119.

87. In contrast to Engels, Marx never used the metaphor of the state

withering away (*Anti-Dühring*), while it was carried further with emphasis by Lenin in *State and Revolution*. Marx only said that the state would lose its compulsory character (*Zwangscharakter*) and assume the form of an association. Many of his interpreters have observed this. See for example Schieder, *Karl Marx als Politiker*, p. 19.

88. Stein, *Der Sozialismus und Kommunismus des heutigen Frankreichs.* Schieder, *Karl Marx als Politiker*, pp. 20ff. *Socialism: Utopian and Scientific* is reproduced in Aveling's translation in CW 24, pp. 281–325. Marx's foreword, MEW 19, pp. 181–5, CW 24, pp. 335–9.

89. Schieder, *Karl Marx als Politiker*, p. 22.

90. Both Marx and Engels used the term 'our party' many times – Marx did so, for example, in the very central document *Critique of the Gotha Programme*; see MEGA I/25, p. 15, MEW 19, p. 22, CW 24, p. 87, and Schieder, *Karl Marx als Politiker*, p. 139.

14 Statues, Malicious Portraits, and the Work

1. Jean-Paul Sartre, *Orden* (Stockholm: Bonniers, 1964), pp. 200f.

2. Leszek Kołakowski, *Main Currents of Marxism: Its Rise, Growth, and Dissolution* (Oxford: Clarendon, 1976).

3. Predrag Vranicki, *Geschichte des Marxismus* (Frankfurt am Main: Suhrkamp, 1972–74).

4. Perry Anderson, *Considerations on Western Marxism* (London: Verso, 1976).

5. A draft of the speech at Marx's grave is reproduced in MEW 19, pp. 333f, CW 24, pp. 463f; the article in *Der Sozialdemokrat*, 22 March 1883, ibid., pp. 335–9 and 467–71 respectively. Liebknecht's brief speech is also reproduced in this text. Engels published an additional article in the same newspaper on 3 May 1883 in which he reproduced a long series of other honours from various corners of the world, ibid., pp. 340–7 and 473–81 respectively.

6. Engels's speech in Zürich, MEGA I/32, p. 375, CW 27, pp. 404f; on the painting that depicted Marx, in the corresponding Apparatband, 1289, as far as is known, the painting has not been preserved. Margarete Greulich was the daughter of Hermann Greulich, the vice-chair of the organizational committee of the congress. On Eleanor Marx's reluctance, see Rachel Holmes, *Eleanor Marx: A Life* (London: Bloomsbury, 2014), p. 316.

7. The socialist William Diack reproduces the scene with Eleanor and the man who thought he knew better in *History of the Trades Council and the Trade Union Movement in Aberdeen* (Aberdeen: Aberdeen Trades Council, 1939), p. 62. Since then, the scene has

been reproduced many times, the latest in Holmes, *Eleanor Marx*, p. 351.

8. *Die Jungen* are dealt with in Dirk H. Müller, *Idealismus und Revolution: zur Opposition der Jungen gegen den sozialdemokratischen Parteivorstand* (Berlin: Spiess, 1975) and Peter Wienand, 'Revoluzzer und Revisionisten', *Politische Vierteljahresschrift* 17 (1976), among other works. In his autobiography *Jünglingsjahre*, Paul Ernst wrote that, bored by Schmoller's lectures in Berlin, he bought the first volume of *Capital* and found in it an intellectual clarity that Schmoller lacked. 'Ich kam von Schmoller zu Marx und kam wie in den himmel', he wrote and continued: 'Ja, das war der Führer den ich brauchte' (Yes, that was the leader I needed); Paul Ernst, *Jünglingsjahre* (München: G. Muller, 1931), p. 166. Ernst's enthusiasm was brief, however, and he gradually moved far to the right on the political scale. In 1933, the year in which he would die, he became a member of the Prussian Akademie der Künste after the purge of the Jews.

9. Engels to Joseph Bloch, 21 September 1890, MEW 37, pp. 462–5, CW 49, pp. 33–7.

10. Eugen Dühring, *Cursus der Philosophie als streng wissenschaftlicher Weltanschauung und Lebensgestaltung* (Leipzig: Erich Koschny, 1875), pp. 2 and 14f. On eternal ethical truths, ibid., p. 192ff. Engels on platitudes, MEW 20, p. 83, CW 25, p. 83.

11. Engels to von Boenigk, 21 August 1890, MEW 37, pp. 447f, CW 49, pp. 18ff.

12. Engels to Kautsky, 13 December 1890, MEW 37, pp. 522f. Marxist orthodoxy in Karl Kautsky, *Karl Marx' oekonomische Lehren gemeinverständlich dargestellt und erläutert* (Stuttgart: J. H. W Dietz, 1910), p. viii. Marx's *Critique of the Gotha Programme* was published in *Die Neue Zeit*, no. 18, vol. 9.

13. On the Erfurt programme, Karl Kautsky, *Das Erfurter Programm in seinem grundsätzlichen Theil erläutert* (Stuttgart: J. H. W. Dietz, 1899). On ethics in the materialist conception of history, Karl Kautsky, *Ethik und materialistische Geschichtsauffassung: ein Versuch* (Stuttgart: J. H. W. Dietz, 1910).

14. On intellectual maturity, Eduard Bernstein, *Die Voraussetzungen des Sozialismus und die Aufgaben der Sozialdemokratie* (Hamburg: Rowohlts Klassiker, 1969), p. 11; on the changeability of theory, p. 39. The standard work on revisionism and its development is Helga Grebing's work on the subject. She begins with a very broad determination of the concept, and then follows a meandering road from Bernstein, Austro-Marxism, and Lukács up to the Prague Spring of 1968; Helga Grebing, *Der Revisionismus von Bernstein bis zum 'Prager Frühling'* (München: Beck, 1977). A somewhat

older, all-round anthology of articles on various aspects of revisionism is Leopold Labedz, *Revisionism: Essays in the History of Marxist Ideas* (London: George Allen and Unwin Ltd, 1962), with interesting contributions from scholars such as Christian Gneuss, Leszek Kołakowski, and Sibnarayan Ray.

15. Georgi Plekhanov, 'Zu Hegel's sechzigstem Todestag', *Die Neue Zeit* (1891/92). Engels's assessment of Plekhanov's article in a letter to Kautsky, 3 December 1891, MEW 38, p. 235, CW 49, p. 317.

16. Engels wrote about Labriola in a letter to Friedrich Adolph Sorge, 30 December 1893: 'Er ist strikter Marxist' (He is a strict Marxist), MEW 39, p. 188, CW 50, p. 250. Labriola's letters to Engels are published in Antonio Labriola, *Lettere a Engels* (Rome: Rinascita, 1949). Labriola's views on historical materialism are seen in Labriola, *Saggi sul materialism storico* (Rome: Editori Riunati, 1977).

17. Lenin is an extraordinarily controversial figure; this marks the great amount of literature about him, which is difficult to grasp. A rather new biography, characterized by sound criticism of sources and nuanced assessments, is Robert Service, *Lenin: A Biography* (Cambridge, Mass.: Harvard University Press, 2000). In *What Is to Be Done?* (1902), Lenin violently attacks what he calls the 'worship of spontaneity' (Lenin, *Collected Works* 5, p. 367), by which he meant the belief that 'the masses' could achieve a social revolution without leadership. He argued that on their own, workers could develop a trade union consciousness but not a political one. This required a well-organized party under the leadership of professional revolutionaries (see in particular pp. 464ff).

18. On Lenin as the creator of the theory of the party, see Ralph Miliband, *Marxistisk politik: en analyserande discussion kring den marxistiska inställningen till politisk praktik* (Stockholm: Bonnier, 1980), pp. 107–10 and Schieder, *Karl Marx als Politiker*, pp. 130ff.

19. Lenin, 'The Three Sources and Three Component Parts of Marxism', *Collected Works* 19, 1913, pp. 24–8.

20. Ernst Mach, *Beiträge zur Analyse der Empfindungen* (Jena: G. Fischer, 1886). On the conflict between Mach and Einstein, see Gerald J. Holton, 'Mach, Einstein and the Search for Reality', *Boston Studies in the Philosophy of Science*, vol. 6 (1970), pp. 165–99.

21. Lenin's letters from this period create complete clarity in the background for *Materialism and Empirio-Criticism*: the opposition between Mensheviks and Bolsheviks, in which the Bolsheviks were the followers of Lenin's theory of the party. To his sorrow, Lenin now saw that Plekhanov, the leading theoretician of the Mensheviks, sided against Mach, while Bogdanov and a number of other Bolsheviks on the contrary abandoned the realist theory of knowledge in favour of Mach's standpoint; see Lenin's letter to Anatoly

Lunacharsky, 1 August 1905, Lenin, *Collected Works*, 43, pp. 161f. Lenin found this upsetting; his opponents could not be the only ones with what he saw as a correct Marxist understanding. He corresponded with revolutionary author Maxim Gorky on the subject. In a long letter, he said that he had read a manuscript by Bogdanov and had been gripped by an 'unbelievable fury'. The Bolsheviks had gone philosophically astray. On top of all this *Die Neue Zeit* – the leading theoretical journal for Marxists – had published an announcement that said that Bogdanov represented the Bolsheviks, and Plekhanov on the other hand the Mensheviks. Letter to Gorky, 25 February 1908, Lenin, *Briefe* (Berlin: Dietz Verlag, 1967), pp. 138–45. (The letter is not reproduced in Lenin's *Collected Works*; neither is the following.) Gorky did not find the matter so crucial, proposing reconciliation between the quarrelling parties. Lenin replied angrily that reconciliation was not possible on such an issue. It was a matter of either/or, the Mensheviks were on the point of winning. Letter from Lenin to Gorky, 24 March 1908, Lenin, *Briefe*, pp. 149ff. A meeting nevertheless took place at Gorky's estate on the island of Capri. Lenin's biographer Robert Service gives an account of the meeting, which was without result regarding the issue of contention. The opposing parties mostly played chess with each other. Lenin became furious when he lost. Service does not realize, however, why the issue of Mach seemed so important for Lenin, who absolutely wanted to see doctrines from metaphysics to political tactics as a unity, a monolith. Service, *Lenin*, pp. 190–6. On a Marxist left with a weakness for Nietzsche's philosophy, see Seth Taylor, *Left-Wing Nietzscheanism: The Politics of German Expressionism* (Berlin: De Gruyter, 1990).

22. Lenin made his notes between September and December 1914 – that is, during the first autumn of the war. They were not published until 1929. Here I have started out from V. I. Lenin, *Materialismus und Empiriokritzismus* (Berlin: Dietz Verlag, 1962), pp. 95–238. On Machism, p. 132.

23. 'On the Question of Dialectics', ibid., pp. 355–63.

24. An exhaustive, partially sympathetic depiction of the revolution and the period up until 1923 is Edward Hallett Carr, *A History of the Soviet Union*, 14 vols (London: Palgrave Macmillan, 1950–78). One outstanding description of the entire history of the Soviet Union is Manfred Hildermeier, *Geschichte der Sowjetunion, 1917–1991* (München: C. H. Beck, 1998).

25. Isaac Deutscher's three-volume biography of Trotsky is written by a sympathizer who was also a good historian. Deutscher does not try to tone down the massacre in Kronstadt, even if he is eager to emphasize that Trotsky only unwillingly let it happen. Isaac Deutscher, *The*

Prophet (London: Verso, 2014), pp. 522ff.

26. A few of the most important contributions in the battle over the dialectic have been gathered in the anthology Abram Deborin and Nikolaj Bukharin, *Kontroversen über dialektischen und mechanischen Materialismus* (Frankfurt am Main: Suhrkamp, 1969). Oskar Negt, 'Marxismus als Legitimationswissenschaft: zur Genese der stalinistischen Philosophie', in ibid., is a valuable introduction. More detail about Deborin in particular can be found in René Ahlberg, *Dialektische Philosophie und Gesellschaft in der Sowjetunion* (Berlin: Osteuropainstitut, 1960). Stephen F. Cohen, *Bucharin och den ryska revolutionen: en politisk biografi 1888–1938* (Lund: Arkiv förlag, 1971), pp. 129–45, which attempts to show that Bukharin cannot be called a mechanist in this context. It is clear that he was not extreme in his viewpoints, but he was the most influential opponent of the interpretation that Deborin advocated. Mark Mitin, 'Uber die Ergebnisse der philosophischen Diskussion', in Deborin and Bucharin, *Kontroversen über dialektischen und mechanischen Materialismus*, in particular pp. 330–42. On Stalin in the philosophers, see further Wladislav Hedeler, 'Stalin und die Philosophen', *Deutsche Zeitschrift für Philosophie*, vol. 39 (1991). On Lysenko, see ibid., p. 524.

27. Eric Hobsbawm, *Ytterligheternas tidsålder: det korta 1900-talet 1914–1991* (Stockholm: Rabén Prisma, 1997), pp. 106–31.

28. John Peter Nettl, *Rosa Luxemburg* (London: Oxford University Press, 1966), remains the standard biography of Luxemburg.

29. Helga Grebing, *Der Revisionismus von Bernstein bis zum 'Prager Frühling'* (München: Beck, 1977), pp. 70–92 on Lukács. An interesting and important collection of articles on Lukács, written by a number of his most outstanding students, is Agnes Heller, *Lukács Revalued* (Oxford: Basil Blackwell, 1983). Karl Korsch, *Marxism och filosofi* (Stockholm: Rabén & Sjögren, 1972) is a book with obvious points in common with Lukács. Korsch, however, made no apologies.

30. Ernst Bloch, *Das Prinzip Hoffnung* (Frankfurt am Main: Suhrkamp, 1959).

31. Michael Löwy, *Förlossning och utopi* (Göteborg: Daidalos, 1992).

32. On Riazanov and his fate, see Jakov Rokitjanskij, 'Das tragische Schicksal von David Borisovič Rjazanov', *Beiträge zur Marx-Engels-Forschung: Neue Folge* (Hamburg: Argument, 1993) and Volker Külow and André Jaroslawski, *David Rjasanov: Marx-Engels-Forscher Humanist Dissident* (Berlin: Dietz Verlag, 1993).

33. There is a large amount of literature on the Frankfurt School and its members. Rolf Wiggershaus, *Die Frankfurter Schule: Geschichte, Theoretische Entwicklung, Politische Bedeutung* (München: Dt.

Taschenbuch Verlag, 1997) and Martin Jay, *The Dialectical Imagination: A History of the Frankfurt School and the Institute of Social Research* (Berkeley: University of California Press, 1973) are excellent. Jürgen Habermas, *Zur Rekonstruktion des historischen Materialismus* (Frankfurt am Main: Suhrkamp, 1976). A rather fresh example of Axel Honneth's struggle with the Marxian world of ideas is 'Die Moral im 'Kapital': Versuch einer Korrektur der Marxschen.konomiekritik', in Rahel Jaeggi and Daniel Loick, *Nach Marx: Philosophie, Kritik, Praxis* (Frankfurt am Main: Suhrkamp, 2013).

34. Michel Foucault, *Dits et écrits*, vol. 1 (Paris: Gallimard, 2001), pp. 1405ff. Jean-Paul Sartre, *Critique of Dialectical Reason*, vol. 1 (London: Verso, 2004). The incomplete continuation was published posthumously: Sartre, *Critique of Dialectical Reason*, vol. 2 (London: Verso, 2006).

35. The critical edition of the Prison Notebooks is Antonio Gramsci, *Quaderni di cercere* (Turin: Einaudi, 1975). Selections in English are *Selections from the Prison Notebooks*, edited and translated by Quintin Hoare and Geoffrey Nowell Smith (New York: International Publishers, 1971) and *Antonio Gramsci: Further Selections from the Prison Notebooks*, edited and translated by Derek Boothman (London: Lawrence & Wishart, 1995). The literature about Gramsci is difficult to survey, but Norberto Bobbio, *Saggi su Gramsci* (Milano: Feltrinelli, 1990) and Peter Ives, Language and Hegemony in Gramsci (London: Pluto Press, 2004), are interesting and rewarding.

36. On Eurocommunism, see Richard Kinderley, *In Search of Eurocommunism* (London: MacMillan, 1981).

37. Agnes Heller, *The Theory of Need in Marx* (London: Alison & Busby, 1976).

38. Karel Kosík, *Det konkretas dialektik: en studie i människans och världens problematik* (Göteborg: Röda Bokförlaget, 1963). On Kosík in his context, see Grebing, *Der Revisionismus von Bernstein bis zum 'Prager Frühling'*, pp. 218–21.

39. Mao Zedong's writings are found in English translation in a number of selections. Mao Tse-tung, *Mao Tse-tung Unrehearsed* (Harmondsworth: Penguin, 1974) is interesting. The publisher of the book, Stuart Schram, has himself authored a number of important books on Mao; the latest is Stuart Schram, *The Thought of Mao Tse-tung* (Cambridge: Cambridge University Press, 1989).

40. One important person for the dissemination of Guevara's ideas – especially in Europe – was the young French academic Régis Debray, who was with him in Bolivia.

41. Leopold Schwarzschild, *Den röde preussaren: Karl Marx – liv och*

legend (Stockholm: Bonniers, 1949).

42. Johan Lagerkvist, *Tiananmen redux: den bortglömda massakern som förändrade världen* (Stockholm: Bonniers, 2014), depicts China's development over the last few decades with expert knowledge and biting acuity.

43. A rather new and quite comprehensive presentation of the dialectic is Fredric Jameson's 2010 work *Valences of the Dialectic*. Jameson not only looks for the modern roots back to Hegel and Marx but also captures a long series of current studies of the concept, for example in Derrida, Foucault, and Deleuze. The book also sweeps over contemporary development, the capitalism of today, and the possibilities of utopian thinking. He still uses the term 'Marxism' without more detailed clarifications, and speaks in a rather ambivalent fashion about developments in the Soviet Union and the reasons for its collapse. On the other hand, he does not try to critically limit the reasonable use of the concept of the dialectic. Jameson, *Valences of the Dialectic* (London: Verso, 2010), above all chapters 2–5 and 15 ('Actually Existing Marxism'), there in particular pp. 397ff.

44. Marx on the kitchen of the future, MEGA II/6, p. 704, CW 35, p. 17.

45. A fine analysis of Marx's views of criticism is Emmanuel Renault, *Marx et l'idée de critique* (Paris: P.U.F., 1995).

46. Marx's 'Confessions' are reproduced in MEW 31, p. 597, CW 42, pp. 567f.

47. There is a very great amount of literature on nationalism. Benedict Anderson, *Imagined Communities: Reflections on the Origin and Spread of Nationalism* (London: Verso, 1983) and Eric Hobsbawm, *Nations and Nationalism since 1790: Programme, Myth, Reality* (Cambridge: Cambridge University Press, 1992) are important works on the subject.

48. Sigmund Freud 1948, *Das Unbehagen der Kultur*, in *Gesammelte Werke, chronologisch geordnet*, vol. 14, edited by Anna Freud (London: Imago, 1948), pp. 241ff.

49. August Bebel, *Kvinnan och socialismen* (Göteborg: Dokument Partisan, 1972), English translation *Women Under Socialism*.

50. Clara Zetkin, *Zur Geschichteder proletarischen Frauenbewegung Deutschlands* (Frankfurt am Main: R. Stern, 1975).

51. Rosa Luxemburg, *Reform or Revolution: And Other Writings*, introduction by Paul Buhle (New York: Dover, 2006), p. 215.

52. Anne Fairchild Pomeroy, *Marx and Whitehead: Process, Dialectics, and the Critique of Capitalism* (Albany: State University of New York Press, 2004).

Index

The index contains names and central concepts. Marx and Engels's central writings are also included, as are a number of important historical events. The names in the postscript are not included; nor are purely bibliographical references in the notes to the text.

Duchamp, Marcel (1887–1968),
French artist – 464
Dudevant, Aurore, *see* Sand, George
Duncan, Graeme, contemporary
British political scientist – 108
Duncker, Franz (1822–88), German
newspaperman, publisher, and
politician – 372, 382, 687, 697, 715
Dühring, Eugen (1833–1921), German
philosopher and political economist
– 402, 493, 496, 525, 590, 690, 719

Eagleton, Terry (b. 1943), British
literary scholar – 11, 683
Eccarius, Johann Georg (1818–89),
German tailor active in unions,
member of the *Bund der
Kommunisten* and the International
– 532
*Economic and Philosophic
Manuscripts* (or the *Paris
Manuscripts*) – 13, 15, 130, 131,
133, 341, 399, 607
Eichhorn, Karl Friedrich (1781–1854),
German professor of law, Prussian
censor – 61, 643
Eichmann, Franz August (1793–1879),
Prussian civil servant – 252, 699
d'Eichthal, Gustave (1804–86) French
journalist and ethnologist, follower
of Saint-Simon's doctrines, with
the ambition of founding a utopian
society – 86
*Eighteenth Brumaire of Louis
Bonaparte*, Marx's 1852 work on
Napoleon III – 300, 303, 306, 309f,
312, 336, 556, 591, 618, 676
Einstein, Albert (1879–1955), German
physicist – 103, 515, 597, 708, 720
Elbe, Ingo (b. 1972), German
philosopher and social scientist –
429, 692f
Elster, Jon (b. 1940), Norwegian
sociologist and political philosopher
– 9, 637
emergence, a more complex structure

arises from a less complex one –
491f
Endemann, Wolfgang, contemporary
German historian of mathematics –
471
energy principle (originally called
the theory of the indestructibility
of energy), the first law of
thermodynamics, which says that
energy can neither be created nor
destroyed – 26, 127, 196, 461, 487f,
525
Engels, Friedrich *père* (1796–1860),
cotton manufacturer, father of the
following – 126, 259, 277, 671
Engels, Friedrich (1820–95), German
socialist author and politician – 8,
passim
Engelsism – alternative term for
Marxism, from the idea that Engels
more than Marx put his stamp
on the more orthodox Marxist
traditions – 12, 497, 637, 692, 705
Epicurus (341–270 BCE), Greek
philosopher – 69f, 72f, 644
Ermen, Godfrey, partner in the firm of
Ermen & Engels in Manchester –
126
Ermen, Peter, partner in the firm of
Ermen & Engels in Manchester –
126
Ernst, Paul (1866–1933), German
author – 589, 709, 718f, 723
Essbach, Wolfgang (b. 1944), German
sociologist – 642f
essence, human, according to Marx
before 1845 it emerged as the final
goal of history – 99, 143, 148f, 178,
408, 523
Ewerbeck, August Hermann (1816–
60), Franco-German doctor,
communist and writer – 109, 200,
649, 661
exactitude, Marx's striving for
scientific – 192, 418, 442f, 449, 695
exchange as a direct relation between

Freiligrath, Ferdinand (1810–76), German author and translator, close friend of Karl Marx – 349, 532f, 685, 710

French Revolution of 1789–94 – 21, 31, 33, 41, 98, 115, 164, 177, 187, 217, 252, 267f, 271, 274, 297, 311, 333, 337, 441, 462, 538, 556, 588, 621, 640, 656, 667

Frenhofer, a fictitious painter in Balzac's story 'The Unknown Masterpiece' – 396, 463–466

Freud, Sigmund (1856–1939), Austrian doctor and author, founder of psychoanalysis – 29, 103, 123, 606, 621, 639, 651, 707, 724

Freyberger, Louise (1860–1950), Austrian social democrat, married first to Karl Kautsky and then to Ludwig Freyberger; Engels's housekeeper during his final years – 286–288, 673

Friedman, Milton (1912–2006), American economist – 5, 230

Friedrich Wilhelm II (1744–97), king of Prussia from 1786 – 251

Friedrich Wilhelm II, Prussian soldier and Prussian minister, president 1848–50 – 251f, 257, 265

Friedrich Wilhelm IV (1795–1846), Prussian king – 42, 62, 79, 122f, 190, 251, 269, 338, 682

Friedrich, Caspar David (1774–1840), German artist – 53

Furet, François (1927–97), French historian – 656f

Galileo Galilei (1564–1642), Italian (Tuscan) natural scientist – 26

Gall, Ludwig (1791–1863), social reformer and inventor – 40, 640

Gans, Eduard (1798–1839), German lawyer, Hegelian – 642

Garaudy, Roger (1913–2012), French philosopher and author – 134, 653

Garibaldi, Guiseppe (1807–82), Italian

freedom fighter – 338, 551

Gaudí, Antoni (1852–1926), Spanish-Catalonian architect – 16

de Gaulle, Charles (1890–1970), French general, president of France 1959–69 – 553, 649

Geddes, Patrick (1854–1932), British sociologist, biologist, and city planner – 638

Gemkow, Heinrich (b. 1928), German historian – 9, 637, 645, 657

George, Stefan (1868–1933), German poet – 94

Gerhardt, Charles-Frédéric (1816–56), French chemist – 486

German Ideology, manuscript Marx and Engels wrote in 1845 but never had published – 161, 171–174, 178, 179, 182–184, 186–188, 191–193, 195f, 198f, 205, 210, 214, 216, 264, 304, 347, 350, 366, 375f, 392, 428, 435, 452, 455, 504, 514, 523, 590, 631, 637, 657f, 660, 685, 698

Gigot, Philippe-Charles (1819–60) Belgian communist, close to Marx and Engels during their years in Brussels – 198, 661

Gladstone, William Ewart (1809–98), British liberal politician – 316, 323, 325, 680

globalization in Marx – 301, 381

Gneuss, Christian, contemporary German political scientist and journalist – 719

Gödel, Kurt (1906–78), Austrian logician and mathematician – 451, 697

von Goethe, Johann Wolfgang (1749–1832), German author – 31, 53, 68, 155f, 182, 229, 237, 329, 463, 619f, 641, 659

Götrek, Per (1798–1876), Swedish bookseller and communist – 242, 667

Godwin, William (1756–1836), British philosopher, social critic

and all for one' – 24, 113, 254, 538, 627, 711
Sombart, Werner (1863–1941), German political economist and sociologist – 697
Soros, George (b. 1930), Hungarian-American financier – 2, 636
specialization, scientific, the process by which researcher obtain an increasingly limited field of competence – 30, 207, 429, 515f, 518, 708
Spencer, Herbert (1820–1903), British philosopher – 28, 32, 508, 517f, 707f
Sperber, Jonathan (b. 1952), American historian – 10, 183, 192, 287, 314, 398, 482, 637, 657, 659f, 667, 673, 677, 679, 682, 689
Spinoza, Baruch (1632–77), Dutch philosopher – 82, 117, 148, 164, 654, 657
Spivak, Gayatri Chakravorty (b. 1942), Indian philosopher and literary theorist – 386, 688
Sraffa, Piero (1898–1973), Italian-British political economist – 696f
Stalin, Josef (Iosif Dzhugashvili, 1878–1953), leader of the Soviet Union – 3, 385, 427, 515, 602–604, 609, 612, 623, 721f
Standing, Guy (b. 1948), British economist – 4, 636
Stedman Jones, Gareth (b. 1942), British political scientist – 482, 573, 665, 682, 695, 706f, 716
Steedman, Ian (b. 1941), British political economist – 697
Steffens, Henrik (or Heinrich, 1773–1845), Norwegian-German natural philosopher – 144, 474
vom Stein zum Altenstein, Karl (1757–1831), German (Prussian) politician, worked for political modernization of Prussia – 66
von Stein, Lorenz (1815–90), German

political scientist – 581, 648
Stern, Daniel, *see* d'Agoult, Marie
Steuart, James (1712–80), British economist – 379
Stieber, Wilhelm (1818–82), Prussian chief of police – 270
Stirner, Max (pseudonym for Johann Caspar Schmidt, 1806–56), German philosopher – 61, 171, 180–185, 188–191, 656, 659f
Strauss, David Friedrich (1808–74), German theologian – 60, 643
Strindberg, August (1849–1912), Swedish author – 156, 231, 303, 573
subject and predicate in the logical sense – 95
substance, form and content – 205, 368, 409, 437–439, 597, 696
Sue, Eugène (1804–57), French author – 165
supernatural, society as something above nature ('supernatural') in relation to it – 439f, 569, 696
surplus value, the increase in value that labour achieves – 288, 343, 408, 417, 454ff, 462, 464, 472, 486f, 495, 670, 672, 723
Süssmayr, Franz Xavier (1766–1803), Austrian composer – 189
Sweezy, Paul (1910–2004), American political economist – 427, 446, 693, 696
Szeliga, *see* von Zychlinski

Tacitus, Publius Cornelius (55–120), Roman historian – 58
Taiping rebellion, a more or less popular uprising in China, 1850–64, directed against imperial power; crushed with the help of British and French troops, the rebellion is most likely the bloodiest war in history – 331
Tait, Peter Guthrie (1831–1901), British physicist – 476, 701